ENCYCLOPEDIA OF
AMERICAN
FOLKLORE

LINDA S. WATTS

Facts On File
An imprint of Infobase Publishing

Encyclopedia of American Folklore

Facts On File, Inc.
An imprint of Infobase Publishing
132 West 31st Street
New York NY 10001

ISBN-13: 978-0-7394-8442-5

Text design by Erika K. Arroyo
Cover design by Cathy Rincon/Dorothy M. Preston

Printed in the United States of America

CONTENTS

ACKNOWLEDGMENTS

While I have contributed entries to many encyclopedias and works of subject bibliography, I had never before undertaken a single-author reference work. I hope that in some sense this book serves as a tribute to, and expression of thanks for, all the help and encouragement I received during its production. Clearly, there are many individuals and organizations to thank for realization of this project: Henry Rasof, for advising on the volume proposal; Jeff Soloway and Facts On File, for their stewardship of the product and patience in the process; my program and academic home, Interdisciplinary Arts and Sciences, for supporting my participation in the venture; the University of Washington (UW) Office of Undergraduate Research, for connecting me with student bibliographers; my institution, the University of Washington, Bothell (UWB) and its academic leaders, for approving the sabbatical leave during which much of the work was completed; the UW's professional librarians, especially those at the UWB/Cascadia Community College (CCC) Library, for their tireless efforts on my behalf; undergraduate bibliographers from the Seattle and Bothell campuses of the University of Washington, including Sammie Bossert, Sam Hannum, Jamie Jones, Jennifer Mau, Erik Shephard, and Kelly Wahlstrom; all my teachers, students, and colleagues over the years (and with especially tender gratitude to those individuals who have proved themselves to be all three), for their willingness to listen to stories about the research and for shaping its process; and, finally, the members of my family, to whom I dedicate this book, for making education and research activities possible in the first place.

PREFACE

While there are numerous dictionaries and encyclopedias of American folklore available for scholars in the discipline, the goal of this work is to provide information in a highly approachable manner for readers who are newcomers, novices, and nonspecialists in folklore. This volume addresses the needs of multiple audiences, including high school, college, and public libraries; archive and museum collections; and independent researchers. Furthermore, the entries here address a wide range of subjects, rather than focusing on a single population, region, genre, or topic within folklore studies.

In preparing the book, I sought to create a reference work that simultaneously takes seriously and speaks clearly to the needs of a general audience of readers. The volume's configuration recognizes the needs of collectors/collections requiring an accurate and accessible, compact, and economical source of frequently sought information about American folklore. Especially where a large collection of specialized volumes would prove prohibitive, this work consolidates user needs within one reference volume. Its categories reflect the kinds of material students require for K–12 and college assignments featuring American folklore. It also considers the kinds of clarifying questions readers might pose when consulting the encyclopedia for other inquiries and purposes. That is, the encyclopedia anticipates needs of secondary-school and college students, teachers, and librarians, as well as folklorists and other researchers, storytellers, and general readers interested in American folklore.

In keeping with the term *folklore*, with its dual denotation, this volume addresses folklore as both a body of information (data) and set of methods for its study (inquiry). The work combines attention to U.S. folk forms with consideration of their cultural origin, historical context, and social function. Curricular links for the book's contents include the disciplines of folklore and folklife, history, literature, cultural anthropology, sociology, art history, and material culture.

As a one-volume encyclopedia, this work aids readers exploring topics, terms, themes, figures, and issues within the study of American folklore. Folklore has sometimes been described as the unwritten literature of a culture: its songs, stories, sayings, games, rituals, beliefs, and ways of life. For the purposes of this work, the term *American folklore* refers to transmitted traditional beliefs, myths, tales, language practices, and customs of the people of the United States, whether that transmission takes place orally, observationally, or through writing about such lore. That being said, the emphasis here remains on verbal (narrative) genres of folklore. It deals chiefly in expressive domains where language acts play a major part. What this means is that while forms such as legends and tales figure prominently, other folk forms (visual art, dance, music, costume, and the like) are less the focus here.

Because many courses, especially within K–12 education, tend to fold folklore into a language-arts curriculum, this volume's content and organization correspond to the ways educators integrate folklore within literacy and wider learning objectives for language arts at the secondary level. In support of such research at all levels, the volume offers such entry categories as FOLK HEROES/LEGENDARY FIGURES, FABLES/FAIRY TALES/MYTHS, and FOLKLORE IN AMERICAN LITERATURE.

Many courses, particularly high-school lower-division college folklore courses, tend to ask students to identify and analyze patterns across texts, explore links between folk forms and the surrounding sociohistorical context, situate themselves in terms of cultural populations, and practice gathering data in the ways folklorists do. For that reason, entry categories such as FOLKLORE IN EVERYDAY LIFE appear.

By the time students reach upper-division-university-level or graduate-level study, their instructors require more varied and sophisticated forms of folklore study. Entries here speak to such needs. For readers wishing to research their own or another's folk heritage, entries on CULTURAL GROUPS, HISTORICAL EVENTS, TERMS, and organizations/agencies (under OTHER ENTRIES) are included.

Finally, because those engaged in lifelong learning, whether curricular or self-initiated, long to understand the relevance of folklore study to their own lives, categories of entries such as HOLIDAYS AND OBSERVANCES assist readers of any age in discovering how much folklore surrounds common customs and behavior, as well as how folklorists understand these elements of received culture and practice.

I have informed the encyclopedia's contents with the most current and sound folklore research available. Headword selection aligns with prevailing practice within folklore pedagogy and research. References and bibliographic material provided highlight primarily recently published and commonly available materials for further study.

The book's working definition of *folklore*, the content choices, and the categories of their arrangement reflect the reading situation of the prospective user of this encyclopedia. Most desire quick and clear guidance on the meaning and implications of American folklore.

Entry-level students of folklore, whether at the high school or college level, typically consult reference volumes in the context of assigned coursework. The volume's design reflects this fact. After surveying introductory-level texts on folklore and course assignments currently in use within secondary-school and college courses featuring American folklore, I framed the encyclopedia accordingly—around the specific folklore reference needs that emerge from that investigation.

While there are many ways of defining folklore and characterizing its meanings, sometimes the most plainspoken descriptions prove the most vivid. In prefacing her anthology of folktales and folk songs for young readers, *From Sea to Shining Sea: A Treasury of American Folklore and Folk Songs* (1993), Amy Cohn evoked the nature of folklore study in this way:

> Simply, folklore is a story, a rhyme, a song, a saying passed down orally through the generations. In some ways folklore is a lot like the popular party game, telephone. Each time someone hears a story or song and repeats it, he or she changes it slightly. … Each teller infuses in the tale a part of himself or herself, filling it with his or her ideas about the world, its people, and its creatures. (xiii)

In this familiar image of a children's game, with its embedded reminder of the ways human transmission shapes the content of a message with each retelling, Cohn captures both the experience and the lasting value of folklore study. She also evokes the importance of active listening, thoughtful speech, and keen observation for the aspiring folklorist. Finally, she reminds us that the process under investigation in the study of American folklore is never complete, and so its unfolding proves a story of generations. In sharing this encyclopedia, I invite you to join in—enrich and be enriched by—the game's endlessly fascinating play. If folklore study, as is folklore itself, is analogous to a game of telephone, then, this call is for you.

INTRODUCTION: WHY STUDY FOLKLORE?

The real power of folklore becomes clearest when happenings in a culture demand deep contemplation and considered response. My case in point is the historic events of September 11, 2001.

The events of 9/11 represent the kind of shared experience that requires not only an individual response but one that reckons all the wisdom of the collective, including the forms most closely associated with folklore: oral history, memoir, children's drawings, tales, songs, tributes, and, yes, even the disaster jokes that help some of us go on with our lives—all the while remembering those who are not lucky enough to survive and face the predicament of determining a fitting response to the events.

As I took in the real-time accounts of 9/11 and monitored subsequent reactions to the events, I was reminded anew—perhaps surprisingly so—of how important folklore really can be within our lives together. In other words, if conflict is the natural consequence of lives conducted in the company of others, and if folk culture functions as one of the ways people process conflict and act to meet that conflict constructively (through understanding, reconciliation, consequence, or change), then cultural traumas playing out on the world stage may offer the clearest picture of the part folklore plays in contending with conflict on a more global scale.

Better, perhaps, than any other example I can summon, 9/11 dramatizes how every aspect of folklore forms a part of the public response to adversity. Witness such examples as:

- makeshift tributes to those who died in the attacks, memorials that surfaced almost immediately at Ground Zero and throughout the streets of New York City;
- artworks that people of all ages used to express and come to terms with the attacks on the World Trade Center and Pentagon;
- collections of first-person narratives that have found publication in the years since 9/11;
- songs, sermons, and speeches delivered in commemoration of the attacks and in raising of funds to give some measure of financial relief to survivors and family members of those who perished; and
- oral histories that have since been collected by the American Folklife Center.

Of course, I am not the only, or even the first, person to notice. As early as the fall–winter 2001 issue of *Voices*, the online *Journal of New York Folklore*, Steven Zeitlin and Ilana Harlow wrote about the connection between folk culture and 9/11. Referencing their book, *Giving a Voice to Sorrow: Personal Response to Death and Mourning*, published on November 11, 2001, these folklorists described how poignantly people had already begun to use folk forms, such as storytelling, personal ritual, and commemorative art, as a means to analyze and react to the 9/11 tragedy.

While we might hope to be spared the point's demonstration through such traumatic means, 9/11 underscores the relevance of folklore research. Although folklore is not the only source of healing, understanding, and renewal, its study has proved a crucial component of the 9/11 aftermath. Folklore is more than a coping mechanism in the face of tragedy; its study helps us inform our responses, choices, and actions. It also challenges us to determine how folklore studies can contribute meaningfully to a post-9/11 America.

Surely, then, any working definition of the term *folklore* must prove robust enough to contend with the realities of the 21st century—and beyond. Just as folk culture has helped Americans come to grips with 9/11, so may the study of folklore help reckon the human consequences of that day and its implications for both the country and the world. It may be impossible at this point to arrive at a vision of this landmark event that perfectly combines the insight of direct testimony with the benefit of hindsight. Still, unless we are steadfast in the attempt to see cultural events for what they are and how they mean, we risk a form of symbolic violence perpetrated by faulty or selective historical representations. Such a response only serves to deepen the wounds opened (or reopened) by 9/11.

During the process of writing this book, other traumatic events such as Hurricane Katrina served once again to dramatize for me the value and vitality of folk culture. The hardships faced by the communities of the Gulf Coast region, in Louisiana and Mississippi, underscore both the threats disasters pose to folk traditions and the power of folklore to sustain us in times of crisis. As I prepared encyclopedia entries on topics such as MARDI GRAS and CAJUN FOLKLORE, it became clearer to me why some residents of New Orleans found a forced departure from their beloved hometown unthinkable and a nation without that historic city unacceptable.

Therefore, if the word *folklore* summons in your mind only quaint, decorative, nostalgic, celebratory, and nationalistic notions of the American past, I would suggest that the historical moment we occupy requires us to imbue the term with valences more apt to the age's challenges and to use it to offer acts of remembrance more worthy of our complex cultural legacies. In this way, we might aspire to a folklore practice consonant with a more profoundly human

(and humane) world, one that reminds us that the safest environment for us all (or homeland, as today's security-speak would have it) is a fully just world—peaceable, inclusive, and in right balance. May it be so.

For Further Reading:

American Folklife Center. September 11, 2001, a Documentary Project. Available online. URL: http://memory.loc.gov/ammem/collections/911_archive/index.html. Accessed March 6, 2006.

Borum, Jennifer P., and Lisa Ross. "In Sorrow and Hope: Creative Responses to Tragedy," *Folk Art* 26, no. 4 (winter 2001): 16–19.

Carithers, David R. "Romantic/Pragmatic Rhetoric after 9/11: Poetry, Prose, and Song," *Dissertation Abstracts International*, Section A: The Humanities and Social Sciences, 65, no. 8 (February 2005): 2,972.

Ellis, Bill. "Making a Big Apple Crumble: The Role of Humor in Constructing a Global Response to Disaster." In *Of Corpse: Death and Humor in Folklore and Popular Culture*, edited by Peter Narváez, 35–79. Logan: Utah State University Press, 2003.

Frank, Russel. "When the Going Gets Tough, the Tough Go Photoshopping: September 11 and the Newslore of Vengeance and Victimization," *New Media & Society* 6, no. 5 (October 2004): 633–658.

Haddad, Yvonne. "Defaming Islam and All Religious Belief," *Chronicle of Higher Education* 51, no. 9 (October 22, 2004): B9.

Hufford, Mary. "A Spontaneous Memorial Near the Pentagon," *Folklife Center News* 23, no. 4 (fall 2001): 5–7.

Jankowski, Nicholas, Steve Jones, and Jeah Lievrouw. "New Media after 9/11," *New Media and Society* 6, no. 5 (October 2004): 587–673.

Juergensmeyer, Mark. "Is Religion the Problem?" *Hedgehog Review* 6, no. 1 (spring 2004): 21–33.

Juergensmeyer, Mark. "Thinking about Religion after September 11," *Journal of the American Academy of Religion* 72, no. 1 (March 2004): 221–234.

Kirschenblatt-Gimblett, Barbara. "Kodak Moments, Flashbulb Memories: Reflections on 9/11," *The Drama Review* 47, no. 1 (spring 2003): 11–48.

Kuipers, Giselinde. "Media Culture and Internet Disaster Jokes: Bin Laden and the Attack on the World Trade Center," *European Journal of Cultural Studies* 5, no. 4 (November 2002): 450–470.

Lofgren, Stephen L. "The Status of Oral History in the Army: Expanding a Tradition," *Oral History Review: Journal of the Oral History Association* 30, no. 2 (summer–fall 2003): 81–97.

Ludwig, Sämi. "Thin Pluralism: Some Observations on American Multiculturalism," *REAL: The Yearbook of Research in English and American Literature* 19 (2003): 225–245.

9/11 Digital Archive. "September 11 Digital Archive: Saving the Histories of September 11, 2001." Available online. URL: http://911digitalarchive. org. Accessed March 6, 2006.

Thornburg, John. "From Rubble to Hope: Texts and Tunes after September 11, 2001," *Hymn* 53, no. 3 (July 2002): 18–21.

White, Geoffrey M. "National Subjects: September 11 and Pearl Harbor," *American Ethnologist* 31, no. 3 (August 2004): 293–310.

Willis, Susan. "Old Glory." In *Dissent from the Homeland: Essays after September 11*, edited by Stanley Hauerwas and Frank Lentricchia, 121–130. Durham, N.C.: Duke University Press, 2003.

Zeitlin, Steven, and Ilana Harlow. Downstate. "9/11: Commemorative Art, Ritual, and Story." *Voices: The Journal of New York Folklore* 27 (fall–winter 2001). Available online. URL: http://www.nyfolklore.org/pubs/voic27-3-4/dnstate. html. Accessed March 6, 2006.

Zeitlin, Steven, and Ilana Harlow. *Giving a Voice to Sorrow: Personal Response to Death and Mourning.* New York: Perigee Books, 2001.

A

Acadian and Creole folklore See CAJUN FOLKLORE.

Administrative Professionals' Day/Week Since 1952, American workplaces have been honoring office staff members with an annual holiday designed to recognize their daily contributions.

The event began as the concept of the National Secretaries Association, an organization now the International Association of Administrative Professionals. The purposes of the celebration were to recognize the value of members' work and to attract newcomers to the profession. It began as Secretary's Day, later became Professional Secretaries Day/Week, and now goes by the name of Administrative Professionals' Day/Week. The current title not only proves more apt to today's job titles and organizational strategies but also encourages appreciation of a wider spectrum of employees. The date for this observance varies, but it usually occurs during the month of April.

Typical gestures associated with Administrative Professionals' Day/Week include cards, gifts, luncheons, and other acknowledgments of the vital duties office members perform within an organization. Some individuals working in these capacities have ventured that it would be preferable to have raises rather than roses, or at least a paid day off in consideration for their efforts. The International Association of Administrative Professionals recommends that the occasion be recognized with workplace investments in continuing education for staff members.

While there are few public observances of Administrative Professionals' Day/Week apart from marketing displays targeted at gift buyers, it is common practice for a boss, supervisor, or office team member to take measures on this day to celebrate the accomplishments of all those who keep a workplace successful and congenial.

As do other workplace holidays, such as Boss Day and Labor Day, Administrative Professionals' Day/Week seeks to recognize the dignity of a job well done.

See also: BOSS DAY; HOLIDAYS/OBSERVANCES; INDUSTRIALIZATION AND FOLKLORE; LABOR DAY; OCCUPATIONAL FOLKLORE.

For Further Reading:
"9 Out of 10 Administrative Professionals Say They Contribute More at Work Than 5 Years Ago: Suggestions for Administrative Professionals Week April 24–30." *Business Wire*, April 25, 2005, 1.

International Association of Administrative Professionals. Administrative Professionals' Week and Day. Available online. URL: http://www.iaap-hq.org/apw/apwindex.htm. Accessed March 6, 2006.

McIntire, Alison. "Commentary: No Cards, Boss, Just Fill the Fax: How to Celebrate Administrative Professionals Day," *Los Angeles Times*, April 27, 2005, B-15.

Trinity University. A Sociological Tour through Cyberspace. Available online. URL: http://www.trinity.edu/~mkearl/secretary.html. Accessed March 6, 2006.

Aesop   See "ANDROCLES AND THE LION;" ANIMALS; "BOY WHO CRIED WOLF, THE"; FABLES; "TORTOISE AND THE HARE, THE."

African-American folklore   Since the inception of the American Folklore Society (AFS) and its founding charge to members of the profession, the study of African-American folklore has been a major focus within folklore scholarship in the United States.

In 1888, the founders of the AFS identified Native Americans and African Americans as two populations whose lore and customs deserved special attention. This public commitment by a professional organization intensified folklorists' interest in study of this target population. Collection of African-American folklore by white folklorists has been going on since the 19th century. Folklore, however, has always been a vital force at work within African-American culture. From the first stories to the latest, images, terms, concepts, and narrative forms drawn from folk culture frame African-American literature and inform its study.

In order to examine African-American folklore, it is first necessary to arrive at a definition of the term. The activist Stokely Carmichael once said that people who can define are masters. Carmichael's assertion couches cultural mastery in terms of language, a notion of naming that undergirds the struggle to write, disseminate, preserve, study, and develop African-American folklore. Defining any term, including one so resonant as folklore, in its relation to a cultural group, is an act that holds the power to frame understandings of, as well as the prospects for

empowerment through, African-American cultural survivals.

The history of African Americans, in terms of both literature and culture, then, is rich with works that reference African-American folklore, whether in terms of style, content, or message. For instance, in his autobiographical narratives, the abolitionist and former slave Frederick Douglass wrote about an experience during which he was given a piece of root to carry in his pocket, a prescribed practice suggestive not only of a lucky charm, but of a particular reference to one's literal and figurative roots, as applied within cultural practices such as conjuring. While Douglass conveyed skepticism about its magic, that bit of root, tucked away however reluctantly in his pocket, made the journey into freedom with Douglass. Much as this root stored in a pocket, folklore—in the form of the language and lessons of a shared cultural past—has accompanied African-American writers ever since.

For many readers today, it is unfortunately still the case that all that is known of African-American storytelling traditions is filtered through the work of people such as Joel Chandler Harris, whose book *Uncle Remus: His Songs and Sayings* (1880) came to represent—or one might more accurately say, misrepresent—African-American storytelling traditions. It was Harris's claim that in relating stories, he provided those stories in their original and unadulterated form. Harris's language proves revealing, though, for when he refers to other people and their cultures as "simple" or "picturesque," he trivializes them.

The works of Zora Neale Hurston, and in particular, her tales collected in *Mules and Men*, prove an illuminating case study, as well as a counterpoint to work by Harris. Hurston's education took her to Columbia and Barnard, where she became a formally trained collector of African-American folklore. Hurston rebutted depictions of African-American lore that attempted to suggest a culture's deficiency or pathology, and so Hurston focused on the integrity of the culture taken as a whole and, as much as possible, on its own terms.

It is difficult, then, to appreciate fully the social world Hurston depicts so richly in both her folklore and her fiction without a sense of the traditions of boasting, the dozens, and storytelling to which it corresponds, and to which it pays tribute. For instance, any reader of Hurston's work notices the role dialect plays within her collections of folklore, and perhaps even wonders why it is that Hurston retains a typographical practice of phoneticizing speech. By rendering on the page the sounded language of African Americans, Hurston hoped to let them speak for themselves.

As the case study of Hurston's writings suggests, folklore contributes to African-American culture a host of memorable and textured characters, both real and imagined. From the Trickster to Brer Rabbit, John Henry to Nat Turner, these fictional and historical personages surface repeatedly in lore in ways both instructive and engaging. It is through the help of these characters, occupying beloved narrative forms such as fables, fairy tales, myths, and tales, that African-American youth enter literacy. In so doing, these readers establish contact with a literary inheritance and cultural legacy shaped to an important extent by folklore.

Many contemporary fiction writers incorporate folkloric elements in substantive ways within their literary works and, in so doing, both honor and extend mother wit—the legacy of lore within African-American cultural expression. From Charles Chesnutt's *The Conjure Woman* and Ralph Ellison's *Invisible Man*, to Toni Morrison's *Tar Baby* and Toni Cade Bambara's *The Salt Eaters*, tales and their tellers find grounding in the soil of folk traditions. Whether one is reading Jean Toomer's *Cane* or Paule Marshall's *The Chosen Place, The Timeless People*, there is a clear and resounding sense that the collective past does not—and ought not—pass away, but rather needfully accompanies one in the efforts to fight for and find a desired future, both on the page and in the lived world.

See also: Anansi; Attucks, Crispus; Bambara, Toni Cade; Brer Rabbit; Brown, Sterling Allen; Chesnutt, Charles Waddell; Christmas, Annie; Civil Rights movement; Civil War; Colonial Williamsburg; conjure/conjuring; cultural groups; Douglass, Frederick; DuBois, W. E. B.; Dunbar, Paul Laurence; Ellison, Ralph Waldo; Emancipation (Proclamation) Day; fables; folklore; folklore in American literature; folkloristics; folktales; Harris, Joel Chandler; Henry, John; Hughes, James Mercer Langston; humor, folk; Hurston, Zora Neale; Ibo Landing; immigration and folklore; Johnson, James Weldon; Juneteenth; Kwanzaa; Locke, Alain Le Roy; luck/fortune; magic; Martin Luther King Day; minstrelsy; Morrison, Toni; Parks, Rosa; proverbs, religion, folk; Remus, Uncle; Revolutionary War; Robinson, Jack Roosevelt; slavery; Smithsonian Institution; speech, folk; Stowe, Harriet Beecher; Styron, William; Tar Baby; toasts/drinking; Toomer, Jean; trickster; Truth, Sojourner; Tubman, Harriet; Turner, Nat; Underground Railroad; vernacular culture; voodoo/hoodoo; Washington, Booker Taliaferro; wedding/marriage folklore; women's suffrage.

For Further Reading:

Byerman, Keith. *Fingering the Jagged Grain: Tradition and Form in Recent Black Fiction.* Athens: University of Georgia Press, 1985.

Courlander, Harold. *A Treasury of Afro-American Folklore.* New York: Crown, 1976.

Dance, Daryl Cumber, ed. *For My People: 400 Years of African American Folklore.* New York: Norton, 2002.

Dundes, Alan. *Mother Wit from the Laughing Barrel: Readings in the Interpretation of Afro-American Folklore.* Jackson: University Press of Mississippi, 1973.

Gates, Henry Louis. *The Signifying Monkey: A Theory of Afro-American Literary Criticism.* New York: Oxford University Press, 1988.

Harris, Joel Chandler. *Told by Uncle Remus: New Stories of the Old Plantation.* New York: Grosset and Dunlap, 1903.

Levine, Lawrence. *Black Culture, Black Consciousness: Afro-American Thought from Slavery to Freedom.* Oxford: Oxford University Press, 1977.

Pryse, Marjorie, and Hortense J. Spillers, eds. *Conjuring: Black Women, Fiction, and Literary Tradition.* Bloomington: Indiana University Press, 1985.

afterbirth See CHILDBIRTH/PREGNANCY FOLKLORE.

afterworld See DEATH; RELIGION AND FOLKLORE.

Agee, James (1909–1955) During his relatively short life and career as a writer, James Agee composed fiction, nonfiction, poems, and screenplays that reflect his commitment to social justice. He attended Exeter Academy and Harvard University and received much recognition for his work, including a posthumous Pulitzer Prize for *A Death in the Family*.

Among his most acclaimed works is a volume entitled *Let Us Now Praise Famous Men* (1941). This text began as an assignment for the business magazine, *Fortune*. Along with his collaborator, the photographer Walker Evans, Agee began work in 1936 on an assignment to depict the lives and struggles of tenant farmers in Hale County, Alabama. This effort grew so extensive that the two produced a book-long product of their experience portraying the lives of poor rural families during the Great Depression. Their work centered on three families in particular, who appeared in the book with pseudonyms. This was the only gesture toward protecting privacy, however, since in every other respect their likenesses, households, and relationships were documented in minute detail. Agee, in his effort to capture the fullness of the lives he portrayed through his prose, even lived with the families who form the subject of his writing.

In prolonged passages of scrupulous detail, Agee reconstructs for his readers every aspect of the lives seen through his fieldwork. The book includes the narrative equivalent of household inventories, as Agee describes even the contents of drawers in the homes he studies. In this respect, Agee admits his envy for the camera's unflinching eye and what he perceives as the photographic medium's power to portray a subject with absolute veracity.

In his writings, Agee had no intention of giving an account whose chief value would be literary or artistic. Instead, he sought to bear witness to the human condition, in all of its nuance. For this reason, Agee strove to make a personal connection with his human subjects. Through the pages of *Let Us Now Praise Famous Men*, Agee anguishes over the choices he makes, both as a man and as a writer, and the book documents his own travails at least as fully as it does those of tenant farm families.

While it was likely not his intention to conduct fieldwork as a folklorist might, Agee nonetheless left behind a chronicle of the lives of ordinary Americans, itself an example of the kind of project oral historians and ethnographers would later undertake in their attempts to document and analyze folklife.

Folklorists find in the work of Agee and Evans documentary evidence of considerable interest as it reveals poverty during 1930s America. Those concerned with material culture take particular note of the strength of *Let Us Now Praise Famous Men* as a record of the objects associated with everyday life.

See also: DEPRESSION, THE GREAT; DOCUMENTARY; ETHICS IN FOLKLORE; FIELDWORK, FOLKLORE; FOLKLORE IN AMERICAN LITERATURE; FRENCH-AMERICAN FOLKLORE; INSIDER/OUTSIDER; JOAD, TOM; PUBLIC FOLKLORE; REGION, FOLK; ROOSEVELT, FRANKLIN DELANO; SOUTHERN REGIONAL FOLKLORE; STEINBECK, JOHN.

For Further Reading:

Boger, Astrid. *Documenting Lives: James Agee's and Walker Evans's* Let Us Now Praise Famous Men. New York: Peter Lang, 1994.

Maharaidge, Dale, and Michael Williamson. *And Their Children after Them: The Legacy of* Let Us Now Praise Famous Men: *James Agee, Walker Evans, and the Rise and Fall of Cotton in the South.* New York: Pantheon Books, 1989.

Sims, Norman, ed. *Literary Journalism in the Twentieth Century.* New York: Oxford University Press, 1990.

Spears, Ross, and Jude Cassidy, eds. *Agee: His Life Remembered.* New York: Holt, Rinehart & Winston, 1985.

Spiegel, Alan. *James Agee and the Legend of Himself: A Critical Study.* Columbia: University of Missouri Press, 1998.

aging and folklore   In their study of humans and their traditions, folklorists are necessarily concerned with all stages of the life cycle.

Therefore, while some might regard the study of aging in its relation to folklore to be concentrated on the old, it is more fitting to say that all humans are part of the aging and maturation process.

Of course, a community's elders are important members of, and contributors to, its folklore. They are its culture bearers and the source of much of its wisdom. In their own experiences, seniors embody history, and their memories represent a treasure trove of lore. For this reason, oral historians have devoted a good deal of attention to interviews with older Americans. The nation's elders can help shape folk histories and promote intergenerational learning when they share their knowledge with younger members of the society. Their testimony lends the perspective of experience, as older citizens have firsthand knowledge of the greatest number of life's stages, transitions, and developmental landmarks. Oral histories and memory projects help preserve these understandings for generations to come.

Items of verbal lore, such as proverbs, can reveal a culture's attitudes toward aging. Sayings in use during conversation in America, such as "There is no fool like an old fool" and "You can't teach an old dog new tricks," suggest the nation's preoccupation with youth and anxiety about the aging process. Rather than portraying the society's elders as a source of wisdom, guidance, and example, the use of such expressions suggests that aging does not dignify individuals or add to their competence. Some of this perception of lost status through aging is likely due to the culture's dread of death and dying. Even in folk-influenced American literature, such as Washington Irving's "Rip Van Winkle," the author portrays aging as a process of loss.

Aging occurs throughout life, however, and so the full examination of aging's connection to folklore must attend to the full demographic spectrum. Its study yields insights into traditions, rites of passage, and landmarks that occur throughout the life course.

See also: DEATH, FOLKLORE IN EVERYDAY LIFE; HISTORY, FOLK; IRVING, WASHINGTON; ORAL HISTORY; PROVERBS; RITES OF PASSAGE; VAN WINKLE, RIP.

For Further Reading:

Ashliman, D. L. "Aging and Death in Folklore." University of Pittsburgh. Available online. URL: www.pitt.edu/-dash/aging.html. Accessed March 6, 2006.

Cutler, Neal E., Nancy A. Whitelaw, and Bonita L. Beattie. *American Perceptions of Aging in the 21st Century : A Myths and Realities of Aging Chartbook.* Washington, D.C.: National Council on the Aging, 2002.

Haber, Carole. *Beyond Sixty-five: The Dilemma of Old Age in America's Past.* New York: Cambridge University Press, 1983.

Johnston, Priscilla, ed. *Perspectives on Aging: Exploding the Myth.* Cambridge, Mass.: Ballinger, 1981.

Jones, Michael Owen, ed. *Putting Folklore to Use.* Lexington: University Press of Kentucky, 1994.

Kausler, Donald H., and Barry C. Kausler. *The Graying of America: An Encyclopedia of Aging, Health, Mind, and Behavior*. Urbana: University of Illinois Press, 2001.

Mullen, Patrick. *Listening to Old Voices: Folklore, Life Stories, and the Elderly*. Bloomington: Indiana University Press, 1992.

Shuldiner, David P. *Folklore, Culture, and Aging: A Research Guide*. Westport, Conn.: Greenwood, 1997.

Vennum, Thomas, ed. *Festival of American Folklife Program Book*. Washington, D.C.: Smithsonian Institution, 1984.

AIDS folklore AIDS folklore suggests that one function folklore can serve is to express the otherwise unspoken beliefs and misgivings of a population regarding its public health.

The challenges posed by the acquired immunodeficiency syndrome (AIDS) epidemic have inspired many people to reconsider their attitudes and behavior, especially as pertains to sexuality. Particularly because for some time researchers could not establish the source of AIDS and the manners in which human immunodeficiency virus (HIV) might be transmitted, Americans tended early on in the history of this condition to fashion their own explanations for the illness and its associated perils.

When illnesses spread rapidly and without a clear understanding of their epidemiological characteristics, popular explanations favor assignments of blame, however ill informed these initial judgments may be. Consider the lore once surrounding the figure Typhoid Mary, for instance. Many of the folk narratives surrounding AIDS concern theories regarding the causes and culpabilities in this modern health crisis. These tales, sometimes hurtful and accusatory, tend to target whole groups of people as implicated in a new health crisis. In some instances, the tales also posit outright conspiracies to infect people intentionally with the virus. While more is now known about how AIDS spreads and how people may protect themselves and their partners from infection, such folk explanations of the problem have not entirely receded.

In fact, a number of urban legends still circulate about AIDS. These legends include a story in which an individual knowingly infects someone with the virus through unprotected sex, and then leaves behind a message written with lipstick on the victim's bathroom mirror: "Welcome to the World of AIDS." Such tales not only express the teller's and listener's shared terror of AIDS, but also reveal apprehensions about moral conduct and risky behavior such as unprotected sex.

Because the initial outbreaks of AIDS were concentrated in historically disenfranchised populations such as homosexuals, people of color, and intravenous drug users, some Americans have felt justified in engaging in something akin to profiling in assessing the relative risks of contact with particular individuals. Whether warranted or not, such inferences can still be observed among people who are trying to estimate their risk of HIV infection. The persistence of these beliefs has also perpetuated the tendency to blame cultural groups for the health dangers involved in AIDS.

Despite the seriousness of the AIDS crisis, there is a category of folk humor devoted specifically to the fears and anxieties that surround the issue. Often, these stories and jokes reflect the teller's assumptions about the condition and its source. Homophobic elements are common in AIDS folklore and are especially prevalent in narratives offered anonymously, as is usually the case in Xerox/fax lore.

From conspiracy lore to urban legends, the AIDS crisis has yielded a whole range of folk expressions of dread and suspicion.

See also: CONSPIRACY FOLKLORE; DISABILITY AND FOLKLORE; FOLKLORE IN EVERYDAY LIFE; GAY/LESBIAN FOLKLORE; HUMOR, FOLK; LEGENDS, FOLK; MEDICINE, FOLK; PROTEST IN FOLKLORE; QUILT, AIDS; URBAN LEGENDS; XEROX/FAX FOLKLORE.

For Further Reading:

Goldstein, Diane E. *Once upon a Virus: AIDS Legends and Vernacular Risk Perception.* Logan: Utah State University Press, 2004.

Goodwin, Joseph. *More Man Than You'll Ever Be: Gay Folklore and Acculturation in Middle America.* Bloomington: Indiana University Press, 1989.

Patton, Cindy. *Inventing AIDS.* New York: Routledge, 1990.

Sontag, Susan. *AIDS and Its Metaphors.* New York: Farrar, Straus & Giroux, 1989.

AIDS Quilt   See QUILT, AIDS.

Alabama folklore   See AGEE, JAMES; APPALACHIAN FOLKLORE; CIVIL RIGHTS MOVEMENT; DOCUMENTARY; GERONIMO; OZARKS FOLKLORE; PARKS, ROSA; SOUTHERN REGIONAL FOLKLORE; WASHINGTON, BOOKER TALIAFERRO.

Alaska folklore   See EARP, WYATT BERRY STAMP; GHOST TOWNS; GOLD RUSH, THE; NORTHWESTERN REGIONAL FOLKLORE.

Alger, Horatio, Jr. (1832–1899)   Horatio Alger, Jr.'s name summons images of rags-to-riches stories in which poor boys rise to financial and social success through pluck, responsibility, and persistence.

As the author of more than 100 popular juvenile novels, Alger was a best-selling writer of his day. Although most of his titles remain out of print today, the message of his "strive and succeed" stories endures, and it continues to inform, however indirectly, the aspirations of many born to humble beginnings.

Alger himself was born in 1832 and, unlike the heroes of his pages, enjoyed sufficient privileges in youth to enable him to attend Harvard and cultivate his talents as a writer. He went on to Harvard Divinity School, emerging from that study to combine his work as a preacher with freelance efforts as a fledgling writer, establishing himself as the pastor of a Unitarian church in Cape Cod.

Amid allegations of undue familiarity with young men in his charge, Alger was forced out of the clergy but nonetheless sought a way to promote the religious ideals that first drew him to the spiritual life. Resituating himself for this purpose in New York City, Alger looked for a way to atone for his misconduct and exert a more positive influence on others.

Nineteenth-century New York afforded Alger a host of social ills to address through such good works. At that time, city children had to contend with poverty, child labor, crime, squalor, homelessness, and, in many cases, insufficient adult influence on their moral maturation. Many children were mistreated or abandoned by their parents. It was in this context that reformers established philanthropic ventures such as the Children's Aid Society, dedicated to securing the safety and affirming the worth of urban youth.

Alger traversed the streets of New York's slums, conversing with such waifs and reflecting on their future prospects. Convinced that one's outlook could do much to counteract worldly misfortune, Alger resolved to devote his work as a writer to promoting the values he felt most salutary to the salvation of these unfortunates. For adult readers, Alger hoped to expose the nature and magnitude of the problem. For young readers, he hoped to point toward its solution.

Hence, Alger's young male protagonists—newsboys, bootblacks, match boys, and the like—combine luck with industry to escape their unfortunate station as street urchins. In a sense, Alger's stories popularized the moral and ethical messages of earlier American writers such as Benjamin Franklin, whose autobiography espoused the practices of hard work and thrift. Through Alger's novels, a whole new generation of readers watched characters resist temptation and vice and, in this way, prevail through the consequences of sound values and prudent choices.

Alger's life ended in 1899, as the century his fiction characterized drew to a close. His writing's impact, however, would extend well beyond the 19th century. In recognition of the values his works represent, enthusiasts founded the Horatio Alger Association of Distinguished Heroes in 1947 and the Horatio Alger Society in 1961. These organizations celebrate the messages of Alger's fiction and applaud their realization in the lives of readers. In 1982, a commemorative 20-cent stamp acknowledged Alger by paying tribute to his ties to the historic urban figure of the newsboy.

Alger's influence on American culture remains pervasive, as frequent references to raising oneself "by the bootstraps" recall the struggles of his fiction's urban youth to reject vice, take responsibility for their own circumstance in life, and make the most of the nation's much-touted possibilities for social mobility.

See also: CITY FOLKLORE; FOLK HEROES/LEGENDARY FIGURES; FOLKLORE IN AMERICAN LITERATURE; FRANKLIN, BENJAMIN; LUCK/FORTUNE; NORTHEASTERN REGIONAL FOLKLORE; OCCUPATIONAL FOLKLORE; REGION, FOLK.

For Further Reading:

Hoyt, Edwin Palmer. *Horatio's Boys: The Life and Works of Horatio Alger, Jr.* Radnor, Pa.: Chilton Books, 1974.

Nackenoff, Carol. *The Fictional Republic: Horatio Alger and American Political Discourse.* New York: Oxford University Press, 1994.

Scharnhorst, Gary. *Horatio Alger, Jr.* Boston: Twayne, 1980.

————. *The Lost Life of Horatio Alger, Jr.* Bloomington: Indiana University Press, 1985.

Tebeel, John William. *From Rags to Riches: Horatio Alger, Jr. and the American Dream.* New York: Macmillan, 1963.

Allen, Ethan (1738–1789) Ethan Allen is a figure from Vermont folklore and military history, but he is best remembered as part of the state's initial formation.

Born in Connecticut in 1738, Allen matured to become a grassroots leader in New England and fought in the French and Indian Wars. He also helped start the Green Mountain Boys, a group who contested territorial disputes with New York and New Hampshire. During the American Revolution, Allen and the Green Mountain Boys served as soldiers. Their efforts helped defeat the British at Fort Ticonderoga, setting the stage for a pivotal victory at Saratoga. Allen served in the Continental Army, but his 1775 capture by the British caused him to miss portions of the war until he was released in a 1778 prisoner exchange. Before his death in 1789, Allen was also associated with Vermont's quest for statehood.

Allen is a prominent figure in local Vermont lore, heralded for his courage and effectiveness, especially in accounts appearing within literature for young people. In one such colorful tale, he is purported to have intervened in a chivalric manner when a woman felt reluctant to undergo dentistry. To reassure her that she would be safe, he had one of his own teeth pulled just to ease her fears. Allen's Burlington, Vermont, residence has been preserved as a historic site. In addition, in the 1890s, a Colchester and Essex, Vermont, fort was named in his honor. Today, the area is maintained as an attraction, the Fort Ethan Allen Historic District.

Ethan Allen lives on in the stories told and tributes paid to this early American soldier and figure associated with the Revolutionary War era.

See also: ATTUCKS, CRISPUS; FOLK HEROES/LEGENDARY FIGURES; HISTORICAL EVENTS; NORTHEASTERN REGIONAL FOLKLORE; REGION, FOLK; REVOLUTIONARY WAR.

For Further Reading:

Bellesiles, Michael A. *Revolutionary Outlaws: Ethan Allen and the Struggle for Independence on the Early American Plain.* Charlottesville: University Press of Virginia, 1993.

Coffin, Tristram Potter. *Uncertain Glory: Folklore and the American Revolution.* Detroit: Folklore Associates, 1971.

De Puy, Henry W. *Ethan Allen and the Green-Mountain Heroes of '76, with a Sketch of the Early*

History of Vermont. Freeport, N.Y.: Books for Libraries Press, 1970.

Haugen, Brenda. *Ethan Allen: Green Mountain Rebel.* Minneapolis: Compass Point Books, 2005.

Jellison, Charles A. *Ethan Allen: Frontier Rebel.* Syracuse, N.Y.: Syracuse University Press, 1969.

Allen, Paula Gunn (1939–) As a writer and leading scholar of Native American literature, Paula Gunn Allen is best known for her essays and nonfiction, although she has also published several volumes of poetry and a novel.

Allen was born in 1939 in Cubero, New Mexico. Before embarking on her career as an educator and critic, she earned a B.A. and M.F.A. from the University of Oregon (1966, 1968), and a Ph.D. from the University of New Mexico (1975). She has since worked as a college professor, most recently as professor of Native American studies and ethnic studies at the University of California, Los Angeles.

Paula Gunn Allen's writings and teachings draw heavily from Native American traditions, from rituals to myths. Allen portrays not only the importance of the past, but the continuing need to reinvent such cultural legacies. In order for such survivals to retain their resonance, the cultural references need to be renewed and reinvigorated for the contemporary situation. She refers to this process as "remythologizing." Taking her cues from her literary colleague Audre Lorde, who entitled her autobiography *Zami: A New Spelling of My Name; A Biomythography* (1983), Allen engages in corresponding processes of recovery she has described as family biomythography.

In both her literary and her scholarly presentations, Allen incorporates a great deal of Native American lore. She asks her readers to recognize (and/or remember) the rich web of cultural meanings that precede the modern writer's life. Typically, she also challenges readers to rethink their understandings of Native American history and life. One example of such an effort is Allen's

Grandmothers of the Light: A Medicine Woman's Sourcebook (1991), in which she engages in retellings of mythic tales and legends.

Allen's 1983 novel, *The Woman Who Owned the Shadows*, is a substantial work. It pieces together various literary forms and cultural narratives to convey the life story of its central character, Ephanie Atencio. The protagonist struggles to unify both aspects of her family heritage, Spanish and Indian. The novel is moreover a story of personal discovery, as Ephanie works to achieve self-knowledge and self-acceptance.

As a scholar, Allen is among the most accomplished analysts of Native American literature and culture. She is particularly interested in feminist issues, taking inspiration from matrilineal societies' emphasis on understanding one's identity as derived from one's mother and other female ancestors. Allen's *Sacred Hoop: Recovery of the Feminine in American Indian Traditions* (1986) represents her commitment to venerating the contributions of women to Native American culture.

A recent volume, *Pocahontas: Medicine Woman, Spy, Entrepreneur, Diplomat* (2003), investigates both the experiences and the perceptions of one of the most widely known women from the Native American past. Never one to shrink from controversy, Allen takes on the legends surrounding Pocahontas, most of which figure her as a tragic figure.

Allen's other works include several books of poetry and numerous edited anthologies. She has helped create a climate in which the work of other Native American women writers may be read and valued. Beneficiaries of this effort include Leslie Marmon Silko, Louise Erdrich, Joy Harjo, and Linda Hogan.

Paula Gunn Allen's ability to reclaim and extend the cultural survivals of Native America make her work of particular interest to folklorists, who find in her poems, novels, and essays a resource for study and understanding. From her attention to worldview, spirituality, and healing practices, readers gain a greater awareness of the complex and robust cultural inheritance of today's Native American writers.

See also: CREATION/ORIGIN STORIES; FOLK-LORE IN AMERICAN LITERATURE; MEDICINE, FOLK; NATIVE AMERICAN FOLKLORE; POCA-HONTAS.

For Further Reading:
Allen, Paula Gunn. *Grandmothers of the Light: A Medicine Woman's Sourcebook.* Boston: Beacon Press, 1991.
———. *Pocahontas: Medicine Woman, Spy, Entrepreneur, Diplomat.* San Francisco: HarperSanFrancisco, 2003.
———. *The Sacred Hoop: Recovering the Feminine in American Indian Traditions.* Boston: Beacon Press, 1986.
Allen, Paula Gunn, ed. *Spider Woman's Granddaughters: Traditional Tales and Contemporary Writing by Native American Women.* Boston: Beacon Press, 1989.
Allen, Paula Gunn. *The Woman Who Owned the Shadows.* San Francisco: Spinsters, Ink, 1983.
Hanson, Elizabeth. *Paula Gunn Allen.* Boise, Idaho: Boise State University, 1990.
Keating, AnaLouise. *Women Reading Women Writing: Self-Invention in Paula Gunn Allen, Gloria Anzaldúa, and Audre Lorde.* Philadelphia: Temple University Press, 1996.

All Fools' Day   See APRIL FOOL'S DAY.

All Hallows' Eve   See HALLOWEEN/ALL HALLOWS' EVE.

almanacs   See FRANKLIN, BENJAMIN; WEATHER FOLKLORE.

Americana   See INDEPENDENCE DAY/FOURTH OF JULY; LIBERTY, MISS; ROSS, BETSY; UNCLE SAM.

American Folk Art Museum   See ART, FOLK; CRAFTS, FOLK.

American Folklife Center   As established in 1976 by United States Public Law 94-201, the American Folklife Center has the charge of documenting, preserving, and presenting American folklife. In 1998, Congress granted a permanent authorization for the American Folklife Center to continue its important work.

The center receives supervision from the librarian of Congress in Washington, D.C. It also accepts direction from a board of trustees. This body's members are appointed by agreement among the president, the librarian of Congress, and Congress.

The American Folklife Center advances its mission through a variety of programs and services. These activities include supporting community organizations, educators, and government agencies. The center is involved in concerts, conferences, lectures, publications, public programs, equipment loans, and online outreach.

Within the purview of the American Folklife Center is the Archive of Folk Culture, established in 1928 at the Library of Congress in Washington, D.C. This resource features an extensive archive of American field materials, as well as recordings of songs and performances.

See also: AMERICAN FOLKLIFE PRESERVATION ACT; ARCHIVE OF FOLK CULTURE; FOLKLIFE; FOLKLIFE MOVEMENT; FOLKLORE; FOLKLORE ARCHIVES; HISTORIC PRESERVATION; MUSEUMS, FOLK; PUBLIC FOLKLORE.

For Further Reading:
American Folklife Center. American Folklife Center. Available online. URL: http://www.loc.gov/folklife/. Accessed February 17, 2006.
Lloyd, Timothy, and Hillary Glatt. *Folklife Resources in the Library of Congress.* Washington, D.C.: American Folklife Center, Library of Congress, 1994.
Zumwalt, Rosemary. *American Folkloristics: The Literary and Anthropological Roots.* Berkeley: University of California Press, 1982.

American Folklife Preservation Act The American Folklife Preservation Act of 1976, also known as Public Law 94-201, has played an important part in protecting the nation's folk heritage.

For the purposes of this law, the members of Congress defined American folklife as

the traditional expressive culture shared within the various groups in the United States: familial, ethnic, occupational, religious, regional, expressive culture includes a wide range of creative and symbolic forms such as custom, belief, technical skill, language, literature, art, architecture, music, play, dance, drama, ritual, pageantry, handicrafts; these expressions are mainly learned orally, by imitation, or in performance, and are generally maintained without benefit of formal instruction or institutional direction.

Upon the basis of this definition, the congressional mandate was designed to recognize the importance of folklife to the nation's vitality and history.

One chief outcome of the American Folklife Preservation Act was establishment of the American Folklife Center at the Library of Congress in Washington, D.C. The center was placed under the guidance of the librarian of Congress, in consultation with a government-appointed board of trustees.

The American Folklife Center is a leader in folklife scholarship in terms of preservation, conservation, and dissemination. From providing an appropriate home to the spoken- and sounded-word analog recordings of the Archive of Folk Culture, established in 1928, to engaging with digital and Web projects reflecting the possibilities of new media for their mission, the American Folklife Center protects and promotes folklife as a vital national resource.

Legislation has established the American Folklife Center as a permanent facility, dedicated to demonstrating the value of folk traditions to America's thriving.

See also: AMERICAN FOLKLIFE CENTER; ARCHIVE OF FOLK CULTURE; FOLKLIFE; FOLKLIFE MOVEMENT; HISTORIC PRESERVATION; LIVING HISTORY MUSEUMS; PUBLIC FOLKLORE.

For Further Reading:
American Folklife Center. About the American Folklife Center. Available online. URL: http://www.loc.gov/folklife/aboutafc.html. Accessed February 17, 2006.
American Folklife Center. American Folklife: A Commonwealth of Cultures. Available online. URL: http://www.loc.gov/folklife/cwc/. Accessed February 17, 2006.
American Folklife Center. The Creation of the American Folklife Center. Available online. URL: http://www.loc.gov/folklife/public_law.html. Accessed February 17, 2006.

American Folklore Society The American Folklore Society (AFS) is the central professional association of persons engaged in the study of American folklore.

The organization began in 1888. Its founders included such leaders in the field as Francis James Child, Franz Boas, Daniel Garrison Brinton, and William Wells Newell. The central purpose of this organization is to promote the systematic and scientific investigation of folklore. American writers such as Samuel Langhorne Clemens, Joel Chandler Harris, and George Washington Cable became members of the AFS during their careers, signaling their enthusiasm for folklore and its study.

The American Folklore Society fulfills its organizational mission through a wide range of professional activities, including sponsorship of publications exemplifying the group's exacting standards of academic rigor. The American Folklore Society publishes the *Journal of American Folklore*, a quarterly periodical that has been the premier source on the subject of American folklore since 1888; the *American Folklore Society*

Newsletter, issued bimonthly since 1971; the *Centennial Index;* and a multitude of scholarly monographs.

In addition to these publishing projects, the American Folklore Society supports folklore research through such means as interest groups, conferences, workshops, prize competitions, and other programs.

The American Folklore Society also maintains a Web site, which features online resources and position statements on issues of consequence for the group's more than 2,200 members worldwide, such as human subjects and ethnographic research, professional ethics, and compensation for self-employed folklorists.

See also: AMERICAN FOLKLIFE CENTER; BRER RABBIT; CABLE, WASHINGTON GEORGE; CLEMENS, SAMUEL LANGHORNE; ETHICS IN FOLKLORE; FOLKLORE; FOLKLORE STUDIES; HARRIS, JOEL CHANDLER; REMUS, UNCLE.

For Further Reading:

American Folklore Society. About the American Folklore Society. Available online. URL: http://afsnet.org/aboutAFS/aboutAFS.cfm. Accessed March 10, 2006.

Clements, William, ed. *One Hundred Years of American Folklore Studies: A Conceptual History.* Washington, D.C.: American Folklore Society, 1988.

Dwyer-Shick, Susan. "The American Folklore Society and Folklore Research in America, 1888–1940." Ph.D. diss., University of Pennsylvania, 1979.

Newell, William Wells. "On the Field and Work of a Journal of American Folk-Lore," *Journal of American Folklore* 1, no. 1 (spring 1888): 1–7.

Zumwalt, Rosemary. *American Folklore Scholarship: A Dialogue of Dissent.* Bloomington: Indiana University Press, 1988.

American Indian folklore See NATIVE AMERICAN FOLKLORE.

American Memory Project The American Memory Project (AMP) is an electronic service and resource provided by the U.S. Library of Congress.

The Memory Project is a platform for historical collections in the National Digital Library and is available to users as an online gateway through the Internet. Through this mechanism, the American Memory Project overcomes the barriers of distance and other impediments to public access to the nation's rich heritage.

By scanning and digitizing items relating to the history and culture of the United States, staff of the project offer to visitors to their Web site ready and convenient access to a wide range of source material for teaching and learning. At present, the electronic archive provides users with more than 7 million digital items of interest to American culture researchers.

In addition to gratifying public interest, this vast resource gives the public unprecedented opportunities to view primary historical documents from their computers at home, school, or elsewhere. While the Library of Congress has always opened its doors to the American people, the American Memory Project makes virtual visits possible for a dramatically larger group of people, including those unable to travel to Washington, D.C., to examine the evidence in person.

In this way, individuals have the chance to see the cultural materials for themselves and make their own firsthand critical assessments of what those items mean and what they help one understand about the American past. More than 100 distinct collections of documents are featured there. The material available through the American Memory Project includes written and pictorial evidence. The AMP makes the richness and diversity of the Library of Congress collections work to the benefit of more constituents.

For the folklore researcher, such items inform the study of folk culture, situate folk traditions within a wider context, and hold the potential to inspire folklorists in designing projects.

See also: AMERICAN FOLKLIFE CENTER; AMERICAN FOLKLIFE PRESERVATION ACT; CUL-

TURE, FOLK; FOLKLIFE; FOLKLIFE MOVEMENT; FOLKLORE; MUSEUMS, FOLK.

For Further Reading:

Arms, C. R. "Available and Useful: OAI at the Library of Congress," *Library Hi Tech* 21, no. 2 (June 25, 2003): 29–40.
Library of Congress/American Folklore Center. September 11, 2001, Documentary Project. Available online. URL: http://memory.loc.gov/ammem/collections/911_archive. Accessed March 10, 2006.
Library of Congress. American Memory Project. Available online. URL: http://memory.loc.gov/ammem/ammemhome.html. Accessed March 10, 2006.
Meeks, Brock. "The Crown Jewels of Content Go Digital," *InterActive Week* 1, no. 1 (October 10, 1994): 62.
Rottman, F. K. "History Comes Alive: The American Memory Project," *School Library Journal* 38, no. 11 (November 1992): 33–36.
Tsou, Judy. "American Memory: Historical Collections for the National Digital Library," *Notes* 57, no. 12 (December 2000): 424–431.

American Red Cross See BARTON, CLARA.

American Revolution See REVOLUTIONARY WAR.

Amish folklore See PENNSYLVANIA DUTCH/PENNSYLVANIA GERMAN FOLKLORE.

amulet See MAGIC.

Anansi (legendary) The name *Anansi* refers to the West African, Central African, and African diasporic character of a spider, one who also appears in American folk tales.

Anansi, or Aunt Nancy, as the character is also called, functions as a trickster figure within traditional animal tales. Although typically taking the form of a spider, Anansi is a shape shifter and so can transform himself into other creatures, such as a rabbit, as the situation demands. It is believed that Anansi is a precursor for the figure of Brer Rabbit in the Uncle Remus tales collected by Joel Chandler Harris.

Anansi tales typically portray battles of wits between the spider and other forces, whether human or animal. He marshals all his resources, including physical advantages, wile, and a little magic now and then, to prevail over an opponent. It should be noted, however, that Anansi does not always win. What does remain consistent across the tales is the fundamental nature of the character placed at their center. Anansi is a self-interested being who often considers himself above or outside social strictures or moral standards.

In one of the better known Anansi tales, the spider encounters another figure from folklore, Tar Baby. As the story goes, a farmer became so outraged by Anansi's pilfering from his garden that he placed a figure made of tar there to deter Anansi's theft. The next time Anansi visits the farmer's garden, the spider greets the Tar Baby. When the salutation is not returned, Anansi strikes the tar figure and in efforts to extricate himself, only becomes more firmly stuck to the Tar Baby. Through this device, the farmer catches Anansi and then beats him to the ground. It is said that this beating explains how spiders got their flat shape.

Although the story of Anansi and the Tar Baby represents a tale in which Anansi's efforts in battle are unsuccessful, many other stories establish Anansi as a capable opponent.

In addition to providing entertainment, the Anansi stories present to readers fictional situations in which a small and seemingly helpless creature often triumphs over a larger and apparently more powerful force or foe. It is not difficult to imagine why such stories might have held great appeal for American slaves, who found in the trickster a model for subversive victory.

See also: AFRICAN-AMERICAN FOLKLORE; ANIMALS; BRER RABBIT; CHANGELINGS; FOLK

HEROES/LEGENDARY FIGURES; FOLKTALES; HARRIS, JOEL CHANDLER; REMUS, UNCLE; TAR BABY; TRICKSTER.

For Further Reading:
Bascom, William. *African Folktales in the New World.* Bloomington: Indiana University Press, 1992.
Bennett, Martin. *West African Trickster Tales.* Oxford: Oxford University Press, 1994.
Davidson, Hilda. *The Hero in Tradition and Folklore.* London: Folklore Society, 1984.
Jekyll, Walter. *Jamaican Song and Story: Annancy Stories, Digging Sings, Ring Tunes, and Dancing Tunes.* New York: Dover, 1966.
McDermott, Gerald. *Anansi the Spider: A Tale from the Ashanti.* New York: Holt, Rinehart & Winston, 1972.
Makhanlall, David. *Brer Anansi Strikes Again!* Glasgow: Blackie, 1976.

Andersen, Hans Christian (1805–1875) The Danish author Hans Christian Andersen has become closely associated with the literary genre of the fairy tale.

Although Andersen also wrote plays and novels, it is his classic retellings of traditional stories that have earned him a place in literature and folklore. He is responsible for the familiarity of many such tales, including "The Little Mermaid," "Inchworm," "The Princess and the Pea," "The Ugly Duckling," "The Emperor's New Clothes," and "Thumbelina." Andersen was less concerned to preserve folktales intact than to find in them inspiration for his own literary imagination. His versions are remarkable for the presence of an overt narrator to provide audience members with direction and comment.

The contributions of Hans Christian Andersen to world literature, but in particular children's works, are recognized in a variety of ways today. These tributes include the prestigious children's literature award that bears his name, the Andersen Medal, and the fact that each year, International Children's Book Day is observed on Andersen's birthday, April 2. The beloved storyteller was also the focus of a 1952 feature-length film, *Hans Christian Andersen*, in which Danny Kaye played the storyteller.

Hans Christian Andersen's retellings of classic tales have had remarkable longevity, and Andersen's name still conjures images of the magical realm of fairy tales, where anything can happen and audiences return again and again, trusting that it will.

See also: CHILDREN'S FOLKLORE; "EMPEROR'S NEW CLOTHES, THE"; FABLES; FOLKLORE IN AMERICAN LITERATURE; "MERMAID, THE LITTLE"; "PRINCESS AND THE PEA, THE"; "UGLY DUCKLING, THE".

For Further Reading:
Bredsdorff, Elias. *Hans Christian Andersen: An Introduction to His Life and Works.* Copenhagen: Hans Reitzels Forlag, 1987.
Mylius, Johan de, Aage Jorgensen, and Viggo Hjornager Pedersen, eds. *Hans Christian Andersen: A Poet in Time.* Odense: Odense University Press, 1999.
Rossel, Sven Hakon, ed. *Hans Christian Andersen: Danish Writer and Citizen of the World.* Amsterdam: Rodopi, 1996.
Wullschlager, Jackie. *Hans Christian Andersen: The Life of a Storyteller.* Chicago: University of Chicago Press, 2002.

"Androcles and the Lion" (legendary) "Androcles and the Lion" is Aesop's beloved fable in which a man forges an unlikely alliance with a lion, a friendship that in turn produces another unexpected result.

Androcles is a mistreated Christian slave in Rome. With hopes of eluding his cruel master, the slave becomes a fugitive. In his flight from captivity, Androcles loses his way in the forest. While trying to find a path to liberty, he encounters a lion. Although his first impulse is to retreat from the beast, somehow Androcles manages to discern that the lion is too sorely distressed to pose an immediate danger to him. After assessing the lion's wound, he manages to relieve the creature from pain by removing a thorn buried in its paw. The lion, of course, is grateful to be rid of the thorn, and they part amicably, as Androcles continues on his way.

Subsequently, Androcles is seized and returned to face the consequences with the emperor. In punishment for his escape, Androcles is cast before a lion in the Coliseum. As it happens, the lion charged with tormenting Androcles on this occasion turns out to be the same creature to whom he had extended the earlier kindness. Recognizing in Androcles the very slave who had plucked the painful thorn from his paw, the lion spares him. The tale ends agreeably for both title characters, as the lion is returned to the forest and Androcles is released.

As with other of Aesop's fables, "Androcles and the Lion" is a survival of earlier folklore, but one that is nonetheless embraced within American culture. It is frequently featured in collections and performances directed to young audiences. Children find delight in the story's surprising events and satisfying outcome.

This story culminates in the framing of a moral or lesson, a plot characteristic and narrative strategy commonly associated with the genre of fables. Androcles owes his very survival to the sound values he displayed with a prior deed, but one he never supposed would prove his salvation. As is so often the case in fables, virtuous behavior, especially in instances when it would be just as easy, if not easier, to conduct oneself otherwise, is the hallmark of good character.

Indeed, it is little wonder that readers appreciate a figure capable of such conduct. Androcles demonstrates an admirable quality in his ability to empathize even with a creature that might pose a physical threat to him. In addition, Androcles is willing to act on that insight, even when that good deed may prove to be to his detriment. He pauses, even in his haste to find freedom, to perform an act of benevolence toward

the lion. He does so even though he might have no reason to expect to see the creature again. For this act of compassion, Androcles is ultimately well rewarded.

This tale has undergone many retellings, most notably an adaptation for the stage by the acclaimed author and dramatist George Bernard Shaw. Aesop's fables have also been arranged in verse and recast as comic tales.

Whatever its version, the basic story of "Androcles and the Lion" delivers a compassionate message that selfless acts matter, and that they will not go unrecognized, even if one cannot at the moment readily imagine how.

See also: ANIMALS; CHILDREN'S FOLKLORE; FABLES; FOLKTALES; SLAVERY.

For Further Reading:

Bettelheim, Bruno. *The Uses of Enchantment: The Meaning and Importance of Fairy Tales.* New York: Knopf, 1976.

French, Vivian. *Aesop's Funky Fables.* New York: Viking, 1998.

Paxton, Tom. *Androcles and the Lion, and Other Aesop's Fables Retold in Verse.* New York: Morrow Junior Books, 1991.

Zafiropoulos, Christos. *Ethics in Aesop's Fables: The Augustana Collection.* Boston: Brill, 2001.

Anglo-American folklore The folklore of Anglo-Americans has a long and complex history.

During the 17th century, this group accounted for the largest population of settlers. Anglo-Americans took many practices, customs, and traditions with them to the New World. It proved a complicated legacy, however, during the Revolutionary War period, when Americans prided themselves on rejecting Britain and its claim to just authority over the colonies. For this reason, Anglo heritage was something of a deficit and became understated in favor of an allegiance to formation of a new nation. The War of 1812 also placed America and England at odds. It would not be until World War I that the

United States and the United Kingdom would become allies, leading to friendlier relations between the nations.

Both because Anglo-Americans were such a dominant force in early America, and because they downplayed British heritage at times when American patriotism seemed to require it, they have sometimes been described as invisible immigrants. Even these days, many Anglo-Americans do not live in a manner that seems mindful of their cultural heritage. They tend not to be self-consciously traditional, understanding their own ways as somehow generic. Anglo-Americans are given to thinking they are somehow less ethnic than other cultural groups in the United States. They may not self-identify as British at all, instead calling themselves Americans by heritage.

There are many ways in which American culture is indebted to British traditions, from Christmas carol singing to aspects of the legal system. Even American folklore owes much to Anglo-American practices. Indeed, when the American Folklore Society was formed in 1888, one of its three main objectives was to collect and study Old English lore. For instance, Appalachian culture has been said to derive from British folk culture.

Even if they do not view themselves as having a distinct cultural identity, Anglo-Americans have an extensive folklore of their own.

See also: AMERICAN FOLKLORE SOCIETY; APPALACHIAN FOLKLORE; BALLADS; CHRISTMAS; CULTURAL GROUPS; ETHNICITY; HILLBILLIES; IMMIGRATION AND FOLKLORE; IRISH-AMERICAN FOLKLORE; REVOLUTIONARY WAR; SCOTTISH-AMERICAN FOLKLORE.

For Further Reading:

Abrahams, Roger, and George Foss. *Anglo-American Folksong Style*. Englewood Cliffs, N.J.: Prentice-Hall, 1968.

Block, Ruth. *Gender and Morality in Anglo-American Culture, 1650–1800*. Berkeley: University of California Press, 2003.

Dugaw, Dianne, ed. *The Anglo-American Ballad: A Folklore Casebook*. New York: Garland, 1995.

Erickson, Charlotte. *Invisible Immigrants: The Adaptation of English and Scottish Immigrants in Nineteenth-Century America*. Coral Gables, Fla.: University of Miami Press, 1972.

Fischer, David Hackett. *Albion's Seed: Four British Folkways in America*. New York: Oxford University Press, 1989.

Walsh, S. Padraig. *Anglo-American General Encyclopedias: A Historical Bibliography, 1703–1967*. New York: Bowker, 1968.

Whisnaut, David. *All That Is Native and Fine: The Politics of Culture in an American Region*. Chapel Hill: University of North Carolina Press, 1983.

animals   Animals populate many folk genres, from fables to proverbs, often serving as the protagonists of such narratives.

Perhaps the best-known American animal narrative genre is the tale. Recent analysts of African-American folktales have interpreted the form's functions variously. Some see folktales as vehicles for self-affirmation, social protest, and psychological release. Others see folktales as reiterating, inculcating, and complementing cultural values, although many would warn against too literal an interpretation of values as depicted in the stories, because of their playful and frequently ironic tone. For instance, many scholars believe that animal tales, and the paradigms those tales provide, had their origin in substitutions of animal names for specific people's names. A literal approach, then, could mask or miss important subtextual meanings of such texts.

In addition to animal tales, Americans share many animal fables. Within these fables, animals are the primary or sole characters and often appear in personified form. When that is the case, although the animals may retain the appearance of creatures, they also possess attributes or abilities of their human counterparts, such as the power of speech. In this way, animals stand in for humans in the unfolding stories. Accordingly, the animals featured in fables may be selected for their characteristic properties, such as rabbits for speed or pigs for greed.

Likely the most famous of all fabulists was Aesop, a legendary figure of sixth-century Greece. Just as the best-known fairy tales in the United States are the Grimm brothers' tales, the most familiar fables are those of Aesop. Aesop's fables, although not American, are commonly told to American children. Among the fables attributed to Aesop are "Androcles and the Lion," "The Boy Who Cried Wolf," "The Golden Goose," and "The Tortoise and the Hare." All provide apt examples of the way fables transmit a lesson as well as a plot and for that reason have long been used to teach precepts to children.

Another name associated with animal fables is America's Joel Chandler Harris. Harris became known for collecting and retelling in print a category of African-American orally transmitted folktales known as Uncle Remus stories. In published form, these animal tales were based on oral narratives documented by the journalist turned folklorist Joel Chandler Harris. Harris, as a member of the American Folklore Society, sought to record the dialect stories told by slaves. He published his work under the guise of a fictional narrator figure who is quoting the accounts of the storyteller Uncle Remus.

Animal figures pervade American folklore, in fables to legends. Mythological and mysterious creatures populate animal legends and lore. Examples include Bigfoot, werewolves, mermaids, and changelings. Folk humor in America includes many jokes involving animals. Children's stories, both oral and written, feature animals. Characters such as Chicken Little, the Three Pigs, Goldilocks and the Three Bears, the Three Billy Goats Gruff, and the Ugly Duckling appear in these stories. American literature is also replete with animal characters and figures, most notably Herman Melville's epic story of the white whale, *Moby-Dick*. Animals figure in many of the nation's celebrations, including the stork with newborn babies, the Thanksgiving turkey, and the weather lore surrounding Groundhog Day. Finally, animals function as symbols throughout American culture, from the patriotic image of the bald eagle

to the animals employed as mascots for sports teams.

Whether used as symbols of human characters or for their own attributes, animals appear throughout American folk narratives.

See also: Anansi; Andersen, Hans Christian; "Androcles and the Lion"; Babe the Blue Ox; beliefs, folk; Bigfoot/Sasquatch; "Boy Who Cried Wolf, The"; Brer Rabbit; changelings; "Chicken Little"; childbearing/pregnancy; Colonial Williamsburg; Coyote; Easter; Easter Bunny; fables; fairy tales; folklore in everyday life; folktales; Frog Prince/Frog King; "Golden Goose, The"; Groundhog Day; Loup-Garou; Harris, Joel Chandler; Melville, Herman; mermaids; "Mermaid, The Little"; monsters; myths, folk; Pecos Bill; "Pied Piper of Hamelin, The"; proverbs; Remus, Uncle; rodeo; Silko, Leslie Marmon; "Sleeping Beauty"; stork, the; "Three Bears, Goldilocks and the"; "Three Billy Goats Gruff, The"; "Three Little Pigs, The"; "Tortoise and the Hare, The"; trickster; "Ugly Duckling, The"; weather folklore; werewolf; witchcraft, Salem.

For Further Reading:

Dorson, Richard. *Man and Beast in American Comic Legend.* Bloomington: Indiana University Press, 1982.

Gillespie, Angus K., and Jay Mechling, eds. *American Wildlife in Symbol and Story.* Knoxville: University of Tennessee Press, 1987.

Ilomäki, Henni. "Animals in People's Mind and in the Language of Folklore," *Folklore: Electronic Journal of Folklore* 21 (August 2002): 92–100.

Porter, Joshua R., and William M. S. Russell. *Animals in Folklore.* Totowa, N.J.: Brewer, Rowman & Littlefield, 1978.

Stoutenberg, Adrien. *American Tall-Tale Animals.* New York: Viking Press, 1968.

anniversaries Anniversaries mark the date of prior significant events, including private occasions such as weddings and public commemorations such as key dates in history. These days of memory may be festive or solemn, but all attempt to measure the lasting impact of past human events for Americans today.

Dates of marriage are the anniversaries most widely celebrated in the United States, with spouses recognizing the wedding date as a means of honoring the interval of years since they began married life. Typical anniversary customs include the husband and wife's dining out and exchanging gifts. Other friends and family members may also pay tribute, particularly at landmark anniversaries such as the 25th, 50th, and 75th. The traditional practice for wedding anniversary gifts involves selecting presents fashioned of specific material corresponding to the number of years a couple has been married: paper for the first anniversary, wood for the fifth, tin for the 10th, crystal for the 15th, china for the 20th, and so forth. As the marriage grows in length, the gifts increase in monetary value.

Adherence to this anniversary custom has loosened over the years, however, and relatively few Americans today remember the proper gift category for a particular wedding anniversary. This custom, however, remains the basis for the still-common reference to the 25th year as the silver anniversary, the 50th year as the gold anniversary, and the 75th as the diamond anniversary.

A counterpart list, reflecting a modernization of the gift tradition, calls for clocks for the first anniversary, silverware for the fifth anniversary, diamond for the 10th anniversary, watches for the 15th, platinum for the 20th, and so on. These updates may coincide with the rise in American divorce rates, as the suggested modern gifts attach a higher monetary value for years of married life, such as china as the gift for the second year rather than the 20th. At the same time, the modern list reflects a measure of optimism in terms of its implication of longer life expectancies. Whereas the traditional list culminates in the 75th anniversary, its modern counterpart projects gift possibilities through the 100th year

of married life, for which a 10-carat diamond is suggested as appropriate.

Whether the rite of passage represents a private celebration of wedded life or another, more public occasion marking a span of years since a key event in the nation's history, anniversaries seek to recall the importance of such moments and to stimulate reflection on their influence in subsequent years.

See also: FAMILY FOLKLORE; HOLIDAYS/ OBSERVANCES; RITES OF PASSAGE; RITUALS, FOLK; WEDDING/MARRIAGE FOLKLORE.

For Further Reading:

Chicago Public Library Information Center. Wedding Anniversaries Gift List. Available online. URL: http://www.chipublib.org/008subject/ 005genref/giswedding.html. Accessed February 17, 2006.

Cohen, Hennig, and Tristram Potter Coffin, eds. *The Folklore of American Holidays.* Detroit: Gale, 1987.

Cotner, June, ed. *Wedding Blessings: Prayers and Poems Celebrating Love, Marriage, and Anniversaries.* New York: Broadway Books, 2003.

Hazeltine, Mary Emogene. *Anniversaries and Holidays, A Calendar of Days and How to Observe Them.* Chicago: American Library Association, 1944.

Myers, Robert. *Celebrations: The Complete Book of American Holidays.* Garden City, N.Y.: Doubleday, 1972.

Ray, Rayburn. *Wedding Anniversary Idea Book: A Guide to Celebrating Wedding Anniversaries.* Brentwood, Tenn.: JM Publications, 1985.

Santino, Jack. *All Around the Year: Holidays and Celebrations in American Life.* Urbana: University of Illinois Press, 1994.

The World Almanac and Books of Facts. Mahwah, N.J.: World Almanac Books, 1997.

Anthony, Susan Brownell (1820–1906) Susan Brownell Anthony was born on February 15, 1820, in Massachusetts. She was Quaker educated, and while she was growing up, her progressive family hosted such reformers as Frederick Douglass. Anthony joined the faculty at a Quaker seminary and subsequently became a school headmistress. In her late 20s, Anthony became actively involved in the causes that would make her both famous and notorious: abolition, pacifism, women's rights, women's suffrage, and labor rights.

Early on, Anthony championed the cause of women's rights. In 1848, she attended the historic Seneca Falls Convention. In 1868, she helped found *Revolution*, an advocacy newspaper. She fought for constitutional standing for women, including the right to cast ballots in elections. Toward this end, she was instrumental in the formation of many organizations: the American Equal Rights Association (1866), the National Woman Suffrage Association (1869), and the International Council of Women (1888). In service of the goal of gaining the franchise for women, Anthony contended that the Constitution already provided that right. Probably her single most noteworthy act of protest, however, was her decision to test that interpretation by casting a ballot in the 1872 presidential election. For this offense, Anthony was convicted and fined. She neither paid the sum nor was pursued for nonpayment. Working in partnership with Elizabeth Cady Stanton, a skilled orator, Anthony advanced the cause of women, even if she would not live long enough to be welcomed at a polling place.

While Susan B. Anthony is most closely associated with women's causes, she actively promoted a whole host of political convictions. For example, Anthony was also an advocate for the abolition of U.S. slavery. During the Civil War, she helped organize the Women's Loyal National League, a populist movement for emancipation. She promoted unionization for laborers and sought equal pay for equal work. Later, she emerged as an opponent of war.

Over the years, Anthony's perspectives on equality have proved controversial on several levels. In her own era, the notion that women were to be accorded proportionate privileges to men's was in itself offensive to many. In the years since Anthony's 1906 death, readers of her works and papers have also questioned how inclusively the activist envisioned such equality. Some have been troubled, for example, by disparaging comments about immigrants and people of color. In particular, Anthony took exception to the Fourteenth Amendment's granting of the vote to African-American men while white women remained disenfranchised.

Whatever the concerns about her social views, however, Anthony continues to be celebrated for her leadership and accomplishments. Along with her counterparts in the cause, such as Elizabeth Cady Stanton and Sojourner Truth, Susan B. Anthony has come to represent the historic struggle for the rights of American women. On February 15 each year, many celebrate the anniversary of Anthony's birth. At the Susan B. Anthony House in Rochester, New York, travelers may visit the National Historic Landmark, both residence and site of Anthony's arrest. In fact, a nine-block area around that house has been designated as a historic district and maintained in the manner of a 19th-century neighborhood. Anthony has appeared as a reference or a character in countless narratives, including Gertrude Stein's play *The Mother of Us All*. In 1979, the U.S. Mint debuted a dollar coin commemorating Anthony's life and work.

Susan Brownell Anthony, better known as Susan B. Anthony, is an icon in the history of American reform, and her contributions to the status of the nation's women are still celebrated today.

See also: Civil Rights movement; Civil War; Douglass, Frederick; folk heroes/ legendary figures; gender and folklore; Labor Day; occupational folklore; politics and folklore; protest and folklore; Quaker folklore; slavery; Stanton, Elizabeth Cady; Truth, Sojourner; women's movement; women's suffrage.

For Further Reading:

Anthony, Susan B., and Ida Husted Harper, eds. *History of Woman Suffrage*. Rochester, N.Y.: Susan B. Anthony, 1902.

DuBois, Ellen Carol, ed. *Elizabeth Cady Stanton, Susan B. Anthony, Correspondence, Writings,
Speeches.* New York: Schocken Books, 1981.

Flexner, Eleanor. *Century of Struggle.* Cambridge,
Mass.: Harvard University Press, 1959.

Gurko, Miriam. *The Ladies of Seneca Falls: The Birth
of the Woman's Rights Movement.* New York:
Schocken, 1976.

Harper, Ida Husted. *The Life and Work of Susan
B. Anthony (1896–1908).* 3 vols. Salem, N.H.:
Ayer Co., 1983.

Sherr, Lynn. *Failure Is Impossible: Susan B. Anthony
in Her Own Words.* New York: Times Books,
1995.

Appalachian folklore Appalachian folklore
has been a popular subject among scholars.

The term *Appalachia* refers not to a people,
but rather to a geographical region. It is defined
by a mountainous area that includes portions of
Alabama, Georgia, Maryland, North and South
Carolina, Kentucky, Tennessee, Virginia, and
West Virginia. One reason the region commands such attention among American folklorists is its distinctive relation to cultural tradition.
As a topographically remote and relatively culturally isolated space well into the 20th century,
Appalachia retained a greater share of its traditions and customs than it might have if its people
had had more contact with other populations
and their ways of life. During the first part of
the 20th century, some believed that Appalachia
represented survivals of Anglo-American and
Irish-American folk traditions that had faded
elsewhere.

Vernacular forms associated with Appalachia
include log houses and other elements of folk
architecture. The region has also been home
to rich traditions in folk music, dance, speech,
and crafts. Appalachian folk festivals have been
taking place since the 1920s. The publication
of Allen Eaton's influential book *Handicrafts of
the Southern Highlands* helped increase awareness of Appalachian folk culture. Agencies such
as the Southern Highland Handicrafts Guild

have also helped publicize the way of life once
insular to Appalachia. Furthermore, the mountainous region, and its identification with folk
traditions, was immortalized in the composer
Aaron Copland's piece *Appalachian Spring.*

In American popular culture, Appalachia has
become unfortunately associated with the figure
of the hillbilly. The term *hillbilly* is a derogatory name for rural residents in general, and for
mountain people of the Appalachian region in
particular.

The description first appeared in print in
1900. Whether spoken or written, the word is
usually a pejorative reference to the perceived
lack of sophistication or worldliness among rural
people. In many instances, the person called
a hillbilly is cast through a stereotype whose
attributes include uninhibited behavior including drinking, shooting, and, in some depictions,
a lack of restraint in sexual contact, even with
close relatives.

The overall image of a hillbilly involves
someone engaged in a backward, inbred, shiftless, and insular way of life. Rather than recognizing the richness of mountain culture, then,
the term *hillbilly* (and its successor term, *redneck*)
suggests coarseness and deficiency. Although
popular culture has muted some of the image's
hostility to create cartoon or television characters portraying the figure of the hillbilly, most
of the humor in these presentations remains at
the expense of mountain people. For instance,
a situation comedy series, *The Beverly Hillbillies,*
based its humor on a fish-out-of-water story
involving a displaced family of hillbillies. Contrary to the unflattering picture of the "hillbilly,"
even the most remote mountain settlements
have folklife traditions that deserve a more fair
assessment. From bluegrass music to down-
home cooking, mountain people have their own
cultural legacies.

Appalachian folklore includes many robust
customs, crafts, and practices, such as distinctive
forms of folk speech and folk building.

See also: ANGLO-AMERICAN FOLKLORE;
BOONE, DANIEL; COPLAND, AARON; CRAFTS,

FOLK; CULTURAL GROUPS; FOLKTALES; HILLBIL-
LIES; IRISH-AMERICAN FOLKLORE; MUSIC, FOLK;
OZARKS FOLKLORE; REGION, FOLK.

For Further Reading:
Becker, Jane. *Selling Tradition: Appalachia and the
Construction of an American Folk, 1930–1940.*
Chapel Hill: University of North Carolina
Press, 1998.
Bial, Raymond. *Mist over the Mountains: Appalachia
and Its People.* Boston: Houghton Mifflin, 1997.
Bogart, Barbara Allen, and Thomas Schlereth.
Sense of Place: American Regional Cultures. Lex-
ington: University Press of Kentucky, 1990.
Conway, Cecilia. *African Banjo Echoes in Appalachia:
A Study of Folk Traditions.* Knoxville: University
of Tennessee Press, 1995.
Drake, Richard. *A History of Appalachia.* Lexington:
University Press of Kentucky, 2001.
Horwitz, Elinor, Joshua Horwitz, and Anthony
Horwitz. *Mountain People, Mountain Crafts.*
Philadelphia: Lippincott, 1974.
McNeil, W. K., ed. *Appalachian Images in Folk and
Popular Culture.* Ann Arbor, Mich.: UMI Press,
1989.
Noe, Kenneth and Shannon Wilson. *The Civil
War in Appalachia: Collected Essays.* Knoxville:
University of Tennessee Press, 1997.
Obermiller, Phillip J., Thomas E. Wagner, and E.
Bruce Tucker, eds. *Appalachian Odyssey: Histori-
cal Perspectives on the Great Migration.* Westport,
Conn.: Praeger, 2000.
Rehder, John. *Appalachian Folkways.* Baltimore:
Johns Hopkins University Press, 2004.
Whisnant, David. *All That Is Native and Fine: The
Politics of Culture in an American Region.* Chapel
Hill: University of North Carolina Press, 1983.

apples   See CHAPMAN, JOHN (JOHNNY APPLE-
SEED); HALLOWEEN/ALL HALLOWS' EVE.

Appleseed, Johnny   See CHAPMAN, JOHN.

April Fool's Day   This holiday's origins are
uncertain, for it most likely derived from multiple sources. As an anonymously authored verse
on the subject would have it, "The first of April,
some do say / Is set apart for All Fools' Day; /
But why the people call it so / Nor I, nor they
themselves, do know, / But on this day are
people sent / On purpose for pure merriment."
For example, April Fool's Day may have had its
beginnings in Hilaria, an ancient Roman festival
of the vernal equinox. The season change from
winter to spring has been known to fool people
with its fluctuating weather and shifting conditions. Another potential influence was the Feast
of Fools, a New Year's celebration dating from
the Middle Ages. It involved rejection of authority and often took the form of a pageant that
inverted the normal social power. In particular,
citizens satirized the church. The day became
linked to rule breaking and irreverence.

It is believed that the reason All Fools' Day
now falls in April is related to the 1582 implementation of the Gregorian calendar reform
in France, which shifted the marking of the
new year's arrival from a week-long gift-giv-
ing celebration spanning March 25 to April 1
to a single-day observance on January 1. When
some people, whether out of stubbornness or
lack of information, persisted in celebrating the
new year at the end of March, others started to
mock the celebrants (fools or "fish," as they are
still known in France) with gag gifts and other
teasing gestures. Images of fish are still associated with this holiday in some countries, just as
in the United States hearts are associated with
Saint Valentine's Day. French children are fond
of taping a picture of a fish to a playmate's back.
When the child discovers the trick, its perpetrator cries out triumphantly, "April fish!" Today's
familiar "Kick me" sign, placed on an unsuspecting person's back for humorous purposes, probably owes its invention to this day.

In modern times, this unofficial holiday is
observed on the first day in April. While today's
holiday practice may seem remote from its origins, when April Fool's Day arrives, U.S. children and adults alike take license in their daily
activities and communications, initiating pranks,

practical jokes, and fool's errands. Participants must split their energies between implementing their own pranks and avoiding becoming the object of others' jokes. From calling a classmate's attention to a supposedly untied shoe, to slipping salt into the family sugar bowl, to duping a friend with false information, to sending a colleague on an impossible task, April Fool's Day is a time for mischief and rebellion against usual social and interpersonal inhibitions. The holiday retains the element of its challenge to social power to the extent that impertinent humor between, say, a student and a teacher is permissible on this day. Tall tales, deliberately improperly set clocks, and spurious reports of events abound. Even in the workplace, April Fool's Day often occasions playful e-mails, hoaxes, and coworker miscues of other kinds. Although somewhat minor among the American holidays, April Fool's Day remains a favorite among those with impish tendencies. The day affords an annual opportunity to laugh at ourselves, for, as Mark Twain once wrote, "The first of April is the day we remember what we are the other 364 days of the year."

See also: CHILDREN'S FOLKLORE; CLEMENS, SAMUEL LANGHORNE; FRENCH-AMERICAN FOLKLORE; GAMES/PASTIMES; HOLIDAYS/OBSERVANCES; HUMOR, FOLK; NEW YEAR'S EVE/DAY; SAINT VALENTINE'S DAY.

For Further Reading:
Cohen, Hennig, and Tristram Potter Coffin, eds. *The Folklore of American Holidays.* Detroit: Gale, 1987.
Myers, Robert. *Celebrations: The Complete Book of American Holidays.* Garden City, N.Y.: Doubleday, 1972.
Santino, Jack. *All around the Year: Holidays and Celebrations in American Life.* Urbana: University of Illinois Press, 1994.

Arbor Day Arbor Day, an original American holiday, owes its existence to a single individual's efforts within a larger 19th-century progressive movement toward social reform.

The holiday later found its champions in the nation's environmental and conservation movements. Dedicated to the planting of trees, Arbor Day began as an effort to forest America's plains but survives in modern times as a day to appreciate the beauty of our environment and honor the contribution of trees to our lives. As an 1854 settler in the Nebraska territory, J. Sterling Morton was quick to make plantings a feature of his new flatland residence. He realized that in addition to their aesthetic value, trees helped retain the soil, offered windbreaks, and furnished fruit, fuel, and materials and provided shade in his new region and home. Morton was also mindful that Americans needed to care for the nation's natural resources and landscape. Morton became a spokesperson for forests and woodlands, declaring "The cultivation of trees is the cultivation of the good, the beautiful, and the ennobling in man."

On April 10, 1872, Morton led the first observance of the holiday, on the basis of his conviction that we should replenish the plants and trees we consume or displace. Arbor Day began as a state holiday in Nebraska, with more than 1 million trees planted during that first celebration in 1872. Arbor Day was legalized as a Nebraska holiday and adopted as a national observance in 1882 and is now even celebrated in some areas beyond the United States. In America, Arbor Day has remained largely a school holiday, charged with educating youth about the importance of nature's stewardship through planting, tree care, and forestation. Morton furthered the holiday by advocating the ceremonial planting of trees to honor individuals of note or events of consequence in the area. In time, the national holiday became associated with the planting of memorial trees, a practice that continues to this day. The observance carries the support of naturalists, educators, and agriculturalists. Each year, the U.S. president plants a tree in conjunction with Arbor Day, and the White House boasts a variety of such trees as a result. Along with Bird Day, which began in the 1890s, Arbor Day seeks to join the love of nature with the love of country. Recitations, songs, skits, and other civic lessons help children understand and articulate the value of trees to our nation's future.

Arbor Day is observed on various dates by state and region, depending upon favorable planting conditions, but is celebrated nationally on the last Friday in April as a gesture to J. Sterling Morton, whose birthday was April 22. The lore of Arbor Day continues through instructional materials and other forms of tradition updated for today's purposes. At the Web site for the National Arbor Day Foundation, for instance, one can read the history of the holiday, download a play for school-age children on the theme, and get ideas for celebrating Arbor Day in one's own community. Given the emphasis on tree planting involved with Arbor Day, it is no surprise that lore surrounding this holiday often makes connections to the folk figure of John "Johnny Appleseed" Chapman (1774–1845), known best for his reputed habit of traveling the frontier planting apple trees.

See also: CHAPMAN, JOHN (JOHNNY APPLESEED); EARTH DAY; FLOWERS; GARDENING; HOLIDAYS/OBSERVANCES; MIDWESTERN REGIONAL FOLKLORE.

For Further Reading:
Beaty, Sandy, J. L. Wilkerson, and Jami Parkison, eds. *Champion of Arbor Day: J. Sterling Morton.* New York: Acorn Books, 1999.

Cohen, Hennig, and Tristram Potter Coffin, eds. *The Folklore of American Holidays.* Detroit: Gale, 1987.

Everard, Lewis. *Arbor Day: Its Purpose and Observance.* Washington, D.C.: U.S. Department of Agriculture, 1926.

Myers, Robert. *Celebrations: The Complete Book of American Holidays.* Garden City, N.Y.: Doubleday, 1972.

Olson, James. *J. Sterling Morton.* Lincoln: Nebraska State Historical Society, 1972.

Santino, Jack. *All around the Year: Holidays and Celebrations in American Life.* Urbana: University of Illinois Press, 1994.

Schauffler, Robert Haven. *Arbor Day: Its History, Observance, Spirit and Significance: With Practical Selections on Treeplanting and Conservation, and a Nature Anthology.* Detroit: Omnigraphics, 1990.

architecture, folk Sometimes described as buildings constructed without benefit of architects, structures associated with folk architecture represent an intriguing feature of folklore studies in the United States.

While art historians concern themselves chiefly with buildings designed by professional architects, folklorists are more interested in those envisioned and set in place by ordinary people. These structures, whether houses or buildings intended to perform other functions, reflect the traditional customs and practices of everyday Americans.

J. B. Jackson, a noted American geographer and landscape historian, was among the first to study this homemade architecture. He distinguished vernacular architecture from its official counterparts by describing it as informed by the world of users rather than the world of planners. They are seldom the product of elaborate blueprints, but they nonetheless match closely the needs of those who will make use of them.

While these "unsigned" buildings may not be the product of famous architects, they provide valuable insights into the lives of America's ancestors. Folk buildings demonstrate cultural values, regional identities, ethnic origins, and specific features of utility. Perhaps the most familiar image of all American folk architecture is the event known as a barn raising, with its connotations of communal cooperation and festivity in shared labor. In the context of folklore research, architecture can play a key part within community studies. From the hex sign on a Pennsylvania Dutch barn to a shotgun house in the South, ordinary buildings reveal aspects of the American past.

In the United States, buildings of particular note, whether by known architects or not, find their way onto the National Register of Historic Places. Locations with this status enjoy some rights and protections others may not. Registered places also tend to undergo historic preservation so that visitors can see the most historically accurate and intact representation possible. Many such historical structures bear markers signaling their part in American history.

In other instances, although a site has strong associations with key moments of the American past, its original historical structures have deteriorated or vanished, falling victim to the ravages of time or neglect. Where old buildings do not survive, reproductions of historical structures are sometimes placed at or near the site where they first stood. The usual objective of such reconstructed buildings is to portray the environment and ways of life previously known at a given location.

Such projects tend to be linked to historical museums and/or living history sites, at which costumed personnel speak in character as members of a past era and community. These "interpreters" interact with visitors and demonstrate trades and crafts characteristic of the periods they portray. The effort of this immersion approach to the past is to bring a location's history to life. By permitting tourists to enter a bygone era, open-air museums invite today's visitors to engage with a three-dimensional experience of the past.

Whether the buildings are original or authentic reproductions, works of folk architecture help folklorists and members of the public alike imagine the way of life for another culture, region, or time.

See also: ART, FOLK; COLONIAL WILLIAMS-BURG; FOLKLIFE; FOLKLIFE MOVEMENT; FOLKLORE IN EVERYDAY LIFE; GREENFIELD VILLAGE, HENRY FORD MUSEUM AND; HISTORIC PRESERVATION; LIVING HISTORY MUSEUMS; MATERIAL CULTURE; MUSEUMS, FOLK; MYSTIC SEAPORT AND PRESERVATION SHIPYARD; OCCUPATIONAL FOLKLORE; PENNSYLVANIA DUTCH/PENNSYLVANIA GERMAN FOLKLORE; SOUTHERN REGIONAL FOLKLORE; STURBRIDGE VILLAGE, OLD; TERMS; VERNACULAR CULTURE.

For Further Reading:

Feintuch, Burt, ed. *The Conservation of Culture: Folklorists and the Public Sector*. Lexington: University Press of Kentucky, 1988.

Jackson, J. B. *Discovering the Vernacular Landscape*. New Haven, Conn.: Yale University Press, 1984.

Jenkins, Geraint, ed. *Studies in Folklife*. New York: Barnes & Noble, 1969.

Meinig, D. W. *The Interpretation of Ordinary Landscape: Geographical Essays*. New York: Oxford University Press, 1979.

Pawar, R. S. *Rural Geography of Folk Houses*. Jaipur: Pointer, 1992.

Pilsbury, Richard, and Andrew Kardos. *A Field Guide to the Folk Architecture of the Northeastern United States: Special Edition on Geographical Lore*. Dartmouth, N.H.: Geography Publications, 1970.

Upton, Dell, and John Michael Vlalch. *Common Places: Readings in American Vernacular Architecture*. Athens: University of Georgia Press, 1986.

Archive of Folk Culture The Archive of Folk Culture (AFC), located in Washington, D.C.'s, Library of Congress, houses a national collection of American folk materials.

The Archive of Folk Culture was established in 1928 as the Archive of Folk Song. It became the depository for a variety of items, including folk music recordings, spoken word recordings, field documents, manuscripts, and related items. In 1980, the facility was renamed the Archive of Folk Culture to reflect the growth of the collection and the full range of folk materials retained there more accurately.

From live recordings of tunes performed by Woody Guthrie to taped interviews with performers conducted by the folklorist Alan Lomax, the AFC preserves folk traditions and practitioner reflections about them that might otherwise have vanished when the informants died.

In addition to collecting material, the Archive of Folk Culture has shaped the direction of folklore studies. For instance, through their example and their advocacy, the staff of AFC helped promote collection of oral history as a field technique for folklorists. The AFC also issued record albums that made excerpts from the holdings available to the public for purchase, increasing visibility for the archive and its contents.

In 1978, as a consequence of the American Folklife Preservation Act, the AFC became part of the American Folklife Center. Today, the Archive of Folk Culture consists of more than 1 million items reflecting American folk traditions.

See also: AMERICAN FOLKLIFE PRESERVATION ACT; FIELDWORK; FOLKLIFE; FOLKLIFE MOVEMENT; LIVING HISTORY MUSEUMS; MATERIAL CULTURE; MUSEUMS, FOLK; MUSIC, FOLK; ORAL HISTORY; RESEARCH, FOLKLIFE.

For Further Reading:

Bartis, Peter Thomas. *A History of the Archive of Folk Song at the Library of Congress: The First Fifty Years.* Ann Arbor, Mich.: UMI Research Press, 1987.

Hall, Stephanie. *The Ethnographic Collections of the Archive of Folk Culture: A Contributor's Guide.* Washington, D.C.: American Folklife Center, Library of Congress, 1995.

Hickerson, Joseph Charles. *Folklore and Folk Music Archives and Related Collections in the United States and Canada.* Washington, D.C.: The Archive, 1978.

Lloyd, Timothy. *The Archive of Folk Culture: The National Collection of American and World Folklore.* Washington, D.C.: American Folklife Center/Library of Congress, 1992.

Archive of Folk Song   See ARCHIVE OF FOLK CULTURE.

Arizona folklore   See CHAVEZ, CÉSAR ESTRADA; CHICANO FOLKLORE; EARP, WYATT BERRY STAMP; GHOST TOWNS; JAPANESE-AMERICAN INTERNMENT; MOMADAY, NAVARRE SCOTT; RODEO; SILKO, LESLIE MARMON; SOUTHWESTERN REGIONAL FOLKLORE; SPANISH-AMERICAN FOLKLORE.

Arkansas folklore   See FLOYD, CHARLES ARTHUR (PRETTY BOY); JAPANESE-AMERICAN INTERNMENT; JOAD, TOM; OZARKS FOLKLORE; STARR, BELLE; STEINBECK, JOHN.

Armistice Day   See VETERANS DAY.

art, folk   Within artistic expression, the category of folk art includes all work by self-taught and informally taught (or so-called naïve, indigenous, vernacular, untutored, primitive, or outsider) producers.

In other words, while elite artists typically develop their skills through formal academic instruction, including university or art institute education, folk artists often enough conduct their entire careers without such official credentials. No matter how proficient their skills or recognized their work may be, folk artists do not enjoy the standing in the so-called serious art community conferred by art degrees or similar status indicators.

That is not to say that folk artists have not honed their techniques and refined their results. Indeed, they often learn a great deal about artistic media and methods through such means as observation, experimentation, and apprenticeship. Their classification as "folk artists," then, merely signals that they conduct their careers outside the elite art scene and its accolades.

Folk arts span a wide range of forms and materials. While some folk artists work chiefly in the "flat arts" (painting, drawing, prints, and the like) traditionally associated with high art, others fashion more utilitarian pieces. These items can be everything from weather vanes and baskets to carvings and musical instruments, and their makers are far from famous. Indeed, sometimes the artists are unknown or anonymous. In this sense, folk arts and folk crafts may prove overlapping categories of study.

While the earliest celebrations of American folk art concentrated on the rural and remote populations of the nation, today folk art exists as a much broader category. It is no longer limited to preindustrial society or its centuries-old artistic forms. It does, however, remain a term associated with artistic media that do not lend themselves easily to mass production. Consequently, folk art retains a connotation of handmade and homemade work.

In fact, while the divide between artists and craftspeople within the elite art world might seem both wide and deep, the line separating art from craft, or folk artists from folk artisans, is blurry at best. Utilitarian items are most often described as folk crafts, but collections of folk art may include any of the products, decorative and/or practical, of folk artistry. In other words, American folk art is a category that encompasses the expressive products of a wide range of ordinary Americans.

One of the best-known examples of America's folk artists is Edward Hicks (1780–1849), who created a series of now-familiar images known as the *Peaceable Kingdom* paintings (1834). Hicks was a Bucks County, Pennsylvania, sign painter and carriage decorator by trade, and his work often featured pictorial, historical, and patriotic elements. Hicks began painting as a form of artistic and spiritual expression his daily work could not always afford. In an articulation of his faith, for he was also a Quaker clergyman, Hicks painted images inspired by Scripture. His *Peaceable Kingdom* paintings appeared framed with quotations from the Bible (Isa. 11:6). In these works, Hicks combined his experience with graphics with his convictions as a Quaker to produce symbolic works depicting spiritual harmony.

Collections of American folk art can be found throughout the world. Indeed, folk art entered American museums chiefly through the interests demonstrated by professional artists, such as Charles Sheeler, and private collectors, such as Abby Aldrich Rockefeller. United States museum collections of folk art include Old Sturbridge Village, Greenfield Village, and Colonial Williamsburg. High art museums, such as the Metropolitan Museum of Art, the Whitney Museum, and the Museum of Modern Art, have devoted numerous exhibitions to the subject of American folk art. In 1963, New York City's Museum of American Folk Art (now the American Folk Art Museum) opened its doors to the public, and this organization has devoted itself to the topic ever since.

When folklorists refer to folk art, they typically allude to the efforts of artists who, without the benefits of formal art training or modern technology, produce artistic works that prove decorative, functional, or a combination of the two.

See also: ARTS AND CRAFTS MOVEMENT; COLONIAL WILLIAMSBURG; CRAFTS, FOLK; FOLKLORE IN EVERYDAY LIFE; GREENFIELD VILLAGE; INDUSTRIALIZATION AND FOLKLORE; LIVING HISTORY MUSEUMS; MATERIAL CULTURE; MUSEUMS, FOLK; QUAKER FOLKLORE; STURBRIDGE VILLAGE, OLD; VERNACULAR CULTURE.

For Further Reading:
Cardinal, Roger. *Outsider Art*. New York: Praeger, 1972.

Cerney, Charlene, and Suzanne Seriff. *Recycled, Re-Seen: Folk Art from the Global Scrap Heap*. New York: Harry N. Abrams, 1996.

Hall, Michael D., and Eugene W. Metcalf, Jr., eds. *The Artist Outsider: Creativity and the Boundaries of Culture*. Washington, D.C.: Smithsonian Institution Press, 1994.

Jones, Michael Owen. *Exploring Folk Art: Twenty Years of Thought on Craft, Work, and Aesthetics*. Ann Arbor, Mich.: UMI Research Press, 1987.

Quimby, Ian, and Scott Swant, eds. *Perspectives on American Folk Art*. New York: W. W. Norton, 1980.

Sellen, Betty-Carol. *Self-Taught, Outsider, and Folk Art: A Guide to American Artists, Locations and Resources*. Jefferson, N.C.: McFarland, 2000.

Vlach, John Michael, and Simon J. Bronner, eds. *Folk Art and Art Worlds*. Ann Arbor, Mich.: UMI Research Press, 1986.

artifacts, folk   The term *folk artifact* refers to any human-made or human-modified object used as an object of cultural investigation. Although such items seldom consist of verbal material, they can nonetheless speak to the scholar prepared to attend to their encoded cultural messages.

Unlike works of art, artifacts need not be items of intrinsic costliness or great beauty to interest scholars. In fact, an artifact can be any item that, whether created or altered for a purpose, reveals practices or values of the culture in which it was fashioned and/or used. Consequently, such objects are collected not necessarily for their market or aesthetic value, but chiefly for their power as historical evidence.

The discipline of archaeology, a kindred inquiry to folklore, relies extensively on artifacts for its study of the past. Such materials are typically unearthed on digs or through similar fieldwork. Other disciplines, such as folklore, have also come to refer to a variety of their objects of examination as artifacts, even if these materials were not uncovered through the classic archaeological method of excavation.

The premise of artifact study for folklorists is that these specimens, as products of human effort, bear the traces of the culture where they originate. If a folklorist can understand the objects, then it may also be possible to gain insight into the way of life of which they formed a part. That is, folklorists take special interest in material objects that embody regional differences, demonstrate distinctive methods of fabrication, or illuminate the human relationships within a society. For example, a folklore researcher might look at a wood carving not only to determine when, how, and by whom it was carved, but also to gain access to the subtle meanings a carving conveyed to members of a specific community.

Artifacts need not be artistic or decorative in aspect, then. Folklorists often also study utilitarian items such as buildings, utensils and vessels, tools and devices, furniture and apparel. For instance, specialists in folk architecture might look at the geographic diffusion over time of a particular framing technique for barn construction.

Artifacts, as the residue of human action within a cultural setting, hold both overt and tacit meanings for the members of a society. Through careful research, folklorists seek to understand both what and how such objects—whether plain or precious—convey meaning within the context of a given historical setting.

See also: ARCHITECTURE, FOLK; FOLKLIFE; FOLKLIFE MOVEMENT; FOLKLORE IN EVERYDAY LIFE; HISTORIC PRESERVATION; MATERIAL CULTURE; MUSEUMS, FOLK; RESEARCH, FOLKLIFE; TERMS.

For Further Reading:

Babcock, Barbara. "Artifact." In *Folklore, Cultural Performances, and Popular Entertainments: A Communications-Centered Handbook*, edited by Richard Bauman, 204–216. New York: Oxford University Press, 1992.

Deetz, James. *In Small Things Forgotten: An Archaeology of Early American Life*. New York: Anchor/Doubleday, 1996.

Prown, Jules, and Kenneth Haltman, eds. *American Artifacts: Essays in Material Culture*. East Lansing: Michigan State University Press, 2000.

Schlereth, Thomas. *Artifacts and the American Past*. Nashville, Tenn.: American Association for State and Local History, 1980.

arts and crafts movement The arts and crafts trend within domestic design, while originally launched in England, also became popular in America during the period from 1880 to 1920.

Arts and crafts design is currently enjoying renewed public interest in America, especially among those wishing to renovate older homes and furnish them with items inspired by the arts and crafts movement.

Both in England and in America, the arts and crafts movement began as a reaction to the industrial age and its threats of an increasingly dehumanized (and dehumanizing) environment. As an antidote to that force, the arts and crafts aesthetic placed great emphasis on human touch, artisanal qualities, and handiwork. Some, though not all, craftspeople associated with this movement eschewed machinery in fashioning their work. Influences of the movement appear in such expressive forms as architecture, pottery, lighting, furniture, and glass. Most of these elements were envisioned for the home, making it a refuge from the harsh and cold atmosphere of the modern workplace, with its impersonal office buildings, plants, and factories. The arts and crafts home answered these settings with a warmth and scale that provided a refuge.

Several famous figures were associated with the movement, including Frank Lloyd Wright, Gustav Stickley, and Louis Comfort Tiffany. Their work—in architecture, furniture, and glasswork, respectively—represented the high end of arts and crafts homes. The majority of houses inspired by the movement, however, were more modest examples created by artisans laboring in relative anonymity. Such homes can still be found throughout the United States, with many original architectural elements intact. The now-familiar architectural form known as the "bungalow" had its origins in this movement. Single-family residences, along with some of their furnishings, are now sought after for their clean lines and homey details. Whether the style is referred to as craftsman, prairie, or mission, such houses take their cues from the arts and crafts movement.

Today's homeowners, particularly those concerned with historic preservation, are often involved in painstaking restoration of an arts and crafts look. Even those with new-construction houses rather than historical homes often look for ways to incorporate arts and crafts touches within their decorating schemes. Toward that end, today's consumers can choose from an array of do-it-yourself books, stencils, and period reproductions intended to help them achieve the spare but cozy, fresh but folksy, feel of an arts and crafts household.

See also: ARCHITECTURE, FOLK; ART, FOLK; ARTIFACT; CRAFTS, FOLK; HISTORIC PRESERVATION; INDUSTRIALIZATION AND FOLKLORE; LIVING HIS-

TORY MUSEUMS; MATERIAL CULTURE; MUSEUMS, FOLK.

For Further Reading:
Denker, Bert, ed. *Substance of Style: Perspectives on the American Arts and Crafts Movement.* Winterthur, Del.: Henry Francis du Pont Winterthur Museum, 1996.

Kaplan, Wendy. *The Arts and Crafts Movement in Europe and America: Design for the Modern World.* New York: Thames & Hudson, 2004.

Sommer, Robin Langley, ed. *The Arts and Crafts Movement.* Edison, N.J.: Chartwell Books, 1995.

Stansky, Peter. *Redesigning the World: William Morris, the 1880s, and the Arts and Crafts.* Princeton, N.J.: Princeton University Press, 1985.

Todd, Pamela. *The Arts and Crafts Companion.* New York: Bulfinch, 2004.

atomic/nuclear era folklore   The advent of the atomic era can be traced to the point at which most Americans began to associate the world's end with the atomic bomb, or—simply—"the bomb," as it came to be known.

Most trace this period to the 1945 bombings of Hiroshima and Nagasaki, Japan, that occurred near the end of World War II. These destructive events helped sober the world about the nature of modern warfare. Fear concerning the bomb threat led to a new kind of world dynamic, couched as a struggle to prevent other countries from developing or using such bomb capacity. This situation was usually referred to as the cold war, an era characterized by fear regarding the impending threat of nuclear destruction in a World War III. Home bomb shelters and school air raids reflected the nation's efforts at emergency preparedness. In America, the cold war was configured as a stark and self-justifying struggle between the forces of good and evil. This manifestation of the nuclear arms race era also gave America such terms of folk speech as *Communist menace* and *iron curtain*, the latter representing the division between Western democracy and Eastern Europe.

The anxieties surrounding this level of atomic and nuclear threat produced a wide range of apocalyptic lore, from rumors and jokes to stories and urban legends. More recent events, such as the fall of the Berlin Wall, have caused this mood to subside somewhat, although its residue remains in American thought and lore.

See also: CITY FOLKLORE; CONSPIRACY FOLKLORE; FOLKLORE IN EVERYDAY LIFE; INDUSTRIALIZATION AND FOLKLORE; LEGENDS, FOLK; SPEECH, FOLK; UFO FOLKLORE; URBAN LEGENDS.

For Further Reading:
Boyer, Paul. *By the Bomb's Early Light: American Thought and Culture at the Dawn of the Atomic Age.* New York: Pantheon, 1985.

Henriksen, Margot. *Dr. Strangelove's America: Society and Culture in the Atomic Age.* Berkeley: University of California Press, 1997.

Lipsitz, George. *Class and Culture in Cold War America: A Rainbow at Midnight.* New York: Praeger, 1983.

Schwartz, Richard. *Cold War Culture: Media and the Arts, 1947–1990.* New York: Facts On File, 1997.

Seed, David. *Imagining Apocalypse: Studies in Cultural Crisis.* New York: Macmillan-St. Martin's, 2000.

Weart, Spencer. *Nuclear Fear: A History of Images.* Cambridge, Mass.: Harvard University Press, 1988.

Whitfield, Stephen. *The Culture of the Cold War.* Baltimore: Johns Hopkins University Press, 1991.

Wojcik, Daniel. *The End of the World as We Know It: Faith, Fatalism, and Apocalypse in America.* New York: New York University Press, 1997.

Zamora, Louis Parkinson. *The Apocalyptic Vision in America: Interdisciplinary Essays on Myth and Culture.* Bowling Green, Ohio: Popular Press, 1982.

Attucks, Crispus (1723–1770) Crispus Attucks is regarded by many historians to be the first to die in America's Revolutionary War.

Attucks perished in the 1770 incident that would subsequently become known as the Boston Massacre. On that day, a conflict between residents of the colonies and British soldiers (or "redcoats," as they were also called by colonists) escalated to a riot. By the end of the skirmish, several were wounded and five fatally so: Crispus Attucks, James Caldwell, Patrick Carr, Samuel Gray, and Samuel Maverick.

Tensions ran high between residents of Boston and the British soldiers who had been posted in 1768 to maintain order in the colonies. The altercation on March 5, 1770, on the Boston Commons began with name calling, progressed to a snowball fight, and culminated in Captain Preston's order to fire on the colonists. Attucks died on the scene of two musket shots to the chest.

Attucks is believed to have been a runaway slave from Framingham, Massachusetts, who had spent the time since his escape working as a seaman on a whaling ship. He was in Boston leading a march against the Townshend Acts, legislation that provoked opposition to its indirect taxation of the colonies, when the Boston Massacre took place. The events of that day were documented by newspapers and in a variety of visual records, such as the contemporaneous engraving rendered by Paul Revere and subsequent depictions, such as John Bufford's 1856 chromolithograph and on-site dramatic reenactments.

The remains of Crispus Attucks were interred at the Old Granary Burial Ground on Boston's Tremont Street and not far from where Attucks was killed. He shares his resting place not only with the others who died in the Boston Massacre, but with some of the best-known patriots of his day, including Samuel Adams, John Hancock, and Paul Revere.

Since his murder by British troops in 1770, Crispus Attucks has been commemorated through various public acts. In 1998, on the 275th anniversary of his birth, the U.S. Mint issued a silver coin in honor of Attucks. In Boston, a 25-foot obelisk stands as a memorial to

Attucks and the others who died in the Boston Massacre. Beginning in 1858, partly in tribute to the patriot and partly in protest of the Dred Scott decision, Attucks celebrations were held annually at Boston's African Meeting House, and in this connection, March 5 has sometimes been referred to as Crispus Attucks Day. Attucks also appears in public art at other locations, including a Works Progress Administration (WPA) mural in the District of Columbia's Recorder of Deeds Office. In addition, efforts are currently under way to erect a Black Patriots Memorial on Washington, D.C.'s, National Mall. This figural sculpture would pay tribute to distinguished figures of the American past such as Frederick Douglass, Harriet Tubman, and Crispus Attucks.

Meanwhile, the memory of Crispus Attucks is preserved through written tributes, which include novels and historical fiction, such as Arthur Hughes's *Crispus Attucks* (2002) and Edmund Curley's *Crispus Attucks: The First to Die* (1973). There are also numerous works, both fiction and nonfiction, that introduce young readers to the deeds of Crispus Attucks, including Dharathula Millender's novel *Crispus Attacks, Boy of Valor* (1965). Attucks has also been the subject of several works written for the stage, among them Thomas Pawley's *Son of Liberty* (1975) and *Crispus Attucks* (2000). Through these and similar works, the historical contributions of Crispus Attucks remain before American audiences.

As an African-American patriot, Crispus Attucks represents more than 5,000 African-American soldiers who fought in the battle for the nation's independence.

See also: AFRICAN-AMERICAN FOLKLORE; DEPRESSION, THE GREAT; DOUGLASS, FREDERICK; FOLK HEROES/LEGENDARY FIGURES; NORTHEASTERN REGIONAL FOLKLORE; PATRIOTS' DAY; PAUL REVERE'S RIDE; REVOLUTIONARY WAR; SLAVERY; TUBMAN, HARRIET.

For Further Reading:
Boston City Council. *A Memorial of Crispus Attucks, Samuel Maverick, James Caldwell, Samuel Gray, and Patrick Carr, from the City of Boston.* Miami: Mnemosyne, 1969.

Lanning, Lt. Col. Michael Lee. *The African-American Soldier: From Crispus Attucks to Colin Powell.* New York: Citadel Press, 1999.

Nell, William. *The Colored Patriots of the American Revolution [electronic resource]: With Sketches of Several Distinguished Colored Persons: To Which Is Added A Brief Survey of the Condition and Prospects of Colored Americans.* Chapel Hill, N.C.: Academic Affairs Library, 1999.

Neyland, James. *Crispus Attucks: Patriot.* Los Angeles: Holloway House, 1995.

auctions   An auction, while it may take several formats, involves the process by which a buyer and a seller arrive at a competitive price for a good or service, thereby finalizing a purchase.

In traditional auctions, an auctioneer of considerable verbal prowess manages to entertain attendees as well as transact the business of transferring property. Some auctioneers became known for their banter and the way they used remarks, stories, and jokes to punctuate the community-based event.

Differences in bidding procedures distinguish the types of auction. An English auction, for example, involves an item's consideration for purchase through rising bids in contention for the prospect of ownership. Participants raise their bids by turn until a bidder reaches a price no one else attending the auction wishes to exceed. This format, coordinated by an auctioneer, is probably the most familiar form of in-person auction in America.

In a "silent auction," often used for charity events, participants offer bids for an item until a predetermined time at which the auction closes. Within this process, those contending usually do not know what others have bid for the item in question. At the conclusion of the process, the person who has made the highest bid becomes the successful bidder for an item or lot of items. This kind of auction was once called a candle auction, for when the candle was spent, the silent auction ended.

Two other, less commonly employed auction styles, are the so-called Dutch auction and the Japanese auction. In a Dutch auction, an item's seller starts the bidding with a highest price. Then, the seller lowers the cost by steps until the first bidder accepts the seller's price. A Japanese auction involves simultaneous actions and bids, for example, in stock market transactions.

In a digital age, the most frequently engaged medium for auction may be the computer-mediated one. Through this means, both sellers and buyers may contact a wider set of opportunities than face-to-face interactions for auction might permit.

The popular image of bidders with nonverbal signals or numbered paddles, presided over by a fast-talking auctioneer who puts one in mind of a square-dance caller, might be largely a thing of the past. Nonetheless, today's electronic environments, including the Internet, have increased American participation in auctions as a means of exchange.

See also: COMPUTER FOLKLORE; FOLKLORE IN EVERYDAY LIFE; OCCUPATIONAL FOLKLORE; RITUALS, FOLK; SPEECH, FOLK.

For Further Reading:

Cassady, Ralph, Jr. *Auctions and Auctioneering.* Berkeley: University of California Press, 1967.

Dilworth, Leah. *Acts of Possession: Collecting in America.* New Brunswick, N.J.: Rutgers University Press, 2003.

Harrison, Phyllis. "Indiana Auctioneering: No Two Sales the Same," *Indiana Folklore* 12 (1979): 101–119.

Jansen, William Hugh. "Down Our Way: Who'll Bid Twenty?" *Kentucky Folklore Record* 2 (1956): 113–121.

Marsh, Anne, and William Aspinall, Jr. "Harold E. Leightley: Portrait of an Auctioneer and His Craft," *Keystone Folklore Quarterly* 16 (1971): 133–150.

McConachie, Bruce. "Slavery and Authenticity: Performing a Slave Auction at Colonial Williamsburg," *Theatre Annual: A Journal of Performance Studies* 51 (fall 1998): 71–81.

Smith, Charles. *Auctions: The Social Construction of Value.* New York: Free Press, 1989.

Aunt Nancy tales   See ANANSI.

Babe the Blue Ox (legendary)   As one of a relatively few animals to be referenced by name within the tall tales of the American frontier, Babe the Blue Ox is a familiar character within the nation's folklore.

To some extent, this awareness is due to Babe's close association with one of the country's best known folk heroes, Paul Bunyan. As a popular icon of the lumberjack of the American West, Bunyan was known for feats of strength and endurance. In such depictions, the legendary logger often appears accompanied by his loyal companion, Babe the Blue Ox. Paul Bunyan is typically included in collections of American tall tales, and the stories of his exploits reflect that genre's tendency toward hyperbole and improbable occurrence. In one such tale, Paul Bunyan fashioned the Great Lakes to serve as Babe's watering hole.

Babe began life as a white ox but became a blue one in the "Winter of the Blue Snow." As was her human companion, Babe the Blue Ox was a giant in size and appetites. This hunger proved Babe's undoing when she consumed a cookstove along with the food being prepared in it. It is said that Paul Bunyan then buried the beloved creature, creating South Dakota's Black Hills to mark her resting place.

While Paul Bunyan and Babe the Blue Ox may be contrived characters, and their stories manufactured for fakelore rather than collected as folklore, both remain among the most widely recognized icons of American tall tales.

See also: ANIMALS; BUNYAN, PAUL; FAKE-LORE; FOLK HEROES/LEGENDARY FIGURES; FOLKLORE IN AMERICAN LITERATURE; FOLKTALES; OCCUPATIONAL FOLKLORE.

For Further Reading:

Hutchinson, W. H. "The Cesarean Delivery of Paul Bunyan," *Western Folklore* 22 (1963): 1–15.
Leary, James, ed. *Wisconsin Folklore*. Madison: University of Wisconsin Press, 1998.
Stekert, Ellen J. "The False Issue of Folklore vs. 'Fakelore': Was Paul Bunyan a Hoax?" *Journal of Forest History* 30, no. 4 (1986): 180–181.

ballads   Ballads are brief texts set to tunes that have regularly repeated movements. Folk ballads typically relate stories with dramatic content, often set forth in rhymed stanzas.

The ballad is quite a long-standing tradition, and a staple of several folk groups, notably the Anglo-American culture. Child ballads, broadside ballads, and other formal variations have captured the interest of folklorists for centuries.

Most American folk ballads are story-driven narratives that commemorate an event, whether real or imagined, that the composers wish others to remember long afterward. Most traditional ballads feature a single voice, with or without musical accompaniment. Many spirituals, chain gang songs, and work songs are constituted with this pattern. Ballads are a staple of numerous American musical genres, including pop, rock and roll, and country music. They may be sad tales of lost love or grief, or celebrations of triumph and the human spirit. Folk heroes and legendary figures such as Belle Starr, Joe Hill, Nat Turner, Jesse James, and Billy the Kid have all been the subjects of folk ballads.

As sung verses, ballads form a valuable part of the folk literature of the United States.

See also: ANGLO-AMERICAN FOLKLORE; BASS, SAM; BROWN, STERLING ALLEN; CHICANO FOLKLORE; CIVIL WAR; COPLAND, AARON; DEPRESSION, THE GREAT; FIELDWORK, FOLKLORE; FLOYD, CHARLES ARTHUR (PRETTY BOY); FOLKLORE; GOLD RUSH, THE; HILL, JOE; JAMES, JESSE; JONES, JOHN LUTHER; LONGFELLOW, HENRY WADSWORTH; MARITIME FOLKLORE; McCARTY, WILLIAM HENRY (BILLY THE KID); MUSIC, FOLK; OUTLAWS; PRISON FOLKLORE; REVOLUTIONARY WAR; SCOTTISH-AMERICAN FOLKLORE; SPEECH, FOLK; STARR, BELLE; TELL, WILLIAM; TURNER, NAT.

For Further Reading:

Coffin, Tristram Potter. *The British Traditional Ballad in North America*. Austin: University of Texas Press, 1977.

Laws, G. Malcolm, Jr. *Native American Balladry*. Philadelphia: American Folklore Society, 1964.

Leach, MacEdward, and Tristram Coffin. *The Critics and the Ballad*. Carbondale: Southern Illinois University Press, 1973.

Lomax, John, and Alan Lomax. *American Ballads and Folk Songs*. New York: Macmillan, 1934.

Seeger, Pete. *American Favorite Ballads*. New York: Oak, 1961.

Silber, Irwin, and Ethel Raim, eds. *American Favorite Ballads: Tunes and Songs as Sung by Pete Seeger*. New York: Oak, 1961.

Baltic-American folklore See LATVIAN-AMERICAN FOLKLORE; LITHUANIAN-AMERICAN FOLKLORE.

Bambara, Toni Cade (1939–1995) As an educator, author, and activist, Toni Cade Bambara incorporated folk references throughout her work, from her classroom practice to her essays and fiction, such as her historical novel of the Civil Rights era, *The Salt Eaters*.

Bambara's career as a writer had its basis in literary study. In her literary antecedents, Bambara found strength rather than constraint, a rich literary past in which to bask and on which to build. In much the same way that African-American folklore calls for a population to know its past, so in African-American literature must writers know their precursors. Although Alice Walker popularized this view through such writings as "In Search of Our Mothers' Gardens," she was not the only writer of her day to reach this conclusion. Through her studies, Bambara became acquainted with the work of such authors as Zora Neale Hurston and James Mercer Langston Hughes, whose work had an impact on Bambara's language and style.

In interviews and essays, Toni Cade Bambara discussed the importance of story forms as cultural strategies in themselves. With her 1971 publication of *Tales and Stories for Black Folk*, Bambara pointed out how fables and parables enabled storytellers (both in Africa and in American slavery) to encode culturally specific and sensitive meanings even within conventional narrative forms to instruct and enliven listeners. She explained how this folkloristic technique of talking back to a cultural narrative is called signifying. The retold, revised, and sometimes reversed stories she then presented, including "The Three Little Panthers," showed characters and storytellers signifying on familiar tales. In this case, she revisited the traditional children's tale of "The Three Little Pigs."

In her retelling, three panthers move into a neighborhood where residents, responding to differences discerned in the newcomers, seek to eradicate those distinctions. The story concludes with the panthers' affirming rather than erasing their differences, and so deflecting the norma-tive expectations and intrusive conformity needs of a host culture.

The tale demonstrates how the panthers regarded folk practices from attire to literature as integral to their communal and historical identity and so declined the demand to assume the practices of their new neighbors. As did Zora Neale Hurston and Alice Walker, Toni Cade Bambara recognized the importance of interrogating the tales that surround and precede one's cultural position.

Elements derived from folklore also find expression within the domains of much recent African-American literary theory and criticism. For example, in *The Signifying Monkey: A Theory of Afro-American Literary Criticism* (1988), the critic Henry Louis Gates uses the same practice of signifying about which Bambara wrote as a means to characterize the way African-American literature contests the master narratives of American culture. Just as W. E. B. DuBois argued that African-American thought was characterized by "double consciousness" (self/other), Gates suggests that African-American literature is double voiced, as it speaks both to and beyond existing cultural scripts. In much the same way that Bambara's three panthers dared to talk back to the insistent voices that threatened their traditions, so do signifying texts throughout African-American literature challenge the assumptions behind traditional literary and cultural stories that would silence or slight the ancestral knowledge of historically disenfranchised populations.

See also: ANIMALS; AFRICAN-AMERICAN FOLK-LORE; CIVIL RIGHTS MOVEMENT; DuBois W. E. B.; FABLES; FAIRY TALES; FOLKLORE IN AMERICAN LITERATURE; FOLKTALES; HUGHES, JAMES MERCER LANGSTON; HURSTON, ZORA NEALE; SLAVERY; "THREE LITTLE PIGS, THE."

For Further Reading:

Bambara, Toni Cade. *The Salt Eaters*. New York: Vintage Books, 1992.

Bambara, Toni Cade. "What It Is I Think I'm Doing Anyhow." In *The Writer on Her Work: Contemporary Women Writers Reflect on Their Art and Situation*, edited by Janet Sternburg, 153–169. New York: W. W. Norton, 1980.

Butler-Evans, Elliott. *Race, Gender, and Desire: Narrative Strategies in the Fiction of Toni Cade Bambara, Toni Morrison, and Alice Walker*. Philadelphia: Temple University Press, 1989.

Byerman, Keith. *Fingering the Jagged Grain: Tradition and Form in Recent Black Fiction*. Athens: University of Georgia Press, 1985.

Gates, Henry Louis. *The Signifying Monkey: A Theory of Afro-American Literary Criticism*. New York: Oxford University Press, 1988.

Guy-Sheftall, Beverly. "Commitment: Toni Cade Bambara Speaks." In *Sturdy Black Bridges: Vision of Black Women in Literature*, edited by Roseann Bell, Bettye J. Parker, and Beverly Guy-Sheftall, 230–249. Garden City, N.Y.: Doubleday, 1979.

Pryse, Marjorie, and Hortense J. Spillers, eds. *Conjuring: Black Women, Fiction, and Literary Tradition*. Bloomington: Indiana University Press, 1985.

Barker, Ma   See CLARK, ARIZONA DONNIE.

bar mitzvah/bat mitzvah   The occasion of a bar mitzvah or bat mitzvah is a pivotal point in the individual's entry into adulthood within Judaism.

These rites mark the point at which the youth becomes subject to the commandments of a faith, a heightened level of responsibility within religious life. The bar mitzvah, typically conducted when the child is 13, is the traditional rite of passage for males. In recent times, the bat mitzvah, at age 12, has come to be the parallel process for females in the faith.

At this time, a ceremony is conducted to accomplish several purposes. The preparations by the person initiated represent a signal of maturity and conviction. The presence of extended family and spiritual community conveys acceptance of the youth into religious adulthood. The service communicates the tradition by which Jewish heritage continues across generations.

Taken together, these elements produce a major event within one's spiritual journey.

It is customary during the bar/bat mitzvah service for the featured individual to be accorded the honor of reciting sacred text. There may also be a ritual involving the scrolls of the Torah, when the Scripture is both literally and figuratively passed to a new generation. The featured youth may also take the opportunity to pay tribute to family members for their love and support.

At the completion of this solemn ceremony, guests celebrate the bar/bat mitzvah with a festive meal and/or party. It is usual to recognize the individual bar/bat mitzvah with the presentation of cards and gifts to celebrate the occasion.

The bar/bat mitzvah is a traditional way of welcoming Jewish youth into the responsibilities of spiritual adulthood, while taking care to preserve the heritage of Judaism for future generations.

See also: AGING AND FOLKLORE; BIRTHDAYS; CHILDREN'S FOLKLORE; FAMILY FOLKLORE; GENDER AND FOLKLORE; HOLIDAYS/OBSERVANCES; JEWISH-AMERICAN FOLKLORE; RELIGION, FOLK.

For Further Reading:

Cardoza, Arlene Rossen. *Jewish Family Celebrations: Shabbat Festivals and Traditional Ceremonies.* New York: St. Martin's, 1982.

Greenspoon, Leonard J., and Ronald Simkins. *Spiritual Dimensions of Judaism.* Omaha, Nebr.: Creighton University Press, 2003.

Kaplan, Dana Evan. *The Cambridge Companion to American Judaism.* New York: Cambridge University Press, 2005.

Maslin, Simeon J., ed. *Gates of Mitzvah=Shaarei Mitzvah: A Guide to the Jewish Life Cycle.* New York: Central Conference of American Rabbis, 1979.

Myers, Robert. *Celebrations: The Complete Book of American Holidays.* Garden City, N.Y.: Doubleday, 1972.

Neusner, Jacob. *The Enchantments of Judaism: Rites of Transformation from Birth through Death.* New York: Basic Books, 1987.

Trepp, Leo. *The Complete Book of Jewish Observance.* New York: Behrman House, 1980.

barns See ARCHITECTURE, FOLK; ARTIFACTS, FOLK.

Barrow, Clyde See BONNIE AND CLYDE.

Bart, Black See BOLES, CHARLES E.

Barton, Clara (1821–1912) Clara Barton was an influential reformer and humanitarian, and her efforts continue to benefit people in need or distress.

Barton began her life in Oxford, Massachusetts, on December 25, 1821. She worked quite successfully as a teacher at a free school she herself had opened until others recommended that a male principal be appointed, causing her to resign.

Barton was later occupied as a patent office clerk when she learned that the Union army needed assistance. In response to this cause, Barton immediately established an agency and began visiting the Civil War's front lines. There, she nursed the wounded and provided medical supplies where needed. This courageous work for any civilian, and highly unconventional work for a woman of that era, earned Barton a reputation as "the angel of the battlefield."

The related accomplishment for which Barton is widely known today is her founding in 1881 of the American chapter of the International Red Cross, now the American Red Cross. She was the founding president of the fledgling relief organization.

Barton also wrote the American Amendment to the Geneva Convention, permitting the Red Cross to provide aid during any disaster, rather than only during times of war.

Clara Barton stands as a distinguished precedent for American women entering previously male-dominated fields and, in the process, effecting social change. Her story is part of the lore of the U.S. women's movement.

See also: CIVIL RIGHTS MOVEMENT; CIVIL WAR; FOLK HEROES/LEGENDARY FIGURES; MEDICINE, FOLK; NORTHEASTERN REGIONAL FOLKLORE; PROTEST IN FOLKLORE; WOMEN'S SUFFRAGE; WOMEN'S MOVEMENT.

For Further Reading:
Burton, David Henry. *Clara Barton: In the Service of Humanity.* Westport, Conn.: Greenwood Press, 1995.

King, David C. *First Facts about American Heroes.* Woodbridge, Conn.: Blackbirch Press, 1996.

Oates, Stephen B. *A Woman of Valor: Clara Barton and the Civil War.* New York: Free Press, 1994.

Sloate, Susan. *Clara Barton: Founder of the American Red Cross.* New York: Fawcett Colombine, 1990.

baseball   See SPORTS FOLKLORE.

basketry   See CRAFTS, FOLK.

Bass, Sam (1851–1878)   Sam Bass is a legendary southwestern outlaw figure who originated in Texas folklore. As the legend would have it, Sam Bass was born on July 21, 1851, in Mitchell, Indiana. Early in life, indeed before he reached the age of 13, Bass was orphaned and left to the care of a relative. This stingy uncle mistreated and exploited Bass to such a degree that he made the decision to raft down the Mississippi River in order to escape him. He worked for a time in a Mississippi sawmill. Bass then resided in Denton, Texas. There, he became active in horse racing during the 1870s. Bass also drove cattle for a while and developed an association with Joel Collins, who would serve as his partner in crime.

In approximately 1877, Bass and Collins became involved with criminals and joined a gang in the Black Hills of the Dakota Territory. As were many other western bandits, he was romanticized as "Robin Hood on a fast horse," robbing the rich to give to the poor. There is little evidence to support this image of Bass,

however. He participated in such offenses as stagecoach, bank and train robberies, as well as murders throughout Texas and its environs. Bass conducted a short but noteworthy life as an outlaw until, thanks to the betrayal of a fellow criminal, he was mortally wounded in a July 19, 1878, ambush in Round Rock, Texas. Bass died a few days later, on his 27th birthday. He was buried there, with a stone inscribed with a message from his sister: "A brave man reposes in death here. Why was he not true?" When souvenir seekers destroyed the Bass tombstone, the Sam Bass Centennial Commission placed a memorial granite obelisk in its place.

The figure of Sam Bass has been the subject of cowboy songs, stories, ballads, and other lore and provided inspiration to such writers as Samuel Langhorne Clemens. John Denton's "Ballad of Sam Bass" is among the songs paying tribute to his exploits. He was also remembered with a statue in his likeness at Madam Tussaud's Waxworks of London.

See also: CLEMENS, SAMUEL LANGHORNE; COWBOYS; OUTLAWS; ROBIN HOOD; SOUTHWESTERN REGIONAL FOLKLORE.

For Further Reading:
Gard, Wayne. *Sam Bass.* Boston: Houghton Mifflin, 1936.

Martin, Charles L. *A Sketch of Sam Bass, the Bandit: A Graphic Narrative: His Various Train Robberies, His Death, and Accounts of the Deaths of His Gang and Their History.* Norman: University of Oklahoma Press, 1997.

McEntire, Nancy Cassell. "Sam Bass: The Ballad and the Man," *Western Folklore* 62, no. 3 (summer 2003): 189–214.

O'Neal, Bill. *Encyclopedia of Western Gunfighters.* Norman: University of Oklahoma Press, 1979.

Reed, Paula, and Grover Ted Tate. *The Tenderfoot Bandits: Sam Bass and Joel Collins, Their Lives and Hard Times.* Tucson, Ariz.: Westernlore Press, 1988.

Smith, Helena Huntington. "Sam Bass and the Myth Machine," *American West* (January 1970): 31–35.

"Battle Hymn of the Republic" See BROWN, JOHN; CIVIL WAR; MOTHER'S DAY.

"Beauty and the Beast" (legendary) "Beauty and the Beast" is a widely known version of the unlikely marriage tale in which two individuals of vastly different or contrary aspects nonetheless find happiness together.

This story begins with a father and his three daughters. On one occasion, when the father had to travel, he asked each child what she wished him to take home to her at the end of his journey. While the first two daughters asked for lavish gifts, the youngest requested only a small token to be found in nature, such as a flower or a piece of fruit.

Upon the father's return, he realizes that he has forgotten the promised token. He sets about a remedy and in the process of plucking a flower from someone's garden, finds himself confronted by the beast to whom the garden belongs. In order to negotiate this conflict, the desperate father makes a deal with the angry beast. He promises to return with one of his daughters to provide companionship for the beast. Upon returning home, the father secures the compliance of his youngest daughter in this demand.

After she has lived with the beast for a time, the daughter becomes quite homesick. Consequently, she arranges a visit home. The young lady is so grateful to be with her own family that her visit home exceeds the agreed-upon duration. Finally, she has a dream that some harm has befallen the beast, and so she returns to him and consents to marry him.

It is at this point that a spell placed on the beast is broken, and he is transformed back into what he once was: a prince.

This familiar tale has important elements in common with other fairy tales, such as the bewitched creature of "The Frog Prince" and the self-effacing beauty of "Cinderella."

The story of "Beauty and the Beast" has been the subject of many retellings, including a feature-length animated Disney film. The tale carries valuable lessons about generosity, sacrifice, and the ability to see beyond personal appearance to the deeper nature of an individual. In a world where doubt, superficiality, and the desire for immediate gratification seem to dominate human conduct, audiences find such moral teachings timely.

See also: CHILDREN'S FOLKLORE; "CINDERELLA"; FLOWERS; FABLES; FAIRY TALES; FROG PRINCE/FROG KING; MYTHS, FOLK.

For Further Reading:
Ashliman, D. L. *Folk and Fairy Tales: A Handbook.* Westport, Conn.: Greenwood Press, 2004.
Hallett, Martin, and Barbara Karasek. *Folk and Fairy Tales.* 3d ed. New York: Broadview Press, 2002.
Hearne, Betsy Gould. *Beauty and the Beast: Visions and Revisions of an Old Tale.* Chicago: University of Chicago Press, 1989.
Tatar, Maria, ed. *The Annotated Classic Fairy Tales.* New York: W. W. Norton, 2002.
Zipes, Jack. *Breaking the Magic Spell: Radical Theories of Folk and Fairy Tales.* Lexington: University Press of Kentucky, 2002.
Zipes, Jack, ed. *The Great Fairy Tale Tradition: From Straparola and Basile to the Brothers Grimm: Texts, Criticism.* New York: W. W. Norton, 2001.

beliefs, folk Folk beliefs are those convictions that are held and transmitted by ordinary people. Such beliefs span every aspect of American life.

Most folk narratives are predicated on some givens, or ideas that are held in common between the speaker and listeners—these beliefs generally concern what is true, right, natural, honorable, fortunate, beautiful, or ideal. Such beliefs contribute immeasurably to the creation of culture.

The folklorist Wayland Hand's "cycle of life" categorization of a society's folk beliefs aptly describes their diversity, including popular beliefs concerning (1) animals/animal husbandry; (2) birth, infancy, and childhood; (3)

cosmic phenomena, including times, numbers, and seasons; (4) death and funeral customs; (5) economic and social relationships; (6) fishing and hunting; (7) home and domestic pursuits; (8) human body and folk medicine; (9) love, courtship, and marriage; (10) plants and plant husbandry; (11) travel and communication; (12) weather; and (13) witchcraft, ghosts, and magical practices. Taken together, these distinct forms of folk belief constitute a set of values to inform individual and group behavior.

Consequently, folk beliefs are a key to understanding the folklore in everyday life in America. Beliefs about the supernatural in the United States have included conjuring, evil eye, Bloody Mary, ghosts, the devil, werewolves, urban legends, witchcraft, voodoo, and the unlucky nature of Friday the thirteenth. Beloved figures of holiday lore, such as Santa Claus and the Easter Bunny, are pivotal to American children's folklore. Most ideas about good and bad luck are matters of folk belief, including weather lore and wedding/marriage folklore. The same is true for ideas concerning health, from folk medicine to childbirth/pregnancy folklore. Efforts at prediction, such as dowsing, divination, clairvoyance, and fortune-telling, all rely on folk beliefs for their potency. In addition, ideas about magic and folk religion are incorporated in folk beliefs. Proverbs, with their pithy lessons of conduct and consequence, may represent the most succinct statements of folk belief.

Another powerful example of a folk belief is a taboo, a notion not of what should happen or be done, but rather what should not. Taboos exist in any culture and may involve any number of prohibitions. In some faiths practiced by Americans, for example, spiritual beliefs prohibit behavior such as dancing and rule out any but the most modest attire. Such beliefs order daily life and shape or constrain folklife.

Even the smallest matters can carry whole sets of folk beliefs. Fingernail parings, for instance, are sometimes used in magic as charms, amulets, or ingredients in witchcraft. Indeed, even the day on which one trims fingernails can be considered significant. As one folk saying goes, someone who cuts his or her fingernails on Saturday will see a lover on Sunday. The very appearance of fingernails has been used as a device to predict one's future luck.

In addition to functioning as a fundamental aspect of American folklore and folklife, folk beliefs offer a lens through which better to view and understand human behavior. Such beliefs also help define a culturally specific worldview.

See also: Bloody Mary; Chesnutt, Charles Waddell; childbirth/pregnancy folklore; Christmas; conjure/conjuring; devil, the; Douglass, Frederick; Easter; Easter Bunny; evil eye; folklore in everyday life; Friday the thirteenth; ghost; magic; May Day; medicine, folk; prediction; proverbs; religion, folk; supernatural; superstition; toasts/drinking; Tooth Fairy; urban legends; vampire; voodoo/hoodoo; weather folklore; wedding/marriage folklore; werewolf; witchcraft, Salem; worldview.

For Further Reading:

Bonfanti, Leo. *Strange Beliefs, Customs, and Superstitions.* Burlington, Mass.: Pride, 1980.

Browne, Ray, ed. *Forbidden Fruits: Taboos and Tabooism in Culture.* Bowling Green, Ohio: Bowling Green State University Popular Press, 1984.

Castle, Sue. *Mother Knows Best? The Truth about Mom's Well-Meaning (but Not Always Accurate) Advice.* Secaucus, N.J.: Citadel Press, 1995.

Engle, Peter. *Sneezing after Sex Prevents Pregnancy.* New York: St. Martin's Press, 1996.

Hand, Wayland, ed. *Popular Beliefs and Superstitions: A Compendium of American Folklore.* Boston: Hall, 1981.

Motz, Marilyn. "The Practice of Belief," *Journal of American Folklore* 111, no. 441 (summer 1998): 339–355.

Mullen, Patrick. "Belief and the American Folk," *Journal of American Folklore* 113, no. 448 (spring 2000): 119–143.

Randall, Margaret. "'Unsubstantiated Belief': What We Assume as Truth, and How We Use Those

Assumptions," *Journal of American Folklore* 117, no. 465 (summer 2004): 288–295.

Bigfoot/Sasquatch (legendary)   This mysterious creature has been sighted throughout the United States and represents one of the most enduring curiosities of American folklore.

As are the creature's lesser-known counterparts, such as the Jersey devil or Abominable Snowman, Bigfoot is an unexplained phenomenon. Some believe firmly in the existence of Bigfoot, while others regard him as an imaginary being. As the werewolf does, Bigfoot combines attributes of both humans and animals. Bigfoot, however, while strange in appearance and physically intimidating, is rarely described as an aggressor.

Although sightings of Bigfoot have been reported across America, the region most closely associated with this mysterious creature is the Pacific Northwest. Many stories of Bigfoot originate in the wooded areas of Washington State and British Columbia. For this reason, Bigfoot is forever tied to the region's folklore, including its history of logging.

The explanation for this creature's name is straightforward. Investigators of Bigfoot sightings search for evidence, including marks purporting to be massive foot impressions left behind on the ground. Some witnesses have even claimed to have still photographs, film, or video footage proving the existence of Bigfoot. The richer lore by far, however, is anecdotal and involves eyewitness testimony.

Most sightings characterize Bigfoot as a hairy figure walking upright and rather ape-like in aspect. While witness accounts vary, most cast Bigfoot as a tall figure, somewhere between seven and 10 feet tall. The creature is hefty, weighing in anywhere from 300 to 1,000 pounds. As the name implies, Bigfoot's signature feature, however, are the large footprint tracks left behind. Trackers have recorded the length of his prints as between 14 and 22 inches long, with a correspondingly long stride. Testimony

suggests that Bigfoot's other name, Sasquatch (a Salish term, meaning wild man), befits the creature's earthy and pungent odor.

Recent resurgence in the enthusiasm for the Bigfoot/Sasquatch intrigue has inspired some hoaxes and some commercial ventures in the Northwest that invoke the creature as a kind of regionally based mascot.

Bigfoot remains a modern monster mystery, and Americans continue to debate actively whether the mythic beast is the product of nature or of imagination.

See also: ANIMALS; BELIEFS, FOLK; CONSPIRACY FOLKLORE; FOLK HEROES/LEGENDARY FIGURES; FOLKTALES; JERSEY DEVIL; LEGENDS, FOLK; MONSTERS; NATIVE AMERICAN FOLKLORE; NORTHWESTERN REGIONAL FOLKLORE; SUPERNATURAL; WEREWOLF.

For Further Reading:
Bord, Janet, and Colin Bord. *The Bigfoot Casebook.* Harrisburg, Pa.: Stackpole Books, 1982.
Hunter, Don, with Rene Dahinden. *Sasquatch/Bigfoot: The Search for North America's Incredible Creature.* New York: Firefly Books, 1993.
Long, Greg. *The Making of Bigfoot: The Inside Story.* Amherst, N.Y.: Prometheus Books, 2004.
Napier, John. *Bigfoot: The Yeti and Sasquatch in Myth and Reality.* New York: E. P. Dutton, 1973.
Pyle, Robert Michael. *Where Bigfoot Walks: Crossing the Dark Divide.* Boston: Houghton Mifflin, 1995.

Billy the Kid   See McCARTY, WILLIAM HENRY.

Bird Day   See ARBOR DAY.

birth   See CHILDBIRTH/PREGNANCY FOLKLORE.

birthdays   Birthdays represent celebrations, often among family members and close friends, marking the anniversary of an individual's birth.

It is said that the earliest birthday parties were conducted because of a belief that evil spirits visit on one's birthday. The gathering of friends and family, along with the lighting of candles, represent methods of protection from the threat posed by these evil forces. Today, however, birthdays are largely festive occasions, when the customs of parties, candles, and the like, are observed with little connection to their earliest meanings. The trend is toward celebrating the individual having a birthday, particularly when that individual is a child.

Although it is the mother whose efforts in delivery might logically be celebrated, the usual practice is to focus attention instead on the child born. Indeed, even before they are old enough to understand what such festivities mean, American children are celebrated on the anniversaries of their birth. Customs include the ceremonial presentation of decorated cakes, inscribed with best wishes for the birthday boy or girl. Birthday cakes are typically served at the conclusion of a special meal or at the culminating moment of a birthday party. These cakes are traditionally adorned with a sufficient number of candles to equal the recipient's age and, in some cases, a bonus candle for luck or "to grow on." When these candles are lit, those celebrating sing in unison to the person. The usual song for this occasion is "Happy Birthday," a tune whose lyrics children have modified over the years for their own amusement. As one such version goes, "Happy Birthday to you / You belong in the zoo / You look like a monkey / And smell like one too." Once the song has concluded, the birthday boy or girl is to make a silent wish and then blow out all of the birthday candles. It is said that the person who is successful in extinguishing the candles in this way can expect the birthday wish to come true. If, however, the birthday wish is not kept a secret, it will not.

Childhood parties often involve rooms or backyards decorated with balloons and crepe paper streamers. Children's parties involve games, such as Pin the Tail on the Donkey. Sometimes the parties also feature a piñata, a treat-filled paper sculpture, designed for use in a game in which blindfolded children take turns trying to break through to the treats by striking at the form with a stick. Additional novelties and trinkets for guests may include confetti, horns, noisemakers, and goody bags containing toys, candies, and other remembrances of the day.

As annual celebrations, birthdays mark the stages of a life's journey. Some birthdays carry additional significance. For example, within Jewish communities, the 13th birthday is special for males and the 12th for females. These birthdays mark a coming of age, as the youth become eligible for religious adulthood through bar mitzvah/bat mitzvah. For American girls, the 16th birthday is observed as a landmark of sorts and is referred to as "Sweet 16." In addition, birthdays that render the individual eligible for new privileges, such as driving, voting, and drinking carry added significance.

Just as young people look forward to birthdays, as these occasions mark the maturation process, older ones come to dread the public signs of aging. By custom, birthdays starting from the age of 30 may begin to remark such regrets with "over the hill" motifs and jokes about being old. This is particularly true in years during which an individual's birthday marks a new decade in his or her life.

At birthdays across the lifespan, friends and loved ones convey their affection for the guest of honor by joining in festivities, as well as offering greeting cards and gifts in honor of the day.

See also: AGING AND FOLKLORE; ANNIVERSARIES; BAR MITZVAH/BAT MITZVAH; CHILDREN'S FOLKLORE; FAMILY FOLKLORE; FOOD/FOODWAYS; HOLIDAYS/OBSERVANCES; HUMOR, FOLK; RITES OF PASSAGE; TOYS, FOLK.

For Further Reading:

Cohen, Hennig, and Tristram Potter Coffin, eds. *The Folklore of American Holidays.* Detroit: Gale, 1987.

Goldschneider, Gary. *The Secret Language of Birthdays: Personology Profiles for Each Day of the Year.* New York: Viking Studio Books, 2003.

Humphrey, Theodore C., and Lin T. Humphrey, eds. *We Gather Together: Food and Festival in American Life*. Ann Arbor, Mich.: UMI Research Press, 1988.

Myers, Robert. *Celebrations: The Complete Book of American Holidays*. Garden City, N.Y.: Doubleday, 1972.

Santino, Jack. *All around the Year: Holidays and Celebrations in American Life*. Urbana: University of Illinois Press, 1994.

Turner, Judith. *The Hidden World of Birthdays*. New York: Simon & Schuster, 1999.

Black Bart See BOLES, CHARLES E.

black magic See WITCHCRAFT, SALEM.

Black Patriots Memorial See ATTUCKS, CRISPUS.

blood See BLOODY MARY; VAMPIRE.

Bloody Mary (legendary) "Bloody Mary" represents both the title and the central figure within a familiar urban legend that has for years terrified youth, especially females, poised before their mirrors in the dark.

"Bloody Mary," also known as "Mary Worth" or "Mary Jane," is an apparition whose appearance youngsters seek to summon with a specific mirror ritual. Routinized in something of the way a séance might be, the steps for invoking this spirit are widely known. Although the details of this ritual vary somewhat in practice, most descriptions of it involve a procedure of entering an unlit room (usually a bathroom) at night, staring at the mirror, and repeating the name "Bloody Mary" three or more times in succession. Sometimes, a declaration of belief ("I believe in you") is required to accompany this incantatory naming process. Frequently, there is also an interaction among participants, such as a finger-pricking and blood-commingling step, to hasten the result. The corresponding expectation is that this series of steps will make the image of "Bloody Mary"—typically, the bloodied figure of an adult female who died an unnatural death—visible in the mirror where one's own reflection would usually appear.

This folk ritual has been prevalent among American preteens, and its elements suggest that the "Bloody Mary" legend both expresses and addresses anxieties associated with puberty. Specific elements of the ritual, such as the setting (bathroom), the instrument (the mirror), and the spectacle (blood), have suggested to folklorists that this legend is linked to body consciousness in general and menarche in specific, corresponding as it does to age-appropriate fears surrounding the onset of menses.

Folklorists have also drawn parallels between "Bloody Mary" and other urban legends, such as the figure of the Vanishing Hitchhiker who disappears from a car's backseat, leaving behind a puddle of blood. Similar images of horror associated with blood appear throughout popular youth culture, such as the climactic stigma scene in the film *Carrie* (1976), during which a bucket of blood is ritually poured on the title character during a school dance. These concerns of viscera and defilement seem close to the surface for teens, whose physical transformations make them acutely conscious of their own bodies and the potential distress such changes might occasion.

See also: CHILDREN'S FOLKLORE; FOLK HEROES/LEGENDARY FIGURES; RITES OF PASSAGE; URBAN LEGENDS.

For Further Reading:

Dundes, Alan. *Bloody Mary in the Mirror: Essays in Psychoanalytic Folkloristics*. Jackson: University Press of Mississippi, 2002.

Langlois, Janet. "'Mary Whales, I Believe in You': Myth and Ritual Subdued," *Indiana Folklore* 11 (1978): 5–33.

Ray, Linda McCoy. "The Legend of Bloody Mary's Grave," *Indiana Folklore* 9 (1976): 175–186.

Summers, Wynee L. "Bloody Mary: When Ostension Becomes a Deadly and Destructive Teen

Ritual," *Midwestern Folklore* 26, no. 1 (spring 2000): 19–26.

boasts   See SPEECH, FOLK.

bodylore   *Bodylore* is a contemporary term used in folklore studies to refer to all human modifications of the physical form undertaken for cultural reasons.

For the folklorist, presentation of the body is a treasure trove of information concerning a society's values, aesthetics, and embodied practices. The term *bodylore* was coined by the scholar Katherine Young in anticipation of the 1989 meetings of the American Folklore Society. It is more inclusive than other terms in use, such as *body art* or *body ornamentation*. Indeed, this aspect of folklore can involve virtually any aspect of physical being, including posture, movement, and appearance. It can incorporate attire, adornment, markings, piercings, tintings and colorings, or tattoos and other bodily inscriptions. It can also include treatments of the body's hair, including shaving, dying, plucking, clipping, cutting, and bleaching. Finally, it may involve cosmetics and even plastic surgery.

Even within a single nation, bodily ideals and metaphors can vary widely, as can the circumstances under which body modifications may be common such as during initiations. There are countless perspectives on the human body and its condition. For example, the medical view of a woman's body likely proves distinct from the maternal view of it by a child. Such values, then, are context sensitive, and uncovering the reasons for such divergent perspectives can be fruitful work for folklorists. For example, some faith communities require body modifications, while others prohibit them. The latter is more common within the United States.

Tattoos and piercings are aspects of bodylore enjoying a resurgence in contemporary America. Also popular are temporary tattoos and ephemeral markings affixed to the skin with pigments such as henna. Tattoos may be placed virtually anywhere on the surface of the skin. Piercings are most commonly done on earlobes but may also be placed in the septum, navel, eyebrow, and tongue. While both tattoos and piercings were once considered subcultural, associated in the popular imagination mostly with those in prisons and gangs, they are now more common in all American populations. There are also methods for removing tattoos when individuals determine that they no longer wish to bear the markings.

Taken together, the practices studied as bodylore can afford insights into American notions of beauty, gender, sexuality, taboos, identity, privacy, profanity, and sanctity as expressed through actions on the bodily self.

See also: AMERICAN FOLKLORE SOCIETY; ART, FOLK; CRAFTS, FOLK; FOLKLORE IN EVERYDAY LIFE; RITES OF PASSAGE; RITUALS, FOLK.

For Further Reading:
DeMello, Margo. *Bodies of Inscription: A Cultural History of the Modern Tattoo Community*. Durham, N.C.: Duke University Press, 2000.

Rubin, Arnold, ed. *Marks of Civilization: Artistic Transformations of the Human Body*. Los Angeles: Museum of Cultural History/University of California, 1988.

Sklar, Deirdre. "Can Bodylore Be Brought to Its Senses?" *Journal of American Folklore* 107, no. 423 (winter 1994): 9–22.

Stewart, Susan. *On Longing: Narratives of the Miniature, the Gigantic, the Souvenir, the Collection*. Baltimore: Johns Hopkins University Press, 1984.

Wojcik, Daniel. *Punk and Neo-Tribal Bodylore*. Jackson: University of Mississippi, 1995.

Young, Katherine, ed. *Bodylore*. Knoxville: University of Tennessee Press, 1993.

Young, Katherine, and Barbara Babcock, eds. "Bodylore," *Journal of American Folklore* 107, no. 423 (winter 1994): 3–196.

Bogeyman   See MONSTERS.

Boles, Charles E. (Black Bart) (1832–c. 1917)   As the "Gentleman Bandit," Black Bart lived a mysterious but notorious life as a 19th-century outlaw in America.

This famous gunfighter and criminal was born Charles E. Boles in New York in 1832. He later moved to Illinois, then volunteered to serve in the Civil War. He attained the rank of sergeant in Illinois's infantry. Once the war concluded, Boles made his way west, where he attempted several activities, including prospecting, in hopes of acquiring wealth. When these efforts did not avail, Boles began his life of crime.

He began a string of stagecoach robberies that would earn him a reputation as a desperado. The first such holdup took place on July 26, 1875, when he robbed a Wells Fargo stage in California. Over the next few years, he would rob some 28 more stagecoaches. Boles became known as "Black Bart," a thief who often accomplished his work alone. His habit of treating passengers, especially women riders, well caused him also to be called the "Gentleman Bandit." He carried, but did not use, a shotgun. He refused to rob stagecoach passengers of their personal effects, instead concentrating on the cash carried within the vehicle strongboxes. This choice probably contributed to his popularity with the public, since he targeted impersonal entities such as banks and left individuals alone.

The strongbox thefts would also lead to another of Black Bart's criminal trademarks. He would take the money and then flee on foot, leaving behind the strongboxes, now containing original verses he had written. These poems added to Black Bart's mystique, as they brazenly recounted his deeds and sentiments about them:

Here I lay me down to sleep
To wait the coming morrow,
Perhaps success, perhaps defeat
And everlasting sorrow.
Yet come what will, I'll try it once,
My conditions can't be worse,
And if there's money in that box,
'Tis money in my purse.

The image of a thief as poet (or "PO-8," as his missives were signed) was nearly irresistible to an American public already fascinated with the Wild West and its outlaws. Journalists chronicled his robberies and rewards were issued for his arrest.

Black Bart's robberies came to a halt in 1883, when a November 3 heist ended in an injury. While leaving the scene, Bat left behind a blood-soaked handkerchief that eventually helped authorities track him down. Bart wound up serving four years in San Quentin Prison. After he emerged from his jail sentence in January 1888, not much is known about the whereabouts of the "Gentleman Bandit." Newspaper reporters clamored for information, but even they could not uncover the truth. Some claimed Bart had resumed his string of stagecoach robberies. On at least one occasion, a poem was left behind in an empty strongbox, but no one was sure whether this was the work of Bart or an imitator. It is believed that Black Bart died in approximately 1917, although rumors that he was still alive persisted as long as Wells Fargo stagecoaches traversed the nation's West.

As a rather unusual criminal, Black Bart was a romantic figure whose exploits became legend in American crime lore.

See also: CIVIL WAR; FOLK HEROES/LEGENDARY FIGURES; OUTLAWS; SPEECH, FOLK; WESTERN REGIONAL FOLKLORE.

For Further Reading:

Axelrod, Alan, and Harry Oster, with Walton Rowls. *The Penguin Dictionary of American Folklore.* New York: Penguin Reference, 2000.

O'Neal, Bill. *Encyclopedia of Western Gunfighters.* Norman: University of Oklahoma Press, 1979.

Bonnie and Clyde (1910–1934, 1909–1934) Born as Clyde Barrow (1909) and Bonnie Parker (1910), this bank robber and his partner in crime were known to the world simply as "Bonnie and Clyde." Their lives as criminals and fugitives inspire many to consider the fate of otherwise ordinary individuals who become part of extraordinary and memorable events, in this case ranging from bank robbery to murder. Their end occurred predictably, as they perished together in a hail of bullets fired at their getaway car during a Louisiana ambush on May 23, 1934.

The pair originally met while both were in their 20s. They made each other's acquaintance in their mutual home state of Texas in 1930, just four years before both would meet a violent end. Despite the fact that Parker was already married, and to a convicted murderer at that, she and Barrow formed a strong bond—often described by others as a romance—that compelled the two to conspire in a series of illegal activities. While one or the other might be incarcerated for a time, they remained connected for the rest of their short lives. For example, when Barrow, who idolized William F. Cody (Buffalo Bill), was sentenced to jail for burglary shortly after meeting Parker, she smuggled a gun to him in prison. Although he escaped for a time, he was retrieved and the two were reunited in February 1932 when Barrow was placed on parole.

Once Bonnie and Clyde were together again, they involved themselves in a variety of criminal activities including burglaries and bank robberies. They were also prime suspects in over a dozen murders. When Clyde's brother, Ivan "Buck" Barrow, along with his wife, Blanche, joined the notorious duo, their foursome commenced a truly historic crime spree. As a consequence of that activity, the fugitives found themselves the subject of an extended pursuit across several states, punctuated by exchanges of gunfire and failed attempts at capture. Law enforcement personnel remained dogged as they sought to arrest members of the Bonnie and Clyde gang. Finally, in May 1934, during an attempt to flee in an automobile, Parker and Barrow were shot to death by area police officers in a Louisiana stakeout.

Often romanticized both as lovers and as robbers, Bonnie and Clyde figure prominently within America's fascination with criminal cul-

ture. From fashion merchandising of "gun moll chic" to Arthur Penn's critically acclaimed 1967 feature film, *Bonnie and Clyde*, the signs remain clear that Americans continue to be curious about the lives and deeds of this outlaw couple, a pair so often the subject of story and song that even the narratives of their autopsies have commanded the attention of folklorists.

See also: CODY, WILLIAM F. (BUFFALO BILL); FOLK HEROES/LEGENDARY FIGURES; OUTLAWS; REGION, FOLK; WESTERN REGIONAL FOLKLORE.

For Further Reading:
Knight, James R., and Jonathan Davis. *Bonnie and Clyde: A Twenty-first-Century Update.* New York: Eakin Press, 2003.

Milner, E. R. *The Lives and Times of Bonnie and Clyde.* Carbondale: Southern Illinois University Press, 1996.

Owen, Richard, and James Owen. *Gangsters and Outlaws of the 1930's: Landmarks of the Public Enemy Era.* New York: White Mane, 2003.

Phillips, John Neal, and André L. Gorzell. "'Tell Them I Don't Smoke Cigars': The Story of Bonnie Parker." In *Legendary Ladies of Texas*, edited by Francis Edward Abernathy, 163–172. Dallas: E. Heart, 1981.

Rich, Carroll Y. "The Autopsy of Bonnie and Clyde," *Western Folklore* 29 (1970): 27–33.

Treherne, John. *The Strange History of Bonnie and Clyde.* London: Jonathan Cape, 1984.

Boone, Daniel (1734–1820) As a pioneer and explorer on the American frontier, Daniel Boone found his place as an icon of westward expansion.

Boone was born in 1734 in Reading, Pennsylvania. He was raised in a large Quaker family and learned early on about how to perform a range of farm chores. As a youth, Boone established his credentials as an outdoorsman, developing as a sharpshooter and hunter. He helped meet the needs of his family through what he caught and what supplies he secured through careful trading. Some of Boone's early adventures included participation in the French and Indian War, during which he drove supply wagons.

His later life and career would carry him west. Most memorable was Boone's role in opening the Cumberland Gap, a route to the area west of the Appalachian Mountains, in 1767. His Wilderness Road became the main route west. He would subsequently participate in a number of such expeditions. In time, Boone constructed a fort, dubbed Boonesborough, in the area that is now Kentucky. Along with his wife and 10 children, he lived in the wilderness. The Boone family became the target of several Indian attacks and captures, in one of which one of Boone's sons died.

Boone became a legend even during own lifetime, widely regarded for his talents as a hunter, trapper, and woodsman. He was also practiced in such trades as blacksmithing and surveying. During the American Revolution, Boone served as an officer in the Virginia militia. He later entered the state legislature and served several terms. He died in 1820, and his body would eventually be laid to rest in Kentucky, where he had distinguished himself as a frontiersman.

Daniel Boone became a popular figure of American lore, in part because he was featured as a character in literature and other media. For example, Boone's life provided the basis for James Fenimore Cooper's well-known Leatherstocking Tales, including *The Last of the Mohicans*. Boone's depictions in such a variety of expressive forms, with their tendency to mythologize even historical figures, make it difficult to determine fact from fiction in terms of Boone's career and exploits.

Known then as now as an accomplished trailblazer and statesman, Daniel Boone joins other icons of the American West, from Davy Crockett to Meriwether Lewis and William Clark.

See also: APPALACHIAN FOLKLORE; COOPER, JOHN FENIMORE; CROCKETT, DAVY; FOLK HEROES/LEGENDARY FIGURES; FRONTIER; LEWIS, MERIWETHER, AND WILLIAM CLARK; QUAKER FOLKLORE; REGION, FOLK; REVOLUTIONARY WAR; WESTERN REGIONAL FOLKLORE.

For Further Reading:

Bakeless, John Edwin. *Daniel Boone, Master of the Wilderness.* Lincoln: University of Nebraska Press, 1989.

Faragher, John Mack. *Daniel Boone: The Life and Legend of an American Pioneer.* New York: Holt, 1992.

Hammon, Neal, ed. *My Father, Daniel Boone: The Draper Interviews with Nathan Boone.* Lexington: University Press of Kentucky, 1999.

Lawlor, Mary. *Recalling the Wild: Naturalism and the Closing of the American West.* New Brunswick, N.J.: Rutgers University Press, 2000.

Lofaro, Michael. *Daniel Boone: An American Life.* Lexington: University Press of Kentucky, 2003.

Borden, Lizzie (1860–1927) Legendary for the two brutal murders she was alleged to have committed, Lizzie Borden (1860–1927) takes her place as one of relatively few women counted among America's most notorious criminals.

The fact that she was tried and acquitted of these homicides has done little to counter the memory of Borden as an infamous hatchet murderer. The controversy surrounding both deaths and their alleged perpetrator persists, along with a singsong children's rhyme still heard on playgrounds in the United States today: "Lizzie Borden took an ax and gave her mother forty whacks. / When she saw what she had done, she gave her father forty-one."

Some matters are not in dispute. As grisly crime scene photographs attest, there is no question that Lizzie Borden's father and stepmother, Andrew and Abby Borden, met horribly violent deaths. Discovered on August 4, 1892, in the private residence they shared with 32-year-old Lizzie in Fall River, Massachusetts, both bore the marks of repeated blows from an ax or similar sharp object.

But other aspects of the events have become the subject of extended debate. Was Borden in fact guilty of the murders? (She claimed to have been in the barn at the time.) Who else, such as Bridget Sullivan, the Borden family's housemaid, might have had sufficient access and motive to commit the crimes? What was the household's untold story? What torments might compel someone, particularly a family member, to such physical violence? The deep controversy surrounding Borden likely owes to the crime's affront to Victorian era sensibilities about womanhood and propriety. A hatchet murder would draw attention in and of itself, then or now, but the notion that an otherwise unremarkable "spinster" (Lizzie was not married) could be implicated in double parricide and, in its commission, in acts of brazen mutilation, was almost impossible for the public to fathom.

The trial itself is the subject of lore, particularly because, despite incriminating circumstantial evidence, Lizzie Borden was acquitted of both the deaths. Although legally exonerated of the crimes, Borden would find herself forever identified with the murders, stigmatized by accusations that she was responsible for brutally ending two innocent lives. She finished up her own life as a pariah at the age of 67, still living in the "Hill" district of Fall River, neither vindicated in public perception nor forgiven by her community.

Borden remains a recognizable figure within popular culture, and the deeds she is said to have committed still capture the nation's imagination. Contemporary retellings of the Borden tale abound, from spooky stories passed among children, to novels, films, plays, operas, and ballets dramatizing Borden's life and unfortunate end. As with other macabre tales, the Borden incident also finds its way into tourism, with eerie sites opened in Fall River, such as the "Lizzie Borden Bed and Breakfast" and its accompanying museum. Guests may stay overnight in the house where the murders occurred; more squeamish visitors, however, may opt to take the daytime tour. Lizzie Borden is likewise the subject, predictably enough, of many Internet sites. At least one "virtual Borden house" invites online guests to experience graphically the bloody scene of the crimes. Other Web sites, somewhat less sensational and morbid in purpose, offer digital archives of trial evidence, serving as curricular units for students posing as historical detectives sleuthing for the truth. That search continues.

See also: FOLK HEROES/LEGENDARY FIGURES; GENDER AND FOLKLORE; MUSEUMS, FOLK; NORTHEASTERN REGIONAL FOLKLORE; OUTLAWS; REGION, FOLK.

For Further Reading:

Bellesiles, Michael A., ed. *Lethal Imagination: Violence and Brutality in American History.* New York: New York University Press, 1999.

Brown, Arnold. *Lizzie Borden: The Legend, the Truth, the Final Chapter.* Nashville, Tenn.: Rutledge Hill Press, 1991.

Kent, David. *Forty Whacks: New Evidence in the Life and Legend of Lizzie Borden.* New York: St. Martin's, 1992.

Kent, David, and Robert A. Flynn. *The Lizzie Borden Sourcebook.* Boston: Branden, 1992.

Williams, Joyce. *Lizzie Borden: A Case Book of Family and Crime in the 1890s.* Bloomington, Ind.: TIS, 1980.

Boss Day (Boss's Day) One of the more recent holidays to appear in the United States is an annual tribute to the boss.

The observance began with Patricia Bays Haroski, a secretary employed in a State Farm Insurance office in Deerfield, Illinois. In 1958, she first paid tribute to her boss on October 16, which also happened to be his birthday. Haroski's enthusiasm for her boss's virtues may have owed something to the fact that her boss was also her father, Bays Haroski. Haroski advocated that the holiday be widened to recognize the accomplishments of other bosses, and that the day of celebration remain October 16 each year. She wanted to acknowledge and encourage leadership and cultivate appreciation between employees and employers.

As a consequence, greeting card companies, novelty retailers, and florists offer a variety of gift items with which employees may honor the boss on this occasion. Hallmark issued its first Boss Day card in 1979. Most common recognitions include greeting cards, balloons, workplace treats, or lunches out with the boss.

Lore concerning this wholly unofficial holiday suggests that workers greet the day with ambivalence. To make too much of the day is to risk being perceived as a sycophant. To ignore it entirely might prove impolitic. Typically, coworkers arrive at a consensus about what celebration is most suitable. In private, however, many may share the sentiment of a baffled employee who, upon learning of the unofficial observance known as National Boss Day, asked, "Isn't every day Boss Day?" It is doubtful that Boss Day will ever rival Secretaries Day (now also commonly known as Administrative Professionals' Day) in scale or visibility, since most employers see it as a time to make amends for a year's worth of missteps with their support staff. Even employees who admire the boss, in other words, may feel that employers receive adequate compensation and recognition of other sorts.

See also: ADMINISTRATIVE PROFESSIONALS' DAY/WEEK; HOLIDAYS/OBSERVANCES; INDUSTRIAL FOLKLORE; MIDWESTERN REGIONAL FOLKLORE; OCCUPATIONAL FOLKLORE; REGION, FOLK.

For Further Reading:

American Greetings Corporate Website. Boss Day. Available online. URL: http://corporate. americangreetings.com/topstories/boss_day01. html. Accessed March 10, 2006.

Brandt, John. "Dumb Bosses Day." *Industry Week* 253, no. 6 (June 2004): 22–23.

Hallmark Cards Corporate Website. Boss Day Fact Sheet. Available online. URL: http://hotnews.hallmark.com/boss_day_fact_sheet.html. Accessed March 10, 2006.

Norrell, Debbie. "Lifestyles Report: Workers' Day." *New Pittsburgh Courier*, October 24, 2004, 95: 85, B1.

Schropp, Mary. "Day for Bosses Finding a Few More Celebrants." *News Journal*, (Daytona Beach) October 16, 2003, 4A.

Boston Massacre See ATTUCKS, CRISPUS; REVOLUTIONARY WAR.

"Boy Who Cried Wolf, The" (legendary)

The Boy Who Cried Wolf" proves an apt example of how fables can be used to inculcate values in a folk audience, whether old or young.

The story centers on a shepherd boy. As he attends to his responsibility for watching over the village flock, the boy becomes restless. To entertain himself, then, he calls out to the villagers as if a wolf is threatening the sheep.

The people of the village dutifully climb the hillside to render assistance. When they arrive, however, they can find no wolf. The villagers, having discovered the boy's prank, caution the shepherd boy and then resume their places in the village.

A bit later, the boy repeats the cry for help, and once again the villagers rally to his aid by mounting the slope. This time, when they learn that there is still no wolf, the villagers speak more sternly to the boy and direct him to abandon his ploy. The boy remains unchastened, though, and enjoys his second stunt as much as the first.

It is not much later that the shepherd boy really does observe a wolf posing a danger to the village sheep. This time, however, the people of the village ignore his cries as false and do not stir from their activities.

That evening, when the boy has not returned their sheep from the hillside as is customary at day's end, they climb the hill a final time.

When they reach the boy, they find him weeping that his authentic call for help was ignored. Now the sheep must be retrieved, but the boy finally understands that people will learn to discount the statements of a liar, even when they are truthful.

This fable by Aesop makes the point that fun should not be had at others' expense, duties should be conducted seriously, and requests for help should be sincere. Failure to realize as much will compromise one's reputation and jeopardize one's well-being. Even today, when someone makes false or fanciful demands of others, that individual risks being characterized as a person who is only "crying wolf."

Literally hundreds of variants and retellings of "The Boy Who Cried Wolf" are available in print, including a whimsical reversal of the tale in Bob Hartman's *The Wolf Who Cried Boy*. In this fractured fable, a young wolf, one who has grown tired of dining on lamb burgers and musratatouille, instead develops a taste for Boys-n-Berry Pie. His parents promise they will prepare such a repast just as soon as the main ingredient can be found. After several mischievous shouts of "Boy!" however, the wolf discovers that once an entire troop of boy scouts finally does come into view, his hungry calls are unheeded.

See also: ANIMALS, CHILDREN'S FOLKLORE; "CHICKEN LITTLE"; FABLES; FAIRY TALES; MYTHS, FOLK; HUMOR, FOLK; LOUP-GAROU; "RED RIDING HOOD, LITTLE"; WEREWOLF.

For Further Reading:

Bernheimer, Kate, ed. *Mirror, Mirror, on the Wall: Women Writers Explore Their Favorite Fairy Tales*. New York: Anchor, 1998.

Cashdan, Sheldon. *The Witch Must Die: The Hidden Meaning of Fairy Tales*. New York: Basic Books, 1999.

Hartman, Bob. *The Wolf Who Cried Boy*. New York: Putnam Juvenile, 2002.

Tatar, Maria, ed. *The Annotated Classic Fairy Tales*. New York: W. W. Norton, 2002.

Brer Fox See BRER RABBIT; HARRIS, JOEL CHANDLER; UNCLE REMUS.

Brer Rabbit (legendary) Brer Rabbit is a recurring character in a series of traditional folk American tales. The most widely recognized among these are tales associated with a fictional storyteller, Uncle Remus, and were collected, published, and popularized by Joel Chandler Harris.

Brer Rabbit is primarily a trickster figure, and the character's exploits usually consist of battles of wits with other forces, whether human or animal. He marshals all his resources, including physical advantages, wiles, and a little magic now and then, to prevail over an opponent such as Brer Fox. The character remains a self-interested being who often considers himself above or outside social strictures or moral standards.

Brer Rabbit is an unlikely hero in this sense but endears himself to audiences with his humor and sense of mischief. As other trickster figures do, Brer Rabbit typically triumphs through unexpected turns of events, whether by chance or design. On this basis, he is related to other figures within folklore who rely upon subterfuge, such as outlaws, magicians, and changelings.

In addition to the traditional stories, Brer Rabbit resurfaces in recent American fiction, such as Ralph Ellison's *Invisible Man*, as an emblem of the African-American narrative legacy. In contemporary American culture, Bugs Bunny is likely the most recognizable descendant of the Brer Rabbit figure, always outwitting and eluding the hunter or rival.

See also: ANANSI; ANIMALS; CHANGELINGS; ELLISON, RALPH WALDO; FOLK HEROES/LEGENDARY FIGURES; HARRIS, JOEL CHANDLER; MAGIC; OUTLAWS; REMUS, UNCLE; SOUTHERN REGIONAL FOLKLORE; TRICKSTER.

For Further Reading:

Brasch, Walter. *Brer Rabbit, Uncle Remus, and the "Cornfield Journalist": The Tale of Joel Chandler Harris*. Macon, Ga.: Mercer University Press, 2000.

Brennan, Jonathan, ed. *When Brer Rabbit Meets Coyote: African-Native American Literature*. Urbana: University of Illinois Press, 2003.

Faulkner, William J. *The Days When the Animals Talked: Black American Folktales and How They Came to Be*. Trenton, N.J.: Africa World Press, 1993.

Reesman, Jeanne Campbell. *Trickster Lives: Culture and Myth in American Fiction*. Athens: University of Georgia Press, 2001.

Brown, John (1800–1859) As a committed leader in the movement to abolish American chattel slavery, John Brown earned a place within the nation's antebellum history and lore.

John Brown, born in 1800, was one of many antislavery activists in the United States during the 19th century. Few were more committed to the cause. He is best known as the leader of an October 1859 raid on the Harpers Ferry, Virginia, arsenal. Brown and his band of followers held slaveholders hostage there for 10 days before the raid was thwarted. The goal was both to chasten slave owners and to incite a slave rebellion. Along with other events demonstrating unrest during this era, such as Nat Turner's 1831 revolt in Southampton, Virginia, the action on Harpers Ferry confirmed southern fears about the potential for violent resistance. As a white northerner, Brown drew especially harsh criticism from southerners, who deemed him an outside agitator. For that role, he was tried for treason. His 1859 death by hanging for involvement in the raid rendered him a martyr for the cause of freeing the slaves. Events such as the Brown-led raid did help set the scene for the Civil War and the subsequent emancipation of slaves.

As with the leaders of other protests against American slavery, such as Nat Turner and Denmark Vesey, John Brown became the subject of a great deal of lore. Various songs responded to the events that made Brown famous. An 1860 lyric describing his sacrifice, "John Brown's Body," was sung to the tune of "The Battle Hymn of the Republic" by Union troops during the Civil War. A mural of the raid, painted by John Steuart Curry and entitled *The Tragic Prelude*, also fixed Brown's image firmly in the public imagination. At the center of this composition stands John Brown, wild eyes and arms outstretched. In one hand is a Bible, in the other a rifle.

Regarded as passionate by his supporters and fanatical by his opponents, John Brown lost his life in the attempt to end U.S. slavery.

See also: CIVIL WAR; FOLK HEROES/LEGENDARY FIGURES; LINCOLN, ABRAHAM; PROTEST IN FOLKLORE; REGION, FOLK; RELIGION, FOLK; SLAVERY; SOUTHERN REGIONAL FOLKLORE; TURNER, NAT; VESEY, DENMARK.

For Further Reading:

Finkelman, Paul, ed. *His Soul Goes Marching On: Responses to John Brown and the Harpers Ferry Raid.* Charlottesville: University Press of Virginia, 1995.

Flanagan, John. "Folk Elements in John Brown's Body," *New York Folklore* 20 (1964): 243–256.

Joyner, Charles W. *Shared Traditions: Southern History and Folk Culture.* Urbana: University of Illinois Press, 1999.

Oates, Stephen. *Our Fiery Trial: Abraham Lincoln, John Brown, and the Civil War Era.* Amherst: University of Massachusetts Press, 1979.

Oates, Stephen. *To Purge This Land with Blood: A Biography of John Brown.* New York: Harper & Row, 1970.

Peterson, Merrill. *John Brown: The Legend Revisited.* Charlottesville: University of Virginia Press, 2002.

Brown, Margaret Tobin (Unsinkable Molly Brown) (1867–1932) Denver's Margaret Tobin Brown became known as the Unsinkable Mrs. Brown after her passage on a fateful voyage on the RMS *Titanic*.

Brown was born to modest circumstances in Hannibal, Missouri, the region made famous in the writings of the American author Samuel Langhorne Clemens (Mark Twain). Her father was an abolitionist, purported to have worked with the antislavery activist John Brown.

As a self-proclaimed "daughter of adventure" and the wife of an affluent Colorado miner, James Joseph "J. J." Brown (also known as Leadville Johnny), Margaret Brown led a colorful life. The best known incident in it involved her survival of the sinking of the *Titanic*, which struck an iceberg on its maiden voyage in 1912. The vessel had been promoted as "unsinkable," a claim that proved more bold than accurate on the basis of its fate.

More than 1,500 people lost their lives in the *Titanic* incident. Brown, however, was one of the passengers who managed to escape death on that occasion. Biographies of Brown indicate that she rowed for hours to help the group reach safety. The lore surrounding her survival further suggests that she took charge of the occupants of her lifeboat, clothing others in her finery and using a gun to threaten anyone who declined to help row.

When interviewed about her good fortune in enduring the crash, Brown thanked family luck, terming the Browns "unsinkable." As a play on the marketing claim for the *Titanic* and as a comment on her fortitude, others dubbed the Denver socialite and philanthropist the Unsinkable Mrs. Brown.

Her sensational experience later inspired a production for musical theater entitled *The Unsinkable Molly Brown* and a 1964 motion picture of the same name, in which the actress Debbie Reynolds portrayed the leading role of Margaret (Molly) Brown. Today, visitors to the Denver residence of the Browns can tour a Victorian house museum and learn about the woman who renovated it and, through her own fame, helped preserve it for future generations.

Her part in the rescue of the 24 occupants of Lifeboat 6 of the *Titanic*, the details of which are thought by some to be more legend than strict historical fact, established Margaret Brown's place in the popular imagination surrounding this episode in disaster folklore.

See also: BROWN, JOHN; CLEMENS, SAMUEL LANGHORNE; FOLK HEROES/LEGENDARY FIGURES; MARITIME FOLKLORE; MUSEUMS, FOLK; REGION, FOLK; WESTERN REGIONAL FOLKLORE.

For Further Reading:

Caroline Bancroft. *The Unsinkable Mrs. Brown.* Boulder, Colo.: Johnson Books, 1963.

Iversen, Kristen. *Molly Brown: Unraveling the Myth: The True Life Story of the Titanic's Most Famous Survivor.* Boulder, Colo.: Johnson Books, 1999.

Landau, Elaine. *The Heroine of the Titanic: The Real Unsinkable Molly Brown.* New York: Clarion, 2001.

Molly Brown House. Molly Brown House Museum. Available online. URL: http://mollybrown.org/. Accessed March 10, 2006.

Tallman, Marjorie. *Dictionary of American Folklore.* New York: Philosophical Library, 1960.

Walters, Charles. *The Unsinkable Molly Brown.* Warner Home Video, 1964/2000.

Brown, Sterling Allen (1901–1989) Best remembered for his association with the Harlem Renaissance, the African-American author and educator Sterling Brown sustained a long and productive writing career. Brown was widely acclaimed as a poet, but he also generated a distinguished body of writings in other forms: essays, reviews, criticism, and folklore.

Born Sterling Allen Brown in 1901, the author grew up in the intellectually stimulating environment of Howard University. There, his father, the Reverend Sterling N. Brown, served as a dean of religion. Reverend Brown's profession exposed his son not only to an academic environment, but also to an atmosphere of racial consciousness. This world was populated by such figures as Frederick Douglass and Booker Taliaferro Washington. As a youngster, Sterling Brown became aware of the need to contest racial inequality, stereotypes, and segregation.

Given his father's connection to Howard, it may be unsurprising that Sterling Brown looked to education as a pursuit by which to advance the cause of racial equality. Brown earned degrees from Williams College (1922) and Harvard University (1923). While still a student, Brown became immersed in the work of such poets as Robert Frost and Carl Sandburg. He then embarked on a project to develop a poetry of the people, verse capable of reflecting the rich experiences and painful legacies of African Americans.

In so doing, Sterling Brown took energy and inspiration from his encounters with ordinary people, but particularly with rural residents. Brown's poems, often framed in dialect, sought to capture not only the perspectives but also the voices of black America. For these efforts, Brown would ultimately be hailed by such figures as Alain Le Roy Locke and James Weldon Johnson, who praised him as a folk poet.

In addition to his commitment to rendering sounded language on the page, Sterling Brown attended closely to the cultural forms emerging from African-American music and performance: blues, jazz, work songs, and the like. Brown functioned as something of a social historian, putting in print the lyrical signatures of contemporary African American song.

Later, during the Great Depression, Brown joined other writers and artists employed through programs in the New Deal. As editor of Negro affairs for the Works Progress Administration's Federal Writers' Project, Brown continued his work toward an inclusive American history by coordinating collections of cultural narratives such as former slaves' interviews. These first-person accounts, precursors of today's oral histories, attempted to honor and preserve the direct testimony of those who emerged from U.S. slavery.

Brown's publications, both during that era and subsequently, were plentiful. He labored to challenge the racial stereotypes and contest the marginalization of artistic work by African Americans. Examples of his book-length works include *Southern Road* (1932), *The Negro in American Fiction* (1937), and *Negro Poetry and Drama* (1937). In works such as his poem "Remembering Nat Turner," Brown challenged readers simultaneously to reckon with the power of historical memory and question its omissions.

Meanwhile, Brown conducted a lengthy career as a university educator. Early in his teaching career, he worked at Virginia Seminary, Lincoln University, and Fisk University. He found his most lasting intellectual home, however, by returning to Howard University, where he remained until his 1969 retirement.

Brown's commitment to a black aesthetic linked his writings to those of a generation of authors such as Claude McKay, Jean Toomer, and James Mercer Langston Hughes. These figures contributed to an explosion of works examining and reflecting upon African-American expressive culture. Together, they were termed the Harlem Renaissance and would set in place the foundation for later black aesthetic movements. Poets from Gwendolyn Brooks to Sonia Sanchez bear the influence and extend the legacy of Sterling Brown. By replacing the flat perceptions of such stock characters as the tragic mulatto with more fully dimensional and nuanced representations of African Americans, Sterling Allen Brown offered a corrective to the prior and pejorative images of a whole population's cultural inheritance.

See also: AFRICAN-AMERICAN FOLKLORE; DEPRESSION, THE GREAT; DOUGLASS, FREDERICK; FOLKLORE IN AMERICAN LITERATURE; HISTORY, FOLK; HUGHES, JAMES MERCER LANGSTON; LOCKE, ALAIN LE ROY; MUSIC, FOLK; REGION, FOLK; SANDBURG, CARL; SOUTHERN REGIONAL FOLKLORE; TOOMER, JEAN; TURNER, NAT; WASHINGTON, BOOKER TALIAFERRO.

For Further Reading:

Alexander, Elizabeth. "Listen Up: Sterling Brown's Folk Remedies," *Village Voice Literary Supplement* 85 (May 1990): 23.

Brown, Sterling. "The Approach of the Creative Artist to Studies in Folklore," *Journal of American Folklore* 59, no. 234 (fall 1946): 506–507.

———. "The Blues as Folk Poetry." In *Folk-Say: A Regional Miscellany*. Vol. 1, edited by Benjamin A. Botkin, pp. 324–329. Norman: University of Oklahoma Press, 1930.

———. "Negro Folk Expression: Spirituals, Seculars, Ballads, and Worksongs," *Phylon* 14 (winter 1953): 45–61.

Gabbin, Joanne. *Sterling A. Brown: Building the Black Aesthetic Tradition*. Westport, Conn.: Greenwood Press, 1985.

Rowell, Charles H. "Sterling A. Brown and the Afro-American Folk Tradition." In *The Harlem Renaissance Re-Examined*, edited by Victor A. Kramer, 315–337. Georgia State Literary Studies 2. New York: AMS, 1987.

Wright, John S. "Sterling Brown's Folk Odyssey." In *American Literature, Culture, and Ideology: Essays in Memory of Henry Nash Smith*, edited by Beverly R. Voloshin, 331–343. New York: Peter Lang, 1990.

Buffalo Bill   See CODY, WILLIAM F. (BUFFALO BILL).

Bunyan, Paul (legendary)   Paul Bunyan is the mythic American woodsman and folk hero.

There is some debate concerning the origins of this figure. Some contend that the character of Paul Bunyan was inspired by an actual 19th-century Canadian logger. Others believe that Bunyan was a literary creation rather than the basis for a folk tradition.

Some facts are known about the history of this mythic hero. The first print reference to Bunyan appears in 1910 in the works of the journalist James McGillivray. Soon after that, Bunyan was featured prominently in a series of advertisements for the Red River Lumber Company. This concept for promotion began with W. B. Laughead, a former lumberjack then working in the advertising field. From 1914 to 1922, booklets for Red River Lumber included content about the adventures of Paul Bunyan. Because there is not a clearly documented oral tradition for Bunyan stories, and because he may then be the invention of writers and advertisers, folklorists have suggested that Bunyan may be an example of fakelore, or invented lore.

Whether or not that is the case, Paul Bunyan is a popular icon of the logging West. As do other occupational heroes, Bunyan possessed superhuman characteristics. He had a strong work ethic, and so the results of his labor span many states, although he is most closely associated with Minnesota. As a lumberjack, Bunyan was known for feats of strength and endurance. The image of Bunyan, clad in his plaid shirt and stocking cap, appears in a wide variety of stories, roadside tributes, and area festivals. In such depictions, the legendary logger often appears accompanied by his loyal companion, Babe the Blue Ox.

Paul Bunyan is typically included in collections of American tall tales, and the stories of his exploits reflect that genre's tendency toward hyperbole and improbable occurrence. In one such tale, Paul Bunyan fashioned the Great Lakes to serve as Babe's watering hole.

Along with comparable figures, from Febold Feboldson to Pecos Bill, Paul Bunyan appears in fanciful accounts of the nation's settlement.

See also: ANIMALS; BABE THE BLUE OX; FAKELORE; FEBOLDSON, FEBOLD; FOLK HEROES/LEGENDARY FIGURES; FOLKLORE IN AMERICAN LITERATURE; FOLKTALES; MIDWESTERN REGIONAL FOLKLORE; OCCUPATIONAL FOLKLORE; PECOS BILL; REGION, FOLK.

For Further Reading:

Fowke, Edith, and Carole Carpenter, eds. *Explorations in Canadian Folklore*. Toronto: McClelland and Stewart, 1985.

Hutchinson, W. H. "The Cesarean Delivery of Paul Bunyan," *Western Folklore*, 22 (1963): 1–15.

Stekert, Ellen J. "The False Issue of Folklore vs. 'Fakelore': Was Paul Bunyan a Hoax?" *Journal of Forest History* 30, no. 4 (1986): 180–181.

Stewart, K. Bernice, and Homer A. Watt. "Legends of Paul Bunyan, Lumberjack." In *Wisconsin Folklore*, edited by James Leary, 139–148. Madison: University of Wisconsin Press, 1998.

burial customs   Over the course of America's history, customs surrounding the treatment of the deceased have changed considerably.

During the earliest periods in America, the treatment of the deceased reflected the heritage colonists took with them to the New World. These customs were largely European, but the actual graves and stones were befitting the religions Anglo-American settlers observed. For example, it was typical during the early phases of American history for the burial site to be a church graveyard rather than a cemetery.

By the 19th century, cemeteries became the standard burial site. Burial customs became more elaborate, with obelisks and crypts joining traditional headstones as memorial tributes in most cemeteries. During the 20th century, other methods for handling human remains became more common. Of these alternatives, cremation is likely the most common, but cryogenics found its advocates and some revisited such practices as mummification.

With millions of Americans dying annually and land for burial at a premium, it may be that customs will continue to change. What is unlikely to change, however, is the extent to which these folk beliefs and practices reveal American attitude toward religion, death, and mourning.

See also: CEMETERY FOLKLORE; DEATH; FOLKLORE IN EVERYDAY LIFE; RELIGION, FOLK.

For Further Reading:
Coffin, Margaret. *Death in America: The History and Folklore of Customs and Superstitions of Early Medicine, Funerals, Burials, and Mourning.* Nashville, Tenn.: Thomas Nelson, 1976.

Coleman, Penny. *Corpses, Coffins, and Crypts: A History of Burial.* New York: Henry Holt, 1997.

Sloane, David Charles. *The Last Great Necessity: Cemeteries in American History.* Baltimore: Johns Hopkins University Press, 1991.

Cable, George Washington (1844–1925) Along with other well-known American writers with strong associations to region, such as Samuel Langhorne Clemens, William Faulkner, and Sarah Orne Jewett, George Washington Cable stands among those of the nation's authors whose texts manage to capture both the power of a place and the texture of that locale's folk cultures. As a writer of fiction, essays, history, and journalism, Cable used as his signature subject matter the culture of Louisiana and, in particular, the lore emerging from its diverse racial and ethnic communities. Indeed, Cable was a member of the American Folklore Society.

When a writer addresses the landscape of a specific area, readers can be quick to dismiss the work as local color writing, a characterization that amounts to faint praise in the harshly exclusive realm of literary criticism. Cable's works are often consigned to the local and the author in turn cast as a minor writer of realist prose. If one considers the power of his writing to evoke the rich folklore and customs of that region, however, Cable's works generate both a renewed literary and social interest.

From its spicy cuisine and spirited music to its mysterious tales of voodoo and magic, Cajun country has long enjoyed a reputation for creatively combining the customs and practices of its many cultural influences. The very term by which many cultural expressions and products of the area are now described, *Creole*, hints at these complex mixtures of cultural origin and ancestry. First used in a linguistic context to denote a hybrid language combining elements of French and West African speech, the word *Creole* and its now-widening of usage to describe an array of other expressive forms tied to the region suggest that Louisiana, as does its famous gumbo, consists of a cultural and ethnic mélange. From the standpoint of the folklorist, Louisiana was an irresistible resource.

Cable was himself a native of New Orleans, born in 1844. He left school when he was just 14 and subsequently joined the Civil War as a member of the Confederate Cavalry. He sustained two injuries from his involvement in that conflict. Such beginnings might predispose any writer to a strong association with the South; in Cable's case, that loyalty amounted to an allegiance to subject matter more than politics. His devotion to the area's traditions should not be mistaken for a wholesale endorsement of the assumptions underlying that past. With his prose, George Washington Cable simultaneously worked to capture the experience of life in the American South and to challenge its views on such area practices as racial segregation.

Over the years of his writing career, most of which he spent performing other duties such as bookkeeping and clerkships to make a living, Cable nonetheless proved an indefatigable

writer. Working in the tradition of realist fiction, Cable published numerous book-length
works, including novels, collections of short
stories, and anthologies of essays. The very titles
of these works typically signal the author's preoccupation with his Louisiana roots: *Old Creole
Days* (1879), *Strange Stories of Louisiana* (1889),
and the work that is likely his best regarded,
The Grandissimes: A Story of Creole Life (1880).
Cable proved an avid collector of Creole tales
and other lore and drew inspiration for his own
imaginative work from the lush tapestry of Louisiana storytelling traditions. For these efforts,
Cable earned a niche within the annals of both
southern writing and American literature.

In his writings, Cable displayed a compelling
interest not only in the content of Louisiana's
stories, but the manner of their telling. Readers of his fiction benefit from more than the
writer's eye for area scenery; Cable's work, with
its attention to the region's distinctive manifestations of both story forms and dialect, reveals a
writer with an equally keen ear. Accent, inflec-
tion, pacing, and interplay of voices all figure in
the way Cable's Creole tales unfold on the page,
approximating the nuances of sounded language.
With such features as dialect, Cable's writings
evoke the important differences in voice and
vision among Louisiana's denizens.

Cable's enthusiasm for the cultural legacies
of the bayou, however, did not render him inca-
pable of criticism. In the process of establishing
his literary profile, Cable managed to position himself as something of a social reformer,
especially on the matter of race relations. Cable
opposed racial segregation and so devoted a portion of his written works to explorations of the
"Negro Question," as it was then posed. Cable
rejected the role of apologist for the South's
legacy of discrimination.

Therefore, while Cable documented the culture of the South, he asked his audience to engage
with difficult and deeply controversial questions
about the region's past, including its residues of
attitudes and assumptions about race dating back
to the antebellum period in America. While his

unpopular stance on racial integration made the
author something of a heretic in the very land he
held dear, Cable's love of the South, and Louisiana in particular, along with his convictions
about race proved profound enough to weather
such criticism. Indeed, his work dared to invite
that response to promote needed reform.

See also: CAJUN FOLKLORE; CIVIL WAR; CLE-
MENS, SAMUEL LANGHORNE; CULTURE, FOLK;
FAULKNER, WILLIAM; PROTEST IN FOLKLORE;
REGION, FOLK; SLAVERY; SOUTHERN REGIONAL
FOLKLORE; SPEECH, FOLK; VOODOO/HOODOO.

For Further Reading:
Biklé, Lucy Leffingwell Cable. *George W. Cable: His
     Life and Letters.* New York: Scribners, 1928.
Butcher, Philip. *George W. Cable.* New York:
     Twayne, 1962.
Cleman, John. *George Washington Cable Revisited.*
     New York: Twayne, 1996.
Rubin, Louis, Jr. *George W. Cable: The Life and
     Times of a Southern Heretic.* New York: Pegasus,
     1969.
Turner, Arlin. *Critical Essays on George W. Cable.*
     Boston: G. K. Hall, 1980.
Wilson, Edmund. *Patriotic Gore.* New York: Oxford
     University Press, 1962.

Cajun folklore Cajun folklore has its origins in the 1755 British expulsion of a group of
French-speaking Canadians, known as Acadians, from what is now Nova Scotia during the
French and Indian War.

These French-speaking exiles made a new
home in southern Louisiana, and some settled in
Texas and California. The culture that resulted
among settlers in the Gulf Coast region, sometimes known as Cajun country, is a distinctive
mélange of Native American, Basque, European,
and French folk traditions. With its spicy cuisine
and spirited music, mysterious tales of voodoo
and magic, and celebrations such as Mardi Gras,
Cajun country has long enjoyed a reputation for
creatively combining the customs and practices
of its many cultural influences.

Most residents of the United States are most aware of Cajun folklore as expressed through food and foodways. The very term by which many cultural expressions and products of the area are now described, *Creole*, hints at these complex mixtures of cultural origin and ancestry. First used in a linguistic context to denote a hybrid language combining elements of French and West African speech, the word *Creole* and its now-widening of usage to describe an array of other expressive forms tied to the region suggest that Louisiana, as does its famous gumbo, consists of a cultural and ethnic mélange. From the standpoint of the folklorist, Louisiana is an irresistible resource to those involved in culture, literature, and the arts.

For instance, Cajun music is rich with cultural influences. It combines Caribbean, German, Scots-Irish, Spanish, Native American, and Anglo musical traditions to create new combinations of sound, rhythm, and movement. An example is the form zydeco, an energetic genre featuring fiddles and accordions. Cajun music achieved national visibility during the 1960s, when enthusiasm for folk music was high and the 1964 Newport Folk Festival featured Cajun musicians on the bill.

Along with other well-known American writers with strong associations to region, several famous authors have chosen Cajun history as their subject matter. For instance, in an 1847 piece, *Evangeline: A Tale of Acadie*, Henry Wadsworth Longfellow explored the plight of the Acadians. As a writer of fiction, essays, history, and journalism, George Washington Cable employed as his signature subject matter the culture of Louisiana and, in particular, the lore emerging from its diverse racial and ethnic communities. The very titles of these works typically signal the author's preoccupation with his Louisiana roots: *Old Creole Days* (1879), *Strange Stories of Louisiana* (1889), and the work that is likely his best regarded, *The Grandissimes: A Story of Creole Life* (1880). Cable, a New Orleans native, proved an avid collector of Creole tales and other lore and

drew inspiration for his own imaginative work from the lush tapestry of Louisiana storytelling traditions.

Cajun people are often stereotyped as a fun-loving, freewheeling group with appetites for food, drink, music, and good company. Their multicultural folklore and folklife inspire many researchers to explore their nuances and meanings.

See also: CABLE, WASHINGTON, GEORGE; CULTURAL GROUPS; FOLKLORE IN AMERICAN LITERATURE; FOOD/FOODWAYS; FRENCH-AMERICAN FOLKLORE; LONGFELLOW; HENRY WADSWORTH; MARDI GRAS; REGION, FOLK; SOUTHERN REGIONAL FOLKLORE; VOODOO/HOODOO.

For Further Reading:
Ancelet, Barry Jean. *Cajun and Creole Folktales: The French Oral Tradition of South Louisiana*. New York: Garland, 1994.
———. *Cajun Music: Its Origins and Development*. Lafayette: Center for Louisiana Studies/University of Southwest Louisiana, 1985.
Ancelet, Barry Jean, Jay D. Edwards, and Glen Pitre. *Cajun Country*. Jackson: University Press of Mississippi, 1991.
Bernard, Shane. *The Cajuns: Americanization of a People*. Jackson: University Press of Mississippi, 2003.
Brasseaux, Carl. *The Founding of New Acadia: The Beginnings of Acadian Life in Louisiana, 1765–1803*. Baton Rouge: Louisiana State University Press, 1987.
Conrad, Glenn, ed. *The Cajuns: Essays on Their History and Culture*. Lafayette: University of Southwestern Louisiana, 1985.
Dreyer, Edward. *Gumbo Ya-Ya: A Collection of Louisiana Folktales*. Boston: Houghton Mifflin, 1945.
Fortier, Alcée. *Louisiana Folk-Tales*. Boston: Houghton, Mifflin, 1895.
Gutierrez, C. Paige. *Cajun Foodways*. Jackson: University Press of Mississippi, 1992.
Hallowell, Christopher. *People of the Bayou: Cajun Life in Lost America*. New York: Dutton, 1979.
Reneaux, J. J. *Cajun Folktales*. Little Rock, Ark.: August House, 1992.

———. *Haunted Bayou and Other Cajun Folk Stories.* Little Rock, Ark.: August House, 1994.

cakewalk   See MINSTRELSY.

Calamity Jane   See CANNARY-BURKE, MARTHA.

California folklore   See BOLES, CHARLES E. (BLACK BART); CAJUN FOLKLORE; CARSON, KIT; CHAVEZ, CÉSAR ESTRADA; CHICANO FOLKLORE; DEPRESSION, THE GREAT; DISNEY, WALTER ELIAS; EARHART, AMELIA MARY; EARP, WYATT BERRY STAMP; FOLKLORE STUDIES; GHOST TOWNS; GOLD RUSH, THE; HAUNTED HOUSES; HIPPIES; JOAD, TOM; JAPANESE-AMERICAN INTERNMENT; KINGSTON, MAXINE HONG; KOREAN-AMERICAN FOLKLORE; KWANZAA; MUSIC, FOLK; NEW YEAR'S EVE/DAY; PARADES; POPLORE; PORTUGUESE-AMERICAN FOLKLORE; SMITH, WINDWAGON; SPANISH-AMERICAN FOLKLORE; STEINBECK, JOHN; WESTERN REGIONAL FOLKLORE.

camp folklore   America's camp lore has been thriving since the camping craze of the 1890s. The 19th century's enthusiasm for frontier and wilderness resulted in a fascination with the outdoors. The nation's fledgling conservation movement also fueled this interest. At the same time that industrialization and urbanization began to estrange people from the natural landscapes, early 20th-century national organizations such as the Young Men's Christian Association (YMCA) and the Boy Scouts and Girl Scouts of America emerged with programs designed to help youth reconnect with the Earth. The late 20th century's environmental movement made such opportunities even more attractive to Americans, and visitor counts at the nation's campgrounds and national parks are testimony to the importance of camping to American culture.

Camp folklore most often deals with the practices and customs associated with structured camps for youth, such as are frequented during summer months. Since many children attend the same camps each summer, these activities become family traditions. For example, boys in America may join scouting organizations and attend the same annual jamborees that their older brothers and fathers participated in. Camp experiences have a big influence on the childhood memories of boys and girls. The process often begins with orientation games and the assignment of camp nicknames. Each day and evening at summer camp has its routines, such as early rising rituals and the usual tales and songs around the campfire at night. Letters written home from camp are another tradition, as children adjust to being away from their families and the comforts of home. As their time at camp unfolds, youth engage in a nearly endless variety of jokes and pranks, such as shortsheeting and snipe hunts. Competitions with rival camps are also common, helping to unite campers in their desire to emerge victorious. The camping session often concludes with talent shows, skits, and other culminating performances. Finally, young people return home from camp with troves of stories about romances and adventures recalled from the previous summer.

Camp folklore is a fairly situation-specific element of children's folklore, but it is a widely experienced one for young Americans.

See also: CHILDREN'S FOLKLORE; EARTH DAY; FOLKLORE IN EVERYDAY LIFE; FRONTIER; GAMES AND PASTIMES; GHOSTS; GHOST STORIES; NAMING/NAMES.

For Further Reading:
Bronner, Simon. *American Children's Folklore*. Little Rock, Ark.: August House, 1988.
Ellis, Bill. "The Camp Mock-Ordeal: Theater as Life," *Journal of American Folklore* 94, no. 374 (fall 1981): 486–505.
Ellis, Bill. "'Ralph and Rudy': The Audience's Role in Re-creating a Camp Legend," *Western Folklore* 41 (1982): 169–191.
Mechling, Jay. "The Magic of the Boy Scout Campfire," *Journal of American Folklore* 93, no. 367 (winter 1980): 35–56.

―――. *On My Honor: Boy Scouts and the Making of American Youth*. Chicago: University of Chicago Press, 2004.

―――. "Patois and Pardox in a Boy Scout Treasure Hunt," *Journal of American Folklore* 97, no. 383 (winter 1984): 34–42.

campus folklore The college enviroment sometimes referred to as an "ivory tower" or world unto itself, has its own forms of traditions and folklore.

As academic organizations, campuses represent places where a folklorist can gather a host of oral folklore. Stories about topics such as tough professors, easy classes, and disastrous experiences with exams circulate widely. In addition, these are usually jokes and tales familiar to anyone who has spent time at colleges. These include humor and talk about cafeteria food, dating/mating prospects, and characteristic attributes of the campus community. Most campuses also have a number of terms and phrases that compose the local student slang.

Colleges and universities have some customs that are equally associated with high schools: team mascots, school colors, songs, cheers, mottoes, and the like. Sports teams and other groups on campus may have their distinctive lore, such as games, rivalries, and parties.

Those colleges functioning as residential educational settings often have additional lore related to student life and the local setting. These items include tales about buildings, annual events, landmarks, and symbolic objects. Any campus with sororities, fraternities, or other nationally-affiliated affiliations also has its signature features: pledge customs, initiation rituals, pranks, drinking practices, and the like. Most colleges and university students have also heard some tale tales, or urban legends, about unusual situations on campus. For example, many students have been told stories about the student who supposedly was granted an automatic 4.0 (or perfect grade average) for the semester when a roommate committed suicide.

Furthermore, college campuses have some distinctive rituals marking the opening and closing of the academic year, along with other key moments in the life of the institution. These occasions include convocations, graduations, and other ceremonies. Academic regalia, processions, caps and gowns, and other formal elements are usual at these times. Surrounding even such offical events are some folk customs, such as graduates' decorating the tops of their mortarboards with personally meaningful symbols and messages.

From formal dances to homecoming weekends, campus lore offers a full range of folk narratives and traditions that characterize American higher learning.

See also: AGING AND FOLKLORE; COURTSHIP/DATING FOLKLORE; CUSTOMS, FOLK; FOLKLORE IN EVERYDAY LIFE; GAMES AND PASTIMES; HUMOR, FOLK; ORAL FOLKLORE; RITES OF PASSAGE; SPORTS FOLKLORE; TOASTS/DRINKING; URBAN LEGENDS.

For Further Reading:

Bronner, Simon. *Piled Higher and Deeper: The Folklore of Student Life*. Little Rock, Ark.: August House, 1995.

Dorson, Richard. *American Folklore*. Chicago: University of Chicago Press, 1959.

Eble, Connie. *Slang and Sociability: In-Group Language among College Students*. Chapel Hill: University of North Carolina Press, 1996.

Horowitz, Helen Leftkowitz. *Campus Life: Undergraduate Cultures from the End of the Eighteenth Century to the Present*. New York: Alfred A. Knopf, 1987.

Oring, Elliott, ed. *Folk Groups and Folklore Genres: A Reader*. Logan: Utah State University Press, 1989.

Toelken, Barre. "The Folklore of Academe." In *The Study of American Folklore: An Introduction*, edited by Jan Harold Brunvand, 502–528. New York: W. W. Norton, 1986.

Cannary-Burke, Martha (Calamity Jane) (1852–1903) Martha Jane Cannary-Burke, born in 1852, went on to be known to folklore as "Calamity Jane."

Along with other women of the frontier, such as Phoebe Annie Oakley and Cattle Kate, Calamity Jane took on the adventures associated with life in the Wild West. From the 1870s on, she was known for her exceptional skills in riding and shooting, two fields that were otherwise dominated by her male counterparts. During her career, Calamity Jane became associated with a variety of individuals who would themselves emerge as frontier folk heroes, including Wild Bill Hickok.

Calamity Jane's image was singularly unconventional for a woman of her era. Whether for reasons of practicality or pose, she often dressed in men's clothing. Her nickname derived from Jane's contention that she promised calamity for any suitors. Nonetheless, she married a man named Cannary in 1885. This renowned wild woman of the frontier died in 1903, at the age of 51.

Calamity Jane figures as an important example of a female hero in the American folklore of westward expansion.

See also: FOLK HEROES/LEGENDARY FIGURES; FRONTIER; HICKOK, JAMES BUTLER; NORTHWEST REGIONAL FOLKLORE; OAKLEY, PHOEBE ANNIE.

For Further Reading:

Aikman, Duncan. *Calamity Jane and the Lady Wildcats.* Lincoln: University of Nebraska Press/Bison Books, 1987.

Coffin, Tristan. *The Female Hero in Folklore and Legend.* New York: Seaburg, 1975.

Faber, Doris. *Calamity Jane: Her Life and Her Legend.* Boston: Houghton Mifflin, 1992.

Glass, Andrew. *Bad Guys: True Stories of Legendary Gunslingers, Sidewinders, Fourflushers, Drygulchers, Bushwhackers, Freebooters, and Downright Bad Guys and Gals of the Wild West.* New York: Doubleday Books for Young Readers, 1998.

Capone, Alphonse Gabriel (Al) (1899–1947)   Al Capone is likely the most widely rec-ognized organized crime figure from Chicago's Prohibition era.

Alphonse Gabriel "Al" Capone was born to Italian immigrant parents in Brooklyn, New York, on January 17, 1899. After dropping out of school at age 14, Capone worked odd jobs in retail and industry until joining Manhattan's Five Points gang. Capone acquired the nickname "Scarface" while in his teens, so named after injuries sustained in a scuffle while working in a gangster-owned New York bar.

A still-young Capone fathered a son, born Albert "Sonny" Francis (December 4, 1918), by Mary "Mae" Coughlin, whom he married later that year. Untamed by family life, Capone involved himself in any number of violent crimes in gangland New York. In 1919, Capone relocated to Chicago, where he became something of an apprentice in the gang-dominated bootlegging business. Capone eventually rose to command the illicit business and was dubbed "The Big Fellow" by those who served him in an expanding industry of vice. Capone presided over a host of illegal activities in the late 1920s, including gambling, prostitution, and illegal brewing.

In his heyday, Al Capone is reputed to have dominated the Chicago crime scene, a reign that contributed to the city's reputation for corruption. While some have questioned the degree of such dominance, there is little question that Capone was a player within the crime world who eluded capture and most charges, in part by eliminating both rivals and potential informants. Perhaps the best known such incident was the February 14, 1929, mass killing known as the "Saint Valentine's Massacre," in which Capone's men murdered members of a rival gang. Headquartered at the Metropole Hotel, Capone's operation employed bribery, fraud, and threats to retain and build its power. Capone himself committed crimes, including murder, but more often delegated such activities to those in his service. He also relied upon the silencing powers of intimidation to shield him from prosecution.

In this way, Capone avoided all but the most minor consequences of his criminal activity. In the end, it would be tax evasion and violations of Prohibition laws that led to Capone's first felony conviction in 1931. Capone won his release in 1939 but emerged from incarceration in poor health as a consequence of syphilis. After a series of illnesses, Capone succumbed to a stroke on January 25, 1947. The self-made mobster's life had reached its end, but his tale had only begun.

Capone has not been forgotten, as can be demonstrated by any number of popular allusions, both direct and indirect, to the man's exploits. For example, Robin Callander and Mitch Murray invoke Al Capone by name in their 1974 song "The Night Chicago Died," made popular by Paper Lace in a number 1 *Billboard* hit. Mobsters of Capone's ilk are also recalled more obliquely in contemporary cultural references from the musical form of "gangsta" rap to the fictional saga of television's *The Sopranos*. For those interested in Capone's Chicago, today's visitors may participate in the "Untouchable Gangster Tour," a theatrical presentation and sightseeing presentation. The tour borrows its name from the moniker used to describe the group of federal agents charged with apprehending figures such as Capone. Led by Eliott Ness, they were called "The Untouchables" for their boast claim that they could not be bribed. The saga of Al Capone and his pursuit by Ness is retold in a 1987 feature film directed by Brian DePalma, *The Untouchables*.

See also: FOLK HEROES/LEGENDARY FIGURES; IMMIGRATION AND FOLKLORE; OUTLAWS; TOASTS/DRINKING; URBAN FOLKLORE.

For Further Reading:
Barra, Allen. "Gangster," *American Heritage Online* 50, no. 3 (May 1999): 1. Available online. URL: http://www.americanheritage.com/articles/magazine/ah/1999/3/1999_3_55.shtml. Accessed February 22, 2006.

Hoffman, Dennis E. *Scarface Al and the Crime Crusader: Chicago's Private War*. Carbondale: Southern Illinois University Press, 1993.

Kind, David C. *Al Capone and the Roaring Twenties*. Woodbridge, Conn.: Blackbirch Press, 1999.

Schoenberg, Robert J. *Mr. Capone*. New York: Morrow, 1992.

Yancey, Diane. *Al Capone*. San Diego: Lucent Books, 2003.

Carson, Kit (Christopher Houston Carson) (1809–1868)   Kit Carson is remembered as an American soldier and frontiersman of note.

Carson was born in Kentucky in 1809 but raised in Missouri. His father died when Kit was just nine years old, and so the young man was entrusted with considerable responsibility while still a youth. When he came of age, Carson relocated to New Mexico, the place from which his subsequent adventures would be launched.

As were other figures associated with the western frontier, Carson was active in outdoor activities. He was a hunter and trapper, rancher, mountain man, and guide. It was for these abilities that John Frémont secured Carson's services for expeditions west over the Rockies to reach Oregon and California. This role, and what it implied about his knowledge of survival in the wilderness, first called Carson to public attention.

He rose to even greater popularity for his contributions to the Mexican War. Among his contributions to the war effort was a heroic 1846 journey behind enemy lines to secure help, during which he traveled some 30 miles miraculously quickly. Carson continued his work as a soldier in the New Mexico Volunteer Infantry of the Union Army during America's Civil War. At this time, his duties involved Indian removal, most memorably portrayed by the "Long Walk," during which Navaho people were moved from Arizona to New Mexico on foot. Carson died in 1868.

In addition to appearing in popular cultural depictions of the American Southwest, Kit Carson is recalled as an explorer and warrior in the names given to numerous western towns, such as Carson City, Nevada.

See also: CIVIL WAR; FOLK HEROES/LEGENDARY FIGURES; FRONTIER; GOLD RUSH, THE; SOUTHWESTERN REGIONAL FOLKLORE.

For Further Reading:

Guild, Thelma, and Harvey Carter. *Kit Carson: A Pattern for Heroes.* Lincoln: University of Nebraska Press, 1984.

Krupat, Arnold. "American Autobiography: The Western Tradition," *Georgia Review* 35, no. 2 (summer 1981): 307–317.

Moody, Ralph. *Kit Carson and the Wild Frontier.* New York: Random House, 1955.

Roberts, David. *A Newer World: Kit Carson, John C. Frémont, and the Claiming of the American West.* New York: Simon & Schuster, 2000.

Schwartz, Henry. *Kit Carson's Long Walk and Other True Tales of Old San Diego.* LaMesa, Calif.: Associated Creative Writers, 1980.

carving   See ART, FOLK; ARTIFACTS, FOLK.

Cassidy, Butch   See PARKER, ROBERT LEROY.

cemetery folklore   Cemetery folklore is an important indicator of American attitudes toward death and dying.

From the customs used for burial to the manner in which graves are marked, groomed, and decorated, cemeteries reveal a great deal about the cultural beliefs regarding the dead and the afterlife. Cemeteries came into common use during the 19th century, when they displaced church graveyards as the typical burial site. Gravestones or headstones, so named because they extend vertically from the head of the grave plot, identified the deceased's name and life dates. Decorative motifs from winged death's heads to cherubs adorn early American headstones. Victorian gravesites were adorned with visual elements more in keeping with the era's neoclassical aesthetic, featuring urns, vines, and bits of verse. Today, the slate and marble of previous centuries have been displaced by polished and carved granite.

As an aspect of death lore, practices surrounding the siting, arrangement, and adornment of cemeteries reflect folk beliefs concerning the nature of faith, death, and grieving.

See also: AGING AND FOLKLORE; BURIAL CUSTOMS; DEATH; FOLKLORE IN EVERYDAY LIFE; RELIGION, FOLK.

For Further Reading:

Jackson, Kenneth, and Camillo José Vergara. *Silent Cities: The Evolution of the American Cemetery.* New York: Princeton Architectural Press, 1989.

Meyer, Richard. *Cemeteries and Gravemarkers: Voices of American Culture.* Logan: Utah State University Press, 1992.

———. *Ethnicity and the American Cemetery.* Bowling Green, Ohio: Bowling Green State University Popular Press, 1993.

Sloan, David Charles. *The Last Great Necessity: Cemeteries in American History.* Baltimore: Johns Hopkins University Press, 1991.

Wallis, Charles. *Stories on Stone: A Book of American Epitaphs.* New York: Oxford University Press, 1954.

centennial, American   See COLONIAL WILLIAMSBURG; FLAG DAY; HICKOK, JAMES BUTLER (WILD BILL); INDEPENDENCE DAY/FOURTH OF JULY; LIBERTY, MISS; SPORTS FOLKLORE; TRANSCONTINENTAL RAILROAD.

changelings   Changelings, characters capable of altering their form and/or appearance to meet the needs of a situation, are a motif within folk tales.

Shape shifters are a staple of folk storytelling, and they are especially frequent within heroic tales in which a figure triumphs against the odds. The ability to transform oneself often represents the key advantage in the struggle to prevail over a villain or other obstacle. The trickster tradition, as exemplified by Coyote and Anansi, pro vides one example of a story genre in which the changeling becomes a signature feature.

Such transmogrification typically occurs in response to specific desires or challenges the character faces within a tale. In some cases, the ardor of courtship causes a character to become more pleasing to a potential mate. Sometimes a contest calls for a character to draw from resources that include the magical. In still other instances, a character undertakes transformation for the purposes of concealment or escape, as when it becomes necessary to disguise or remove oneself.

Such folk characters manifest desires for self-modification that all readers/listeners have felt at one time or another. Changelings demonstrate in dramatic ways the power of appearances to shape the outcome of events. Those who can alter their appearance can also exert some control over their environments and interactions with others.

See also: ANANSI; COYOTE; DEVIL, THE; FOLKTALES; STAGOLEE; TRICKSTER; VAMPIRE; WEREWOLF.

For Further Reading:

Eberly, Susan Schoon. "Fairies and the Folklore of Disability: Changelings, Hybrids and the Solitary Fairy," *Folklore* 99, no. 1 (1988): 58–77.

Jones, Dudley, and Tony Watkins, eds. *A Necessary Fantasy? The Heroic Figure in Children's Popular Culture.* New York: Garland, 2000.

Landay, Lori. *Madcaps, Screwballs, and Con Women: The Female Trickster in American Culture.* Philadelphia: University of Pennsylvania Press, 1998.

Reesman, Jeanne Campbell. *Trickster Lives: Culture and Myth in American Fiction.* Athens: University of Georgia Press, 2001.

Skjelbred, Ann Helene Bolstad. "From Legends of the Past to Timeless Stories about Man: The Changeling at All Times," *Arv: Nordic Yearbook of Folklore* 55 (1999): 93–103.

chanteys, sea   See MARITIME FOLKLORE.

Chapman, John (Johnny Appleseed) (1774–1845) Johnny Appleseed is among the best known figures in all of American folklore.

The character of Johnny Appleseed was inspired by the life and career of John Chapman (September 1774–March 1845). Born in Massachusetts, Chapman/Appleseed was an unconventional person. He followed the teachings of a philosopher named Emmanuel Swedenborg, who promoted benevolence and denounced materialism. Chapman was a vegetarian, a naturalist, and, purportedly, a soothsayer. He lived simply and cared deeply about spirituality, the Earth, and its creatures.

As many Americans living during his era did, Chapman decided to venture west and explore the country's frontier. His trek began in his home state of Massachusetts and passed through the states of Pennsylvania, Ohio, Illinois, and Indiana.

According to most accounts, Chapman busied himself during his journey by planting apple seeds along his route. This activity caused others to begin referring to him as "Johnny Appleseed," the name by which he is now remembered. His efforts as an agriculturalist provided the basis for a legend, and many apple orchards today claim to owe their beginnings to Johnny Appleseed. Chapman's grave is located in Fort Wayne, Indiana, nestled within Johnny Appleseed Park. Appleseed has been celebrated ever since with stories, songs, apple festivals, postage stamps, and a film vignette within Walt Disney's 1948 film, *Melody Time.*

Folklorists such as Richard Dorson contend that the lore surrounding this individual became distorted and exaggerated through the misdeeds of profiteers who wished to exploit the post–World War I enthusiasms for national culture. Such opportunism, usually by anthologists and authors of children's books, threatened to turn a genuine folk figure into an icon of fakelore, such as Febold Feboldson.

Today, it is difficult to discern definitively where John Chapman ends and Johnny Appleseed begins. The cartoonlike figure of an eccentric, walking barefoot and wearing a cooking pot for a hat, is likely an embellishment. The basic idea of a man responsible for the planting of apple trees during pioneer times, however, seems to coincide with the historical record.

Whether he is called John Chapman or Johnny Appleseed, there is little question that he introduced apple seeds to the American frontier, an occupation that established him as a legendary figure in American lore. Along with Paul Bunyan and John Henry, Johnny Appleseed helps define the hero in occupational folklore.

See also: ARBOR DAY; BUNYAN, PAUL; DISNEY, WALTER ELIAS; FAKELORE; FEBOLDSON, FEBOLD; FOLK HEROES/LEGENDARY FIGURES; FRONTIER; HENRY, JOHN; LEGENDS, FOLK; OCCUPATIONAL FOLKLORE; WORLD WAR I.

For Further Reading:

Hillis, Newell Dwight. *The Quest of John Chapman: The Story of a Forgotten Hero.* New York: Macmillan, 1904.

Holberg, Ruth Langland. *Restless Johnny: The Story of Johnny Appleseed.* New York: Crowell, 1950.

Le Sueur, Meridel. *Little Brother of the Wilderness: The Story of Johnny Appleseed.* New York: A. A. Knopf, 1947.

Moses, Will. *Johnny Appleseed: The Story of a Legend.* New York: Philomel Books, 2001.

Osborne, Mary Pope. *American Tall Tales.* New York: Alfred A. Knopf, 1991.

Price, Robert. *Johnny Appleseed: Man and Myth.* Bloomington: Indiana University Press, 1954.

charms See MAGIC.

Chavez, César Estrada (1927–1993) César Chavez was a well-known activist for the cause of labor in America.

Chavez was born César Estrada Chavez in Arizona in 1927. As a youth, he traveled with his family as they, with other migrant farm workers, followed the harvests across the country. They moved from state to state, region to region, picking fruit and vegetable crops that had reached maturity.

Not only was this a rootless life for the workers, they were paid little, asked to work under difficult circumstances, and afforded few legal protections as temporary employees. Landowners regarded migrants as a cheap labor force and often exploited them as such. Conditions for migrant workers and their families were adverse, and Chavez became sensitized as a young person to this group of laborers and their plight. Among his accomplishments was the establishment of the first labor union for farm workers, the United Farm Workers of America (UFW).

Many Americans learned about the problems facing labor firsthand during the Great Depression, when unemployed adults scrambled to find any way to meet their expenses and feed their families. Such a situation is dramatized in the dust bowl saga of the Joad family in John Steinbeck's *Grapes of Wrath*.

As a champion of the farm workers, and organizer of the union that sought to protect their interests, Chavez used several methods to address the problems facing migrant laborers. He led marches, conducted hunger strikes, and spearheaded consumer boycotts of products when situations indicated the need.

While the title of Steinbeck's novel was figurative, the difficulties Chavez faced with the grape industry were all too literal. For example, in 1968, Chavez led a boycott against California grapes on the basis that the landowners did not treat their field workers appropriately. A second boycott, this time in 1984, sought to reduce the amount of pesticides routinely applied to crops of California grapes.

Up until his death in 1993, César Estrada Chavez advocated effectively for the civil rights of ordinary workers in America, and he is revered as a friend to whole groups of laborers who would otherwise have found little support for their cause.

See also: CHICANO FOLKLORE; CIVIL RIGHTS MOVEMENT; DEPRESSION, THE GREAT; FOLK HEROES/LEGENDARY FIGURES; FOOD/FOODWAYS;

OCCUPATIONAL FOLKLORE; PROTEST IN FOLK-
LORE; STEINBECK, JOHN; TOASTS/DRINKING;
WESTERN REGIONAL FOLKLORE.

For Further Reading:

Ferriss, Susan, and Ricardo Sandoval. *The Fight in the Fields: César Chavez and the Farmworkers Movement.* New York: Harcourt Brace, 1997.

Levy, Jacques. *César Chavez: Autobiography of La Cause.* New York: W. W. Norton, 1975.

London, Joan, and Henry Anderson. *So Shall Ye Reap: The Story of César Chavez and the Farm Workers' Movement.* New York: Thomas Y. Crowell, 1970.

Matthiessen, Peter. *Sal si Puedes: César Chavez and the New American Revolution.* New York: Dell, 1969.

Taylor, Ronald B. *Chavez and the Farm Workers.* Boston: Beacon Press, 1975.

Villarino, José, and Arturo Ramírez, eds. *Astlán Chicano Culture and Folklore: An Anthology.* New York: McGraw Hill, 1997.

Chesnutt, Charles Waddell (1858–1932) As a storyteller, biographer, and novelist, Charles Waddell Chesnutt left behind an important body of work for students of both African-American literature and American folklore.

In 1858, Chesnutt was born to middle-class parents who were members of different races. His mother had taught North Carolina slaves in secret, and his father served in the Union Army during the Civil War. The social and racial circumstances of Chesnutt's childhood set in place many of the concerns of his later fiction.

As a youth, Chesnutt attended a school established in 1865 by the Freedman's Bureau. His mixed racial heritage sensitized the young man to issues of social justice and cultural heritage. He taught school in North Carolina for a time. As were his parents, Chesnutt was clearly interested in advancing the quality of life for the next generation of African Americans.

Accordingly, when he became an author, Chesnutt chose topics that promoted historical awareness and cultural pride. In 1899, Chesnutt published *The Conjure Woman*, a collection of stories rooted firmly in the oral culture of African-American slaves. The tales he presented in this tradition both honored and revealed the importance of folk beliefs and practices, such as conjure, to the survival of African Americans. By working in close connection to this cultural legacy, Chesnutt did his part to preserve folk culture and transmit it to a new and wider audience.

In another work of fiction, *The Marrow of Tradition* (1901), Chesnutt presented a historical novel inspired by the 1898 Wilmington race riot and coup. By taking racial conflict, and a specific historical event, as his theme, Chesnutt presented a people's history of African-American resistance. This, too, is a part of a folk legacy. Chesnutt's other works include *The Wife of His Youth and Other Stories of the Color Line* (1899), *The House behind the Cedars* (1900), *The Colonel's Dream* (1905), and a biography of Frederick Douglass.

By incorporating traditional narrative elements into his writing, as well as by framing the folk history of his time, Charles Waddell Chesnutt signaled the lasting importance of folklore to American culture.

See also: AFRICAN-AMERICAN FOLKLORE; BELIEFS, FOLK; CIVIL WAR; CONJURE/CONJURING; DOUGLASS, FREDERICK; FOLKLORE IN AMERICAN LITERATURE; MAGIC; MEDICINE, FOLK; PROTEST IN FOLKLORE; SLAVERY; SOUTHERN REGIONAL FOLKLORE; SUPERNATURAL; SUPERSTITION; TRICKSTER.

For Further Reading:

Dixon, Melvin. "The Teller as Folk Trickster in Chesnutt's *The Conjure Woman*," *College Language Association Journal* 18 (1974): 186–197.

Hemenway, Robert. "The Functions of Folklore in Charles Chesnutt's *The Conjure Woman*," *Journal of the Folklore Institute* 13 (1976): 283–309.

Jaskoski, Helen. "Power Unequal to Man: The Significance of Conjure in Works by Five Afro-American Authors," *Southern Folklore Quarterly* 38 (1974): 91–108.

Webb, Bernice Larson. "Picking at 'The Goophered Grapevine,'" *Kentucky Folklore Record: A Regional Journal of Folklore and Folklife* 25 (1979): 64–67.

Winkelman, Donald M. "Three American Authors as Semi-Folk Artists." *Journal of American Folklore* 78, no. 308 (spring 1965): 130–135.

Chicano folklore   Chicano folklore pertains to immigrants to the United States from Mexico and/or persons born in the United States of Mexican ancestry.

Given Mexico's proximity, immigration to the United States has been a long-standing pattern. Mexican immigrants have favored the American Southwest and the areas along the southern border. Many have made their homes in the states of Arizona, California, Colorado, New Mexico, and Texas.

Chicano folklore spans many genres, including folk music, folk beliefs, folk crafts, and folk customs. Secular or sacred yard art and household shrines are both forms commonly found in Chicano communities. An example of Chicano traditional music are the *corridos*, or folk ballads. Traditional Mexican foodways are quite popular in the United States, where family restaurants and fast-food establishments commonly serve Americanized versions of such dishes as fajitas, tamales, and tacos.

Verbal lore is also a robust part of Chicano folklore. For instance, the figure of the Weeping Woman, also known as "La Llorona," is a character well known within Chicano narrative folklore. As this legend of the American Southwest would have it, the character at the center of this story was a widow who, in her eagerness to remarry, went to the river and drowned her children of her first marriage. Now a ghost herself, the Weeping Woman is said to be a restless spirit one can still encounter at the side of a river. According to the lore, mothers warn their sons and daughters not to linger by the river after dusk, for it is at night that the Weeping Woman searches by the river for her own children, and there is no telling what she might do if she encountered children who are not her own. Generally speaking, a sighting of the Weeping Woman by adults is regarded as a portent of sorrow, misfortune, or even death. Spoken rituals are sometime used to fend off ill effects of the Weeping Woman.

In addition to celebrating many of the same holidays other Americans do, Chicano communities observe some celebrations that originated in Mexico, such as Cinco de Mayo. Celebrated on May 5 each year, Cinco de Mayo is a day devoted to commemorating a historic Mexican victory: the Mexican army's victory, however fleeting, over the French in 1862's battle of Puebla. In Mexico, the observance represents unity, freedom, and national pride. Celebrations of this occasion in the United States have, in some ways, outstripped those conducted in Mexico. With the help of the commercialization typical of U.S. holidays, Cinco de Mayo has become inflated into a general celebration of Mexican culture. Contemporary American observances include Mexico-themed festivals, parades, food, music, and dancing.

Organizations dedicated to the preservation and study of Chicano culture include Santa Barbara, California's, Center for Chicano Studies; Austin, Texas's, Center for Mexican American Studies; and Los Angeles's Chicano Studies Research Center. Major collections of Chicano cultural material include Chicago's Mexican Fine Arts Center Museum; San Antonio, Texas's, Guadalupe Cultural Arts Center; and Albuquerque, New Mexico's, Southwest Hispanic Research Institute.

As part of a border culture, Chicano folklore documents centuries of interplay between Mexican and American folk cultures. Chicano Americans are among the most extensively explored folk groups within American folklore studies.

See also: CHAVEZ, CÉSAR ESTRADA; CINCO DE MAYO; CULTURAL GROUPS; ETHNICITY; FOOD/FOODWAYS; HOLIDAYS/OBSERVANCES; IMMIGRATION AND FOLKLORE; SOUTHWESTERN REGIONAL FOLKLORE; WEEPING WOMAN.

For Further Reading:

Cantú, Norma E., and Olga Nájera-Ramírez, eds. *Chicana Traditions: Continuity and Change.* Chicago: University of Illinois Press, 2002.

Castro, Rafaela G. *Chicano Folklore: A Guide to the Folktales, Traditions, Rituals and Religious Practices of Mexican Americans.* New York: Oxford University Press, 2001.

Castro, Rafaela G. *Dictionary of Chicano Folklore.* Santa Barbara, Calif.: ABC-CLIO, 2000.

Herrera-Sobek, Maria. *Northward Bound: The Mexican Immigrant Experience in Ballad and Song.* Bloomington: Indiana University Press, 1993.

Maestas, José Griego, and Rudolfo A. Anaya. *Cuentos: Tales from the Hispanic Southwest.* Santa Fe: Museum of New Mexico Press, 1980.

Martin, Patricia Preciado. *Songs My Mother Sang to Me: An Oral History of Mexican American Women.* Tucson: University of Arizona Press, 1992.

Robb, John. *Hispanic Folk Music of New Mexico and the Southwest: A Self-Portrait of People.* Norman: University of Oklahoma Press, 1980.

Trotter, Robert T., and Juan Antonia Chavira. *Curanderismo: Mexican American Folk Healing.* Athens: University of Georgia Press, 1997.

Waugh, Julie Nott. *The Silver Cradle: Las Posadas, Los Pastores, and Other Mexican American Traditions.* Austin: University of Texas Press, 1988.

Weigle, Marta, ed. *Two Guadalupes: Hispanic Legends and Magic Tales from New Northern New Mexico.* Santa Fe, N. Mex.: Ancient City Press, 1987.

West, John O., ed. *Mexican-American Folklore.* Little Rock, Ark.: August House, 1988.

"Chicken Little" (legendary) As simple a story as can be found, "Chicken Little" reminds audiences of the risks of sounding a false alarm. In this respect, it resembles the fable "The Boy Who Cried Wolf."

This animal tale narrates a fateful experience in the life of the title character. While walking in the woods one day, Chicken Little is unexpectedly struck on the head by a falling acorn. The bird is startled by this blow and reaches the immediate though incorrect conclusion that the sky is falling. She departs the woods to notify the king.

On the journey to warn the king, Chicken Little meets a series of her friends, including Henny Penny, Ducky Lucky, Goosey Loosey, and Turkey Lurkey. Each one asks Chicken Little what the matter is. She explains to each that she has determined through the direct evidence of her own senses that the sky is falling. One friend after another accepts Chicken Little's assertion and joins in the hurried trip to tell the king.

They are all moving briskly when they encounter Foxy Loxy, who, as the other creatures have, inquires about the reason for their hurry. Once again, Chicken Little explains that the sky is falling. The fox replies with an offer to help by leading the way to the king.

The chicken, the hen, the duck, the goose, and the turkey accept this offer, but the fox directs them not to the castle, but rather to his den. None of the birds is heard from again.

This story has a strong set of moral messages. First, the audience is advised against reaching uninformed conclusions, as Chicken Little does regarding the acorn. Second, the story cautions against inciting needless fear. Finally, the tale warns audience members about the danger of accepting others' judgments uncritically and assuming others' integrity without basis.

In addition to its many retellings over the years, including most recently a 2005 feature-length film from Disney, "Chicken Little" has achieved the status of an epithet, which is applied to any person who proves to lack caution or be an alarmist.

See also: ANIMALS; "BOY WHO CRIED WOLF, THE"; CHILDREN'S FOLKLORE; DISNEY, WALTER ELIAS; FABLES; FAIRY TALES; MYTHS, FOLK.

For Further Reading:

Bernheimer, Kate, ed. *Mirror, Mirror, on the Wall: Women Writers Explore Their Favorite Fairy Tales.* New York: Anchor, 1998.

Cashdan, Sheldon. *The Witch Must Die: The Hidden Meaning of Fairy Tales.* New York: Basic Books, 1999.

Garner, James Finn. *Politically Correct Bedtime Stories.* New York: Macmillan, 1994.

Tatar, Maria, ed. *The Annotated Classic Fairy Tales.* New York: W. W. Norton, 2002.

childbirth/pregnancy folklore No stage in the human life course inspires more folklore than the experience of pregnancy and childbirth.

In American folklore, as in that of other nations, there are many folk beliefs, customs, and practices surrounding gestation. These notions could be said to begin with people's efforts to promote or limit fertility. Similarly, there are ideas about how best to conceive boys or girls, depending upon the wishes of the parents. After conception takes place, Americans have numerous beliefs about the pregnancy term. Probably the best known among these is the concept that a woman's experiences during pregnancy can influence the child carried, in ways either fortunate or unfortunate. For example, a scare experienced by a pregnant woman could become a fear or aversion transmitted to the baby. In addition, there are cultural beliefs about the implications associated with specific nutritional habits of a pregnant woman.

Other childbearing lore concentrates on forecasting whether an expected child will be a girl or a boy. When it comes to predicting the sex of the fetus a woman is carrying, there are many supposed methods. For instance, in one such technique, the woman's wedding ring is hung from a string and held over her belly. Depending upon the way the suspended ring begins to swing, she is expected to have a boy or a girl. This sort of activity is frequently a part of baby showers, parties at which the pregnancy is celebrated by the pregnant woman's friends and family members. At these gatherings, it is customary for each guest to present the woman with a gift for the baby's care or use. The décor at such parties often includes the figure of a stork, the character who very small children are customarily told carries newborn babies to families. Within such tales, the stork, rather than the pregnant mother, delivers the child.

Folk beliefs also accompany a woman into the birthing process. Whether the delivery takes place at home with a midwife or in a hospital with an obstetrician, families often try to aid the process by using traditional ideas from folk medicine. One such practice is the placement of scissors or a similar sharp object under the woman's bed pillow during labor, done with the intent to "cut" the woman's pain. There is also considerable folklore surrounding midwives, including the tale of the Jersey devil's birth, in which the newborn creature murders the midwife attending to his mother. Once the delivery is complete, there are traditional ideas about disposal or treatment of the afterbirth, one of many ideas about how to confer luck on both the mother and her baby.

The folklore of childbirth and pregnancy in America consists mostly of attempts to predict or protect the outcomes of childbearing.

See also: BODYLORE; CHILDREN'S FOLKLORE; FAMILY FOLKLORE; FOLKLORE IN EVERYDAY LIFE; GENDER AND FOLKLORE; JERSEY DEVIL; LUCK/FORTUNE; MEDICINE, FOLK; PREDICTION; RITES OF PASSAGE; STORK, THE.

For Further Reading:
Campbell, Marie. *Folks Do Get Born.* New York: Rinehart, 1946.

Coleman, Chrisena. *Mama Knows Best: African-American Wives' Tales, Myths, and Remedies for Mothers and Mothers-to-Be.* New York: Simon & Schuster, 1997.

Davis-Floyd, Robbie E. *Birth as an American Rite of Passage.* Berkeley: University of California Press, 1992.

Franklin, Rosalind. *Baby Lore: Superstitions and Old Wives Tales from the World Over Related to Pregnancy, Birth, and Baby Care.* West Sussex, England: Diggory Press, 2005.

68

Pollock, Della. *Telling Bodies Performing Birth: Everyday Narratives of Childbirth*. New York: Columbia University Press, 1999.

Roach, Joyce. "Baby Lore: The Why and Wherefore of It." In *2001: A Texas Folklore Odyssey*, edited by Francis Edward Abernathy and Shannon R. Thompson, 106–121. Denton: University of North Texas Press, 2001.

children's folklore   American childhood is an abundant source of folklore, and its many features have been well studied by folklorists.

Although the experiences of the nation's children change considerably over time, what is remarkable is how universal some components of children's lore remains. Some of the same jokes, games, and sayings in circulation 50 years ago are still popular today. These traditions, if not universal, are certainly persistent aspects of U.S. social life and customs.

Most of these folk elements are related to children's playtime practices and amusements. Particularly rich is the verbal lore among children. Folk speech categories among children include slang and euphemisms, riddles and jokes, insults, tongue twisters, invented languages, stories and legends, games and rhymes, and handmade toys.

One of the most fascinating forms of children's folklore are rhymes. These can include hand clapping, jump rope, ball bouncing, and counting rhymes. As the name suggests, hand-clapping rhymes are used to accompany patterned and partnered movements among children. Typically, a pair of children work together to perform these routines of touching and clapping hands in time to the music of a sung rhyme. An example of a popular hand-clapping rhyme is "Miss Mary Mack." Jump rope rhymes are quite similar, as they are used to accompany rope turning and jumping. An example of a well-known jump rope rhyme is "All in Together." Ball-bouncing rhymes can turn the simple act of dribbling of a ball into a game. In one such rhyme, each player takes a turn reciting a rhyme, traveling through the alphabet using the same scaffolding verse: "*A* my name is *Alice*, / My husband's name is *Al*, / We come from *Alabama*, / And we sell *apples*." Counting rhymes are most often used to choose turns, and the person speaking the rhyme typically counts rounds by touching toes or fists. The speaker typically touches his or her own chin in turn if hands are busy doing the counting. A sample of a counting rhyme, this one used to decide who will be "it" in a game, follows: "Engine, engine, number nine / Going down Chicago line / If the train falls off the track / Do you get your money back?" Depending upon the answer received, the rhymer would proceed with the appropriate reply, such as "*Y-E-S* spells *yes* and you are not it" or "*N-O* spells *no* and out you go."

In addition to folk rhymes, American children's folklore includes slang and euphemisms. As might be predicted, much of this slang is devoted to the topics that interest young children, such as body functions and insults. Words and phrases such as *cooties* (lice), *booger* (mucus), and *tinsel teeth* (braces) are common. There are also folk sayings, both to taunt and to rebuff such verbal behavior. A typical saying addressed to someone accused of speaking less than the truth is as follows: "Liar, liar, pants on fire, hang them up on a telephone wire." Such a saying acknowledges a falsehood, exposes it to others, and ridicules the fibber. The person accused of lying might reply with sayings such as "Sticks and stones may break my bones, but words will never hurt me," or "Make like a tree and leave."

Other verbal lore among children includes tongue twisters and invented languages. Tongue twisters are usually alliterative phrases or statements that are designed to confound a speaker, or even to make him or her utter taboo words by mistake. Examples include two traditional tongue twisters: "Rubber baby buggy bumpers," and "How much wood would a woodchuck chuck if a woodchuck could chuck wood?" Invented languages include such make-believe tongues as pig latin or private ones such as twin languages.

Children's stories and legends can also be formulaic, such as campfire tales, ghost and spooky stories, camp lore, and urban legends. As boys and girls become old enough to tell, as well as be told, stories, they enjoy delivering tales to audiences of their friends. Games are also popular entertainments among children. Examples of children's folk games are Hide and Seek, Kick the Can, Ghost in the Graveyard, Freeze Tag, Marco Polo; Mother, May I?; Red Light, Green Light, Spud, and Hopscotch. These games rely heavily on children's imagination and usually involve few props or items of equipment.

Finally, folk toys, while largely eclipsed today by mass-produced playthings, still play a role in the recreational lives of America's children. As with folk games, folk toys are homemade and require few supplies beyond those on hand, such as paper. Typical folk toys include origami, chewing gum wrapper chains, daisy chains, sand sculptures, snow sculptures, and slingshots.

Rounding out children's folklore are all the narrative forms provided youth in this country, including fables, fairy tales, and folktales of other kinds. American children's folklore is a robust field of study, in terms of both the traditions it preserves and the ones it updates.

See also: AGING AND FOLKLORE; CAMP FOLKLORE; CITY FOLKLORE; FABLES; FAIRY TALES; FAMILY FOLKLORE; FOLKLORE IN EVERYDAY LIFE; GAMES AND PASTIMES; JUMP ROPE RHYMES; MYTHS, FOLK; RHYMES, FOLK; TOYS, FOLK; URBAN LEGENDS.

For Further Reading:

Blatt, Gloria T. *Once Upon a Folktale: Capturing the Folklore Process with Children.* New York: Teachers College Press, 1992.

Bronner, Simon J. *American Children's Folklore.* Little Rock, Ark.: August House, 1988.

Knapp, Mary, and Herbet Knapp. *One Potato, Two Potato ...": The Secret Education of American Children.* New York: W. W. Norton, 1976.

Motz, Marilyn J. et al., eds. *Eye on the Future: Popular Culture Scholarship into the Twenty-first Century.* Bowling Green, Ohio: Bowling Green State University Popular Press, 1994.

Oring, Elliott, ed. *Folk Groups and Folklore Genres: An Introduction.* Logan: Utah State University Press, 1986.

Schoemaker, George H., ed. *The Emergence of Folklore in Everyday Life: A Fieldguide and Sourcebook.* Bloomington, Ind.: Trickster Press, 1990.

Sherman, Josepha, and T. K. F. Weisskopf. *Greasy Grimy Gopher Guts: The Subversive Folklore of Childhood.* Little Rock, Ark.: August House, 1995.

Sutton-Smith, Brian, and David Abrams. *The Folkstories of Children.* Philadelphia: University of Pennsylvania Press, 1981.

Sutton-Smith, Brian, and Jay Mechling, eds. *Children's Folklore: A Sourcebook.* Logan: Utah State University Press, 1999.

Young, Terrell A., ed. *Happily Ever After: Sharing Folk Literature with Elementary and Middle School Students.* Newark, N.J.: International Reading Association, 2004.

Chinatown   See CHINESE-AMERICAN FOLKLORE; CITY FOLKLORE; ETHNICITY.

Chinese-American folklore   Chinese Americans have played an instrumental part in the settlement of the frontier and the development of the nation's resources and services.

Chinese immigration to the United States began in the 1840s, when newcomers began to arrive in the western states of California, Colorado, Idaho, Montana, Oregon, and Washington. In this way, Chinese Americans contributed to the nation's westward expansion, including the building of the transcontinental railroad and the gold rush.

At this point in American history, most Chinese people in America were men, who had immigrated to establish themselves economically. They would only later be joined by women and children. Together, these immigrants often settled in urban ethnic neighborhoods, sometimes known as Chinatowns. These districts helped immigrants access one another and shielded them from hostility directed from other groups in America. Chinatowns still exist across America, from San Francisco to New York City.

By the middle of the 19th century, anti-Chinese sentiment resulted in added restrictions on immigration and naturalization, as well as curtailment of legal rights for Chinese Americans. Most notable among these changes in policy was the 1882 Chinese Exclusion Act, a restrictive law that was not repealed until 1943. Immigration laws passed during the 1960s finally removed all quotas pertaining to Chinese immigration to America.

Chinese-American folklore has many aspects, the most publicly recognizable of which involve holidays and observances. The celebration of Chinese New Year, for instance, is marked annually in some American cities. The event features processions, parades, and other festivities. Such New Year's celebrations are a favorite among residents and tourists alike. Giant artificial figures of dragons and lions are presented at this time, accompanied by music, dance, and fireworks. All of these measures are taken in the hope that by making enough movement and noise they can fend off evil spirits. By custom, it represents a time of renewal, when luck is sought, debts are repaid, and visits are exchanged.

Other folk traditions involve foodways, construction of temples, and seasonal festivals such as those honoring ancestors. Chinese medicine features folk beliefs about health, illness, and healing. Herbs, acupuncture, and homeopathic treatments are associated with this tradition.

The history of Chinese people in America is an embattled one, in which folklore provides comfort, reaffirmation, and community solidarity.

See also: CULTURAL GROUPS; ETHNICITY; GOLD RUSH, THE; IMMIGRATION AND FOLKLORE; KINGSTON, MAXINE HONG; MEDICINE, FOLK; PARADES; TRANSCONTINENTAL RAILROAD; WESTERN REGIONAL FOLKLORE.

For Further Reading:

Chan, Sucheng, ed. *Entry Denied: Exclusion and the Chinese Community in America, 1882–1943.* Philadelphia: Temple University Press, 1991.

Chang, Iris. *The Chinese in America: A Narrative History.* New York: Penguin, 2004.

Chen, Shehong. *Being Chinese, Becoming Chinese American.* Urbana: University of Illinois Press, 2002.

Chun, Gloria Heyung. *Of Orphans and Warriors: Inventing Chinese American Culture and Identity.* New Brunswick, N.J.: Rutgers University Press, 2000.

Lai, Him Mark. *Becoming Chinese American: A History of Communities and Institutions.* Walnut Creek, Calif.: AltaMira, 2004.

Louie, Andrea. *Chineseness across Borders: Renegotiating Chinese Identities in China and the United States.* Durham, N.C.: Duke University Press, 2004.

Lyman, Stanford Morris. *Chinatown and Little Tokyo: Power, Conflict, and Community among Chinese and Japanese Immigrants in America.* Millwood, N.Y.: Associated Faculty Press, 1986.

Mark, Diane Mei Lin, and Ginger Chih. *A Place Called Chinese America.* Dubuque, Iowa: Kendall/Hunt, 1982.

Takaki, Ronald. *Ethnic Islands: The Emergence of Urban Chinese America.* New York: Chelsea House, 1994.

Tsai, Shih-shan Henry. *The Chinese Experience in America.* Bloomington: Indiana University Press, 1986.

Wong, K. Scott, and Sucheng Chan, eds. *Claiming America: Constructing Chinese American Identities during the Exclusion Era.* Philadelphia: Temple University Press, 1998.

Christmas At once one of the most sacred and most commercialized events of the calendar year, Christmas is observed by Christians on December 25 annually.

The holiday is older than the United States, and America nearly did not establish it as such because of the disapproval of such faith groups as the Puritans of its pagan origins. In the latter part of the 17th century in Massachusetts, for example, a financial penalty could be levied against anyone found observing Christmas. Over the years, however, those with profound spiritual objections to Christmas yielded to the views of those who embraced the holiday. The timing of the current holiday seems to combine the Dutch custom of celebrating Saint Nicholas's Day on December 6 with the interpolated date on which the events of the nativity are believed to have occurred. The present timing of the holiday also coincides more or less with the winter solstice. By 1890, all states and the District of Columbia afforded legal recognition to Christmas, a somewhat unusual status for a religious observance.

Folk customs for Christmas abound, and each has its own story. Even the names used to characterize this holiday's season are steeped in lore. Yuletide, for instance, derives from both a Celtic feast held in November and Scandinavia's Yule feast. The familiar custom of burning the yule log dates back to earlier solstice celebrations and their tradition of bonfires. The Christmas practice calls for burning a portion of the log each evening until Twelfth Night (January 6). The log is subsequently placed beneath the bed for the coming year for luck, and particularly for protection from the household threats of lightning and, with some irony, fire. Many have beliefs based on the appearance of the yule log as it burns, and by counting the sparks and such, they seek to discern their fortunes in the new year and beyond.

As an emblem of divine light, illumination is an important symbol within this winter holiday, and along with the yule fire, those celebrating Christmas display candles. The yule candle, as does the yule log, burns from December 24 to either January 1 or January 6. Today's electric candles used as window decorations recall an Irish tradition of setting candles in the window to guide Mary and Joseph to a place of shelter and welcome.

Other Christmas practices, such as the customs of caroling and exchanging cards, originate in England. Although the practice is somewhat less prevalent than it once was in the United States, groups of carolers still go door to door in some areas sharing songs of the season. Innovations in printing and, especially, lithography, made the exchange of Christmas cards fashionable during the latter portion of the 19th century. A German native, Louis Prang, who rose to prominence for his card designs during the 1870s, is widely regarded as the chief originator of this practice in America.

Among the most dearly—and long-held—traditions of Christmas are the foods and foodways used in its celebrations. Feasts are traditional, with roast pig, mince pie, and plum pudding representing some of the standard fare. Christmas cookies, prepared in holiday-themed shapes, appear to have been a contribution from the Pennsylvania Dutch, but today cookies from a wide range of countries may be found at meals or cookie exchanges at Christmastime. Some food and drink rituals have undergone substantial updating over the years. Wassail, an English drink containing nutmeg, sugar, eggs, apples, and ale, is largely replaced by today's eggnog, prepared with cream, sugar, eggs, spices, and either brandy or whiskey.

Plant lore has a key place in American celebrations of Christmas. Mistletoe, for example, has ancient significance and lore that dates back at least to Norse legend. Today, sprigs of mistletoe are employed in a specific household use that is not merely decorative. This U.S. custom may recall the Scandinavian custom establishing mistletoe as the plant of peace and suggesting that those who meet beneath the plant will not fight. American custom around mistletoe takes one genial step further, suggesting that those who meet beneath mistletoe hung in a doorway at Christmas must exchange a kiss. Years ago, a man so engaged was expected to remove a berry from the display each time he stole a kiss.

Other plants featured in Christmas celebrations include holly and poinsettia. Holly has long served as a Christian symbol, with the red berries representing the blood of Christ and the pointed leaves representing the crown of thorns. In medieval times, holly was also believed to protect against black witchcraft and the evil eye. It is a common decoration at holiday time in American homes, as are poinsettia plants. These flowers take their name from Dr. Joel Poinsett, who introduced the vibrantly colored plants to the United States. Previous to that, poinsettias figured within Mexican folklore. With their distinctive appearance, the plants were thought to resemble the star of Bethlehem, and so were characterized as the "Flower of the Holy Night." Poinsettias also figure in a Mexican legend of the nativity, in which a boy without a present kneels to pray for the Christ child. Where he knelt, the poinsettia grows in tribute to the birth.

The most prominent decoration taken from the outdoors inside at Christmas is the evergreen tree, with its symbolism of hardiness and continuous renewal. Trees were once a part of pagan observances of winter solstice, as the tree was regarded as a place where a spirit dwells. There are various legends about how Christmas trees came into favor, but the first mention of one in America dates from 1821 in Pennsylvania, likely the introduction of German settlers there familiar with a holiday tree tradition. Since then, decorated and illuminated trees have adorned family homes and the ceremonial lightings of community trees in such locations as Boston Common, New York City's Rockefeller Center, and the White House signal the arrival of the Christmas season. Over the years, there have been many folk beliefs about the placement and disposal of Christmas trees, usually indicating which practices produce the best luck. Although such cautions have receded, there was once a time when bad luck could be expected if a tree was taken inside before December 24, left in the house too long, or burned while still green.

While America hardly originated the celebration of Christmas, its residents have maintained many older traditions from other lands,

modified others, and added still more practices of their own to the day's observance.

See also: EVIL EYE; FLOWERS; FOOD/FOODWAYS; HOLIDAYS/OBSERVANCES; PENNSYLVANIA DUTCH/ PENNSYLVANIA GERMAN FOLKLORE; RELIGION, FOLK; SANTA CLAUS; SOLSTICE; TOASTS/DRINKING.

For Further Reading:
Coffin, Tristram P. *The Book of Christmas Folklore.* New York: Seabury Press, 1973.
Horsley, Richard, and James Tracy, eds. *Christmas Unwrapped: Consumerism, Christ, and Culture.* Harrisburg, Pa.: Trinity Press International, 2001.
Myers, Robert J. *Celebrations: The Complete Book of American Holidays.* Garden City, N.Y.: Doubleday, 1972.
Restad, Penne L. *Christmas in America: A History.* New York: Oxford University Press, 1995.
Santino, Jack. *All around the Year: Holidays and Celebrations in American Life.* Urbana: University of Illinois Press, 1994.

Christmas, Annie (legendary) As one of the relatively few female protagonists appearing in American tall tales, Annie Christmas offers a powerful image of female agency.

Christmas first appeared in print in *Gumbo Ya-Ya*, an anthology published in 1945. As were her male counterparts in such stories, such as Paul Bunyan and John Henry, she was hailed for her feats of physical strength. Christmas worked the Mississippi River, and the name of her craft was *Big River's Daughter.* No stranger to manual labor, she is reputed to have pulled a vessel out of harm's way herself during a particularly heroic rescue. Her prowess on the keelboats was such that, according to the tales, when people accomplished something impressive, they were praised for proving "as strong as Annie Christmas."

Christmas was a memorable character, including in terms of her appearance and manner. Standing six feet eight inches and weighing in at over 250 pounds, this legendary figure had an imposing presence. Christmas often dressed in men's apparel and tucked a red turkey feather in her hatband. In some accounts, she had a mustache. Around her neck, she wore a string of pearls, one for each man she had subdued in a fight. It is said that her necklace was some 20 feet long at the time of her death.

According to the lore, Annie Christmas even managed to keep the legendary Mike Fink in check. She was a hard-working, hard-drinking woman with a deep and booming voice. She was the widowed mother of 12 sons, and while the stories of her exploits vary, all attest to the woman's unusual fortitude.

In addition, Christmas earned a reputation as a fearless woman and a skilled gambler. In fact, as the story goes, Christmas eventually fell in love with a riverboat gambler. After he died at the card table, Christmas died of grief for her lost love.

Those who buried Christmas arranged a fitting recognition of her life on the water. For her funeral, Christmas's body was loaded onto a barge, with other boats whistling a tribute, and she made her way down the river and out to sea.

While this larger-than-life character is less widely known today than some of the legendary men who worked the river with her, Annie Christmas stands out as a folk portrait of African-American womanhood as being brave and capable and living life to its fullest.

See also: AFRICAN-AMERICAN FOLKLORE; BUNYAN, PAUL; CAJUN FOLKLORE; FINK, MIKE; FOLK HEROES/LEGENDARY FIGURES; GENDER AND FOLKLORE; HENRY, JOHN; MARITIME FOLKLORE; OCCUPATIONAL FOLKLORE; REGION, FOLK; SOUTHERN REGIONAL FOLKLORE.

For Further Reading:

Cohn, Amy L., comp. *From Sea to Shining Sea: A Treasury of American Folklore and Folk Songs.* New York: Scholastic, 1993.

Dorson, Richard. *American Folklore.* Chicago: University of Chicago Press, 1959.

Hamilton, Virginia. *Her Stories: African American Folktales, Fairy Tales, and True Tales.* New York: Blue Sky Press, 1995.

San Souci, Robert D. *Cut from the Same Cloth: American Women of Myth, Legend, and the Tall Tale.* New York: Philomel Books, 1993.

Saxon, Lyle, Robert Tallant, and Edward Dreyer. *Gumbo Ya-Ya: A Collection of Louisiana Folktales.* Boston: Houghton Mifflin, 1945.

Cinco de Mayo Celebrated on May 5 each year, Cinco de Mayo is a day devoted to commemorating a historic Mexican victory.

In the face of demands to repay mounting international debt immediately, Mexico had to contend with countries that wished to collect on their loans through one means or another. Cinco de Mayo commemorates the Mexican army's victory, however fleeting, over the French in 1862's Battle of Puebla. In Mexico, the observance represents unity, freedom, and national pride. Its celebration is largely regional, concentrated in the area where the battle took place.

Celebrations of this occasion in the United States have, in some ways, outstripped those conducted in Mexico. With the help of commercialization typical of U.S. holidays, Cinco de Mayo has become inflated into a general celebration of Mexican culture. Contemporary American observances include Mexico-themed festivals, parades, food, music, and dancing. It is joined by modern American observances of the Day of the Dead, or Dia de los Muertos.

Sometimes mistaken for Mexico's Independence Day (September 16, 1810), Cinco de Mayo has evolved in the United States into a broadly cultural holiday, with little reference to its specific Mexican origins.

See also: CHICANO FOLKLORE; ETHNICITY; FOOD/FOODWAYS; HOLIDAYS/OBSERVANCES; PARADES.

For Further Reading:

Boggs, Ralph S. *Bibliography of Latin American Folklore: Tales, Festivals, Customs, Arts, Magic, Music.* Detroit: Blaine Ethridge Books, 1940/1971.

Carlson, Alvar. "America's Growing Observance of Cinco de Mayo," *Journal of American Culture* 21, no. 2 (summer 1998): 7–16.

Littwicki, Ellen. *America's Public Holidays, 1865–1920.* Washington, D.C.: Smithsonian Institute Press, 2000.

Menard, Valerie. *The Latino Holiday Book: From Cinco de Mayo to Dia de los Muertos: The Celebrations and Traditions of Hispanic-Americans.* New York: Marlowe, 2000.

Santino, Jack. *New Old-Fashioned Ways: Holidays and Popular Culture.* Knoxville: University of Tennessee Press, 1996.

Sommers, Laura Kay. "Inventing Latinismo: The Creation of 'Hispanic' Panethnicity in the United States," *Journal of American Folklore* 104, no. 411 (winter 1991): 32–53.

———. "Symbol and Style in Cinco de Mayo," *Journal of American Folklore* 98, no. 390 (fall 1985): 476–482.

"Cinderella"   In what may be the most widely known of all fairy tales, "Cinderella," an unfortunate young woman magically escapes mistreatment and finds true love with a prince.

Details of the plot vary across tellings, but the basic contours of the tale remain. When the wife of a rich man lay dying, she called upon her daughter and directed her to be virtuous. When the father remarries, two stepdaughters enter the family's home. The three new arrivals to the household are beautiful but cruel, particularly where it concerns the man's daughter. The girl is made into a servant to the three newcomers and finds no rest. She finds herself insulted, punished, and left to sleep in the hearth cinders. This is how she comes to be known as Cinderella.

When the man leaves home on some travels, he asks the children what they wished him to give them upon his return. Cinderella requests a hazel branch, which she grows as a tree, watered with her own tears, on her mother's grave. One day, a white bird appears at the gravesite and offers to grant Cinderella three wishes.

Shortly thereafter, the king announces a three-day festival, intended for the purpose of identifying a bride for his son. The stepmother asserts that that if Cinderella retrieves a dish of lentils the stepmother casts into the fireplace, she may attend the festival. With the help of the bird, Cinderella complies with this condition, only to have the stepmother insist that she then retrieve two dishes of lentils from the flames. Again, Cinderella and the bird fetch the beans. Again, the stepmother says no, indicating that Cinderella lacks proper attire for the ball. Finally, the white bird magically grants Cinderella garments in which to attend each night of the event.

So great is Cinderella's transformation that even her stepsisters do not recognize her as she arrives at the ball. While there, Cinderella attracts the prince's attention. To the consternation of others present, particularly the stepsisters, this pattern repeats for the next two days of the festival. The prince finds himself captivated by Cinderella, whose identity remains a mystery to him even as the festival concludes.

Because in her haste of departure Cinderella leaves behind one of her slippers, the prince conducts a lengthy search through the kingdom, trying to find the young woman he admires. At the conclusion of this quest, Cinderella and the prince become betrothed.

The ending is not happy for everyone, though. Birds peck out one of the eyes of each of Cinderella's stepsisters. As with many Grimm brothers tales, wrongdoers do not escape unscathed. The stepsisters' cruelty leads them to a cruel fate, while Cinderella's humility and forbearance are rewarded with romance.

Such a tale has wide appeal, and "Cinderella" has been retold countless times in books, plays, and films. Audiences identify with the title character's plight and root for her to find a way out of the wretched circumstances of her existence.

"Cinderella" stands as an icon of triumph and transformation, and along with other stories in which worthy young women win the hearts of handsome princes, serves as a parable about the importance of right conduct.

The story is not without detractors, however, and today's references to Cinderella are as often cautionary as celebratory. Contemporary readers of "Cinderella" have focused in the rigid gender roles depicted within this story, as in other fairy tales, and many modern retellings shift the characters to make them more agreeable to current sensibilities. Such "politically correct" versions of tales such as "Cinderella" envision her with greater agency and less reliance upon rescue by others. This same impulse underlies a term within popular psychology that warns against the "Cinderella complex," in which women forfeit independence and wait for men to save, redeem, or complete their lives.

See also: CHILDREN'S FOLKLORE; FABLES; FAIRY TALES; GRIMM BROTHERS; MYTHS, FOLK.

For Further Reading:

Dowling, Colette. *The Cinderella Complex: Women's Hidden Fear of Independence.* New York: Pocket Books, 1982.

Dundes, Alan, ed. *Cinderella: A Casebook.* Madison: University of Wisconsin Press, 1982.

Garner, James Finn. *Politically Correct Bedtime Stories.* New York: Macmillan, 1994.

Huang, Mei. *Transforming the Cinderella Dream: From Frances Burney to Charlotte Bronte.* New Brunswick, N.J.: Rutgers University Press, 1990.

Philip, Neil. *The Cinderella Story: The Origins and Variations of the Story Known as "Cinderella."* New York: Penguin, 1989.

Tatar, Maria, ed. *The Annotated Classic Fairy Tales.* New York: W. W. Norton, 2002.

Citizenship Day Citizenship Day was first declared a holiday on February 29, 1952, when President Harry Truman signed it into law. This observance took the place of two prior and kindred holidays: Constitution Day and I Am an American Day. Constitution Day, previously observed on September 17 each year, recalled the date in 1787 when the Constitution was signed by its authors. Some Americans still elect to remember this historic event each year during Constitution Week, September 17–23. The second observance, I Am an American Day, was instituted by Congress in 1940, took place on the third Sunday each May, and paid tribute to immigrants recently naturalized as American citizens. The new holiday, Citizenship Day, combined these themes and their public observance into a single occasion.

Citizenship Day was designed to mark an annual recognition of the rights and responsibilities of all the nation's citizens, with special emphasis on those who have secured American citizenship during the previous year. Although some continue to mark the holiday in May, a residue of I Am an American Day customs, Citizenship Day's official date is September 17, selected to coincide with commemorations of the Constitutional Congress and the lasting importance of its culmination in a signed document. Because of the day's ceremonial nature, Citizenship Day festivities tend toward reverence and restraint. Nearly all activities surround oath ceremonies for new American citizens and typically include speeches, plays, pageants, and special presentations. On September 17, 2002, for instance, the U.S. Immigration and Naturalization Service delivered the oath of allegiance to more than 15,000 persons granted citizenship that day.

On this day each year, it is standard practice for government buildings to display the U.S. flag. In addition, to honor the event's personal significance for participants, newly sworn-in citizens often bear or receive small U.S. flags or other objects symbolic of their newly attained national status.

Citizenship Day means most to those who have just become citizens or have just witnessed loved ones' being awarded that status, and other Americans may not take much note of the occasion each year.

See also: ETHNICITY; HOLIDAYS/OBSERVANCES; IMMIGRANT AND FOLKLORE; LIBERTY, MISS; PLEDGE OF ALLEGIANCE; ROSS, BETSY; UNCLE SAM.

For Further Reading:
Holiday Origins. Holiday Origins for Citizen-
    ship Day. Available online. URL: http://www.
    holidayorigins.com/html/citizenshipday.html.
    Accessed March 10, 2006.
Myers, Robert J. *Celebrations: The Complete Book of
    American Holidays.* Garden City, N.Y.: Double-
    day, 1972.

city folklore   Although rural and preindustrial
society was long the central focus for the study
of American folklore, urban lore has increasingly
been a source of interest for folklorists.

Both specific to a site and inflected by the
people who arrive there, a city's folklore can be
a complex combination of folk traditions from
both within and beyond the United States. Such
influences are noticeable in ethnic enclaves
within America's major cities, such as New
York's Little Italy and San Francisco's Chinatown. These cultural hearths help immigrants
from similar areas locate one another and con-
gregate. They also help reinforce shared cultural
identities and preserve folk practices. Continuity
of folkways can be important to prevent loss of
traditions in the process of cultural assimilation.

Expressive forms associated with city life
can vary considerably from those customary in
more agricultural landscapes. For instance, yard
and porch culture in the country may take the
more spatially concentrated shapes of street and
stoop culture possible in the densely built and
populated city. Sidewalk chalk, jump rope and
counting rhymes, and stickball may take the
place of children's entertainments that rely upon
spacious lawns and playgrounds. The hex signs
on barns and whitewashed fences of farmland
may take the form of the graffiti and murals of
urban life.

Urban folklore and industrial folklore often
overlap. For example, during eras with high rates
of urban migration, whereby underemployed
farm workers relocated for jobs in factories,
mills, and other urban workplaces, the American
people learned to shed ways not appropriate to
an urban or urbane environment. This adjust-
ment involved everything from foodways to
courtship practices. Generally speaking, cities
offered additional personal freedom to immigrant and migrant alike. In addition, the cities
provided a safe harbor for those whose lives and
ways were not accepted in less cosmopolitan
settings such as farms and small towns. This has
traditionally been the case for gay, lesbian, and
transgender persons, who frequently gravitate to
thriving subcultures within urban centers.

The folk heroes of America's cities are distinct from those who typify other portions of
the nation. Instead of Paul Bunyan and Johnny
Appleseed, cities produce such figures as Mose
the Fireman and Joe Magarac. Legends set in
forests and fields began to stand beside new ones
taking place in locales more consonant with the
lives of city dwellers. These contemporary tales
became known as urban legends. Cities also
became associated in the popular imagination
with other and less positive phenomena, including notorious figures reputed to be active within
organized crime. The crime lore of America's
cities began to include Chicago's Al Capone and
mafia kingpins of New York City.

See also: BUNYAN, PAUL; CAPONE, ALPHONSE
GABRIEL (AL); CHINESE-AMERICAN FOLKLORE;
ETHNICITY; FOLKLORE IN EVERYDAY LIFE; FOLK-
LORE STUDIES; GAY/LESBIAN FOLKLORE; GRAF-
FITI; IMMIGRATION AND FOLKLORE; INDUSTRI-
ALIZATION AND FOLKLORE; ITALIAN-AMERICAN
FOLKLORE; JUMP ROPE RHYMES; MAGARAC, JOE;
MOSE THE FIREMAN; OUTLAWS; RHYMES, FOLK;
URBAN LEGENDS.

For Further Reading:
Abrahams, Roger D., and Michael Robert Evans,
    ed. *Fields of Folklore.* Bloomington, Ind.: Trick-
    ster, 1995.
Botkin, Benjamin. *New York City Folklore: Legends,
    Tall Tales, Anecdotes, Stories, Sagas, Heroes and
    Characters, Customs, Traditions, and Sayings.*
    New York: Random House, 1956.
Botkin, B. A. *Sidewalks of America; Folklore, Legends,
    Sagas, Traditions, Customs, Songs, Stories, and*

Sayings of City Folk. Indianapolis: Bobbs-Merrill, 1954.

Dundes, Alan, and Carl R. Pagter. *Sometimes the Dragon Wins: Yet More Urban Folklore from the Paperwork Empire*. Syracuse, N.Y.: Syracuse University Press, 1996.

Hamer, David. *History in Urban Places: The Historic Districts of the United States*. Columbus: Ohio State University Press, 1988.

Jones, Michael Owen, ed. *Putting Folklore to Use*. Lexington: University Press of Kentucky, 1994.

Paredes, Américo, and Ellen Stekert, eds. *The Urban Experience and Folk Tradition*. Austin: University of Texas Press, 1971.

Civil Rights movement The struggle for civil rights in America centers on the notion that no one in a society is free until everyone in it is free. Throughout the nation's history, any grassroots effort to secure, preserve, or restore the equality of rights and conditions for a group of people might be considered part of this far-reaching movement.

In this sense, a great many causes have been championed on the basis of a claim to civil rights. Examples include movements to end slavery, extend the franchise to women, release Japanese Americans from internment camps, ensure legal rights for gay/lesbian/transgender persons, and provide accessible schools and services for the disabled. For the most part, however, when Americans speak of the Civil Rights movement, they refer to a broad-based effort over at least the past century to protect the human and constitutional rights of African Americans.

Although it is difficult to pinpoint a precise beginning for a long-term grassroots action, the push for legal rights for African Americans could be said to have commenced with the Civil War, a conflict that put an end to U.S. slavery. Unlike other cultural groups who voluntarily became immigrants to the United States, many persons of African descent arriving in America were transported against their will through the international slave trade. Inhuman working arrangements and deplorable living conditions characterized this era in African-American history, and ever since, the Civil Rights movement has endeavored to redress these historical wrongs and give institutional recognition to the dignity and inherent rights of all human life.

The Civil Rights movement reached its peak during the period from 1955 to 1975. A landmark moment within this process of social change was an incident in Montgomery, Alabama, in December 1955. In the still-segregated American South, members of different races were expected to use separate facilities or designated areas of shared ones. When the women of Montgomery staged a bus boycott, spearheaded by Rosa Parks, a new era in the Civil Rights movement began. During the late 1950s and 1960s, protesters marched, staged sit-ins, and otherwise challenged racial segregation as a practice. Activists also worked to address poverty, joblessness, and low rates of voter registration among historically disenfranchised populations. While it is true that leaders such as Dr. Martin Luther King, Jr., rose to prominence in these efforts, most of the work of inception and implementation was conducted anonymously by ordinary Americans of every race who believed in the cause of racial equality.

The folklore of the Civil Rights movement includes virtually every category of expression. Dissenters such as Rosa Parks became folk heroes within the movement. Songs that had once been sung by slaves, such as hymns and spirituals whose lyrics communicated in code to informed listeners about the journey to liberty, were now reused and adapted to build solidarity of feeling, message, and result at rallies and other gatherings. Stories of the "freedom rides" and other campaigns to put an end to racial segregation and discrimination were plentiful. Even print literature evoked the complexity of the struggle, from memoirs such as Anne Moody's *Coming of Age in Mississippi* (1968) to novels such as Alice Walker's *Meridian* (1976) and Toni Cade Bambara's *The Salt Eaters* (1992).

Resulting laws, such as the Civil Rights Act of 1964 and the Voting Rights Act of 1965, helped advance racial equality and ensure civil rights for all Americans.

See also: AFRICAN-AMERICAN FOLKLORE; BAMBARA, TONI CADE; BRER RABBIT; CIVIL WAR; DISABILITY AND FOLKLORE; DOUGLASS, FREDERICK; EMANCIPATION (PROCLAMATION) DAY; GAY/LESBIAN FOLKLORE; HISTORICAL EVENTS; JAPANESE-AMERICAN FOLKLORE; JAPANESE-AMERICAN INTERNMENT; JUNETEENTH; MARTIN LUTHER KING DAY; PARKS, ROSA; POLITICS AND FOLKLORE; PROTEST IN FOLKLORE; REGION, FOLK; SLAVERY; SOUTHERN REGIONAL FOLKLORE; UNDERGROUND RAILROAD; WOMEN'S MOVEMENT; WOMEN'S SUFFRAGE.

For Further Reading:

Carawan, Guy, and Candie Carawan, eds. *Sing for Freedom: The Story of the Civil Rights Movement through the Songs.* Bethlehem, Pa.: Sing Out Publications, 1990.

Cohn, Amy L., comp. *From Sea to Shining Sea: A Treasury of American Folklore and Folk Songs.* New York: Scholastic, 1993.

Joyner, Charles W. *Shared Traditions: Southern History and Folk Culture.* Urbana: University of Illinois Press, 1999.

McKinney, Don S. "Brer Rabbit and Brother Martin Luther King, Jr.: The Folktale Background of the Birmingham Protest," *Journal of Religious Thought* 46, no. 2 (1989–90): 42–52.

Mechling, Jay. "The Failure of Folklore in Richard Wright's *Black Boy*," *Journal of American Folklore* 104, no. 413 (summer 1991): 275–294.

Mieder, Wolfgang. "'Do Unto Others as You Would Have Them Do Unto You': Frederick Douglass's Proverbial Struggle for Civil Rights," *Journal of American Folklore* 114, no. 453 (summer 2001): 331–357.

Civil War The American Civil War was one of the most trying events in the history of a still-young nation. The secession of the South from the entity previously known as the "United States" put the American founders' democratic experiment to the test. Today, it also poses a challenge to folklorists seeking to study its traditions and lasting impact.

Of all events in American history, the Civil War seems to be the topic that lingers most in the nation's popular imagination, interesting the greatest numbers of hobby historians or history buffs. There is a booming industry in Civil War books, tours, and commemorative objects. In addition, some Americans still enjoy joining in reenactments of events associated with the Civil War. For these reenactments, participants conduct research into the battles they feature and the uniforms and identities of soldiers and use their findings to make their work more accurate.

It is possible to argue that the war began with various antebellum conflicts, such as the insurrections led by Nat Turner and Denmark Vesey, or the raid on Harpers Ferry by John Brown. Even practices used to transport slaves to freedom in the North, such as the Underground Railroad, could be said to be a part of Civil War folklore. These events helped change the climate of race relations in slavery, as well as the discourse about the place of slavery in the nation's future.

Because the war required so much of people's energies and attention, relatively little folklore was collected at the time. Most of what is known about Civil War folklore was gathered in retrospect. Nonetheless as the military conflict that first threatened and then restored the Union, the Civil War holds a special place within the nation's lore. As with any major war, this event produced an extensive oral tradition of stories about military service, battle, tending to the wounded, and grieving for the dead. Tall tales, legends of heroism, and ghost stories are also a part of this legacy. The era produced such ballads as "The Cumberland" and "The Battle of Shiloh." In addition to other forms of folk music, the Civil War produced such popular tunes as "Dixie" and "Battle Hymn of the Republic."

The Civil War was also the first American conflict to receive extensive photographic documentation. As a new technology at the time, photography became an indelible part of the way the Civil War etched itself on popular memory. Because of the long exposures needed to create photographs, most shots were taken after battles. Often, they forced viewers to confront the brutal reality of entire scenes of fallen soldiers. Because half-tone methods were not yet used, most Americans encountered the daguerreotypes rendered as lithographs and engravings in sources such as *Harper's Weekly*. Photographers such as Mathew Brady, Alexander Gardner, and Timothy O'Sullivan created photographs that still illustrate American history books.

The mortality rate associated with the war, in terms of both fatalities from injury and illness, caused an era of national grief only compounded with the assassination of President Abraham Lincoln. The carnage of the Civil War led to the creation of military cemeteries, as well as developments in treatment of the dead, such as embalming, so that the war dead could be transported back to their places of residence.

Other important aspects of Civil War folklore could be said to extend into the period following the war's conclusion. Various annual celebrations and observances resulted from the war's end. For instance, Memorial Day had its origins in the era's deep grief over Civil War deaths. This observance has been held since 1866, and while it was once fixed on May 30 each year, it has since been changed to the last Monday in May. Customs associated with Memorial Day are accordingly patriotic ones. Parades, ceremonies, and reenactments at Civil War sites are usual forms of remembrance.

Emancipation (Proclamation) Day, marked in the United States each year on various dates, but most typically on January 1, recalls Abraham Lincoln's signing of the Emancipation Proclamation at the close of the American Civil War. While the Emancipation Proclamation sought to free slaves after the Civil War, the Thirteenth Amendment also carried great importance insofar as it addressed not just the status of individuals, but also the institution of slavery itself. This amendment did so by rendering unlawful all slavery and involuntary servitude, except that administered as punishment for a convicted offense.

Juneteenth, also known as Jun-Jun Freedom Day, or National Freedom Day, is among the oldest African-American observances. This holiday is celebrated each year on June 19. After the Civil War concluded and the Emancipation Proclamation was signed by President Abraham Lincoln, it took time for the "freedom message" to cross the country. The occasion of Juneteenth takes it name from a specific date in history—June 19, 1865. On this date, news of the Emancipation Proclamation reached Galveston, Texas. Customs for Juneteenth vary, but typical events include meals, picnics, parties, and public readings of key freedom documents, such as the Emancipation Proclamation. As does its companion holiday, Emancipation (Proclamation) Day, usually marked on January 1 each year, Juneteenth ensures that the indignities and injustices of American slavery are not forgotten. Juneteenth marks the historical moment that represents to slaves something analogous in a sense to what the Declaration of Independence meant to colonists. The meaningful difference, however is that although colonists experienced a lack of autonomy and representation, slaves endured torture and suffered a complete lack of liberty.

As the example of Juneteenth demonstrates, localities observe emancipation on various dates. These variations usually result from distinctions in the specific event commemorated. In Richmond, Virginia, for example, the date corresponding to the fall of Richmond during the Civil War proves most salient with the locals. In Washington, D.C., emancipation is celebrated on April 16 each year, in remembrance of the date (April 16, 1862) on which Abraham Lincoln signed the District of Columbia Emancipation Act, and so ever since 1866, residents of the District have observed a private holiday at this time.

In the United States, the Civil War, as a dispute that threatened to split the nation in two, remains a part of the national consciousness, as well as its folklore and regional traditions. As a highly divisive conflict even within families, the Civil War has often been depicted as one in which brother was made to fight against brother. In some areas of the country, particularly the Deep South, there are still bad feelings about their defeat in a contest some still describe as the War between the States.

See also: ANTHONY, SUSAN BROWNELL; APPALACHIAN FOLKLORE; BARTON, CLARA; BALLADS; BROWN, JOHN; CABLE, WASHINGTON GEORGE; CARSON, KIT; CHESNUTT, CHARLES WADDELL; CIVIL WAR; CODY, WILLIAM F. (BUFFALO BILL); DEATH; DOUGLASS, FREDERICK; DRAMA, FOLK; DUNBAR, PAUL LAURENCE; ELLISON, RALPH WALDO; EMANCIPATION (PROCLAMATION) DAY; FATHER'S DAY; FAULKNER, WILLIAM; REGION, FOLK; HICKOK, JAMES BUTLER (WILD BILL); HISTORIC PRESERVATION; HISTORICAL EVENTS; JAMES, JESSE; JUNETEENTH; LIBERTY, MISS; LINCOLN, ABRAHAM; LIVING HISTORY MUSEUMS; MEMORIAL DAY; MOSE THE FIREMAN; MOTHER'S DAY; MUSEUMS, FOLK; MUSIC, FOLK; PRESIDENTS' DAY; REMUS, UNCLE; SLAVERY; SOUTHERN REGIONAL FOLKLORE; STARR, BELLE; STOWE, HARRIET BEECHER; STYRON, WILLIAM; TRANSCONTINENTAL RAILROAD; TRUTH, SOJOURNER; TUBMAN, HARRIET; TURNER, NAT; UNDERGROUND RAILROAD; VESEY, DENMARK; WASHINGTON, BOOKER TALIAFERRO; WASHINGTON, GEORGE; WHITMAN, WALT; YANKEE DOODLE; YANKEE PEDDLER.

For Further Reading:
Anderson, Jay. *Time Machine: The World of Living History.* Nashville, Tenn.: American Society for State and Local History, 1984.
Blight, David. *Race and Reunion: The Civil War in American Memory.* Cambridge, Mass.: Harvard University Press, 2002.
Botkin, B. A., ed. *A Civil War Treasury of Tales, Legends, and Folklore.* New York: Promontory Press, 1993.

Davis, William C. "Tall Tales of the Civil War," *Civil War Times Illustrated* 35, no. 4 (1996): 48–55.
Gallagher, Gary W., and Alan T. Nolan, eds. *The Myth of the Lost Cause and Civil War History.* Bloomington: Indiana University Press, 2000.
Grant, Susan-Mary, and Peter J. Parish, eds. *Legacy of Disunion: The Enduring Significance of the American Civil War.* Baton Rouge: Louisiana State University Press, 2003.
Heeps, William Allison. *The Singing Sixties: The Spirit of the Civil War Days Drawn from the Music of the Times.* Norman: University of Oklahoma Press, 1960.
McNeil, Keith, and Rusty McNeil. *Civil War Songbook with Historical Commentary.* Riverside, Calif.: WEM Records, 1999.
Roberts, Nancy. *Civil War Ghosts and Legends.* Columbia: University of South Carolina Press, 1992.
Silber, Irwin. *Songs of the Civil War.* New York: Dover, 1960.
Townsend, E. D. *Anecdotes of the Civil War in the United States.* New York: D. Appleton, 1884.
Turner, Rory. "The Play of History: Civil War Reenactments and Their Use of the Past," *Folklore Forum* 22, nos. 1–2 (1989): 54–61.

Clark, Arizona Donnie (Ma Barker) (1872–1935) Whether as a partner or as merely a protector to her sons and their associates in criminal activity, "Ma" Barker gained a nationwide reputation as a matriarch outlaw in the era of 1920s and 1930s, replete with its images of gangsters and government agents (G-men). Her girlhood admiration for figures such as Jesse James led Barker to a career that, with its updated props of machine guns and automobiles, would prove the modern equivalent of that bandit's life. Her involvement in the Barker-Karpis gang, known for crimes ranging from theft and robbery to murder and abduction, made her a legend in America's history of women outlaws.

Arizona "Arrie" Donnie Clark, better known by her alias as Kate "Ma" Barker, was born in Ash Grove, Missouri, in 1872. She spent most of her life in the Midwest, primarily in Missouri, Oklahoma, and Minnesota. Her September 14, 1892, marriage to George E. Barker, from whom she separated in 1926, produced four sons within the space of 10 years: Herman (b. 1894), Lloyd (b. 1896), Arthur "Doc" (b. 1899), and Fred (b. 1902). These sons, along with their associates, such as Alvin "Creepy" Karpis, Harry Campbell, and Volney Davis, formed the core of a criminal band that would subsequently become known to authorities as the Barker-Karpis Gang.

Although "Ma" Barker would claim that her sons worked in "insurance," their young interests instead turned to burglary and, later, more violent forms of transgression, including the murder of their coconspirator A. W. "Old Man" Dunlop, and the kidnappings of two businessmen, William A. Hamm, Jr., in 1933 and Edward Bremer in 1934. The latter abduction earned the gang's members wide notoriety, as their faces and stories began to appear on wanted posters and in magazine accounts.

Barker's sons were periodically apprehended, and occasionally sentenced, for their involvements in crimes, but it was not until a January 16, 1935, standoff and shootout in Florida that "Ma" Barker's crime spree would reach its end. As the agents raided the hideout, they discovered "Ma," along with her son Freddie, shot dead while still gripping their firearms. This violent end caused the Federal Bureau of Investigation (FBI) to describe this public enemy as "Bloody Mama." Barker's exploits and, in particular, her brazen persistence in them distinguished her as a fearless and unrepentant figure. She is reputed to have extended hospitality to criminal contemporaries from John Dillinger to Baby Face Nelson. Alternately described as the mastermind of the criminal band and merely the manipulator of the justice system in her gang's defense, Barker was not above subterfuge to elude the law or, if members of her group were made to stand trial, extreme courtroom displays of emotion

intended to reduce their sentences or spare them from imprisonment. The "Ma" Barker legend pivots around this devious image, a reputation for loose living, a willingness to indulge her taste for luxury with the proceeds of the gang's crime, and, perhaps most shocking of all, the idea that she gave birth to and raised her own crime gang. The lore surrounding Barker's life and violent death has become the subject of numerous feature films, documentaries, and other representations in American popular culture.

See also: DILLINGER, JOHN; FOLK HEROES/LEGENDARY FIGURES; JAMES, JESSE; MIDWESTERN REGIONAL FOLKLORE; OUTLAWS; OZARKS FOLKLORE.

For Further Reading:
Breuer, William. *J. Edgar Hoover and his G-Men.* Westport, Conn.: Praeger, 1995.
Burrough, Bryan. *Public Enemies: America's Greatest Crime Wave and the Birth of the FBI, 1933–1934.* New York: Penguin Press, 2004.
DeFord, Miriam. *The Real Ma Barker.* New York: Ace, 1970.
Durden-Smith, Jo. *100 Most Infamous Criminals.* New York: MetroBooks, 2004.
Hamilton, Sue L., and John Hamilton. *Public Enemy Number One: The Barkers.* Bloomington, Ind.: Abdo and Daughters, 1989.
Jones, Richard. *The Mammouth Book of Women Who Kill.* New York: Carroll & Graf, 2002.
MacNee, Marie, and Jane Hockner. *Outlaws, Mobsters, and Crooks: From the Old West to the Internet.* Detroit: UXL, 1998.
Winter, Robert. *Mean Men: The Sons of Ma Barker.* Danbury, Conn.: Routledge, 2000.

Clemens, Samuel Langhorne (1835–1910)
Samuel Langhorne Clemens is the birth name of the 19th-century American writer also known by his pen name, Mark Twain.

Samuel Langhorne Clemens was born on November 30, 1835, and grew up in Hannibal, Missouri, the setting for some of his subsequent fiction. After Clemens's father died when the boy was just 12, it became necessary for Clemens to secure employment and help contribute to the family's support. He worked as a printer's apprentice and an itinerant printer. He went on to become a Mississippi riverboat pilot, failed prospector, journalist, and member of the Confederate militia. It is for his literary career—as a local color writer, travel author, teller of tall tales, and folk humorist—that Clemens is remembered.

Clemens was a folk enthusiast and member of the American Folklore Society. His works invoke folk speech and folk types. In addition, his fiction, especially his short stories, often mimics folk tales. Some of his stories were firmly grounded in lore, such as the well-known tale "The Notorious Jumping Frog of Calaveras County." Indeed, the pseudonym Clemens chose was itself inspired by the chanted call of steamboat leadmen: "Mark twain."

As a former riverboat pilot, Clemens had an abiding interest in maritime lore. This fascination is reflected in some of his literary subject matter choices, for instance, *Life on the Mississippi* (1883). In works such as *Roughing It* (1872), Clemens also explored the folklore of the frontier and the American West. He recorded the quintessential figure of a confidence man in *The Man Who Corrupted Hadleyburg* (1900). Even the term *gilded age*, now commonly used to describe the lattermost portion of the 19th century in America, had its origins in Clemens's story of postwar corruption, *The Gilded Age: A Tale of To-Day* (1873).

Among Clemens's most widely read works are *The Adventures of Tom Sawyer* (1876), *Adventures of Huckleberry Finn* (1884), *The Tragedy of Pudd'nhead Wilson* (1894), and *A Connecticut Yankee in King Arthur's Court* (1889). These works are replete with folk beliefs, dialect, and other elements of regional lore. Clemens's most familiar literary images, such as Huck Finn's floating down the river on his raft or Tom Sawyer's tricking his friends into whitewashing a fence for him, are favorites among readers and have been referenced in countless stage productions and popular culture depictions. Characters such as Tom and Huck remain staples of American children's reading lives and lore.

To meet the interest of a national audience, Clemens and George Washington Cable joined forces for a speaking tour during the mid-1880s. Together, they were able to address the popular appetite for folklore-influenced literature and discussion of its context and background. Even before his death in 1910, Clemens was a highly acclaimed author and was hailed as one of the nation's finest fiction writers. While his later works, such as *The United States of Lyncherdom* (1901), *The Mysterious Stranger* (1916), and various unfinished and unpublished pieces, seem bitter or dark, Clemens is nonetheless recalled as a wit and purveyor of Americana.

Whether known as Samuel Langhorne Clemens or Mark Twain, this American author helped celebrate the nation's folk traditions, characters, and regions. In an important sense, Huck Finn and Tom Sawyer captured the popular imagination as fully as their legendary counterparts from oral lore, Mike Fink, Annie Christmas, and Sam Bass.

See also: BASS, SAM; CABLE, WASHINGTON GEORGE; CHILDREN'S FOLKLORE; CHRISTMAS, ANNIE; FINK, MIKE; FOLKLORE IN AMERICAN LITERATURE; FOLKTALES; HUMOR, FOLK; MARITIME FOLKLORE; REGION, FOLK; SOUTHERN REGIONAL FOLKLORE; YANKEE, CONNECTICUT;.

For Further Reading:

Botkin, B. A., ed. *A Treasury of Mississippi River Folklore: Stories, Ballads, and Folkways of the Mid-American River Country*. New York: Crown, 1955.

Brunvand, Jan Harold. "Western Folk Humor in *Roughing It*." In *The Western Folklore Conference: Selected Papers*, edited by Austin Fife and J. Golden Taylor, 53–65. Logan: Utah State University Press, 1964.

Cohen, Hennig. "Twain's Jumping Frog: Folktale to Literature." *Western Folklore* 22 (1963): 17–18.

Devoto, Bernard. *Mark Twain's America*. Boston: Little, Brown, 1932.

Frantz, Ray W. "The Role of Folklore in *Huckleberry Finn*," *American Literature* 28, no. 3 (November 1956): 314–327.

Kaplan, Justin. *Mister Clemens and Mark Twain: A Biography*. New York: Simon & Schuster, 1966.

LeMaster, J. R., and James D. Wilson. *The Mark Twain Encyclopedia*. New York: Garland, 1993.

West, Victor Royce. *Folklore in the Works of Mark Twain*. Lincoln: University of Nebraska Press, 1930.

Winkelman, Donald. "Goodman Brown, Tom Sawyer, and the Oral Tradition," *Keystone Folklore* 10 (1965): 43–48.

clichés. See SPEECH, FOLK.

clowns See TRICKSTER.

Cody, William F. (Buffalo Bill) (1846–1917) William F. "Buffalo Bill" Cody was born in 1846. When his father died in an 1857 stabbing incident, the youth needed to help support the family his father left behind.

Stories about Cody's life are plentiful, although separating truth from fancy in such tales proves challenging. By some accounts, Cody worked as a messenger for the Pony Express. He appears also to have worked as a trapper and prospector. During the Civil War, Cody served in the Seventh Kansas Cavalry. He married Louisa Frederici, with whom he fathered four children.

It was not as a family man, however, that Cody would become best known. Rather, his adventures on the American frontier defined his fame. Cody was a stagecoach driver, buffalo hunter, and Indian fighter. He is said to have sold buffalo meat to the Union Pacific workers constructing the transcontinental railroad. As if this were not enough to secure his place in Western lore, Cody spent the years from 1883 to 1913 presiding over Buffalo Bill's Wild West Show. This commercialized version of a rodeo involved hundreds of cowboys engaged in exhibitions and dramatizations. Cody also featured folk icons of the American West, such as Phoebe Annie Oakley and Wild Bill Hickok. This traveling show helped define the popular perception of the cowboy among Americans, just as it added to the mythology of the West's regional folklore.

Famous as a showman and adventurer even during his lifetime, William F. "Buffalo Bill" Cody remains a widely recognized promoter of cowboy culture long after his death in 1917.

See also: BONNIE AND CLYDE; CIVIL WAR; COWBOYS; FOLK HEROES/LEGENDARY FIGURES; FRONTIER; HICKOK, JAMES BUTLER (WILD BILL); MIDWESTERN REGIONAL FOLKLORE; OAKLEY, PHOEBE ANNIE; REGION, FOLK; RODEO; TRANSCONTINENTAL RAILROAD.

For Further Reading:
Blackstone, Sarah. *Buckskins, Bullets, and Business: A History of Buffalo Bill's Wild West*. Westport, Conn.: Greenwood Press, 1986.

Bridger, Bobby. *Buffalo Bill and Sitting Bull: Inventing the Wild West*. Austin: University of Texas Press, 2002.

Carter, Robert. *Buffalo Bill Cody: The Man behind the Legend*. New York: Wiley, 2000.

Cody, William F. *The Adventures of Buffalo Bill*. New York: Harper, 1904.

Rosa, Joseph, and Robin May. *Buffalo Bill and His Wild West*. Lawrence: University Press of Kansas, 1989.

cold war See ATOMIC/NUCLEAR ERA FOLKLORE.

college folklore See CAMPUS FOLKLORE.

Colonial National Historical Park See COLONIAL WILLIAMSBURG.

colonial revival See COLONIAL WILLIAMSBURG.

Colonial Williamsburg Colonial Willamsburg, a site opened to visitors in 1926, is likely the nation's best known living history museum.

As the location name suggests, this attraction offers tourists a restoration of the 18th-century capital of Virginia during the time it was still a British colony. Colonial Williamsburg covers 301 acres, making it the largest outdoor living history museum in the United States.

The project began as the concept of Bruton Parish Church's rector, Reverend William Goodwin. It would not have proceeded, however, without sponsors. These donors were found through cultivation of interest from John D. Rockefeller and holders of Standard Oil wealth. With such support, it became possible to establish a private concern, the Colonial Williamsburg Foundation. The foundation makes possible this rare presentation of an entire town as it might have been found during 1790.

This location may represent the culmination of the colonial revival movement, which commenced with America's centennial in 1876. A centerpiece of Colonial Williamsburg is the restoration of Carter's Grove plantation. The property includes many structures spared from demolition, as well as some reconstructed buildings. For example, in 1988 the Department of African-American Interpretations and Presentations was established. In this way, previously unseen aspects of the built environment, such as slave quarters, were reintroduced at Colonial Williamsburg.

As a living history museum, Williamsburg employs historical interpreters. The site uses approximately 600 reenactors, who are attired in period costume performing functions associated with life in prerevolutionary America. They also interact with visitors through the technique of first-person dramatizations. Such embodiments of social history seek to make the experience of everyday life in colonial America more immediate and accessible than a conventional museum display might. Through both the live-action facility and the Colonial Williamsburg Web site, visitors may learn about the realities of daily life

for early Americans, including manners, politics, religion, holidays, and family. Information is also available concerning the material world, with elements such as animals, gardening, tools, trades, clothing, and food.

In addition to maintaining the site and underwriting the museum, Colonial Williamsburg promotes scholarship concerned with early America. Such research includes archaeological excavations that help reveal the material culture of another time. The museum also partners with elementary and secondary education, higher education institutions such as the College of William and Mary, and Colonial National Historical Park.

Along with other living history museums, such as Old Sturbridge Village, Greenfield Village, and Mystic Seaport, Colonial Williamsburg invites Americans to "let the past speak to us."

See also: African-American folklore; art, folk; folklore in everyday life; Greenfield Village, Henry Ford Museum and; historic preservation; holidays/observances; living history museums; material culture; museums, folk; Mystic Seaport and Preservation Shipyard; region, folk; Revolutionary War; slavery; Southern regional folklore; Sturbridge Village, Old.

For Further Reading:

Greenspan, Anders. *Creating Colonial Williamsburg.* Washington, D.C.: Smithsonian Institution Press, 2002.

Handler, Richard. *The New History in an Old Museum: Creating the Past at Colonial Williamsburg.* Durham, N.C.: Duke University Press, 1997.

Hood, Graham. *The Governor's Palace in Williamsburg: A Cultural Study.* Williamsburg, Va.: The Colonial Williamsburg Foundation, 1991.

Rossano, Geoffrey, ed. *Creating a Dignified Past: Museums and the Colonial Revival.* Savage, Md.: Rowman & Littlefield, 1991.

Tyler, Lyon Gardiner. *Williamsburg: The Old Colonial Capital.* Richmond, Va.: Whittet and Shepperson, 1907.

Walsh, Lorena Seebach. *From Calabar to Carter's Grove: The History of a Virginia Slave Community*. Charlottesville: University Press of Virginia, 1997.

Colorado folklore See BROWN, MARGARET TOBIN (UNSINKABLE MOLLY BROWN); CHICANO FOLKLORE; CHINESE-AMERICAN FOLKLORE; GHOST TOWNS; GOLD RUSH, THE; JAPANESE-AMERICAN INTERNMENT; WESTERN REGIONAL FOLKLORE.

Columbian Exhibition See COLUMBUS DAY.

Columbian Exposition See COLUMBUS, CHRISTOPHER; COLUMBUS DAY.

Columbus, Christopher (1451–1506) For good or for ill, the explorer Christopher Columbus may be the world explorer best known to America's schoolchildren.

Although his expeditions took place during the 15th century, Columbus did not figure in American folklore until the 18th century. At about the time that the United States gained independence from England, Christopher Columbus emerged as a national icon. He became a prominent figure within the nation's myth of origin. Now that the country has passed the quincentenary of the Columbus voyage that figures most in American lore, both Columbus and his claim to historical importance are matters of contestation.

For many years, Columbus stood at the center of a mythos of America's discovery. In addition to being credited, erroneously or not, with the insight that the world was round rather than flat, Columbus was long identified as the explorer who first discovered America as the New World. This attribution made him an icon for the American people and an ethnic hero for Italian Americans. During the 18th and 19th centuries, Columbus was a popular subject for writers and storytellers, including Washington Irving. Columbus also became the theme for Chicago's World's Fair in the 1890s. In the first half of the 20th century, President Franklin Delano Roosevelt formally designated Columbus Day as a national holiday in the explorer's honor. Each autumn, elementary schoolchildren were greeted with stories, whether accurate or note, of the Columbus legacy, including a rhyme that most American youth learned to recite: "In fourteen hundred ninety-two / Columbus sailed the ocean blue."

By the 1960s, however, a time of cultural questioning generally, the celebration of Columbus and Columbus Day became a controversial issue. Detractors challenged the appropriateness of a public-school curriculum that so mythologized the explorer's fortuitous arrival in North America (he was bound for Asia) and a national holiday honoring a colonizer of indigenous people.

At this point in history, the image of Christopher Columbus is, if not tarnished, a controversial part of the way American history is retold and its heroes celebrated.

See also: COLUMBUS DAY; FOLK HEROES/LEGENDARY FIGURES; HOLIDAYS/OBSERVANCES; IMMIGRATION AND FOLKLORE; IRVING, WASHINGTON; ROOSEVELT, FRANKLIN DELANO.

For Further Reading:

Bushman, Claudia. *America Discovers Columbus: How an Italian Explorer Became an American Hero*. Hanover, N.H.: University Press of New England, 1992.

Jones, Mary Ellen. *Christopher Columbus and His Legacy: Opposing Viewpoints*. San Diego: Greenhaven Press, 1992.

Phillips, William, Jr. *Before 1492: Christopher Columbus's Formative Years*. Washington, D.C.: American Historical Association, 1992.

Royal, Robert. *1492 and All That: Political Manipulations of History*. Washington, D.C.: Ethics and Public Policy Center, 1992.

Sale, Kirkpatrick. *The Conquest of Paradise: Christopher Columbus and the Columbia Legacy*. New York: Knopf, 1990.

Summerhill, Stephen, and John Alexander Williams. *Sinking Columbus: Contested History, Cultural Politics, and Mythmaking during the Quincentenary.* Gainesville: University Press of Florida, 2000.

Taylor, David, and John Alexander Williams. *Old Ties and New Attachments: Italian American Folklife in the West.* Washington, D.C.: American Folklife Center, 1993.

Thompson, Gunnar. *American Discovery: The Real Story.* Seattle: Misty Isles Press, 1992.

Columbus Day   Held in honor of the 1492 "discovery" of the New World by Christopher Columbus, Columbus Day is marked on the second Monday in October each year.

Columbus has long had a place within the national imagination, and writings devoted to his life and career, such as Washington Irving's 1828 biography of the explorer, did much to keep his memory alive. Nonetheless, despite the event's remoteness in time and claimed significance to America's history, the national observance of this day is a relatively recent phenomenon.

Although there had been countless tributes to Columbus, including the naming of Columbia University, the identification of the nation's capital as the District of Columbia, and even the symbolic designation of the nation itself as Columbia, the holiday itself did not take hold until the 20th century. Efforts to make such celebrations an annual event began near the end of the 19th century, concurrently with the 500th anniversary of the Columbus voyage. It was with this concept in mind that Chicago's World's Fair (set for 1892, but delayed in opening until 1893) bore the official title of the World's Columbian Exposition. It would not be until the 1930s, however, that President Franklin Delano Roosevelt would approve designation of a national holiday to honor Christopher Columbus.

In the current cultural climate, there is considerable controversy concerning the justness of Columbus's claim given the presence of indigenous peoples. For this reason, there is a corresponding sensitivity about the Columbus Day holiday. Some think the day should not be celebrated at all, while others continue to support its recognition of the explorer.

Today's observances of Columbus Day include parades, charitable banquets, ethnic festivals, and religious services.

See also: COLUMBUS, CHRISTOPHER; ETHNICITY; HOLIDAYS/OBSERVANCES; IMMIGRATION AND FOLKLORE; IRVING, WASHINGTON; PARADES; ROOSEVELT, FRANKLIN DELANO.

For Further Reading:
Cohen, Hennig, and Tristram Potter Coffin, eds. *The Folklore of American Holidays.* Detroit: Gale, 1987.

Herman, Viola J., and Carolyn Margolis. *Seeds of Change: A Quincentennial Commemoration.* Washington, D.C.: Smithsonian Institution Press, 1991.

Myers, Robert J. *Celebrations: The Complete Book of American Holidays.* Garden City, N.Y.: Doubleday, 1972.

Sale, Kirkpatrick. *The Conquest of Paradise: Christopher Columbus and the Columbia Legacy.* New York: Knopf, 1990.

Santino, Jack. *All around the Year: Holidays and Celebrations in American Life.* Urbana: University of Illinois Press, 1994.

Speroni, Charles. "The Development of the Columbus Day Pageant of San Francisco," *Western Folklore* (1948) 7: 325–335.

Summerhill, Stephen, and John Alexander Williams. *Sinking Columbus: Contested History, Cultural Politics, and Mythmaking during the Quincentenary.* Gainesville: University Press of Florida, 2000.

Vorsey, Louis de. *Keys to the Encounter: A Library of Congress Resource Guide for the Study of the Age of Discovery.* Washington, D.C.: Library of Congress, 1992.

computer folklore   The folklore of computers is an emerging genre of American folk practice, and there are many aspects available for study.

In the nation's popular imagination, as well as in representations in popular film, computer lore is dominated by the image of the hacker. This figure typically refers to a disaffected youth, usually male, who wields prowess with technology against an unfit society. This malevolent image emblematizes American culture's fears about technology and its dangers.

Although in popular culture the word *hacker* summons images of a computer outlaw or evil-doer, among programmers, adherence to a hacker ethic is a strong expectation. Computing workers who choose to transgress that behavioral code find themselves spurned by other programmers. Those who violate systems or break security are not upholding the hacker ethic. For using their computer capacities either to harm people or to profit unfairly at others' expense, such individuals are known as "crackers" rather than hackers. They are rejected, rather than revered, for their misdeeds.

Among the computer savvy, then, there is a narrative culture of programmers and their exploits. The protagonist of such tales is typically a heroic hacker, someone known for prodigious knowledge of computing. This character represents a modern form of trickster figure.

For the rest of American culture, computer folklore involves the ways regular users experience the computing environment. In recent years, there has been an explosion of interest in the tales surrounding the power computers seem to exert within society. From the millennium bug scare that many thought threatened to disrupt services and systems at the advent of the 21st century (year 2000 or Y2K), to the steady flow of other security alerts, most computer users are aware of cautionary tales associated with personal computing. Even if one does not use a computer, it is impossible to avoid having one's private information online as banks, credit card companies, and insurance carriers keep records on computer networks.

In addition, "cyberlore," a set of stories surrounding the Internet, is a growing body of narrative. Most Americans are aware of the threats of spy ware, identity theft, or other forms of abuse of the Internet's tremendous reach into the lives of ordinary citizens. While the Internet holds the potential to reunite sweethearts, classmates, and long lost friends, it also opens the possibility of undesired contact with strangers. Tales of specific incidents or scares about newly identified risks of the Internet are deemed newsworthy and so circulate briskly through the electronic media as well as through word of mouth.

Finally, "e-lore," the folk practices associated with e-mail, offers another new medium for communication. The correspondence that used to travel through the U.S. mail (now known as "snail mail" to users of e-mail, with its heightened expectations for rapid relay of content from sender to recipient) has been replaced by e-mail. From love letters to chain letters, the system of e-mail has displaced much of the communication that used to move through the postal service and now takes place through the paperless format of e-mail. The low cost and quick conveyance of such messages, along with the ease of sending to multiple recipients, have resulted in a high volume of electronic mail. Such communications are replete with virus alerts, hoaxes, and attempts at humor.

As is the companion form of Xerox/fax folklore, computer lore is a prominent feature of life in America during the information age, complete with both new promises and perils.

See also: CITY FOLKLORE; CONSPIRACY FOLKLORE; FOLKLORE IN EVERYDAY LIFE; INDUSTRIALIZATION AND FOLKLORE; LUCK/FORTUNE; OCCUPATIONAL FOLKLORE; OUTLAWS; TRICKSTER; URBAN LEGENDS; XEROX/FAX FOLKLORE.

For Further Reading:
Brunvand, Erik. "The Heroic Hacker: Legends of the Computer Age." In *The Truth Never Stands in the Way of a Good Story*, edited by Jan Harold Brunvand, 170–198. Urbana: University of Illinois Press, 2000.

Dorst, John. "Tags and Burners, Cycles and Networks: Folklore in the Telectronic Age," *Journal of Folklore Research* 27 (1990): 179–190.

Fernback, J. "Legends on the Net: An Examination of Computer-Mediated Communication as a Locus of Oral Culture," *New Media and Society* 5, no. 1 (March 1, 2003): 29–45.

Fox, William. "Computerized Creation and Diffusion of Folkloric Materials," *Folklore Forum* 16 (1983): 5–20.

Jennings, Karla. *The Devouring Fungus: Tales of the Computer Age.* New York: W. W. Norton, 1990.

Roszak, Theodore. *The Cult of Information: The Folklore of Computers and the True Art of Thinking.* New York: Pantheon, 1986.

Shapiro, Fred R. "Etymology of the Computer Bug: History and Folklore," *American Speech: A Quarterly of Linguistic Usage* 62, no. 4 (1987): 376–378.

conjure/conjuring   Conjure, or the art of conjuring, is the practice of securing or hastening desired results through the use of magic.

The concept of conjuring describes a wide array of magical feats, deeds producing results for which there is otherwise no ready explanation. A conjurer is someone who appeals for the help of unseen and supernatural forces to accomplish goals. In most cases, this work involves the summoning of a spirit through ritual acts such as the use of charms, invocations, or incantations.

Within the context of African-American culture, conjure typically refers to a more specific activity, also known as rootwork or root medicine. Zora Neale Hurston, a writer formally trained in anthropology, both collected and adapted such folk material in her print works. A root doctor's business includes determining whether a client has been the subject of conjuring, reversing its effects, and curing the patient. A conjure doctor may complete the treatment by furnishing the client with an object that is meant as a magical item of protection, shielding the individual from further tricks.

Folk traditions for conjuring are linked closely to beliefs about medicine and health. For instance, conjure plays a significant role in voodoo. Hoodoo, its American incarnation, blends influences from African, Judeo-Christian, and Native American traditions.

Many scholars believe that conjure is largely an African cultural influence that became an enduring part of African-American slave culture. For example, in his slave narrative, Frederick Douglass writes about how another slave offers him a magical root (possibly High John the Conqueror root, reputed to be especially powerful in helping slaves) to carry in his pocket as a way to fend off violence from his slave master. Douglass regards this manner of protection skeptically but accepts it nonetheless. The same suspicious tone toward conjuring appears in other artistic works, such as Scott Joplin's ragtime opera *Treemonisha*, in which folk beliefs are cast as superstitious and backward. More accepting depictions of conjuring can be found in literary works such as Charles Waddell Chesnutt's *The Conjure Woman* and Gloria Naylor's *Mama Day*.

Conjuring represents any application of magic, but most especially the employment of roots and herbs for magical effects. Believers consider plant use by conjurers effective in efforts to shield against, counter, or initiate spells.

See also: AFRICAN-AMERICAN FOLKLORE; BELIEFS, FOLK; CHESNUTT, CHARLES WADDELL; DOUGLASS, FREDERICK; FOLKLORE IN EVERYDAY LIFE; GARDENING; HURSTON, ZORA NEALE; MAGIC; MEDICINE, FOLK; SLAVERY; SOUTHERN REGIONAL FOLKLORE; SUPERSTITION; VOODOO/HOODOO.

For Further Reading:

Ashanti, Kwabena. *Root Doctor.* Durham, N.C.: Sarafina Books, 1992.

Beardslee, Karen E. *Literary Legacies, Folklore Foundations: Selfhood and Cultural Tradition in Nineteenth- and Twentieth-Century American Literature.* Knoxville: University of Tennessee Press, 2001.

Billingslea-Brown, Alma. *Crossing Borders through Folklore: African American Women's Fiction and Art.* Columbia: University of Missouri Press, 1999.

Bird, Stephanie Rose. *Sticks, Stones, Roots, and Bones: Hoodoo, Mojo, and Conjuring with Herbs.* St. Paul, Minn.: Llewellyn, 2004.

Dundes, Alan, ed. *Mother Wit from the Laughing Barrel: Readings in the Interpretation of Afro-American Folklore.* Jackson: University Press of Mississippi Press, 1990.

Jaskoski, Helen. "Power Unequal to Man: The Significance of Conjure in Works by Five Afro-American Authors," *Southern Folklore Quarterly* 38 (1974): 91–108.

Pryse, Marjorie, and Hortense J. Spillers, eds. *Conjuring: Black Women, Fiction, and Literary Tradition* Bloomington: Indiana University Press, 1985.

Connecticut folklore See ALLEN, ETHAN; CLEMENS, SAMUEL LANGHORNE; ELECTION DAY; MARITIME FOLKLORE; MYSTIC SEAPORT AND PRESERVATION SHIPYARD; NAMING/NAMES; NORTHEASTERN REGIONAL FOLKLORE; SHAKER FOLKLORE; STEPHENS, ANN SOPHIA; YANKEE, CONNECTICUT.

conspiracy folklore The phrase *conspiracy lore* refers to a wide range of theories concerning misfortunes, disasters, mysteries, or unexplained phenomena.

Most conspiracies of this kind suggest that there are secret forces at work to influence human events or experiences. The resulting lore purports to expose these hidden truths. In this sense, the narratives claim to perform a public service similar to that of investigative journalisms. Typically, these stories are presented as the untold truth others attempt to conceal from America.

Extraterrestrial and unidentified flying object (UFO) lore represents one category of conspiracy. Stories of alien encounters and abductions abound, and accounts of flying saucer sightings

have been fairly common since the mid-20th century. The intrigue surrounding the so-called Area 51, a location near a New Mexico U.S. air base about which there is endless speculation about alien activity, provides a relevant example.

Other rumors relate to similar suspicions that the federal government stands behind false information or misleading accounts. In one such case, tellers contend that the U.S. Moon landing never really happened. Within these tales audiences can encounter the notion that an elaborate hoax was perpetrated on the nation and world. Likewise, there exist alternative theories surrounding major assassinations in America, from Abraham Lincoln's to John Fitzgerald Kennedy's.

Still other conspiracies involve mysterious events, from crop circles to computer viruses. For every phenomenon that goes unexplained, there will be folk accounts of what "really" happened. Whether the topic is the whereabouts of kidnapped children, the fate of prisoners of war, the source of acquired immunodeficiency syndrome (AIDS), or the activities of fraternal organizations, secret societies, and cults, conspiracy lore gratifies the popular desire to have insider information. It also reflects feelings of powerlessness in the face of such impersonal forces as bureaucracy and technology.

Conspiracy lore usually states outright, or at least hints, that matters of consequence are not quite as they appear or are reported.

See also: AIDS FOLKLORE; ATOMIC/NUCLEAR ERA FOLKLORE; COMPUTER FOLKLORE; FOLKLORE IN EVERYDAY LIFE; LINCOLN, ABRAHAM; LINDBERGH, CHARLES; OCCUPATIONAL FOLKLORE; OUTLAWS; POLITICS AND FOLKLORE; UFO FOLKLORE; XEROX/FAX FOLKLORE.

For Further Reading:

Barkun, Michael. *A Culture of Conspiracy: Apocalyptic Visions in Contemporary America.* Berkeley: University of California Press, 2003.

Curry, Richard Orr, and Thomas M. Brown, eds., *Conspiracy: The Fear of Subversion in American*

History. New York: Holt, Rinehart & Winston, 1972.

Fine, Gary Alan. "Among Those Dark Satanic Mills: Rumors of Kooks, Cults, and Corporations," *Southern Folklore* 47, no. 2 (1990): 133–146.

Goldberg, Robert Alan. *Enemies Within: The Culture of Conspiracy in Modern America*. New Haven, Conn.: Yale University Press, 2001.

Constitutional Congress See Citizenship Day.

Constitution Day See Citizenship Day.

conversation See speech, folk.

Cooper, James Fenimore (1789–1851) James Fenimore Cooper was a prolific 19th-century American writer with keen interests in the nation's history and lore.

Cooper was born James Cooper on September 15, 1789, in Burlington, New Jersey. He was the youngest of six children. He grew up in Cooperstown, New York. He did not take the middle name of Fenimore, his mother's maiden name, until he was 37 and already a known author. Cooper's father had resolved that James would prepare for a career in law. At 13, Cooper began a college education at Yale University in Connecticut, but he was expelled after two years for unruly behavior. He went on to become a midshipman in the U.S. Navy, where he remained until the age of 20 when his father died.

He did not become a writer until approximately 1820. Cooper's purported entry into authorship occurred when he became disgusted with the poor quality of a volume he was reading. As the story goes, he pitched the book in a fit of pique and vowed that he could do better. He then set about proving it by creating a literature of the American frontier.

Cooper's series of five Leatherstocking Tales were beloved among readers, especially those intrigued by stories of the American West. This wilderness series featured protagonists drawn broadly from the historical adventures of the frontiersman Daniel Boone. It was in this set of tales that Cooper presented his most famous fictional protagonist, Natty Bumppo.

Bumppo, the figure of a skilled outdoorsman, recurred in Cooper's fiction. Cooper's stories of the fictional hero would later be translated to popular culture, such as film westerns. As the author of 32 novels, including *The Last of the Mohicans: A Narrative of 1757* (1826), Cooper became a widely read writer of fiction, stories of the sea, and travel literature before he died September 14, 1851.

As literary tastes and critical fashions have shifted, Cooper's reputation has not rivaled that of other writers to whom he is compared. Still, his historical romances are a window into the 19th century's fascination with the nation's expansion and its heroes' exploits.

James Fenimore Cooper remains a classic American writer, and in the pages of his work today's readers can encounter the stories of a country still being traversed and a national literature still being formed.

See also: Boone, Daniel; folklore in American literature; frontier; maritime folklore; Northeastern regional folklore; region, folk; Western regional folklore.

For Further Reading:

Baker, Martin, and Roger Sabin. *The Lasting of the Mohicans: History of an American Myth*. Jackson: University Press of Mississippi, 1995.

Baumbarten, Linda. "Leather Stockings and Hunting Shirts." In *American Material Culture: The Shape of the Field*, edited by Ann Smart Martin and J. Ritchie Garrison, 251–276. Winterthur, Del.: Winterthur Museum, 1997.

Clagett, John H. "The Maritime Works of James Fenimore Cooper as Sources for Sea Lore, Sea Legend, and Sea Idiom," *SFQ* 30 (1966): 323–331.

Fink, Robert. "Harvey Birch: The Yankee Peddler as an American Hero," *New York Folklore Quarterly* 30 (1974): 137–152.

Long, Robert Emmet. *James Fenimore Cooper*. New York: Continuum, 1990.

McWilliams, John P. *The Last of the Mohicans: Civil Savagery and Savage Civility*. New York: Twayne, 1995.

Test, George. *James Fenimore Cooper: His Country and His Art*. Oneonta, N.Y.: SUNY, 1981.

Vlach, John. "Fenimore Cooper's Leatherstocking as Folk Hero," *New York Folklore Quarterly* 27 (1971): 323–338.

Copland, Aaron (1900–1990) Very possibly the American composer most immersed in folk material, Aaron Copland wrote some of the best-known compositions among the nation's classical music.

Copland was born to immigrant parents in Brooklyn, New York, on November 14, 1900. Although he was not raised in an especially musical household, by his teens Copland resolved to become a composer. This aspiration took the young man to France, where he developed his skills with a musical expert of the day, Nadia Boulanger. Paradoxically, though, once Copland conducted his training in France, he returned to the United States determined to create uniquely American pieces.

This objective inspired Aaron Copland to familiarize himself with America's indigenous musical traditions. While he made a study of such musical forms as blues, jazz, and ragtime, in time, it was American folklore that would hold the greatest promise for Copland's work. His body of writing would bear the influence of such genres as cowboy ballads, church hymns, and a variety of other folk forms. By incorporating elements from this music as themes or motifs within his classical compositions, Copland brought to fruition the works for which he is remembered today. In his three ballets, Copland demonstrated a fondness for the American West and its lore. These works are the popular pieces *Billy the Kid* (1938), *Rodeo* (1942), and *Appalachian Spring* (1944). Copland composed additional pieces celebrating America's heritage

and heroes, including "Fanfare for the Common Man" (1942) and "A Lincoln Portrait" (1942). He also created the musical scores for several Hollywood films, including screen adaptations of literary works by such American authors as John Steinbeck and Thornton Wilder. These films included *Of Mice of Men* (1939), *Our Town* (1940), and *The Red Pony* (1948).

In addition to being a successful composer, Copland delivered lectures, taught, conducted, and wrote popular books about musical appreciation, including *What to Listen For in Music* (1939). Copland died on December 2, 1990.

With his music, Aaron Copland effectively bridged the distances among classical music, popular culture, and folk melodies.

See also: APPALACHIAN FOLKLORE; LINCOLN, ABRAHAM; McCARTY, WILLIAM HENRY (BILLY THE KID); MUSIC, FOLK; RODEO; SHAKER FOLKLORE.

For Further Reading:

Copland, Aaron, and Vivian Perlis. *Copland: 1900 through 1942*. New York: St. Martin's/Marek, 1984.

Copland, Aaron, and Vivian Perlis. *Copland: Since 1943*. New York: St. Martins/Marek, 1989.

Kostelanetz, Richard, ed. *Aaron Copland: A Reader: Selected Writings, 1923–1972*. New York: Routledge, 2004.

Oja, Carol J., and Judith Tick, eds. *Aaron Copland and His World*. Princeton, N.J.: Princeton University Press, 2005.

Pollack, Howard. *Aaron Copland: The Life and Work of an Uncommon Man*. New York: Henry Holt, 1999.

courtship/dating folklore Within American society, dating has chiefly been understood as the social process by which individuals form romantic relationships that might result in formation of couples and/or marriages.

Dating and courtship practices are not necessary within societies where marriages are arranged by third parties, such as the couple's parents. Since arranged marriages have never been the standard in the United States, courtship customs have a long and evolving history. Such behavior is generally understood as a process of mutual selection of partners. In a society where the divorce rate is high, dating occurs not only among the never married, but also among those who are separated, divorced, or in open (nonexclusive) relationships.

Traditionally, Americans chose their dating partners on the basis of a variety of factors. The desired attributes may be different for one individual and the next, but most people dating in America employ such criteria in order to assess and compare prospective partners. Characteristics such as religion, occupation, wealth, appearance, or other status markers help guide individual choices of dates. In early America, dating was considered a step in contemplation of marriage, with the bride's father granting the groom consent. During the 19th century, courtship remained formal, with gentleman callers paying visits to the family homes of marriageable women.

The 20th century proved a more freewheeling phase in the history of American courtship. As urbanization caused many youths to relocate to cities to pursue employment, they were no longer subject to the same level of family and hometown scrutiny once experienced in rural areas and small towns. As young women entered the paid workforce in increasing numbers, they also relied less upon their suitors for the resources to secure a residence and maintain a household. Both of these shifts, urban migration and women's paid employment, also served to increase the number of prospective dates for America's single women. The 1950s marked an era in the United States during which dating couples were less likely to delay physical contact until engagement or marriage. Customs such as "going steady" might represent a sufficiently committed relationship for participants to consent mutually to sexual intimacy. It was still usual for young people to interact in groups or, alternatively, as couples attending such wholesome and chaperoned events as school dances or ice cream socials. With the women's movement and the availability of oral contraceptives during the 1960s, the so-called sexual revolution began. The stigma of premarital sex, and the risk of unwanted pregnancies, diminished. Consequently, more casual attitudes about, and practices regarding, sexual contact began to prevail in America. This era also produced an increase in the rate of nonmarital pregnancies, perhaps because of such factors as unwed pregnancies by choice and increased rates of sexual contact.

Today, courtship practices involve the exchange of both verbal and nonverbal cues, used to signal availability and interest. Flirtations may involve extended looks at the potential partner or approach with a verbal overture, often described as an opening line. Dating is not automatically considered to be a step closer to commitment for participants, and while mating scripts (such as a kiss on the first date) persist to some degree, the predictability of such sequences is much lower today than it once was.

Folklorists, along with other social scientists, have attended to many aspects of dating and courtship in the United States. Such matters as rituals associated with first dates and romantic customs across the years reveal attitudes about gender, sexuality, mating, and marriage. From the image of a lover's leap, a precipice from which rejected or otherwise aggrieved lovers jump to their death, to the self-help and advice literature of dating of the 21st century, there are many nuances to this field within folklore.

The folklore of dating/courtship, as a rite of passage, has changed over time but remains a highly charged subject in the lives of ordinary Americans.

See also: CUSTOMS, FOLK; FAMILY FOLKLORE; FOLKLORE IN EVERYDAY LIFE; GENDER AND FOLKLORE; RITES OF PASSAGE; WEDDING/MARRIAGE FOLKLORE.

For Further Reading:
Bailey, Beth L. *From Front Porch to Back Seat: Courtship in Twentieth Century America*. Baltimore: Johns Hopkins University Press, 1989.

Cate, Rodney. *Courtship*. Newbury Park, Calif.: Sage, 1992.

Gourse, Leslie. *Native American Courtship and Marriage Traditions*. New York: Hippocrene Books, 2000.

McEntire, Nancy Cassell. "The American Play-Party in Context," *Voices: The Journal of New York Folklore* 28, nos. 1–2 (spring–summer 2002): 30–33.

Rothman, Ellen. *Hands and Love: A History of Courtship in America*. New York: Basic Books, 1950.

Tally, Frances. "American Folk Customs of Courtship and Marriage: The Bedroom." In *Forms upon the Frontier: Folklife and Folk Arts in the United States*, edited by Austin E. Fife, Alta Stephens Fife, and Henry H. Glassie, 138–158. Logan: Utah State University Press, 1969.

Turner, E. S. *A History of Courting*. New York: Dutton, 1955.

cowboys As the archetypal image of Americans, both in the United States and abroad, cowboys function as icons of the days and doings of the frontier.

A cowboy is a character from occupational folklore, a person working the land of the American West. Central activities of the cowboy in this regard involve cattle driving, roping, and riding. While cowboys are tied in a specific sense to the cattle industry, over time they have come to represent the spirit of American independence.

During the period of westward expansion, cowboys endured long hours, difficult work, rough terrain, and a notoriously lawless environment. Nonetheless, the life of the cowboy is frequently romanticized in the nation's folklore. The figure of a rough-hewn man clad in denim, chaps, boots, bandana, and 10-gallon hat dominates this image. His poetry, stories, sayings, and way of life are celebrated in everything from pulp novels to western movies. Entertainment figures including Will Rogers, Gene Autry, Roy Rogers, and Tex Ritter have perpetuated this concept of the cowboy as autonomous, noble, and adventurous. Cowboy songs, such as "Bury Me Not on the Lone Prairie," are campfire favorites.

While the actual life of the cowboy was likely more gritty and less virtuous than the myth might suggest, cowboy culture continues to be regarded as an emblem of sorts for the national character.

See also: CANNARY-BURKE, MARTHA (CALAMITY JANE); CODY, WILLIAM F. (BUFFALO BILL); EARP, WYATT BERRY STAMP; FOLK HEROES/LEGENDARY FIGURES; FRONTIER; GHOST TOWNS; HICKOK, JAMES BUTLER (WILD BILL); HUMOR, FOLK; MUSIC, FOLK; OAKLEY, PHOEBE ANNIE; OCCUPATIONAL FOLKLORE; PECOS BILL; REGION, FOLK; RODEO; SOUTHWESTERN REGIONAL FOLKLORE; STARR, BELLE; WESTERN REGIONAL FOLKLORE.

For Further Reading:
Felton, Harold. *Cowboy Jamboree: Western Songs and Lore*. New York: Knopf, 1951.

Martin, Russell. *Cowboy, the Enduring Myth of the Wild West*. New York: Stewart, Tabori & Chang, 1983.

Price, B. Byron. *Cowboys of the American West*. San Diego: Thunder Bay Books, 1996.

Rollins, Philip Ashton. *The Cowboy: An Unconventional History of Civilization on the Old-Time Cattle Range*. New York: Scribners, 1936.

Savage, William W., Jr. *The Cowboy Hero*. Norman: University of Oklahoma Press, 1979.

Savage, William W., Jr., ed. *Cowboy Life: Reconstructing an American Myth*. Norman: University of Oklahoma Press, 1975.

Taylor, Lonn, and Ingrid Maar. *The American Cowboy*. Washington, D.C.: American Folklife Center, 1983.

Coyote (legendary) Alternately assuming the shape of a man or a wild canine, Coyote is a trickster figure from Native American folklore.

In much the manner that Raven is a trickster figure linked to Northwestern regional folklore,

Coyote is connected to Southwestern regional folklore. As with other trickster figures, Coyote functions as a picaresque hero. He transgresses cultural expectations and societal rules, often to great effect. Tricksters are playful creatures, given to pranks and misdirection, and so their victories are often accomplished through deception and sly humor.

Although there are many variations, probably the most famous tale of Coyote involves the power of fire. Demonstrating the true spirit of a trickster, Coyote steals fire from the gods and gives it to humans. In this sense, Coyote exerts considerable power. He, as many tricksters do, operates as a creator figure rather than simply a manipulator. Tricksters alter the human world with their feats of guile and strength.

Other trickster figures in American folklore include Anansi, Brer Rabbit, and the Yankee Peddler. Each is featured in tales of surprising turns of events, in which tricksters usually emerge the victors. As with Coyote, these tricksters are known for getting the better of those who are otherwise mightier or more powerful within the social structure. Those who would seek to exploit the trickster are likely to find themselves painfully reminded that social power has a way of shifting, especially when figures such as Coyote are on scene.

As an element of Native American folklore, Coyote continues to be featured within North American turnabout narratives.

See also: ANANSI; ANIMALS; BRER RABBIT; CHANGELINGS; FOLK HEROES/LEGENDARY FIGURES; FOLKTALES; MAGIC; NATIVE AMERICAN FOLKLORE; NORTHWESTERN REGIONAL FOLKLORE; REMUS, UNCLE; SOUTHWESTERN REGIONAL FOLKLORE; TAR BABY; TRICKSTER; YANKEE PEDDLER.

For Further Reading:

Ballinger, Franchot. *Living Sideways: Tricksters in American Indian Oral Traditions.* Norman: University of Oklahoma Press, 2004.
Brennan, Jonathan, ed. *When Brer Rabbit Meets Coyote: African-Native American Literature.* Urbana: University of Illinois Press, 2003.
Bright, William. *A Coyote Reader.* Berkeley: University of California Press, 1993.
Dobie, J. Frank. *The Voice of the Coyote.* Boston: Little, Brown, 1949.
Hymes, Dell. *Now I Know Only So Far.* Lincoln: University of Nebraska Press, 2003.
Toelken, Barre. "Beauty behind Me, Beauty before Me (AFS Address)," *Journal of American Folklore* 117, no. 466 (fall 2004): 441–445.

crafts, folk   When folklorists speaks of folk crafts, the reference generally suggests handmade items constructed by using traditional materials and fabrication methods.

Within American folklore studies, the initial emphasis was nearly exclusively on the artifacts produced and used within rural, preindustrial cultures. Such craft genres include toys, basketry, weaving, quilting, pottery, needlework, and woodworking. More recently, folklorists have widened the scope of their investigations of folk crafts to include more contemporary forms associated with urban and industrial culture. Nonetheless, the majority of folklore scholarship dealing with American crafts continues to focus on the older traditions.

The early years of the American Folklore Society as an organization coincided with the arts and crafts movement, a revival of interest in domestic handicrafts. Both in England and in America, the arts and crafts movement began as a reaction to the industrial age and its threats of an increasingly dehumanized (and dehumanizing) environment. As an antidote to that force, the arts and crafts aesthetic placed highest value on human touch, artisanal qualities, and handiwork. Some, though not all, craftspeople associated with this 1880–1920 movement eschewed machinery in fashioning their work. Influences of the movement appear in such expressive forms as architecture, pottery, lighting, furniture, and glass. Most of these elements were envisioned for the home, making it a refuge from the harsh and cold atmosphere of the modern workplace, with its impersonal office buildings, plants, and factories. The arts and crafts home answered these settings with a warmth and scale that provided a refuge.

During the 1920s, the nation began to be especially interested in the folk crafts of the Appalachian region. One reason the region commands such attention among American folklorists is its distinctive relation to cultural tradition. As a topographically remote and relatively culturally isolated space well into the 20th century, Appalachia has retained a greater share of its traditions and customs than it might have if its people had had more contact with other populations and their ways of life. During the first part of the 20th century, some believed that Appalachia represented survivals of Anglo-American and Irish-American folk traditions that had faded elsewhere.

Vernacular forms associated with Appalachia include log houses and other elements of folk architecture. The region has also been home to rich traditions in folk music, dance, speech, and crafts. Appalachian folk festivals have been taking place since the 1920s. The publication of Allen Eaton's influential book *Handicrafts of the Southern Highlands* helped increase awareness of Appalachian folk culture.

By the 1930s, a host of government agencies were formed to counter the effects of the Great Depression. This "New Deal," as the effort was known, employed artists such as mural painters and photographers. It also financed the work of folklorists who set about collecting oral histories and documenting the customs and crafts of the American people, generating an unprecedented record of the nation's folklore. For example, the *Index of American Design* chronicled the ingenuity of the country's artists and both the beauty and the utility of their forms.

By the 1960s, the folk revival highlighted not only folk music, but also folk arts and crafts. This enthusiasm produced a folklife movement. The term *folklife* refers to nonverbal traditions of a population, as well as to their study in social and cultural context. *Folklore* and *folklife* are kindred terms in the sense that both explore the way of life experienced by ordinary members of a cul-

tural group. While the two are interlocking categories of analysis, it is usually the case that the word *folklore* is used to emphasize the narrative lore of a people, while *folklife* concentrates more on their nonnarrative, nonverbal practices. In this respect, folklorists have close ties to linguistics, while folklife researchers have more in common with anthropologists. The emphasis within this study is on cultural patterns of expression learned without benefit of formal education or institutional support. In other words, folklife includes the customs, beliefs, and practices that are transmitted interpersonally. Typically, this transfer of knowledge and capacity is achieved through oral communication, performance, or demonstration. Folk crafts are a central part of American folklife and its study.

Signs of widening acceptance for this approach to the study of American folk traditions include the establishment of high-profile folk festivals such as the Festival of American Folklife, established in 1967. In addition, the National Endowment for the Arts established a program for folk crafts in 1974. Another important sign of support was the decision by Congress to approve the American Folklife Preservation Act of 1976, which promoted the nation's efforts to research and educate folklife. It also provided for establishment within the Library of the Congress of the American Folklife Center.

The folklife movement, though controversial with those who favor the earlier emphasis on verbal performance within folklore studies, has broadened the scope of research and documentation of American folk culture. It has also helped develop a trend in the configuration of folk museums, wherein demonstrations, reenactments, hands-on workshops, interactive exhibits, and living history presentations have become more prevalent. Such organizations frequently incorporate first-person interpreters of American folk history, who assume the role of actual or composite members of past societies. Often positioned within restored historical buildings or reconstructed historical districts, these figures conduct the traditional way of life.

They also interact with visitors, usually speaking with the dialect, idiom, and delivery associated with the era they represent. In this way, visitors may ask questions and engage with the past in an embodied, more personal form than artifact display alone would afford.

The folklife movement had its origins in regional ethnology and calls for a holistic approach to the study of American culture. This shift in the study of folk traditions introduced more anthropological and ethnographic approaches than had previously typified folklore study. Advocates for the folklife movement placed relatively less emphasis on verbal and narrative forms of folk culture, and more on custom, foodways, and architecture.

American folk crafts are now recognized by curators and collectors alike for their artful combinations of form and function. Displays of particularly accomplished examples of folk crafts appear in museums and galleries across the nation, such as the American Folk Art Museum. These handmade and homemade artifacts embody the way of life of the Americans who produced and used them. They also contribute to the sense of identity of folk groups and the sense of place across the nation's regions.

See also: APPALACHIAN FOLKLORE; ARCHITECTURE, FOLK; ART, FOLK; ARTS AND CRAFTS MOVEMENT; CHICANO FOLKLORE; CREATION/ORIGIN STORIES; DANISH-AMERICAN FOLKLORE; FOLKLIFE; FOLKLORE IN EVERYDAY LIFE; HILLBILLIES; HUNGARIAN-AMERICAN FOLKLORE; INDUSTRIALIZATION AND FOLKLORE; LIVING HISTORY MUSEUMS; MUSEUMS, FOLK; NORWEGIAN-AMERICAN FOLKLORE; OCCUPATIONAL FOLKLORE; OZARKS FOLKLORE; PENNSYLVANIA DUTCH/PENNSYLVANIA GERMAN FOLKLORE; POLISH-AMERICAN FOLKLORE; PRISON FOLKLORE; RESEARCH, FOLKLIFE; SCOTTISH-AMERICAN FOLKLORE; SHAKER FOLKLORE; TOYS, FOLK.

For Further Reading:
Bronner, Simon. *Grasping Things: Folk Material Culture and Mass Society in America.* Lexington: University Press of Kentucky, 1986.

Cooper, Patricia, and Norma Buferd, *The Quilters: Women and Domestic Art.* New York: Doubleday, 1977.

Denker, Bert, ed. *The Substance of Style: Perspectives on the American Arts and Crafts Movement.* Winterthur, Del.: Winterthur Museum, 1996.

Dorson, Richard. *Folklore and Folklife: An Introduction.* Chicago: University of Chicago Press, 1972.

Ferris, William R., ed. *Afro-American Folk Art and Crafts.* Boston: Hall, 1983.

Lucie-Smith, Edward. *The Story of Craft: The Craftman's Role in Society.* Ithaca, N.Y.: Cornell University Press, 1981.

Crazy Horse (c. 1838–1877) Crazy Horse was a Sioux warrior and chief during the 19th century.

He was born in South Dakota around 1838. During this time in the nation's history, westward expansion by Anglo-Americans during the 1860s and 1870s created conflicts over land rights and challenges to the liberty of indigenous populations. In the era of Indian removal, Native Americans were often driven onto reservations. As did many Native Americans of his time, Crazy Horse had to contend with encroachments on the land he occupied in the western territories.

Crazy Horse became part of the resistance to such threats, painting a lightning streak on his cheek as he readied for battle. Anxious to avoid life on the reservation, Crazy Horse and his warriors stood up to those who expected Native Americans to yield. In his most famous such encounter, Crazy Horse faced off with George Armstrong Custer and the Seventh Cavalry. The problem seems to have begun when an 1874 discovery of gold in Black Hills, South Dakota, prompted white fortune seekers to flood into the area. In 1875, an order was issued for Indian removal. Custer and his men had been dispatched in response to tensions that had erupted in the region. This June 1876 contest became known to history as the battle of Little

Bighorn. Some today also refer to it as "Custer's Last Stand."

Crazy Horse withstood this battle, but later hardships led his people to relent and they agree to live on the reservation. When he sustained fatal stab wounds at the hands of a guard in 1877, Crazy Horse was paid tribute and laid to rest. It is believed that he was buried at Wounded Knee, South Dakota, the location of the 1890 massacre. A large mountainside sculpture, similar to Mount Rushmore's tributes to American presidents, is currently in progress.

Crazy Horse became a historical figure as he emerged as a Native American leader, and within folklore he became a symbol of the determination and agency of his people.

See also: ANGLO-AMERICAN FOLKLORE; CUSTER, GEORGE ARMSTRONG; FOLK HEROES/ LEGENDARY FIGURES; FRONTIER; GOLD RUSH, THE; NATIVE AMERICAN FOLKLORE; NORTHWESTERN REGIONAL FOLKLORE; REGION, FOLK.

For Further Reading:

Ambrose, Stephen. *Crazy Horse and Custer: The Parallel Lives of Two American Warriors*. Garden City, N.Y.: Doubleday, 1975.

Hardorff, Richard, ed. *The Surrender and Death of Crazy Horse: A Source Book about a Tragic Episode in Lakota History*. Spokane, Wash.: Arthur H. Clarke, 1998.

Marshall, Joseph III. *The Journey of Crazy Horse: A Lakota History*. New York: Viking, 2004.

Masson, Jean-Robert. *The Great Indian Chiefs: Cochise, Geronimo, Crazy Horse, Sitting Bull*. Hauppauge, N.Y.: Barron's, 1994.

Sajna, Mike. *Crazy Horse: The Life behind the Legend*. New York: Wiley, 2000.

creation/origin stories Most folk cultures have stories that account for the world's creation or its origins. These tales of cosmogony interest the folklorist because they suggest meanings underlying the human condition.

Because folk groups the world over have immigrated to the United States, American creation stories reflect this international range of culturally based explanations. These world origin narratives vary widely by population but may generally be classified into several categories by type. Examples include stories of divine creation, by one or more deities; stories in which human life originates from the waters of the world; and stories in which human life emerges from the Earth's core.

In terms of American folklore, some of the most closely studied creation stories are those of Native Americans. These accounts for the world's or human life's origin differ across tribes and regions. They may also detail the source of other natural phenomena such as the origin of fire, corn, or the thunderbird. Most embody fundamental beliefs that help form a folk group's worldview. Some even constitute central folk myths for a culture.

For example, the figure of Grandmother Spider functions in a symbolic manner for Native Americans comparable to that of the figure of Anansi the Spider for those of West African descent. Groups such as the Choctaw and Hopi feature Grandmother Spider in stories in which she weaves the world out of her own web. Native American folk crafts also reflect this myth, such as the use of myth-driven designs for sandpainting rituals and textiles.

Creation tales reveal fundamental beliefs a people hold regarding divinity, the Earth, and the source and purpose of human life. From the Judeo-Christian story of Genesis to the Native American tales of Grandmother Spider, stories or cosmogonies appear all over the world. Regardless of which model of world origin they employ, creation stories function as cherished narratives and telling statements of belief within a folk group.

See also: ANANSI; ANIMALS; CHILDREN'S FOLKLORE; CRAFTS, FOLK; FABLES; FAIRY TALES; MOMADAY, NAVARRE SCOTT; MYTHS, FOLK; NATIVE AMERICAN FOLKLORE; RELIGION, FOLK; SILKO, LESLIE MARMON.

For Further Reading:

Caduto, Michael J. *Earth Tales from around the World*. Golden, Colo.: Fulcrum, 1997.

Erdoes, Richard, and Alfonso Ortiz. *American Indian Myths and Legends*. New York: Pantheon Books, 1984.

Gish, Robert F. "Voices from Bear Country: Leslie Silko's Allegories of Creation," *FEMSPEC* 2, no. 2 (2001): 48–55.

Hamilton, Virginia. *In the Beginning: Creation Stories from around the World*. San Diego: Harcourt Brace Jovanovich, 1988.

Leeming, David A., and Margaret Leeming. *A Dictionary of Creation Myths*. New York: Oxford University Press, 1995.

Moss, Maria. *We've Been Here Before: Women in Creation Myths and Contemporary Literature of the Native American Southwest*. Münster, Germany: Lit, 1993.

Neulander, Judith S. "Creating the Universe: A Study of Cosmos and Cognition," *Folklore Forum* 25, no. 1 (1992): 3–18.

Weigle, Marta. *Creation and Procreation: Feminist Reflections on Mythologies of Cosmogony and Parturition*. Philadelphia: University of Pennsylvania Press, 1989.

crime folklore   See OUTLAWS.

Crockett, Davy (1786–1836)   As a frontiersman of extraordinary talents, Davy Crockett joins the pantheon of America's tall tale heroes.

His superhuman strengths accompany a larger-than-life physical presence. According to the tales of his life, Crockett was some 200 pounds at the time of his backwoods birth in 1786. He was so large that a giant turtle's shell served as his cradle. As he grew, he proved to be a bold outdoorsman. He excelled as a lumberjack, hunter, and trapper.

As was Mike Fink, Davy Crockett was not above boasting about his powers. He claimed to be a better shot, rider, fighter, and all-around sportsman than anyone in America. Many folk tales are devoted to dramatizing the basis for such claims. His can-do attitude served him well on the frontier, and images of Crockett in his famous coonskin cap permeate children's folklore. His character also starred in a popular television program, *The Legends of Davy Crockett*, produced during the 1950s and re-aired in the 1960s, in which Crockett was hailed as "king of the wild frontier." Youngsters donned caps reminiscent of the Crockett costume, playing out their fantasies of the wilderness.

Davy Crockett's motto was "Be sure you're right, then go ahead." In addition to his exploits on the land, he is reputed to have fought with Andrew Jackson in the War of 1812. He later cultivated his public image by serving in the United States House of Representatives. From 1835 until 1856, a Nashville imprint also published a Crockett-inspired almanac. Crockett's life, though not his lore, ended at the Alamo in 1836.

As an icon of the American frontier, Davy Crockett persists as part of the nation's folklore and historical imagination.

See also: APPALACHIAN FOLKLORE; DISNEY, WALTER ELIAS; FINK, MIKE; FOLK HEROES/LEGENDARY FIGURES; FOLKTALES; FRONTIER; SOUTHERN REGIONAL FOLKLORE; WHIRLWIND, SALLY ANN THUNDER ANN.

For Further Reading:

Derr, Mark. *The Frontiersman: The Real Life and Many Legends of Davy Crockett*. New York: W. Morrow, 1993.

Dorson, Richard, ed. *Davy Crockett, American Comic Legend*. New York: Rockland Editions, 1939.

Hauck, Richard Boyd. *Davy Crockett, a Handbook*. Lincoln: University of Nebraska Press, 1986.

Lofaro, Michael, ed. *Davy Crockett: The Man, the Legend, the Legacy, 1786–1986*. Knoxville: University of Tennessee Press, 1985.

Lofaro, Michael, and Joe Cummings, eds. *Crockett at Two Hundred: New Perspectives on the Man and the Myth*. Knoxville: University of Tennessee Press, 1989.

Osborne, Mary Pope. *American Tall Tales*. New York: Knopf, 1991.

Rourke, Constance. *Davy Crockett*. Lincoln: University of Nebraska Press, 1998.

crying woman   See WEEPING WOMAN.

cultural groups   Because there is not one single and uniform American culture, it becomes necessary to consider how members of various cultural groups (by region, religion, race, or ethnicity) engage folklore. Whether studying one's own cultural heritage or another's, knowledge of patterned folk practice and narrative proves important.

It has sometimes been said that America is a nation of immigrants. While that characterization fails to include important populations such as Native Americans and African Americans whose ancestors were taken to America involuntarily through the slave trade, it is true that the United States is an ever more multicultural nation. Because people often transmit folkways within families and family traditions vary culturally, it is important to consider cultural groups as one of the important factors shaping American folklore and folklife.

Whether likened to a melting pot, salad bowl, quilt, or mosaic, the folk culture of the United States combines many elements from its myriad cultural groups.

See also: AFRICAN-AMERICAN FOLKLORE; ANGLO-AMERICAN FOLKLORE; APPALACHIAN FOLKLORE; CAJUN FOLKLORE; CHICANO FOLKLORE; CHINESE-AMERICAN FOLKLORE; DANISH-AMERICAN FOLKLORE; DUTCH-AMERICAN FOLKLORE; FILIPINO-AMERICAN FOLKLORE; FINNISH-AMERICAN FOLKLORE; FRENCH-AMERICAN FOLKLORE; GERMAN-AMERICAN FOLKLORE; GREEK-AMERICAN FOLKLORE; HUNGARIAN-AMERICAN FOLKLORE; ICELANDIC-AMERICAN FOLKLORE; ITALIAN-AMERICAN FOLKLORE; JAMAICAN-AMERICAN FOLKLORE; JAPANESE-AMERICAN FOLKLORE; JEWISH-AMERICAN FOLKLORE; KOREAN-AMERICAN FOLKLORE; LATVIAN-AMERICAN FOLKLORE; LITHUANIAN-AMERICAN FOLKLORE; MEXICAN-AMERICAN FOLKLORE; MORMON FOLKLORE; NATIVE AMERICAN FOLKLORE; NORWEGIAN-AMERICAN FOLKLORE; OZARKS FOLKLORE; PENNSYLVANIA DUTCH FOLKLORE; POLISH-AMERICAN FOLKLORE; PORTUGUESE-AMERICAN FOLKLORE; QUAKER FOLKLORE; SCOTTISH-AMERICAN FOLKLORE; SHAKER FOLKLORE; SPANISH-AMERICAN FOLKLORE; SWEDISH-AMERICAN FOLKLORE.

For Further Reading:
Katz, William Loren. *A History of Multicultural America*. Austin, Tex.: Raintree Steck-Vaughn, 1993.
Lehman, Jeffrey, ed. *Gale Encyclopedia of Multicultural America*. Detroit: Gale, 2000.
Lippard, Lucy R. *Mixed Blessings: New Art in a Multicultural America*. New York: New Press, 2000.
Mechling, Jay. "On Sharing Folklore and American Identity in a Multicultural Society," *Western Folklore* 52, nos. 2–4 (April–October 1994): 271–280.
Takaki, Ronald T. *A Different Mirror: A History of Multicultural America*. Boston: Little, Brown, 1993.
Takaki, Ronald T., ed. *From Different Shores: Perspectives on Race and Ethnicity in America*. New York: Oxford University Press, 1987.

culture, folk   *Folk culture* is a term that refers to a group of people who have folk traditions in common. It typically refers to a group's local and traditional way of life.

There was a time when culture was considered to include only elite examples of human expression, what E. B. Tylor called "the best thought and said." During the 20th century, however, a more inclusive definition of culture came into usage. Culture became a less restrictive or elevated category of analysis, encompassing a fuller spectrum of human performances and products. In this sense, folk culture may be juxtaposed with high culture or elite culture.

In this way, populations once known only as folk groups in America began to be referred to as folk cultures or subcultures. Such populations could be identified on the basis of any number of common attributes, such as geographic, religious, or economic similarities. Examples include Appalachian folk culture, Shaker folklore, or working-class lore.

The use of a term such as *folk culture* helps bridge the gaps created by arbitrary distinctions among folk, popular, and elite traditions.

See also: APPALACHIAN FOLKLORE; POPLORE; SHAKER FOLKLORE; TERMS; VERNACULAR CULTURE.

For Further Reading:

Berger, Harris, and Giovanna Del Negro, eds. *Identity and Everyday Life: Essays in the Study of Folklore, Music, and Popular Culture.* Middletown, Conn.: Wesleyan University Press, 2004.

Cantwell, Robert. *Ethnomimesis: Folklife and the Representation of Culture.* Chapel Hill: University of North Carolina Press, 1993.

Degh, Linda. *American Folkore and the Mass Media.* Bloomington: Indiana University Press, 1994.

Eagleton, Terry. *The Idea of Culture.* Oxford: Blackwell, 2000.

Harris, Neil. *Cultural Excursions: Marketing Appetites and Cultural Tastes in Modern America.* Chicago: University of Chicago Press, 1990.

Kurin, Richard. "Folklife in Contemporary Multicultural Society (1990)." In *Folk Nation: Folklore in the Creation of American Tradition,* edited by Simon Bronner, 249–263. Wilmington, Del.: Scholarly Resources, 2002.

Narvaez, Peter, and Martin Laba, eds. *Media Sense: The Folklore–Popular Culture Continuum.* Bowling Green, Ohio: Bowling Green State University Popular Press, 1986.

Paredes, Americo, and Ellen Stekert, eds. *The Urban Experience and Folk Tradition.* Austin: University of Texas Press. 1971.

Williams, Brett, ed. *The Politics of Culture.* Washington, D.C.: Smithsonian Institution Press, 1991.

Cumberland Gap   See BOONE, DANIEL.

Curry, John Steuart   See BROWN, JOHN.

curses   See EVIL EYE; MAGIC; WITCHCRAFT, SALEM.

cursing   See SPEECH, FOLK.

Custer, George Armstrong (1839–1876)   George Armstrong Custer was born in Ohio in 1839. He attended West Point, where he earned more of a reputation for mischief than for scholastics.

Custer emerged as the "boy general," and something of a legend as a soldier. Within these tales, he is frequently depicted with long, flowing hear and carrying the sword that was his favorite weapon, his "Toledo Blade." He is probably best remembered for the battle of Little Bighorn, in which he led the Seventh Cavalry in a conflict with Native Americans. This event, also known as "Custer's Last Stand," occurred on June 25, 1876. In an approach to this skirmish by Custer that many today deem reckless on Custer's part, 266 cavalry men lost their lives.

Nonetheless, Custer has entered the popular imagination as something of a martyr. His career forms the basis of many stories, legends, and visual images.

See also: CRAZY HORSE; FOLK HEROES/LEGENDARY FIGURES; FRONTIER; HISTORICAL EVENTS; MIDWESTERN REGIONAL FOLKLORE; NATIVE AMERICAN FOLKLORE; REGION, FOLK; SITTING BULL.

For Further Reading:

Ambrose, Stephen. *Crazy Horse and Custer: The Parallel Lives of Two American Warriors.* Garden City, N.Y.: Doubleday, 1975.

Ben-Amos, Dan, and Liliane Wissberg, eds. *Cultural Memory and the Construction of Identity.* Detroit: Wayne State University Press, 1999.

Deloria, Vine, Jr. *Custer Died for Your Sins: An Indian Manifesto.* New York: Macmillan, 1969.

Frost, Lawrence A. *Custer Legends.* Bowling Green, Ohio: Bowling Green State University Popular Press, 1981.

Reader, Ian, and Tony Walter, eds. *Pilgrimage in Popular Culture.* London: Macmillan, 1993.

Rosenberg, Bruce. *Custer and the Epic of Defeat.* University Park, Pa.: Penn State University Press, 1974.

Welch, James. *Killing Custer: The Battle of the Little Bighorn and the Fate of the Plains Indians.* New York: W. W. Norton, 1994.

customs, folk   Folk customs are the practices that have, through repetition and over time, become usual within a group or population. Items of folk custom can attend virtually any form of human action, from the way a meal is prepared to the manner in which greetings are exchanged upon meeting someone new.

Customs can also be subtle aspects of a population's behavior, nuances and differences across cultural groups that are informative. They may only become noticeable or visible as customs, even to members of the group, when these expectations are transgressed or overlooked. It is for this reason that a knowledge of folk customs is so crucial to intercultural and international contacts. What might be considered routine or respectful in one cultural context might prove rude, even hostile, in another.

One relatively conspicuous category of folk customs involves standards of politeness. While etiquette experts might be the official arbiters of protocol, nearly every individual in America has an understanding of the distinction between good manners and poor manners. These concepts are transmitted both in words and by demonstration, from one generation to the next. While each generation may modify those rules of conduct, basic traditions of appropriate behavior, such as the golden rule (Do unto others as you would have them do unto you) endure.

Ideas of morality represent another category of folk customs. Concepts of what is sacred and profane, pure and unclean, chaste and depraved help set the climate for a folk culture. These values can be manifested in such choices as attire, adornment, and deportment.

Examining folk customs helps a folklorist to uncover those tacit aspects of a culture that can be discerned in no other way.

See also: FOLKLORE IN EVERYDAY LIFE; FOOD/ FOODWAYS; ORAL FOLKLORE; RITES OF PASSAGE; RITUALS, FOLK.

For Further Reading:
Bronner, Simon, ed. *Folklife Studies from the Gilded Age: Object, Rite, and Custom in Victorian America.* Ann Arbor, Mich.: UMI Research Press, 1987.

Caldwell, Mark. *A Short History of Rudeness: Manners, Morals, and Misbehavior in Modern America.* New York: Picador USA, 1999.

Collis, Harry. *101 American Customs: Understanding Language and Culture through Common Practices.* New York: McGraw-Hill, 1999.

Long, Lucy, ed. *Culinary Tourism.* Lexington: University Press of Kentucky, 2003.

Pillsbury, Richard. *No Foreign Food: The American Diet in Time and Place.* Boulder, Colo.: Westview, 1998.

Shortridge, Barbara, and James Shortridge. *The Taste of American Place: A Reader on Regional and Ethnic Foods.* Lanham, Md.: Rowman & Littlefield, 1998.

D

Danish-American folklore Danish-American folklore includes all the popular beliefs and traditions associated with Danish immigrants and those persons of Danish descent born in the United States.

Immigration from Denmark to the United States began in the 17th century and peaked in the late 19th century. Many newcomers settled in portions of midwestern America associated with agriculture, the livelihood many Danish immigrants hoped to continue to practice in their new home. This area, sometimes referred to as the Danish belt, included the states of Illinois, Iowa, Nebraska, South Dakota, and Wisconsin.

Danish-American foodways are the product of long-standing practices from the old country. The everyday cuisine features potatoes, cabbage, port, filled pastries, and other hearty fare. On special occasions, Danish Americans may follow customs specific to the holiday or observance. For example, on Christmas Eve, a meal of roasted goose is traditional, followed by a dessert of rice pudding. Concealed within the pudding is a whole almond, and according to folk belief, the diner who discovers the nut will have good luck throughout the coming year. Holiday baking is also a cherished tradition among Danish Americans. Assortments of Christmas cookies are presented as gifts, and many households have porcelain plates featuring holiday designs for

the purpose of receiving and serving such treats. Before going to sleep on Christmas Eve, it is also customary to leave out a bowl of porridge for the benefit of Denmark's magical creatures known as little people. Traditional holiday decorations draw from Danish-American folk crafts, including paper cutting, basket making, and fashioning items from straw. Danish traditional songs and folk dances still play a part in some Danish-American celebrations.

Other Danish-American holidays reflect a combination of those retained from Denmark and those associated with the United States. For example, they celebrate Danish Constitution Day on June 5 each year. The people of Denmark also celebrate America's independence annually on July 4, forming the largest such observance held beyond the United States. As this pair of observances demonstrate, Danish Americans observe special days of both their old country and their new one.

Danish verbal lore is extensive, and likely the best-known Danish storyteller internationally is Hans Christian Andersen. Andersen has become closely associated with the literary genre of the fairy tale. Although Andersen also wrote plays and novels, it is his classic retellings of traditional stories that have earned him a place in literature and folklore. He is responsible for the familiarity of many such tales, including "The Little Mermaid," "Inchworm," "The Princess and the Pea," "The Ugly Duckling," "The Emperor's New Clothes," and "Thumbelina." Andersen was less concerned to preserve folk tales intact than to find in them inspiration for his own literary imagination. His versions are remarkable for the presence of an overt narrator to provide audience members with direction and comment.

Organizations in the United States dedicated to the preservation and study of Danish and/or Danish-American culture include the Danish American Heritage Society and the Danish Brotherhood in America.

Denmark is a Nordic country, and so folklorists also compare Danish-American lore to that of Finnish Americans, Icelandic Americans, Norwegian Americans, and Swedish Americans.

See also: ANDERSEN, HANS CHRISTIAN; CHILDREN'S FOLKLORE; CHRISTMAS; CULTURAL GROUPS; FAIRY TALES; FINNISH-AMERICAN FOLKLORE; ICELANDIC-AMERICAN FOLKLORE; INDEPENDENCE DAY/FOURTH OF JULY; NORWEGIAN-AMERICAN FOLKLORE; SWEDISH-AMERICAN FOLKLORE.

For Further Reading:

Dal, Erik. *Danish Ballads and Folk Songs.* New York: American-Scandinavian Foundation, 1967.

Hansen, Thorvald, ed. *Danish Immigrant Archival Listing: A Guide to Source Materials Related to the Danish Immigrant in America to Be Found in Repositories in the United States, Canada, and Denmark.* Des Moines, Iowa: Grand View College/Danish American Heritage Society, 1988.

Lovoll, Odd S., ed. *Nordics in America: The Future of Their Past.* Northfield, Minn.: Norwegian American Historical Association, 1993.

Mortensen, Enok. *Schools for Life: Grundtvigian Folk Schools in America.* Junction City, Oreg.: Danish-American Heritage Society, 1977.

Olrik, Alex. *The Heroic Legends of Denmark.* New York: American-Scandinavian Foundation, 1919.

Paulston, Rolland G., ed. *Other Dreams, Other Schools: Folk Colleges in Social and Ethnic Movements.* Pittsburgh: University Center for International Studies/University of Pittsburgh, 1980.

death   Among all common fears, death is the most pervasive. The folklore of death and dying represents a way of coping with that dread.

In addition to burial customs and cemetery folklore, the verbal lore surrounding death is extensive. At funerals, for example, eulogists deliver spoken tributes to the deceased. Memorial verses may also be read aloud or printed on cards and programs. Hymns, songs, and items from sacred texts can also be included in services accompanying funerals, wakes, and viewings. Tombstone inscriptions, such as quips, lines from poems, and other literature, represent another form of death lore.

Mourning customs can vary greatly across cultures and eras. A case in point would be the Civil War era, during which an unprecedented number of Americans, more than 600,000, lost their lives. In a single day at Antietam, the Union forces withstood more than 2,000 fatalities. So grave was the risk of death that, in a time before imprinted fatigues or dog tags, soldiers fastened information about their identities within their uniforms. Even greater than the danger of death by combat was death by diseases such as typhoid and smallpox as they swept through camps and hospitals. It was at this time that embalming was developed as a means to preserve corpses long enough that they could be transported back to their places of residence and families.

Such high casualty rates produced a new culture of mourning. During the postbellum period in America, death often occasioned such ritual objects of grief as death masks, death photographs, and jewelry made with or containing bits of the deceased's hair. Numerous acts of public memory also represent responses to death. Holidays such as Memorial Day and Veterans Day, for instance, commemorate the lives of those who perished during war and military service. Memorial Day had its origins in the entire nation's deep grief over Civil War deaths.

Henry C. Welles, a Waterloo, New York, pharmacist, made the suggestion that these graves be adorned annually with flower tributes. New York was the first to formalize the practice at the state level in 1873. Memorial Day has since been identified as a national day of remembrance for all men and women lost in service. Customs associated with Memorial Day are accordingly patriotic ones. Parades, ceremonies, and reenactments at Civil War sites are usual.

The scale of Civil War fatalities also led to the establishment of military cemeteries on American soil. The Robert E. Lee estate, located near the nation's capital, became Arlington National Cemetery. This national burial site was dedicated to those who served the nation in the armed forces. Each year on Memorial Day, the U.S. president participates in a solemn recognition held at Arlington National Cemetery.

When other famous personages pass away, the public may mourn them collectively. For example, after Abraham Lincoln's assassination in 1865, not long after the Civil War came to a close, the American people joined together in their grief at his untimely death. The Lincoln Memorial in Washington, D.C., not far from Arlington National Cemetery, was dedicated on Memorial Day 1922. This monument is inscribed with words Lincoln spoke in his Gettysburg Address, on the battlefield where so many Civil War soldiers perished. Similarly, many famous people are remembered for their parting thoughts and last words, especially if they were literary figures, orators, epigrammists, or wits.

From the way the dying say good-bye to the way the survivors bid them farewell, the folklore of death reflects anxieties about mortality and attitudes toward the afterlife.

See also: AGING AND FOLKLORE; BURIAL CUSTOMS; CEMETERY FOLKLORE; CIVIL WAR; FOLKLORE IN EVERYDAY LIFE; GHOSTS; GHOST STORIES; HAUNTED HOUSES; LINCOLN, ABRAHAM; MEMORIAL DAY; PARADES; PRESIDENTS' DAY; RITES OF PASSAGE; RITUALS, FOLK; SUPERNATURAL; SUPERSTITION; VETERANS DAY.

For Further Reading:

Bisport, Alan. *Famous Last Words: Apt Observations, Pleas, Curses, Benedictions, Sour Notes, Bon Mots, and Insights from People on the Brink of Departure.* San Francisco: Pomegranate, 2001.

Brandreth, Gyles Daubeney. *Famous Last Words and Tombstone Humor.* New York: Sterling, 1989.

Farrell, James. *Inventing the American Way of Death, 1830–1920.* Philadelphia: Temple University Press, 1980.

Faust, Drew Gilpin. "The Civil War Soldier and the Art of Dying," *Journal of Southern History* 67, no. 1 (2001): 3–40.

Jackson, Charles O., ed. *Passing: The Vision of Death in America.* Westport, Conn.: Greenwood, 1977.

Laderman, Gary. *The Sacred Remains: American Attitudes toward Death, 1799–1883.* New Haven, Conn.: Yale University Press, 1996.

Linenthal, Edward. *Sacred Ground: Americans and Their Battlefields.* Urbana: University of Illinois Press, 1991.

MacCloskey, Monro. *Hallowed Ground: Our National Cemeteries.* New York: Richards Rosen, 1969.

Montell, William Lynwood. *Ghosts along the Cumberland: Deathlore in the Kentucky Foothills.* Knoxville: University of Tennessee Press, 1975.

Narváez, Peter. *Of Corpse: Death and Humor in Folklore and Popular Culture.* Logan: Utah State University Press, 2003.

O'Kill, Brian. *Exit Lines: Famous (and Not-So-Famous) Last Words.* Harlow, England: Longman, 1986.

Robinson, Ray. *Famous Last Words, Fond Farewells, Deathbed Diatribes, and Exclamations upon Expiration.* New York: Workman, 2003.

Sloane, David Charles. *The Last Great Necessity: Cemeteries in American History.* Baltimore: Johns Hopkins University Press, 1991.

Vinovskis, Maris A., ed. *Toward a Social History of the American Civil War: Exploratory Essays.* Cambridge: Cambridge University Press, 1990.

"Declaration of Independence" See FRANKLIN, BENJAMIN; INDEPENDENCE DAY/FOURTH OF JULY; STANTON, ELIZABETH CADY.

"Declaration of Sentiments" See ANTHONY, SUSAN BROWNELL; STANTON, ELIZABETH CADY; SUFFRAGE, WOMEN'S.

Decoration Day See MEMORIAL DAY.

decoys See FOLK CRAFTS.

Delaware folklore See NORTHEASTERN REGIONAL FOLKLORE; SWEDISH-AMERICAN FOLKLORE.

Depression, the Great The Great Depression is the name given to the era of economic adversity in America that followed the 1929 stock market crash.

On October 29, 1929, a date sometimes referred to as "Black Tuesday," stock values fell so precipitously that the investment world was severely tested. As the stories go, many people who lost all their money fell into despair. In fact, stories circulated that some dejected businessmen ruined in the crash committed suicide by leaping to their death from skyscraper building windows.

The whole nation was plunged into an economic downturn that was unparalleled in American history. Images of the era show the signs of such difficulty, with street vendors trying to sell apples and citizens standing in breadlines for food. In popular songs, such as "Brother, Can You Spare a Dime?" lyrics lamented the plight of hard-working Americans down on their luck.

As if the fiscal crisis was not enough, the nation was experiencing extraordinary climate challenges. The American Plains, the so-called bread basket of the country's food supply, experienced drought and dust storms that damaged farm crops. The dust bowl, as this phenomenon

was termed, drove families off their farms and westward in search of work that would help them get back on their feet.

The author John Steinbeck characterized this situation aptly in his fiction, particularly in his epic novel *The Grapes of Wrath*. In this text, Steinbeck told the story of a fictional family, the Joads, who left behind their farm in Oklahoma to become migrant workers in the California fields. In the process, they discovered the challenges most of the nation faced during the Depression.

Similarly, photographers from the Farm Security Administration (FSA), an offshoot of the Resettlement Administration, documented the living and working conditions of Depression era Americans. World-class photographers, such as Dorothea Lange and Walker Evans, turned their cameras in the direction of ordinary citizens and the worlds they occupied. The FSA photographers left behind a vast archive of the everyday experiences of Americans throughout the nation. In what is, perhaps, the most recognizable image from this archive, Lange's *Migrant Mother*, a woman and infant take shelter under a tent while the woman stares into the middle distance. This modern-day Madonna emerged as a kind of icon of American suffering during the 1930s. The FSA pictures documented the hardships of Americans while celebrating their strength, forbearance, and values.

The FSA was but one of many national agencies established to employ Americans and aid in the nation's recovery. This set of initiatives by President Franklin Delano Roosevelt became known as the "New Deal," so named for a reference made within one of Roosevelt's speeches. Other public works organizations, such as the Tennessee Valley Authority (TVA) and Civilian Conservation Corps (CCC) targeted environmental projects, such as irrigation, intended to improve the fortunes of American agriculture.

In addition to these New Deal agencies, Roosevelt promoted many federal arts projects. Beyond the documentary efforts of the FSA photographers, his establishment of the Works Progress Administration (WPA) and the Federal

Writers' Project (FWP) yielded many artistic works and cultural resources for the nation. The many public art installations included countless murals painted in public buildings such as capitals, state houses, and post offices. Researchers conducted historic interviews with America's former slaves, making their testimony available to posterity. Meanwhile, writers such as Sterling Allen Brown produced texts expressing the era's hopes and yearnings. Figures such as the author Ralph Waldo Ellison joined in folklore collection efforts. Many regard this historical period as the true beginning of public folklore in the United States.

From the dust bowl ballads of the folksinger Woody Guthrie to the lore surrounding hoboes traveling the nation by freight train, the Great Depression proved a time of both crisis and creativity.

See also: AGEE, JAMES; BROWN, STERLING ALLEN; CHAVEZ, CÉSAR ESTRADA; ELLISON, RALPH WALDO; FLOYD, CHARLES ARTHUR (PRETTY BOY); FOOD/FOODWAYS; HISTORICAL EVENTS; HOBOES; JOAD, TOM; LUCK/FORTUNE; MIDWESTERN REGIONAL FOLKLORE; MUSIC, FOLK; OCCUPATIONAL FOLKLORE; ORAL HISTORY; PHOTOGRAPHY, FOLK; PROTEST IN FOLKLORE; PUBLIC FOLKLORE; REGION, FOLK; ROOSEVELT, FRANKLIN DELANO; SLAVERY; STEINBECK, JOHN.

For Further Reading:
Billington, Ray Allen. "Government and the Arts: the WPA Experience," *American Quarterly* 13 (1961): 466–479.

De Hart, Jane Sherron. *The Federal Theatre*. Princeton, N.J.: Princeton University Press, 1967.

Hobson, Archie, ed. *Remembering America: A Sampler of the WPA American Guide Series*. New York: Columbia University Press, 1985.

McDonald, William. *Federal Relief Administration and the Arts*. Columbus: Ohio State University Press, 1969.

Park, Marlene, and Gerald E. Markowitz. *Democratic Vistas: Post Offices and Public Art in the New Deal*. Philadelphia: Temple University Press, 1984.

Shindo, Charles J. *Dust Bowl Migrants in the American Imagination*. Lawrence: University of Kansas Press, 1997.

devil, the (legendary) Known by many names—Lucifer, Beelzebub, and so forth—the devil is a prominent figure within folklore, including but not limited to, American lore.

The devil embodies evil, both in a worldly and in a metaphysical sense. Depending upon one's religious beliefs, the devil came into being through various processes. Some believe that the devil is the malevolence that resides somewhere within all human life. Others believe the devil represents the world's temptations to betray higher impulses. Still others consider the devil to be a fallen angel who turned all energies to countering the virtuous and the spiritually sound impulses within humanity. In any case, the devil appears across eras, cultures, and folk genres.

The devil seeks to influence people, events, and consequences, turning all to evil result. The chief method employed by the devil is temptation, although mischief and trickery are other techniques invoked from time to time. The archetypal victory for the devil involves laying claim to a human being's immortal soul. In the context of folklore, as distinct from theology, the devil appears more commonly as a quintessential trickster figure, manipulating others for his own gain.

The classic folktale featuring the devil depicts a protagonist or other character so desperate for fulfillment of a wish that he or she admits, usually aloud, that he or she would do anything to gratify the desire. This confession is enough to summon the devil, who appears to accept the person's soul in exchange for the desired outcome. The remaining plot derives its drama from attempts to rescind the offer and reclaim the character's soul.

Most folktales in which the devil figures prominently involve either this Faustian transaction or another so-called deal with the devil. In some cases, the character is offered an opportunity to reverse the situation by prevailing in a feat of skill or guessing game, such as solving a riddle. Within individual stories, the devil may take another shape, such as a malevolent person or creature. Mild examples from children's stories include "Rumpelstiltskin" and "The Three Billy Goats Gruff." Daunting and mysterious creatures may also be termed devils, as with the figure of the Jersey devil. Whether understood as high-stakes morality lessons or merely as tall tales, stories featuring the devil continue to appear within American folklore.

More fanciful images of the devil occur in popular culture. Some are related to difficult choices individuals face between competing impulses. Such a person is described, and often depicted, as having an angel on one shoulder and a devil on the other and so must decide which voice to listen to and so which impulse will prevail. It may be because of the air of mischief involved in the holiday of Halloween that trick-or-treaters and partygoers alike often costume themselves as some version of the devil. Similarly, when a treat is deemed so good it is sinful, it may be figuratively connected to the devil, as with the chocolate cake known as "devil's food."

The folk meanings associated with the figure of the devil should not be confused with folk devils. The term *folk devil* was coined in 1972 by the sociologist Stanley Cohen in his work *Folk Devils and Moral Panics*. In this context, folk devils are social outsiders or deviants who are demonized for whatever reason. Examples would include those accused of witchcraft in 17th-century Salem. Although folk beliefs associated witches with dark arts connected to the devil, a folk devil can be anyone who falls outside the norms of a folk group.

Depending upon the context, then, folk images of the devil may be as mild in suggestion as the tendency toward naughty behavior or as powerful as the decision to yield to evil as a guiding energy.

See also: EVIL EYE; FOLK HEROES/LEGENDARY FIGURES; HALLOWEEN/ALL HALLOWS' EVE; JERSEY DEVIL; MAGIC; MONSTERS; NORTHEASTERN REGIONAL FOLKLORE; RELIGION, FOLK; "RUMPLESTILTSKIN"; "THREE BILLY GOATS GRUFF, THE"; TRICKSTER; WITCHCRAFT, SALEM; VOODOO/HOODOO.

For Further Reading:

Abrahams, Roger D., ed. *Fields of Folklore: Essays in Honor of Kenneth S. Goldstein*. Bloomington, Ind.: Trickster Press, 1995.

Delbanco, Andrew. *The Death of Satan: How Americans Have Lost the Sense of Evil*. New York: Farrar, Straus & Giroux, 1995.

Ellis, Bill. *Raising the Devil: Satanism, New Religions, and the Media*. Lexington: University Press of Kentucky, 2000.

Jacoby, Mario, Verena Kast, and Ingrid Riedel. *Witches, Ogres, and the Devil's Daughter: Encounters with Evil in Fairy Tales*. Boston: Shambhala, 1992.

Limón, José Eduardo. *Dancing with the Devil: Society and Cultural Poetics in Mexican American South Texas*. Madison: University of Wisconsin Press, 1994.

Martin, Malachi. *Hostage to the Devil: The Possession and Exorcism of Five Living Americans*. San Francisco: Harper, 1992.

Dillinger, John (1903–1934) John Dillinger's life of infamy, conducted largely as a midwestern gangster and bank robber, was short, spanning just over 30 years. Nonetheless, the number and nature of Dillinger's violent crimes captured the imagination of a 1930s public preoccupied with outlaws and prone to make celebrities of notorious wrongdoers such as the mobster Al Capone.

John Dillinger was born in 1903 in the Oak Hill section of Indianapolis, Indiana, to middle-class parents. Dillinger's mother died when her son was only three. As a youth, Dillinger dropped out of school and worked in a machine shop. To shield his son from the perils of urban crime, Dillinger's father relocated the family to a rural area. Nonetheless, Dillinger would soon have a brush with the law over an auto theft and removed himself from the situation by enlisting in the navy. Here, too, Dillinger found trouble, and he ultimately went absent without leave from naval service. By 1924, he was married to 16-year-old Beryl Hovius, and the pair returned to Dillinger's hometown of Indianapolis.

It was not long thereafter that Dillinger was implicated in another criminal offense, to which he confessed, and for which he was incarcerated in Indiana State Prison. On May 10, 1933, after serving eight and one-half years of his original sentence, Dillinger was granted parole, and he exited prison a bitter young man. So began a Midwest rampage that would land him in an Ohio jail by September 22. In this way, Dillinger's career as a criminal unfolded, as he and his gang engaged in a series of robberies, jailbreaks, and murders.

Although some romanticized Dillinger and his fellow outlaws as modern-day Robin Hoods, their methods were considerably more brutal and shameless, as when they stole weapons and bulletproof vests from a police station. In Dillinger's most personally costly crime, he broke out of the supposedly "escape-proof" county jail in Crown Point, Indiana, on March 3, 1934. This jailbreak drew him to the attention of the Federal Bureau of Investigation (FBI), as he made the fateful error of crossing the Indiana-Illinois state line in a car he had stolen from the sheriff. This act elevated the crime to a federal offense and set in place the forces of scrutiny that eventually would put an end to Dillinger's misdeeds.

The very limelight surrounding Dillinger's crimes would lead to his capture. Although surveillance had not yet brought Dillinger to justice, it was not long until an informant, Anna Sage, eager to trade information on the man she recognized as the notorious Dillinger, tipped the authorities. She cooperated to prevent her own deportation as an undesirable. Sage alerted agents she would be accompanying Dillinger to a movie theater on Sunday, July 22, 1934. She planned to wear a red dress for the occasion in order to assist officers in spotting the fugitive,

a move that later established Sage as herself a figure in the public imagination, termed "the Lady in Red." On the basis of this information, law enforcement officers stood poised outside Chicago's Biograph Theater, and when the viewing party emerged that evening from a screening of Clark Gable's *Manhattan Melodrama*, authorities were ready to take the fugitive into custody.

Dillinger sensed the danger, produced a firearm, and was gunned down in the alley beside the theater. He would die of these injuries, and this violent end would make him the last fatality to occur as a direct result of his criminal activities. His body was buried in the place of his birth, Indianapolis, Indiana, but his legend lives on in countless songs, stories, and films. In addition, the Biograph Theater remains as a Chicago landmark and stands as a physical reminder of Dillinger's tale of infamy as his era's "Public Enemy Number One."

See also: CAPONE, ALPHONSE GABRIEL (AL); CITY FOLKLORE; FOLK HEROES/LEGENDARY FIGURES; MIDWESTERN REGIONAL FOLKLORE; OUTLAWS; ROBIN HOOD.

For Further Reading:

Cromie, Robert. *Dillinger: A Short and Violent Life.* New York: McGraw-Hill, 1962.

Girardin, George Russell. *Dillinger: The Untold Story.* Bloomington: Indiana University Press, 1994.

Hamilton, Sue L. *Public Enemy Number One: John H. Dillinger.* Bloomington, Ind.: Abdo and Daughters, 1989.

Kooistra, Paul. *Criminals as Heroes: Structure, Power, and Identity.* Bowling Green, Ohio: Bowling Green State University Popular Press, 1989.

A List of Songs Concerning John Dillinger. Washington, D.C.: Archive of Folk Song, 1970.

Matera, Dary. *John Dillinger: The Life and Death of America's First Celebrity Criminal.* New York: Carroll & Graf, 2004.

Nash, Jay Robert. *Dillinger: Dead or Alive?* Chicago: H. Regnery, 1970.

disability and folklore Whether by conditions of birth, injury, or illness, many Americans live with one or more disabilities.

Disabilities may be defined as any circumstances that interfere with or affect major activities of daily life, such as healthiness, mobility, and self-care. Generally speaking, disabilities fall into the categories of cognitive, neurological, physical, psychological, and sensory conditions. A given individual may have more than one disability and so may cross these categories. At present, one of the most rapidly growing populations in the United States, whether by increased rates of incidence or diagnosis, are persons who have learning disabilities.

While not the same sort of folk group as an ethnic, racial, or regional population, disabled people in America share similar challenges. These needs include accessing sites and services, securing education and employment opportunities, and promoting understanding of disability among the general population.

While treatment of people with disabilities in the United States has improved over time, there are still many misperceptions about the nature of disability and the contributions of people with disabilities. In fact, for many years, such individuals were referred to as *handicapped* or *crippled*, terms that have generally fallen out of favor. Today, the emphasis is on the person rather than the condition, making *persons with a disability* or *persons who are differently able* more widely accepted terms for those whose activities of daily life require modifications or accommodations. These phrases are preferable to others, such as *disabled person* or *the disabled*, which put the disability first and the person second. In fact, some populations, such as the deaf community, often prefer to think of themselves as a culture rather than a diagnostic category.

Depending upon the nature of one's disability, the stigma experienced can be either slight or substantive. While the national trend has been toward inclusion, many older persons who have disabilities still remember a time when such individuals were kept out of the social mainstream because of fear, shame, or misunderstanding. Today, the pervasive problem is a set of uninformed and unexamined assumptions Americans may still have about people with disabilities.

For this reason, a set of folk customs, sometimes described as disability etiquette, help guide people through interactions that might otherwise prove difficult. Employees may attend trainings or read primers on how best to engage persons with disabilities, and family members or classmates of persons with newly diagnosed disabilities may receive similar coaching. For the most part, disability etiquette cautions against assumptions about others, especially premature decisions regarding whether help is needed, what kind of help should be provided, and in what manner persons with disabilities may perform their duties and responsibilities. The overarching principle is to ask persons who have a disability what, if anything, they wish or need from others, thereby according them a measure of both control and respect in the situation.

Folklore surrounding disability ranges from verbal lore to protest culture. People with disabilities in America have numerous folk icons, such as Helen Keller and Christopher Reeve. These individuals with disabilities not only became highly accomplished, but also contributed greatly to the standard of living for people with disabilities by becoming effective advocates for understanding, inclusion, and research. The disability rights movement of the 1970s, inspired by other grassroots efforts such as those for civil rights and women's rights, took on symbolic as well as literal meanings as it won changes in the society's infrastructure and policies.

The fight for civil rights for people with disabilities in America is far from over. People who have conditions such as schizophrenia, for example, are still regarded with ridicule, suspicion, or both. Submerged, but not banished, such attitudes toward people with disabilities resurface in expressive domains including "sick jokes" or joke cycles in which figures such as Helen Keller appear. These items of folk belief and folk humor portray the lingering fears and misgivings many Americans still harbor regarding persons with disabilities.

Through such civil rights legislation as the Americans with Disabilities Act of 1990, persons with disability in the United States have gained specific protections against discrimination or exclusion. Over time, the trend has been toward emphasizing what individuals can accomplish rather than what activities disabilities limit or prohibit. As with other campaigns for constitutional rights and protections, the disabilities rights movement may be chronicled and understood in part through its surrounding folklore.

See also: AIDS FOLKLORE; BELIEFS, FOLK; BODYLORE; FOLKLORE IN EVERYDAY LIFE; HUMOR, FOLK; MEDICINE, FOLK; QUILT, AIDS.

For Further Reading:
Atkinson, Dorothy. "Research and Empowerment: Involving People with Learning Difficulties in Oral and Life History Research," *Disability and Society* 19, no. 7 (December 2004): 691–702.

Cunningham, Keith. "'He Gits around Pretty Good Once He Gits on a Horse': Traditional Views of Disability: Rehabilitation in Paradise," *Western Folklore* 48, no. 1 (January 1989): 58–61.

Eberly, Susan Schoon. "Fairies and the Folklore of Disability: Changelings, Hybrids and the Solitary Fairy," *Folklore* 99, no. 1 (1988): 58–77.

Hollis, Susan Tower, Linda Pershing, and M. Jane Young, eds. *Feminist Theory and the Study of Folklore*. Urbana: University of Illinois Press, 1993.

Naráez, Peter, ed. *The Good People: New Fairylore Essays*. New York: Garland, 1991.

Rutherford, Susan Dell. *Study of American Deaf Folklore*. Burtonsville, Md.: Linstok Press, 1993.

disaster folklore See AIDS FOLKLORE; ATOMIC/NUCLEAR ERA FOLKLORE; BARTON, CLARA; BROWN, MARGARET TOBIN (UNSINKABLE MOLLY); DEPRESSION, THE GREAT.

Disney, Walter Elias (Walt Disney) (1901–1966) Walter Elias Disney adapted many folktales, fairy tales, and classic stories to the screen, making him an influential force in American folklore.

Walt Disney was born December 5, 1901, in Chicago, Illinois. He grew up on a Missouri farm, where he demonstrated a talent for and interest in the visual arts. By the time he was in high school, Disney started attending night classes at Academy of Fine Arts. When World War I broke out, a still-teenage Disney became a volunteer ambulance driver. He covered the vehicle with his own cartoon drawings. This decoration anticipated Disney's career in visual comedy and entertainment.

Upon his return, Walt found work as an advertising cartoonist in Kansas City. Meanwhile, Disney pursued his passion for animation. In 1920, he sold his first animated cartoons. He also developed a technique for creating films that commingle animation with live action. By 1923, he went to California to join his brother, Roy Disney, and together they embarked on a career in comedy films. It would not be for another five years that Walt Disney would devise the character that would become the most widely recognized film star in the world: Mickey Mouse. Later that year, he released the first feature-length animated musical on film: *Snow White and the Seven Dwarfs*. This film would be followed by many other successful animated features, making it possible for Disney to build a studio in California, where he began conducting business in 1940. During World War II, the Disney Studio devoted a good deal of its time to developing training films and prowar propaganda.

In 1955, Disney opened Disneyland, a theme park in Anaheim, California. Later, he began work on a second location, Disney World, in Orlando, Florida. These would be the first of many Disney-themed amusement parks, from Tokyo to Paris. By featuring the narratives and characters appearing in Disney films, these parks reinforced Disney's depictions of such figures as Sleeping Beauty, Chicken Little, Pinocchio, Peter Pan, Pocahontas, and Snow White. Disney's retellings of such classics as "The Little Mermaid," "The Three Little Pigs," and "The Emperor's New Clothes" may now be better known than the tales on which they were based. His forays into television programming exposed a new generation of Americans to the tales of Davy Crockett, Daniel Boone, John Chapman (Johnny Appleseed), Windwagon Smith, Pecos Bill, and Uncle Remus.

Walt Disney died on December 15, 1966, but his fame and his entertainment empire did not end there. The Disney family name went on to become synonymous with family entertainment in America and throughout the world. When it comes to children's folklore, everything from Grimm's fairy tales to American folk heroes such as Johnny Appleseed, it is the Disney version that audiences tend to know and recognize.

See also: "BEAUTY AND THE BEAST"; BOONE, DANIEL; CHAPMAN, JOHN (JOHNNY APPLESEED); "CHICKEN LITTLE"; CROCKETT, DAVY; "EMPEROR'S NEW CLOTHES, THE"; GREENFIELD VILLAGE, HENRY FORD MUSEUM AND; GRIMM BROTHERS; HARRIS, JOEL CHANDLER; LINCOLN, ABRAHAM; MERMAIDS; "MERMAID, THE LITTLE"; MUSEUMS, FOLK; NAMING/NAMES; PECOS BILL; POCAHONTAS; POPLORE; REMUS, UNCLE; "SLEEPING BEAUTY"; SMITH, WINDWAGON; "SNOW WHITE"; "THREE LITTLE PIGS, THE."

For Further Reading:

Evans, Harold, Gail Buckland, and David Lofer. *They Made America: From the Steam Engine to the Search Engine: Two Centuries of Innovation.* New York: Little, Brown, 2004.

Giroux, Henry. *The Mouse That Roared: Disney and the End of Innocence.* Lanham, Md.: Rowman & Littlefield, 1999.

Mannheim, Steve. *Walt Disney and the Quest for Community.* Burlington, Vt.: Ashgate, 2002.

Sammond, Nicholas. *Babes in Tomorrowland: Walt Disney and the Making of the American Child, 1930–1960.* Durham, N.C.: Duke University Press, 2005.

Schickel, Richard. *The Disney Version: The Life, Times, Art, and Commerce of Walt Disney.* New York: Simon & Schuster, 1985.

Smoodin, Eric, ed. *Disney Discourse: Producing the Magic Kingdom.* New York: Routledge, 1994.

Watts, Steven. *The Magic Kingdom: Walt Disney and the American Way of Life.* Boston: Houghton Mifflin, 1997.

District of Columbia folklore See AMERICAN FOLKLIFE CENTER; AMERICAN MEMORY PROJECT; ATTUCKS, CRISPUS; CHRISTMAS; CIVIL WAR; COLUMBUS, CHRISTOPHER; EMANCIPATION (PROCLAMATION) DAY; GHOST STORIES; INAUGURATION DAY; LABOR DAY; NAMING/NAMES; NORTHEASTERN REGIONAL FOLKLORE; PUBLIC FOLKLORE; SMITHSONIAN INSTITUTION.

divination See PREDICTION.

divorce See COURTSHIP/DATING FOLKLORE; WEDDING/MARRIAGE FOLKLORE.

Dixie See CIVIL WAR.

documentary The term *documentary* describes both a perspective and a medium in terms of folklore studies—both characterized by an effort to investigate and convey the truth of human experience.

In the context of American folklore, documentary efforts generally focus on practitioners or expressive forms that are at risk of vanishing from experience and memory. Documentarians use any number of techniques and technologies for recording such endangered manifestations of folklore. Through these documentaries, folklorists seek to preserve and interpret the phenomena studied.

The documentary tradition in America spans many media but usually fits a basic profile. Documentaries typically involve nonfiction accounts, although informants and documentarians may bring their perspectives to bear in the presentation. Documentaries are most often designed to inform audiences and, in some cases, to increase cultural understanding or effect social change. People depicted in documentary photographs and motion pictures appear as themselves, rather than being portrayed by actors. Documentary films are almost always shot on location, where the figures featured live or work. The expectation with documentary evidence is that it neither misrepresents nor manipulates the subject matter it treats.

The 20th century marked a time of keen interest in documenting and preserving the American past. Folklorists such as Alan Lomax conducted fieldwork to collect folk songs. Zora Neale Hurston rendered for the page the "lies" or tall tales of the American South's oral traditions. Field researchers with federal agencies during the Great Depression interviewed former slaves about their lives and experiences. In that same era, documentary photographers such as Dorothea Lange and Arthur Rothstein crossed the nation to create images of dust bowl refugees and migrant laborers. Similarly, the writer James Agee and the photographer Walker Evans went to Hale County, Alabama, during the 1930s to live with and document sharecropper families in their book *Let Us Now Praise Famous Men*. Later in the century, figures from Studs Terkel to Robert Coles continued the documentary tradition with their efforts to make a record of the lives of ordinary Americans.

From oral history to nonfiction films, documentarians contribute evidence and insight into American folklore and folklife. While audiences today realize that documentary writings, photographs, films, and videos are hardly neutral, there is still a tendency to suspend disbelief when encountering a work produced in the documentary tradition.

See also: AGEE, JAMES; ETHICS AND FOLKLORE; FESTIVALS, FOLKLORE; FIELDWORK, FOLKLORE; FOLKLIFE; FOLKLORE STUDIES; INSIDER/OUTSIDER; ORAL HISTORY; RESEARCH, FOLKLIFE; TERMS.

For Further Reading:
Bascom, William. "Four Functions of Folklore," *Journal of American Folklore* 67, no. 266 (fall 1954): 333–349.
Dundes, Alan. *Analytical Essays in Folklore*. Berkeley: University of California, 1975.
———. *Interpreting Folklore*. Bloomington: Indiana University Press, 1980.
Goldstein, Kenneth S. *A Guide for Field Workers in Folklore*. Hatboro, Pa.: Folklore Association, 1964.
Jackson, Bruce. *Fieldwork*. Chicago: University of Illinois Press, 1987.
Toelken, Barre. *The Dynamics of Folklore*. Logan: Utah State University, 1996.

Douglass Frederick (1818–1895) As a former slave and self-made man, Frederick Douglass developed a national profile as an abolitionist and orator during the 19th century.

Douglass was born a slave in Maryland in 1818. As a child, he withstood harsh treatment from his masters, which included separation from his mother when she was sold to a different master.

In 1838, Douglass became a fugitive from slavery as he journeyed into northern free states. Once out of captivity, Douglass became an author, lecturer, and advocate for abolition. He published his autobiography in 1845 and founded *The North Star*, an antislavery publication.

In his life story, *Narrative of the Life of Frederick Douglass: An American Slave*, Douglass recounted the horrors of slavery, his efforts to achieve literacy, and his struggle to secure his freedom. In the context of telling that story, Frederick Douglass comments on the folk practices and beliefs of African Americans during this era.

In one such anecdote, Douglass recalls a fellow slave, Sandy Jenkins, who gave him a piece of plant root to carry for luck. In particular, the object is meant to have magical power to protect Douglass from beatings. Douglass was ambivalent about such a gift, for he did not believe in the magic of such a talisman, but he recognized the sustaining power of such beliefs as conjuring to people who, as slaves, had little conventional power over the conditions of their lives.

Not content to rely upon magic for his well-being, however, Frederick Douglass argued for the social, economic, and civic enfranchisement of African Americans. In the 1852 text, "What to the Slave is the Fourth of July?" Douglass drew parallels between the cause of the colonists and the plight of the slaves. He challenged America to make good on its egalitarian claims and, much as Patrick Henry had before him, described liberty as one of the attending conditions of an authentically human condition.

Douglass emerged as a kind of celebrity during the 1850s and had dealings with many of the most famous people of his time. Harriet Beecher Stowe, author of *Uncle Tom's Cabin*, hosted him for a discussion of strategies for helping the slaves. The antislavery spearhead John Brown also conferred with Frederick Douglass concerning his plans to catalyze slave revolts. Although Douglass declined any part in Brown's raid on Harpers Ferry, the fact that he was in demand among figures such as Stowe and Brown suggests he was a central figure in the cause of abolition.

Douglass went on to become an advocate for a range of human rights causes, including the fight for women's rights. He served his country in a variety of capacities, from United States marshal of the District of Columbia to the minister resident consul-general to the Republic of Haiti.

When he died in 1895, Frederick Douglass concluded what was by any standard an extraordinary life, beginning as a slave and ending as an international statesman.

Frederick Douglass achieved the status of a cultural hero. His legacy is recognized with biographies, scholarly monographs, plays, and documentary films.

See also: AFRICAN-AMERICAN FOLKLORE; ANTHONY, SUSAN BROWNELL; ATTUCKS, CRIS-PUS; BELIEFS, FOLK; BROWN, JOHN; BROWN, STERLING ALLEN; CIVIL RIGHTS MOVEMENT; CIVIL WAR; CONJURE/CONJURING; FOLKLORE IN AMERICAN LITERATURE; HENRY, PATRICK; INDEPENDENCE DAY/FOURTH OF JULY; PROTEST IN FOLKLORE; REVOLUTIONARY WAR; SLAVERY; STOWE, HARRIET BEECHER; STYRON, WILLIAM; UNDERGROUND RAILROAD.

For Further Reading:
Andrews, William. *To Tell a Free Story: The First Century of Afro-American Autobiography, 1760–1865.* Urbana: University of Illinois Press, 1986.

Douglass, Frederick. *Narrative of the Life of Frederic Douglass: An American Slave.* Boston: Anti-Slavery Office, 1845.

Fisher, Dexter, and Robert Stepto, eds. *Afro-American Literature: The Reconstruction of Instruction.* New York: Modern Language Association of America, 1979.

Martin, Waldo E., Jr. *The Mind of Frederick Douglass.* Chapel Hill: University of North Carolina Press, 1984.

Sundquist, Eric, ed. *Frederick Douglass: New Literary and Historical Essays.* New York: Cambridge University Press, 1990.

dowsing See PREDICTION.

dozens, or dirty dozens See SPEECH, FOLK; TOASTS/DRINKING.

drama, folk As distinct from other forms of theater, folk drama reflects the theatricality of everyday life.

Folk drama involves role play employed in a narrative context. The situation of a folk drama gathers together performers and audience members who are part of the same folk population, such as members of a faith community. The action of folk drama is self-conscious for both participants and spectators, and both understand their part in the performance.

Such drama can take many forms, from puppetry to pantomime, and does not require professional training so much as intimacy and immediacy of exchange. The performances can be spontaneous or planned, formal or informal, but delivery is generally live. Performers can be of any age, and school pageants, children's theater, and camp skits are all common forms of folk drama. Performances can be seasonal or annual events, such as Mardi Gras, costume parties, trick-or-treating, passion plays, Easter pageants, Christmas mumming, nativity scenes, or Purim stories enacted within religious settings. Popular dramas adapted from literature, such as the works of Harriet Beecher Stowe and James Mercer Langston Hughes, can also be regarded as folk dramas. Therapeutic uses of role play, such as those utilized in individual, group, or family therapy, could be considered folk drama. Street theater, from the dramatic portions of parades to the guerrilla theater of direct-action activists, represent additional forms of folk drama, as are ethnic theater and local and community performances, such as battle or slave auction reenactments. Living history interpreters, posing as people of another time at museums or other historically based sites, engage in a form of folk drama. Even the rituals of play or the repertoires of storytelling and conversation can involve a kind of folk drama.

Folk drama typically involves traditional narratives offered through enactment or other dramatic performance. It may be playful, somber, strident, or satirical, depending upon the circumstance and the intent of a given drama.

See also: CAMP FOLKLORE; CHRISTMAS; CIVIL WAR; EASTER; ETHNICITY; FOLKLORE IN AMERICAN LITERATURE; FOLKLORE IN EVERYDAY LIFE; HALLOWEEN/ALL HALLOWS' EVE; HOLIDAYS/OBSERVANCES; HUGHES, JAMES MERCER LANGSTON; LIVING HISTORY MUSEUMS; MARDI GRAS; MINSTRELSY; MUSEUMS, FOLK; PARADES; POLITICS IN FOLKLORE; PROTEST IN FOLKLORE; RELIGION, FOLK; SLAVERY; STOWE, HARRIET BEECHER.

For Further Reading:
Ben-Amos, Dan, and Kenneth S. Goldstein, eds. *Folklore: Performance and Communication*. The Hague: Mouton, 1975.
Charyk, John. *The Biggest Day of the Year: The Old Time Christmas School Concert*. Saskatoon, Canada: Western Producer–Prairie Books, 1985.
Dickinson, Thomas. *The Case of American Drama*. Boston: Houghton Mifflin, 1915.
Glassberg, David. *American Historical Pageantry: The Use of Tradition in the Early Twentieth Century*. Chapel Hill: University of North Carolina Press, 1990.
Koch, Frederick, and Archibald Henderson. *American Folk Plays*. New York: D. Appleton-Century, 1939.
McConachie, Bruce. "Slavery and Authenticity: Performing a Slave Auction at Colonial Williamsburg," *Theatre Annual: A Journal of Performance Studies* 51 (fall, 1998): 71–81.
McLaren, Joseph. *Langston Hughes, Folk Dramatist in the Protest Tradition, 1921–1943*. Westport, Conn.: Greenwood Press, 1997.
Tillis, Steven. *Rethinking Folk Drama*. Westport, Conn.: Greenwood Press, 1999.
Turner, Rory. "The Play of History: Civil War Reenactments and Their Use of the Past," *Folklore Forum* 22, nos. 1–2 (1989): 54–61.

drinking   See TOASTING/DRINKING.

DuBois, W. E. B. (William Edward Burghardt DuBois) (1868–1963)   W. E. B. DuBois is one of the most distinguished figures in African-American letters, and he helped readers recognize the vitality of folklore and folklife to the thriving of American culture.

DuBois was born February 23, 1868, in Great Barrington, Massachusetts. He attended Fisk University, where he received a bachelor of arts in 1888. DuBois then attended Harvard University, where he earned a second bachelor's degree in 1890 and a master of arts degree in 1891. In 1896, DuBois became the first African American to receive a Ph.D. from Harvard. His doctoral dissertation, "The Suppression of the African Slave Trade to the United States of America, 1638–1870," treated a crucial phenomenon in African-American history. Later, he conducted additional studies at the University of Berlin.

DuBois was a prolific writer and published plays, poems, novels, autobiography, and critical articles. He was also a skilled editor and correspondent. DuBois's published writings include *The Philadelphia Negro* (1899), *The Star of Ethiopia* (1913), *The Negro* (1915), *Dark Water: Voices from within the Veil* (1920), *The Brownies' Book* (1920), *Black Reconstruction* (1935), *Black Folk Then and Now* (1939), and *Dusk of Dawn* (1946). DuBois also composed nonfiction. In 1909, for example, he published a biography of the abolitionist John Brown. By far his most famous work, however, was *The Souls of Black Folk* (1903). This landmark work deals with the value of cultural consciousness. It is within this text that DuBois articulated his concepts of "twoness" and "double consciousness": That is, he contended that in terms of survival, African Americans had no choice but to cultivate awareness of both African-American and white cultural outlooks. The final chapter of this book employs the African-American folk song to symbolize a rich heritage of folk traditions. In fact, DuBois argued that this music, such as spirituals, represented the only true national legacy in America. Although this approach separated DuBois from more conciliatory figures such as Booker Taliaferro Washington, his celebratory view of African-American folk culture was shared by many of DuBois's contemporaries, from Alain Locke to James Mercer Langston Hughes.

DuBois's notion of double consciousness also finds expression within the domains of recent African-American literary theory and criticism. For example, in *The Signifying Monkey: A Theory of Afro-American Literary Criticism* (1988), the critic Henry Louis Gates uses the same practice of signifying about which Bambara wrote as a way to characterize the way African-American literature contests the master narratives of American culture. Just as W. E. B. DuBois argued that African-American thought was characterized by "double consciousness," Gates suggests that African-American literature is double voiced, as it speaks both to and beyond existing cultural scripts. In much the same way that African-American singers dared to talk back to the insistent voices that threaten their traditions, so do signifying texts throughout African-American literature challenge the assumptions behind traditional literary and cultural stories that would silence or slight the ancestral knowledge of historically disenfranchised populations.

In addition to his life as a published author, DuBois achieved distinction as editor of *Crisis*, a publication of the National Association for the Advancement of Colored People (NAACP), from approximately 1910 to 1935. In time, DuBois would be named to the faculty of several institutions, including Wilberforce College, the University of Pennsylvania, and Atlanta University. His work helped inform subsequent writers, such as Ralph Waldo Ellison and Toni Cade Bambara.

During his final years, DuBois became discouraged about the prospects for racial equality and understanding in America. In 1961, he joined the Communist Party of the United States. He also became more actively interested in such ideas as Pan-Africanism. He ultimately relocated to Ghana, where he became a naturalized citizen. W. E. B. DuBois died on August 27, 1963, in Accra, Ghana.

See also: AFRICAN-AMERICAN FOLKLORE; BAMBARA, TONI CADE; BROWN, JOHN; ELLISON, RALPH WALDO; FOLKLORE IN AMERICAN LITERATURE; HUGHES, JAMES MERCER LANGSTON; LOCKE, ALAIN LE ROY; MUSIC, FOLK; WASHINGTON, BOOKER TALIAFERRO.

For Further Reading:

Andrews, William L., ed. *Critical Essays on W. E. B. DuBois.* Boston: Hall, 1985.

Byerman, Keith. *Seizing the Work: History, Art, and Self in the Work of W. E. B. DuBois.* Athens: University of Georgia Press, 1994.

Hopkins, Dwight N. "Social Justice Struggle." In *Spirituality and the Secular Quest*, edited by Peter H. Van Ness, 356–384. New York: Crossroad, 1996.

Lemelle, Sidney J., and Robin D. G. Kelley. *Imagining Home: Class, Culture, and Nationalism in the African Diaspora*. London: Verso, 1994.

Moore, Jack. *W. E. B. DuBois*. Boston: Twayne, 1981.

Rampersad, Arnold. *The Art and Imagination of W. E. B. DuBois*. Cambridge, Mass.: Harvard University Press, 1976.

Zamir, Shamoon. *Dark Voices: W. E. B. DuBois and American Thought, 1888–1903*. Chicago: University of Chicago Press, 1995.

Dunbar, Paul Laurence (1872–1906) Paul Laurence Dunbar was probably the most widely known and acclaimed African-American writer of his day; part of his signature as a writer was an attention to folk culture and, in particular, sounded language.

Paul Laurence Dunbar was born in Dayton, Ohio, on June 27, 1872. His parents were both former slaves. Dunbar's father had escaped slavery, later fighting as a soldier in the Civil War. Both parents stimulated Dunbar with narrative culture. His mother read him poems and his father told him stories of life on the plantation. Each of these literary forms would have a profound effect on the young Dunbar, helping to shape his subsequent career as a writer.

As a young man, Dunbar was a voracious reader, who devoted his time to such authors as Henry Wadsworth Longfellow, whose work was itself influenced greatly by American folklore. Dunbar graduated from high school in 1891 and went on to hold positions such as elevator operator and reading room assistant in the Library of Congress. Still, it would be writing that would emerge as Dunbar's calling. For a time, Dunbar served as editor of Dayton's first African-American newspaper, which was printed at the Wright Brothers' shop, Wright and Wright Job Printers. This location is now preserved as part of Aviation Heritage National Historical Park. Dunbar's experiences as an editor proved apt for a budding literary career.

Over the course of his life, Dunbar wrote essays, songs, plays, stories, and, most interesting, poems. His publications include *Folks from Dixie* (1898), *Sport of the Gods* (1902), *The Strength of Gideon and Other Stories* (1900), and *The Fanatics* (1901). Dunbar's folk-inspired plays include *Clorindy, or the Origin of the Cakewalk* (1898), and *In Dahomey: A Negro Musical Comedy* (1902). His works reflected the history of African-American slavery. Dunbar wrote plantation stories and dialect poems. These works in particular bore the mark of folklore and folklife. In something of the way Samuel Langhorne Clemens captured the essence of southern white culture during the 19th century, Dunbar evoked the lives of African Americans of that era in the American South. His work is sometimes compared to that of Charles Waddell Chesnutt and James Weldon Johnson.

Dunbar drew a racially diverse audience of readers for his work. It is fitting, then, that the text that is perhaps his most famous single poem, "We Wear the Mask," protests the circumstances of African Americans, particularly the need for African Americans to contend with external perceptions and expectations. With its image of the mask, which both presents a public face and shields a private one, Dunbar anticipated the concept of double consciousness later articulated by W. E. B. DuBois.

Although later African-American writers, such as those of the Harlem Renaissance, would write more overtly about the color line, writers such as Dunbar made those protests possible. His work could be said to find its echoes in the writings of later African-American authors, including Zora Neale Hurston, Richard Wright, and Ralph Waldo Ellison.

Dunbar's literary activity would continue throughout his life. Dunbar died of tuberculosis in 1906. His life and works are remembered at Ohio's Dunbar State Memorial, which includes

Oak and Ivy Park, which was named after one of Dunbar's texts.

From folk drama to dialect poetry, Paul Laurence Dunbar inflected his writings with the forms and nuances of African-American folk traditions.

See also: AFRICAN-AMERICAN FOLKLORE; CLEMENS, SAMUEL LANGHORNE; CHESNUTT, CHARLES WADDELL; CIVIL WAR; DRAMA, FOLK; DUBOIS, W. E. B.; ELLISON, RALPH WALDO; FOLKLORE IN AMERICAN LITERATURE; HUGHES, JAMES MERCER LANGSTON; HURSTON, ZORA NEALE; JOHNSON, JAMES WELDON; LONGFELLOW, HENRY WADSWORTH; MIDWESTERN REGIONAL FOLKLORE; SLAVERY; SOUTHERN REGIONAL FOLKLORE; SPEECH, FOLK; WRIGHT BROTHERS.

For Further Reading:

Best, Felton. "Paul Laurence Dunbar's Protest Literature: The Final Years," *Western Journal of Black Studies* 17, no. 1 (spring 1993): 54–63.

Dunbar, Paul Laurence. *In Old Plantation Days.* New York: Dodd, Mead, 1903.

———. *Poems of Cabin and Field.* New York: Dodd, Mead, 1901.

Gentry, Tony. *Paul Laurence Dunbar.* New York: Chelsea House, 1989.

Keeling, Joe. "Paul Dunbar and the Mask of Dialect," *Southern Literary Journal* 25, no. 2 (spring 1993): 24–38.

Martin, J. *A Singer in the Dawn: Reinterpretations of Paul Laurence Dunbar.* New York: Dodd, Mead, 1975.

Dutch-American folklore Dutch-American folklore involves immigrants to the United States from those portions of the Netherlands where Dutch is spoken, as well as those persons born of Dutch descent in America.

Dutch immigration to the United States began during the colonial era, with settlements concentrated in the northeastern states such as New York and New Jersey. A second major wave of arrivals took place during the 19th century, this time with the emphasis on finding homes in the American Midwest, including the states of Iowa, Michigan, and Minnesota. These are not the only places where Dutch Americans settled, and Dutch-influenced folklore can be found across the United States.

Today, folklorists face the considerable challenge of distinguishing between the version of Dutch culture that exists in the popular mind and authentic cultural expressions. In many parts of the nation, perceptions of Dutch Americans have been shaped by a festival culture that may reinterpret folklore for an external audience. These events, held in places from Pella, Iowa, to Holland, Michigan, characterize the culture symbolically with Dutch letter pastries, windmill cookies, and tulip blooms. These public presentations do not necessarily capture the real nuances of Dutch-American culture and folklore, as they are tailored to appeal to cultural outsiders.

Similarly, Americans may form impressions of Dutch and Dutch-American culture on the basis of their depictions in literature and the arts. For example, the author Washington Irving's folk-influenced short stories, from "Rip Van Winkle" to "The Legend of Sleepy Hollow," feature Dutch-American characters. The playful and satiric tone of these tales, however, results in characterizations that are cartoonish at best. This effect does little to inform readers accurately about the nature of Dutch-American folkways. What is known about actual Dutch-American folklore suggests a largely agricultural lore, keeping people close to the land that nourishes them and provides their livelihoods. Folktales, folk songs, and folk dances play a part within that cultural inheritance.

Dutch Americans also celebrate some holidays and conduct some observances that are not universally recognized in the United States. An example is the annual tribute to Saint Nicholas, the patron saint of Amsterdam. This tradition has shifted somewhat over the years. At some point during the 19th century, the link formed between the historical Saint Nicholas and the legendary Santa Claus (also known as Saint Nick) resulted in some conflations of the two holidays. Although those in the Netherlands honor Saint Nicholas on December 6 each year, Dutch Americans tend to incorporate Saint Nicholas Day customs in their celebrations of Christmas on December 25. These practices include filling children's shoes with small treats and gifts.

American folk speech includes several unfortunate references to the Dutch within its slang. For example, when someone falls out of favor or into trouble, the predicament is sometimes described as "getting in Dutch." "Dutch treat" is a phrase that implies that social companions pay for the cost of shared meals and entertainments separately. These oddities of usage appear to have little if anything to do with Dutch heritage or custom. As with the folk festivals and fanciful depictions of the Dutch appearing in literature, these phrases only serve to obscure the actual culture of Dutch Americans. Further complicating the situation is the fact that Dutch Americans are sometimes confused with the Pennsylvania Dutch, who despite the reference are in fact of German origin.

Organizations preserving and promoting Dutch-American heritage include New York's Holland Society and Nertherland-American Foundation. Major collections of Dutch-American cultural material may be found at such locations as the Dutch Heritage Center in Palos Heights, Illinois, and the Association for Advancement of Dutch-American Studies in Holland, Michigan.

Despite many false impressions, Dutch Americans have a set of folk traditions that may only be glimpsed in popular culture images of them. Their folklore combines the customs of their homeland with those of their country of residence.

See also: AUCTIONS; CHRISTMAS; CULTURAL GROUPS; FESTIVALS, FOLKLORE; FOLKLORE IN AMERICAN LITERATURE; FOLKTALES; IMMIGRATION AND FOLKLORE; IRVING, WASHINGTON; MIDWESTERN REGIONAL FOLKLORE; MUSIC, FOLK; NORTHEASTERN REGIONAL FOLKLORE; PENNSYLVANIA DUTCH/PENNSYLVANIA GERMAN FOLKLORE; SANTA CLAUS; VAN WINKLE, RIP.

For Further Reading:

Brinks, Herbert J. *Dutch American Voices: Letters from the United States, 1850–1930.* Ithaca, N.Y.: Cornell University Press, 1995.

De Jong, Gerald F., ed. *The Dutch in America.* Boston: Twayne, 1975.

Krabbendan, Hans, and Larry J. Wagenaar, eds. *The Dutch-American Experience: Essays in Honor of Robert P. Swierenga.* Amsterdam: VU Uitgeverij, 2000.

Lucas, Henry S. *Dutch Immigrant Memoirs and Related Writings.* Grand Rapids, Mich.: W. B. Eerdmans, 1997.

Lucas, Henry S. *Netherlanders in America: Dutch Immigration to the United States and Canada.* Grand Rapids, Mich.: W. B. Eerdmans 1989.

Mulder, Arnold. *Americans from Holland.* Philadelphia, J. B. Lippincott, 1947.

Rose, Peter G., ed. *The Sensible Cook: Dutch Foodways in the Old and the New World.* Syracuse, N.Y.: Syracuse University Press, 1989.

Swierenga, Robert P., ed. *The Dutch in America: Immigration, Settlement, and Cultural Change, 1609–1974.* New Brunswick, N.J.: Rutgers University Press, 1985.

Yoder, Don. *Discovering American Folklife: Studies in Ethnic, Religious, and Regional Culture.* Ann Arbor, Mich.: UMI Research Press, 1989.

E

eagle See ANIMALS.

Earhart, Amelia Mary (1897–1937) As a pioneer of aviation and an early woman pilot, Amelia Mary Earhart became an American cultural hero.

Earhart was born on July 24, 1897, in Atchison, Kansas. Hers was an affluent family, and she enjoyed many privileges as a consequence. Earhart trained as a nurse's aide and worked in a military hospital until 1918. The next year, she began conducting medical studies. It was in 1920, after she left her premed program, that Earhart took her first flight. After a 10-minute biplane excursion, Earhart vowed to learn to fly for herself.

Toward that end, she began lessons with Anita Snook, a woman aviator. Eventually, Earhart acquired a plane of her own, which she named *The Canary*. She became involved in the field of aviation and established herself as one of that endeavor's female pioneers. Earhart became active in the National Aeronautic Association and invested in forming an aviation company.

In 1927, Earhart was approached about becoming the first woman to make a transatlantic flight. Earhart embraced the challenge and so was nicknamed "Lady Lindy" after the famed aviator Charles Lindbergh. Although she was a passenger rather than a pilot on this particular journey, Earhart found herself at the center of a media frenzy. She gave many lectures and interviews for the benefit of a curious and admiring public.

Earhart piloted a solo flight across the Atlantic on May 30, 1932. She also flew the first trans-Pacific flight, departing Hawaii and landing in California, before traveling on to Washington, D.C. In 1935, she began to attempt a record-breaking flight around the world. In 1937, Earhart's plane went down off the coast of Howland Island. The circumstances of the crash were unknown, and although searches of the area were conducted, Earhart's body was never found.

The mystery of Amelia Mary Earhart's disappearance resulted in intrigue and a number of unconfirmed sightings of the aviation hero.

See also: FLIGHT; FOLK HEROES/LEGENDARY FIGURES; LINDBERGH, CHARLES; MIDWESTERN REGIONAL FOLKLORE; OCCUPATIONAL FOLKLORE; REGION, FOLK; WRIGHT BROTHERS.

For Further Reading:
Earhart, Amelia. *The Fun of It*. New York: Brewer, Warren, and Putnam, 1932.
———. *Last Flight*. New York: Harcourt Brace, 1937.
———. *20 Hours 40 Minutes*. New York: G. P. Putnam's Sons, 1929.
King, Thomas, Randall Jacobson, and Karen Ramey Burns. *Amelia Earhart's Shoes: Is the*

Mystery Solved? Walnut Creek, Calif.: Alta Mira Press, 2001.

Earp, Wyatt Berry Stamp (1848–1929) Wyatt Earp, legendary figure from the American West, was a lawman, stagecoach driver, marksman, and frontiersman.

Earp was born in Monmouth, Illinois, in 1848. He is best remembered for a single event in which he participated, the October 26, 1881, shootout at the O.K. Corral. This conflict took place in the mining boomtown of Tombstone, Arizona. Along with his brothers Virgil and Morgan, and their associate John "Doc" Holliday, Wyatt Earp faced off with Billy Clanton, Frank McLaury, and Tom McLaury. Wyatt Earp left this skirmish unharmed, adding to his mystique. While Virgil Earp was ambushed and Morgan Earp murdered in the wake of the shootout, Wyatt Earp went on to further exploits. Some accounts suggest that he worked on the transcontinental railroad. Others describe him as a gambler. Still others suggest that he joined several phases of the gold rush—Black Hills, California, and Alaska. Wyatt Earp died in 1929.

Earp's career is recalled and romanticized in various popular representations. These depictions include the movies *My Darling Clementine* and *Tombstone*. He was also the focus of a television series, *The Life and Times of Wyatt Earp*. In addition, Earp was featured within a set of western-themed U.S. postage stamps in 1993. At the Wyatt Earp Museum, visitors can learn about the man and witness reenactments of the 1881 shootout. Earp is also the subject of countless folk narratives.

Along with such figures as William F. Cody (Buffalo Bill), Phoebe Annie Oakley, "Wild Bill" Hickok, and Kit Carson, Wyatt Berry Stamp Earp is one of the best-known legends of the American West.

See also: CARSON, KIT; CODY, WILLIAM F. (BUFFALO BILL); COWBOYS; FOLK HEROES/LEGENDARY FIGURES; FRONTIER; GHOST TOWNS; GOLD RUSH, THE; HICKOK, JAMES BUTLER (WILD BILL); MUSEUMS, FOLK; OAKLEY, PHOEBE ANNIE; OUTLAWS; REGION, FOLK; TRANSCONTINENTAL RAILROAD; WESTERN REGIONAL FOLKLORE.

For Further Reading:

Barra, Allen. *Inventing Wyatt Earp: His Life and Many Legends*. New York: Carroll & Graf, 1998.

Braendlin, Bonnie, and Hans Braendlin, eds. *Authority and Transgression in Literature and Film*. Gainesville: University Press of Florida, 1996.

Corkin, Stanley. *Cowboys as Cold Warriors: The Western and U.S. History*. Philadelphia: Temple University Press, 2004.

Lake, Stuart. *Wyatt Earp, Frontier Marshal*. New York: Houghton Mifflin, 1931.

Lubet, Steven. *Murder in Tombstone: The Forgotten Trial of Wyatt Earp*. New Haven, Conn.: Yale University Press, 2004.

Tefertiller, Casey. *Wyatt Earp: The Life behind the Legend*. New York: John Wiley, 1997.

Earth Day Earth Day, held on April 22 each year, represents a celebration of the Earth's vitality, accompanied by a pledge to thoughtful stewardship of its resources.

Earth Day was conceptualized during the environmentally minded 1960s. Americans were concerned about degradation of the natural environment through pollution, waste, and other human practices injurious to the Earth. It was an era of social movements, including environmentalism, and Earth Day offered a way to garner national attention annually for the importance of conservation and care of the Earth.

It began when the late Senator Gaylord Nelson, an environmental activist and the day's founder, called for a grassroots demonstration of the principles of environmentalism. Events for the day were to follow the general example of the counterculture's "teach-ins," where protest was combined with public education on a topic.

The first observance took place in 1970, and Nelson was surprised by the depth of feeling and the breadth of participation in it.

In addition to its educational agenda, Earth Day dramatizes that environmental causes have sufficient constituent support to command the attention of lawmakers and policy framers. During the era following the first observance of Earth Day, such rulings as the Clean Air Act, Occupational Safety and Health Act, Endangered Species Act, Federal Land Policy and Management Act, Federal Environmental Pesticide Control Act, Safe Drinking Water Act, Water Pollution and Control Act Amendments, Resource Conservation and Recovery Act, Resource Recovery Act, and Water Quality Improvement Act were all ratified. The public attention created by Earth Day, along with other forms of activism and lobbying, probably contributed to such outcomes.

Starting in 1971, the United Nations began celebrating its own version of Earth Day. This global holiday is tied to the March equinox, or the first day of spring, and calls for international cooperation and unity in caring for the Earth.

Earth Day combines a range of activities related to the day's theme. Such elements as recycling programs, conservation projects, and community service activities all play a part in recognizing the occasion.

See also: CAMP FOLKLORE; GARDENING; HOLIDAYS/OBSERVANCES; OCCUPATIONAL FOLKLORE; PROTEST IN FOLKLORE.

For Further Reading:

Activity Book: Earth Day Everyday: "For the Benefit of All." Cleveland: NASA/Lewis Research Center, 1997.

Ansary, Mir Tamim. *Earth Day.* Chicago: Heinemann Library, 2002.

Gardner, Robert. *Celebrating Earth Day: A Sourcebook of Activities and Experiments.* Brookfield, Conn.: Millbrook Press, 1992.

Hayes, Denis. *The Official Earth Day Guide to Planet Repair.* Washington, D.C.: Island Press, 2000.

Mowry, Marc. *Not in Our Backyard: The People and Events That Shaped America's Modern Environmental Movement.* New York: W. Morrow, 1993.

Nelson, Gaylord, with Susan Campbell and Paul Wozniak. *Beyond Earth Day: Fulfilling the Promise.* Madison: University of Wisconsin Press, 2002.

Steffoff, Rebecca. *The American Environmental Movement.* New York: Facts On File, 1995.

Easter   Easter is marked on the first Sunday after the full Moon that follows the vernal equinox each year, which typically falls during the month of March or April. This sacred Christian holiday is timed as an annual celebration of the resurrection of Jesus Christ.

Although world traditions for observing Easter have varied widely over the years, contemporary practices by believers residing in the United States include attendance at worship, feasts of celebration, and other more fanciful and secular festivities such as parades, egg coloring, egg hunts, and gifts of candy and gift baskets. Folk custom allows the number of treats delivered to children by the Easter Bunny (or Easter Rabbit), who is to Easter what Santa Claus is to Christmas. In addition, new attire is often reserved for this day as a gesture toward good luck, a custom that probably recalls earlier baptism rites.

As with many holidays celebrated in the United States, participants know more about the holiday practices associated with Easter than with their cultural and social origins. Eggs and hares, for instance, both carry associations with a goddess of spring, and, further, symbolize fertility. By the same logic, the baskets—or in some cases, nests—children prepare and leave to be filled by the Easter Bunny represent nurture and rebirth. Games, such as the egg roll, also have a reference to the religious past, harkening back hundreds of years to earlier games in which the rolling of the egg symbolizes the removal of the stone from the entry to Christ's tomb.

Despite the separation of church and state in America, some Easter-related celebrations are still customary in the nation's capital. Since at least the days of President James Madison, Washington, D.C., has hosted an egg roll for children at Easter. At first, the event was held on the grounds of the Capitol, but later it moved to the lawn of the White House, where it continues to this day. Although the tradition has typically been suspended during inclement weather and during some times of war, the White House Egg Roll remains a cherished tradition, which culminates in the appearance of a White House staff member costumed as the Easter Bunny.

Families often enjoy a large meal together on Easter, often including specific foods each year, such as ham or other family favorites. Within households, Easter's arrival is frequently marked by egg hunts, during which children are provided with baskets and encouraged to seek out eggs and other goodies concealed in the yard or an area park. Often, children join in the activity of dressing hard-boiled eggs for this purpose, using a range of dyes and decorative techniques. Many children wake on Easter to find a collection of treats left for their enjoyment by the Easter Bunny. Customary items for this purpose include such confections as chocolate molded into the shape of rabbits, marshmallow chicks, and jelly eggs.

Many communities also celebrate the day with a parade or themed procession. The best known of these in America is probably New York City's Easter Parade down Fifth Avenue. By tradition, here as elsewhere, parade participants show off their holiday finery and join in festivities of the day. Paying tribute to this custom are the familiar Irving Berlin tune "Easter Parade" and the 1948 film musical of the same name. Most distinctive about this parade is the emphasis on millinery, for between the custom for ladies to wear hats in church and the temptation to accessorize new Easter ensembles, the most remarked piece of holiday clothing is, by tradition, the so-called Easter bonnet.

Perhaps it is due to the importance of new clothes and outdoor activities at Easter that numerous folk beliefs related to the holiday concern weather lore. It is supposed by some that rain on Easter Sunday will be followed by seven more rainy Sundays. Another folk belief posits a link between the weather on Christmas and Easter in a given year. This belief holds that snow at Christmas indicates a green Easter; by the same token, clear weather at Christmas calls for snow on the following Easter.

Although traditionally celebrated as a holy day, Easter, as has Christmas, has also come to be associated with a great many customs and practices that, while festive, prove less directly tied to the sacred occasion.

See also: CHRISTMAS; DRAMA, FOLK; EASTER BUNNY; HOLIDAYS/OBSERVANCES; LUCK/FORTUNE; PARADES; RELIGION, FOLK; SANTA CLAUS; WEATHER FOLKLORE.

For Further Reading:

Aveni, Anthony F. *The Book of the Year: A Brief History of Our Seasonal Holidays.* New York: Oxford University Press, 2004.

Cohen, Hennig, and Tristram Potter Coffin, eds. *The Folklore of American Holidays.* Detroit: Gale, 1987.

Haceltine, Alice Isabel. *The Easter Book of Legends and Stories.* New York: Lothrop, Lee, & Shepard, 1947.

Myers, Robert J. *Celebrations: The Complete Book of American Holidays.* Garden City, N.Y.: Doubleday, 1972.

Newall, Venetia. *An Egg at Easter: A Folklore Study.* London: Routledge and Kegan Paul, 1971.

Santino, Jack. *All around the Year: Holidays and Celebrations in American Life.* Urbana: University of Illinois Press, 1994.

Watts, Alan. *Easter: Its Story and Meaning.* New York: Henry Schuman, 1950.

Easter Bunny (legendary)   The figure of the Easter Bunny (or Easter Rabbit) is loosely linked to the doctrinal meanings of the Christian holy day of Easter but plays a greater part in secular folk practices conducted in conjunction with the day's celebration each year.

Although the image of a hare does not relate directly to the sacred purpose of Easter, the resurrection of Jesus Christ, it does carry an association with a pre-Christian goddess of spring. It also symbolizes fertility. Both ideas are tied, however tenuously, to Easter's general theme of renewal and rebirth.

It is believed that the concept of the Easter Bunny originated in Germany, and that the image was first introduced to the United States by German settlers in Pennsylvania Dutch communities. As a result, many American children began to look forward to the treats the Easter Bunny would give when visiting the homes of good boys and girls each Easter.

By custom, the Easter Bunny pays an annual visit to contribute to the holiday enjoyment of children at this time of year. It is the Easter Bunny who many children believe fills the empty baskets, nests, or hats boys and girls leave out before Easter. Consequently, the candy and treats made available at this season often pay tribute to the Easter Bunny, especially in terms of the traditional confection of chocolate molded into the shape of a rabbit. Some children also consider that the items in use at special Easter festivities, such as egg rolls and egg hunts, were provided or hidden by the Easter Bunny for their benefit.

It appears that the specific notion of the Easter Bunny's delivering eggs as gifts is a relatively recent one and emerged as something of a marketing strategy for promoting the sale of eggs. Therefore, while other animals such as chicks (whose relations to eggs would otherwise seem more direct) play a part in holiday decorations for Easter, the figure of the rabbit remains most prominent in the imaginations of children.

As with his Christmas counterpart, Santa Claus, in addition to the annual visit itself, the Easter Bunny appears at special events and makes himself available during the weeks before Easter to greet children at shopping centers and malls. As does Santa, though, on the holiday itself, the Easter Bunny typically travels unseen, leaving behind tokens and trinkets of his visit and setting in place items to engage youngsters in the holiday's merriment.

Unlike more conventional Christian iconography associated with Easter, such as the cross, the lily, and the lamb, the Easter Bunny has a more oblique relationship to Scripture. He is nonetheless awaited fondly each year by children eager for the sweets he gives, and so has emerged as an important component of holiday lore.

See also: ANIMALS; CHRISTMAS; EASTER; HOLIDAYS/OBSERVANCES; RELIGION, FOLK; SANTA CLAUS.

For Further Reading:

Degh, Linda, Henry Glassie, and Felix Oinas, eds. *Folklore Today: A Festschrift for Richard M. Dorson.* Bloomington: Indiana University Press, 1976.

Myers, Robert J. *Celebrations: The Complete Book of American Holidays.* Garden City, N.Y.: Doubleday, 1972.

Santino, Jack. *All around the Year: Holidays and Celebrations in American Life.* Urbana: University of Illinois Press, 1994.

Edison, Thomas Alva (1847–1931) As a prolific inventor, Thomas Alva Edison emerged as a folk icon for American ingenuity.

Edison was born in Milan, Ohio, on February 11, 1847. His family moved to Michigan, where he attended a one-room schoolhouse. Edison's intellectual curiosity began early in life, and he became a voracious reader and independent learner. The young man took a special interest in the sciences and challenged many of the then-new notions about such topics as electricity. Edison had all the makings of an inventor.

With more than 1,000 patents to his credit, Edison was an unquestionable success in his field, and not just as the inventor of electric illumination. Innovations involving such materials as ethanol, rubber, and concrete, such devices as the telegraph, dictaphone, mimeograph, telephone, storage battery, electric railcar, phonograph, and kinetoscope (a precursor to motion picture technology) made Edison a virtuoso of scientific discovery. Edison was hardly the only talented inventor of his era, but some consider him among the most creative, in terms of both his research and its promotion. Even today, an incandescent light bulb depicted as appearing above a person's head remains the icon of a startlingly good idea. Edison's fame as a scientist cast him as something of a celebrity. Consequently, although he was a driven individual with an unrivaled work ethic, he socialized with other noted figures of his day, from Henry Ford to Charles Lindbergh.

Since 1962, the Edison National Historic Site, located in the New Jersey township that bears his surname, on the ground where the original Edison buildings once stood, has been an area attraction in the form of a re-creation of the Edison research facility, including a lab museum and memorial tower. Visitors can see artifacts and memorabilia related to the inventor.

The automobile baron and Edison admirer Henry Ford constructed a tribute to the New Jersey inventor on the premises of Greenfield Village, Ford's living history museum located in Dearborn, Michigan. Here, in the company of homages to figures such as Orville Wright and Wilbur Wright, visitors can see a re-creation of the residence and early lab of "The Wizard of Menlo Park." This scene recalls the Menlo Park, New Jersey, "Invention Factory," where Edison worked before he moved to the much larger West Orange location.

Here, as elsewhere, Edison is remembered not just as a gifted mind, but also as an agent of technological—and ultimately cultural—change. Edison died in October 18, 1931, at which time the U.S. president asked the nation to dim their lights in his memory. The impact of Edison's inventions, however, continues to burn today with undiminished light.

See also: EINSTEIN, ALBERT; FOLK HEROES/ LEGENDARY FIGURES; FORD, HENRY; GREEN-FIELD VILLAGE, HENRY FORD MUSEUM AND; INDUSTRIALIZATION AND FOLKLORE; LIND-BERGH, CHARLES; MUSEUMS, FOLK; OCCUPATIONAL FOLKLORE.

For Further Reading:
Baldwin, Neil. *Edison, Inventing the Century.* New York: Hyperion, 1995.

Essig, Mark Regan. *Edison and the Electric Chair: A Story of Light and Death.* New York: Walker, 2003.

Israel, Paul. *Edison: A Life of Invention.* New York: Wiley, 1998.

Josephson, Matthew. *Edison: A Biography.* New York: Wiley, 1992.

Wachhorst, Wyn. *Thomas Alva Edison, an American Myth.* Cambridge, Mass.: MIT Press, 1981.

Einstein, Albert (1879–1955) Albert Einstein was born on March 14, 1879, in Germany. He was reputed to have been an intelligent and inquisitive child, with an early interest in scientific principles. He studied math and physics in Switzerland and earned a Ph.D. at the University of Zurich in 1901.

It is telling that Einstein, a famous researcher, found his first job as a clerk in a patent office. In 1933, he accepted a position on staff at Princeton's Institute of Advanced Study. This relationship would last throughout Einstein's life. He became professor of theoretical physics at Princeton, where he remained on the faculty until he retired in 1945. Einstein became widely known for his scientific insights, and his greatest fame resulted from his theory of relativity. The equation he developed to express the equivalence of mass and energy is quoted, although not understood, widely. With this and other accomplishments, Einstein changed the face of physics as a discipline. He was able to think beyond Newtonian mechanics and to reach understandings of aspects of science no one had. As a result, Albert Einstein received many accolades, including the 1923 Nobel Prize in physics.

Einstein's objections to Hitler led him to renounce his German citizenship in 1933. Although he had opposed militarism in the past,

Einstein's outrage at Hitler's deeds caused him to rethink that view. He ultimately persuaded President Franklin Delano Roosevelt to authorize the Manhattan Project in 1939, a program to advance research into the atomic bomb, in order to counter any similar research being done by the Nazi scientists. Consequently, Einstein became associated in the public imagination with the atomic age. He became a United States citizen in 1940. Einstein died April 18, 1955, in Princeton, New Jersey. His passing occurred just as the cold war peaked.

Although the substance of Albert Einstein's findings exceeded the grasp of most laypeople, he nonetheless represented the figure of a scientific genius in the popular imagination. In Washington, D.C., on the grounds of the National Academy of Sciences, stands the Robert Berks Albert Einstein Memorial, where the man is honored with a figural bronze sculpture that humanizes a great mind by depicting him in his casual and rumpled glory. While his ideas may have eluded the American public, the memorial makes Einstein friendly and approachable. Visitors daily pose draped on the monument, and children routinely climb Einstein's figure as commemorated there.

See also: ATOMIC/NUCLEAR ERA FOLKLORE; FOLK HEROES/LEGENDARY FIGURES; FORD, HENRY; GREENFIELD VILLAGE, HENRY FORD MUSEUM AND; MUSEUMS, FOLK; WORLD WAR II.

For Further Reading:

Brian, Denis. *Einstein: A Life*. New York: Wiley, 1997.
Sayen, Jamie. *Einstein in America: The Scientist's Conscience in the Age of Hitler and Hiroshima*. New York: Crown, 1985.

Election Day   Election Day affords American citizens the opportunity to participate in the democratic process by casting their ballots for candidates and making their opinions known on referendum items.

Uniform national elections have been held since 1845 in the United States. Every two years, on even-numbered years, a national election is held on the first Tuesday after the first Monday occurring in the month of October. Presidential elections occur every four years, in years whose numbers are evenly divisible by 4.

Long ago, Election Day was the occasion for many attempts to influence the voting outcome, even within polling places. Lobbyists for candidates sought to ply voters with strong drink or other enticements. Today, polling places and voters have protections that include restrictions on campaigning and surveying activities within a specified distance of polling locations.

Modern folklore surrounding elections includes urban legends. Prominent among these are information-age pranks or hoaxes in which e-mails advise voters—or groups of voters, depending on the perpetrator's desired outcome—that for one reason or another, voting has been rescheduled to an alternate date. If taken seriously, such messages could constitute fraud as they seek to deny otherwise qualified voters the legally protected right to exercise the franchise.

Although Election Day is not a legal holiday, the event nonetheless is associated with folk customs. For example, in New England, there is a tradition of preparing Election Day cake. This yeast-raised cake, prepared with spices, raisins, and nuts, dates back to the 1700s in Connecticut. It is tied to an era in which the trip to cast one's vote was a journey punctuated with visits to friends and family. By the 19th century, polling places were more accessible, and the customs of Election Day cake and callers waned.

Election Day finds its companion observances in Independence Day/Fourth of July and Inauguration Day. Election Day provides citizens with a procedure for exercising the autonomy celebrated each Fourth of July. Inauguration Day represents the public affirmation of the results of each presidential election. Both in fact and in symbol, Election Day enables Americans to play a part in civic decision making, including selection of local, state, and federal leaders.

See also: FOOD/FOODWAYS; HOLIDAYS/
OBSERVANCES; INAUGURATION DAY; INDEPEN-
DENCE DAY/FOURTH OF JULY; POLITICS AND
FOLKLORE.

For Further Reading:

Dinkin, Robert J., ed. *Election Day: A Documentary History*. Westport, Conn.: Greenwood Press, 2002.

Fabre, Genevieve. "Election Day Celebrations." In *Slavery in the Americas*, edited by Wolfgang Binder, 403–420. Würzburg: Königshausen & Neumann, 1993.

Grossberg, Michael, and Hendrik Hartog, eds. *American Public Life and the Historical Imagination*. Notre Dame, Ind.: University of Notre Dame Press, 2003.

Patterson, Thomas. *The Vanishing Voter: Public Involvement in an Age of Uncertainty*. New York: Vintage Books, 2003.

Santino, Jack. *All around the Year: Holidays and Celebrations in American Life*. Urbana: University of Illinois Press, 1994.

Sarvis, William R. "The Folklore and Oral History of Election Fraud in Rural Postwar Missouri," *Mid-America Folklore* 26, nos. 1–2 (spring–fall 1998): 42–70.

Schudson, Michael. *The Good Citizen: A History of American Civic Life*. New York: Martin Kessler Books, 1998.

White, Joyce M. "Meaning and Cultural Expression: New England Election Day Cake," *Digest: A Review for the Interdisciplinary Study of Food* 13, nos. 1–2 (1993): 9–15.

Ellis Island See IMMIGRATION AND FOLK-
LORE; LIBERTY, MISS.

Ellison, Ralph Waldo (1914–1994) Ralph Ellison distinguished himself as a writer of essays, short stories, and one completed novel, all of which bear the influences and convey the importance of African-American folklore and folk culture.

Born in Oklahoma in 1914, Ellison seemed destined for a career in music when he arrived at Tuskegee Institute, founded by Booker Taliaferro Washington. While there, however, Ellison became more involved in literature and writing. The man who was himself named after another writer, Ralph Waldo Emerson, soon became an author. While he would continue to twine musical themes and motifs into his works for the rest of his career, literature won out over music for his attention.

Ellison may have developed his appetite for folklore during the Great Depression, during which he joined the Federal Writers' Project (FWP). His affiliation with FWP lasted from 1938 to 1942. During that time, his assignments included collecting children's folklore with the noted folklorist B. A. Botkin.

Ellison's greatest triumph, at least in the estimation of many readers and critics, is the single novel he produced, *Invisible Man* (1952). This monumental text, both in length and in implication, secured Ellison's place within American literature. It also provided a tapestry of allusions to African-American folklore and history. Attentive readers of Ellison's texts can find countless references to fables, folktales, stories, and tunes from American lore.

Invisible Man recounts the tragic story of an unnamed protagonist. In this sense, it complicates the heroic conventions of the novel as genre, denying the reader a name by which to reference or know the central character. This technique also implies that Ellison's novel is not a story of one, but rather of many. The figure at the center of *Invisible Man* begins his journey of discovery a young and hopeful person, filled with the conviction that hard work will win his objectives in life. As he matures, the character becomes both more worldly and more cynical about the possibilities available to him. As he ventures from his southern community of Greenwood north to Harlem, the character conducts a quest for identity, only to find what a vexed question identity is for African Americans. This grandson of a slave realizes that he, as did his ancestors, faces a dangerous, perplexing, and deadly world where perceptions become destinies. In keeping with this theme, Ellison's novel is replete with terms that emphasize the language of perception, especially visual perception, as signaled by the work's title. The novel is full of references to sight, visibility, and visual miscues. These sensory images link closely to the themes of identity within the novel, for matters are not as they appear and people are not who they appear. Ellison makes this point with figurative language regarding masks, doubles, and paradoxes.

Ellison's writings, including *Invisible Man* in particular, demonstrate a preoccupation with cultural survivals within African America. The author populates his work with the ghosts of African-American history, such as Booker Taliaferro Washington and W. E. B. DuBois. Elements of American folklore abound in his work, from the spirituals that sustained slaves to the Sambo and minstrel images that have threatened to reduce African Americans to cultural stereotypes. In confronting the influences of folk culture, both affirmative and negative, Ellison reconnects his readers to a ravaged and maligned cultural legacy. Only by embracing the complexities and the confounding nature of this folk culture inheritance, Ellison seems to suggest, can African Americans become whole.

Ellison's own journey ended in 1994 with his death. *Juneteenth*, an unfinished novel published posthumously in 1999, underscored his message about the relationship between one's individual identity and one's collective history.

While citing literary influences such as Herman Melville, James Fenimore Cooper, James Mercer Langston Hughes, James Weldon Johnson, and Samuel Langhorne Clemens, Ralph Ellison also drew considerable inspiration for his work from the oral traditions and enduring customs of African Americans.

See also: AFRICAN-AMERICAN FOLKLORE; CITY FOLKLORE; CIVIL RIGHTS MOVEMENT; CIVIL WAR; CLEMENS, SAMUEL LANGHORNE; COOPER, JAMES FENIMORE; DEPRESSION, THE GREAT; DUBOIS, W. E. B.; FOLKLORE IN AMERICAN LITERATURE; HUGHES, JAMES MERCER LANGSTON; HUMOR, FOLK; JOHNSON, JAMES WELDON; JUNETEENTH; LOCKE, ALAIN LE ROY; MINSTRELSY; MUSIC, FOLK; NORTHEASTERN REGIONAL FOLKLORE; POLITICS AND FOLKLORE; PROTEST IN FOLKLORE; REGION, FOLK; SLAVERY; SOUTHERN REGIONAL FOLKLORE; VERNACULAR CULTURE; WASHINGTON, BOOKER TALIAFERRO.

For Further Reading:

Blake, Susan L. "Ritual and Rationalization: Black Folklore in the Works of Ralph Ellison," *PMLA: Publications of the Modern Language Association of America* 94 (1979): 121–136.

Graham, Maryemma, and Amritjit Singh, eds. *Conversations with Ralph Ellison.* Jackson: University of Mississippi, 1995.

O'Meally, Robert G. "Riffs and Rituals: Folklore in the Work of Ralph Ellison." In *Afro-American Literature: The Reconstruction of Instruction*, edited by Dexter Fisher and Robert B. Stepto, 153–169. New York: MLA, 1979.

Roberts, John W. "'… Hidden Right Out in the Open': The Field of Folklore and the Problem of Invisibility: 1998 American Folklore Society Presidential Address," *Journal of American Folklore* 112, no. 444 (spring 1999): 119–139.

Sundquist, Eric. *Cultural Contexts for Ralph Ellison's Invisible Man.* New York: Bedford/St. Martin's, 1995.

Wiggins, William H., Jr. "The Folklore Elements in Ralph Ellison's *Invisible Man*," *Selected Proceedings of the Third Annual Conference on Minority Studies*, 4 (April 1975): 39–44.

Emancipation (Proclamation) Day   Emancipation (Proclamation) Day, marked in the United States each year on various dates, but most typically on January 1, recalls Abraham Lincoln's January 1, 1863, signing of the Emancipation Proclamation at the close of the American Civil War.

While the Emancipation Proclamation sought to free slaves after the Civil War, the Thirteenth Amendment also carried great importance insofar as it addressed not just the status of individuals, but also the institution of slavery itself. This amendment did so by rendering unlawful all slavery and involuntary servitude, except that administered as punishment for a convicted offense.

As the example of Juneteenth, a June 19 Texas observance, demonstrates, localities observe emancipation on various dates. These variations usually result from distinctions in the specific event commemorated. In Richmond, Virginia, for example, the date corresponding to the fall of Richmond during the Civil War proves most salient with the locals. In Washington, D.C., emancipation is celebrated on April 16 each year, in remembrance of the date (April 16, 1862) on which Abraham Lincoln signed the District of Columbia Emancipation Act, and so ever since 1866, residents of the District have observed a private holiday at this time.

Whatever the date reserved to mark the occasion, Emancipation Day in the United States, as do comparable observances in other places worldwide, communicates the importance of human freedom and the right of self-determination. In the United States, Emancipation Day also commemorates the ultimate outcome of the nation's Civil War.

See also: AFRICAN-AMERICAN FOLKLORE; CIVIL RIGHTS MOVEMENT; CIVIL WAR; HOLIDAYS/OBSERVANCES; JUNETEENTH; LINCOLN, ABRAHAM; PRESIDENTS' DAY; PROTEST IN FOLKLORE; SLAVERY.

For Further Reading:

Anyike, James C. *African American Holidays: A Historical Research and Reference Guide to Cultural Celebrations.* Chicago: Popular Truth, 1991.

Dazey, Mary Ann. "Eight o'May, 1865–1980," *Mississippi Folklore Register* 14, no. 1 (spring 1980): 36–39.

Santino, Jack. *All around the Year: Holidays and Celebrations in American Life.* Urbana: University of Illinois Press, 1994.

Wiggins, William. *O Freedom! Afro-American Emancipation Celebrations.* Knoxville: University of Tennessee Press, 1987.

emic/etic   See INSIDER/OUTSIDER.

"Emperor's New Clothes, The"   A fairy tale popularized by Hans Christian Andersen, the story centers on a vain emperor who delights in his own appearance. He loves to acquire new garments and show them off to his public.

One day, two unscrupulous businessmen arrived at the emperor's home. Describing themselves as weavers of distinction, the two men make an unusual pitch to the clothes-hungry monarch. As salespeople do, they claim that the clothes they produce are of the highest quality and visual appeal. In addition, however, they contend that their garments have a distinctive advantage over other finery. The clothes they make are so exceptional that only the worthy are capable of even seeing them. Others, who are fools or unworthy of their roles, will gaze upon the clothiers' work and see nothing at all.

This approach intrigues the emperor on two levels. He will have the finest clothes in the land, and he will also acquire, through the magical properties of the new attire, insights into those around him. Pleased on both counts, the emperor engages the weavers to fashion an outfit for him. For these goods, he pays handsomely with money, gold, and expensive fabrics such as silk.

Determined to carry out their lucrative ruse, the imposters set about their work. They spend countless hours miming work with scissors and loom, periodically requesting more materials and compensation. Finally, they declare the work finished and remark on the exceptional color and craftsmanship of the new clothing. In fact, they characterize the garments as so light that the emperor will feel as though he is wearing nothing at all!

The time arrives for the emperor to display his purchases, and it is decided that a procession will afford the proper occasion for such an unveiling. The preparations get under way, with the charlatans miming the gestures of fitting and arranging the clothes. As the event begins, the townspeople are shocked and amazed, but not by the clothes. Instead, they see an unclad emperor striding proudly through the streets of the land. Fearful that they will be found out and thought incompetent for their inability to see the new garments, the onlookers instead offer their emperor praise or silent appreciation. As the display continues, a child speaks out and declares the emperor to be naked. Taking notice of the child's bravery, others confirm that finding until even the emperor recognizes the child's exclamation as true. For the sake of appearances, however, he completes the procession with even more regal bearing.

This fairy tale extolls a whole set of virtues but most lauds the innocence and frankness of children, who neither distrust nor conceal the evidence of their own senses. The story warns against deceit and excessive pride, without which the story could not occur.

To this day, during conversation, when people wish to expose the truth of a situation, especially one involving a false claim or appearance by someone in power, they, as does the youth from the story, pronounce that "the emperor has no clothes."

"The Emperor's New Clothes" has been retold many times over the years, including an update of the story in Disney's feature-length animated film released in 2000, *The Emperor's New Groove*.

See also: ANDERSEN, HANS CHRISTIAN; CHILDREN'S FOLKLORE; FABLES; FAIRY TALES; MYTHS, FOLK; TRICKSTER; YANKEE PEDDLER.

For Further Reading:

Ashliman, D. L. *Folk and Fairy Tales: A Handbook*. Westport, Conn.: Greenwood, 2004.

Bredsdorff, Elias. *Hans Christian Andersen: An Introduction to His Life and Works*. Copenhagen: Hans Reitzels Forlag, 1987.

Jones, Steven Swann. *The Fairy Tale: The Magic Mirror of Imagination*. New York: Twayne, 1995.

Mylius, Johan de, Aage Jorgensen, and Viggo Hjornager Pedersen, eds. *Hans Christian Ander-*

sen: A Poet in Time. Odense: Odense University Press, 1999.

Rossel, Sven Hakon, ed. *Hans Christian Andersen: Danish Writer and Citizen of the World*. Amsterdam: Rodopi, 1996.

Tatar, Maria, ed. *The Annotated Classic Fairy Tales*. New York: W. W. Norton, 2002.

Wullschlager, Jackie. *Hans Christian Andersen: The Life of a Storyteller*. Chicago: University of Chicago Press, 2002.

esoteric/exoteric   See INSIDER/OUTSIDER.

ethics in folklore   As public scholars, folklorists must consider not only the consequences of their research for the collective, but also the effects of such scholarship on the individual informants and respondents contacted through their study.

Over and above considerations of academic integrity that apply to all scholarly endeavors, folklorists must work with human subjects. Consequently, they need to observe standards of conduct, inquiry, and impact management that come into play with human informants. In this and other respects, ethical practice in folklore parallels the behavior required or recommended in other social sciences.

Virtually every professional organization for social scientists creates and seeks to uphold a document delineating the fundamental expectations for ethical conduct. Examples include the American Anthropological Association's "Code of Ethics," the American Sociological Association's "Code of Ethics," the Modern Language Association's "Statement of Professional Ethics," and the Oral History Association's "Oral History Evaluation Guidelines."

Oral history is a good example of the care needed in conducting ethical folklore research. The work of ethical research begins long before interviews take place. The project design must be informed by current codes of conduct, such as those listed. Depending upon institutional policies, such as university regulations, it may also be necessary to submit the project design to a review panel charged with authorizing human subject research. In addition, with oral history it is customary to prepare documents that help gain informed consent among participants and release forms that permit the researcher to transcribe, cite, publish, or preserve in an archive the recordings of informant interviews. During interactions with interview participants, a folklorist must be respectful, prepared, forthright, and trustworthy in fulfilling the terms of any agreements. Issues of accuracy and confidentiality must be clearly articulated, mutually understood, and fully honored in any resulting work.

As with any inquiry involving human subjects, folklore studies require practitioners to behave thoughtfully in terms of the effect such work has on participants' and readers' lives.

See also: FIELDWORK, FOLKLORE; FOLKLORE IN EVERYDAY LIFE; FOLKLORE STUDIES; FOLKLORISTICS.

For Further Reading:

Adler, Patricia A., Peter Adler, and E. Burke Rochford, Jr., eds. "The Politics of Participation in Field Research," *Urban Life* 14, no. 4 (1986): 363–376.

Appell, G. N. *Ethical Dilemmas in Anthropological Inquiry: A Case Book.* Los Angeles, Calif.: Crossroads Press, 1978.

Beauchamp, T. L. et al., eds. *Ethical Issues in Social Science Research.* Baltimore: Johns Hopkins University Press, 1982.

Buckley, Thomas. "Dialogue and Shared Authority: Informants as Critics," *Central Issues in Anthropology* 7, no. 1 (1987): 13–23.

Bunch, John B. "The Legal Consideration of Privacy, Property, Copyright, and Unfair Practices, in the Publication of Folklore Material," *Folklore Forum* 6, no. 4 (1973): 211–216.

Farrer, Claire. "Fieldwork Ethics." In *Trends and New Vistas in Contemporary Native American Folklore Study*, edited by Stephen Mannenbach, 59–63. Bloomington, Ind.: Folklore Forum, 1976.

Jansen, William Hugh. "Ethics and the Folklorist." In *Handbook of American Folklore*, edited by Richard M. Dorson et al., 533–539. Bloomington: Indiana University Press, 1983.

Kirsch, Gesa E. *Ethical Dilemmas in Feminist Research: The Politics of Location, Interpretation, and Publication.* Albany: State University of New York Press, 1999.

Schoemaker, George H., ed. *The Emergence of Folklore in Everyday Life: A Fieldguide and Sourcebook.* Bloomington, Ind.: Trickster Press, 1990.

ethnicity   *Ethnicity* refers to the way of life and folk traditions associated with a given population.

Such a group typically consists of members with a common collective history and a shared homeland. An ethnic group may coincide with the practitioners of a particular faith, often one outside Judeo-Christian traditions. Awareness of this shared legacy shapes identity and informs behavior.

In this sense, ethnic identity can play a key role in a the life of a folk group and the self-concept of its members. Members of the same ethnic group recognize one another as kindred and celebrate that connection through actions of daily life. For instance, many major American cities boast ethnic neighborhoods established by immigrant groups. These areas bear names such as Chinatown, Little Italy, and Little Tokyo, depending upon the ancestry of the immigrants residing and working there. By concentrating a population, districts of this kind help preserve ethnic traditions in the face of pressures for cultural assimilation. Through means of home-language newspapers and periodicals, members of an ethnic group can maintain awareness of cultural perspectives and events. Ethnic neighborhoods also become sites for import shops, homeland-inspired celebrations, cultural museums, and ethnic restaurants serving both area residents and tourists.

Ethnicity can be expressed in any number of customs and practices. Examples include foodways, music, holidays and observances, festivals, recreations, and other events. Some folk groups in America have strong traditions of ethnic theater and ethnic parades, both of which reinforce shared identity and assert a group's pride in public. These practices can also introduce young members of the community to aspects of ethnic tradition, such as attire, music, dance, and pageantry.

Ethnicity helps unify members of a group while underscoring the important cultural distinctions between insiders and outsiders of that population, from inside jokes to folk festivals.

See also: CULTURAL GROUPS; FOLKLORE IN EVERYDAY LIFE; IMMIGRATION AND FOLKLORE; INSIDER/OUTSIDER; LIBERTY, MISS; MUSEUMS, FOLK; TERMS.

For Further Reading:

Brown, Linda Keller, and Kay Mussell, eds. *Ethnic and Regional Foodways in the United States: The Performance of Group Identity*. Knoxville: University of Tennessee Press, 1984.

Danielson, Larry, ed. *Studies in Folklore and Ethnicity*. Los Angeles: California Folklore Society, 1978.

Georges, Robert, and Stephen Stern. *American and Canadian Immigrant and Ethnic Folklore: An Annotated Bibliography*. New York: Garland, 1982.

Oring, Elliott, ed. *Folk Groups and Folklore Genres: A Reader*. Logan: Utah State University Press, 1989.

Royce, Anya Peterson. *Ethnic Identity: Strategies of Diversity*. Bloomington: Indiana University Press, 1982.

Sanna, Ellyn. *Ethnic Folklore*. Broomal, Pa.: Mason Crest, 2003.

Schoemaker, George H., ed. *The Emergence of Folklore in Everyday Life: A Fieldguide and Sourcebook*. Bloomington, Ind.: Trickster Press, 1990.

Stern, Stephen, and John Allan Cicala, eds. *Creative Ethnicity: Symbols and Strategies of Contemporary Ethnic Life*. Logan: Utah State University Press, 1991.

Thernstrom, Stephan, Ann Orlov, and Oscar Handlin, eds. *Harvard Encyclopedia of American Ethnic Groups*. Cambridge, Mass.: Belknap Press, 1980.

Wynar, L. R., and L. Buttlar. *Guide to Ethnic Museums, Libraries, and Archives in the United States*. Kent, Ohio: Program for the Study of Ethnic Publications/School of Library Science, 1978.

Young, Bernard. *Art, Culture, and Ethnicity*. Reston, Va.: National Art Education Association, 1990.

euphemisms   See SPEECH, FOLK.

everyday life, folklore of   See FOLKLORE IN EVERYDAY LIFE.

evil eye   In folklore, the "evil eye" is related to the belief that an ill-wishing gaze can cause harm to the person in its path.

In this respect, the evil eye, sometimes called "the look" or "the wounding eye," is one aspect of the larger concept of malevolence, in which bad feelings can actually harm the recipient. Most Americans recognize this idea most readily through phrases of common usage. For example, when a harsh glance is cast at someone, it is not unusual for onlookers to speculate on the consequence of such a view, "If looks could kill." The sender's act of giving someone the evil eye is also known as "overlooking."

The evil eye, then, is a fairly immediate form of exacting justice or revenge for wrongdoing. It is similar to a trick in conjuring, a spell in witchcraft, or a curse in other lore. By giving the evil eye, one actively seeks to harm the person on view or, in some cases, causes such harm inadvertently by acting as a detractor. The evil eye, an ancient danger to be guarded against, is usually the result of envy, but it can also be provoked when one receives a compliment or boasts of one's fortune. It appears to target pride as well as to redress other forms of misdeeds. For this reason, one approach to avoiding the evil eye is to understate one's qualities or fortunes.

Also known in immigrant lore as *malocchio* or *matiasma*, the evil eye is an aspect of superstition in many cultures. Folk beliefs vary about whether anyone can be a sender of the evil eye, or whether only people with specific physical attributes or manners of disposition are able to deliver the evil eye.

The evil eye's effects are most severe, even life-threatening, for the very young. For the rest of the population, the evil eye can cause illness or bad luck but is generally not more dangerous. As with most matters of superstition, the goal is to avoid evil eye; that way, there is no need of cure.

There are a variety of folk practices intended to prevent it, detect it, and reverse it as necessary. Because the evil eye is widely regarded as a consequence of envy or bad feeling, those wishing to avoid its effects may abstain from bragging or speaking ill of others. Beliefs about averting the evil eye also include the hanging of plants such as camel's needle, the burning of seeds such as cumin, spoken ritual of protection, and the use of amulets or lucky objects. Some believe that the bridal veil is itself a shield against such evil.

While not originating in America, the concept of the evil eye is believed to have reached this country with its populations of immigrants, who introduced their cultural traditions, including notions of risk and protection, along with them.

See also: BELIEFS, FOLK; CHRISTMAS; CONJURE/CONJURING; DEVIL, THE; FOLKLORE IN EVERYDAY LIFE; GREEK-AMERICAN FOLKLORE; IMMIGRATION AND FOLKLORE; LUCK/FORTUNE; MAGIC; MEDICINE, FOLK; MORRISON, TONI; PREDICTION; RELIGION, FOLK; SUPERNATURAL; SUPERSTITION; VOODOO/HOODOO; WEDDING/MARRIAGE FOLKLORE; WITCHCRAFT, SALEM.

For Further Reading:

Browne, Ray B., ed. *Forbidden Fruits: Taboos and Tabooism in Culture.* Bowling Green, Ohio: Bowling Green State University Popular Press, 1984.

Distasi, L. *Mal Occhio: The Underside of Vision.* San Francisco: North Point Press, 1981.

Dundes, Alan, ed. *The Evil Eye: A Folklore Casebook.* New York: Garland, 1981.

Griego, Linda. "The 'Ojo,'" *Southwest Folklore* 1, no. 4 (1977): 35.

Hartman, Peter, and Karyl McIntontosh. "Evil Eye Beliefs Collected in Utica, New York," *New York Folklore Quarterly* 4 (1978): 61–69.

Kirkland, James. "'The Tell-Tale Heart' as Evil Eye Event," *Southern Folklore* 56, no. 2 (1999): 135–147.

Koperski, Katherine J. "Imagining Evil in Polish-American Culture," *New York Folklore Quarterly* 12, nos. 3–4 (summer–fall 1986): 137–141.

Maloney, Clarence, ed. *The Evil Eye.* New York: Columbia University Press, 1976.

F

fables Animal tales are a vast body of folktales, both in America and around the world. Generally speaking, fables are animal stories of a very particular sort: They are narratives pointing a moral for audience members. In this sense, the ultimate message of the fable takes precedence over the details of the story, although these, too, can be quite engaging.

Within these fables, animals are the primary or sole characters and often appear in personified form. When that is the case, while the animals retain the appearance of creatures, they also possess attributes or abilities of their human counterparts, such as the power of speech. In this way, animals stand in for humans in the unfolding stories. Accordingly, the animals featured in fables may be selected for their characteristic properties, such as rabbits for speed or pigs for greed.

Probably the most famous of all fabulists was Aesop, a legendary figure of sixth-century Greece. Although there are different accounts of who Aesop was, there is no disputing that his name has become nearly synonymous with the fable as narrative form. Just as the best-known fairy tales in the United States are the Grimm brothers' tales, the most familiar fables are those penned by Aesop. Among the best-known fables attributed to Aesop are "Androcles and the Lion," "The Golden Goose," and "The Tor-

toise and the Hare." All provide apt examples of the way fables transmit a lesson as well as a plot and for that reason have long been used to teach precepts to children. In some cases, fables also incorporate elements of satire as tellers make their moral points.

American retellings of Aesop's fables along with other traditional tales, such as those originating within Native American culture and African-American lore, make fables a vital form of narrative lore in the United States.

See also: African-American folklore; "Androcles and the Lion"; animals; Bambara, Toni Cade; "Boy Who Cried Wolf, The"; children's folklore; Ellison, Ralph Waldo; folktales; "Golden Goose, The"; Greek-American folklore; Native American folklore; "Tortoise and the Hare, The."

For Further Reading:

Aesop. *The Classic Treasury of Aesop's Fables.* Philadelphia: Courage Books, 1999.

Blackham, J. J. *The Fable as Literature.* London: Athlone, 1985.

Carnes, Pack. *Folk Scholarship: An Annotated Bibliography.* New York: Garland, 1985.

Hoffman, Daniel. *Form and Fable in American Fiction.* New York: Oxford University Press, 1961.

fairies See CINDERELLA; FAIRY TALES; GRIMM BROTHERS; SAINT PATRICK'S DAY; TOOTH FAIRY.

fairy tales While fairy tales do not originate in the United States, each familiar story is a staple of the country's folklore.

Borrowed from European lore, fairy tales permeate American culture. Particularly in the lives of children these texts, from "Little Red Riding Hood" to "The Princess and the Pea," appear prominently. Later in life, one sees these familiar tales reworked countless times in ways specific to rhetorical occasions.

Most of the fairy tales familiar to Americans stem from the collections of the Grimm brothers, two early folklorists who were interested in recording traditional tales for posterity. Jacob Grimm (1785–1863) and Wilhelm Grimm (1786–1859) were influential collectors of 19th-century European folklore, especially fairy tales. American readers have made these didactic stories their own through rereadings and retellings over the years. The folk tales the Grimm brothers committed to paper include many of the most beloved tales now offered to children the world over: "The Golden Goose," "Hansel and Gretel," "Sleeping Beauty," "Snow White," and more. The Grimms' main anthology, *Children's and Household Tales* (1812), also included such well-known characters as Rumpelstiltskin and the Frog King. This key volume of European magical tales proved so welcome among readers that it went through numerous editions. Along with Charles Perrault and Hans Christian Andersen, the brothers Grimm figure among the most important figures in rendering traditional folktales for children.

While the word *fairy* brings to mind images of magical beings with extraordinary abilities, such as the fairy godmother in "Cinderella," not all fairy tales involve such supernatural elements. The term *fairy tale* is now used to describe a whole range of children's stories that may or may not have fairies. In fact, most of the best known known fairy tales do not. Examples include "Rapunzel," "The Three Little Pigs," and "Goldilocks and the Three Bears."

From "The Princess and the Pea" to "Jack and the Beanstalk," fairy tales are among the most widely told—and retold—folktales in America.

See also: ANDERSEN, HANS CHRISTIAN; "BEAUTY AND THE BEAST"; CHILDREN'S FOLKLORE; FABLES; "CINDERELLA"; "EMPEROR'S NEW CLOTHES, THE"; FOLKTALES; FROG PRINCE/FROG KING; "GOLDEN GOOSE, THE"; "THREE BEARS, GOLDILOCKS AND THE"; "HANSEL AND GRETEL"; "JACK AND THE BEANSTALK"; MYTHS, FOLK; NURSERY RHYMES; "PRINCESS AND THE PEA, THE"; "RAPUNZEL"; "RED RIDING HOOD, LITTLE"; "RUMPELSTILTSKIN"; "SLEEPING BEAUTY"; "SNOW WHITE"; "THREE BILLY GOATS GRUFF, THE"; "THREE LITTLE PIGS, THE."

For Further Reading:

Bettelheim, Bruno. *The Uses of Enchantment: The Meaning and Importance of Fairy Tales.* New York: Knopf, 1976.

Bottigheimer, Ruth, ed. *Fairy Tales and Society: Illusion, Allusion, and Paradigm.* Philadelphia: University of Pennsylvania Press, 1986.

Hand, Wayland. "European Fairy Lore in the New World," *Folklore* 92 (1981): 141–148.

Lindahl, Carl, ed. *Perspectives on the Jack Tales and Other North American Märchen.* Bloomington: Folklore Institute/Indiana University, 2001.

Narváez, Peter, ed. *The Good People: New Fairylore Essays.* New York: Garland, 1991.

Scieszka, Jon, and Lane Smith. *The Stinky Cheese Man and Other Fairly Stupid Tales.* New York: Viking, 1992.

Wolf, Joan. *The Beanstalk and Beyond: Developing Critical Thinking through Fairy Tales.* Englewood, Colo.: Teacher Ideas Press, 1997.

Zipes, Jack. *The Oxford Companion to Fairy Tales.* New York: Oxford University Press, 2000.

fakelore This term, coined in 1950 by the noted American folklorist Richard M. Dorson, had its origins in a concern for the rigor and authenticity of folklore books published in the 1940s.

In his writings on the subject, including *American Folklore and the Historian* and *Folklore and Fakelore: Essays toward a Discipline of Folk Studies*, Dorson describes his coining of the term *fakelore* as a response to what he considered the uncritical and irresponsible methods he saw emerging in anthologies and collections designed to cash in on the post–World War I enthusiasm for tales of American national identity.

He deemed such works frivolous and unduly commercial. Moreover, Dorson contended that editors, including otherwise noteworthy academics, were engaged in publishing works that did not uphold standards associated with field collection. The result was wide circulation of flawed, spurious, or even synthetic content under the guise of genuine folklore.

Whether rewriting the tales others collected or contriving heroic figures such as Joe Magarac and Febold Feboldson, fakelorists were exploiting the public interest in the nation's heritage by disseminating sentimental, sanitized, or ersatz tales. Dorson's objections had their basis in the need for folklore publications to meet usual academic standards of integrity, as well as additional ethical obligations researchers incur when presenting the testimony of cultural informants contacted through work in the field.

See also: BABE THE BLUE OX; BUNYAN, PAUL; CHAPMAN, JOHN (JOHNNY APPLESEED); ETHICS IN FOLKLORE; FEBOLDSON, FEBOLD; FOLKLORE IN EVERYDAY LIFE; FOLKLORISM; HENRY, JOHN; MAGARAC, JOE; OCCUPATIONAL FOLKLORE; PECOS BILL; POPLORE; SMITH, WINDWAGON; STYRON, WILLIAM; TERMS.

For Further Reading:

Bluestein, Gene. *Poplore: Folk and Pop in American Culture*. Amherst: University of Massachusetts Press, 1994.

Dorson, Richard M. *Folklore and Fakelore: Essays toward a Discipline of Folk Studies*. Cambridge, Mass.: Harvard University Press, 1976.

Fox, William S. "Folklore and Fakelore: Some Sociological Considerations," *Journal of the Folklore Institute* 17 (1980): 244–261.

Riley, Sam G. "A Search for the Cultural Bigfoot: Folklore or Fakelore?" *Journal of Popular Culture* 10 (1976): 377–387.

Sullenberger, Tom. "Ajax Meets the Jolly Green Giant: Some Observations on the Use of Folklore and Myth in American Mass Marketing," *Journal of American Folklore* 87, no. 343 (winter 1974): 53–65.

family folklore   Family folklore is one of the most pervasive forms of American tradition, as it can be found in every household and era.

Every family has its own traditions, customs, and rituals. These practices, along with understanding of them, bind relatives to one another and reinforce those connections over time. Family folklore begins with a working definition of who may be considered a member of the family unit. While it may be a straightforward matter who one's blood relatives are, the circumstances of contemporary social relations make the definition of family more difficult to assume. With families of divorce, blended families, and families of choice more common than ever in America, each family unit determines its membership.

Within virtually every family exists a set of rules, whether explicit or implicit, setting out the expectations of conduct for members. Sometimes described as house rules or ground rules, these requirements help a family thrive and live harmoniously. Family rules can address such matters as privacy, loyalty, honesty, and honor. A family's rules often embed notions of child rearing, morality, and civility. These rules can also help establish the power dynamic within a family, including intergenerationally.

Foodways within families are similarly widespread aspects of family lore. Every aspect of food preparation, presentation, and consumption can help summon family memories and cultural traditions. Although American foodways associated with long-held traditions such as holidays and formal occasions such as weddings may come first to mind in this regard, scholars of foodways take equal note of the less formal and everyday ways in which food and meals communicate values, connections, and symbolic meanings.

Foodways analysts collect the lore surrounding food's service, customs in its fashioning from ingredients, procedures for its consumption, and understandings surrounding food's power to suggest shared identity in the lives of families and communities. While foodways cannot be separated entirely from other cultural practices, such as conversation and song, which often accompany the enjoyment of food, they represent a growing area of interest among students of family folklore who find themselves intrigued by the intricacies of food behavior. Although some foodways are common in given cultural groups such as members of a particular immigrant population, others are highly specific to an individual family. These customs include family recipes, idiosyncratic details of holiday observance (such as permitting the birthday girl or boy to choose a favorite dish for dinner), and practices for ritual occasions (such as bar mitzvahs and bat mitzvahs, anniversaries, and weddings) passed down from one generation to the next.

Another element of family folklore, and one of the most celebrated ones, is photography. When fires and other disasters threaten a family home, the first artifact many Americans seek to retrieve is the family photo collection. Photographs may act as visual cues to the persons connected with those images; that is, they frequently encourage an intimate viewer to engage in a dialogue specifically corresponding to the imagery. Additionally, pictures may serve as a catalyst to viewer-listener sharing of a visual narrative, as is common in the ritual act of presenting the contents of a family album. Without such organization, as years pass family photographs risk becoming a pedestrian and meaning-devoid collection of depictions of persons and their circumstances, artifacts whose specific impor-

tance resides in their function within social and historical memory. In this sense, the study of photographs concerns itself with the history of ordinary life. Once the hand camera freed photographers of some of the costly and cumbersome tripods and flash units once required, more travel and quicker exposures became possible. This revolution in technology had an impact on both the photographic subjects and the manner of their presentation. Pictures became affordable, and plentiful, and so less formal and posed. Scholars from Marianne Hirsch to Jerald Maddox approach home-mode photography as a folk medium, concerned more with document than technology or high art.

Whatever the form it takes, from house rules to home-mode photography, family folklore helps codify family identity and build a legacy for future family members.

See also: ANNIVERSARIES; BIRTHDAYS; CHILDREN'S FOLKLORE; COURTSHIP/DATING FOLKLORE; DEATH; FATHER'S DAY; FOLKLORE IN EVERYDAY LIFE; FOOD/FOODWAYS; GRANDPARENTS DAY; HOLIDAYS/OBSERVANCES; MATERIAL CULTURE; MOTHER'S DAY; PHOTOGRAPHY, FOLK; WEDDING/MARRIAGE FOLKLORE.

For Further Reading:

Baker, Holly Cutting, Amy Kotkin, and Margaret Yocom. *Family Folklore: Interviewing Guide and Questionnaire.* Washington, D.C.: Smithsonian Institution, 1978.

Boatright, Mody, ed. *The Family Saga and Other Phases of American Folklore.* Urbana: University of Illinois Press, 1958.

Cutting Baker, Holly, Amy J. Kotkin, and Margaret Yocum. *Family Folklore: Interviewing Guide and Questionnaire.* Washington, D.C.: Smithsonian Institution, 1976.

Danielson, Larry. "Family Folklore Studies 1994," *Southern Folklore* 51, no. 1 (1994): 11–16.

Frederick, Charles R. "Family Folklore." In *The Emergence of Folklore in Everyday Life: A Field Guide and Sourcebook,* edited by George H. Schoemaker, 171–173. Bloomington, Ind.: Trickster Press, 1990.

Gillis, John R. *A World of Their Own Making: Myth, Ritual, and the Quest for Family Values.* Cambridge, Mass.: Harvard University Press, 1996.

Hanson, Debbie A. "Transmission by Customary Subscription: Popular Women's Magazine and Family Folklore," *Southern Folklore* 51, no. 1 (1994): 49–60.

Miller, Kim. "All in the Family: Family Folklore, Objectivity, and Self-Censorship," *Western Folklore* 56, nos. 3–4 (1997): 331–345.

Pleck, Elizabeth H. *Celebrating the Family: Ethnicity, Consumer Culture, and Family Rituals.* Cambridge, Mass.: Harvard University Press, 2000.

Stone, Elizabeth. *Black Sheep and Kissing Cousins: How Our Family Stories Shape Us.* New York: Times Books, 1988.

Zeitlin, Steven J., Amy J. Kotlin, and Holly Cutting Baker. *A Celebration of American Family Folklore: Tales and Traditions from the Smithsonian Collection.* New York: Pantheon, 1982.

farming See Agee, James; Chavez, César Estrada; Depression, the Great; Joad, Tom; occupational folklore; Steinbeck, John.

Father's Day Father's Day is a holiday that follows Mother's Day, both in terms of chronology of origin and in the sequence on the calendar each year. As for many holidays, its beginnings are somewhat unclear, and more than one name and locality have been credited with its design. Around 1900, there appear to have been several local movements toward declaration of a day to honor America's fathers, including efforts in Illinois and West Virginia. Perhaps the most widely known among these efforts, whether or not it was truly the first, was spearheaded by Washington State's Sonora Louise Smart Dodd. As the story goes, a Mother's Day sermon inspired Dodd to build and promote an equivalent holiday for fathers. Dodd sought to pay formal tribute to fathers, especially her own. William Jackson Smart, a Civil War veteran, raised Dodd, along with five other children, on a Spokane farm after the death of his wife during childbirth. In 1910, Spokane, Washington, celebrated the holiday on the third Sunday in June, the birth month of Dodd's beloved father. At that time, Dodd sought to establish the custom of Father's Day celebrants' wearing a red rose to thank a living father, and a white rose to honor a deceased one.

Formal designation of Father's Day as a holiday in the United States took time. From Spokane, the celebration spread through Washington State. At that point, several states appear to have been marking Father's Day. In 1916, President Woodrow Wilson signaled public approval for the concept, and in 1924, President Coolidge encouraged states to hold their own observances. It was not until 1966 that President Lyndon Johnson made the third Sunday in June a national father's holiday by annual presidential proclamation, and not until 1972 that President Nixon made June's third Sunday a permanent holiday like its counterpart, Mother's Day. Now other countries, such as Canada and the United Kingdom, annually devote this same day to appreciation of fathers.

Customs surrounding this holiday are few, but cards, gifts, and special meals are usual tributes. The single most traditional gift for the day is a necktie. Indeed, this present is so strongly associated with Father's Day that one frequently encounters Father's Day cards and cakes decorated to resemble dress shirts worn with ties. While fathers remain the focus, anyone who plays a fatherly role may be celebrated on this occasion each year, as sons and daughters, whether children or adults, offer their compliments and thanks.

See also: Civil War; family folklore; Grandparents Day; holidays/observances; Mother's Day; Northwestern regional folklore.

For Further Reading:

Cohen, Hennig, and Tristram Potter Coffin, eds. *The Folklore of American Holidays.* Detroit: Gale, 1987.

McCann, Jim, and Jeanne Benedict. *Celebrations: A Joyous Guide to the Holidays from Past to Present.* New York: HPBooks/Penguin, 2001.

Meyers, Robert. *Celebrations: The Complete Book of American Holidays.* Garden City, N.Y.: Doubleday, 1972.

Santino, Jack. *All around the Year: Holidays and Celebrations in American Life.* Urbana: University of Illinois Press, 1994.

Father Time   See NEW YEAR'S EVE/DAY.

Faulkner, William (1897–1962)   William Faulkner's writing has come to be closely associated with the region in which so many of his stories are set, the American South.

The author was born William Cuthbert Faulkner in New Albany, Mississippi, on September 25, 1897. In portraying the South, Faulkner devoted considerable energy to its folklore. These elements not only set the climate for his writing, but added a layer of suggestions made through folk songs, poetry, and legends. By rendering folk speech and lore within his poetry and prose, Faulkner afforded a wide audience the opportunity to hear credibly rendered voices of the American South.

Faulkner was a prolific writer and worked across literary genres throughout his career. Early on, most of his energy went to poetry, but he later turned to the fiction for which he is now better known. Among his most famous novels are *The Sound and the Fury* (1929), *Absalom! Absalom!* (1936), *Light in August* (1932), and *As I Lay Dying* (1930). Throughout his life, Faulkner also produced short stories, including such frequently anthologized examples as "A Rose for Emily" and "The Bear."

Faulkner's literary landscape is noteworthy for his creation of a fictional Southern locale, Yoknapatawpha County, Mississippi, where many of his tales unfold. By creating a mythical setting for his Southern tales, Faulkner can allude to the region's characteristics without being limited by them. That is, he can make the folklore elements recognizably Southern, while avoiding the specificity of an actual cultural and geographical reference point. In some respects, Yoknapatawpha resembles the place where Faulkner grew up, Oxford, Mississippi.

Faulkner's birth near the end of the 19th century and in the Deep South meant that he came of age in a time when the region was still recovering from the Civil War and the conflicts precipitating it. During this era in history, the American South had to contend with the aftermath of a bitter loss, and Faulkner seemed fascinated by the ways that reckoning took shape. His writings explore the dark side of Southern culture, as well as of human nature. The effect, both socially and psychologically, is that of a fire left to smolder unattended. Flash points spark everywhere, from race relations to gender roles, economics to politics. In Faulkner's fictional world, all the layers of both individual and collective consciousness bear exploration. Within that context, folklore forms both the expression and the encryption of those unresolved conflicts that plague Faulkner's characters and their communities. All the enmity, bigotry, and self-doubt that characterized the worst parts of the era of Reconstruction surface in Faulkner's tales. Usually mapped over the lives of specific families, these dramas prove to be stories told in generations as much as by chapters. His work draws much of its energy from the historic tensions that Southerners experienced in the years following the Civil War.

Faulkner was that curious combination of aspects as an author; in literary terms, he was an internationally attuned modernist, while culturally, he seemed preoccupied with a region and its traditions. As a result, his works often evoke the internal experience of human consciousness, with all its impulses and misgivings, bridging the local and the global. In so doing, his writing tends toward the ample and often employs techniques such as stream-of-consciousness writing. Faulkner's prose tends so much toward the character-driven, psychologically shaped, and long-winded that some have caricatured these attributes in his work. In fact, in an annual write-alike contest, contestants write in the manner of Faulkner in hopes of winning the chance to read their work aloud at that year's Faulkner and

Yoknapatawpha Conference at the University of Mississippi. Nonetheless, for his achievements as a writer, Faulkner received many literary accolades, including the Nobel Prize, prior to his death in 1962 in his native Mississippi.

By directing readers to the history and culture of the postbellum American South, Faulkner characterized a fictional world fraught with the legacies of U.S. slavery and the Civil War.

See also: CIVIL WAR; CLEMENS, SAMUEL LANGHORNE; FOLKLORE IN AMERICAN LITERATURE; REGION, FOLK; SLAVERY; SOUTHERN REGIONAL FOLKLORE.

For Further Reading:

Boswell, George W. "The Legendary Background in Faulkner's Work," *Mississippi Folklore Register* 21, nos. 1–2 (spring–fall 1987): 29–39.

Flanagan, James T. "The Mythic Background of Faulkner's Horse Imagery," *North Carolina Folklore Journal* 13, nos. 1–2 (1965): 135–145.

Hoffman, Daniel. *Faulkner's Country Matters: Folklore and Fable in Yoknapatawpha.* Baton Rouge: Louisiana State University Press, 1989.

McHaney, Thomas L. "What Faulkner Learned from the Tall Tale." In *Faulkner and Humor: Faulkner and Yoknapatawpha*, edited by Doreen Fowler and Ann J. Abadie, 110–135. Jackson: University Press of Mississippi, 1986.

Milledge, Luetta Upshur. "Light Eternal: An Analysis of Some Folkloristic Elements in Faulkner's *Go Down Moses*," *Tennessee Folklore Society Bulletin* 29 (1963): 86–93.

Montenyohl, Eric L. "Folklore and Faulkner: Toward an Expansion of the Relations of Folklore and Literature," *Motif: International Review of Research in Folklore & Literature* 7 (February 1989): 1, 4–6.

Peavy, Charles. "Faulkner's Use of Folklore in *The Sound and the Fury*," *Journal of American Folklore* 79, no. 313 (summer 1966): 437–447.

Feboldson, Febold (legendary) Febold

Feboldson is a legendary Nebraska plainsman featured in collections of American and Canadian folktales.

In the available accounts, Feboldson appears as a Scandinavian-American farmer. The authenticity of this Nebraska plainsman as occupational hero is somewhat suspect. Some believe Feboldson was a mythic figure inspired by an actual historic personage, Olaf Berstrom, a Swedish immigrant whose deeds appeared in newspapers and comics. Others contend that Feboldson is strictly an invention, devised by writers with the Gothenberg (Nebraska) *Times*, with the central force usually identified as the *Times* employee Paul Beath. If this was the case, the circumstances of Feboldson's origin would cast the stories of this figure as fakelore rather than folklore, more the product of print culture than oral tradition.

In any case, Febold Feboldson functions as a folk hero, although one far less known than such figures as Paul Bunyan or John "Johnny Appleseed" Chapman. As with those icons, Feboldson figures within the history of American tall tales. Most Feboldson stories are related to his work as a farmer. For instance, in one tale, Feboldson attaches an eagle-sized bee to his plow, with the thought that the insect will guide his plow on a straight path, or "bee line." The resulting plowline corresponds to the state border of Kansas and Nebraska. In another story, he buries the fog beneath the Earth so that farmers can conduct their work under clear skies. He is also credited with inventing, or being present at the spontaneous occurrence of, the first popcorn ball.

Whether authentic or synthetic, the figure of Febold Feboldson can be associated with many entertaining tales of agriculture during the settler times in the American Midwest.

See also: BUNYAN, PAUL; CHAPMAN, JOHN (JOHNNY APPLESEED); FAKELORE; FOLK HEROES/ LEGENDARY FIGURES; FOLKTALES; MIDWESTERN REGIONAL FOLKLORE; OCCUPATIONAL FOLKLORE; REGION, FOLK.

For Further Reading:

Beath, Paul. *Febold Feboldson: Tall Tales from the Great Plains.* Lincoln: University of Nebraska Press, 1948.

Botkin, Benjamin A., ed. *A Treasury of American Folklore*. New York: Crown, 1944.

Coffin, Tristram Potter, and Hennig Cohen, eds. *The Parade of Heroes: Legendary Figures in American Lore*. Garden City, N.Y.: Anchor Press/Doubleday, 1978.

Leach, Maria, ed. *Funk and Wagnall's Standard Dictionary of Folklore, Mythology, and Legend*. London: New English Library, 1975.

Osborne, Mary Pope. *American Tall Tales*. New York: Knopf, 1991.

festivals, folklore   Of all the presentations of American folklore, festivals are likely the most widely attended events.

Some festivals are organic to a population and so serve purposes internal to that particular group. Others are approached as educational, spectatorial, or promotional and so are geared toward including a wide spectrum of participants and/or attendees. These festivals tend to be arranged as popular entertainments, emphasizing recreation and tourism.

As symbolic events, festivals can involve everything from enactments associated with holidays to performance-based rituals of other kinds. There is a sense in which even such familiar events as Mardi Gras, May Day festivals, Halloween trick or treating, and rodeos could be regarded as folk festivals. These occasions involve carnivals, concerts, dances, pageants, parades, feasts, or other forms of festivity associated with traditions in American social life and customs.

The folklife movement in the United States both signaled and stimulated a popular appetite for displays of traditional culture and ways of life. Even those who would not venture to a museum or historical society can often be tempted by a one-time or annual opportunity to sample folk cultural expression. Festivals tend to focus public attention on the vitality of American folk traditions and typically engage those who attend in a celebration of those practices. Folk music festivals are popular, but so are events at which folk arts, crafts, dance, and foodways are featured. Within these informal venues, people may experience aspects of other cultures, generally without having to leave their home regions or comfort zones.

Two festivals with national visibility, which exemplify spectacles of American folklore, are the American Folk Song Festival and the Festival of American Folklore. These national folk festivals are examples of public sector folklore, conducted as a form of outreach to engage the widest possible audience for American folkways and traditions. The Festival of American Folklore is sponsored by the Smithsonian Institution and takes place in Washington, D.C., each year since 1967. It is accompanied by public displays arranged on the Mall for visitors to the festival. The American Folk Song Festival features an annual concert at which a wide range of performances of traditional music from different areas, populations, and musical genres may be heard. More local versions of this event can be found nationwide, from Philadelphia, Pennsylvania, to Portland, Oregon. The folk revival of the 1960s and 1970s increased the interest in such showcases for folk music and folk-influenced performance.

Folk festivals can serve to celebrate and underscore commonality or diversity of cultural understandings, convictions, and identities. In addition, festivals satisfy otherwise unmet needs by suspending ordinary activities and creating a time of special possibilities, as for members of a democratic society to play at aristocratic titles, such as "Rhubarb Princess" or "Strawberry Queen."

See also: DRAMA, FOLK; ETHNICITY; FOLKLORE OF EVERYDAY LIFE; FOOD/FOODWAYS; HALLOWEEN/ALL HALLOWS' EVE; HOLIDAYS/OBSERVANCES; LIVING HISTORY MUSEUMS; MARDI GRAS; MAY DAY; MUSEUMS, FOLK; MUSIC, FOLK; PARADES; PUBLIC FOLKLORE; RODEO; SMITHSONIAN INSTITUTION.

For Further Reading:
Bauman, Richard, ed. *Folklore, Cultural Performances, and Popular Entertainments: A Commu-*

nications-Centered Handbook. New York: Oxford University Press, 1992.

Bauman, Richard, and Roger Abrahams, eds. *"And Other Neighborly Names": Social Process and Cultural Image in Texas Folklore*. Austin: University of Texas Press, 1981.

Bauman, Richard, Patricia Sawin, and Inta Gale Carpenter. *Reflections on the Folklife Festival: An Ethnography of Participant Experience*. Indiana University Special Publications of the Folklore Institute, no. 2. Bloomington: Indiana University Press, 1992.

Camp, Charles, and Timothy Lloyd. "Six Reasons Not to Produce Folk Festivals," *Kentucky Folklore Record* 26 (1980): 1–2, 67–74.

Carlson, Barbara. *Food Festivals: Eating Your Way from Coast to Coast*. Detroit: Invisible Ink Press, 1997.

Gillespie, Angus. "Folk Festival and Festival Folk in Twentieth-Century America." In *Time out of Time: Essays on the Festival*, edited by Alessandro Falassi, 152–161. Albuquerque: University of New Mexico Press, 1987.

Hill, Kathleen Thompson. *Festivals USA*. New York: Wiley, 1988.

Manning, Frank, ed. *The Celebration of Society*. Bowling Green, Ohio: Bowling Green State University Popular Press, 1983.

Merin, Jennifer, with Elizabeth B. Burdick. *International Directory of Theatre, Dance and Folklore Festivals: A Project of the International Theatre Institute of the United States*. Westport, Conn.: Greenwood Press, 1979.

Peterson, Betsy, ed. *The Changing Faces of Tradition: A Report on the Folk and Traditional Arts in the United States*. Washington, D.C.: National Endowment for the Arts, 1996.

Schoemaker, George H., ed. *The Emergence of Folklore in Everyday Life: A Fieldguide and Sourcebook*. Bloomington, Ind.: Trickster Press, 1990.

Wasserman, Paul, and Edmond L. Appelbaum, eds. *Festivals Sourcebook*. Detroit: Gale Research, 1984.

West, Amanda. *Main Street Festivals: Traditional and Unique Events on America's Main Events*. New York: Wiley, 1998.

fieldwork, folklore   Fieldwork is the process by which folklorists apply their concepts and put their theories of the discipline to the test.

That is, most folklorists do more than utilize existing archives of source material or collections of folklore gathered by other scholars. Through observation, research, and documentation, they also generate their own folk material. Within folklore studies, there are various theories and methods for the conduct of this work. Despite these wide variations, some characteristics are inherent in most, if not all, folklore fieldwork.

Most folklorists learn to do original research in which they collect folklore and explore its context. In doing so, they seek to document their findings not only for their own use, but for the benefit of other researchers. Such documentation can take numerous forms, including tape recording, photography, videotaping, and ethnography. In this way, the phenomenon undergoing folklore study can be preserved for further and future reference. It can also provide corroboration for interpretations and analyses resulting from fieldwork.

Because the majority of fieldwork in this discipline involves interaction with live informants, folklorists must devote thorough consideration to the ethics of their research with human subjects. Care is taken to prevent unnecessary interference in a population under study, distortion of its ways and customs, or damage to its members. Respect, forthrightness, and reciprocity are the key guidelines for those conducting fieldwork of this kind. For example, improvements in recording technology have raised the expectations and standards for full and accurate transcription of informant speech.

Fieldwork in folklore may finds its focus in a traditional form (such as the ballad), a population (such as Anglo Americans), a period (such as since 1945), or some combination thereof. Once the material has been documented, the folklorist uses it to test reasonable hypotheses and arrive at meaningful conclusions. With appropriate consent of participants and records of circumstances of collection, the documents from a field project can be housed in an archive or other facility where the material can be cared for and reviewed by future scholars.

Only by conducting the work of a folklorist in the field, whether the project's scale is grand or small, is it possible to understand the full implications of folklore in action.

See also: DOCUMENTARY; ETHICS IN FOLK-LORE; FOLKLORE OF EVERYDAY LIFE; FOLKLORE STUDIES; FOLKLORISTICS; INSIDER/OUTSIDER; ORAL HISTORY; RESEARCH, FOLKLIFE; TERMS.

For Further Reading:

Bartis, Peter. *Folklife and Fieldwork: A Layman's Introduction to Field Techniques.* Available online. URL: http://www.loc.gov/folklife/fieldwork/index.html. Accessed March 10, 2006.

Georges, Robert A., and Michael Owen Jones. *People Studying People: The Human Element in Fieldwork.* Berkeley: University of California Press, 1980.

Goldstein, Kenneth S. *A Guide for Fieldworkers in Folklore.* Hatboro, Pa.: Folklore Associates, 1964.

Jackson, Bruce, and Edward D. Ives, eds. *The World Observed: Reflections on the Fieldwork Process.* Urbana: University of Illinois Press, 1996.

Lindahl, Carl, J. Sanford Rikoon, and Elaine J. Lawless. *A Basic Guide to Fieldwork for Beginning Folklore Students.* Folklore Publication Group Monograph Series, no. 7. Bloomington: University of Indiana Press, 1979.

Schoemaker, George H., ed. *The Emergence of Folklore in Everyday Life: A Fieldguide and Sourcebook.* Bloomington, Ind.: Trickster Press, 1990.

Filipino-American folklore Filipino American folklore consists of the traditions and customs of immigrants to the United States from the Philippines, as well as those born in America of Filipino descent.

Immigration to the United States from the Philippines has occurred since the early 20th century. The first arrived to attend institutions of higher education, to work on the sugar plantations of Hawaii, or to labor in other forms of agriculture on the Pacific coast.

Filipino folklore takes many forms. Verbal lore includes stories and comic anecdotes about migrant Filipino laborers and their misadventures or mistreatment by others. Filipino Americans also have an active festival culture, celebrating their heritage or special occasions with feasts, music, dancing, and parades. Foodways include rice dishes and boiled meats, such as pork or chicken, prepared with a seasoned soy sauce.

Organizations dedicated to the preservation and study of Filipino-American culture include Seattle, Washington's, Filipino American National Historical Society. Major collections of Filipino-American cultural material include Oakland, California's Oakland Museum and Honolulu, Hawaii's Social Science Research Institute.

Through their maintenance of traditions and folkways, Filipino Americans remain connected to their cultural heritage.

See also: CULTURAL GROUPS; ETHNICITY; FOOD/FOODWAYS; IMMIGRATION AND FOLK-LORE.

For Further Reading:

Almirol, Ewin. *Ethnic Identity and Social Negotiation: A Study of Filipino Communities.* New York: AMS, 1985.

Bautista, Veltisezar. *The Filipino Americans (1763–Present): Their History, Culture, and Traditions.* 2d ed. Naperville, Ill.: Bookhaus, 2002.

Cordova, Fred. *Filipinos: Forgotten Asian Americans: A Pictorial Essay, 1763–c. 1963.* Dubuque, Iowa: Kendall/Hunt, 1983.

Hart, Donn Vorhis. *Riddles in Filipino Folklore: An Anthropological Analysis.* Syracuse, N.Y.: Syracuse University Press, 1964.

Meñez, Herminia Quimpo. *Explorations in Philippine Folklore.* Quezon City: Ateneo de Manila University Press, 1996.

———. *Folk Communication among Filipinos in California.* New York: Arno Press, 1980.

Root, Maria, ed. *Filipino Americans: Transformation and Identity.* Thousand Oaks, Calif.: Sage, 1997.

Takaki, Ron. *Strangers from a Different Shore: A History of Asian Americans.* New York: Penguin Books, 1989.

Fink, Mike (c. 1775–1823)   Mike Fink is the legendary figure of a 19th-century Mississippi, Missouri, and Ohio river keelboat man.

As do other characters related to America's occupational lore, such as Annie Christmas and Old Stormalong, Mike Fink captures the romantic image of America's waterways. Mike Fink stories accomplished in oral lore something parallel to what Samuel Langhorne Clemens's stories did in print and George Caleb Bingham's did in painting—making mythic the great river's history.

Unlike some of the figures featured in America's tall tales, however, Fink appears to have been based upon an actual person. Relatively little is known about the historical figure on which the character of Mike Fink was based, but he appears to have been a 19th-century outdoorsman. As Fink traveled into lore, he took on the larger-than-life qualities that befit folktales. Depending upon which accounts one hears, he is part horse, part alligator, part turtle, and so forth. As with any trickster figure in folklore, Fink was also given to pranks and practical jokes.

He was known for piloting flatbeds south to New Orleans, transporting goods and passengers. Through his adventures, he demonstrated that he was a talented marksman, hunter, and scout. For this reason, he is sometimes compared to figures such as Davy Crockett and Daniel Boone. In addition, however, Mike Fink earned a strong reputation as a fighter, storyteller, and braggart. He emerged as a classic bad man, as wild as the West itself.

As is often the case for legends of occupational lore, the arrival of new technology marked the close of Mike Fink's career. Steamships changed the waterways, and with them Fink's bragging rights.

Although not as widely known as some other American legends, Mike Fink continues to appear in children's books and collections of American folktales as the last of the great boatmen.

See also: Boone, Daniel; Christmas, Annie; Clemens, Samuel Langhorne; Crockett, Davy; folk heroes/legendary figures; folklore in American literature; frontier; Stormalong, Old; trickster; Western regional folklore; Whirlwind, Sally Ann Thunder Ann.

For Further Reading:
Blair, Walter, and Franklin Meine. *Half Horse, Half Alligator: The Growth of the Mike Fink Legend.* New York: Arno Press, 1956.

Blair, Walter, and Franklin Meine. *Mike Fink: King of Mississippi Keelboatmen.* New York: H. Holt, 1933.

Dorson, Richard. *American Folklore.* Chicago: University of Chicago Press, 1959.

Kellogg, Steven. *Mike Fink: A Tall Tale.* New York: Morrow, 1992.

Leeming, David, and Jake Page. *Myths, Legends, and Folktales of America: An Anthology.* New York: Oxford University Press, 1999.

Finn, Huck   See Clemens, Samuel Langhorne; folklore in American literature.

Finnish-American folklore   Finnish-American folklore involves the traditions and customs of immigrants to the United States from Finland and portions of Norway, Russia, and Sweden in which Finnish is spoken. It also describes the lore of persons born in America with these ancestries.

Finnish immigration to the United States has occurred since the 17th century. While they settled throughout the nation, some of the densest concentrations of population occurred in the American Midwest, where Finnish immigrants could practice some of the forms of life and work associated with an agricultural economy. Folklorists have been collecting verbal lore of Finnish America since at least the 1920s, at which time the Works Progress Administration interviewed many members of this population for documentary purposes.

In addition to observing some of the usual American holidays, Finnish Americans retain some holiday tradition of their own. For example, on December 6 each year, many Finnish Americans join people in their homeland by celebrating Finnish Independence Day. Furthermore, in at least one instance, Finnish Americans devised a holiday that is original to them, without precedent in Finland or America. Taking cues from the role Saint Patrick's Day plays in the lives of Irish Americans, Finnish Americans developed a holiday called Saint Urho's Day. This occasion, observed on March 16 each year, honors the saint who has been credited with ridding Finland of grasshoppers.

Perhaps the most widely recognized custom of Finnish Americans is their use of the sauna, or steam bath. It is also one of the most enduring elements of Finnish-American folk culture. This method has been used to maintain health or, in a form of folk medicine, to treat minor illnesses. Others outside the Finnish-American population have also embraced the use of saunas for purposes of recreation and relaxation.

Organizations created to promote study and philanthropy concerning Finnish-American culture include Seattle, Washington's Finlandia Foundation and Fitchburg, Massachusetts's, Finnish American League for Democracy. Major collections of Finnish-American cultural material are available to researchers at Suomi College's Finnish American Heritage Center, the Finnish-American Historical Society of the West, and the University of Minnesota's Immigration History Research Center, located in Hancock, Michigan; Portland, Oregon; and Saint Paul, Minnesota, respectively.

Through folklore, both that transplanted and that developed since arrival in the United States, Finnish Americans nurture a sense of cultural identity and pride.

See also: CULTURAL GROUPS; HOLIDAYS/ OBSERVANCES; IMMIGRATION AND FOLKLORE; MEDICINE, FOLK; SAINT PATRICK'S DAY.

For Further Reading:

Danielson, Larry, ed. *Folklore and Ethnicity*. Los Angeles: California Folklore Society, 1977.

Dorson, Richard. *Bloodstoppers and Bearwalkers: Folk Traditions of the Upper Peninsula*. Cambridge, Mass.: Harvard University Press, 1952.

———. "Dialect Stories of the Upper Peninsula: A New Form of American Folklore," *Journal of American Folklore* 61, no. 240 (spring 1948): 113–150.

Hoglund, A. William. *Finnish Immigrants in America, 1880–1920*. Madison: University of Wisconsin Press, 1960.

Jarvenpa, Robert. "Visual Expression in Finnish-American Ethnic Slurs," *Journal of American Folklore* 89, no. 351 (winter 1976): 90–91.

Lockwood, Yvonne Hiipakka. "The Sauna: An Expression of Finnish-American Identity," *Western Folklore* 36 (1977): 71–84.

Ross, Carl. *The Finn Factor in American Labor, Culture, and Society*. New York Mills, Minn.: Parta, 1977.

Ross, Carl, and K. Marianne Wargelin Brown, eds. *Women Who Dared: The History of Finnish American Women*. Saint Paul: Immigration History Research Center/University of Minnesota, 1986.

Stern, Steven, and Allan Cicala. *Creative Ethnicity*. Logan: Utah State University Press, 1991.

fish See ANIMALS; APRIL FOOL'S DAY; FOOD/ FOODWAYS.

fishing folklore See MARITIME FOLKLORE; OCCUPATIONAL FOLKLORE.

Flag Day On August 3, 1949, U.S. President Harry Truman signed a bill formally designating

June 14 each year as Flag Day. This civic holiday pays tribute to one of America's most prominent symbols, its national flag. A great deal of folklore surrounds the American flag, from tales of its design by George Washington, to its legendary stitching by Betsy Ross, to its featured role within the lyrics of Francis Scott Key's "Star-Spangled Banner," the song that now stands as our national anthem. Flag Day observances first began informally in 1877, with the centennial of the June 14, 1777, Flag Resolution by the Continental Congress. Public display of the "stars and stripes," or "Old Glory," as the U.S. flag came to be known, remains the central act of observance on this day.

American public schools began to fly the flag and offer programs to mark Flag Day during the later half of the 19th century. Children participated in flag drills, patriotic exercises, and recitation of verses suitable to the occasion. By the 1890s, it became a daily practice for schoolchildren to recognize the flag each morning with the Pledge of Allegiance. Class members would stand, place their right hand over their heart, and recite the pledge. The text of this pledge has shifted several times over the years but has, since President Eisenhower's 1954 addition of "under God," read as follows: "I pledge allegiance to the flag of the United States of America and to the Republic for which it stands, one Nation under God, indivisible, with liberty and justice for all."

The holiday attempts to educate youth about proper flag display, care, and etiquette. The nation has identified standards of respect and required procedures for the flag's indoor and outdoor display, parading, raising and lowering, salute, and use of a half-staff flag position when a tragedy, such as a president's death, occurs.

Flag Day is the time each year when organizations such as the American Legion hold appropriate ceremonies for those wishing to retire worn flags from service. Although flags figure prominently within the observances of many national holidays, Flag Day directs attention to the flag itself as the national emblem of democracy.

See also: DEATH; HOLIDAYS/OBSERVANCES; PLEDGE OF ALLEGIANCE; REVOLUTIONARY WAR; ROSS, BETSY; WASHINGTON, GEORGE.

For Further Reading:
Cohen, Hennig, and Tristram Potter Coffin, eds. *The Folklore of American Holidays.* Detroit: Gale, 1987.
Litwicki, Ellen M. *America's Public Holidays: 1865–1920.* Washington, D.C.: Smithsonian Institution Press, 2000.
Myers, Robert. *Celebrations: The Complete Book of American Holidays.* Garden City, N.Y.: Doubleday, 1972.
Quaife, Milo M., Melvin J. Weig, and Roy E. Appleman. *The History of the United States Flag.* New York: Harper & Row, 1961.
Santino, Jack. *All around the Year: Holidays and Celebrations in American Life.* Urbana: University of Illinois Press, 1994.

flag folklore See FLAG DAY; PLEDGE OF ALLEGIANCE; ROSS, BETSY.

flight Americans have played a prominent role in the history of aviation, and so there is a good deal of folklore surrounding the figures active in pioneering flight.

Most notably, Orville Wright and Wilbur Wright are generally regarded as the first people to fly. More specifically, they were the first to be successful with a controlled flight powered by an engine rather than wind alone. For this achievement, they are considered among the nation's greatest inventors.

The Wrights, with their landmark achievement in 1903, set the scene for other pioneers of aviation. Other famous flyers include Charles Lindbergh and Amelia Mary Earhart. Together with the Wright brothers, these individuals symbolize the nation's progress in technology and transportation and launched aviation as a world-bridging tool for travel.

In honor of the accomplishments of inventors and pilots such as these, Americans devised

National Aviation Day. This lesser-known American holiday has been observed on August 19 ever since a congressional resolution in 1939. The initial impetus for the observance was to honor the Wright brothers and other pioneers of aviation. Consequently, the date selected for the holiday coincides with Orville Wright's birthday.

Today, the groundbreaking contributions of American aviators are widely regarded as the precedent for later triumphs of science and technology, including space travel.

See also: DUNBAR, PAUL LAURENCE; EARHART, AMELIA MARY; FOLKLORE OF EVERYDAY LIFE; HOLIDAYS/OBSERVANCES; LINDBERGH, CHARLES; OCCUPATIONAL FOLKLORE; WRIGHT BROTHERS.

For Further Reading:

Bilstein, Roger. *Flight in America: From the Wrights to the Astronauts.* Baltimore: Johns Hopkins University Press, 2001.

Crouch, Tom. *First Flight: The Wright Brothers and the Invention of the Airplane.* Washington, D.C.: Harpers Ferry Center National Park Service, 2002.

McCurdy, Howard. *Space and the American Imagination.* Washington, D.C.: Smithsonian Institution Press, 1997.

White, Elwood. *Winged Crusade: The Quest for American Aerospace Power.* Colorado Springs, Colo.: United States Air Force Academy, 2003.

Florida folklore   See CLARK, ARIZONA DONNIE (MA BARKER); DISNEY, WALTER ELIAS; GERONIMO; HURSTON, ZORA NEALE; JOHNSON, JAMES WELDON; SOUTHERN REGIONAL FOLKLORE; SPANISH-AMERICAN FOLKLORE.

flowers   Of all the forms of plant lore in the United States, lore related to flowers is probably the most popular.

In addition to the folklore surrounding the medicinal properties of flowers and the customs surrounding gardening, an extensive symbol-ism exists for flowering plants. This enthusiasm reached its peak during the Victorian era, when the "language of flowers" was articulated in etiquette manuals and specialized guides or dictionaries. For the most part, these symbols pertain to romantic situations, current or contemplated, but flowers can communicate wordless messages in a wide range of contexts.

First, there is the meaning associated with the flower in itself. Some of these connotations, often derived from English lore, are obvious from the name of the bloom. An example of such a direct relationship between a flower and its cultural meaning would include the way a bachelor button represents celibacy. Other plant and flower symbolisms are logical, though perhaps not obvious, connections between name and meaning. For instance, bittersweet symbolizes truth. In other cases, the meanings connected to a form of flower are not intuitive, but are so widely known within a culture as to seem evident. Such a message is the way, within flower language, mistletoe says, "Kiss me." Consequently, the traditional meanings must be studied if one is to use flowers effectively and communicate the intended message to a recipient.

Colors of flowers prove important within the language of symbols. For example, daisies and other white flowers typically connote purity and innocence. Red flowers tend toward more passionate connotations. For this reason, it is not sufficient to think only in terms of the flower selection. Its hue must also be considered, for a white tulip and a red tulip send different signals to the recipient, and it is wise to know when a declaration of love might be construed on the basis of a flower's color as well as type.

A familiar example of this nuance is illustrated by the rose, which is available in many shades as well as colors. Each has its own distinct suggestion. Therefore, within the language of flowers, presentation of a rose can signal everything from mourning to desire. Needless to say, such subtleties have resulted in some misunderstandings, particularly in cases when gift givers remain unaware of flower symbolism and choose their gifts on other bases.

Perhaps the height of the use of flower symbolism was in the Victorian era's fondness for "tussie-mussies," or small bouquets that were assembled to convey secret messages between giver and recipient. The combinations and arrangements of flowers, taken together, were designed to speak for themselves.

Additional flower folklore extends beyond the variety and color of the flower to include a host of other factors, each capable of sending an encoded message. Not only the size of flowers, but the way they were grouped or sent could be significant. If offered in person, the position of the flower might matter, as an upward pointing flower is the most hopeful sign. In instances when the flowers are offered in response to an invitation or request, the hand from which the flowers are offered makes a difference. By customs, flowers offered with the right hand suggest an affirmative reply, while those offered with the left hand suggest a negative response.

Today, however, many of these fine points of flower lore have receded, and it is only a vague symbolism of flower form that remains in current gift practices and ceremonial occasions. This may be welcome news for well-meaning suitors who, oblivious to the language of flowers, fail to realize that the blossoms they choose might prove an insult rather than tender tribute to the intended recipient.

See also: CHRISTMAS; COURTING/DATING FOLKLORE; DEATH; FOLKLORE IN EVERYDAY LIFE; GARDENING; HOLIDAYS/OBSERVANCES; LUCK/FORTUNE; MAY DAY; MEDICINE, FOLK; VERNACULAR CULTURE; WEDDING/MARRIAGE FOLKLORE.

For Further Reading:
Chesanow, Jeanné. *Honeysuckle Sipping: The Plant Lore of Childhood*. Camden, Me.: Down East Books, 1987.
Durant, Mary. *Who Named the Daisy? Who Named the Rose? A Roving Dictionary of North American Wildflowers*. New York: Dodd, Mead, 1976.
Lehner, Ernst, and Johanna Lerner. *Folklore and Symbolism of Flowers, Plants, and Trees*. Detroit: Omnigraphics, 1990.
Loy, Susan. *Flowers, the Angels' Alphabet: The Language and Poetry of Flowers with an American Floral Dictionary*. Moneta, Va.: CSL Press, 2001.
Powell, Claire. *The Meaning of Flowers: A Garland of Plant Lore and Symbolism from Popular Custom and Literature*. London: Jupiter Books, 1977.
Sanders, Jack. *The Secrets of Wildflowers: A Delightful Feast of Little-Known Facts, Folklore, and History*. Guilford, Conn.: Lyons Press, 2003.
Seaton, Beverly. *The Language of Flowers: A History*. Charlottesville: University Press of Virginia, 1995.

Floyd, Charles Arthur (Pretty Boy) (1904–1934)   Widely recognized for his prowess as a highway robber, bank robber, and killer, "Pretty Boy" Floyd had a reputation as a friend to the common man that rendered him a somewhat fondly regarded legend among America's so-called bad men.

The outlaw who would gain notoriety with his most famous alias, "Pretty Boy" Floyd, was born Charles Arthur Floyd on February 3, 1904. Floyd arrived as the fourth child in an Oklahoma farm family. As a boy, young Floyd dreamed of figures such as Jesse James. By his midteens, he began to emulate his outlaw heroes of America's "Wild West." Floyd acquired his nickname when a victim in one of his payroll robberies described the culprit to the authorities as a "pretty boy with apple cheeks." To Floyd's considerable dismay, the name stuck, and he carried it throughout his life.

After charming the women of his acquaintance with his looks and wit, Floyd married 16-year-old Ruby Hargraves in 1924. The birth of a son, Charles Dempsey Floyd, followed that same year. Floyd worked as a laborer but entertained notions of more remote regions and prospects. Eventually leaving his family behind, Floyd embarked on a journey that would be dotted with his crimes, a series of actions that ultimately landed him in the penitentiary. By the time Floyd was released on March 7, 1929, he learned that his wife had filed for divorce.

Floyd found a new start, although not a new way of life, in Kansas City, Missouri. By 1930, Floyd had become affiliated with a criminal gang, an association that would result in a 15-year sentence in the Ohio State Penitentiary. Floyd escaped while being transported to prison, only to resume his life of crime while a fugitive.

Over time, Floyd found himself enjoying notoriety. He began to develop a profile as an enemy of the rich and a friend to the poor. He also came to be called "The Phantom of the Ozarks" and "Robin Hood of Oklahoma" for his acts of generosity toward ordinary citizens who had fallen on hard times. Floyd's reputation as a criminal capable of humbling financial institutions and dodging the law endeared him to a Depression era public. Rather than side with the bankers, who were already unpopular among the dust bowl farmers, so many of whom stood to lose their homes to the banks, displaced midwestern farmers or "Okies" began to root for the outlaws, especially one known to leave behind cash and groceries for hungry farm families.

Meanwhile, Floyd tracked down his former wife, who, although remarried and living in Kansas with their son, nonetheless agreed to join him in hiding. They set up housekeeping together in Arkansas, and later in Oklahoma, under an assumed name. Rumors began to threaten their fragile anonymity, however, and Floyd had to leave his wife and son behind once more. Floyd had grown weary of being hunted when on June 17, 1933, an incident in which four Missouri police officers were murdered sealed Floyd's fate.

This event, later known as the "Kansas City Massacre," placed Floyd high among the Federal Bureau of Investigation's (FBI's) arrest priorities. Although there is considerable doubt Floyd was involved in the massacre, his presence in Kansas City that day was enough to implicate him. In his flight from justice, Floyd would continue his criminal activity, and it is believed that

he even joined forces with his fellow gangster John Dillinger for a time. Floyd met his death on October 22, 1934, when he was shot dead while resisting arrest in Ohio. He was returned to Oklahoma, where some 20,000 mourners attended his funeral.

A downtrodden public's enthusiasm for Floyd's bravado ensured that his tale would find many retellings, most notably in a ballad (entitled "Pretty Boy Floyd") composed and performed by the Depression era folk singer Woody Guthrie. Floyd also figures in John Steinbeck's classic novel of the Depression, *The Grapes of Wrath*.

See also: DEPRESSION, THE GREAT; DILLINGER, JOHN; FOLK HEROES/LEGENDARY FIGURES; FOLKLORE IN AMERICAN LITERATURE; JAMES, JESSE; MIDWESTERN REGIONAL FOLKLORE; MUSIC, FOLK; OUTLAWS; OZARKS FOLKLORE; REGION, FOLK; ROBIN HOOD; STEINBECK, JOHN.

For Further Reading:

Bruns, Roger A. *The Bandit Kings: From Jesse James to Pretty Boy Floyd*. New York: Crown, 1995.

Hamilton, Sue L. *Public Enemy Number One: Pretty Boy Floyd (America's Most Wanted)*. New York: Abdo and Daughters, 1989.

King, Jeffery S. *The Life and Death of Pretty Boy Floyd*. Kent, Ohio: Kent State University Press, 1998.

Wallis, Michael. *Pretty Boy: The Life and Times of Charles Arthur Floyd*. New York: St. Martin's Griffin, 1994.

folk art   See ART, FOLK.

folk artifacts   See ARTIFACTS, FOLK.

folk beliefs   See BELIEFS, FOLK.

folk culture   See CULTURE, FOLK.

folk customs   See CUSTOMS, FOLK.

folk drama See DRAMA, FOLK.

folk festivals See FESTIVALS, FOLK.

folk heroes/legendary figures American folklore has a host of memorable characters, both real and imagined.

From Paul Bunyan to Yankee Doodle, these personages surface in stories, songs, and other lore. They reach audiences in ways both instructive and engaging. Their persistence suggests that each is a resonant figure for the people of the United States. If a nation's heroes embody its aspirations, villains portray its fears, and classic tales dramatize its struggles, then America's folk heroes and legendary figures, taken together, reveal a great deal about American history through its lore. It is through the help of these characters, occupying beloved narrative forms such as fables, fairy tales, myths, and tales, that youth enter literacy. In so doing, these readers establish contact with a literary inheritance and cultural legacy shaped to an important extent by folklore.

Whether appearing in children's literature, historical works, or other forms of storytelling, America's folk heroes and legendary figures express the ideals to which the nation's people aspire and, in some cases, the notorious lives they struggle to avoid.

See also: ALGER, HORATIO, JR.; ALLEN, ETHAN; ANANSI; ANTHONY, SUSAN BROWNELL; ATTUCKS, CRISPUS; BARTON, CLARA; BIGFOOT/SASQUATCH; BLOODY MARY; BONNIE AND CLYDE; BOONE, DANIEL; BORDEN, LIZZIE; BRER RABBIT; BROWN, JOHN; BROWN, MARGARET TOBIN (UNSINKABLE MOLLY); BUNYAN, PAUL; CANARY-BURKE, MARTHA (CALAMITY JANE); CAPONE, ALPHONSE GABRIEL (AL); CARSON, KIT; CHAPMAN, JOHN (JOHNNY APPLESEED); CHAVEZ, CÉSAR ESTRADA; CHRISTMAS, ANNIE; CLARK, ARIZONA DONNIE; CODY, WILLIAM F. (BUFFALO BILL); COLUMBUS, CHRISTOPHER; COWBOYS; COYOTE; CRAZY HORSE; CROCKETT, DAVY; CUSTER, GEORGE ARMSTRONG; DEVIL, THE; DILLINGER, JOHN; EARHART, AMELIA MARY; EARP, WYATT BERRY STAMP; EASTER BUNNY; EDISON, THOMAS ALVA; EINSTEIN, ALBERT; FEBOLDSON, FEBOLD; FINK, MIKE; FLOYD, CHARLES ARTHUR (PRETTY BOY); FRANKLIN, BENJAMIN; GERONIMO; HENRY, PATRICK; HIAWATHA; HICKOK, JAMES BUTLER (WILD BILL); HILL, JOE; HORSEMAN, HEADLESS; HOUDINI, HARRY; JAMES, JESSE; JERSEY DEVIL; JOAD, TOM; JONES, JOHN LUTHER (CASEY); JONES, JOHN PAUL; JOSEPH, CHIEF; KILROY; LEWIS, MERIWETHER AND WILLIAM CLARK; LIBERTY, MISS; LINCOLN, ABRAHAM; LOUP-GAROU; MAGARAC, JOE; McCARTY, WILLIAM HENRY (BILLY THE KID); MOSE THE FIREMAN; MOTHER GOOSE; OAKLEY, PHOEBE ANNIE; PARKS, ROSA; PECOS BILL; "PIED PIPER OF HAMELIN, THE"; POCAHONTAS; REMUS, UNCLE; ROBIN HOOD; ROBINSON, JACK ROOSEVELT (JACKIE); ROOSEVELT, THEODORE; ROSS, BETSY; SACAJAWEA; SANTA CLAUS; SEATTLE, CHIEF; SHELLEY, KATE; SMITH, WINDWAGON; STAGOLEE; STANTON, ELIZABETH CADY; STORMALONG, OLD; LONGABAUGH, HARRY (SUNDANCE KID); TAR BABY; TELL, WILLIAM; TOOTH FAIRY; TRUTH, SOJOURNER; TUBMAN, HARRIET; TURNER, NAT; TRICKSTER; UNCLE SAM; VAN WINKLE, RIP; VESEY, DENMARK; WASHINGTON, BOOKER TALIAFERRO; WASHINGTON, GEORGE; WEEPING WOMAN; WHIRLWIND, SALLY ANN THUNDER ANN; WRIGHT BROTHERS; YANKEE, CONNECTICUT; YANKEE DOODLE; YANKEE PEDDLER.

For Further Reading:

Battle, Kemp P. *Great American Folklore: Legends, Tales, Ballads and Superstitions from All across America.* New York: Doubleday, 1986.

Bierhorst, John. *The Mythology of North America.* New York: Morrow, 1985.

Blair, Walter. *Tall Tale America: A Legendary History of Our Humorous Heroes.* New York: Coward-McCann, 1944.

Clough, Ben C., ed. *The American Imagination at Work: Tall Tales and Folk Tales.* New York: Knopf, 1947.

Coffin, Tristram Potter. *The Female Hero in Folklore and Legend.* New York: Seabury Press, 1975.

Coffin, Tristram Potter, and Hennig Cohen, eds. *The Parade of Heroes: Legendary Figures in American Lore.* Garden City, N.Y.: Anchor Press/Doubleday, 1978.

Leeming, David, and Jake Page. *Myths, Legends, and Folktales of America: An Anthology.* New York: Oxford University Press, 1999.

San Souci, Robert D. *Cut from the Same Cloth: American Women of Myth, Legend, and the Tall Tale.* New York: Philomel Books, 1993.

———. *Larger than Life: The Adventures of American Legendary Heroes.* New York: Delacorte Press, 1991.

Seal, Graham. *Encyclopedia of Folk Heroes.* Santa Barbara, Calif.: ABC-CLIO, 2001.

Shapiro, Ira. *Heroes in American Folklore.* New York: J. Messner, 1962.

Spies, Karen. *Our Folk Heroes.* Brookfield, Conn.: Millbrook Press, 1994.

folk history   See HISTORY, FOLK.

folk humor   See HUMOR, FOLK.

folklife   The term *folklife* refers to nonverbal traditions of a population, as well as to their study in social and cultural context.

Folklore and *folklife* are kindred terms in the sense that both explore the way of life experienced by ordinary members of a cultural group. While the two are interlocking categories of analysis, it is usually the case that the word *folklore* is used to emphasize the narrative lore of a people, while the word *folklife* concentrates more on their nonnarrative, nonverbal practices. In this respect, folklorists have close ties to linguists, while folklife researchers have more in common with anthropologists.

In studying American folklife, scholars consider a wide range of topics, pursued through various forms of evidence. The tendency in folklife study is to prioritize artifacts over texts.

Rather than collecting and analyzing anecdotes, stories, legends, and lyrics, a student of American folklife would be much more likely to notice how objects, occupations, pastimes, and alterations of the landscape reveal the nature of a specific group's outlook and worldview.

That is, folklife studies might take careful note of material culture and the behavior associated with everyday life. Such studies might consider how tools are fashioned and used, how meals are prepared and served, how houses are placed and built, how musical instruments are designed and played, how gardens are arranged and tended, and the like. Through close attention to the physical environment as modified by members of a population, folklife scholars hope to discern the values, beliefs, and assumptions of that population as a cultural group.

Signs of widening acceptance for this approach to the study of American folk traditions include the legislative support conveyed by Congress through the American Folklife Preservation Act of 1976, which promoted the nation's efforts to research and educate people about folklife. This law also provided for establishment within the Library of the Congress of the American Folklife Center.

The folklife movement, though controversial with those who favor the earlier emphasis on verbal performance within folklore studies, has broadened the scope of research and documentation of American folk culture. It has also helped develop a trend in the configuration of folk museums, wherein demonstrations, reenactments, hands-on workshops, interactive exhibits, and living history presentations have become more prevalent. Such organizations frequently incorporate first-person interpreters of American folk history, assuming the role of actual or composite members of past societies. Often positioned within restored historical buildings or reconstructed historical districts, these figures conduct the traditional way of life. They also interact with visitors, usually speaking with the dialect, idiom, and delivery associated with the era they represent. In this way, visitors may ask questions and engage with the past in an embodied, more personal form than artifact display alone would afford.

While both folklorists and folklife scholars look at traditional culture, those working with folklife devote most of their energies to the customs and traditions that are demonstrated in areas outside sounded or printed language.

See also: AGEE, JAMES; AMERICAN FOLKLIFE CENTER; AMERICAN FOLKLIFE PRESERVATION ACT; FOLKLIFE MOVEMENT; FOLKLORE OF EVERYDAY LIFE; FOLKLORISTICS; HISTORIC PRESERVATION; LIVING HISTORY MUSEUMS; MATERIAL CULTURE; MUSEUMS, FOLK; TERMS; WORLDVIEW.

For Further Reading:

Carney, George. *Baseball, Barns, and Bluegrass: A Geography of American Folklife.* Lanham, Md.: Rowman & Littlefield, 1998.

Dorson, Richard, ed. *Folklore and Folklife: An Introduction.* Chicago: University of Chicago Press, 1972.

Hufford, Mary. *American Folklife: A Commonwealth of Cultures.* Washington, D.C.: American Folklife Center, 1991.

Roberts, Warren. *Viewpoints on Folklife: Looking at the Overlooked.* Ann Arbor, Mich.: UMI Research Press, 1988.

Yoder, Don, ed. *American Folklife.* Austin: University of Texas Press, 1976.

Yoder, Don. *Discovering American Folklife: Studies in Ethnic, Religious, and Regional Culture.* Ann Arbor, Mich.: UMI Research Press, 1989.

folklife movement   As a kindred enterprise to the study of folklore, folklife research calls for investigation of the traditional culture of all populations of the United States.

The emphasis within this study is on cultural patterns of expression learned without benefit of formal education or institutional support. In other words, *folklife* refers to the customs, beliefs, and practices that are transmitted interpersonally. Typically, this transfer of knowledge

and capacity is achieved through oral communication, performance, or demonstration.

The folklife movement had its origins in regional ethnology, and calls for a holistic approach to the study of American culture. This shift in the study of folk traditions introduced more anthropological and ethnographic approaches than had previously typified folklore study. Advocates for the folklife movement placed relatively less emphasis on verbal and narrative forms of folk culture, and more on custom, foodways, and architecture.

See also: AMERICAN FOLKLIFE CENTER; FOLKLIFE; FOLKLORE OF EVERYDAY LIFE; LIVING HISTORY MUSEUMS; MATERIAL CULTURE; MUSEUMS, FOLK; SMITHSONIAN INSTITUTION; TERMS.

For Further Reading:

Bartis, Peter. *Folklife and Fieldwork: A Layman's Introduction to Field Techniques.* Washington, D.C.: Library of Congress, 2002.

Bartis, Peter, and Hilary Glatt. *Folklife Sourcebook: A Directory of Folklife Resources in the United States.* Washington, D.C.: Library of Congress, 1994.

Cantwell, Robert. *Ethnomimesis: Folklife and the Representation of Culture.* Chapel Hill: University of North Carolina Press, 1993.

Hall, Patricia and Charlie Seemann, eds. *Folklife and Museums: Selected Readings.* Nashville, Tenn.: American Association for State and Local History, 1987.

Schlereth, Thomas. *Cultural History and Material Culture: Everyday Life, Landscapes, Museums.* Ann Arbor, Mich.: UMI Research Press, 1989.

Yoder, Don. "The Folklife Studies Movement," *Pennsylvania Folklife* 13 (1963): 43–56.

folklore   *Folklore* is a complex term, alternately defined as a body of knowledge, a mode of thought, a kind of art, and a communicative process.

For the most part, folklorists have concerned themselves with unofficial and informal aspects of culture. These local outlooks and habits, rarely written down, reach the next generation chiefly through oral transmission, demonstration, or observation. As the definition suggests, oral culture proves fundamental to folklore—whether as sermons, jokes, rumors and gossip, stories, or speeches.

The term *folklore* was introduced by William John Thoms, a British antiquarian, in 1846. Up until that time, the subject matter associated with what is now considered folklore was described as "popular antiquities." As that name suggests, antiquities were thought of as curiosities—remarkable, even unlikely, cultural survivals of bygone times. Antiquarians made a study of traditional culture, largely because its elements appeared to be endangered, less common, or vanishing.

Thoms coined the term *folklore* to describe a wide array or beliefs, practices, and artifacts associated with traditional culture. Examples include superstitions, proverbs, observances, ballads, tales, manners, and customs. Because the emphasis was on those aspects of culture widely practiced, Thoms resisted a definition of culture that focused only on a cultural elite. Instead, he directed attention to ordinary, often anonymous, people whose usual way of life proved characteristic of the group and time in which they lived. Although the term *folklore* did not come into use until 1846, the subject matter and originating traditions studied by folklorists often predate that time. In America, for instance, folk heroes, tall tales, beliefs, and sayings were always a part of the culture.

In 1888, the American Folklore Society (AFS) was founded, creating a locus of scholarly energy and a professional organization for folklore researchers in the United States. The society is a scholarly association of persons participating in the advancement of folklore studies.

The AFS founders included such leaders in the field as Francis James Child, Franz Boas, Daniel Garrison Brinton, and William Wells Newell. The central purpose of this organization is to promote the systematic and scientific investigation of folklore. American writers such as Samuel Langhorne Clemens, Joel Chandler Harris, and George Washington Cable became members of the AFS during their careers, signaling their enthusiasm for folklore and its study. In the AFS foundational writings placed special emphasis on collecting and preserving folklore from two populations: African Americans and Native Americans. Both groups had embattled histories that threatened to erode or even to erase their distinctive folk traditions.

Today, the American Folklore Society fulfills its organizational mission through a wide range of professional activities, including sponsorship of publications exemplifying the group's exacting standards of academic rigor. The American Folklore Society publishes the *Journal of American Folklore*, a quarterly periodical that has been the premier source on the subject of American folklore since 1888; the *American Folklore Society Newsletter*, issued bimonthly since 1971; the *Centennial Index;* and a multitude of scholarly monographs. In addition to these publishing projects, the American Folklore Society supports folklore research through such means as interest groups, conferences, workshops, prize competitions, and other programs.

Because of the circumstance under which the term *folklore* developed, the initial tendency among American folklorists was to focus on folk traditions that were rural, remote, local or regional, old-fashioned, and preindustrial. It was not until the 20th century that folklorists widened their field of investigation to integrate more thoroughly urban, densely populated, national, modern, and industrial/postindustrial populations within American folklore scholarship.

For the purposes of this volume, folklore might best be described as the unwritten literature of a culture: its songs, stories, proverbs, parables, riddles, and sayings. More important, the term refers to ancestral understandings culturally transmitted through traditional beliefs, myths, tales, and language practices of people, whether that transmission takes place orally, observationally, or through writing about such lore. As a result, the emphasis remains on verbal (narrative) genres of folklore—chiefly in stories, tales, or customs in which language acts play a major part.

See also: AMERICAN FOLKLORE SOCIETY; CABLE, GEORGE WASHINGTON; CLEMENS, SAMUEL LANGHORNE; FAKELORE; FIELDWORK, FOLKLORE; FOLKLIFE; FOLKLORE STUDIES; FOLKLORISTICS; HARRIS, JOEL CHANDLER; TERMS.

For Further Reading:

Bauman, Richard. "Differential Identity and the Social Base of Folklore," *Journal of American Folklore* 84 , no. 331 (winter 1971): 31–43.

Ben-Amos, Dan. "Toward a Definition of Folklore in Context," *Journal of American Folklore* 84, no. 331 (winter 1971): 3–15.

Ben-Amos, Dan, and Kenneth Goldstein. *Folklore: Performance and Communication*. The Hague: Mouton, 1975.

Dorson, Richard. "Folklore in America vs. American Folklore," *Journal of the Folklore Institute* 15: 97–112.

Dundes, Alan. "The American Concept of Folklore," *Journal of the Folklore Institute* 3 (1966): 226–249.

Dundes, Alan. "What Is Folklore?" In *The Study of Folklore*, edited by Alan Dundes, 1–3. Englewood Cliffs, N.J.: Prentice-Hall, 1965.

Halpert, Herbert. "Folklore: Breadth versus Depth," *Journal of American Folklore* 71, no. 280 (spring 1958): 97–103.

Kelley, Robin D. G. "Notes on Deconstructing 'The Folk,'" *American Historical Review* 97, no. 5 (December 1992): 1400–1408.

folklore fieldwork See FIELDWORK, FOLKLORE.

folklore in American literature American literature has always been attentive to folklore's narratives, and today's readers may first encounter elements of American folklore through the retellings such stories receive in the pages of American literature. Other authors do more than record folktales; they also generate them. For example, Washington Irving's legends of Rip Van Winkle and Sleepy Hollow are still widely read, retold, and incorporated in other cultural practices or stories.

Every region in the United States boasts some authors who have recast oral lore for the page, adapted its themes or motifs, or created stories reminiscent of American folklore. Whether Herman Melvilles in *Moby-Dick*, with its depictions of the whaling industry, or Zora Neale Hurston in *Tell My Horse*, with its accounts of hoodoo as practiced on the Gulf Coast, American literary figures enjoy close ties to the folklore and folklife of the country in which they reside and about which they write.

See also: AGEE, JAMES; ALLEN, PAULA GUNN; ANDERSEN, HANS CHRISTIAN; BAMBARA, TONI CADE; BROWN, STERLING ALLEN; CABLE, WASHINGTON GEORGE; CHESNUTT CHARLES WADDELL; CLEMENS, SAMUEL LANGHORNE; COOPER, JAMES FENIMORE; DUBOIS, W. E. B.; DUNBAR, PAUL LAURENCE; ELLISON, RALPH WALDO; FAULKNER, WILLIAM; GRIMM BROTHERS; HURSTON, ZORA NEALE; IRVING, WASHINGTON; KINGSTON, MAXINE HONG; LOCKE, ALAIN LE ROY; LONGFELLOW, HENRY WADSWORTH; MOMADAY, NAVARRE SCOTT; MORRISON, TONI; SANDBURG, CARL; SILKO, LESLIE MARMON; STEINBECK, JOHN; STOWE, HARRIET BEECHER; STYRON, WILLIAM; TOOMER, JEAN; WHITMAN, WALT.

For Further Reading:

DeCaro, Frank A., and Rosan Augusta Jordan. *Re-Situating Folklore: Folk Contexts and Twentieth-Century Literature and Art*. Knoxville: University of Tennessee Press, 2004.

Dorson, Richard M. *American Folklore and the Historian*. Chicago: University of Chicago Press, 1971.

Flanagan, John, and Arthur Palmer Hudson, eds. *Folklore in American Literature*. Evanston, Ill.: Row, Peterson, 1958.

Hoffman, Daniel. *Form and Fable in American Fiction*. New York: W. W. Norton, 1961.

Jones, Steven Swann. *Folklore and Literature in the United States: An Annotated Bibliography of Studies of Folklore in American Literature.* New York: Garland, 1984.

Rosenberg, Bruce. *Folklore and Literature: Rival Siblings.* Knoxville: University of Tennessee Press, 1991.

folklore in everyday life   Just as holidays reveal beliefs and values, so do everyday activities.

From foodways to jokes, folklore permeates daily lives. It stands behind the ways we costume and adorn ourselves, including body art. It shapes the way we construct, furnish, and decorate our homes. It affects the choice of trees and flowers we cultivate, along with the way we make use of what we grow. It informs the way we bear, birth, and rear children. It helps form our concepts of courtship, marriage, and family life. It even plays a part in how we approach aging, illness, dying, and the afterlife.

At work, play, and rest, American folklore inflects behavior, relationships, and understandings of daily reality. Often without realizing it, we observe traditions and reenact customs that are centuries old. Part of the work folklorists do is to pose questions about the origins and meanings of those practices. Why do brides wear veils? Why are mothers-to-be celebrated at parties called baby showers? Why do walking companions say, "Bread and butter" when they are parted by a fireplug or other obstacle on the street? How is it that well-wishers bless someone who sneezes, but not someone who coughs? Why do people avoid walking under ladders, fear Friday the 13th, or cross their fingers for luck?

By drawing to the surface the customs and reasons behind them, American folklorists help deepen understanding of cultural assumptions and values.

See also: AGING AND FOLKLORE; ANIMALS; ARCHITECTURE, FOLK; ART, FOLK; ATOMIC/NUCLEAR ERA FOLKLORE; CAMP FOLKLORE; CAMPUS FOLKLORE; CHILDBIRTH/PREGNANCY FOLKLORE; CHILDREN'S FOLKLORE; CITY FOLKLORE; COMPUTER FOLKLORE; CONJURE/CONJURING; CONSPIRACY FOLKLORE; COURTSHIP/DATING FOLKLORE; CRAFTS, FOLK; CUSTOMS, FOLK; DEATH; DISABILITY AND FOLKLORE; DRAMA, FOLK; ETHICS IN FOLKLORE; EVIL EYE; FABLES; FAIRY TALES; FAMILY FOLKLORE; FESTIVALS, FOLKLORE; FLIGHT; FLOWERS; FOLKTALES; GAMES AND PASTIMES; GARDENING; GAY/LESBIAN FOLKLORE; GENDER AND FOLKLORE; GESTURES; GHOSTS; GHOST STORIES; GHOST TOWNS; GOSSIP/RUMOR; GRAFFITI; GREETINGS; HAUNTED HOUSES; HILLBILLIES; HIPPIES; HOBOES; HUMOR, FOLK; IMMIGRATION AND FOLKLORE; INDUSTRIALIZATION AND FOLKLORE; JUMP ROPE RHYMES; KITSCH; LEGENDS, FOLK; LIVING HISTORY MUSEUMS; MAGIC; MEDICINE, FOLK; MINSTRELSY; MONSTERS; MUSEUMS, FOLK; MUSIC, FOLK; MYTHS, FOLK; NAMING/NAMES; NURSERY RHYMES; OCCUPATIONAL FOLKLORE; ORAL FOLKLORE; OUTLAWS; PARADES; PHOTOGRAPHY, FOLK; PLEDGE OF ALLEGIANCE; POLITICS AND FOLKLORE; PRISON FOLKLORE; PROTEST IN FOLKLORE; PROVERBS; QUILT, AIDS; REGION, FOLK; RELIGION, FOLK; RIDDLES, FOLK; RHYMES, FOLK; RITES OF PASSAGE; RITUALS, FOLK; RODEO; SPEECH, FOLK; SPORTS FOLKLORE; SUPERNATURAL; SUPERSTITION; TOASTS/DRINKING; TOYS, FOLK; UFO FOLKLORE; VAMPIRE; VOODOO/HOODOO; WEDDING/MARRIAGE FOLKLORE; WEREWOLF; WORLDVIEW; XEROX/FAX FOLKLORE.

For Further Reading:

Berger, Harris, and Giovanna Del Negro. *Identity and Everyday Life: Essays in the Study of Folklore, Music, and Popular Culture.* Middletown, Conn.: Wesleyan University Press, 2004.

Langellier, Kristin, and Eric Peterson. *Storytelling in Daily Life: Performing Narrative.* Philadelphia: Temple University Press, 2004.

Schoemaker, George H., ed. *The Emergence of Folklore in Everyday Life: A Fieldguide and Sourcebook.* Bloomington, Ind.: Trickster Press, 1990.

Thompson, C. J. S. *The Hands of Destiny: The Folk-Lore and Superstitions of Everyday Life.* London: Rider, 1932.

folklore studies Within higher education, the study of American folklore has shaped the curriculum at many campuses.

It is rare that a four-year college or university does not offer at least introductory coursework on folklore, and many schools offer multiple classes in which folklore is either the focus or a substantive component.

In addition, there are quite a few locations where those interested in folklore may earn specialized degrees. Institutions such as University of California, Berkeley; Indiana University; University of North Carolina at Chapel Hill; University of Oregon; University of Pennsylvania; and Western Kentucky University all offer graduate degrees in folklore or folk studies. Many other campuses have configured concentrations in folklore and/or folklife within their undergraduate or graduate degree programs in other disciplines, such as English, anthropology, and American studies; these programs include those of George Washington University and Utah State University. Within these contexts, persons interested in developing their understanding of American folklore and folklife may engage in sustained study while earning advanced degrees.

Individuals who have preparation of this kind often put their learning into practice in teaching, as well as work in cultural agencies such as museums, libraries, and archives.

See also: FIELDWORK, FOLKLORE; FOLKLORE; FOLKLORISTICS; MUSEUMS, FOLK; PUBLIC FOLKLORE; RESEARCH, FOLKLIFE; TERMS.

For Further Reading:

Bendix, Regina. *In Search of Authenticity: The Formation of Folklore Studies*. Madison: University of Wisconsin Press, 1997.

Bronner, Simon. *American Folklore Studies: An Intellectual History*. Lawrence: University Press of Kansas, 1986.

Bronner, Simon. "Exploring American Traditions: A Survey of Folklore and Folklife Research in American Studies," *American Studies International* 31 (1993): 37–59.

Cashion, Gerald, ed. *Conceptual Problems in Contemporary Folklore Study*. Folklore Forum Bibliographic and Special Series, no. 12. Bloomington, Ind.: Folklore Forum Society, 1974.

Clements, William, ed. *One Hundred Years of Folklore Studies*. Washington, D.C.: American Folklore Society, 1988.

Jackson, Bruce, ed. *Teaching Folklore*. Buffalo, N.Y.: Documentary Research, 1989.

Zumwalt, Rosemary. *American Folklore Scholarship: A Dialogue of Dissent*. Bloomington: Indiana University Press, 1988.

folklorism The term *folklorism* describes instances in which elements of folk culture are popularized, but without the necessary cultural context in which they may be understood.

The term *folklorism* was coined by Hans Moser in 1962, as *Volkskunde*. The label was adopted for use within the study of American folklore. Sometimes known as *neofolklorism*, folklorism involves cases in which individuals or organizations, typically those involved in such pursuits as journalism, propaganda, and merchandising, appropriate aspects of folklore in an opportunistic manner. For this reason, they do not concern themselves unduly with the integrity of collection or cultural reference points. These actions may be taken for any number of reasons, including for sport, profit, entertainment, slumming, and exoticism. A typical example would be the staging of a purportedly authentic cultural event for the exclusive purpose of making it available for tourists to view. In other words, *folklorism* was devised as a term to signal that such representations were artificial rather than genuine.

In recent times, there has been a slight shift in folklorists' approach to folklorism. Once viewed as suspect, even counterfeit, such performances and presentations have come to be regarded as interesting phenomena in themselves. Rather than being fooled by cultural counterfeits, many folklorists now believe it might be informative to investigate folklorism in its own right.

Such research might reveal cultural perceptions and value judgments not discernible elsewhere: How are reenactments conceived, designed, and implemented? On what basis are simulations built, and why? What do such displays suggest about the worldview of the spectators, as well as their notions of themselves in relation to what they see?

While such research on folklorism is still a relatively new concept within the study of American folklore, it promises to afford folklorists new insights into human behavior and thought.

See also: FAKELORE; FOLKLORE STUDIES; INSIDER/OUTSIDER; TERMS.

For Further Reading:

Bausinger, Hermann. "Toward a Critique of Folklorism Criticism." In *German Volkskunde: A Decade of Theoretical Confrontation, Debate, and Reorientation (1967–1977)*, edited by James R. Dow and Hannjost Lixfield, 113–123. Bloomington: Indiana University Press, 1966.

Newell, Venetia. "The Adaptation of Folklore and Tradition (Folklorismus)," *Folklore* 98 (1987): 131–151.

Voight, Vilmos. "Confines of Literature, Folklore, and Folklorism," *Neohelikon* 7 (1979–1980): 123–140.

folkloristics   The term *folkloristics* refers to inquiry conducted within the discipline of folklore itself.

That is, the subject matter of folklore—songs, stories, and the like—may receive scholarly attention within many disciplines and may be addressed with various approaches and purposes. A linguist might study conversations. An artist might study wood carving. A sociologist might study urban legends. All three would be examining the material of folklore; still, they would be examining it by using the methods and the objectives of their own respective fields of investigation: linguistics, art history, sociology.

Within folkloristics, however, such subject matter receives attention within the context of folklore studies. That includes folklore methods, objectives, and frameworks of understanding. For example, a folklorist who examines African-American quilts from America's antebellum period could bring to bear a whole set of questions: Who made the quilts? How did they make the quilts? Who used the quilts? What do the quilts reveal about the culture and the era in which they were produced or used? What do the quilts represent? What, in particular, do their patterns and designs suggest? Is it possible, as some have argued, that display of quilts, especially ones with particular visual elements, played a part in the Underground Railroad? What can interviews with the people who now own the quilts help researchers understand about history, customs, and way of life? What is the nature of quilt culture? What does it mean that some contemporary African-American artists, such as Faith Ringgold, have made story quilting their medium of choice? What might it say that the nation's largest acquired immunodeficiency syndrome (AIDS) memorial takes the shape of a giant quilt? Folklorists are interested in the quilts, then, but not merely for their own sake. Rather, they are interested in the social and cultural meanings such objects transmit.

Folkloristics involves scholarship into folk material that balances an interest in the local and the universal, the distinctive and the collective, the significance of a people's social practices, traditions, habits, and customs.

See also: AFRICAN-AMERICAN FOLKLORE; CRAFTS, FOLK; FIELDWORK, FOLKLORE; FOLKLORE; FOLKLORE STUDIES; ORAL HISTORY; QUILT, AIDS; SLAVERY; TERMS; UNDERGROUND RAILROAD.

For Further Reading:

Burns, Thomas A. "Folkloristics: A Conception of Theory," *Western Folklore* 36 (1977): 109–134.

Dundes, Alan. *Essays in Folkloristics*. Meerut, India: Folklore Institute, 1978.

Farrington, Lisa. *Faith Ringgold*. San Francisco: Pomegranate, 2004.

Georges, Robert, and Michael Owen Jones. *Folk-loristics: An Introduction.* Bloomington: Indiana University Press, 1995.

Ruskin, Cindy. *The Quilt: Stories from the NAMES Project.* New York: Pocket Books, 1998.

Tobin, Jacqueline, and Raymond Dobard. *Hidden in Plain View: The Secret Story of Quilts and the Underground Railroad.* New York: Doubleday, 1999.

Zumwalt, Rosemary. *American Folkloristics: The Literary and Anthropological Roots.* Berkeley: University of California Press, 1982.

folklure   See FAKELORE.

folk medicine   See MEDICINE, FOLK.

folk museum   See MUSEUM, FOLK.

folk music   See MUSIC, FOLK.

folk narrative   See NARRATIVE, FOLK.

folk region   See REGION, FOLK.

folk religion   See RELIGION, FOLK.

folk rituals   See RITUALS, FOLK.

folk-say   See SPEECH, FOLK.

folk speech   See SPEECH, FOLK.

folktales   Folktales can be any sort of traditional narratives but usually involve variants of fictional spoken stories.

One of the most pervasive kinds of folktales are animal stories. Populating such stories are such figures as Anansi the spider, Coyote, or other creature protagonists. Por quoi tales are a specific category of animal stories in which various characteristics of those creatures are explained. For example, one por quoi story provides an explanation of how the leopard got its spots.

Trickster tales represent another form of folktale and may feature animal characters, human characters, or both. The figure of the trickster is a common one throughout American folklore, especially in Native American and African-American tales. The trickster is an unlikely hero and appears even less likely to emerge as a victor, yet somehow prevails in a variety of situations portrayed within trickster tales. The trickster typically triumphs through unexpected turns of events, whether by chance or design. On this basis, the trickster is related to other figures in folklore who rely upon subterfuge, such as outlaws, magicians, and changelings.

The human characters of folktales are frequently ordinary people, who have remarkable experiences. In such cases, recognizable characters help listeners relate to the tale, but the unusual events help hold their interest.

An exception to this formula would be tall tales (sometimes called yarns or lies). Tall tales represent a subcategory within the genre of folktales. Within American lore, these 19th-century stories tend toward drama, hyperbole, and exaggeration in depicting the exploits of western expansion. They typically employ a plausible premise but describe incredible events and/or outcomes. Characters include Pecos Bill, Paul Bunyan and Babe the Blue Ox, Mike Fink, and Febold Feboldson. These legendary figures with their exceptional exploits are among the best known characters in all of American folklore.

Other forms of folktales include Jack stories, magic tales, dialect stories, plantation tales, and conjure stories. In addition to amusing audiences, these story forms have inspired many of America's writers, such as Samuel Langhorne Clemens, Charles Waddell Chestnutt, Ralph Waldo Ellison, and Toni Morrison. Whatever the genre, however, folktales help define the narrative history of the American people.

158 folk tradition

See also: AFRICAN-AMERICAN FOLKLORE; ANANSI; ANIMALS; BABE THE BLUE OX; BUNYAN, PAUL; CHESNUTT, CHARLES WADDELL; CHRISTMAS, ANNIE; CLEMENS, SAMUEL LANGHORNE; CONJURE/CONJURING; ELLISON, RALPH WALDO; FEBOLDSON FEBOLD; FINK, MIKE; FOLK HEROES/LEGENDARY FIGURES; MORRISON, TONI; ORAL FOLKLORE; REMUS, UNCLE; TRICKSTER.

For Further Reading:

Lindahl, Carl, ed. *American Folktales: From the Collections of the Library of Congress.* Armonk, New York: M. E. Sharpe, 2004.

Blair, Walter. *Tall Tale America: A Legendary History of Our Humorous Heroes.* New York: Coward-McCann, 1944.

Brown, Carolyn. *The Tall Tale in American Folklore and Literature.* Knoxville: University of Tennessee Press, 1987.

Dorson, Richard. *Man and Beast in American Comic Legend.* Bloomington: Indiana University Press, 1982.

San Souci, Robert D. *Cut from the Same Cloth: American Women of Myth, Legend, and the Tall Tale.* New York: Philomel Books, 1993.

Tall Tales. Austin, Tex.: Steck-Vaughn, 1990.

Walker, Paul Robert. *Big Men, Big Country: A Collection of American Tall Tales.* San Diego: Harcourt, Brace, Jovanovich, 2000.

Wonham, Henry B. *Mark Twain and the Art of the Tall Tale.* New York: Oxford University Press, 1993.

folk tradition See HISTORY, FOLK.

folkways See CUSTOMS, FOLK.

food/foodways Foodways represents an important category of analysis within folklore studies. Through their detailed investigation of foodways, scholars attend to the practices, cultural meanings, and traditions associated with preparing, presenting, and interacting around food and drink.

Therefore, while the foods themselves hold interest to participants and observers alike, researchers of foodways typically examine the way food functions within a web of human behavior, relationships, and communal identities. Although American foodways associated with long-held traditions such as holidays and formal occasions such as weddings may come first to mind in this regard, scholars of foodways take equal note of the less formal and everyday ways in which food and meals communicate values, connections, and symbolic meanings.

Foodways analysts collect the lore surrounding food's service (Why does Thanksgiving feature turkey?), customs in its fashioning from ingredients (What is involved in maintaining a kosher kitchen?), procedures for its consumption (Why is dessert served at the end of a meal's courses?), and understandings surrounding food's power to suggest shared identity in the lives of families and communities (Why are eggs featured in hunts at Easter?).

While foodways cannot be separated entirely from other cultural practices, such as conversation and song, which often accompany the enjoyment of food, it does represent a growing area of interest among students of folklore who find themselves intrigued by the intricacies of food behavior.

See also: CHRISTMAS; CUSTOMS, FOLK; EASTER; ETHNICITY; FOLKLORE IN EVERYDAY LIFE; "GOLDEN GOOSE, THE"; HALLOWEEN/ALL HALLOWS' EVE; HANUKKAH; HOLIDAYS/OBSERVANCES; KWANZAA; NEW YEAR'S EVE/DAY; PASSOVER; RAMADAN; SWEETEST DAY; THANKSGIVING; TOASTS/DRINKING; WEDDING/MARRIAGE FOLKLORE.

For Further Reading:

Brown, Linda Keller, and Kay Mussell. *Ethnic and Regional Foodways in the United States: The Performance of Group Identity.* Knoxville: University of Tennessee Press, 1984.

Camp, Charles. *American Foodways: What, When, Why, and How We Eat in America.* Little Rock, Ark.: August House, 1989.

Humphrey, Theodore C., and Lin T. Humphrey, eds. *We Gather Together: Food and Festival in American Life*. Ann Arbor, Mich.: UMI Research Press, 1988.

Jones, Michael Owen, Bruce Giuliano, and Roberta Krell, eds. *Foodways and Eating Habits: Directions for Research*. Los Angeles: California Folklore Society, 1983.

McIntosh, Elaine N. *American Food Habits in Historical Perspective*. Westport, Conn.: Praeger, 1995.

Pleck, Elizabeth H. *Celebrating the Family: Ethnicity, Consumer Culture, and Family Rituals*. Cambridge, Mass.: Harvard University Press, 2000.

Weaver, William Woys. *American Eats: Forms of Edible Folk Art*. New York: Harper & Row, 1989.

Wilson, David Scofield, and Angus Kress Gillespie. *Rooted in America: Foodlore of Popular Fruits and Vegetables*. Knoxville: University of Tennessee Press, 1999.

foo-fighters See WORLD WAR II.

fools See APRIL FOOL'S DAY; TRICKSTER.

Ford, Henry (1863–1947) With his pioneering efforts in the automobile industry, Henry Ford embodied the American ideal of the self-made capitalist.

Ford was born July 30, 1863. Although he had an enjoyable childhood on the family farm, Ford felt called to pursuits that would take him away from agriculture and toward industrial technology. In 1879, he apprenticed as a machinist in Detroit, where he proved adept at repairing, retooling, and running machinery and instruments. These talents helped him land a position as an engineer with Detroit's Edison Illuminating Company, where he became chief engineer in 1893. This work served as a platform for Ford's own pursuits as an entrepreneur.

The Ford Motor Company had its beginnings in Detroit and Highland Park. In this way, Ford introduced his now-legendary Model T in 1908. His Model T became so popular that by 1918, this vehicle accounted for nearly a 50 percent share of the American auto market. This was the kind of success Ford had envisioned for his industry. He wanted to achieve efficient production of a solid means of transportation for the average American consumer.

Henry Ford's hometown of Dearborn, Michigan, became the site for the Ford Company's industrial complex in the 1920s. At this plant on the edge of the Rouge River, Ford realized his mass production concepts, such as the moving assembly line. His success as a manufacturer helped transform America into a car culture, with a national network of highways, dotted with roadside attractions and amenities such as fuel stations and diners.

Dearborn also served as the location for Ford's Greenfield Village, with something of the reverence Walt Disney would later express for small-town America in his design of such attractions as Main Street USA at Disneyland, Ford sought to make of Greenfield Village "America's Hometown." The building for what is now the Ford Museum, but was then called the Edison Institute, was dedicated in 1928. Ford collected an unusual array of Americana, including both plainspoken objects and such items as a Revolutionary War camp bed used by George Washington and the Ford Theater balcony chair in which Abraham Lincoln was seated at the time of his assassination.

The 13-acre property around the Ford Museum first opened in 1933, featuring reproductions and 80 historical structures. In something of the visual arrangement of a New England village, Ford had created a suite of historic districts for visitors to experience. Perhaps predictably, there was a version of Ford's first assembly plant. Because Ford so admired another American inventor, also available were versions of both Thomas Alva Edison's residence and his Menlo Park, New Jersey, labs. Along with these areas were sites designed to recall the homes of the Wright brothers, George

Washington Carver, Noah Webster, and Robert Frost. Visitors could also see Ford's take on a William Holmes McGuffey school, paying tribute to the man behind the popular readers used by American schoolchildren since 1836. With Greenfield Village, Ford expressed his admiration for his country and its success stories.

Ford did not invent the automobile, but he did help establish it as the dominant form of transportation in the United States. His own rise to wealth and success as an industrialist, along with his reverence for the nation's patriotic heroes, helped establish Henry Ford as a force within America's folklore.

See also: DISNEY, WALTER ELIAS; EDISON, THOMAS ALVA; EINSTEIN, ALBERT; FOLK HEROES/LEGENDARY FIGURES; GREENFIELD VILLAGE, HENRY FORD MUSEUM AND; LINCOLN, ABRAHAM; MUSEUMS, FOLK; REVOLUTIONARY WAR; WASHINGTON, GEORGE; WRIGHT BROTHERS.

For Further Reading:
Brinkley, Douglas. *Wheels for the World: Henry Ford, His Company, and a Century of Progress, 1903–2003.* New York: Viking, 2003.
Segal, Howard. *Recasting the Machine Age: Henry Ford's Village Industries.* Amherst: University of Massachusetts Press, 2005.
Wallace, Max. *The American Axis: Henry Ford, Charles Lindbergh, and the Rise of the Third Reich.* New York: St. Martin's Press, 2003.
Watts, Steven. *The People's Tycoon: Henry Ford and the American Century.* New York: Knopf, 2005.
Wik, Reynold. *Henry Ford and Grass-Roots America.* Ann Arbor: University of Michigan Press, 1972.

Ford Museum See GREENFIELD VILLAGE AND HENRY FORD MUSEUM.

fortune See LUCK/FORTUNE.

fortune-telling See PREDICTION.

four-leafed clover See LUCK/FORTUNE; SAINT PATRICK'S DAY.

Fourth of July See INDEPENDENCE DAY/FOURTH OF JULY.

Franco-American folklore See FRENCH-AMERICAN FOLKLORE.

Franklin, Benjamin (1706–1790) Hailed as one of the nation's Founding Fathers, Benjamin Franklin was both a collector of folk knowledge and a subject of folklore.

Franklin's life began in Boston on January 1, 1706. Hard times and a large family meant that Franklin would enter the workforce while still a youth. Although he started in the tallow trade, he soon and gratefully found his way into an apprenticeship in printing. By the custom of the day, printers were similar to today's publishers, taking an active role in editing work and shaping its statement. Franklin edited the *Pennsylvania Gazette* and, from 1732 until 1757, annually distributed *Poor Richard's Almanack* under the pseudonym Richard Saunders. In these annuals, Franklin collected maxims, proverbs, weather lore, and the like. *Poor Richard's Almanack* is the source of many familiar sayings still in use today, such as "A fool and his money are soon parted" and "Early to bed and early to rise makes a man healthy, wealthy, and wise." Franklin also published a 1771 autobiography, extolling the virtues of thrift, discipline, and self-improvement. This text is alluded to throughout American literature and culture, from the Horatio Alger novels to an ironic reference in F. Scott Fitzgerald's *The Great Gatsby*.

Franklin was accomplished in many arenas: as a businessman, statesman, author, printer, and publisher. He played a central part in two foundational documents of American democracy, the Declaration of Independence and the Constitution. He was a delegate to the Continental Congress, as well as serving as postmaster general.

Most of the folklore surrounding Benjamin Franklin, however, has to do with conduct as an inventor. Franklin is credited with the ideas for the Franklin stove, lightning rod, bifocal eyeglasses, and an ethereal sounding musical instrument he called the glass harmonica. Also attributed to Franklin are the experiments that proved that lightning is electricity. Although there is some doubt about the veracity of this claim, folk narratives portray Franklin out in a thunderstorm, flying a kite attached to a metal key. This image of Franklin persists, regardless of whether it is a bonafide account. In other words, the stories of Franklin's kite experiments may amount to an early American urban legend.

Through both a distinctive autobiography and a carefully cultivated persona, Benjamin Franklin emerged as an icon of America's historical heroes.

See also: ALGER, HORATIO, JR.; FOLK HEROES/LEGENDARY FIGURES; OCCUPATIONAL FOLKLORE; PENNSYLVANIA FOLKLORE; PROVERBS; REVOLUTIONARY WAR; SPEECH, FOLK; URBAN LEGENDS; WEATHER FOLKLORE.

For Further Reading:

Barbour, Frances. *"A Concordance to the Sayings in Franklin's 'Poor Richard.'"* Detroit: Gale, 1974.

Coffin, Tristram Potter, and Hennig Cohen, eds. *The Parade of Heroes: Legendary Figures in American Lore.* Garden City, N.Y.: Anchor Press/Doubleday, 1978.

Dorson, Richard. *American Folklore.* Chicago: University of Chicago Press, 1959.

Meister, Charles. "Franklin as a Proverb Stylist," *American Literature* 24 (1952–1953): 157–166.

Mieder, Wolfgang. *American Proverbs: A Study of Texts and Contexts.* Bern: Peter Lang, 1989.

French-American folklore French-American folklore is derived from the social life and customs of immigrants arriving in the United States from France, French-speaking Canada, and areas such as the West Indies. It also includes the traditions of those persons born in America of French descent.

Immigration to the United States by these populations has occurred since the 17th century. Local place-names taken from the French language, such as Des Plaines, Illinois, and Des Moines, Iowa, mark some of the locations where clusters of French-speaking settlers made their homes. While French Americans were not as likely as some other populations to join ethnic enclaves in major American cities, there are nonetheless some regions demarcated, as the French-Canadian–founded Little Canada, Minnesota's, name indicates, in such a way as to suggest the concentration of a group's heritage.

Several aspects of French-American folklore are widely known in the United States. French cuisines vary by group and region, but generally speaking, French foodways are revered in America for sauces, wines, and other signatures. In fact, numerous cooking terms, phrases, and expressions have been incorporated into American English usage, including *casserole, à la mode, sauté,* and *hors d'oeuvres.* Several French Americans have achieved recognition as authors, including Henry David Thoreau, Henry Wadsworth Longfellow, and John Greenleaf Whittier. Holidays and observances among French Americans include Mardi Gras and Bastille Day, a July 14 commemoration of the events leading to the 1789 formation of the First Republic.

Organizations established for the preservation and study of French-American culture include New York's French American Foundation, New York's French Institute/Alliance Française, and Manchester, New Hampshire's National Association of Franco-Americans. Major collections of French-American cultural material may be found at Louisiana State University's Center for French and Francophone Studies (Baton Rouge), the Henri Peyre French Institute (New York City), and the Society for French Historical Studies (Iowa City, Iowa).

With its tall tales, songs, folk heroes, and foodways, French-American folklore provides cultural continuity for those of French ancestry.

See also: Cajun folklore; cultural groups; Longfellow, Henry Wadsworth; Mardi Gras; Revere, Paul; Roosevelt, Franklin Delano; Roosevelt, Theodore.

For Further Reading:

Cameron, Dan, ed. *Dancing at the Louvre: Faith Ringgold's French Collection and Other Story Quilts.* Berkeley: University of California Press, 1998.

Dean, John, and Jean-Paul Gabilliet, eds. *European Readings of American Popular Culture.* Westport, Conn.: Greenwood, 1996.

DeRoche, Celeste. "'I Learned Things Today That I Never Knew Before': Oral History at the Kitchen Table," *Oral History Review: Journal of the Oral History Association* 23, no. 2 (winter 1996): 45–61.

Glowacka, Dorota, and Stephen Boos, eds. *Between Ethics and Aesthetics: Crossing the Boundaries.* Albany: State University of New York Press, 2002.

Harries, Elizabeth Wanning. *Twice upon a Time: Women Writers and the History of the Fairy Tale.* Princeton, N.J.: Princeton University Press, 2001.

Lane, Brigitte. *Franco-American Folk Traditions.* New York: Garland, 1990.

Poel, Ieme van der, Sophie Bertho, and Ton Hoenselaars, eds. *Traveling Theory: France and the United States.* Madison, N.J.: Fairleigh Dickinson University Press, 1999.

Santelli, Robert, Jim Brown, and Holly George-Warren, eds. *American Roots Music.* New York: Abrams, 2001.

Sexton, Rocky. "Don't Let the Rain Fall on My Face: French Louisiana Gravehouses in an Anthropo-Geographical Context," *Material Culture: Journal of the Pioneer American Society* 23, no. 3 (fall 1991): 31–46.

French and Indian Wars See Boone, Daniel; Cajun folklore; Yankee Doodle.

Friday the thirteenth Unlike many other observances or holidays that occur annually, Friday the thirteenth is, a combination of date and day of the week that occurs between one and several times each year depending upon arrangement of the calendar. It is considered by many a day of bad luck and dark prospect. Only those born on Friday the thirteenth are exempted, as they purportedly enjoy good luck on all incidences of Friday the thirteenth.

There are many competing explanations for the reputation of this particular date in history. The occasion appears to combine two sets of fears: those surrounding the number 13 (triskaidekaphobia) and those associated with Friday. Together, these beliefs produce a formidable level of dread, sometimes genuine and sometimes feigned for entertainment, like screams at a horror movie. There is even a name for the phobia inspired by this day's prospect: *parasketvidekatriaphobia.*

The number 13 has long been regarded as unlucky in American culture. This fear is so prevalent that hotels sometimes skip this number when assigning room or floor numbers, so that an elevator panel may follow floor 12 with floor 14. Christians associate the number 13 with the number of people in attendance at the Last Supper. Some lore still holds that if 13 people sit down to dine together, the first to stand after the meal will die within 12 months. Today's custom of inviting even numbers of people to dinner parties may have some connection to this idea.

Fridays is considered lucky by some and serves as the Sabbath in Judaism. Still, Christians believe that it was a Friday on which Adam ate the apple in the Garden of Eden, and so this day of the week retains the association with misfortune. Friday the thirteenth represents a day of pagan celebration and so this day, with Easter and Christmas, may be a case of Christian cultures' reassigning meanings to a holiday or observance. Whether or not the fear of this day is warranted, it remains common. It is not unusual on Friday the thirteenth to overhear conversations in schools, workplaces, and other places that suggest the sense of foreboding associated with this day.

Lore surrounding this day is not exclusively American, but the dread of this day is implied in such things phenomena as the title of a series of popular horror films, *Friday the Thirteenth*.

See also: BELIEFS, FOLK; CHRISTMAS; EASTER; HOLIDAYS/OBSERVANCES; LUCK/FORTUNE; PREDICTION; RELIGION, FOLK; SUPERNATURAL; SUPERSTITION.

For Further Reading:

Brunvand, Jan Harold. *American Folklore: An Encyclopedia*. New York: Garland, 1998.

Dossey, Donald. *Holiday Folklore, Phobias, and Fun: Mythical Origins, Scientific Treatments, and Superstitious Cures*. Los Angeles: Outcomes Unlimited Press, 1992.

"Friday the Thirteenth Computer Virus," *Foaftale News* 16 (December 1989): 6–7.

Lewis, Jerry M., and Timothy J. Gallagher. "The Salience of Friday the 13th for College Students," *College Student Journal* 35, no. 2 (June 2001): 216–222.

Frog Prince/Frog King (legendary) First published in the Grimm brothers' *Children's and Household Tales*, "The Frog Prince" is a fairy tale that recounts the story of a bewitched prince.

As the story opens, a king has three lovely daughters, and the most beautiful of all is the youngest. The children are happy and love to play outdoors. A favorite location for the girls is in the forest, beside a cool well. The youngest daughter often rests there, tossing into the air and catching again in her hand her favorite plaything, a golden ball. On one occasion, however, she fails to catch the ball on its descent. The golden orb falls to the ground, and then drops deep within the well, much to the dismay of the princess.

While she is weeping over the loss of her plaything, the princess hears a voice inquiring about the source of her sorrow. The voice belongs to a frog, who feels compassion for the girl's distress. The princess, upon catching sight of the frog, realizes that he might prove helpful in retrieving the lost toy. She pleads with the frog to come to her assistance, and he agrees on the condition that the princess become a companion to him. If they may eat, play, and rest in company, he will, in return, fetch her golden ball from deep within the well. With this bargain commences a most unexpected romance, and one akin to that depicted in "Beauty and the Beast" in terms of its unlikely attraction.

The princess is delighted when the frog returns her golden ball from the well, but her gratitude is short-lived. Once she is in possession of her toy again, the princess is quick to overlook her portion of the bargain she struck with the frog. She leaves him behind, consumed once again with her own interests and activities and conducting herself with utter disregard for the lonely frog to whom she made her promise.

Once she is back at the castle, the royal family sits down to a meal. The princess's repast is interrupted by the frog, who wishes to have his good turn toward the girl reciprocated. When the king discovers what the frog has done for his youngest daughter, he insists that the princess honor her commitment. Consequently, the frog is permitted to join her at the table and share the food on her plate.

Once the meal has concluded, the frog is well pleased and indicates that they should now retire for sleep. The princess had endured the offense of the frog as a meal mate, but she is outraged by the prospect of hosting him in her bed. Enraged at the very thought, the princess hurls the frog at the bedchamber wall in defiance of his wish.

When he recovers from this blow, the frog is magically transformed into a handsome prince. As it turns out, a witch had transformed the young man into a frog, but the experience of striking the wall somehow reversed the effects of the spell. As she casts eyes on the prince before her, the princess finds herself able now to fulfill her original promise of companionship. The two become betrothed, and the princess accompanies the prince as he returns to his kingdom.

This fairy tale frames several moral lessons, but two dominate: the importance of living up to one's promises and obligations and the dangers of judging people or things by their appearance. This tale has undergone many variations, and most recent versions replace the moment when the princess throws the frog with a scene in which she kisses the frog instead and so more gently undoes the witch's spell. Contemporary retellings tend to deal playfully with the tale and, in the spirit of fractured fairy tales, make whimsical adjustments to the traditional story. One such example is John Scieszka's *The Frog Prince, Continued*, a sequel in which the prince seeks the help of a witch in order to extricate himself from what proves an unhappy marriage to the princess.

In modern parlance, the story of "The Frog Prince" lingers in the adage that one has to kiss a lot of toads to find one's prince.

See also: ANIMALS; "BEAUTY AND THE BEAST"; CHANGELINGS; CHILDREN'S FOLKLORE; FABLES; FAIRY TALES; MYTHS, FOLK.

For Further Reading:

Bettelheim, Bruno. *The Uses of Enchantment: The Meaning and Importance of Fairy Tales*. New York: Knopf, 1976.

Garner, James Finn. *Politically Correct Bedtime Stories*. New York: Macmillan, 1994.

Scieszka, John. *The Frog Prince, Continued*. New York: Viking, 1991.

frontier   From the concept of manifest destiny to the notion of westward expansion, the American frontier has proved a powerful symbol for the nation's life and development.

The term *frontier* is quite resonant in American history, literature, and lore. A frontier typically denotes the boundary between civilization and savagery. In America, it traditionally represents the westernmost edge of settlement by Anglo-Europeans in the continental United States, and the term was used in this way through the 19th century. This image of plentiful and unsettled land has informed a great deal of the nation's self-characterization and thought. The most celebrated theorist of the American frontier was Frederick Jackson Turner. His now-famous 1893 address to the American Historical Association, entitled "The Significance of the Frontier in American History," helped shape the way many would regard the meaning of a frontier in American life.

The Turner thesis contended that the single most salient factor in American national character was the availability of an expanse of land unsettled by the colonists and their descendants. He argued that the ability to spread out across North America functioned as a safety valve for anxieties that would otherwise have found no expression or resolution. He also warned that once the land had become settled, the national culture would reach a kind of crisis.

Of course, this theory of the American frontier has serious imperfections and therefore has been the subject of controversy. For one thing, American exceptionalism—the notion of the country's national character and its utter uniqueness—is an idea that has become unfashionable over the years. Similarly, a theory so completely focused on Euro-Americans and their conquests has not aged well in the face of a multicultural society. What has remained is the concept of the frontier as a contact zone between two populations and/or two ways of life.

Long after Turner's death, his vision of American history continued to influence the way people think about and understand the story of westward expansion in the United States. Modern applications of Turner's thesis seek to map his ideas onto different kinds of territory, both spatial and temporal. Examples include space exploration and the movement toward 24-four hour commerce.

In addition to its attraction as a topic for historians, the American frontier has become an object of considerable attention among the nation's folklorists. Whether construed as an idea of the West as a region or as the notion of a westward-moving migration, the frontier has contributed a wide array of historical figures, legendary characters, and tall tales that, taken together, help constitute a distinctive American lore.

Although the American frontier is a boundary that can neither be fixed nor mapped definitively, its impact on the popular imagination is inestimable. To the extent that American folklore lends itself to some version of a national character, it is most often the image of the frontier—its settlers, cowboys, prospectors, outlaws, and lawmen—that many still invoke as the quintessential embodiment of an American spirit.

See also: ALLEN, ETHAN; BABE THE BLUE OX; BOONE, DANIEL; BUNYAN, PAUL; CANNARY-BURKE, MARTHA (CALAMITY JANE); CARSON, KIT; CHAPMAN, JOHN (JOHNNY APPLESEED); CHILDBIRTH/PREGNANCY FOLKLORE; CODY, WILLIAM F. (BUFFALO BILL); COOPER, JAMES FENIMORE; COWBOYS; CRAZY HORSE; CROCKETT, DAVY; CUSTER, GEORGE ARMSTRONG; EARP, WYATT BERRY STAMP; GERONIMO; GHOST TOWNS; GOLD RUSH, THE; HICKOK, JAMES BUTLER (WILD BILL); HISTORICAL EVENTS; HISTORY, FOLK; JAMES, JESSE; JOSEPH, CHIEF; LEWIS, MERIWETHER, AND WILLIAM CLARK; LONGABAUGH, HARRY (SUNDANCE KID); McCARTY, WILLIAM HENRY (BILLY THE KID); OAKLEY, PHOEBE ANNIE; OUTLAWS; PECOS BILL; REGION, FOLK; RODEOS; SITTING BULL; SMITH, WINDWAGON; SOUTHWESTERN REGIONAL FOLKLORE; STARR, BELLE; TRANSCONTINENTAL RAILROAD; VIETNAM WAR; WESTERN REGIONAL FOLKLORE; WHIRLWIND, SALLY ANN THUNDER ANN.

For Further Reading:

Cayton, Andrew, and Fredrika Teute, eds. *Contact Points: American Frontiers from the Mohawk Valley to the Mississippi, 1750–1830.* Chapel Hill: University of North Carolina Press, 1998.

Chittick, Victor Lovitt Oakes, ed. *Ring-Taled Roarers: Tall Tales of the American Frontier, 1830–1860.* Caldwell, Idaho: Caxton Printers, 1946.

Cohn, Amy L., ed. *From Sea to Shining Sea: A Treasury of American Folklore and Folk Songs.* New York: Scholastic, 1993.

Davis, William. *The American Frontier: Pioneers, Settlers, and Cowboys, 1800–1899.* Norman: University of Oklahoma Press, 1999.

Erdoes, Richard. *Tales from the American Frontier.* New York: Pantheon, 1991.

Faragher, John Mack, ed. *Rereading Frederick Jackson Turner: "The Significance of the Frontier in American History: and Other Essays." New York: Henry Holt, 1994.*

Fife, Austin, Alta Fife, and Henry Glassie, eds. *Forms upon the Frontier: Folklife and Folk Arts in the United States.* Logan: Utah State University Press, 1969.

Kirshenblatt-Gimblett, Barbara. "The Future of Folklore Studies in America: The Urban Frontier," *Folklore Forum* 16, no. 2 (1983): 175–234.

Klein, Kerwin Lee. *Frontiers of Historical Imagination.* Berkeley: University of California Press, 1997.

Limerick, Patricia Nelson. *The Legacy of Conquest: The Unbroken Past of the American West.* New York: W. W. Norton, 1987.

Melbin, Murray. *Night as Frontier: Colonizing the World after Dark.* New York: Free Press, 1987.

Nobles, Gregory H. *American Frontiers: Cultural Encounters and Continental Conquest.* New York: Hill & Wang, 1997.

Stoeltje, Beverley J. "Making the Frontier Myth: Folklore Processes in a Modern Nation," *Western Folklore* 46, no. 4 (1987): 235–253.

Turner, Frederick Jackson. *The Frontier in American History.* New York: Holt, 1920.

funeral rites See BURIAL CUSTOMS; CEMETERY FOLKLORE; DEATH.

games and pastimes Folk games and pastimes are a vital part of American children's folklore.

Games are popular entertainments among children. Examples of children's folk games are Hide and Seek, Kick the Can, Ghost in the Graveyard, Marco Polo, Mother, May I? and Spud. These games rely heavily on children's imagination and usually involve few props or special equipment. For instance, Cat's Cradle is a traditional game played with the simplest sort of toy: a looped piece of string. Whether played by one or more individuals this game involves making string figures by using the basic loop and careful hand positioning.

Other folk games involve no more than a piece of chalk to draw a gameboard and a stone to mark a place on the board. Hopscotch is one such diversion. Other games call for only a ball, such as the playground favorites Kick Ball and Dodge Ball. Still others require nothing but the players themselves, such as Freeze Tag, Red Light, Green Light, Twenty Questions, and I Spy. These games are entirely verbal in nature and can be played anywhere by participants of any age.

Very young children engage in games that involve movement as the central activity. Examples include Ring-around-a-Rosy, Musical Chairs, and Follow the Leader. Such games help youngsters learn about cooperative play, rhythm, and turn taking. As children grow, they graduate to more structured games that teach coordination, such as Catch and jump rope. As youth mature, they tend to become active in the same games adults play, including such sports as baseball, football, soccer, and tennis.

Games and pastimes, as forms of play without toys, are an enjoyable part of everyday life for most Americans.

See also: CHILDREN'S FOLKLORE; FAMILY FOLKLORE; FOLKLORE IN EVERYDAY LIFE; JUMP ROPE RHYMES; RHYMES, FOLK; SPORTS FOLKLORE; TOYS, FOLK.

For Further Reading:

Bartlett, Vernon. *The Past of Pastimes.* Hamden, Conn.: Archon Books, 1969.

Giordano, Ralph G. *Fun and Games in Twentieth-Century America: A Historical Guide to Leisure.* Westport, Conn.: Greenwood Press, 2003.

Jones, Bessie, and Bess Lomax Hawes. *Step It Down: Games, Plays, Songs, and Stories from the Afro-American Heritage.* Athens: University of Georgia Press, 1987.

Messina, Lynn M. *Sports in America.* New York: H. W. Wilson, 2001.

Nasaw, David. *Going Out: The Rise and Fall of Public Amusements.* New York: Basic Books, 1993.

Sutton-Smith, Brian. *The Folkgames of Children.* Austin: University of Texas Press, 1972.

Vinton, Iris. *The Folkway Omnibus of Children's Games.* Harrisburg, Pa.: Stackpole Books, 1970.

Weingertner, Fannia, and Donna R. Braden, eds. *Leisure and Entertainment in America.* Dearborn, Mich.: Henry Ford Museum and Greenfield Village, 1988.

Wilmeth, Don B. *Variety Entertainment and Outdoor Amusements: A Reference Guide.* Westport, Conn.: Greenwood Press, 1982.

gardening　　At one point, America had a chiefly agrarian economy. In a country still symbolically identified with farming, plant and planting lore remains a noteworthy dimension of folklore.

Residents of the United States have countless tradition practices and beliefs surrounding plants. From backyard gardens to field crops, American plants and their cultivation have inspired all kinds of folk wisdom. These traditions have many aspects, each rich with cultural meaning. These may be beliefs about which plants are healthful and lucky, as well as the reasons why.

Such lore begins with the plants themselves. Some are intended for consumption, others for decoration, and still others for medicinal uses. Edible plants include berries and vegetables. Those growing vegetable gardens may have specific notions about garden design, including layout of rows and placement of different plants. For instance, some plants are believed to be more companionable than others. Potatoes and tomatoes, for example, are said to be poor neighbors. In addition, vegetable gardeners have notions of which plants, such as marigolds, are helpful in terms of protecting the vegetables from insects and other pests. There are even folk beliefs concerning the desirable timing for placing such plants in the earth: potatoes by Saint Patrick's Day, peas by Good Friday, and corn when oak leaves reach the size of squirrel ears.

There are also many folk beliefs about flowering plants. In addition to the folklore surrounding the medicinal properties of flowers and the customs surrounding gardening, an extensive symbolism exists for flowering plants. This enthusiasm reached its peak during the Victorian era, when the "language of flowers" was articulated in etiquette manuals and specialized guides or dictionaries. For the most part, these symbols pertain to romantic situations, current or contemplated, but flowers can communicate wordless messages in a wide range of contexts.

First, there is the meaning associated with the flower itself. Some of these connotations, often derived from English lore, are obvious from the name of the bloom. An example of such a direct relationship between a flower and its cultural meaning would include the way a bachelor button represents celibacy. Other plant and flower symbolism is a logical, though perhaps not obvious, connection between the name and the meaning. For instance, bittersweet symbolizes truth. In other cases, the meanings connected to a form of flower are not intuitive but are so widely known within a culture as to seem evident. Such a message is the way, within flower language, mistletoe says, "Kiss me."

Colors of flowers prove important within the language of symbols. A familiar example of this nuance is the rose, which is available in many shades as well as colors. Each has its own distinct suggestion. Additional flower folklore extends beyond the variety and color of the flower to include a host of other factors, each capable of sending an encoded message. Not only the size of flowers, but the way they were grouped or sent could be significant. Today, however, many of these fine points of flower lore have receded, and only vague symbolism of flower form remains in current gift practices and ceremonial occasions.

Plant lore also surrounds those items believed to have magical or medicinal properties. Such plants may be used as charms, poultices, dressings, tonics, teas, or herbal remedies. Beliefs in protective or fortune-promoting plants are common even among those not actively involved in folk medicine. Examples include the carrying of the four-leafed clover for luck or the practice of eating black-eyed peas at New Year's to ensure prosperity in the coming year.

The folklore of gardening encompasses customs concerning ornamental, edible, and healing plants, and such lore is abundant in the United States.

See also: BELIEFS, FOLK; CONJURE/CONJURING; FLOWERS; FOLKLORE IN EVERYDAY LIFE; FOOD/FOODWAYS; HOLIDAYS/OBSERVANCES; LUCK/FORTUNE; MAGIC; MEDICINE, FOLK; NEW YEAR'S EVE/DAY; OCCUPATIONAL FOLKLORE; PREDICTION; SAINT PATRICK'S DAY; VERNACULAR CULTURE; VOODOO/HOODOO; WEATHER FOLKLORE.

For Further Reading:
Bergen, Fanny D., ed. *Animal and Plant Lore: Collected from the Oral Tradition of English Speaking Folk.* New York: Houghton Mifflin, 1899.
Conan, Michel, ed. *Perspectives on Garden Histories.* Washington, D.C.: Dumbarton Oaks Research Library and Collection, 1999.
Jenkins, Virginia Scott. *The Lawn: A History of an American Obsession.* Washington, D.C.: Smithsonian Institution Press, 1994.
Jones, Pamela. *Just Weeds: History, Myths, and Uses.* New York: Prentice Hall, 1991.
Martin, Laura C. *Garden Flower Folklore.* Chester, Conn.: Globe Pequot Press, 1987.
Otis, Denise. *Grounds for Pleasure: Four Centuries of the American Garden.* New York: Harry N. Abrams, 2002.
Riotte, Louise. *Sleeping with a Sunflower: A Treasury of Old-Time Gardening Lore.* Pownal, Vt.: Storey Communications, 1987.
Schroeder, Fred. *Front Yard America: The Evolution and Meanings of a Vernacular Domestic Landscape.* Bowling Green, Ohio: Bowling Green State University Popular Press, 1993.
Thacker, Christopher. *The History of Gardens.* Berkeley: University of California Press, 1979.
Wesmacott, Richard. *African-American Gardens and Yards.* Knoxville: University of Tennessee Press, 1992.

Wilson, David Scofield, and Angus Kress Gillespie, eds. *Rooted in America: Foodlore of Popular Fruits and Vegetables.* Knoxville: University of Tennessee Press, 1999.

Garou, Loup   See LOUP-GAROU.

gay/lesbian folklore   As with other historically disenfranchised populations in the United States, the culture of gay, lesbian, bisexual, and transsexual persons has a complicated history and its own lore.

For most of American history, members of this group have been socially stigmatized by perceptions that homosexuals were sick, sinful, mentally ill, criminal, or otherwise defective. Such an atmosphere drove many, if not most, persons outside the heterosexual community to conceal the nature of their private lives from such scrutiny. These individuals, sometimes described as "closeted," made a secret of their sexual identities to escape judgment, bias, and discrimination from other members of society.

While there have always been some individuals willing to be open about homosexuality, the pattern for the majority was either to disclose nothing about their personal identities or to conduct their lives as if they were in fact heterosexual. Only a person's closest friends, family members, and associates might be aware of his or her true sexual identity. This atmosphere prevailed well into the 20th century, until the beginnings of the gay liberation movement.

The landmark incident most often cited as the turning point in this movement was a June 1969 riot at the Stonewall Inn, as gay patrons clashed with officers from the New York Police Department. In an era of movements for civil rights and women's rights, this event marked the beginning of a process of radicalization of America's homosexual community. What ensued was a campaign for "gay power," meaning dignity and equality of treatment for the nation's homosexual population. With gay pride rallies, parades, and festivals, the movement promoted acceptance of homosexuals, bisexuals, and transgender persons in America.

Forceful groups within the gay power movement were organizations such as the National Gay Task Force (which later became the National Gay and Lesbian Task Force), the Gay Liberation Front, and the Gay and Lesbian Alliance against Defamation. Public efforts to educate, communicate with, and persuade others were all part of the movement to win fair and equal treatment.

Some specific victories were won along the way. During the 1970s, for example, the American Psychological Association demedicalized homosexuality and removed it from the list of psychological diagnoses in use in the United States. In the face of the human immunodeficiency virus/acquired immunodeficiency syndrome (HIV/AIDS) epidemic, groups such as the Gay Men's Health Crisis and ACT-UP were effective in speeding the process by which treatment drugs, such as azidothymidine (AZT), were approved for use. Other causes, such as legalization of same-sex marriage, continue to this day.

Folklore within the gay community has many aspects. One of the most extensive categories of gay verbal lore consists of personal narratives described as "coming-out stories." To "come out" means to reveal one's sexual identity to others, whether privately to individuals or publicly to the wider world. Most members of the gay community have their own stories of what happened when they confided this information to family members, particularly to parents. As with most subcultures, the gay community also has its share of in-jokes, bits of humor that are funny only if one knows the context and reference for the jokes. The AIDS crisis, for example, resulted in a great many anecdotes and jokes designed to break the tension surrounding health concerns and related personal conflicts. Some of these items relate closely to coming-out stories, since some individuals did not come out to family members until they learned they were HIV positive. In one such joke, a gay man who

is still in the closet with his family describes telling his parents he has AIDS. "The hard part," the joke remarks, "was convincing them I was an intravenous drug user." The humor of such a joke hinges on the comparative stigma of each of several at-risk populations for AIDS.

Because most gay and lesbian youth undergo a time of discovering a wider community associated with their sexual identity, there is an informal but fairly extensive process of acculturation, designed to support those coming out, help individuals cope with conflict and discrimination, and help them understand (as well as be understood within) a subculture. Especially during those periods in American history when homosexuality was most stigmatized, care was necessary to identify those in whom one might confide and with whom one might partner. Today, this set of codes, cues, and signals is still referred to as *gaydar*, a playful turn on the word *radar*, with its connotations of detection and knowing without being told.

Other aspects of gay/lesbian folk culture include theatrical presentations intended to convey self-acceptance and pride. An example would be the process by which gay activists, such as those associated with a group known as Queer Nation, co-opt epithets (such as *queer*) and invert symbols used to insult gays. Such activists may appear at marches defiantly chanting slogans such as "We're here; we're queer; get used to it!" Other folk traditions include masquerade, double entendres, and parody, such as drag and camp. Both phenomena involve efforts to delight in gay/lesbian identity and, at times, to flaunt that pride before the public.

Identity politics helped mobilize a variety of groups to assert their rights and seek social change. Such groups include people of color, women, and gay/lesbian/bisexual/transgender persons. Each group has its own folklore, including that directly connected to the movement for equality.

See also: AIDS FOLKLORE; FOLKLORE IN EVERY-DAY LIFE; GENDER AND FOLKLORE; HUMOR, FOLK; PARADES; PROTEST IN FOLKLORE; QUILT, AIDS.

For Further Reading:

Adam, Barry. *The Rise of a Gay and Lesbian Movement.* Boston: Twayne, 1987.

Bawer, Bruce. *A Place at the Table: The Gay Individual in American Society.* New York: Poseidon Press, 1993.

Bronski, Michael. *Culture Clash: The Making of Gay Sensibility.* Boston: South End Press, 1984.

Bucholtz, Mary, A. C. Liang, and Laurel A. Sutton, eds. *Reinventing Identities: The Gendered Self in Discourse.* New York: Oxford University Press, 1999.

Cruikshank, Margaret. *The Gay and Lesbian Liberation Movement.* New York: Routledge, 1992.

Duberman, Martin, Martha Vicinus, and George Chauncey, Jr., eds. *Hidden from History: Reclaiming the Gay and Lesbian Past.* New York: NAL Books, 1989.

Elledge, Jim. *Gay, Lesbian, Bisexual, + Transgender Myths from the Arapaho to the Zuñi: An Anthology.* New York: Peter Lang, 2002.

Hodes, Martha, ed. *Sex, Love, Race: Crossing Boundaries in North American History.* New York: New York University Press, 1999.

Katz, Johnathan. *Gay American History: Lesbians and Gay Men in the USA.* New York: Thomas Crowell, 1976.

Martinac, Paula. *The Queerest Places: A National Guide to Gay and Lesbian Historic Sites.* New York: Holt, 1997.

Prejudice and Pride: Lesbian and Gay Traditions in America. New York: New York Folklore Society, 1993.

gender and folklore   *Gender* is a term that refers to all those human distinctions between males and females that are not the product of physiological characteristics, birth, or inherent difference. In other words, studies of gender do not address the biological phenomenon of sex; they look beyond the biological foundations to the social relations and ideology that together constitute a gender system within a given culture.

Gender studies focuses on the ways in which a society or a group within it imagines male and female as constructed categories. For instance, in 19th-century America, men and women were expected to occupy opposite gender roles, associated with different social spheres. Within this social framework, women were linked to domestic and private space, while men were linked to external and public fields of action. Such a demarcation between men and women also translated into a juxtaposition between the attributes and arenas of each gender.

Gender meanings and symbols vary across cultures. Depending upon the views within a given society, gender may imply more than two positions, such as male female, and transgender. Furthermore, gender is one of many interrelated categories of social analysis used within folklore studies. Examples of related categories include race, ethnicity, and class. Taken together, these distinctions help define the social relations and ideology within a culture.

Scholars attentive to gender have paid particular attention to the ways in which gender differences in a society result in gender inequalities for its members. Where gender roles are sharply distinguished, there may also be ways in which those roles translate into differences in privilege, access, and status. In terms of the example of 19th-century America's notion of gendered spheres, women's work was contained and devalued as compared to the more visible and celebrated labors of men. That is, folk heroes of that era generally are those whose triumphs and exploits occur outdoors and in male-coded fields of endeavor such as logging, railroading, and seafaring. As often occurs, such gender positions imply power relations and reflect underlying perceptions of the relative value of genders.

For this reason, feminist folklorists are especially interested in the ways that gender images, roles, and perceptions shape everyday experience within a folk group.

All the socially produced expectations, codes, and bifurcations related to gender identity interest the folklorist who studies the relationship between gender and folklore.

See also: BORDEN, LIZZIE; FAMILY FOLKLORE; FOLKLORE IN EVERYDAY LIFE; GAY/LESBIAN FOLKLORE; WOMEN'S MOVEMENT; WOMEN'S SUFFRAGE.

For Further Reading:

Bennett, Tony. *New Keywords: A Vocabulary of Culture and Society.* New York: Blackwell, 2005.

Hollis, Susan Tower, ed. *Feminist Theory and the Study of Folklore.* Urbana: University of Illinois Press, 1993.

Jordan, Rosan, and Susan Kalcik, eds. *Women's Folklore, Women's Culture.* Philadelphia: University of Pennsylvania Press, 1985.

Kodish, Deborah. "Absent Gender, Silent Encounter," *Journal of American Folklore* 100, no. 398 (fall 1987): 583–578.

Radner, Joan Newlon, ed. *Feminist Messages: Coding in Women's Folk Culture.* Urbana: University of Illinois Press, 1993.

Saltzman, Rachelle H. "Folklore, Feminism, and the Folk: Whose Lore Is It?" *Journal of American Folklore* 100, no. 398 (fall 1987): 548–562.

Scott, Joan Wallach. "Gender: A Useful Category for Historical Analysis," *American Historical Review* 91 (1986): 1053–1075.

Thomas, Jeannie Banks. *Naked Barbies, Warrior Joes, and Other Forms of Visible Gender.* Chicago: University of Illinois Press, 2003.

Georgia folklore See APPALACHIAN FOLKLORE; SOUTHERN REGIONAL FOLKLORE.

German-American folklore German-American folklore pertains to immigrants to the United States from Germany, along with those born in America of German heritage.

Immigration to the United States from Germany has been going on since the colonial era. German Americans remain among the nation's largest immigrant groups. The densest concentrations of German-American settlement are inland, including the states of Iowa, Minnesota, Nebraska, North Dakota, South Dakota, and Wisconsin.

Much of what the general public associates with German Americans is actually Bavarian, from German Day festivals to lederhosen. German Americans celebrate many of the same holidays other Americans do but may add their own customs to the festivities. For example, the tradition of discharging firearms at New Year's, known as "shooting in the new year," originates with German culture. During and after World War II, anti-German sentiment made it more difficult for German Americans to express cultural pride, but many folkways continued nonetheless.

Populations of German Americans living in Pennsylvania represent a case in point. The population sometimes known as the Pennsylvania Dutch are more accurately described as the Pennsylvania Germans. The reference to them as Dutch is a misnomer, likely deriving from the German word for "German," *Deutsch.* Therefore, when people speak of Pennsylvania's "Dutch Country," they usually mean the state's residents of German ancestry. In particular, they often mean those subgroups of the Pennsylvania German whose folkways remain the most distinctive, such as the Amish and the Mennonites. These communities have held true to traditional ways and resisted the introduction of new technologies. With their horse and buggy transportation, the Amish represent otherwise lost or vanishing folkways.

The Pennsylvania Germans have earned a wide reputation for signature folklore forms from folk art to folk architecture. Folk crafts associated with the Pennsylvania Germans include paper cutting, quilting, stenciling, illuminated manuscripts, and painted furniture or other domestic objects. Pennsylvania German decorative motifs such as birds, flowers, hearts, and hex signs such as can be seen on traditional barns and farmhouses typify the look of Pennsylvania German handiwork. This folk group is responsible for several holiday customs observed by many Americans beyond their group, including the

Easter Bunny, the adorned Christmas tree, and Groundhog Day. Perhaps the most famous of all Pennsylvania German traditions involve food customs and foodways. Popular dishes originating with the Pennsylvania Germans are pretzels, scrapple, sauerkraut, funnel cakes, and shoofly pie.

With the formation of recognition organizations such as the Pennsylvania German Society, founded in 1891, Americans paid tribute to the folk culture and traditions associated with this small but influential group. Organizations dedicated to the preservation and study of German-American culture include the German American Information and Education Association in Burke, Pennsylvania. Major collections of German-American cultural material include the University of Cincinnati's Society for German American Studies.

German-American folklore takes many forms, all of which maintain the cultural identity and traditional ways of persons of German heritage in the United States.

See also: ARCHITECTURE, FOLK; CHRISTMAS; CRAFTS, FOLK; CULTURAL GROUPS; EASTER; EASTER BUNNY; EINSTEIN, ALBERT; ETHNICITY; FOOD/FOODWAYS; GROUNDHOG DAY; HOLIDAYS/OBSERVANCES; IMMIGRATION AND FOLKLORE; NEW YEAR'S EVE/DAY; PENNSYLVANIA DUTCH/PENNSYLVANIA GERMAN FOLKLORE.

For Further Reading:
Albrecht, Erich A., and J. Anthony Burzle, eds. *Germanica Americana 1976: Symposium on German-American Literature and Culture.* Lawrence: Max Kade Document & Research Center/University of Kansas, 1977.

Barrick, Mac. *German-American Folklore.* Little Rock, Ark.: August House, 1987.

Bohlman, Philip, and Otto Holzapfel, eds. *Land Without Nightingales: Music in the Making of German-America.* Madison: Max Kade Institute for German American Studies/University of Wisconsin, 2002.

Bungert, Heike. "'Feast of Fools': German-American Carnival as a Medium of Identity Formation, 1854–1914," *Amerikastudien/American Studies* 48, no. 3 (2003): 325–344.

Cook, Bernard A., and Rosemary Petralle Cook. *German Americans.* Vero Beach, Fla.: Rourke, 1991.

Farrior, Stephanie. "German Immigrants in America as Presented in Travel Accounts," *Pennsylvania Folklife* 26, no. 2 (1976–1977): 42–48.

Hebel, Udo J., ed. *Sites of Memory in American Literatures and Cultures.* Heidelberg: Carl Winter Universitätsverlag, 2003.

Keel, William. "Was is eine Schnitzelbank? The Tradition behind the Popular German-American Sing-Along," *Missouri Folklore Society Journal* 24 (2002): 21–35.

Yocom, Margaret. "Blessing the Ties That Bind: Storytelling at Family Festivals." In *A Celebration of American Family Folklore: Tales and Traditions from the Smithsonian Collection*, edited by Steven J. Zeitlin, Amy Kotkin, and Holly Cutting Baker, 250–259. New York: Pantheon, 1982.

Geronimo (1829–1909) Geronimo was a famous figure within Native American resistance efforts.

Born in 1829, Geronimo was part of an Apache group, the Chirocahua. His name was a war cry, and the circumstances of his life were difficult. He experienced many tragedies, including the murders of his mother, wife, and children. In addition, as did many Native Americans, Geronimo had to contend with Indian removal campaigns.

As a warrior against efforts to relocate his population, Geronimo led them in resistance. This period, from 1881 to 1886, marked the height of his fame. The events were alternately described as Geronimo's Resistance and the Apache Wars. He and his people struggled mightily against removal, spending some time in hiding and some time on reservations in the process. Finally, in September 1886, Geronimo surrendered to Anglo-American forces and became a prisoner of war. He was then sent into exile in Florida, and later Alabama. He died on an Oklahoma reservation in 1909.

Although he did not escape the fate of life on the reservation, Geronimo became an icon of courage in battle. In face, Theodore Roosevelt invited him to appear in the inaugural parade when Roosevelt assumed the U.S. presidency in 1905. During World War II, Geronimo's name became a jumper's yell, one that is still sometimes exclaimed when someone leaps or falls from a height. He continues to be remembered as a courageous warrior, inspiring others to bravery or, on occasions such as the jumps, bravado.

Along with other memorable figures such as Crazy Horse and Sitting Bull, Geronimo found his place within American history and folklore as a freedom fighter for his people.

See also: ALLEN, PAULA GUNN; CIVIL RIGHTS MOVEMENT; CRAZY HORSE; FOLK HEROES/LEGENDARY FIGURES; FRONTIER; INAUGURATION DAY; NATIVE AMERICAN FOLKLORE; PROTEST IN FOLKLORE; REGION, FOLK; ROOSEVELT, THEODORE; SILKO, LESLIE MARMON; WESTERN REGIONAL FOLKLORE; WORLD WAR II.

For Further Reading:

Allen, Paula Gunn. *As Long as the River Flows: The Stories of Nine Native Americans.* New York: Scholastic, 2001.

Carmony, Neil, and David Brown, eds. *Tough Times in Rough Places: Personal Narratives of Adventure, Death, and Survival on the Western Frontier.* Salt Lake City: University of Utah Press, 2001.

Masson, Jean-Robert. *The Great Indian Chiefs: Cochise, Geronimo, Crazy Horse, Sitting Bull.* Hauppauge, N.Y.: Barron's, 1994.

Roberts, David. *Once They Moved like the Wind: Cochise, Geronimo, and the Apache Wars.* New York: Simon & Schuster, 1993.

Silko, Leslie Marmon. "A Geronimo Story." In *The Man to Send Rain Clouds: Contemporary Stories by American Indians,* edited by Kenneth Rosen, 128–144. New York: Penguin, 1992.

gestures   Gestures are a nonverbal form of communication consisting of bodily movements to which the members of a group has assigned shared meanings. Most gestures involve the face or hands, but the full body may be used in making a gesture.

Probably the most frequently demonstrated gestures in daily life are facial expressions, such as smiles, frowns, or eyebrow raises. These fleeting motions can be subtle or broad in their suggestions, whether substituting for verbal expression, complementing it, or complicating it. As with other forms of folklife, gestures are reliant upon context and culture. Gestural communication, as is spoken language, is idiomatic. In order for a gesture to convey its intended meaning, its symbolism and message must be clear to both the person offering the gesture and the person receiving it. For that reason, many gestures employ pantomime or pictorial elements to ensure understanding.

Most of the hand gestures used in everyday communication seem obvious among cultural insiders, but they are still part of a code just as much as verbal communication. A waved hand is a salutation of greeting or farewell. A pointed finger signals a directional cue. A raised hand is a request for a potential speaker to take the floor. Beyond these routine gestures, most Americans recognize a wide array of other nonverbal messages, such as air quotes, the high five, the victory sign, or a peace sign. The most extensive vocabulary system of gesture used within the United States is American Sign Language (ASL), typically used by and for the hearing impaired.

As an important form of folk speech, gestures inflect a conversation with all the nuances a transcript of the exchange would fail to capture.

See also: DISABILITY AND FOLKLORE; FOLKLORE IN EVERYDAY LIFE; SPEECH, FOLK.

For Further Reading:

Bauman, Richard, ed. *Folklore, Cultural Performances, and Popular Entertainments: A Communications-Centered Handbook.* New York: Oxford University Press, 1992.

Benthall, Jonathan, and Ted Polhemus, eds. *The Body as a Medium of Expression.* New York: Dutton, 1992.

Efron, David. *Gesture, Race and Culture.* The Hague: Mouton, 1972.

Kendon, Adam. *Gesture: Visible Action as Utterance.* New York : Cambridge University Press, 2004.

Kendon, Adam, ed. *Nonverbal Communication, Interaction, and Gesture.* The Hague: Mouton, 1981.

Lock, Andrew, ed. *Action, Gesture, and Symbol: The Emergence of Language.* London: Academic Press, 1978.

Morris, Desmond et al. *Gestures: Their Origins and Distribution.* New York: Stein & Day, 1979.

ghosts Ghosts and their influences on the living prove a popular subject within American folklore.

Ghosts are the disembodied spirits of the dead. They are either the spirits of those who have recently died or those who have returned to travel among the living. Although ghosts are a staple of the horror genre, and closely associated with spooky occasions such as Halloween, they need not be frightening or malevolent. In fact, some accounts suggest that ghosts can exert a positive energy and protective force on those who have contact with them.

The presence of ghosts, however, is usually disconcerting to those who believe themselves to have encountered one. According to the lore, ghosts tend to frequent the places that were important to them in life or in death. Graveyards are commonly said to attract the spirits of those buried there. Of all outdoor locations, cemeteries are the most likely to be the site for reports of ghosts, as for ghost stories.

Residences are another favorite location among ghosts, particularly if the structure was once home to the deceased individual. When a ghost becomes associated with a particular building over time, it is said to be haunted. Such designations usually imply more than one sighting, and usually several witnesses to recount the presence of the dead as sensed there. Many consider the Whaley House, built in 1857 over a cemetery in San Diego, California, to be one of the most haunted houses in the nation on the basis of the volume of paranormal experiences reported there.

In another such instance, a house in Amityville, New York, has been repeatedly claimed to be haunted by ghosts that torment residents. As with many houses deemed haunted, this home was the sight of a tragic event. A young man named DeFeo is alleged to have murdered his entire family on the premises. Among other things, the ghost of the alleged perpetrator is said to speak to the house's residents and urge them to acts of violence similar to his own. Subsequent occupants, most notably the Lutz family, have reported strange happenings. It was on the basis of these experiences that a popular book and film, both titled *The Amityville Horror*, took shape. Debates continue about whether the story of this New York house represents a hoax or an authentic account.

Apparitions vary in appearance as well as disposition. Some are vague and filmy in their manifestation, while others are so detailed and convincing in their presence that they are mistaken for the living. If the ghost takes a form that resembles a human body, it may linger in an area that holds significance or move about the building at will. Some frequently sighted ghosts appear to have habits and characteristic movements or moods, and testimony of those who see them proves fairly consistent. In some cases, the ghost is made restless by guilt, regret, grief, or other unresolved emotions. Ghosts of this sort seem drawn to the same places and the same acts ritualistically, as if to find an answer or resolution. Such is the case with the story of the Weeping Woman, a ghost thought to wander the side of a river after dark, looking for the children she drowned there.

Poltergeists described in folklore vary from the mischievous to the hostile, and their exploits form the subject of many stories and tales in America.

See also: BELIEFS, FOLK; BLOODY MARY; BURIAL CUSTOMS; CEMETERY FOLKLORE; DEATH; FOLKLORE IN EVERYDAY LIFE; GHOST STORIES; GHOST TOWNS; HALLOWEEN/ALL HALLOWS' EVE; HAUNTED HOUSES; MAGIC; MORRISON, TONI; SUPERNATURAL; SUPERSTITION; URBAN LEGENDS; VAMPIRE; WEEPING WOMAN.

For Further Reading:

Bennett, Gillian. *Alas, Poor Ghost! Traditions of Belief in Story and Discourse*. Logan: Utah State University Press, 1999.

Davidson, Hilda, and W. M. S. Russell, eds. *The Folklore of Ghosts*. Cambridge, Mass.: Folklore Society/Brewer, 1981.

Green, Celia, and Charles McCreery. *Apparitions*. Oxford: Institute for Psychophysical Research, 1989.

Guiley, Rosemary. *The Encyclopedia of Ghosts and Spirits*. New York: Facts On File, 1992.

———. *Harper's Encyclopedia of Mystical and Paranormal Experience*. Edison, N.J.: Castle, 1991.

Montrell, William Lynwood. *Ghosts along the Cumberland: Deathlore in the Kentucky Foothills*. Knoxville: University of Tennessee Press, 1987.

ghost stories Stories about spirits are common in both spoken and written lore in America. These tales of ghosts feature manifestations of the recently or long deceased. Specters may make their presence known in any of a variety of a ways, sometimes as subtle as a localized shift in room temperature or property of its lighting. In most cases, however, ghost stories involve more specific changes in the environment haunted, including sights, sounds, and occasionally smells.

Ghost stories belong to a wider genre of folktales, told to entertain with the sensation of fright. These spooky stories can be told at any time of year, but are most commonly recounted around campfires and at Halloween. Tellers and listeners alike delight in the exchange of paranormal stories, populated by ghosts and other frights.

The ghosts who populate these tales typically busy themselves with unfinished business from their time among the living. Some seek clarification, understanding, or connection, while others are said to attend to immortal purposes, such as vindicating themselves, avenging actions whether their own or someone else's, or transmitting a message from beyond the grave.

Perhaps the most famous haunted house in the United States, although for other reasons, is the White House in Washington, D.C. Over the years that this structure has served as residence for the president and his family, quite a few unexplained events have taken place there. Residents, guests, and staff alike have added to the body of lore associated with 1600 Pennsylvania Avenue.

It may stand to reason that a building that has housed the nation's leaders and visiting dignitaries would have its share of such stories. In one set of accounts, the ghost of a British soldier from the War of 1812 is seen around the White House, holding a torch. These stories recall the time in 1814 when the White House was burned by the British. Other ghost stories associated with the White House involve individual staff members, often those of long standing, who are spotted around the house. Usually, they appear to be performing their usual duties, ever the devoted employees.

In addition, there exist many stories about the White House's being haunted by the presidents who once called it home. One first lady, for example, reported hearing a deceased Andrew Jackson cursing on the premises. Others have claimed to have seen the ghosts of Thomas Jefferson or first ladies such as Abigail Adams and Dolley Madison around the historic residence.

Of all the ghost stories surrounding the White House, however, the most persistent involves sightings of Abraham Lincoln. By several accounts, he is purported to still linger around the White House, especially those portions most beloved to him. Indeed, it is said that Winston Churchill refused to stay in the Lincoln Bedroom because he had spotted the ghost of Lincoln in its vicinity. Theodore Roosevelt also believed he sensed Lincoln's presence in the White House, manifested as a knocking at the bedroom door.

Whether it be the urban legends, from Bloody Mary to the Weeping Woman, or figures of national significance, such as Thomas Jefferson or Abraham Lincoln, stories involving the activities of ghosts persist in American lore.

See also: BLOODY MARY; DEATH; FOLKLORE IN AMERICAN LITERATURE; FOLKLORE IN EVERYDAY LIFE; GHOST TOWNS; GHOSTS; IRVING, WASHINGTON; LINCOLN, ABRAHAM; MORRISON, TONI; ROOSEVELT, THEODORE; SUPERNATURAL; SUPERSTITION; WEEPING WOMAN.

For Further Reading:

Cohn, Amy L., ed. *From Sea to Shining Sea: A Treasury of American Folklore and Folk Songs.* New York: Scholastic, 1993.

DeSpain, Pleasant. *Sweet Land of Story: Thirty-Six American Tales to Tell.* Little Rock, Ark.: August House, 2000.

Downer, Deborah, ed. *Classic American Ghost Stories: 200 Years of Ghost Lore from the Great Plains, New England, the South, and the Pacific Northwest.* Little Rock, Ark.: August House, 1990.

National Association for the Preservation and Perpetuation of Storytelling. *Best-Loved Stories Told at the National Storytelling Festival.* Jonesborough, Tenn.: National Storytelling Press, 1991.

Rash, Bryson B. *Footnote Washington: Tracking the Engaging, Humorous, and Surprising Bypaths of Capital History.* McLean, Va.: EPM Publications, 1983.

Schwartz, Alvin. *Ghosts! Ghostly Tales from Folklore.* New York: HarperCollins, 1991.

ghost towns   Ghost towns are like Hollywood stage sets, in that they represent the traces left behind of former glory, or dreams of it.

Many ghost towns originated as a result of the construction of the transcontinental railroad.

As the rails stretched across America, towns began to dot the path it traveled. This effect became heightened around 1849 with the discovery of gold in the Black Hills and elsewhere in the American West. Fortune hunters descended on the locations where prospectors had been rumored to have found gold. Western expansion engaged in these ways was destined to produce some boom-and-bust communities, sometimes at the same locations. Because of the fleeting economies of both railway towns and gold rush settlements, the land alongside the track of the transcontinental railroad became the site of many ghost towns. When freight pathways shifted or railroad stops changed, a once-flourishing town and its residents could find themselves passed, both literally and figuratively, by progress.

Most ghost towns are mining and railroad towns past their prime. Still, there are any number of other reasons a prospering town may experience a reversal, leaving a ghost town in its wake. When mills or military bases close, or when oil wells run dry, the surrounding areas tend to lose population and vitality. If not entirely abandoned, such ghost towns nonetheless fall out of both favor and repair. The majority of America's ghost towns are located in the states of Arizona, California, Colorado, Montana, Nevada, New Mexico, and Utah.

Because of their historical suggestions, some ghost towns are approached as revitalization projects. Usually, however, the goal is not to restore a residential population and economy, but instead to accommodate the interests and appetites of potential tourists. This commercial focus can create artificial or falsified landscapes posing as historically authentic ones.

For instance, the community of Locke, California, was once a thriving town founded by Chinese Americans in 1905. It is the last extant rural Chinatown in the United States. Although a 1913 law prevented anyone but citizens from landholding, they purchased the structures that made up their town. Once settled in Locke, the residents farmed the rich land of the Sacramento Delta. Over time, though, the town lost its young residents to other cities, lost its older residents to death, and failed to attract a new population of residents to maintain its vibrant life as a community. Locke became the site of a struggle for control, as historic preservationists, developers, tourists, and the last few remaining town residents sought to decide its future. In several senses, then, Locke had become a ghost town, its historical resonances in as much peril as its handful of surviving Chinese-American occupants.

Therefore, while the term *ghost town* is figurative, the allure and controversy of such a place lie precisely in its echoes of past lives and their intrigue.

See also: ETHNICITY; FOLKLORE IN EVERYDAY LIFE; GHOSTS; GHOST STORIES; GOLD RUSH, THE; HISTORIC PRESERVATION; NORTHWESTERN REGIONAL FOLKLORE; OCCUPATIONAL FOLKLORE; REGION, FOLK; SUPERNATURAL; TRANSCONTINENTAL RAILROAD; WESTERN REGIONAL FOLKLORE.

For Further Reading:
Adams, Paul, Steven Hoelscher, and Karen Till, eds. *Textures of Place: Exploring Humanist Geographies.* Minneapolis: University of Minnesota Press, 2001.
Carter, William. *Ghost Towns of the West.* Menlo Park, Calif.: Lane Magazine and Book, 1971.
Hanna, Stephen, and Vincent Del Casino, Jr., eds. *Mapping Tourism.* Minneapolis: University of Minnesota Press, 2003.
O'Neal, Bill. *Ghost Towns of the American West.* Lincolnwood, Ill.: Publications International, Ltd., 1995.
Roberts, Nancy. *The Gold Seekers: Gold, Ghosts and Legends from Carolina to California.* Columbia: University of South Carolina Press, 1989.
Silverberg, Robert. *Ghost Towns of the American West.* New York: Crowell, 1968.
Sprague, Marguerite. *Bodie's Gold: Tall Tales and True History from a California Mining Town.* Reno: University of Nevada Press, 2003.
Thompson, Linda Kay. *Alaska's Abandoned Towns: Case Studies for Preservation and Interpretation.* Anchorage: Alaska Division of Parks, 1972.

"Golden Goose, The" "The Golden Goose" is a very familiar fairy tale recorded in print by the Grimm brothers.

The story centers on a man with three sons. The youngest of these, Dummling, is often mocked. Each son is sent into the forest to chop wood. Each young man is provided with food and drink to take on the journey. During those travels, each son is approached by a curious little man. The first two sons refuse to share, and shortly thereafter each meets with an injury while performing his duty.

When the gray man makes the same request of the third son, the young man agrees. Just as Dummling is apologizing for the humble nature of the food and drink, he discovers that his cinder cake has magically become a sweet cake and his sour beer is now good wine. For the generosity the third son has demonstrated, the gray man decides to give him good luck.

When the young man returns to his work, he discovers a strange sight in the roots of a tree he is chopping down. It is a golden goose.

Dummling takes the goose to an inn. The innkeeper's daughters take great notice of the bird's golden feathers, and each begins to conceive of ways to have a gold feather for herself. In their efforts to do so, by some magic turn, the daughters wind up stuck to the goose and to each other.

When Dummling leaves the inn, he carries the goose. Trailing behind them are the innkeeper's three daughters. As others approach to admire the bird or scold the girls, they too adhere to the train. Dummling takes the goose and what turns out to be a string of seven people to a city where it is widely known that the king's daughter cannot smile. The king has announced that anyone who can elicit a smile from the princess will be granted permission to marry her.

Upon seeing the goose and its human entourage, the princess not only smiles, but laughs uncontrollably. Dummling then seeks her hand in marriage, but the king does not approve of the young man and so keeps setting additional conditions on the proposal. After several such exchanges, the king finally relents, and so Dummling and the princess marry. Not long after that, the king dies, Dummling inherits the estate, and he and princess live happily ever after.

As is customary with fairy tales, "The Golden Goose" carries a strong moral or message to its audience. As is also usual to the genre, it functions as a cautionary tale. The chief warning concerns the dangers of avarice and false promise.

It is a testimony to the staying power of this fairy tale that even today, people advise one another not to "kill the golden goose." In so saying, they are warning against being so greedy or duplicitous that they curse their own good fortune.

See also: CHILDREN'S FOLKLORE; FABLES; FAIRY TALES; GRIMM BROTHERS; "JACK AND THE BEANSTALK"; MYTHS, FOLK.

For Further Reading:

Bettelheim, Bruno. *The Uses of Enchantment: The Meaning and Importance of Fairy Tales.* New York: Knopf, 1976.

Radner, Joan Newlon, ed. *Feminist Messages: Coding in Women's Folk Culture.* Urbana: University of Illinois Press, 1993.

Tatar, Maria. *The Hard Facts of the Grimms' Fairy Tales.* Princeton, N.J.: Princeton University Press, 1987.

Ward, Donald. "The German Connection: The Brothers Grimm and the Study of 'Oral' Literature," *Western Folklore* 53, no. 1 (January 1994): 1–26.

Zipes, Jack. *The Complete Fairy Tales of the Brothers Grimm.* New York: Bantam Books, 1992.

"Goldilocks and the Three Bears" See "THREE BEARS, GOLDILOCKS AND THE."

gold rush, the The *gold rush* is an expression that refers to a 19th-century phenomenon during which many Americans sought their fortunes by prospecting and panning for gold.

Children's folklore is replete with tales about the temptations and the dangers of gold. Fables, fairy tales, and myths all caution about the greed gold excites and the wealth, power, and influence that it promises. This is a plot or subplot in such classics as "Rumplestiltskin," "Sleeping Beauty," "King Midas," and "The Golden Goose," and even "Goldilocks and the Three Bears." America's history of gold mining has, in turn, furnished its own complement of adventurous and cautionary tales about the lure of this precious metal.

Although the reference to this phenomenon is typically singular, there were many gold rushes spanning the period from 1803 to 1900. Such events drew hopefuls to the states of North Carolina, Georgia, Nevada, Oregon, Colorado, Utah, and Alaska. The best-known rush, however, is the one that occurred in what was then the California Territory. According to the lore, it was on January 24, 1848, that James Marshall accidentally found gold while preparing to build a sawmill. As news of this find spread, people from all over made their way west in hopes of striking it rich by hitting the "mother lode."

The pattern of such events, whether in California or elsewhere, was fairly consistent. Once the presence of gold was detected or suspected, there would be an influx of prospectors, panners, gamblers, traders, criminals, and other opportunists. These newcomers and their endeavors would displace local residents. The new arrivals would plunder the area of its easily found quantities of gold, ravage the landscape, and move on to their next speculation. The desire for gold is said to account for some of the interest in establishing a transcontinental railroad, whose construction was completed with a final, ceremonial golden spike.

When the craze was over, many of the settlements formed by these fortune hunters were abandoned, and the sites became ghost towns. Some locations, however, such as the area where Marshall made his discovery, have been maintained for visitors. Today, for instance, at the Marshall Gold Discovery State Historical Park, tourists can learn about the forty-niners immortalized in such popular American folk songs such as "Oh My Darling, Clementine." This 1880s folk song is usually attributed to Percy Montrose and sung in the voice of Clementine's grieving suitor. Once a ballad and now a camp song, the tune relates the tragic fate met by his beloved, the daughter of a forty-niner: "Ruby lips above the water / Blowing bubbles, soft and fine / But, alas, I was no swimmer / So I lost my Clementine." At the Klondike Gold Rush National Historic Park, visitors can explore the last major American rush, in which would-be miners ventured northwest to join a gold rush to the Canadian Yukon's Klondike district.

The American gold rush is recalled fondly within popular culture by songs, stories, expressions, and media representations. Such depictions include Charlie Chaplin's silent movie *The Gold Rush* (1925), in which his widely recognizable tramp character catches gold fever in Klondike country at the turn of the century. Although the stories and other lore associated with the gold rush recount the threats posed by prospecting and the misdeeds of bandits, claim jumpers, and others seeking to cash in on the good fortune of others, the gold rush retains a certain cachet within American folklore as a time of seemingly unlimited possibility, if also unreckoned peril. Through characters from Black Bart, a desperado, to Windwagon Smith, an inventor, the story of the American gold rush has undergone countless retellings.

The allure of yesteryear's gold rush is more than a distant historical reference; its legend lives on in today's many get-rich-quick schemes and scams in which it is supposed one can manufacture or borrow good luck.

See also: FRONTIER; GHOST TOWNS; "GOLDEN GOOSE, THE"; HISTORICAL EVENTS; HISTORIC PRESERVATION; LUCK/FORTUNE; MIDAS, KING; NORTHWESTERN REGIONAL FOLKLORE; OCCUPATIONAL FOLKLORE; REGION, FOLK; SMITH, WINDWAGON; "THREE BEARS, GOLDILOCKS AND THE"; TRANSCONTINENTAL RAILROAD; WESTERN REGIONAL FOLKLORE.

For Further Reading:

Bernstein, Peter. *The Power of Gold: The History of an Obsession.* New York: Wiley, 2000.

Black, Eleonora. *The Gold Rush Song Book.* San Francisco: Colt Press, 1940.

Dary, David. *The Oregon Trail: An American Saga.* New York: Random House, 2004.

English, Logan, and Billy Faler. *The Days of '49; Songs of the Gold Rush* (audio recording). New York: Folkways Records, 1957.

James, Ronald M., and C. Elizabeth Raymond, eds. *Comstock Women.* Reno: University of Nevada Press, 1998.

Roberts, Nancy. *The Gold Seekers: Gold, Ghosts and Legends from Carolina to California.* Columbia: University of South Carolina Press, 1989.

Rosenberg, Bruce A. "The Folklore of the Gold Rush," *Huntington Library Quarterly* 44, no. 4 (1981): 293–308.

gossip/rumor   See SPEECH, FOLK.

graffiti   Viewed by some as art and by others as vandalism, graffiti are a common sight in America's towns and cities.

Graffiti include any visual material, whether pictorial or verbal, affixed to public spaces. While the most typical means of applying these messages is spray paint, any number of media may be used. For example, writing on bathroom walls, a popular form of graffiti for many years in America, is usually done with markers rather than paints. Whatever the material used to inscribe the message, however, graffiti represent an ordinary American's attempt to claim a public forum for personal expression. Through graffiti placed in public view, the individual reaches a wide audience. Graffiti are most often a kind of outsider art, advancing the views of the disenfranchised.

Some graffiti operate as a code. In the first half of the 20th century, for instance, hoboes used a language of picture symbols to communicate with other hoboes. Created by transients, these pictographs were a reasonably safe way to leave behind advice for those who arrived next. That the messages were encoded helped shield the writers and readers of such graffiti; only someone familiar with the picture language would have any clue what the messages or their placement might mean.

Writing graffiti is often a territorial act, used to demonstrate that the individual or a group to which she or he belongs has control of a public area. For example, gang markings function in this way. In territorial graffiti, specific visual or verbal elements become signatures recognizable to viewers. These distinctive forms are sometimes called tags. By placing tags on the perimeter of a public space, the graffiti maker signals that the marked area represents a "home" or claimed space. The character of Kilroy provides an illustration of how military, and later civilian, lore asserted power in this way.

Graffiti may also be an expressive medium, used to display the artistry and the vision of the individual at work. In the latter part of the 20th century, even museum artists started to take note of the vitality of graffiti art. Some, such as Keith Haring, both created graffiti and incorporated the aesthetic into his gallery work.

For the most part, however, graffiti represent a kind of folk speech from people who would otherwise be anonymous and unheard in American society.

Graffiti are a long-standing form of folk communication that, while frequently illegal, continue to flourish in the United States.

See also: ART, FOLK; CITY FOLKLORE; FOLKLORE IN EVERYDAY LIFE; HOBOES; KILROY; MUSEUMS, FOLK; OUTLAWS. SPEECH, FOLK.

For Further Reading:

Barrick, Mac. "The Growth of Graffiti," *Folklore Forum* 7 (1974): 273–275.

Castleman, Craig. *Getting Up: Subway Graffiti in New York.* Cambridge, Mass.: MIT Press, 1982.

Reisner, Robert. *Two Thousand Years of Wall Writing.* New York: Cowles Book, 1971.

Roemer, Danielle. "Graffiti as Story and Act." In *Folklore, Literature, and Cultural Theory: Col-lected Essays*, edited by Cathy Lynn Preston, 22–28. New York: Garland, 1995.

Grandparents Day   Like National Boss Day, Grandparents Day is a relatively recent American holiday and one brought about by a dedicated individual. In this case, the holiday's originator was Marian McQuade, of Oak Hill, West Virginia. Married for over 50 years to Joe McQuade, Marian McQuade is the mother of 15 children, grandparent to some 40 grandchildren, and great-grandmother to three. Marian McQuade recalled the value and enjoyment of childhood visits with community elders, and after decades spent as an adult volunteer working with seniors, she sought a way to meet the companionship needs of older people residing in nursing homes. Her short-range goal, then, was to combat the isolation experienced by the aging, particularly persons over 80. Her larger goal was to create a formal way to honor the personal and cultural knowledge seniors contribute to their communities.

McQuade began her campaign in 1973 in West Virginia, and by 1978, U.S. President Jimmy Carter issued a proclamation that the first Sunday after Labor Day each year would be known as Grandparents Day. Although earlier celebrations had taken place in May, September was selected for the national observance to symbolize the autumn of life. The first such observance was in 1979. In 1989, the 10-year anniversary of Grandparents Day, the U.S. Postal Service issued a commemorative stamp bearing McQuade's likeness.

The statute proclaiming the holiday describes its purpose as threefold: "to honor grandparents, to give grandparents an opportunity to show love for their children's children, and to help children become aware of strength, information, and guidance older people can offer." As appropriate to the holiday's theme of familial and cultural memory, the official flower of Grandparents Day is the forget-me-not.

The McQuades themselves have always declined any donations to their efforts on behalf of Grandparents Day and finance their advocacy of the observance personally. In keeping with that wish to prevent commercialization, celebrants may honor grandparents with visits, genealogies, scrapbooks, family portraits, and remembrances of all those who function as grandparents (whether biologically so or not) within their communities. Time and attention, more than merchandise, are most likely to counteract the loneliness too often experienced by aging persons.

Many Americans have formed the habit of recognizing grandparents through already established holidays, paying tribute to grandmothers on Mother's Day and grandfathers on Father's Day. New holidays of this kind, though, no matter how scrupulously arranged to limit commerce, are a boon to greeting card companies, florists, and other organizations that market general gift merchandise. As the holiday has become more widely publicized, again by marketers, specialized cards and gift items have become available. It remains to be seen whether commercial pressure and advertising will transform Grandparents Day into an observance on the order of Mother's or Father's Day. At present, the day is most likely to be celebrated by families of young children, as they are still in the process of establishing family rituals.

In addition to increasing the contact between the community and its elders, Grandparents Day may contribute to American folklore by promoting intergenerational contact necessary to the transmission of family history and cultural traditions.

See also: AGING AND FOLKLORE; FAMILY FOLKLORE; FATHER'S DAY; HOLIDAYS/OBSERVANCES; LABOR DAY; MOTHER'S DAY.

For Further Reading:
Brasset, Jane. *Ideas to Celebrate Grandparents Day: The Second Sunday in September.* Vancouver, Canada: Council for the Family, 1991.
Carlson, Nancy. *Hooray for Grandparent's Day.* New York: Viking, 2000.
Grandparents Day Web site. Grandparents Day. Available online. URL: http://grandparentsday. com. Accessed February 17, 2006.
Legal Information Institute, Cornell University Law School. National Grandparents Day: Proclamation, Designation, and Observance. Available online. URL: http://www4.law.cornell. edu/uscode/36/142b.html. Accessed March 10, 2006.
Logue, Judy. *Celebrate Grandparent's Day: Reflections in Honor of Grandparents.* Liguori, Mo.: Liguori Publications, 1998.
Mathews, Garret. *Grandparents Day and Marian McQuade.* Richwood: West Virginia Press Club, 1983.
National Grandparents Day Web site. Grandparents Day. Available online. URL: http://www. grandparents-day.com. Accessed March 10, 2006.
OakGrove, Artemis. *Dangerous Thoughts.* Seattle: One Rogue Press, 1998.
Tate, Nikki. *Grandparents' Day.* Toronto: Annick Press, 2004.
United States, Congress, Senate, Committee on the Judiciary. *Grandparents Day: Report to Accompany S.J. Res. 24.* Washington, D.C.: U.S. Government Printing Office, 1977.

Great Depression See DEPRESSION, THE GREAT.

Greek-American folklore Greek-American folklore includes the cultural traditions and folkways of immigrants to the United States from Greece, along with those of American-born individuals of Greek descent.

Greeks may have sailed with Christopher Columbus when he reached to North America. Greek immigrants have lived in the United States since at least the 18th century. Initially, they were frequently agricultural workers. Later, many were employed in factories or owned small businesses such as candy stores and restaurants. Most Greek immigration to the United States has taken place since 1910.

Boston, New York City, Chicago, and Pittsburgh have attracted large populations of Greek Americans.

Greek folklore dates back to the mythology of ancient times. It has played a crucial part, especially among youth, in building cultural identity and strengthening affiliations with the homeland. In addition to ethnic festivals, fasts, feasts, and other observances associated with the Greek Orthodox Church help structure the year and its passing seasons. Greek Americans may also celebrate Greece's Independence Day on March 25 each year. Cultural traditions from Greece are also featured within major rites of passage, such as baptisms, weddings, and funerals. The distinctiveness of Greek-American customs and folk beliefs provides much of the humor in a recent feature-length film, *My Big Fat Greek Wedding*, which portrays the marriage of a Greek woman to a non-Greek man. Elements of folklore highlighted within the film include foodways, line and circle dances, music, folk beliefs such as the evil eye, and folk rituals such as knocking on wood to banish misfortune.

Organizations dedicated to the preservation and study of Greek culture include Chicago's United Hellenic American Congress and the District of Columbia's American Hellenic Educational Progressive Association. Major collections of Greek cultural material include Chicago's Hellenic Museum and Cultural Center, New York's Astoria's Greek-American Folklore Society, Saint Paul's Immigration History Research Center, and Salt Lake City's Hellenic Cultural Museum.

Greek Americans typically feel a strong sense of cultural identity, an ethnic pride in which folklore plays a sustaining role.

See also: FOLK BELIEFS; COLUMBUS, CHRISTOPHER; CULTURAL GROUPS; CUSTOMS, FOLK; DEATH; ETHNICITY; EVIL EYE; FESTIVALS, FOLKLORE; FOOD/FOODWAYS; IMMIGRATION AND FOLKLORE; MUSIC, FOLK; MYTHS, FOLK; RELIGION, FOLK; WEDDING/MARRIAGE FOLKLORE.

For Further Reading:

Georgakas, Dan, and Moskos, Charles, eds. *New Directions in Greek American Studies.* New York: Pella, 1991.

Georges, Robert. *Greek-American Folk Beliefs and Narratives.* New York: Arno Press, 1980.

Kunkelman, Gary. *The Religion of Ethnicity: Belief and Belonging in a Greek-American Community.* New York: Garland, 1990.

Lawson, John Cuthbert. *Modern Greek Folklore and Ancient Greek Religion: A Study in Survivals.* New Hyde Park, N.Y.: University Books, 1964.

Mouzaki, Rozanna. *Greek Dances for Americans.* Garden City, N.Y.: Doubleday, 1981.

Rouvelas, Marilyn. *A Guide to Greek Traditions and Customs in America.* Bethesda, Md.: Attica, 1993.

Salutos, Theodore. *The Greeks in the United States.* Cambridge, Mass.: Harvard University Press, 1964.

Greenfield Village, Henry Ford Museum and

At the Henry Ford Museum and Greenfield Village, visitors are afforded a perspective on American folk history that is both a heartfelt and a curious tribute.

The Dearborn, Michigan, attraction was an original concept of the American inventor Henry Ford (1863–1947). With something of the reverence Walt Disney would later express for small-town America in his design of such attractions as "Main Street USA" at Disneyland, Ford sought to make of Greenfield Village "America's Hometown." The building for what is now the Ford Museum, but was then called the Edison Institute, was dedicated in 1928. Ford collected an unusual array of Americana, including both plainspoken objects and such items as a Revolutionary War camp bed used by George Washington and the Ford Theater balcony chair in which Abraham Lincoln was seated at the time of his assassination.

The 13-acre property around the Ford Museum first opened in 1933, featuring reproductions and 80 historical structures. In something of the visual arrangement of a New England village, Ford had created a suite of historic districts for visitors to experience. Perhaps predictably, there was a version of Ford's first assembly plant. Because Ford so admired another American inventor, also available were versions of both Thomas Alva Edison's residence and his Menlo Park, New Jersey, labs. Along with these areas were sites designed to recall the homes of the Wright brothers, George Washington Carver, Noah Webster, and Robert Frost. Visitors could also see Ford's take on a William Holmes McGuffey school, paying tribute to the man behind the popular readers used by American schoolchildren since 1836.

As do some of its living history museum counterparts, such as Colonial Williamsburg and Old Sturbridge Village, Michigan's Greenfield Village seeks to make the American past immediate by surrounding guests with the original buildings and artifacts or accurate reproductions of them.

See also: ART, FOLK; COLONIAL WILLIAMSBURG; DISNEY, WALTER ELIAS; EDISON, THOMAS ALVA; FOLKLIFE; FOLKLORE IN EVERYDAY LIFE; HISTORIC PRESERVATION; INDUSTRIALIZATION AND FOLKLORE; LINCOLN, ABRAHAM; LIVING HISTORY MUSEUMS; MATERIAL CULTURE; MUSEUMS, FOLK; MYSTIC SEAPORT AND PRESERVATION SHIPYARD; REVOLUTIONARY WAR; WASHINGTON, GEORGE; WRIGHT BROTHERS.

For Further Reading:
An American Invention: The Story of Henry Ford Museum and Greenfield Village. Dearborn, Mich.: Henry Ford Museum and Greenfield Village, 1999.
Braden, Donna, and Gretchen Overhiser, eds. *Old Collections, New Audiences: Decorative Arts and Visitor Experience for the 21st Century*. Dearborn, Mich.: Henry Ford Museum and Greenfield Village, 2000.
Jennings, Jan, ed. *Roadside America: The Automobile in Design and Culture*. Ames: Iowa State University for the Society for Commercial Archaeology, 1990.
Upward, Geoffrey. *A Home for Our Heritage: The Building and Growth of Greenfield Village and Henry Ford Museum, 1929–1979*. Dearborn, Mich.: Henry Ford Museum Press, 1979.
Wamsley, James. *American Ingenuity: Henry Ford Museum and Greenfield Village*. New York: Abrams, 1985.

Green Mountain Boys   See ALLEN, ETHAN.

greetings   See SPEECH, FOLK.

gremlins   See MONSTERS.

Gretel   See "HANSEL AND GRETEL."

Grimm brothers (Jacob, 1785–1863; **Wilhelm,** 1786–1859)   The Grimm brothers, Jacob and Wilhelm, were influential collectors of 19th-century European folklore, especially fairy tales. American readers have made these stories their own through rereadings and retellings over the years.

In the early 1800s, this pair arrived at a plan to gather traditional oral tales and publish them. Their central purpose was to preserve Germanic folklore in the face of rapid cultural change. Their collection of tales was an act of national pride rather than direct service to children. Only later would the tales function chiefly as entertainments or moral instruction for children.

As early folklorists, the Grimms presented to their readers hundreds of stories. Most of the storytelling takes place in a darkly enchanted realm, filled with witches and other villains, virtuous but imperiled heroes and heroines, dangerous forests, and creatures possessing curious attributes and magical abilities.

The folktales the Grimm brothers committed to paper include many of the most beloved tales now offered to children the world over: "Cinderella," "The Golden Goose," "Hansel and Gretel," "Rapunzel," "Red Riding Hood," "Sleeping Beauty," "Snow White," and more. The Grimms' main anthology, *Children's and Household Tales* (1812), also included such well-known characters as Rumpelstiltskin and the Frog King. This key volume of European magical tales proved so welcome among readers that it went through numerous editions.

Most conspicuous and consistent about the tales is their strongly didactic style. Bourgeois values dominate this genre, as the tales espouse merits such as hard work, personal and sexual restraint, and responsibility toward others. The stories caution readers dramatically, typically through the fates met by characters within the stories. In addition to decisive, even cruel, punishments for villains, the tales warn against the dangers of milder forms of misbehavior. For instance, characters frequently learn the hard way what happens to any child who lies, disobeys parents, talks to strangers, yields to temptation, or falls short of his or her word.

Modern adaptations, and even later versions from the Grimms, who sensed a rapidly expanding market for the right kind of children's literature, tend to soften the original edges of these folktales. The notable feature of such revisions is their customary effort to mute the severity of outcomes of bad behavior in the tales, retaining their moral consequences while making their imagery and proportionality more palatable to parents.

Although the general plots of the Grimm tales are usually familiar to Americans, most readers are surprised to find the texts themselves rather harsh, and even violent, particularly for consumption by young readers. For example, while most contemporary children believe that the princess turned the "Frog King" into a prince with a kiss, in the actual narrative she casts it at a wall, and the frog reawakens as a prince.

The Grimm stories remain popular today, although most children now encounter the tales in a revised or even sanitized form. In the United States, most children experience Walt Disney's versions of the Grimm tales. Indeed, since Disney's feature-length animation of *Snow White and the Seven Dwarfs* (1937) debuted to acclaim, including a special Oscar award in 1939, Disney has produced films of many Grimm tales, as well as other classic tales from children's literature. The Disney films have given way to another kind of lore, as viewers trade rumors and urban legends about subliminal messages and hidden meanings in the film. In one such exchange, viewers attribute the names of characters in the story (Snow White, Sneezy, and the like) to cocaine or drug references. Such speculations are hotly contested among viewers in terms of their appropriateness, accuracy, or explanatory power.

Numerous efforts have been made to analyze the psychological or social meanings of the Grimm tales. In most cases, this analysis is easier to accomplish with contemporary retellings, as we are closer to the dreads and desires on which such recastings depend. For example, in the late 20th century a number of retellings sought to strengthen the voices and increase the agency of female characters within the traditional tales. Such updates reveal quite a lot about the climate of an era—its hopes, fears, and expectations.

It has been many years since Jacob and Wilhelm gathered the tales now associated with their names. In Kassel, Germany, the Museum of the Brothers Grimm keeps alive the legacy of these early folklorists. With Charles Perrault and Hans Christian Andersen, the brothers Grimm figure among the most important figures in rendering traditional folktales for children. That the characters in these stories remain household names and metaphors for human situations (a female whose fortunes change rapidly may be described as a "Cinderella," while a person who contributes value without exacting cost may be termed a "Golden Goose") suggests the staying power of these centuries-old tales. Although European in origin, the stories have been embraced as part of the lore of American childhood.

See also: "Cinderella"; fables; fairy tales; folklore in American literature; folktales; "Golden Goose, The"; "Hansel and Gretel"; museums, folk; myths, folk; "Rapunzel"; "Red Riding Hood, Little"; "Rumpelstiltskin"; "Sleeping Beauty"; "Snow White."

For Further Reading:

Degh, Linda. "Grimms' Household Tales and Its Place in the Household: The Social Relevance of a Controversial Classic," *Western Folklore* 38 (1979): 83–103.

Dundes, Alan, ed. *International Folkloristics: Classic Contributions by the Founders of Folklore.* Lanham, Md.: Rowman & Littlefield, 1999.

Ellis, John M. *One Fairy Story Too Many: The Brothers Grimm and Their Tales.* Chicago: University of Chicago Press, 1983.

Haase, Donald, ed. *The Reception of Grimms' Fairy Tales.* Detroit: Wayne State University Press, 1993.

McGlathery, James M., ed. *The Brothers Grimm and Folktale.* Urbana: University of Illinois Press, 1988.

Michaelis-Jena, Ruth. *The Brothers Grimm.* New York: Praeger, 1970.

O'Neill, Thomas. "Guardians of the Fairy Tale: The Brothers Grimm," *National Geographic* (December 1999): 102–129.

Radner, Joan Newlon, ed. *Feminist Messages: Coding in Women's Folk Culture.* Urbana: University of Illinois Press, 1993.

Tatar, Maria. *The Hard Facts of the Grimms' Fairy Tales.* Princeton, N.J.: Princeton University Press, 1987.

Ward, Donald. "The German Connection: The Brothers Grimm and the Study of 'Oral' Literature," *Western Folklore* 53, no. 1 (January 1994): 1–26.

Zipes, Jack. *The Complete Fairy Tales of the Brothers Grimm.* New York: Bantam Books, 1992.

Groundhog Day   Groundhog Day has been observed on February 2 each year in America since at least 1841. Falling as it does, roughly at the midpoint between winter solstice and spring equinox, the day promises to indicate, through the behavior of this burrowing creature, the nearness of the coming season of spring.

The holiday has its origins in Germany with the observance of Candlemas, when it is supposed that badgers possess the ability to foretell the timing of spring's arrival. This prognostication belief, while curious, seems to capture the popular imagination. This custom was adapted for the United States in that it features a groundhog in place of the badger.

In a ritual repeated annually, interested parties gather to watch a groundhog emerge from the earth as winter draws to a close and the groundhog concludes hibernation. The notion is that if the creature leaves the hole and sees his shadow, as would be the case on a sunny day, he will be frightened back underground. In that case, the forecast calls for six additional weeks of winter. If the groundhog fails to see his shadow, as would occur on a cloudy day, the creature is expected to venture outside. The accompanying prediction is that spring will arrive without delay.

This folk holiday is unofficial but finds enthusiasts nonetheless. Groundhog clubs exist throughout the country, and particular groundhogs, foremost among them Pennsylvania's Punxsutawney Phil, are highly regarded and monitored especially closely, no matter the reliability of their findings. The record demonstrates that Phil's forecasts from "the weather capital of the world" prove accurate less than half the time. Still, Phil continues to be placed in a heated burrow beneath a simulated hollow tree stump, from which he is roused for the purpose of performing this ritual at the appointed hour each Groundhog Day. Attendees have been known to boo and jeer at Phil when he issues a prediction that calls for six more weeks of winter.

See also: animals; beliefs, folk; holidays/observances; prediction; superstition; weather folklore.

For Further Reading:

Aveni, Anthony F. *The Book of the Year: A Brief History of Our Seasonal Holidays.* New York: Oxford University Press, 2004.

Cohen, Hennig, and Tristram Potter Coffin, eds. *The Folklore of American Holidays.* Detroit: Gale, 1987.

Myers, Robert. *Celebrations: The Complete Book of American Holidays.* Garden City, N.Y.: Doubleday, 1972.

Santino, Jack. *All around the Year: Holidays and Celebrations in American Life.* Urbana: University of Illinois Press, 1994.

Guthrie, Woody   See ARCHIVE OF FOLK CULTURE; DEPRESSION, THE GREAT; JOAD, TOM.

hackers See COMPUTER FOLKLORE.

Halloween/All Hallows' Eve Although far from a national holiday, Halloween is one of the most pervasively and extravagantly celebrated annual holidays in the United States.

The origins of Halloween are probably in the Celtic Day of the Dead or festival of Samhain, an occasion that marks summer's end and the arrival of a new pagan year. Folk belief suggested that all who had died in the previous year entered the next world at this time. Their spirits could be sensed more keenly because of the special importance of this occasion. By tradition, this is a time when mortals are most capable of glimpsing the spirit world. At this time, the pagan gods are believed to respond by playing tricks and making mischief. Humans, in turn, try to hide or shield themselves from such influences. Therefore, Halloween is integrally related to the prospect of contact with spiritual forces, many of which threaten or frighten. Mortals responded to this fear by such means as concealing themselves, attempting to appease such spirits, or trying to deflect harm through such practices as lighting bonfires. This festival gave way to the Feast of All Saints or All Hallows, days on which prayers by the living on behalf of those who died in the past year were customary.

Today, the Halloween holiday, celebrated in the United States on October 31 each year, retains this spooky quality, although with little signal of its source. For most Americans, Halloween is more festive than solemn, and its observance centers on costume rituals. While adults may don costumes for parties and festivals, at Halloween the greatest emphasis is on the children's masquerades.

In the custom of trick-or-treating, popular since the middle of the 20th century, costumed children go from house to house seeking holiday treats. Trick-or-treating appears to derive from the Irish Samhain practice of "rhyming," in which children visit neighboring houses to sing or tell rhymes in return for small favors such as nuts or coins. In some parts of the nation, such as portions of the Midwest, American children perform a joke or riddle in exchange for candy from neighbors. In other regions, youth just appear at the door and say, "Trick or Treat." Usual Halloween goodies include candy bars, gum, cookies, candy corn, and popcorn balls. In other words, it is children rather than demons that Halloween now tries to appease. In fact, some believe that the American practice began as a means to reduce the number or severity of children's pranks during the Halloween season. Still, both Halloween and the night before, known as "Hell Night" or "Mischief Night" in some towns and cities of the United States, remain popular times for vandalism and practical jokes. Some seem to want both tricks and treats for Halloween.

The traces of Halloween's beginnings remain in the costumes favored for this holiday. While costumes may be worn at parties and festivals throughout the year, Halloween costumes tend to include a darker variety of characters, such as witches, vampires, werewolves, mummies, skeletons, ghouls, devils, and other monsters. Themed locations decorated for the holiday are also marketed as "haunted houses," to heighten the suspense associated with Halloween entertainments. Ghost stories also recall the notion of Halloween as a time when spirits are especially close at hand.

Because of the time of year at which Halloween falls, it also functions as a harvest festival of sorts. Common decorations for the home include pumpkins, gourds, indian corn, and autumn leaves. At Halloween parties, seasonal crops figure prominently, as with the drinking of apple cider or the bobbing for apples. The latter activity is a variation on a divination game from Samhain in which girls sought to learn the identity of their future husbands. The popular jack-o-lantern made from a pumpkin is another adaptation of Samhain traditions, in which turnips are hollowed out, carved with faces, and lit from within with candles to form lanterns. The sight of these illuminated faces recalls the spirits of the dead, out on Halloween night to seek rest or consolation.

While some faiths prefer not to celebrate a holiday with pagan origins, Halloween appeals to a wide variety of children and adults for whom the opportunity to assume a playful alternate identity is a welcome festivity.

See also: BELIEFS, FOLK; CHANGELINGS; DEVIL, THE; FESTIVALS, FOLKLORE; FOOD/FOODWAYS; GHOSTS; GHOST STORIES; HAUNTED HOUSES; HOLIDAYS/OBSERVANCES; IRVING, WASHINGTON; MIDWESTERN REGIONAL FOLKLORE; PARADES; REGION, FOLK; SUPERSTITION; VAMPIRE; WEREWOLF.

For Further Reading:

Aveni, Anthony. *The Book of the Year: A Brief History of Our Seasonal Holidays.* New York: Oxford University Press, 2003.

Babbatyne, Leslie Pratt. *Halloween: An American Holiday, An American History.* New York: Facts On File, 1990.

Cohen, Hennig, and Tristram Potter Coffin, eds. *The Folklore of American Holidays.* Detroit: Gale, 1987.

Gallembo, Phyllis. *Dressed for Thrills: 100 Years of Halloween Costume and Masquerade.* New York: Harry N. Abrams, 2002.

Myers, Robert. *Celebrations: The Complete Book of American Holidays.* Garden City, N.Y.: Doubleday, 1972.

Rogers, Nicholas. *Halloween: From Pagan Ritual to Party Night.* New York: Oxford University Press, 2002.

Santino, Jack. *All around the Year: Holidays and Celebrations in American Life.* Urbana: University of Illinois Press, 1994.

———. *Halloween and Other Festivals of Death and Life.* Knoxville: University of Tennessee Press, 1994.

Vlach, John Michael, and Simon J. Bronner, eds. *Folk Art and Art Worlds.* Ann Arbor, Mich.: UMI Research Press, 1986.

"Hansel and Gretel"   "Hansel and Gretel" is a European fairy tale from among the many collected by the brothers Grimm during the 19th century. It recounts the story of a pair of children left to fend for themselves in a fallen world.

This story focuses on an impoverished family. The plot is set in motion when the mother reaches such desperation in the attempt to feed the family that she persuades the father that, in the interest of economy, they must cast their children, a boy and girl, named Hansel and Gretel, into the forest. With fewer mouths to feed, they presume, life will be easier and food more plentiful.

The plan is to leave the children in the forest with the impression that their parents will return for them. When their parents do not retrieve them, Hansel and Gretel find their way home by following a trait of bread crumbs they left.

Once again, however, the parents deliver their children to the forest with the intent of abandoning them there. This time, birds have eaten the bread crumb trail, and so Hansel and Gretel cannot retrace their steps.

As the hungry children wander through the forest, they discover a miraculous sight—a cottage constructed entirely of candies and cake. Under the circumstances, the witch who resides there has little difficulty in enticing the children inside, where she traps them.

As the story proceeds, it becomes clear that the witch's intentions toward the children are not altruistic. It appears that she means to fatten Hansel and then devour him. As the children discover the threat the witch poses, Gretel manages to trick the witch inside the cottage's oven, where she meets a fiery death. Hansel and Gretel then return home bearing their captor's riches. When they arrive, they discover a penitent father and a dead or absent mother, and so their homecoming is a safe and happy one.

The tale of "Hansel and Gretel" carries some cautions standard to fairy tales. In this case, most of the messages cluster around the deadly sin of gluttony. The parents dispose of their children for the prospect of fuller bellies, the children enter harm's way by yielding to the allure of a house made of sweets, and the witch, who wishes to feed on the orphaned children, finds herself cooked in an oven. The moral appears repeatedly within the story's unfolding.

Also suggested by the tale are warnings about greed and failures of responsibility. Both the mother, who disappears by story's end, and the witch, whose graphic end the story narrates, are punished for putting their own desires before the well-being of children in their care.

References within popular culture to this tale include sayings, such as the advice when fearful about becoming lost, to create a bread crumb trail. The other popular connection to the narrative is the custom of decorating gingerbread houses at Christmastime with a candy cottage motif. While the dark atmosphere of the original tale would seem incompatible with the holiday of Christmas, most such confections focus on the excitement of the candy house rather than the events that transpired there. Hansel and Gretel continue to serve as an image of innocents left to their own devices in a sometimes harsh world.

See also: CHILDREN'S FOLKLORE; CHRISTMAS; FABLES; FAIRY TALES; FOLKTALES; FOOD/FOODWAYS; GRIMM BROTHERS; MYTHS, FOLK.

For Further Reading:

Bettelheim, Bruno. *The Uses of Enchantment: The Meaning and Importance of Fairy Tales.* New York: Knopf, 1976.

Cashdan, Sheldon. *The Witch Must Die: The Hidden Meaning of Fairy Tales.* New York: Basic Books, 1999.

Radner, Joan Newlon, ed. *Feminist Messages: Coding in Women's Folk Culture.* Urbana: University of Illinois Press, 1993.

Tatar, Maria. *The Hard Facts of the Grimms' Fairy Tales.* Princeton, N.J.: Princeton University Press, 1987.

Ward, Donald. "The German Connection: The Brothers Grimm and the Study of 'Oral' Literature," *Western Folklore* 53, no. 1 (January 1994): 1–26.

Zipes, Jack. *The Complete Fairy Tales of the Brothers Grimm.* New York: Bantam Books, 1992.

Hanukkah   Hanukkah is the name given to an eight-day winter festival in Judaism, generally occurring during the month of December.

The meaning of the holiday's name is *Dedication*, and in keeping with that theme, Hanukkah remembers the shared past. In so doing, Hanukkah honors practices and ideals of community among Jewish persons the world over.

Customs surrounding this holiday are designed to promote awareness of the historical struggles of Jewish people, and in particular their efforts to keep intact their cultural and religious identity in the face of great challenges within and threats without. Daily readings from the Torah, a sacred text, are a usual part of Hanukkah's celebration. Specific historical incidents of great consequence, such as the dedication of the Temple, the triumph of the Maccabees, and the miracle of the oil, receive special attention within the holiday's remarks, lessons, and rejoicing.

The other name by which the holiday is known, the Festival of Lights, refers to the overarching holiday symbolism of the menorah, a traditional candleholder used prominently in the observance of Hanukkah. The menorah accommodates up to nine candles, including one for each day of Hanukkah and a ninth, or servant candle, used to light each of the others used in the festivities. As part of the celebration, one additional candle is placed (from left to right) and lit (from left to right) on each night of Hanukkah.

As with other winter holidays in America, the illumination of the season's darkness also promises the prospect of the sunshine ahead and longer days to come. In that way, the candles not only kindle remembrance, but also depict hopefulness. Furthermore, their light's lasting power reminds celebrants of the miracle of the oil.

Other customs associated with Hanukkah include specific activities to inform and involve children in the celebration. For instance, the preparation of special foods, such as latkes (potato pancakes) and jelly doughnuts made with oil, reminds participants of the historic miracle of the oil and is frequently incorporated in the celebration. Another such example is the symbolism associated with the dreidel. This wooden or clay top, marked on each of four side with Hebrew letters, is the centerpiece of a child's game and the subject of a familiar song ("The Dreidel Song") describing the joy in its play. Boys and girls playing the dreidel game can win coin and candy rewards, including gelt, a chocolate candy covered in foil in such a way as to resemble coins. Together, the letters inscribed on the dreidel carry the message "A Great Miracle Happened Here," indicating the rich and precious cultural legacy that survives to this day.

Although Hanukkah does not represent one of the highest holidays within the Jewish calendar, its celebration falls close to the central Christian holiday of Christmas. Both because the two holidays are close to each another in the American sequence of holidays and because of a gradual movement toward a multicultural approach to holidays in schools and other organizations each year, some links are made between Hanukkah and Christmas references in the public sphere. In an effort to make sure Jewish children do not feel overshadowed by Christmas or slighted in their experience of Hanukkah, additional practices such as decorations and gift exchanges have become a part of many Hanukkah celebrations. So long as these changes do not threaten the integrity of the distinctive cultural and religious meanings of Hanukkah, such trends can help include a new generation in its observance.

See also: CHRISTMAS; FESTIVALS, FOLKLORE; FOOD/FOODWAYS; HOLIDAYS/OBSERVANCES; JEWISH-AMERICAN FOLKLORE; RELIGION, FOLK.

For Further Reading:

Cohen, Hennig, and Tristram Potter Coffin, eds. *The Folklore of American Holidays.* Detroit: Gale, 1987.

Gaster, Theodor H. *Festivals of the Jewish Year.* New York: William Sloane Associates, 1952.

Greenspoon, Leonard J., and Ronald Simkins. *Spiritual Dimensions of Judaism.* Omaha, Nebr.: Creighton University Press, 2003.

Kaplan, Dana Evan. *The Cambridge Companion to American Judaism.* New York: Cambridge University Press, 2005.

Myers, Robert. *Celebrations: The Complete Book of American Holidays.* Garden City, N.Y.: Doubleday, 1972.

Santino, Jack. *All around the Year: Holidays and Cel-ebrations in American Life*. Urbana: University of Illinois Press, 1994.

Schauss, Hayyim. *The Jewish Festivals: History and Observance*. New York: Schocken Books, 1962.

Harlem Renaissance   See BROWN, STERLING ALLEN; HUGHES, JAMES MERCER LANGSTON; LOCKE, ALAIN LE ROY; TOOMER, JEAN.

Harpers Ferry   See BROWN, JOHN.

Harris, Joel Chandler (1848–1908)   Born on December 8, 1848, Joel Chandler Harris became known for collecting and retelling in print a category of African-American orally transmitted folk tales known as Uncle Remus stories.

In published form, these animal tales and plantation stories were based on oral narratives documented by the journalist-turned-folklorist Joel Chandler Harris. Harris, a member of the American Folklore Society, sought to record the dialect stories told by slaves. He published his work using the device of a fictional storyteller, Uncle Remus. Uncle Remus was the legend-ary narrator of a series of tales dating back to the Civil War and Reconstruction eras in the American South.

In this sense, Harris became a popularizer of such tales, especially for white readers. Harris's books include *Uncle Remus: His Songs and Saying* (1881), *Nights with Uncle Remus* (1883), *Uncle Remus and His Friends* (1892), and *Uncle Remus and the Little Boy* (1905). The upbeat, even idealized, representation of antebellum race relations helped make these stories popular with readers.

It was Harris's claim that in relating stories, he provided them in their original and unadul-terated form. Harris's language proves reveal-ing, though, for when he refers to other people and their cultures as "simple" or "picturesque," he trivializes them. That is, he might not have

consciously set out to inscribe his own attitudes about African Americans, but neither was he self-conscious about the implications of a white observer's serving up African-American culture to a white audience, and all that that could mean.

Today, very few Americans familiar with the Uncle Remus tales, discovered them through oral culture. Contemporary youth probably encounter the Uncle Remus tales indirectly, through storybook adaptations such as those of Walt Disney. In the end, Walt Disney and Joel Chandler Harris may not function as folklorists, but their audiences nonetheless experience and understand folk content through their represen-tations.

Whatever his shortcomings as a transcriber or failings as a folklorist, Joel Chandler Harris nonetheless drew wide attention to the African-American oral tradition that became the focus of his work. Harris died on July 3, 1908.

See also: AFRICAN-AMERICAN FOLKLORE; AMERICAN FOLKLORE SOCIETY; ANANSI; ANI-MALS; BRER RABBIT; DISNEY, WALTER ELIAS; FOLKTALES; HURSTON, ZORA NEALE; MORRISON, TONI; ORAL FOLKLORE; POPLORE; REMUS, UNCLE; SLAVERY; SOUTHERN REGIONAL FOLKLORE; STOWE, HARRIET BEECHER; TAR BABY; TRICKSTER.

For Further Reading:
Brasch, Walter. *Brer Rabbit, Uncle Remus, and the "Cornfield Journalist": The Tale of Joel Chandler Harris*. Macon, Ga.: Mercer University Press, 2000.

Brookes, Stella Brewer. *Joel Chandler Harris, Folk-lorist*. Athens: University of Georgia Press, 1950.

Burrison, John. *The Golden Arm: The Folk Tale and Its Literary Use by Mark Twain and Joel C. Har-ris*. Atlanta: Georgia State College, 1968.

Cousins, Paul. *Joel Chandler Harris: A Biography*. Baton Rouge: Louisiana State University Press, 1968.

Trotman, C. James, ed. *Multiculturalism: Roots and Realities*. Bloomington: Indiana University Press, 2002.

harvest festivals See HALLOWEEN/ALL HALLOWS' EVE; THANKSGIVING.

haunted houses Haunted places in America are most often homes in which unexplained events and experiences occur.

Parapsychologists attribute haunting to the spirits of the dead, whose energies are not at rest. Most appear to have unfinished business, and their hauntings are an expression of this lack of closure. Some are believed to have difficulty accepting their demise, while others have unresolved traumas from the world of the living. Still others seem to engage in protection or direction of the lives of the living on the premises of places known to the ghosts, particularly their former residences. The sites where ghosts appear often bear some connection to the irreconcilable nature of their difficulties in life or losses in death.

Witnesses describe the haunting spirits they have encountered as benevolent, benign, mischievous, or malevolent. Contacts with these energies vary, then, from amusing to terrifying for occupants of the haunted buildings. Individual ghosts frequently have a characteristic appearance, including repeated movements or actions associated with their detected presence. Often, such ghosts are described as resembling bodily forms, but hauntings can also involve mysterious lights, smells, sounds, movements, and changes in area temperature or overall perceived atmosphere.

Some localities, some structures, and even some specific areas within buildings emerge as hubs for haunting. Some owners have been known to befriend the specters, others exploit them for profit, and still others seek to banish the spirits of the dead from their property. Haunted houses are a staple of horror stories in popular culture and are often simulated as a spooky entertainment and attraction for trick-or-treaters at Halloween. The customary location is an older house with several stories, particularly one with distinctive structural features

(hidden staircases and the like) and/or unusual historical references (residences of murder victims and such).

Hauntings are a motif across many genres of American folklore, including ghost stories, camp lore, and urban legends.

See also: CAMP FOLKLORE; DEATH; FOLKLORE IN EVERYDAY LIFE; GHOSTS; GHOST STORIES; GHOST TOWNS; HALLOWEEN/ALL HALLOWS' EVE; SPIRITUALISM; SUPERNATURAL; SUPERSTITION; URBAN LEGENDS.

For Further Reading:
Bailey, Dale. *American Nightmares: The Haunted House Formula in American Popular Fiction.* Bowling Green, Ohio: Bowling Green State University Popular Press, 1999.
Davidson, Hilday, and W. M. S. Russell, eds. *The Folklore of Ghosts.* Cambridge, Mass.: Folklore Society/Brewer, 1981.
Myers, Arthur. *The Ghostly Register: Haunted Dwellings—Active Spirits, a Journey to America's Strangest Landmarks.* Chicago: Contemporary Books, 1986.
Riccio, Dolores, and John Bingham. *Haunted Houses USA.* New York: Pocket Books, 1989.
———. *More Haunted Houses USA.* New York: Pocket Books, 1991.
Winer, Richard, and Nancy Osborn. *Haunted Houses.* New York: Bantam, 1979.

Hawaii folklore See EARHART, AMELIA MARY; JAPANESE-AMERICAN FOLKLORE; JAPANESE-AMERICAN INTERNMENT; KOREAN-AMERICAN FOLKLORE; PEARL HARBOR (REMEMBRANCE) DAY; WESTERN REGIONAL FOLKLORE.

Hawthorne, Nathaniel (1804–1864) With fiction that delved into the moral and mental worlds of characters in historical fiction, Nathaniel Hawthorne developed a reputation as an author whose work both invokes and evokes America's folklore.

Hawthorne was born in Salem, Massachusetts, on July 4, 1804. His family was descended from the Puritans, and that historical consciousness would later help shape his work. Hawthorne attended Maine's Bowdoin College, where his friends included the writer Henry Wadsworth Longfellow. Hawthorne held various jobs, including work at a customhouse, but found it difficult to compose literature during periods of such employment. Other writers revered his abilities; indeed Herman Melville dedicated his epic work, *Moby-Dick*, to his friend and colleague. Nonetheless, the author was not rewarded with great wealth, and received recognition relatively late in his life.

Today, Hawthorne stands among America's most celebrated 19th-century writers. Hawthorne was an accomplished author of fiction whose short stories and novels win over audiences. His works include *Twice-Told Tales* (1837); *The Scarlet Letter, a Romance* (1850); *The House of the Seven Gables, a Romance (1851); and The Blithedale Romance* (1852). Examples of his short fiction, such as "Young Goodman Brown," and "The Minister's Black Veil," routinely appear in anthologies of American literature.

Hawthorne's work demonstrates his fascination with the psychology of human action, and so his stories probe characters in terms of their states of mind and motives. His best-known tales explore the darker side of the human mind; he leads readers into the doubts, secrets, sin, guilt, loneliness, and misdeeds of his literary characters. Through this attention to psychological detail, his fiction derives some of its power and relevance for readers.

Hawthorne died on May 19, 1864. His funeral was attended by such literary luminaries as Ralph Waldo Emerson, John Greenleaf Whitier, and Henry Wadsworth Longfellow. Hawthorne will long be remembered as a fiction writer whose historical works frequently called upon traditional lore, especially that of early American life, for their setting or circumstance.

He also influenced the work of other authors, such as William Faulkner and Herman Melville, who shared his enthusiasm for American folklore and folklife.

See also: FAULKNER, WILLIAM; FOLKLORE IN AMERICAN LITERATURE; LONGFELLOW, HENRY WADSWORTH; MELVILLE, HERMAN; WITCHCRAFT, SALEM.

For Further Reading:
Bercovitch, Sacvan. *The Office of The Scarlet Letter*. Baltimore: Johns Hopkins University Press, 1991.

Gale, Robert L. *A Hawthorne Encyclopedia*. Westport, Conn.: Greenwood Press, 1988.

Miller, J. Hillis. *Hawthorne and History: Defacing It*. Cambridge, Mass.: Blackwell, 1991.

Millington, Richard H. *Practicing Romance: Narrative Form and Cultural Engagement in Hawthorne's Fiction*. Princeton, N.J.: Princeton University Press, 1992.

Moore, Margaret B. *The Salem World of Nathaniel Hawthorne*. Columbia: University of Missouri Press, 1998.

Pfister, Joel. *The Production of Personal Life: Class, Gender, and the Psychological in Hawthorne's Fiction*. Stanford, Calif.: Stanford University Press, 1991.

healing   See MEDICINE, FOLK.

hearts   See PENNSYLVANIA DUTCH/PENNSYLVANIA GERMAN FOLKLORE; SAINT VALENTINE'S DAY.

Henry, John (legendary)   John Henry is the name associated with an African-American railroad legend. His stories are usually set in 19th-century West Virginia.

According to the stories about him, John Henry was unusually strong, even as a child. As he matured, he put this physical power to good use. He became famous for his abilities as a railroad worker, in particular. Henry could work harder, longer, and more productively than just about anyone. His hammer work, as he set and secured railroad track, was exemplary.

When technology began to change the industry, John Henry decided to put his skills as a rail worker to the test. He entered a contest against a steam drill and vowed that he could lay more track faster than any machine.

The contest was a grueling one, and John Henry very nearly reached even his limits as he sought to outperform the mechanized drill. In the end, the famed railroadman prevailed. Although he won the rail contest, Henry died shortly thereafter. The challenge proved too much for him to endure.

Folk stories and songs memorialize this mythic hero, known for his great appetites and even greater prowess on the job. Legend places John Henry prominently among the most celebrated figures—both real and imagined—of occupational folklore, such as Paul Bunyan, Casey Jones, Joe Hill, and Pecos Bill.

Some scholars have challenged the authenticity of this story as genuine folklore, hinting that it might instead be fakelore, a manufactured tale. Either way, however, Henry's story remains a classic among American tall tales.

For contemporary audiences, John Henry's victory over the steam drill symbolizes, among other things, an act of resistance in the face of the industrial revolution. With their steadfastness and vigor, his efforts to excel at his profession dignify the image of the American worker.

See also: AFRICAN-AMERICAN FOLKLORE; BUNYAN, PAUL; FAKELORE; FOLK HEROES/LEGENDARY FIGURES; HILL, JOE; JONES, JOHN LUTHER (CASEY); OCCUPATIONAL FOLKLORE; PECOS BILL; SOUTHERN REGIONAL FOLKLORE.

For Further Reading:

Chappell, Louis. *John Henry: A Folk-Lore Study.* Port Washington, N.Y.: Kennikat Press, 1933.

Johnson, Guy B. *John Henry: Tracking Down a Negro Legend.* New York: AMS Press, 1969.

Keats, Ezra. *John Henry: An American Legend.* New York: Pantheon, 1965.

Osborne, Mary Pope. *American Tall Tales.* New York: Knopf, 1991.

Whitehead, Colson. *John Henry Days.* New York: Anchor, 2002.

Williams, Brett. *John Henry: A Bio-Bibliography.* Westport, Conn.: Greenwood Press, 1983.

Henry, Patrick (1736–1799) Rendered immortal by his famous declaration "Give me liberty or give me death," Patrick Henry is an icon of the early American patriot.

Henry was born in Virginia on May 29, 1736. He worked as a lawyer and later became a delegate to the Continental Congress. Henry developed a reputation as a compelling speaker, particularly in terms of his address to the Virginia convention. Copies of his remarks there, calling for courage in the battle for independence, were printed and widely distributed. The text was one of the forces that helped lead to the framing of the Declaration of Independence.

In this way, Henry played an important part in the nation's struggle for autonomy. He later became Virginia's first governor, and he would serve a total of five terms in that office over the course of his lifetime.

In 1778, Patrick Henry resisted the adoption of the U.S. Constitution. He objected on the basis of his view that the document placed too great limits on individual rights. When it became clear that the Constitution would be ratified, he urged adoption of the Bill of Rights, affording as it does explicit protections for some of the individual rights he wished to preserve.

As an orator and leader, Patrick Henry was a staunch supporter of liberty in America, especially for the individual citizen.

See also: FOLK HEROES/LEGENDARY FIGURES; FRANKLIN, BENJAMIN; POLITICS AND FOLKLORE; PROTEST IN FOLKLORE; REVOLUTIONARY WAR.

For Further Reading:

Beeman, Richard. *Patrick Henry: A Biography.* New York: McGraw-Hill, 1974.

Mayer, Henry. *A Son of Thunder: Patrick Henry and the American Republic.* New York: F. Watts, 1986.

Mayo, Bernard. *Myths and Men: Patrick Henry, George Washington and Thomas Jefferson.* New York: Harper & Row, 1963.

Wirt, William. *Sketches of the Life and Character of Patrick Henry.* Chapel Hill: University of North Carolina at Chapel Hill, 1999.

heroes, folk See FOLK HEROES/LEGENDARY FIGURES.

hex See ARCHITECTURE, FOLK; WITCHCRAFT, SALEM.

Hiawatha (15th century) Hiawatha was a legendary Iroquoian chief whose deeds earned him a place in American folklore.

Hiawatha, whose name means "He Makes Rivers," lived during the 15th century, but his influence continued for centuries. Relatively little is known about the details of Hiawatha's biography, but his role in the history of Native America is firmly etched.

Many Americans first encounter this figure through a work of literature. They perceive Hiawatha through the lens of a poem written by Henry Wadsworth Longfellow, "Song of Hiawatha" (1855). This epic work portrays Hiawatha as a historic and heroic figure to represent Native Americans.

Longfellow favored historical subjects for his verse and may be best known for his poem "Paul Revere's Ride." The scholarship of Henry Schoolcraft, a collector of Native American legends, is believed to be the principal source of information on which Longfellow based his poem.

Hiawatha was a very knowledgeable individual, with expertise in such diverse topics as farming, art, medicine, and navigation. He also imparted this information to others.

Hiawatha contributed meaningfully to the formation of the Iroquois Confederacy. He is credited with uniting some warring tribes, among them the Algonquin, Oneida, Mohawk, Cayuga, and Iroquois people.

Hiawatha was a capable teacher and leader, and his story has become part of the nation's lore.

See also: FOLK HEROES/LEGENDARY FIGURES; LONGFELLOW, HENRY WADSWORTH; NATIVE AMERICAN FOLKLORE; NORTHEASTERN REGIONAL FOLKLORE.

For Further Reading:
Clark, Ella Elizabeth. *Indian Legends of Canada.* Toronto: McClelland and Stewart, 1960.

Coffin, Tristram Potter, and Hennig Cohen, eds. *The Parade of Heroes: Legendary Figures in American Lore.* Garden City, N.Y.: Anchor Press/Doubleday, 1978.

Schoolcraft, Henry R. *The Myth of Hiawatha, and Other Oral Legends, Mythologic and Allegoric, of the North American Indians.* Philadelphia: J. B. Lippincott, 1856.

Seal, Graham. *Encyclopedia of Folk Heroes.* Santa Barbara, Calif.: ABC-CLIO, 2001.

Thompson, Stith., ed. *Tales of the North American Indians.* Bloomington: Indiana University Press, 1929.

Trachtenberg, Alan. *Shades of Hiawatha: Staging Indians, Making Americans, 1880–1930.* New York: Hill & Wang, 2004.

Williams, Mentor L., ed. *Schoolcraft's Indian Legends.* East Lansing: Michigan State University Press, 1956.

Hickok, James Butler (Wild Bill) (1837–1876) James Butler "Wild Bill" Hickok was one of the 19th century's most noted marksmen and lawmen.

Hickok was born on May 27, 1837, in Troy Grove, Illinois. His adventures as a young man foreshadowed the fame that awaited him as a frontier legend. Always a talented shooter, Hickok was known for his exhibitions of quick draw techniques and stunts. He worked for a time as a stagecoach driver. During the Civil War, Hickok worked as both a scout and a spy for the Union Army. In this pursuit, he was imprisoned several times but always managed to escape his captivity.

Later, Hickok became well known as a law enforcer in towns that were known to live up to the image of the Wild West. He was successful as both the sheriff of Hays City, Kansas, and the marshal of Abilene, Kansas. According to lore, Hickok's shooting skills were so revered that he never even needed to draw his gun.

Eventually, the man celebrated as "Wild Bill" would spend several years touring with William F. "Buffalo Bill" Cody's Wild West Show, where his displays of marksmanship were well received. As colorful as the way he lived was the manner in which he died. As the story goes, Hickok was shot in the back during a card game in a Dakota Territory saloon during the nation's centennial year, 1876. He was in a location known as Deadwood, and it is said that he was holding the so-called dead man's hand in poker at the time he was shot: aces and eights.

Famous during his life and long after it, "Wild Bill" Hickok remains a popular figure in American folklore of the West.

See also: CIVIL WAR; CODY, WILLIAM F. (BUFFALO BILL); COWBOYS; FOLK HEROES/LEGENDARY FIGURES; FRONTIER; REGION, FOLK; RODEO; WESTERN REGIONAL FOLKLORE.

For Further Reading:

Glass, Andrew. *Bad Guys: True Stories of Legendary Gunslingers, Sidewinders, Fourflushers, Drygulchers, Bushwhackers, Freebooters, and Downright Bad Guys and Gals of the Wild West.* New York: Doubleday Book for Young Readers, 1998.

Leeming, David, and Jake Page. *Myths, Legends, and Folktales of America: An Anthology.* New York: Oxford University Press, 1999.

Rosa, Joseph G. *They Called Him Wild Bill: The Life and Adventures of James Butler Hickok.* Norman: University of Oklahoma Press, 1964.

———. *Wild Bill Hickok: The Man and His Myth.* Lawrence: University Press of Kansas, 1996.

Hicks, Edward   See ART, FOLK.

hillbillies   The term *hillbilly* is a derogatory name for rural residents in general, and for mountain people of the Appalachian region in particular.

In all likelihood, this term derived from a Scots-Irish term, *Billy boy*. When people of this ancestry immigrated to the United States and settled in its mountainous regions, such as the Appalachias and the Ozarks, they became known as "hill billies." In another explanation of the term's origins, a pro-Union hill person during the Civil War was referred to as *Billy Yank*. This reference may have morphed into *hillbilly* over time.

The description first appeared in print in 1900. Whether spoken or written, the word is usually a pejorative reference to the perceived lack of sophistication or worldliness of rural people. In many instances, the person called a hillbilly is cast through a stereotype whose attributes include uninhibited behavior including drinking, shooting, and, in some depictions, a lack of restraint when it comes to sexual contact with close relatives.

The overall image of a hillbilly involves someone engaged in a backward, inbred, shiftless, and insular way of life. Rather than recognizing the richness of mountain culture, then, the term *hillbilly* (and its successor term, *redneck*) suggests coarseness and deficiency. Although popular culture has muted some of the image's hostility to create cartoon or television characters who portray the figure of the hillbilly, most of the humor in these presentations remains at the expense of mountain people. For instance, a situation comedy series, *The Beverly Hillbillies*, sought humor in a fish-out-of-water-story involving a displaced family of hillbillies. The Clampetts, as they were called, struck oil accidentally and used their newfound wealth to purchase a Beverly Hills mansion. Although the program made the family's members somewhat endearing, the notion of hillbillies as crude and lacking in intelligence remained. While it is true that the characters on this program, which aired first-run episodes from 1962 until 1971, had some positive qualities, such as honesty and filial loyalty, their guileless outlook nonetheless subjected them to ridicule and exploitation.

Contrary to the unflattering picture of the "hillbilly," even the most remote mountain settlements have folklife traditions that deserve a more fair assessment. From bluegrass music to down-home cooking, mountain people have their own cultural legacies.

Therefore, although Appalachian and Ozarks folklore includes many robust customs, crafts, and practices, the image of the hillbilly is at best a caricature of the group's culture.

See also: APPALACHIAN FOLKLORE; FOLKLORE IN EVERYDAY LIFE; FOOD/FOODWAYS; MUSIC, FOLK; OZARKS FOLKLORE; REGION, FOLK; TOASTS/DRINKING.

For Further Reading:

Biggs, Mark. *The Ozarks: Just That Much Hillbilly in Me.* Springfield: Southwest Missouri State University, 1999.

Grundy, Pamela. "'We Always Tried to Be Good People': Respectability, Crazy Water Crystals, and Hillbilly Music on the Air, 1933–1935," *Journal of American History* 81, no. 4 (March 1995): 1581–1620.

Harkins, Anthony. *Hillbilly: A Cultural History of an American Icon.* New York: Oxford University Press, 2004.

Wilgus, D. K., and John Greenway, eds. "Hillbilly Issue," *Journal of American Folklore* 78, no. 309 (summer 1965): 195–287.

Hill, Joe (1879–1915)   Born Joel Emmanuel Hägglund in 1879, the figure best known as Joe Hill is remembered for his labor advocacy.

Hill was a Swedish immigrant who arrived in the United States in 1902. As an adult, he became involved in the cause of labor as a leader, songwriter, and parodist. He participated in worker protest, and engaged in radical politics. Joe Hill, also known as Joe Hillstrom, popularized the phrase "pie in the sky" to suggest that workers ought not to wait for the afterlife for right treatment or reward. Hill gained a reputation as a friend of the American worker. His efforts ended suddenly, when the activist was executed in 1915 for a murder he may or may not have committed. Before meeting his fate, Hill gave some famous words of advice to "Big Bill" Haywood: "Don't mourn—organize." Since that time, this phrase has formed a slogan of sorts for laborers who meet with hardships or discouraging circumstances.

Joe Hill's career as an organizer has been celebrated in countless folk songs composed by everyone from John Luther "Casey" Jones to Alfred Hayes. More recently, in the context of the American folk revival, artists such as Joan Baez, Woody Guthrie, and Pete Seeger have popularized tunes that recall Hill's legacy.

Joe Hill emerged as a martyr of sorts in the history of American labor.

See also: FOLK HEROES/LEGENDARY FIGURES; HENRY, JOHN; IMMIGRATION AND FOLKLORE; INDUSTRIALIZATION AND FOLKLORE; JONES, JOHN LUTHER; MUSIC, FOLK; OCCUPATIONAL FOLKLORE; OUTLAWS; PROTEST IN FOLKLORE.

For Further Reading:

Foner, Philip. *The Case of Joe Hill.* New York: International, 1966.

Hampton, Wayne. *Guerrilla Minstrels: John Lennon, Joe Hill, Woody Guthrie, Bob Dylan.* Knoxville: University of Tennessee Press, 1986.

Hill, Joe. *Don't Mourn—Organize! Songs of Labor Songwriter Joe Hill.* Washington, D.C.: Smithsonian/Folkways, 1990.

Industrial Worker. *Songs of the Workers: On the Road, in the Jungles, and in the Shops/Songs to Fan the Flames of Discontent.* Spokane, Wash.: Industrial Worker, 1917.

Reuss, R. "The Ballad of Joe Hill Revisited," *Western Folklore* 26 (1967): 187–188.

Smith, G. *Joe Hill.* Salt Lake City: Utah University Press, 1969.

Stavis, Barrie. *The Man Who Never Died: A Play about Joe Hill.* New York: Haven Press, 1954.

hippies Hippies, a subcultural label most closely associated with America during the 1960s and 1970s, were considered youth culture's freest spirits.

As America's baby boom generation approached adulthood, they began to challenge—sometimes radically—the way of life their parents embraced. Expressed as a generational conflict between hip youth and a repressive host culture, the American counterculture exploded and reached its peak between 1965 and 1975. The results were both upheaval and rethinking.

As members of the counterculture came of age, hippies challenged virtually all the assumptions of the prevailing society. They contested values such as sexual abstinence as prudish. They defied social and legal prohibitions, such as those against drugs. They advanced new and contrary tastes, such as rock music. They engaged in direct actions to change law, such as those involving racial segregation. Most of all, they questioned policies, such as U.S. involvement in the Vietnam War.

Hippies evinced a willingness to question authority, while espousing a kind of idealism that called for peace, love, and equality. Integral to hippie living was its music, and several of the most memorable events related to the era of the hippies were its massive concerts and festivals, such as Woodstock in 1969.

If the Hippie Nation had a capital, it was San Francisco, California. More specifically, the Haight-Ashbury district was a central location for hippie gatherings. New York's Greenwich Village was another important cultural hub. Many young people looking for like-minded others flocked to such locations for the fellowship and stimulation they afforded.

Although the conclusion of the Vietnam War and the co-optation of hippie culture by mainstream society brought the hippie movement to an end, for a time hippie culture signaled the rebel energy of a generation not willing to defer to previous ones for its convictions or understandings.

See also: AGING AND FOLKLORE; CIVIL RIGHTS MOVEMENT; DEATH; FOLKLORE IN EVERYDAY LIFE; GENDER AND FOLKLORE; POLITICS AND FOLKLORE; PROTEST IN FOLKLORE; VIETNAM WAR; WOMEN'S MOVEMENT.

For Further Reading:

Cain, Chelsea. *The Hippie Handbook.* San Francisco: Chronicle Books, 2004.

Miles, Barry. *Hippie.* New York: Sterling, 2004.

Miller, Timothy. *The Hippies and American Values.* Knoxville: University of Tennessee Press, 1991.

Partridge, William. *The Hippie Ghetto: The Natural History of a Subculture.* New York: Holt, Rinehart & Winston, 1973.

Von Hoffman, Nicholas. *We Are the People Our Parents Warned Us Against.* Chicago: Quadrangle Books, 1968.

Winston, Stephanie. *Hippies, Drugs, and Promiscuity.* New Rochelle, N.Y.: Arlington House, 1972.

historical events While folklore implies an ongoing set of processes, some specific events, such as the Civil War and the gold rush, stimulate an unusual volume of folk stories. Many of these events are recounted, celebrated, and/or commemorated in later narratives.

In some cases, these events involve campaigns for social change. Examples include the abolition, Civil Rights, women's suffrage, women's and gay rights movements. Other historical events that are surrounded with folklore include wars, such as the Revolutionary War, Civil War, World War I, World War II, and Vietnam War. Other events that resonate in this way are crises in the nation's history. Examples include the Great Depression, Salem witch trials, and Japanese-American internment. Events that inspire folklore also involve times of perceived opportunity, such as westward expansion along the frontier or the gold rush.

Through the study of folklore, it is possible to gain insights into the events that have shaped the lives of ordinary Americans.

See also: CIVIL RIGHTS MOVEMENT; CIVIL WAR; DEPRESSION, THE GREAT; FRONTIER; GOLD

RUSH, THE; HISTORIC PRESERVATION; IBO LAND-
ING; JAPANESE-AMERICAN INTERNMENT; LIVING
HISTORY MUSEUMS; PAUL REVERE'S RIDE; REVO-
LUTIONARY WAR; SLAVERY; SUFFRAGE; TRANSCON-
TINENTAL RAILROAD; UNDERGROUND RAILROAD;
VIETNAM WAR; WITCHCRAFT, SALEM; WOMEN'S
MOVEMENT; WORLD WAR I; WORLD WAR II.

For Further Reading:

Dégh, Linda, Henry Glassie, and Felix Oinas, eds. *Folklore Today: A Festschrift for Richard Dorson.* Bloomington: Indiana University Press, 1976.

Dorson, Richard. *American Folklore.* Chicago: University of Chicago Press, 1959.

———. *American Folklore and the Historian.* Chicago: University of Chicago Press, 1971.

———. *America in Legend: Folklore from the Colonial Period to the Present.* New York: Pantheon Books. 1971.

Leeming, David, and Jake Page. *Myths, Legends, and Folktales of America: An Anthology.* New York: Oxford University Press, 1999.

historic preservation The phrase *historic preservation* has many different meanings but usually refers to a process by which a location is retained in its current condition or restored to its former condition.

America's movement toward historic preservation seems motivated chiefly by a concern that the nation's heritage might be lost or distorted through neglect. Part of that legacy can be found in the built environment, whether the landscapes of ordinary life or the sites of specific historical interest.

Buildings and districts of special note may be placed on the National Register of Historic Places, or designated as national parks or national landmarks. In this way, Americans can visit the locations and learn about their historical significance. For instance, some locations take on importance because of single events that proved key in the nation's military history. One example is Gettysburg National Military Park, where President Abraham Lincoln deliv-ered his now-famous "Gettysburg Address" at the close of the Civil War, on November 19, 1865. Another such example is the U.S.S. *Arizona* Memorial, which commemorates the lives lost in the December 7, 1941, attack on Pearl Harbor.

Other sites of historic preservation are determined on the basis of their connection to singular individuals in American history, such as birthplaces and childhood homes of U.S. presidents. Also included in this category might be sites such as Lemhi Pass and Lolo Trail, preserved in their connection to the expeditions of Meriwether Lewis and William Clark.

Still other locations undergo historic preservation because they are related closely to crucial inventions, discoveries, or innovations. Such areas include the Edison labs in West Orange, New Jersey, or the place where the Wright brothers launched their planes.

Finally, there are historic preservation projects that target important shared experiences by ordinary Americans. Samples of these would be the Klondike Gold Rush National Historic Park and the Golden Spike National Historic Site, for both recall landmarks in the lives of America's workers. Locations of this sort are of most central interest to students of folklore and folklife because they reveal something broader about American social history than do those linked only to exceptional individuals and events.

While not all of these places have direct ties to American folklore, they do help build the national consciousness of the past and its lasting resonances. As folk museums and living history museums do, sites of historic preservation help Americans respect the customs, traditions, and folkways that contribute to the nation's culture, both present and future.

See also: ARCHITECTURE, FOLK; CIVIL WAR; COLONIAL WILLIAMSBURG; FOLKLORE IN EVERY-DAY LIFE; GHOST TOWNS; GOLD RUSH, THE; GREENFIELD VILLAGE, HENRY FORD MUSEUM AND; HISTORICAL EVENTS; LEWIS, MERIWETHER, AND WILLIAM CLARK; LINCOLN, ABRAHAM;

LIVING HISTORY MUSEUMS; MUSEUMS, FOLK; MYSTIC SEAPORT AND PRESERVATION SHIPYARD; PEARL HARBOR (REMEMBRANCE) DAY; STURBRIDGE VILLAGE, OLD; TERMS; TRANSCONTINENTAL RAILROAD; VERNACULAR CULTURE; WORLD WAR II.

For Further Reading:

Alanen, Arnold, and Robert Melnick, eds. *Preserving Cultural Landscapes in America.* Baltimore: Johns Hopkins University Press, 2000.

Hufford, Mary, ed. *Conserving Culture: A New Discourse on Heritage.* Urbana: University of Illinois Press, 1994.

Miller, Page Putnam, ed. *Reclaiming the Past: Landmarks of Women's History.* Bloomington: Indiana University Press, 1992.

Murtagh, William. *Keeping Time: The History and Theory of Preservation in America.* New York: Wiley, 1997.

Stipe, Robert, ed. *A Richer Heritage: Historic Preservation in the Twenty-First Century.* Chapel Hill: University of North Carolina Press, 2003.

Wallace, Mike. *Mickey Mouse History and Other Essays on American Memory.* Philadelphia: Temple University Press, 1996.

history, folk Folk history, sometimes also called folk memory, is the version of past events people carry with them. It is the unofficial account rather than the one arrived at by professional historians or other academics.

Folk history may take many forms, and so researchers interested in recovering folk history must be eclectic in their methods and sources. It can appear in such expressive media as murals, quilts, songs, or stories. It can even be detected in the practices surrounding holidays and observances, because what and how people choose to celebrate or remember can reveal the past they most value.

For this reason oral history remains one of the central fieldwork techniques employed by folklorists. It affords researchers a means to study and preserve the voices of the American people.

Oral history employs tape-recorded interviews that document the direct testimony of all the individuals who may serve as historical informants. Before oral history came into use as a field method, most first-person accounts of the American experience were those of the elite. Such evidence focused chiefly on those who were famous enough to be interviewed by journalists, studied in universities, and/or permitted to publish their autobiographies and memoirs.

With the advent of oral history, it became possible to widen the pool of potential witnesses to American history. Oral historians typically devote their energies to social history, or the documentation of daily experiences for ordinary citizens. Rather than concentrating on presidents and generals, then, oral historians find their subjects in the constituencies of such leaders.

Oral histories have contributed in important ways to the way the world perceives and understands the American past. Through oral history, the voices of former slaves, sharecroppers, mill workers, and homemakers help tell a fuller story of the nation's character and development. Oral history proceeds from an understanding that all people have a role to play in the unfolding of the past.

For folklorists, oral history confers dignity on the observations of crasftspeople and practitioners, records oral traditions precisely as their tellers render them, and helps preserve the story of generations that attends the transmission of folk culture.

The value of this form of history is that it honors the perspectives and insights of participants over so-called experts. First-person memories and narratives make folk history a distinctive record of the past.

See also: FOLKLORE IN EVERYDAY LIFE; FOLKTALES; MUSEUMS, FOLK; ORAL FOLKLORE; ORAL HISTORY; TERMS.

For Further Reading:

Anderson, Jay, ed. *A Living History Reader*. Nashville, Tenn.: American Association for State and Local History, 1991.

Henderson, Amy, and Adrienne L. Kaeppler, eds. *Exhibiting Dilemmas: Issues of Representation at the Smithsonian*. Washington, D.C.: Smithsonian Institution Press, 1997.

Karp, Ivan, Christin Mullen Kreamer, and Steven D. Lavine, eds. *Museums and Communities: The Politics of Public Culture*. Washington, D.C.: Smithsonian Institution Press, 1992.

McNeil, W. K. "History in American Folklore: An Historical Perspective," *Western Folklore* 41, no. 1 (1982): 30–35.

Schlereth, Thomas. *Cultural History and Material Culture: Everyday Life, Landscapes, Museums*. Ann Arbor, Mich.: UMI Research Press, 1989.

Wallace, Mike. *Mickey Mouse History and Other Essays on American Memory*. Philadelphia: Temple University Press, 1996.

history, oral   See ORAL HISTORY.

hoboes   The term *hoboes* usually refers to underemployed and unemployed vagabonds, going from town to town and seeking better opportunities of one sort or another.

It was during the late 19th century that the level of public alarm about the growing population of homeless Americans reached an all-time high. Fears about the negative influences of such persons led to stiffer regulations and harsher consequences for vagrants. Communities regarded such newcomers or strangers with suspicion and increasingly criminalized their misfortune.

While hardly the nation's first poor or homeless people, hoboes came to the American public's attention in the early decades of the 20th century. They are most closely associated in the historical imagination with the Great Depression, an era when many Americans fell on hard times. Before establishment of national programs such as social security or unemployment insurance, people who lost their job, health, or homes were left largely to their own devices. During the Depression, a whole subculture of such individuals emerged. These homeless and itinerant individuals, typically men, traveled the country without cost by stowing away on boxcars of freight trains. In this way, tramps sought new communities in which to secure employment as migrant laborers or other forms of aid.

The image of the hobo is often cast in a romantic way as a hard-luck hero who carried his possessions wrapped in a bandana or tied in another sort of bundle, frequently secured at the end of a stick, which he then carried slung over one shoulder. This fanciful depiction explains the other name given to hoboes: *bindlestiffs*, or persons who carry belongings with them as they go. Folk stories and blues songs seek to capture the image of the hobo as a marginal figure in society but a prominent one within railroad lore. Even today, some individuals attempt to catch rides on freight trains to get a sense of what it might be like to be a "Knight of the road." Railroad hobbyists and enthusiasts are especially prone to such exploits. Although there is little to envy about homelessness or poverty, the hobo remains a popular icon of footloose travel.

Because they remained part of a disenfranchised subculture, hoboes developed adaptive strategies for shared survival. Perhaps the best known of these devices was a vocabulary of picture writing with which hoboes inscribed the built environment. With coded messages chalked or otherwise marked on areas visible from public spaces such as fences, walls, and trestles, tramps communicated with one another. Such symbols revealed detailed cues to the informed reader, such as how to avoid danger and where to secure help. Where uninitiated onlookers would see only a graffitilike squiggle, those in the know about hobo markings could find advice about a community with which they might be unfamiliar. Is the town hospitable to hoboes? Are the residents at this home kind to tramps? Is the neighborhood dangerous? Will this doctor treat the indigent? For itinerants, as most hoboes were, such a system of clues for navigation through unknown territory simultaneously masked the message content from others, especially those hostile to the presence of hoboes in a community.

Whether represented as an individual deserving of help because down on his luck or one likely to resort to begging or theft to meet his or her needs, the hobo persists as a folk icon of the open road.

See also: DEPRESSION; THE GREAT; FOLKLORE IN EVERYDAY LIFE; GRAFFITI; SPEECH, FOLK.

For Further Reading:
Allsop, Kenneth. *Hard Travelin: The Hobo and His History.* London: Hodder and Soughton, 1967.
Anderson, Nels. *The Hobo: The Sociology of the Homeless Man.* Chicago: University of Chicago Press, 1923.
Bruns, Roger. *Knights of the Road: A Hobo History.* New York: Methuen, 1980.
DePastino, Todd. *Citizen Hobo: How a Century of Homelessness Shaped America.* Chicago: University of Chicago Press, 2003.
Fox, Charles Elmer. *Tales of an American Hobo.* Iowa City: University of Iowa Press, 1989.
A Selected Bibliography on Hoboes and Their Folklore. Washington, D.C.: Archive of Folk Song, 1983.

Hole in the Wall Gang   See PARKER, ROBERT LEROY (BUTCH CASSIDY).

holidays/observances   Few Americans know all the origins of the nation's holidays or the reasons behind the ways the country observes special dates and occasions. However unexamined these matters may be, they nonetheless reveal a great deal about the culture and its folk customs.

While we may not think of the calendar as a culture bearer, all of the customs associated with holidays and observances represent a familiar form of folklore in practice. These practices raise many questions for careful observers. Why is it that some holidays and observances become formally designated as national holidays, while others do not? Despite the concept of separation of church and state, why is it that some religious days are still accorded special attention by public facilities, such as school closing on Christmas and Easter egg hunts on the White House lawn?

From the decorations and foods used, to the customs and practices associated with each day, holidays and observances can prove culturally informative. Why is it customary to serve a cake with lit candles at birthdays? How is it that traditional anniversary gifts have shifted with shifting trends in marriage and divorce patterns? Where did the annual custom of trick-or-treating at Halloween begin? How do American celebrations of such occasions as Saint Patrick's Day vary from those in Ireland? What is the story behind a holiday such as Groundhog Day? How and when do holidays and associated practices change? For instance, how and why do holidays take shape in the United States?

From the origins of each occasion to its decorations, events, and foods, holidays and observances punctuate the calendar year and prompt our collective memories. When studied closely, they help Americans understand traditions and annual festivities they might otherwise not take notice of or question.

See also: ADMINISTRATIVE PROFESSIONALS' DAY/WEEK; ANNIVERSARIES; APRIL FOOLS' DAY; ARBOR DAY; BAR MITZVAH/BAT MITZVAH; BIRTHDAYS; BOSS DAY (BOSS'S DAY); CHRISTMAS; CINCO DE MAYO; CITIZENSHIP DAY; COLUMBUS DAY; EARTH DAY; EASTER; ELECTION DAY; EMANCIPATION (PROCLAMATION) DAY; FATHER'S DAY; FLAG DAY; FRIDAY THE THIRTEENTH; GRANDPARENTS DAY; GROUNDHOG DAY; HALLOWEEN/ALL HALLOWS' EVE; HANUKKAH; INAUGURATION DAY; INDEPENDENCE DAY/FOURTH OF JULY; JUNETEENTH; KWANZAA; LABOR DAY; MARDI GRAS; MARTIN LUTHER KING DAY; MAY DAY; MEMORIAL DAY; MOTHER'S DAY; NEW YEAR'S EVE/DAY;

Passover; Patriot Day; Pearl Harbor Day; Presidents' Day; Ramadan; Rosh Hashonah; Saint Patrick's Day; Saint Valentine's Day; solstice; Sweetest Day; Thanksgiving; Veterans Day; Yom Kippur.

For Further Reading:

Cohen, Hennig, and Tristram Potter Coffin, eds. *The Folklore of American Holidays*. Detroit: Gale, 1987.

Dupuy, Trevor Nevitt, ed. *Holidays: Days of Significance for All Americans*. New York: Franklin Watts, 1965.

Hutchison, Ruth, and Ruth Adams. *Every Day's a Holiday*. New York: Harper & Bros., 1951.

James, E. O. *Seasonal Feasts and Festivals*. New York: Barnes & Noble, 1961.

Krythe, Maymie. *All about American Holidays*. New York: Harper & Row, 1962.

Murphy, Patricia J. *Our National Holidays*. Minneapolis: Compass Point Books, 2002.

Myers, Robert. *Celebrations: The Complete Book of American Holidays*. Garden City, N.Y.: Doubleday, 1972.

Santino, Jack. *All around the Year: Holidays and Celebrations in American Life*. Urbana: University of Illinois Press, 1994.

Thompson, Sue Ellen. *Holiday Symbols: A Guide to the Legend and Lore*. Detroit: Omnigraphics, 2000.

holly   See Christmas.

home remedies   See medicine, folk.

hoodoo   See voodoo/hoodoo.

Horseman, Headless (legendary)   The Headless Horseman is the nemesis of the schoolteacher Ichabod Crane in Washington Irving's "The Legend of Sleepy Hollow."

Although the tale is nominally a love triangle, it is better known as a tale of Halloween horror. The story's gangly but vain protagonist, Ichabod Crane, is a schoolteacher whose initial response to his new environment is one of delight with the charming and hospitable locale. After his arrival in the northern New York community of Sleepy Hollow, Crane finds himself smitten with Katrina Von Tassel, the daughter of a local farmer. In time, she invites him to her father's Halloween party, causing Crane to suppose his romantic prospects with her to be favorable.

Near the close of the event, the men begin to exchange scary stories. In this context, Brom Bones, a rival for Katrina's affections, tells a vivid story of the Headless Horseman, a dark demon in flowing garments who travels the countryside at night.

As Crane takes his leave from the Halloween celebration, he finds himself confronted in the darkness by a figure meeting Bones's description of the Headless Horseman, with what appears to be his head tucked in an arm. The figure pursues the teacher and, at the culmination of the chase, hurls the severed head at the horrified Crane.

By morning, only a smashed pumpkin remains where the head would have been, leading readers to wonder whether the moonlit encounter was merely a prank to displace Crane as a suitor for Katrina. If so, the ploy succeeds. In the end, Crane flees Sleepy Hollow, leaving Katrina Von Tassel and Brom Bones to marry. As the legend has it, Crane's tormented presence can still be felt in the dark of Sleepy Hollow nights.

Although "The Legend of Sleepy Hollow," with its image of the Headless Horseman, stands as a work of print literature, its presentation as legend and its plentiful retellings in oral and popular culture render it a staple within the folklore of the United States and, in particular, the lore of Halloween. From Mr. Magoo's to Johnny Depp's, screen characterizations of Ichabod Crane's classic confrontation with the Headless Horseman have delighted audiences by recalling a narrative past associated with regional folklore.

See also: folk heroes/legendary figures; Halloween/All Hallows' Eve; Irving, Washington; Northeastern regional folklore; region, folk.

For Further Reading:

Hedges, William L. "The Theme of Americanism in Irving's Writings." In *Washington Irving: A Tribute*, edited by Andres B. Myers, 29–35. Tarrytown, N.Y.: Sleepy Hollow Restorations, 1972.

Hoffman, Daniel G. "Irving's Use of American Folklore in 'The Legend of Sleepy Hollow,'" *Publications of the Modern Language Association of America* 68, no. 3 (June 1953): 425–435.

Irving, Washington. *The Legend of Sleepy Hollow.* Mankato, Minn.: Creative Education, 1990.

MacPhail, Bruce D. *The Wit and Whimsy of Washington Irving.* Tarrytown, N.Y.: Sleepy Hollow, 1979.

Poenicke, Klaus. "Engendering Cultural Memory: 'The Legend of Sleepy Hollow' as Text and Intertext," *Amerikastudien/American Studies* 43, no. 1 (1998): 19–32.

Houdini, Harry (1874–1926)   Born in Hungary on April 6, 1874, as Ehrich Weiss, Harry Houdini became a world-renowned master magician and illusionist.

Houdini developed an early interest in performance and appeared in a home-styled circus as a youth. He resolved to become a showman and worked in vaudeville on the Orpheum circuit. His first appearances were as a contortionist and trapeze artist. He then began a magic act, featured at Chicago's World's Columbian Exposition in 1892. By the turn of the century, he was emerging as a popular entertainer, especially in terms of his work as an escape artist. Promotional materials depict him locked in chains and describe him as the "King of Handcuffs." Houdini went on to perform a wide range of feats, from jailbreaks to escapes from straitjackets. In one of his most famous stage tricks in 1918 he made an elephant disappear at New York's Hippodrome Theater.

Other enthusiasms for Houdini included the history of magic, aviation, and the challenge of discrediting frauds posing as psychics and spiritualists. He hoped to be remembered after his 1926 death for his research into the world of magic.

More than a parlor-trick magician, Houdini excited audiences with the mystery of his stunts and the intrigue of his escapes. The public loved seeing him free himself from the most restrictive and dangerous predicaments, perhaps providing a vicarious sense of agility, freedom, and agency. These talents became so widely recognized that by 1920, Funk and Wagnall's listed Houdini's surname as a verb: *houdanize.*

Today, Harry Houdini has an iconic place in magic lore and has been the subject of many books and dramatizations. In addition, several subsequent magicians have researched and attempted to reenact Houdini's tricks.

See also: FESTIVALS, FOLKLORE; FOLK HEROES/ LEGENDARY FIGURES; MAGIC; SUPERNATURAL.

For Further Reading:

Brandon, Ruth. *The Life and Many Deaths of Harry Houdini.* London: Secker and Warburg, 1993.

Fitzsimons, Raymund. *Death and the Magician: The Mystery of Houdini.* London: H. Hamilton, 1980.

Kellock, Harold. *Houdini: His Life-Story.* London: Heinemann, 1928.

Rukeyser, Muriel. *Houdini: A Musical.* Ashfield, Mass.: Paris Press, 2002.

Silverman, Kenneth. *Houdini! The Career of Erich Weiss: American Self-Liberator, Europe's Eclipsing Sensation, World's Handcuff King, and Prison Breaker.* New York: HarperCollins, 1996.

houses, haunted   See HAUNTED HOUSES.

Hughes, James Mercer Langston (1902–1967)   As one of the most illustrious African-American writers, Langston Hughes helped make visible, enduring, and influential the folklore traditions of a historically disenfranchised population.

Hughes was born James Mercer Langston Hughes in Joplin, Missouri, on February 1,

1902. His grandmother was the last surviving widow of the John Brown raid of 1859 conducted in opposition to American slavery.

As a boy, Hughes became infatuated with books and reading, a portent of his career in the field of writing. He attended Columbia University and Lincoln University. The daughter of the well-known African-American fiction writer Charles Waddell Chesnutt was one of the schoolteachers who worked with Hughes when he was a youth.

Although Hughes became best known for his poetry, he was also an accomplished playwright, editor, fiction writer, scriptwriter, translator, and correspondent. His career spanned the period from the Harlem Renaissance of the 1920s to the black arts movement of the 1960s. Nine of his early poems appeared in Alain Le Roy Locke's landmark collection of Harlem Renaissance writings *The New Negro* (1925). His poems spoke forthrightly to the human condition and the realities of racism. Hughes frequently incorporated in his writings aspects of African-American folk culture, most notably elements derived from jazz, gospel, and blues music. His poems include "The Negro Speaks of Rivers," "Jazzonia," "The Weary Blues," and "Negro Dancer."

Over the course of his life, Langston Hughes associated with many of the century's most celebrated African-American writers, including Zora Neale Hurston, James Weldon Johnson, Arna Bontemps, Margaret Walker, and W. E. B. DuBois. Late in his career, Hughes edited numerous books, including *The Book of Negro Humor* (1966) and *The Book of Negro Folklore* (1955), which he coedited with Bontemps. Hughes died on May 22, 1967, in New York City.

Today, the writings of James Mercer Langston Hughes inspire a new generation of writers, who pay tribute to his literary legacy and attentiveness to African-American folk traditions. In addition, plays such as *Black Nativity* continue to be staged and spoken word recordings with and without music are still being issued to honor the writer's contributions.

See also: AFRICAN-AMERICAN FOLKLORE; BROWN, JOHN; CHESNUTT, CHARLES WADDELL; DuBois, W. E. B.; FOLKLORE IN AMERICAN LITERATURE; HURSTON, ZORA NEALE; LOCKE, ALAIN LE ROY.

For Further Reading:
Bloom, Harold, ed. *Langston Hughes*. New York: Chelsea House, 1989.

Gates, Henry Louis, Jr., and K. A. Appiah. *Langston Hughes: Critical Perspectives Past and Present.* New York: Amistad, 1993.

Mandelik, Peter, and Stanley Schatt. *Concordance to Langston Hughes*. Detroit: Gale Research, 1975.

Mullen, Edward J., ed. *Critical Essays on Langston Hughes*. Boston: G. K. Hall, 1986.

Osofsky, Audrey. *Free to Dream: The Making of a Poet: Langston Hughes*. New York: Lothrop, Lee & Shepard, 1996.

Rampersad, Arnold. *The Life of Langston Hughes*. New York: Oxford University Press, 1986–1988.

Tracy, Steven C. *Langston Hughes and the Blues*. Urbana: University of Illinois Press, 1988.

Trotman, C. James, ed. *Langston Hughes: The Man, His Art, and His Continuing Influence*. New York: Garland Press, 1995.

humor, folk   As is true in any culture, that of the United States relies upon the entertainment and comic relief provided by folk humor.

Folk humor involves any kinds of comedic speech or performance by ordinary people rather than professional comedians. It can include anecdotes, riddles, limericks, stories, tall tales, pranks, practical jokes, or jokes of other kinds. In a few cases, even individuals who make their living through comedy can have close ties to folk humor. Will Rogers (1879–1935) was one of America's best-known folk humorists. His homespun sayings and down-home aphorisms are still remembered today. For example, Rogers became known for plainspoken quips such as "Even if you're on the right track, you'll get run over if you just sit there." As a cowboy everyman, Rogers satirized American politics. "There's no trick to being a humorist," Rogers liked to say, "when you have the whole government working for you." With his sharp wit, colloquial speech, and informal mannerisms, he helped his audiences challenge pretension and claims to sophistication. Although Will Rogers became associated with old-fashioned humor of rural America, there are forms of humor associated with every region and era in the nation's history, such as midwestern or frontier humor.

Oral folklore, and everyday verbal lore more generally, is replete with folk humor. In addition to stories such as tall tales, which are humorous through overstatement and hyperbole, there are humorous anecdotes such as those recounting the teller's most embarrassing moment(s). Most skilled storytellers know and employ the power of humor in holding and rewarding an audience's attention. In fact, even the youngest members of a language community usually tell jokes of one kind or another, from "Knock, Knock" jokes to riddles. Children's jokes usually take a whimsical turn. For example, in one such riddle, the questioner asks, "Why was 6 afraid of 7?" When the listener replies with the customary "I don't know—why was 6 afraid of 7?" the teller can explain, "Because 7-8-9!" As this sample demonstrates, many children's jokes rely upon word play that works only in sounded language, in this case a homophone between the number 8 and the word *ate*.

Quite common in American joke telling are joke cycles, so called because they involve whole categories of jokes related by type or motif. Joke cycles both appeal to joke collectors and permit joke tellers to present a series of jokes in a sequence. Examples of joke cycles include dumb jokes (such as Dumb Dora or Little Moron jokes), sick jokes (such as dead baby, Helen Keller, AIDS, and *Challenger* jokes), occupational jokes (such as lawyer, doctor, and politician jokes). Joke cycles transform single jokes into entire comedic exchanges. Such repertoires are common in schoolyard and campus lore.

Elements of humor are also a part of several American holidays, such as Halloween and April Fool's Day. Halloween, with its traditions of trick or treat activities, is a time not only for masquerade, but also for playful mischief. On April Fool's Day, it is customary to exchange practical jokes, which seek to dupe others. Of course, pranks can be practiced at any time of year. One of the most notorious fool's errands in American lore is the snipe hunt. With this gag, participants convince an unwitting victim that snipes, small creatures of the wild, can only be caught by a team working at night. The group takes their mark, or victim, out in the darkness and positions him or her as a catcher. The others disperse, promising to drive the snipe(s) into the collecting sack of the catcher. In truth, the rest of the participants leave the unsuspecting catcher alone in the night, where the individual either figures out the prank or waits to be retrieved by the pranksters. This trick is a favorite of campers and outdoors enthusiasts. Another popular American prank is the game described as 52 Card Pickup. The prank player asks the victim whether he or she would like to play 52 Pickup. If the mark answers affirmatively, then the prankster throws the entire card deck on the floor and says, "Okay, pick them up!" This prank is usually played on very young children who are seeking to be included in others' play, since it only works if the victim asks no questions about how the game is played.

Contemporary updates on such practical jokes involve new technologies that have become pervasive, such as computer, photocopy, and fax pranks. In the keypunch days of computing, for example, a "lace card," a keypunch card with all slots punched, could be used for mischief, often jamming the computer. More recently, the "black fax" is a prank that targets the fax recipient by expending as much toner as possible, depleting the victim's supply. Other information age pranks involve hoax e-mails and faxes, which bait recipients to respond with alarm.

Although there are many theories about how humor functions and what makes it funny to people in a given situation, it is fair to say that comedy cannot be reduced to a formula or set of rules. Rather, whether the joke relies upon verbal punning, satire, or a playful engagement with social taboos, folk humor's delight is in its endless surprises.

See also: AIDS FOLKLORE; APRIL FOOL'S DAY; BIRTHDAYS; "BOY WHO CRIED WOLF, THE"; BRER RABBIT; CAMPUS FOLKLORE; CLEMENS, SAMUEL LANGHORNE; COMPUTER FOLKLORE; COWBOYS; COYOTE; ELLISON, RALPH WALDO; FOLK HEROES/ LEGENDARY FIGURES; FOLKLORE IN EVERYDAY LIFE; FOLKTALES; GRAFFITI; HILLBILLIES; INAUGURATION DAY; IRVING, WASHINGTON; JONES, JOHN LUTHER (CASEY); JUMP ROPE RHYMES; MOSE THE FIREMAN; REGION, FOLK; RIDDLES, FOLK; SPEECH, FOLK; UNCLE SAM; XEROX/FAX FOLKLORE; YANKEE PEDDLAR.

For Further Reading:
Boatright, Mody. *Folk Laughter on the American Frontier*. New York: Collier, 1946.

Dorson, Richard. *Jonathan Draws the Long Bow*. Cambridge, Mass.: Harvard University Press, 1946.

Dundes, Alan. *Cracking Jokes: Studies of Sick Humor Cycles and Stereotypes*. Berkeley, Calif.: Ten Speed Press, 1987.

Dundes, Alan, ed. *Mother Wit from the Laughing Barrel*. Jackson: University Press of Mississippi, 1990.

Leary, James P. *Midwestern Folk Humor*. Little Rock, Ark.: August House, 1991.

Legman, Gershon. *No Laughing Matter: An Analysis of Sexual Humor*. Bloomington: Indiana University Press, 1967.

Mintz, Lawrence E., ed. *Humor in America: A Research Guide to Genres and Topics*. Westport, Conn.: Greenwood, 1988.

Oring, Elliott. *Jokes and Their Relations*. Lexington: University Press of Kentucky, 1992.

Rourke, Constance. *American Humor: A Study of Our National Character*. Garden City, N.Y.: Doubleday, 1931.

Schoemaker, George H., ed. *The Emergence of Folklore in Everyday Life: A Fieldguide and Sourcebook*. Bloomington, Ind.: Trickster Press, 1990.

Schwartz, Alvin. *Flapdoodle, Pure Nonsense from American Folklore*. New York: Lippincott, 1980.

Tidwell, James Nathan. *A Treasury of American Folk Humor: A Rare Confection of Laughter, Tall Tales, Jests, and Other Gems of Merriment of the American People*. New York: Crown, 1956.

West, John O. *Cowboy Folk Humor: Life and Laughter in the American West*. Little Rock, Ark.: August House, 1990.

Wilson, Christopher. *Jokes: Form, Content, Use, and Function*. New York: Academic Press, 1979.

Humpty Dumpty (legendary)   The brief but memorable nursery rhyme featuring Humpty Dumpty is a standard element of children's narrative culture.

The rhymed verse of this Mother Goose story describes how the title character, a personified egg, topples from his perch atop a wall and cannot be mended:

> Humpty Dumpty sat on a wall,
> Humpty Dumpty had a great fall,
> All the king's horses and all the king's
>   men,
> Could not put Humpty together again.

Although on one level, "Humpty Dumpty" appears to be mostly a nonsensical tale, its fanciful and symbolic quality has captured the imagination of audiences.

The framework and/or phrases of this rhyme have been endlessly adapted. For example, Lewis Carroll's fantasy story of Alice, *Through the Looking Glass and What Alice Found There* (1871), devoted an entire chapter to Humpty Dumpty and his interaction with Alice.

In most such retellings or recastings, "Humpty Dumpty" represents a comic figure who, despite royal connections, cannot be spared the effects of a metaphorical, or perhaps even metaphysical, decline. The concept of the fall of the mighty is a familiar one and reassures audiences that no one is immune to the vagaries of life.

In particular, contemporary writers have used the image of Humpty Dumpty, including Robert Penn Warren in *All the King's Men* (1946), Philip K. Dick in *Humpty Dumpty in Oakland* (1960), and Carl Bernstein and Robert Woodward in *All the President's Men* (1974).

Whether taken as whimsical or cautionary, Humpty Dumpty's tale reminds readers and listeners of some of the most basic folk wisdom of all, concerning the fragility of life and the elusiveness of immortality.

See also: CHILDREN'S FOLKLORE; FABLES; FAIRY TALES; MOTHER GOOSE; MYTHS, FOLK; NURSERY RHYMES; RHYMES, FOLK.

For Further Reading:

Carlock, Mary Sue. "Humpty Dumpty and the Autobiography," *Genre* 3 (1970): 340–350.

Hillman, Ellis. "Dinah, the Cheshire Cat, and Humpty Dumpty," *Jabberwocky: The Journal of the Lewis Carroll Society* 6 (1977): 29.

Knieger, Bernard M. "Humpty Dumpty and Symbolism," *College English* 20, no. 5 (February 1959): 244–245.

Loney, Douglas. "Humpty Dumpty in the Heavens: Perspective in *Out of the Silent Planet*," *Mythlore: A Journal of J. R. R. Tolkien, C. S. Lewis, Charles Williams, and the Genres of Myth and Fantasy Studies* 16, no. 2 (winter 1989): 14–20.

Ruoff, James. "Humpty Dumpty and *All the King's Men*: A Note on Robert Penn Warren's Teleology," *Twentieth Century Literature: A Scholarly and Critical Journal* 3, no. 3 (October 1957): 128–134.

Shannon, George W. B. *Humpty Dumpty: A Pictorial History*. La Jolla, Calif.: Green Tiger/Stars & Elephant, 1980.

Walley, Harold R. "Reconstruction for Humpty Dumpty: The Comparative Concept in Literary Study," *College English* 6, no. 7 (April 1945): 404–408.

Hungarian-American folklore   Hungarian-American folklore reflects the cultural tradition of both immigrants to the United States from Hungary and American-born individuals of Hungarian ancestry.

Waves of immigration to America from Hungary have occurred since the 1860s. Major centers of Hungarian-American population include New Brunswick, New Jersey; Cleveland, Ohio; and Pittsburgh, Pennsylvania. As is the case with other immigrant groups, each generation of Hungarian Americans tends to grow more distant from the homeland and its folkways.

Hungarian-American folk traditions include crafts, dances, and music. Hungarian Americans celebrate American holidays, along with three occasions that recall key dates in the life of their homeland: Saint Stephen's Day, the Revolution of 1848, and the Revolution of 1956. In addition, festivals designed to celebrate Hungarian heritage and raise consciousness among Hungarian Americans are common in areas where large populations reside.

Organizations dedicated to the preservation and study of Hungarian-American culture include Bogota, New Jersey's Hungarian Folklore Centrum; Akron, Ohio's American Hungarian Federation; and Stone Mountain, Georgia's Hungarian Cultural Foundation. Major collections of Hungarian-American cultural material include New Brunswick, New Jersey's American-Hungarian Foundation and Hungarian Institute, as well as Bloomington, Indiana's Institute of Hungarian Studies.

Even though elements of Hungarian culture, such as language, may be remote for many of today's Hungarian Americans, folklore remains a way for them to remember their ethnic and cultural origins.

See also: CULTURAL GROUPS; ETHNICITY; HOUDINI, HARRY; IMMIGRATION AND FOLKLORE.

For Further Reading:

Degh, Linda. "Approaches to Folklore Research among Immigrant Groups," *Journal of American Folklore* 79, no. 314 (fall 1966): 551–556.

Lengyel, Emil. *Americans from Hungary*. Philadelphia: J. B. Lippincott, 1948.

Orring, Elliott. *Folk Groups and Folklore Genres: An Introduction*. Logan: Utah State University Press, 1986.

Puskás, Julianna. *From Hungary to the United States, 1880–1914*. Budapest: Akadémiai Kiadó, 1982.

Tezla, Albert. *The Hazardous Quest: Hungarian Immigrants in the United States, 1895–1920*. Budapest: Corvina, 1993.

———. *The Hungarian-Americans*. Boston: Twayne, 1985.

———. *The Hungarian Americans: The Hungarian Experience in North America*. New York and Philadelphia: Chelsea House, 1990.

Hurston, Zora Neale (c. 1891–1960) In terms of assessing the influence of folklore on African-American literature, the works of Zora Neale Hurston, and in particular, her tales collected in *Mules and Men*, provide an illuminating case study, as well as a counterpoint to work by the collector Joel Chandler Harris.

Although Hurston may be best known for her fiction, including such book-length fiction as *Their Eyes Were Watching God* (1937), she was also a formally trained and published collector of African-American folklore. Hurston's education took her to Columbia and Barnard, where she found a mentor of sorts in the noted anthropologist Franz Boas. In the preface of Hurston's collection *Mules and Men* Boas suggests that in the past, white interest in African-American folklore was both halfhearted and biased. Figures such as Joel Chandler Harris, with his Uncle Remus tales, recorded African-American tales but in the process embedded their own stereotypical views of African-American narrative culture. Boas addresses this issue somewhat diplomatically, by suggesting that efforts such as those by Chandler fail to capture what he calls the intimate setting of those tales.

The language Boas uses to describe the anthropologist's work is telling. He depicts the anthropologist as one who gathers a community's secrets. Within this enterprise, Boas notes the special difficulty of anthropological fieldwork, in which there is the additional dynamic of an observer from the dominant culture who interviews people of an oppressed group. There is more than a scholarly difficulty; there is an interpersonal and intercultural danger that in the process and/or presentation of that anthropology one merely replicates and perpetuates social hierarchies and racial inequalities. In other words, given these circumstances of folklore, a study with an inherently acquisitive and appropriative nature, African Americans have good reasons to shield their heritage. The guarding of one's inner life—whether individual or collective—is not to be taken lightly or abandoned easily.

Mules and Men (1935) represents, at least in part, Hurston's efforts to counter the work and agendas of people such as Joel Chandler Harris. This was no small matter, especially during her era. In order to document her cultural legacy, Hurston herself had to contend with a paternalistic world of white mentors and sponsors. She addressed her teacher as "Papa Franz" and her patron, Charlotte Osgood Mason, as "Godmother." These names were indicative of the social relations of racial, and in the case of Mason, financial deference, upon which even her scholarship about African-American folklore relied. With her studies in the social sciences, though, Hurston was by no means interested in imitating or inculcating white cultural forms or hierarchies. Instead, the discipline of anthropology provided Hurston with the opportunity to introduce her own life world to a reconfigured scholarly study, to put to use what she calls the "spyglass" of anthropology in the preservation and interpretation of authentically rendered African-American folklore. Hurston rebutted depictions of that lore that attempted to suggest a culture's deficiency or abnormality, and so Hurston focused on the integrity of the culture taken as a whole and, as much as possible, on its own terms.

Hurston was also interested in combating the notion of the tragic black as stereotypical figure, and in many ways the stories she shares in *Mules and Men* underscore that point. It was Hurston's firm belief that while the past was important to study, one must not be immobilized by its painful confrontation. One cannot help being the product of tragedy, but one need not fall its victim. In keeping with this outlook, within her own works of fiction, Hurston's characters search for an identity—on the horizon, beneath pear trees, and in a lover's eyes. In other words, she depicts the heroism of daily life. Hurston insists that she is a person and not a problem, an individual rather than a type, and so should her characters be realistic and nuanced. She longed to see ordinary, credible people as characters in both nonfiction and fiction by and about African Americans.

It is difficult, then, to appreciate fully the social world Hurston depicts so richly in both her folklore and her fiction without a sense of the traditions of boasting, the dozens, and storytelling to which it corresponds, and to which it pays tribute. For instance, any reader of Hurston's work notices the role dialect plays within Hurston's collections of folklore and perhaps even wonders why it is that Hurston retains a typographical practice of phoneticizing speech. By rendering on the page the sounded language of African Americans, Hurston hopes to let them speak for themselves. So in this respect as well, Hurston offers a corrective for previous folkloristic abuses. Language could be restorative, and Hurston dedicated herself to that work of cultural regeneration. Hurston's very writing of such a book represents an act of resistance. Hurston not only acquired anthropological training in a white-dominated society and university system but applied that knowledge to a community of people that system overlooked or looked at only as a primitive spectacle. It is noteworthy that Hurston chooses to confront white misconceptions about African-American folklife by telling the community's stories, for in so doing she dramatizes language as in itself a means of environmental and situational mastery, no less powerful because spoken rather than written.

Zora Neale Hurston's own rediscovery by contemporary readers owes much to this process of African-American recovery. Hurston attracted the public's attention posthumously, when the author Alice Walker traveled, as her 1983 book's title would have it, "In Search of Our Mothers' Gardens." Walker rescued Hurston's earlier literary and folkloristic contributions from obscurity by returning Hurston's texts to print and invoking those writings as antecedents to those of contemporary women writers of color from Toni Cade Bambara to Paule Marshall.

See also: AFRICAN-AMERICAN FOLKLORE; BAMBARA, TONI CADE; FIELDWORK, FOLKLORE; FOLKLORE IN AMERICAN LITERATURE; FOLKTALES; HARRIS, JOEL CHANDLER; HUMOR, FOLK; REMUS, UNCLE; SOUTHERN REGIONAL FOLKLORE; SPEECH, FOLK; TAR BABY; VOODOO/HOODOO.

For Further Reading:

Croft, Robert. *A Zora Neale Hurston Companion.* Westport, Conn.: Greenwood Press, 2002.

Duck, Leigh Anne. "'Go There tuh Know There': Zora Neale Hurston and the Chronotype of the Folk," *American Literary History* 13, no. 2 (summer 2001): 265–294.

Peters, Pearlie Mae Fisher. *The Assertive Woman in Zora Neale Hurston's Fiction, Folklore, and Drama.* New York: Garland, 1998.

Wall, Cheryl A., ed. *Zora Neale Hurston: Folklore, Memoirs, and Other Writings.* New York: Library of America, 1995.

I

I am an American Day See CITIZENSHIP DAY.

Ibo Landing As the site for a memorable act of resistance to U.S. slavery, Ibo Landing has taken on symbolic importance within African-American folklore.

Ibo Landing, sometimes known as Ebo Landing, takes its name from Gullah folktales dating back to the 19th century. The specific reference is to an event in May 1803. At this time, a slave ship carrying Ibo people from West Africa arrived to deliver its "cargo" at Saint Simons Island, Georgia. The West Africans, upon assessing their situation, resolved to risk their lives by walking home over the water rather than submitting to the living death that awaited them in American slavery. As the tale has it, the tribespeople disembarked from the ship, and as a group, turned around and walked along the water, traveling in the opposite direction from the arrival port. As they took this march together, the West Africans joined in song. They are reported to have sung a hymn in which the lyrics assert that the water spirit will take them home. While versions of this story vary in nuance, all attest to the courage in rebellion displayed by the enslaved Ibo. By opposing the conditions of chattel slavery in the United States, these tribespeople inspired others to seek alternatives to such oppression.

This Gullah folktale has been retold countless times in African-American culture, and it has also found its way into both print and film. Two prominent examples of adaptations of the Ibo folktale for popular culture are Paule Marshall's 1983 novel *Prasesong for the Widow* and Julie Dash's 1992 feature-length film *Daughters of the Dust*. In Marshall's novel, patterned as the story of a woman's literal and figurative voyage of discovery, the protagonist, Avey Johnson, becomes conscious of her own cultural legacies, including the tale of Ibo Landing. Through such awareness, the character achieves a spiritual rebirth. In Julie Dash's film, the Ibo Landing story is also retold, but this time in the context of the surviving Gullah people in the Sea Islands area. What connects these variations on the folktale is a sense of the power of refusal that rests at the center of the tale. The Ibo people, proud in their cultural identity and courageous in their rejection of enslavement, continue to inspire audiences who face threats to their cultural autonomy.

Gullah folklore is particularly closely associated with the states of North Carolina, South Carolina, and Georgia. The water-walking Ibos, as do the legendary flying Africans, embody the conviction and capacity of both African and African-American folk culture.

See also: AFRICAN-AMERICAN FOLKLORE; BAMBARA, TONI CADE; LEGENDS, FOLK; HIS-

TORICAL EVENTS; HISTORY, FOLK; PROTEST IN
FOLKLORE; SLAVERY; SOUTHERN REGIONAL
FOLKLORE.

For Further Reading:

Bracy, Ibsan. *Ibo Landing: An Offering of Short Stories.* New York: Cool Grove Press, 1998.

Brown, Thomas. *Lessons Learned from the Gullah
Experience: Powerful Forces in Educating African-
American Youth.* Columbia, Md.: Brown and
Associates, 1998.

Countryman, Edward, and Ira Berlin, eds. *How
Did American Slavery Begin? Readings.* Boston:
Bedford/St. Martin's, 1999.

Goodwine, Marquetta, ed. *The Legacy of Ibo Landing: Gullah Roots of African American Culture.*
Atlanta: Clarity Press, 2002.

Jones, Charles. *Gullah Folktales from the Georgia
Coast.* Athens: University of Georgia Press,
2000.

Jones, Charles. *Negro Myths from the Georgia Coast
Told in the Vernacular.* Detroit: Singing Tree
Press, 1969.

Pinckney, Roger. *Blue Roots: African-American Folk
Magic of the Gullah People.* Saint Paul, Minn.:
Llewellyn, 1998.

Icelandic-American folklore

Icelandic-American folklore consists of the cultural tradi-
tions of immigrants to the United States from
Iceland, as well as those of person born in
America of Icelandic heritage.

It could be said that Icelandic Americans have
been immigrating to the United States since
Leif Eriksson became the first white to arrive in
North America in A.D. 1000. Most immigration
by Icelandic Americans, however, has occurred
since the middle of the 19th century. Since that
time, Icelandic-American immigrants have made
homes across the country. A significant portion
of the population is concentrated in the midwestern region, with settlements in North Dakota,
South Dakota, Minnesota, and Wisconsin.

Their early activities in America reflected the
patterns of their homeland, with its emphasis on
seafaring, fishing, and agriculture. Accordingly,
Icelandic-American foodways place an emphasis
on items such as fish, bread, and several forms
of pancakes.

Icelandic narrative lore features numerous
stories of magical creatures such as fairies, elves,
and trolls. Such stories generally depict fairies
and elves as magical in positive ways, while trolls
are more likely to use their powers to harm or
taunt others. At New Year's, elves confer good
luck if invited into the family home with lights
and chants of welcome. Gryla, one of the trolls
featured in Icelandic traditional stories, persists
as a folk myth among Icelandic Americans. Such
characters help connect Icelandic Americans to
their place and culture of origin.

Holidays are often a time when Icelandic
Americans connect with their ethnic heritage.
For example, many immigrants join in celebrations of Icelandic Independence Day each
June 14. The First Day of Summer is also a
very important celebration for Icelandic Americans, featuring festivals, special foods, and gift
exchanges.

In order to help preserve the cultural legacies, Icelandic Americans have formed several
organizations to document traditions, promote
cultural understanding, and affirm shared ethnic
identity. These groups include the Icelandic
National League. Important collections of Icelandic American cultural material are in place
at the University of Wisconsin, University of
North Dakota, Cornell University, and Brigham
Young University.

Although Iceland was once under Danish
rule, and so others may conceive of it as as part
of Scandinavia, Icelandics and Icelandic Americans have distinct traditions and customs.

See also: CULTURAL GROUPS; FOOD/FOOD-
WAYS; HOLIDAYS/OBSERVANCES; IMMIGRATION
AND FOLKLORE; MAGIC; MARITIME FOLKLORE;
NEW YEAR'S EVE/DAY; SUPERNATURAL.

For Further Reading:

Arnason, David, and Michael Olito. *The Icelanders.*
Winnipeg, Canada: Turnstone Press, 1981.

Bjornson, Valdimar. "Icelanders in the United States," *Scandinavian Review* 64 (1976): 39–41.

Bjornsson, Arni. *Icelandic Feasts and Holidays: Celebrations, Past and Present.* Translated by May and Hallberg Hallmundson. Reykjavik: Iceland Review, 1980.

Jonsson, Hjorleifur Rafn. "Trolls, Chiefs and Children: Changing Perspectives on an Icelandic Christmas Myth," *Nord Nytt: Nordisk Tidsskrift for Folkelivsforskning* 41 (1990): 55–63.

Walters, Thorstina Jackson. *Modern Sagas: The Story of Icelanders in North America.* Fargo, N. Dak.: Institute for Regional Studies, 1953.

Idaho folklore See CHINESE-AMERICAN FOLKLORE; JAPANESE-AMERICAN INTERNMENT; JOSEPH, CHIEF; LEWIS, MERIWETHER, AND WILLIAM CLARK; MORMON FOLKLORE; NORTHWESTERN REGIONAL FOLKLORE.

Illinois folklore See CHAPMAN, JOHN (JOHNNY APPLESEED); BOLES, CHARLES E. (BLACK BART); BOSS DAY/BOSS'S DAY; CAPONE, ALPHONSE GABRIEL (AL); DILLINGER, JOHN; DISNEY, WALTER ELIAS; EARP, WYATT BERRY STAMP; FATHER'S DAY; HICKOK, JAMES BUTLER (WILD BILL); LINCOLN, ABRAHAM; MIDWESTERN REGIONAL FOLKLORE; PRESIDENTS' DAY; SANDBURG, CARL.

immigration and folklore Sometimes known as a nation of immigrants, the United States has a rich history and lore of immigration.

America is constantly being referred to as a "melting pot" or "salad bowl" of different nationalities, races, and ethnicities. Whether or not these terms are appropriate ones, there can be little doubt that America is a multiculture. Although indigenous people were not immigrants, and African Americans were taken to the United States involuntarily during American slavery, a great many of the ancestors of those living in the nation now arrived as immigrants. For this reason, immigration stands as a singularly important part of American folklore.

Perhaps the most iconic landscape of American immigration is Ellis Island, located in New York City's harbor. This was the portal through which millions of the nation's new residents, especially those arriving from Europe, entered from 1892 to 1954. At the processing center at Ellis Island, newcomers were given a health examination and interviewed before being granted admission to the United States. During the last 30 years of its operation, this processing center was devoted chiefly to refugees and others who were detained.

Although within the popular imagination the Statue of Liberty and Ellis Island are inextricably linked, the monument stands on Liberty Island nearby. Nonetheless, the statue's image upon arrival is a feature of many immigrant stories, perhaps because of its greeting. The Emma Lazarus verse inscribed on the base of the Statue of Liberty, with its welcome to those others reject, only serves to underscore this impression of acceptance.

Perhaps the most common legend concerning Ellis Island is that immigrant names were routinely Americanized or otherwise modified for the convenience of processing center officials. Although this is a common belief, it belies some of the facts of immigration policies during this era. For example, even illiterate travelers required written proof of their identity, including exit visas in some cases. In addition, arriving vessels needed passenger lists. Consequently, Ellis Island officers were not faced with the task of writing down surnames they did not understand and could not corroborate. Finally, many translators were on hand for conducting interviews with immigrants, so spoken explanations provided by immigrants were more likely to be accurately understood. Therefore, while name changes may have occurred during the period in which Ellis Island operated, it is not likely that this happened very frequently.

At present, Ellis Island is the site of an immigration museum operated by the National Park Service. It can be reached by ferry from New

Jersey or New York. It has become part of the folklore of American immigration.

See also: ANGLO-AMERICAN FOLKLORE; CAPONE, ALPHONSE GABRIEL (AL); CHINESE-AMERICAN FOLKLORE; CITIZENSHIP DAY; COLUMBUS, CHRISTOPHER; COLUMBUS DAY; CULTURAL GROUPS; DUTCH-AMERICAN FOLKLORE; ETHNICITY; EVIL EYE; FILIPINO-AMERICAN FOLKLORE; FOLKLORE IN EVERYDAY LIFE; FRENCH-AMERICAN FOLKLORE; GERMAN-AMERICAN FOLKLORE; GREEK-AMERICAN FOLKLORE; HILL, JOE; HISTORICAL EVENTS; HUNGARIAN-AMERICAN FOLKLORE; IRISH-AMERICAN FOLKLORE; ITALIAN-AMERICAN FOLKLORE; JAPANESE-AMERICAN FOLKLORE; JEWISH-AMERICAN FOLKLORE; KOREAN-AMERICAN FOLKLORE; LIBERTY, MISS; MAGARAC, JOE; MEXICAN-AMERICAN FOLKLORE; MUSEUMS, FOLK; PENNSYLVANIA DUTCH/PENNSYLVANIA-GERMAN FOLKLORE; POLISH-AMERICAN FOLKLORE; PORTUGUESE-AMERICAN FOLKLORE; SAINT PATRICK'S DAY; SCOTTISH-AMERICAN FOLKLORE; TRANSCONTINENTAL RAILROAD.

For Further Reading:

Degh, Linda. "Approaches to Folklore Research among Immigrant Groups," *Journal of American Folklore* 79, no. 314 (fall 1966): 551–556.

Georges, Robart A., and Stephen Stern, eds. *American and Canadian Immigrant and Ethnic Folklore: An Annotated Bibliography.* New York: Garland, 1982.

Köngäs, Elli Kaija. "Immigrant Folklore: Survival or Living Tradition?" *Midwest Folklore* 10 (1960): 117–123.

Pozzetta, George E. *Folklore, Culture, and the Immigrant Mind.* New York: Garland, 1991.

Inauguration Day Every four years, January 20 is the day on which an outgoing U.S. president completes a term and an incoming president's term formally commences.

Inauguration is the ceremonial process by which this transfer of power is accomplished and celebrated. The official act associated with this observance is the swearing-in ceremony that in modern times, with the exception of extenuating circumstances such as presidential assassination, always occurs on this date and through this means.

The nation's first president, George Washington, took his oath of office on April 30, 1789. The date of inauguration later shifted to March 4 until 1933, at which time the Twentieth Amendment to the Constitution fixed the inauguration date as January 20.

While Inauguration Day is a legal holiday only within the District of Columbia, its importance to all citizens cannot be underestimated. If the American presidency represents "leadership of the free world," as is commonly claimed, surely a public ceremony aids in the recognition of this role and its holder. Inauguration signifies the shift in office and, in so doing, affirms both the democratic process and the results of the previous November's general election.

Depending upon which account one reads, either President James Monroe or President Andrew Jackson is responsible for the first use of the Capitol's eastern portico for the swearing-in ceremony, and it continues to serve as the frequent, though not exclusive, location for this event. There, before a gallery of spectators and an electronic audience, each modern president accepts the duties and responsibilities of the nation's highest office. Having done so, the new president delivers an address to the nation marking the occasion of assuming office. It is also standard practice since President Thomas Jefferson's second inaugural in 1805 for the new or newly reelected president, to parade along Washington, D.C.'s, Pennsylvania Avenue from the Capitol to the White House. Historically speaking, the weather for these activities is notoriously inclement, and more than once it has been necessary to cancel outdoor events and conduct the formal ceremony indoors, such as was done in the Capitol Rotunda for the second inaugural of President Ronald Reagan.

Although the swearing-in ceremony itself is the culmination of the official events of

Inauguration Day, several other customs are typically associated with the day. Many such activities are formal events, most of which are located in the nation's capital city. These tributes tend to include processions and parades, which, when held in Washington, D.C., are by custom addressed to the president, who, along with the first family, members of the cabinet, and other special guests, occupies a prominent position at the reviewing stand. Because one of the president's duties as commander in chief is to command the armed forces, military participants in such assemblies pause to salute the president before advancing beyond his or her place at the reviewing station. Patriotic marches, and other music appropriate to the occasion, accompany these processions.

The arrival of the newly inaugurated U.S. president at ceremonial functions is greeted to the sound of the brief composition that serves as musical prelude, "Ruffles and Flourishes," followed closely by the traditional song of recognition and encouragement, "Hail to the Chief" (words by Albert Gamse, music by James Sanderson). This enthusiastic tune has been in use at inaugurations since the 1852 swearing in of President James Polk. It has honored seated presidents since the early 19th century. Other parades or celebrations may be held elsewhere in the nation, including in the hometown and home state of the newly elected president, along with any locality or jurisdiction where he or she has held previous public office.

The evening of Inauguration Day in Washington, D.C., has by custom offered the occasion for first one, and later multiple, inaugural balls held in honor of the new president. These gala black-tie affairs provide guests with an opportunity to mark the arrival of the new president of the United States with food, drink, song, and celebratory remarks. When possible, the president makes brief appearances at all of these events throughout the evening, expressing appreciation for the guests' support.

Folklore about Inauguration Day is scant compared to that for some other holidays, with a few very notable exceptions. As with other civic events, schoolchildren frequently participate in lessons and other activities intended to teach them about the presidency, the electoral process, and the democratic tradition. Another but lesser known bit of folklore is the playing of pranks by outgoing appointed White House staffers on their successors. This is especially the case when the transition transfers the holder of the White House from one political party to the other. Whether prank or urban legend, according to one such account departing staffers for President William Clinton removed or otherwise effaced the letter *W* on White House computer keyboards, presumably as a response to incoming President George W. Bush's habit of going by a nickname based upon a folksy pronunciation of his middle initial: "Dub-ya." The other folk custom tied to Inauguration Day entails the fashioning, collection, and purchase of souvenirs of the occasion. With no small bit of irony, the variety of such Americana rivals the commemorative zeal the British demonstrate on ceremonial occasions of the royal family, such as coronations.

See also: COMPUTER FOLKLORE; ELECTION DAY; HOLIDAYS/OBSERVANCES; HUMOR, FOLK; PARADES; ROOSEVELT, THEODORE; URBAN LEGENDS; WEATHER FOLKLORE.

For Further Reading:

Boller, Paul F. *Presidential Inaugurations*. San Diego: Harcourt, 2002.

Bunch, Lonnie. *The American Presidency: A Glorious Burden*. Washington, D.C.: Smithsonian Institution Press/National Museum of American History, 2000.

Hurja, Emil Edward. *History of Presidential Inaugurations*. New York: New York Democrat, 1933.

Kittler, Glenn D. *Hail to the Chief! The Inauguration Days of Our Presidents*. Philadelphia: Chilton Books, 1965.

Santella, Andrew. *U.S. Presidential Inaugurations*. New York: Children's Press, 2002.

Viola, Joy Winkie. *Presidential Inaugurations: Planning for More than Pomp and Circumstance*.

Washington, D.C.: Council for Advancement and Support of Education, 1993.

Independence Day/Fourth of July Independence Day, or the Fourth of July as it is frequently described, sets aside a time each year at which to remember the events surrounding the nation's formation.

The precursor to this holiday involved a more solemn thematically related occasion, remembering the March 5, 1770, Boston Massacre, in which British forces fired on colonial forces. Independence Day was celebrated for the first time in 1777 in Philadelphia, with candles set in the windows and gun firing providing an exuberant announcement of the day. Philadelphia now observes Freedom Week, devoting seven days, the week surrounding July 4, to commemorating the signing of the Declaration of Independence by John Hancock and Charles Thomson. This enthusiasm is in part the product of Philadelphia's close ties to the Declaration of Independence as the site for the Continental Congress. The rest of the country, however, tends to focus on July 4 itself or, if it falls on or adjacent to a weekend, the resulting three-day holiday.

The timing of the holiday's placement is a point of interest, since there are numerous key dates related to the document the day honors. July 2 was actually the day on which the Continental Congress, except New York, agreed to the declaration. The Declaration of Independence was first read in public on July 8 in Independence Square, Philadelphia. More distant areas received the news later. Williamsburg, for example, was informed on July 25, and so Colonial Williamsburg continues to observe this day as the crucial one in their independence festivities.

Although every year features an Independence Day celebration, particularly elaborate and poignant observances have accompanied nationally meaningful occasions such as the Centennial in 1876 and the Bicentennial in 1976. Both were times of heightened pageantry and increased spectacle surrounding Independence Day.

Annual Independence Day events today include speeches, parades, reenactments, plays, flag displays, barbecues, concerts, and fireworks displays.

Another icon associated with this yearly celebration of freedom is the Liberty Bell, now housed in Philadelphia's Independence Hall. The bell has its own legend, centered on its ringings on high occasions, as well as lore regarding the crack in the vessel and subsequent efforts to restore its structural integrity through recastings. The logical link between the bell and Independence Day sentiments involves the statement inscribed on the bell: "Proclaim Liberty throughout all the land unto all the inhabitants thereof." Therefore, the bell seems to strike the same note the signers of the Declaration wished to strike with their document.

Independence Day/Fourth of July, along with other patriotic holidays, reminds Americans of both their national heritage and their legacy of liberty. Through the flying of flags and other public rituals, Americans demonstrate their pride in and gratitude toward the framers of the Declaration of Independence.

See also: ATTUCKS, CRISPUS; FLAG DAY; FRANKLIN, BENJAMIN; HOLIDAYS/OBSERVANCES; LIBERTY, MISS; PATRIOTS' DAY; REVOLUTIONARY WAR; ROSS, BETSY; UNCLE SAM.

For Further Reading:

Bloom, James D. "Independence Day, Apart from the Fireworks," *Chronicle of Higher Education* 48, no. 43 (July 5, 2002): B10–B11.

Festivals and Holidays. New York: Macmillan Library Reference USA, 1999.

Ford, Richard. *Independence Day.* New York: Knopf, 1995.

Goetsch, Paul, and Hurm, Gerd, eds. *The Fourth of July: Political Oratory and Literary Reactions, 1776–1876.* ScriptOralia, 45. Tübingen: Narr, 1992.

Graham-Barber, Lynda, and Betsy Lewin. *Doodle Dandy! The Complete Book of Independence Day Words.* New York: Bradbury Press, 1992.

Hobby, Teresa Santerre. "Independence Day: Reinforcing Patriarchal Myths about Gender and Power," *Journal of Popular Culture* 34, no. 2 (fall 2000): 39–55.

Myers, Robert. *Celebrations: The Complete Book of American Holidays.* Garden City, N.Y.: Doubleday, 1972.

Santino, Jack. *All around the Year: Holidays and Celebrations in American Life.* Urbana: University of Illinois Press, 1994.

Travers, Len. *Celebrating the Fourth: Independence Day and the Rites of Nationalism in the Early Republic.* Amherst: University of Massachusetts Press, 1997.

Indiana folklore   See DILLINGER, JOHN.

Indian folklore   See NATIVE-AMERICAN FOLKLORE.

industrialization and folklore   Although folklorists in America initially regarded industrialization as putting an end to folk culture, they have since come to understand the sense in which an industrial society could also be said to support a rich range of folklore forms.

The process by which countries such as the United States shifted from an agricultural economy to a manufacturing economy, characterized by mechanization and urbanization, was such a dramatic transformation that it is sometimes termed the Industrial Revolution. This change involved such innovations as mass production, interchangeable parts, and assembly lines.

Up until that point in history, folklorists had defined folk artifacts chiefly as handmade and hand-crafted items produced within preindustrial, and typically rural, societies. For that reason, it appeared that the very inventions that sped technological process would displace the traditions folklorists wished to document and study. If manufactured goods became plentiful, affordable, and of sufficient quality, it appeared that folk objects would disappear from American culture.

While it is true that the nation's movement "from farm to factory" did alter the cultural landscape of the United States, folk arts and crafts did not vanish. Folk groups continue to honor their regional and ethnic heritage and to express themselves through traditional practices, customs, and beliefs, including these manifested through material culture. In fact, modern America's twin emphases on urbanization and industrialization introduced a host of new forms of folklore. Examples include labor lore, organizational folklore, computer lore, and Xerox/fax lore, and urban legends.

Industrialization did not extinguish folk expression in the United States, but it did change the context in which folklorists understood their discipline and its span of concerns.

See also: ADMINISTRATIVE PROFESSIONALS' DAY/WEEK; ARTS AND CRAFTS MOVEMENT; BOSS DAY (BOSS'S DAY); CITY FOLKLORE; COMPUTER FOLKLORE; EDISON, THOMAS ALVA; FOLKLORE IN EVERYDAY LIFE; GREENFIELD VILLAGE, HENRY FORD MUSEUM AND; HENRY, JOHN; HILL, JOE; JONES, JOHN LUTHER; LABOR DAY; MUSEUMS, FOLK; OCCUPATIONAL FOLKORE; STORMALONG, OLD; TRANSCONTINENTAL RAILROAD; URBAN LEGENDS; XEROX/FAX FOLKLORE.

For Further Reading:

Bausinger, Hermann. *Folk Culture in a World of Technology.* Bloomington: Indiana University Press, 1990.

Cochran, Thomas C. *Frontiers of Change: Early Industrialism in America.* New York: Oxford University Press, 1981.

Fine, Gary Alan. *Manufacturing Tales: Sex and Money in Contemporary Legends.* Knoxville: University of Tennessee Press, 1992.

Hounshell, David A. *From the American System to Mass Production, 1800–1932: The Development of Manufacturing Technology in the United States.* Baltimore: Johns Hopkins University Press, 1984.

Jones, Michael Owen, Michael Dane Moore, and Richard Christopher Snyder, eds. *Inside Organizations: Understanding the Human Dimension.* Newbury Park, Calif.: Sage, 1988.

Levine, Lawrence W. "The Folklore of Industrial Society: Popular Culture and Its Audiences." In *The Unpredictable Past: Explorations in American Cultural History*, edited by Lawrence W. Levine, 219–320. New York: Oxford University Press, 1985.

Licht, Walter. *Industrializing America: The Nineteenth Century*. Baltimore: Johns Hopkins University Press, 1995.

McLuhan, Marshall. *The Mechanical Bride: Folklore of Industrial Man*. New York: Vanguard Press, 1951.

Randall, Clarence Belden. *The Folklore of Management*. Boston: Little, Brown, 1961.

Songs of the Workers: To Fan the Flames of Discontent. Chicago: Industrial Workers of the World, 1973.

initiation   See RITES OF PASSAGE.

insider/outsider   Any folklorist conducting fieldwork quickly discovers that the perspectives of insiders and outsiders of a community differ in meaningful ways.

Within the study of cultural systems, the terms *emic* and *etic* are used to describe these two different outlooks. These are labels folklore borrows from anthropology, in which the need to distinguish between the views of insiders and outsiders is central to the investigation of culture. The words *emic* and *etic* are derived from two terms used by linguists, *phonemic* and *phonetic*. Regardless of the academic discipline, those studying cultural phenomena strive to discern important differences between the understandings of members of a population and of those studying that group.

Emic and *etic*, then, represent two distinct approaches to cultural knowledge: Emic perceptions and categories are intrinsic ones, those held valid by natives of a group; etic perceptions and categories are extrinsic ones, arrived at by outsiders or observers. Since both intrinsic and extrinsic, insider and outsider, insights are crucial to a holistic view of cultural systems, most scholarship strives to integrate the two. Within some social science research, there have even been attempts by scholars to merge the two perspectives by functioning as participant-observers. In some cases, this means conducting research about a group to which the scholar already belongs. In other instances, the participant-observer role involves assuming on a temporary basis the role of membership within a group, with the ultimate goal of documenting its practices by using the methods of scholarly investigators.

Whatever the model and method of fieldwork chosen, folklorists have good reason to seek to incorporate the insights of both insiders and outsiders about a cultural phenomenon.

See also: ETHICS IN FOLKLORE; FIELDWORK, FOLKLORE; FOLKLIFE; FOLKLIFE MOVEMENT; FOLKLORE; FOLKLORE STUDIES; FOLKLORISTICS; HISTORY, FOLK; TERMS.

For Further Reading:

Dundes, Alan. "From Emic to Etic in the Structural Study of Folktales," *Journal of American Folklore* 75, no. 296 (spring 1962): 95–105.

Harris, Marvin. "History and Significance of the Emic/Etic Distinction," *Annual Review of Anthropology* 5 (October 1976): 329–350.

Headland, Thomas N., Kenneth Pike, and Marvin Harris, eds. *Emics and Etics: The Insider/Outsider Debate*. Frontiers of Anthropology 7. Summer Institute of Linguistics. Newbury Park, Calif.: Sage Publications, 1990.

Jansen, William Hugh. "The Esoteric and Exoteric Factor in Folklore," *Fabula: Journal of Folktale Studies* 2 (1959): 205–211.

insults   See SPEECH, FOLK.

internment, Japanese-American   See JAPANESE-AMERICAN INTERNMENT.

Iowa folklore   See LEWIS, MERIWETHER, AND WILLIAM CLARK; MIDWESTERN REGIONAL FOLKLORE; SHELLEY, KATE.

Irish-American folklore Irish-American folklore belongs to all immigrants to the United States from Ireland, along with American-born people of Irish ancestry.

Immigration from Ireland to the United States began in the 17th century. Concentration of Irish-American populations formed in the American Northeast and Midwest. They were especially drawn to the nation's urban centers, including Boston, Chicago, New York, Philadelphia, and San Francisco. In these locations, Irish Americans formed ethnic enclaves where residents could affirm their cultural identity and find refuge from nativist sentiments that resulted in discrimination and even violence against Irish Americans, especially during the first decades of the 20th century.

Irish culture has an abundance of folklore. In particular, it features a vibrant tradition of verbal lore. It is known for an array of folk sayings, blessings, and toasts. Irish storytelling forms are especially robust. Irish Americans extend this tradition, enjoying a similar reputation as raconteurs. Several American folk heroes and legendary figures are also Irish American, such as Joe Magarac and Mose the Fireman.

In addition to narrative traditions, Irish-American folklore features customs and foodways associated with holidays and observances. Irish Americans celebrate many of the holidays other Americans enjoy. They are also the source of a saint's day celebration that has become a secular holiday observed widely in the United States, even among those without Irish heritage. This holiday is named for Ireland's patron saint, Patrick. In addition to converting many to Christianity, Saint Patrick founded numerous churches and schools, making him a key religious figure. In Ireland, Saint Patrick's Day began as a religious observance and a tribute to the miracles ascribed to him, such as driving the snakes from Ireland, but the holiday is now more often observed with secular festivities, such as gatherings in area pubs.

Saint Patrick's Day has been celebrated in America since 1737, when Boston became home to the holiday's new incarnation. The first Saint Patrick's Day parade took place in America, with 1762 marking the first such event in New York City, where parades continue annually ever since. Additional holiday-themed events are associated with other cities, such as Chicago's tradition, begun in 1962, of temporarily tinting river water with green food coloring to celebrate the day.

Along with parades and public processions, parties, speeches, dinners, and dancing are typical practices in American observances of Saint Patrick's Day. Only some of the American traditions for this day derive from Irish culture. Others are U.S. inventions or appropriations of elements perceived to be Irish. Celtic symbols and images invoked within American celebrations of Saint Patrick's Day include the leprechaun (fairy) and the shamrock (used to represent and promote fertility in spring rites at this time in the calendar). The shamrock, or trefoil, has an additional connection to Saint Patrick through his use of the plant's three leaves to symbolize the Christian Trinity and its stem to portray their unity in God. Saint Patrick's Day probably is the best known of all aspects of Irish-American folklore.

With its allusions to Irish history and folk belief, Irish-American folklore connects new generations born in the United States to both their ancestors and their homeland.

See also: CHRISTMAS; CROCKETT, DAVY; CULTURAL GROUPS; ETHNICITY; FINNISH-AMERICAN FOLKLORE; HALLOWEEN/ALL HALLOWS' EVE; IMMIGRATION AND FOLKLORE; INDUSTRIALIZATION AND FOLKLORE; LUCK/FORTUNE; MAGARAC, JOE; MOSE THE FIREMAN; PARADES; SAINT PATRICK'S DAY; SCOTTISH-AMERICAN FOLKLORE.

For Further Reading:
Callahan, Bob. *The Big Book of American Irish Culture.* New York: Penguin Books, 1989.
Diner, Hasia. *Erin's Daughters in America: Irish Immigrant Women in the Nineteenth Century.* Baltimore: Johns Hopkins University Press, 1983.

Griffin, William. *The Book of Irish Americans*. New York: Time Books, 1990.

Kenny, Kevin. *The American Irish: A History*. New York: Longman, 2000.

McCaffrey, Lawrence. *Textures of Irish America*. Syracuse, N.Y.: Syracuse University Press, 1992.

Miller, Kerby. *Emigrants and Exiles: Ireland and the Irish Exodus to North America*. New York: Oxford University Press, 1985.

O'Hanlon, Ray. *The New Irish Americans*. Niwot, Colo.: Roberts Rinehart, 1998.

Williams, William H. A. *'Twas Only an Irishman's Dream: The Image of Ireland and the Irish in American Popular Song Lyrics, 1800–1920*. Urbana: University of Illinois Press, 1996.

Irving, Washington (1783–1859) Washington Irving is responsible for two familiar characters in classic American literature, Rip Van Winkle and Ichabod Crane. Drawing from folklore and his travels, Irving framed legends for the page and, in so doing, cast a portrait of the New York scenes and stories he loved.

Irving was born April 3, 1783, to a well-to-do merchant family. As a boy who had frail health, he embraced reading and found area travel therapeutic. Both his love of books and his passion for the New York landscape would later favor his literary career. Irving devoted a portion of his life to working with the family's cutlery business. He would also spend time as a lawyer on Wall Street, a military aide to the New York governor in the War of 1812, and U.S. minister to Spain. It is for his writing, however, that Irving is most remembered.

By the age of 35, Irving was devoting most of his time to that pursuit. Over the course of his career, he wrote essays, poems, and several biographies, including a five-volume life of George Washington. Still, it is for his tales and short stories that Irving is best known, such as those collected in *Knickerbocker's History of New York* (1809) and *The Sketch Book* (1812–20). Here, his vision of a mysterious and occasionally enchant-

ing world of upstate New York took shape. Irving's "Legend of Sleepy Hollow" and "Rip Van Winkle" are two of his most celebrated texts. He is especially appreciated for a comic ability in his work frequently likened to the storytelling craft of Mark Twain. Irving's career ended with his death on November 28, 1859.

As both a reader and a writer of folktales and legends, Irving established his place in both American folklore and literature.

See also: CLEMENS, SAMUEL LANGHORNE; FOLKLORE IN AMERICAN LITERATURE; HORSEMAN, HEADLESS; NORTHEASTERN REGIONAL FOLKLORE; REGION, FOLK; VAN WINKLE, RIP; WASHINGTON, GEORGE.

For Further Reading:
Anderson, Hilton. "A Southern 'Sleepy Hollow,'" *Mississippi Folklore Register* 3 (1969): 85–88.

Clark, James W., Jr. "Washington Irving and New England Witchlore," *New York Folklore Quarterly* 29 (1973): 304–313.

Hoffman, Daniel G. "Irving's Use of American Folklore in 'The Legend of Sleepy Hollow,'" *Publications of the Modern Language Association of America* 68, no. 3 (June 1953): 425–435.

Wess, Robert C. "The Use of Hudson-Valley Folk Traditions in Washington Irving's Knickerbocker History of New York," *New York Folklore Quarterly* 30 (1974): 212–225.

Zug, Charles III. "The Construction of 'The Devil and Tom Walker': A Study of Irving's Later Use of Folklore," *New York Folklore* 24 (1968): 243–260.

Italian-American folklore Italian-American folklore includes the traditions and customs of those immigrating to the United States from Italy, along with persons of Italian descent born in the United States.

Italians have been in America ever since the arrival of Christopher Columbus. For this reason, Columbus remains a cultural figure and folk hero among Italian Americans, who continue to lead the way in such American celebrations as Columbus Day parades. Italian-American immigration peaked in the late 19th to early 20th centuries, when most immigrants were from the south of Italy, where poverty prompted many to leave to seek opportunities elsewhere. Most of these new arrivals settled in urban centers, especially in the northeastern region. Often, they resided in "Little Italy," an ethnic enclave established not just to connect those with common heritage, but also to protect them from the nativist and anti-Italian sentiments of others around them.

During the first half of the 20th century, urban folklore was replete with stories and rumors of organized crime. Gangsters such as Chicago's Al Capone helped solidify perceived connections between Italian Americans and city crime. This perception deepened resentments toward Italian immigrants and their families. It was not until their participation in the Second World War that Italian Americans won wider acceptance in American society.

Italian folktales and fairy tales are an important part of Italian-American culture. "Little Peter" tales, for example, are tales that together compose a story cycle. Within these narratives, a child named Peter contends with ogres and witches as a direct result of his refusal to listen to parental advice.

Italian foodways are well known to Americans, especially since World War II, and Italian cuisine is among the most popular for those dining out at restaurants and bistros. The cuisine most Americans associate with Italian immigrants is southern Italian food, with its rustic tastes of the garden. While many recipes in use in America's Italian restaurants have been adapted for new audiences, the fundamental nature of the foods remains constant. Whole-grain breads, tomato sauces, and pasta are staples, as are spices and garlic to season dishes.

In accordance with religious traditions, many Italians participate in regular appeals and tributes to saints. One example is the observance of Saint Joseph's Day on March 19 each year. Saints may be venerated in the home, as well, with small decorated altars. Holiday traditions also include street festivals to honor saints. In contemporary America, these public festivities often include non-Italians.

Numerous organizations in the United States promote Italian-American culture, including the America-Italy Society, the National Italian American Foundation, and the Order of the Sons of Italy in America. Major collections of Italian-American cultural information include those of the New York Public Library and the University of Minnesota's Immigration History Research Center.

With its array of customs, traditions, and practices, Italian-American folklore represents an enduring cultural legacy.

See also: CAPONE, ALPHONSE GABRIEL (AL); CITY FOLKLORE; COLUMBUS, CHRISTOPHER; COLUMBUS DAY; CULTURAL GROUPS; ETHNICITY; FOLKTALES; FOOD/FOODWAYS; IMMIGRATION AND FOLKLORE.

For Further Reading:

Alba, Richard. *Italian Americans: Into the Twilight of Ethnicity.* Englewood Cliffs, N.J.: Prentice-Hall, 1985.

Del Giudice, Luisa, ed. *Studies in Italian American Folklore.* Logan: Utah State University Press, 1993.

Ferraro, Thomas. *Feeling Italian: The Art of Ethnicity in America.* New York: New York University Press, 2005.

LaGumina, Salvatore John. *The Italian American Experience: An Encyclopedia.* New York: Garland, 2000.

Malpezzi, Frances. *Italian-American Folklore.* Little Rock, Ark.: August House, 1972.

Mangione, Jerre, and Ben Morriale. *La Storia: Five Centuries of the Italian American Experience.* New York: HarperCollins, 1992.

Mathias, Elizabeth, and Richard Raspa. *Italian Folktales in America: The Verbal Art of an Immigrant Woman.* Detroit: Wayne State University Press, 1985.

Richards, David A. J. *Italian American: The Racializing of an Ethnic Identity.* New York: New York University Press, 1999.

J

"Jack and the Beanstalk" (legendary) "Jack and the Beanstalk" is a classic fairy tale commonly presented to American youth.

It is the story of a boy living on a farm with his widowed mother. Life is hard for them and food scarce. Eventually, even the cow that has provided them with dairy products must be sold. It falls to Jack to deliver the cow to market. En route to the marketplace, Jack encounters a little man who wishes to purchase the cow on the spot, and this individual convinces Jack to sell the cow to him in exchange for three magic beans.

When Jack returns home, his desperate mother rages at what her son has done. In disbelief, she casts the beans out the window and into the garden. When Jack awakens the next morning, however, he discovers that the discarded beans have magically grown into a stalk as thick as a tree outside the house. The boy climbs the beanstalk beyond the clouds to a land ruled by an ogre. The ogre's wife becomes an ally to Jack, helping him negotiate this new and perilous environment. From her, Jack also learns of the ogre's two greatest treasures: a magic harp and a golden goose.

Eager to redeem himself with his mother, Jack resolves to steal the ogre's golden goose. As he escapes with the goose, the ogre chops down the beanstalk with an ax. Jack arrives home safely, however, and no harm befalls him, and he can now provide his family with greater security. In time, Jack marries and lives happily ever after.

The story of "Jack and the Beanstalk" represents a familiar tale even for today's children. The moral tone of this fairy tale is somewhat more ambiguous than in most examples of the genre. Contrary to most fairy tales, this one rewards a thief. Jack's story also reminds the audience that even though prudence is important, it is sometimes necessary to take a chance in order to change one's situation.

See also: CHILDREN'S FOLKLORE; FABLES; FAIRY TALES; FOLKTALES; GOLDEN GOOSE, THE; MAGIC; MYTHS, FOLK.

For Further Reading:

Ashliman, D. L. *Folk and Fairy Tales: A Handbook.* Westport, Conn.: Greenwood Press, 2004.

Bacchilega, Cristina. *Postmodern Fairy Tales: Gender and Narrative Strategies.* Philadelphia: University of Pennsylvania Press, 1997.

Wolf, Joan. *The Beanstalk and Beyond: Developing Critical Thinking through Fairy Tales.* Englewood, Colo.: Teacher Ideas Press, 1997.

Jack o' Lantern See HALLOWEEN/ALL HALLOWS' EVE.

Jamaican-American folklore Jamaican-American folklore includes the customs and cultural traditions of both first-generation immigrants and those of Jamaican descent born in the United States.

Immigration to the United States from Jamaica dates back to the early 17th century. At this time, Jamaicans entered the United States as indentured servants. Jamaica would also be an important transportation point in the slave trade to America. Well into the 19th century, American plantation owners continued to send for short-term agricultural workers from Jamaica on a seasonal basis, especially in the harvesting of sugarcane. Thousands of Jamaican laborers were also recruited to help complete the Panama Canal. Regulations governing immigration by Jamaicans have often challenged the integrity of family bonds by restricting simultaneous arrival of entire families, but economic hardships in Jamaica remain an incentive for immigrants to venture to America nonetheless. To build solidarity and community, Jamaicans sometimes established ethnic enclaves in American cities such as Brooklyn, N.Y. and Miami, Fla.

Several Jamaican Americans have made names for themselves as folklorists, including Leonie Forbes, Louise Bennett-Coverly, Marjorie Wiley, and Rannie Williams. The author Claude McKay, a first-generation Jamaican immigrant associated with the Harlem Renaissance, produced fiction inspired by Jamaican-American folklore. As in Jamaica, Jamaican Americans speak variants of English, often including Patois, a Jamaican-based tongue sometimes known as Jamaican talk and generally reserved for use in informal contexts. Although they represent a numerical minority among Jamaica's religious groups, the Rastafarians are well known around the world for such signature characteristics of self-presentation as hair worn in dreadlocks. This Afro-Caribbean faith was established during the 20th century in response to the Pan-Africanism of the black nationalist Marcus Garvey.

Among the most widely recognized expressive traditions of Jamaican Americans is reggae music. Artists including Bob Marley and Jimmy Cliff have achieved international prominence for their musical accomplishments. Such musical forms and performers are famous in their own right and have in turn influenced and infused American musical genres such as jazz.

Other forms of Jamaican-American folklore include verbal lore, such as sayings and proverbs. Distinctive folk celebrations among Jamaican Americans closely match those of Jamaica, such as Boxing Day, Bob Marley's Birthday, National Heroes' Day, and Jamaica's Independence Day. Jamaicans are also known for folk dancing, steel drumming, and "dub" poetry, a musical kind of spoken word performance. Jamaican cuisine features jerk chicken, plantains and other fruits, fish dishes, and the use of seasonings such as ginger and allspice.

A Jamaican folk saying, "Out of Many, One People," bespeaks the strong sense of cultural identity shared among the island's people, as well as its blending of traditional forms of expression.

See also: ANANSI; ANIMALS; CULTURAL GROUPS; FOLKTALES; HURSTON, ZORA NEALE; MUSIC, FOLK; RELIGION, FOLK.

For Further Reading:

Alleyne, Mervyn C. *Roots of Jamaican Culture*. London: Pluto Press, 1988.

Barrett, Leonard. *The Rastafarians*. Boston: Beacon Press, 1997.

———. *The Sun and the Drum: African Roots in Jamaican Folk Tradition*. London: Heinemann, 1976.

Beckwith, Martha. *Jamaican Folk-Lore*. New York: American Folk-Lore Society, 1928.

Carty, Hilary S. *Folk Dances of Jamaica: An Insight*. London: Dance Books, 1988.

Llewellyn, Watson G. *Jamaican Sayings: With Notes on Folklore, Aesthetics, and Social Control*. Tallahassee: Florida A & M University Press, 1991.

Okpewho, Isidore, and Carole Boyce Davies. *The African Diaspora: African Origins and New World Identities*. Bloomington: Indiana University Press, 1999.

Prahlad, Anand. *Reggae Wisdom: Proverbs in Jamaican Music*. Jackson: University Press of Mississippi, 2001.

Walter, Jekyll. *Jamaican Song and Story: Annancy Stories, Digging Sings, Ring Tunes, and Dancing Tunes.* New York: Dover, 1966.

James, Jesse (1847–1882)

James, Jesse (1847–1882) Jesse James was a notorious outlaw of the American West.

Born in 1847 as Jesse Woodson James, he came of age during America's Civil War. He engaged in active service during the war. At some point in his participation in that conflict, James became disenchanted with that service and began his career as an outlaw.

As a member of the Younger-James gang, a crime band combining members of two families and their associates, Jesse James embarked on an infamous spree of train, bank, and stage-coach robberies that would last from the 1860s through the 1880s.

Although such a criminal might seem an unusual choice for a cultural hero, Jesse James was embraced by a public that felt exploited by the elite and mistreated by formidable institutions such as banks and railroads. Criminals who targeted the seemingly faceless force behind the economy began to seem avengers of the plight of ordinary people. Bandits such as James dazzled Americans with their daring and defiance in this regard. In this way, Jesse James became associated with the Robin Hood legend of stealing from the rich to give to the poor. Although stories sometimes cast James as the savior of widows facing eviction at the hands of heartless landlords, there is little evidence in his case to support this stock image of the Robin Hood robber.

While James was capturing public sympathy, law enforcement redoubled their efforts to apprehend him. In a misguided 1875 raid on the home of James's mother and stepfather, Pinkerton detectives hoping to end James's crime spree instead added, in a tragic manner, to his cachet. James was elsewhere at the time of the ill-fated raid, and before it was over, James's eight year-old half brother lay dead and his mother had sustained an injury that cost her most of one arm.

Not only did this event fail to capture James, it also rallied the public in his defense.

In the end, it was the betrayal for bounty by two of his accomplices that put an end to the exploits of Jesse James. On April 3, 1882, Bob Ford shot James in the back of the head. The governor of Missouri would soon pardon Ford for the incident, thus permitting the former partner in crime to net a reward while eluding punitive consequences.

The lore surrounding Jesse James began with his brazen robberies. It continued even after his death, as speculation spread that James was not really dead. The legend of Jesse James persists, with countless depictions in film and stories. Further, Liberty, Missouri, is home to the Jesse James Bank Museum. At this location, a restored bank preserves the site of James's first major robbery, an event reenacted by the museum for visitors and tourists. In addition to his own exploits, James inspired the careers of later bandit figures in crime lore from John Dillinger to Charles Arthur (Pretty Boy) Floyd.

This archetypal "bad man" reappears frequently within popular culture representations in story and film.

See also: Civil War; Dillinger, John; Floyd, Charles Arthur (Pretty Boy); folk heroes/legendary figures; frontier; museums, folk; outlaws; region, folk; Robin Hood; Southwestern regional folklore; Western regional folklore.

For Further Reading:
Breihan, Carl W. *Saga of Jesse James.* Caldwell, Idaho: Caxton Printers, 1991.

Horan, James. *Desperate Men: The James Gang and the Wild Bunch.* Lincoln: University of Nebraska Press, 1997.

Love, Robert. *Rise and Fall of Jesse James.* New York: Blue Ribbon Books, 1939.

Settle, William, Jr. *Jesse James Was His Name.* Columbia: University of Missouri Press, 1966.

Steckmesser, Kent. "Robin Hood and the American Outlaw," *Journal of American Folklore* 79, no. 312 (spring 1966): 348–355.

———. *The Western Hero in History and Legend.* Norman: University of Oklahoma Press, 1965.

Stiles, T. J. *Jesse James: Last Rebel of the Civil War.* New York: Random House, 2002.

Japanese-American folklore Japanese-American folklore includes the cultural traditions of immigrants to the United States from Japan, as well as persons born in America of Japanese ancestry.

Immigration from Japan to the land that now belongs to the United States has occurred since the latter half of the 19th century, when Japanese laborers went to Hawaii to work on the sugarcane plantations. Subsequent settlers made their homes within ethnic neighborhoods in major cities, such as Chicago, San Francisco, and Los Angeles. Prejudice against Japanese Americans was always a problem, and during the nativist 1920s in America, especially with the National Origins Act of 1924, the immigration process nearly ceased.

Anti-Japanese sentiment ran high in the period following the December 1941 bombing at Pearl Harbor. This response culminated in a decision to incarcerate Japanese Americans as national security risks. During the spring and summer of 1942, persons of Japanese descent residing in California, Oregon, and Washington were removed from their homes to internment camps. Over two-thirds of the people to be interned were native-born citizens of Japanese descent. The rest were first-generation Japanese immigrants residing on the West Coast, which had been designated as a "military zone."

Camps were established for this purpose at locations in Arizona, California, Wyoming, Colorado, Idaho, Utah, and Arkansas. Japanese Americans remained in these concentration camps, under guard of armed troops, up to four years until orders allowing them to return home arrived.

Folk traditions were disrupted if not stopped completely. Food and foodways were difficult to maintain under camp conditions. Family and gender roles were disturbed by the living arrangements of the camp. Agriculture, gardening, and other customary practices were left behind. Most of what survives of folklore from this time is verbal lore, consisting of the stories, correspondence, and memoirs of those interned.

Despite this abridgment of civil liberties, Japanese Americans managed to maintain aspects of their shared heritage. Although folk traditions have faded somewhat with each generation, as is often the case within immigrant communities, some folkways survived. Distinctive folk customs and revived traditional practices among today's Japanese Americans span many genres of personal and cultural expression. Examples include flower arrangement, calligraphy, folk music, tea ceremony, and foodways such as sushi preparation.

See also: CIVIL RIGHTS MOVEMENT; CULTURAL GROUPS; ETHNICITY; FOOD/FOODWAYS; IMMIGRATION AND FOLKLORE; JAPANESE-AMERICAN INTERNMENT; PEARL HARBOR (REMEMBRANCE) DAY; WESTERN REGIONAL FOLKLORE. WORLD WAR II.

For Further Reading:
Aihara, Chris. *Nikkei Donburi: A Japanese American Cultural Survival Guide.* Chicago: Polychrome, 1999.

Alder, Susan Matoba. *Mothering, Education, and Ethnicity: The Transformation of Japanese American Culture.* New York: Garland, 1998.

Araki, Nancy, and Jane Horii. *Matsuri: Festival: Japanese American Celebrations and Activities.* San Francisco: Heian International, 1978.

Fugita, Stephen, and David O'Brien. *Japanese American Ethnicity: The Persistence of Community.* Seattle: University of Washington Press, 1991.

Glen, Evelyn Nakano. *Issei, Nisei, War Bride: Three Generations of Japanese American Women in Domestic Service.* Philadelphia: Temple University Press, 1986.

Higa, Kavin M. ed. *The View from Within: Japanese American Art from the Internment Camps,*

1942–1945. Seattle: University of Washington Press, 1992.

Kitano, Harry H. L. *Japanese Americans: The Evolution of a Subculture.* Englewood Cliffs, N.J.: Prentice-Hall, 1969.

Nakagawa, Dana. *The Rice Cooker's Companion: Japanese American Food and Stories.* San Francisco: National Japanese American Historical Society, 2000.

Yanagisako, Sylvia Junko. *Transforming the Past: Tradition and Kinship among Japanese Americans.* Palo Alto, Calif.: Stanford University Press, 1985.

Japanese-American internment During an unfortunate chapter in America's history, more than 110,000 persons of Japanese descent residing in the western states were forcibly interned during World War II.

The event said to precipitate this action was the December 7, 1941, attack on the U.S. fleet at Pearl Harbor, Hawaii. A crew of more than 1,100 was killed when the *Arizona*, a U.S. battleship anchored in the harbor there, was destroyed by a bomb.

On February 19, 1942, some 74 days after the bombing at Pearl Harbor, President Franklin Delano Roosevelt signed Executive Order 9066. This edict was drafted by the U.S. War Department and called for Japanese Americans to report for mandatory relocation on the grounds of national security. The action was defended on the basis of fears of sabotage or attack. The order itself was legally contested. Because American citizens could not be made to submit to military authority without a declaration of martial law, on March 18, 1942, a second order, Executive Order 9102, established the War Relocation Authority, which made the internment of Japanese Americans legal.

As a consequence, during the spring and summer of 1942, persons of Japanese descent residing in California, Oregon, and Washington were removed from their homes to internment camps. More than two-thirds of the people to be interned were native-born citizens of Japanese descent. The rest were first-generation Japanese immigrants residing on the West Coast, which had been designated as a "military zone."

Notification of those who must leave their homes was short, sometimes allowing just two days for Japanese Americans to sell, store, or make arrangements otherwise for their property and businesses. Those made to leave their places of residence were first directed to one of 16 "assembly centers," typically fairgrounds and racetracks where Japanese Americans were forced to reside in animal stalls and other substandard housing. From these sites, they were dispatched to one of many "relocation centers." Camps were established for this purpose at locations in Arizona, California, Wyoming, Colorado, Idaho, Utah, and Arkansas. Here, in concentration camps where troops stood on guard, Japanese Americans remained up to four years until orders allowing them to return home arrived.

The extended and embattled experience of internment took its toll on those held in relocation camps, eroding both cultural traditions and family structures. Those interned lived in barracks and used communal cooking and sanitation facilities. Climate at many of the locations was harsh and unfamiliar to those who had been relocated. While interned, Japanese-American youth attended camp schools, where lessons in patriotism and civic virtue were delivered. Adults were required to complete and sign loyalty questionnaires, swearing loyalty to the United States of America and renouncing any loyalty to the Japanese emperor or foreign powers. Meanwhile, family members were sometimes separated for questioning and subjected to disrespectful treatment both within and beyond the camps.

Folk traditions were disrupted if not ended completely. Food and foodways were difficult to maintain under camp conditions. Family and gender roles were disturbed by the living arrangements of the camp. Agriculture, gardening, and other customary practices were left behind. Most of what survives of folklore from this time is verbal lore, consisting of the stories, correspondence, and memoirs of those interned.

Internment camps operated similarly to Indian reservations, where people remained against their individual and collective will. Those who protested rules at the internment camps were shot by troops. Men in the camps eligible for military service continued to be drafted. Many who were interned volunteered or were drafted and served with distinction, but those who resisted the draft on the basis of denial of their civil liberties at home were placed in prison.

There is no evidence that anyone placed in World War II internment camps posed a threat to the United States, but it was many years before this fact was acknowledged publicly. The 1948 Japanese American Claims Act afforded some compensation for property losses incurred as a result of relocation. With the Civil Liberties Act of 1988, some 80,000 survivors received letters of apology and individual reparation payments in the amount of $20,000.

Although internment had been used as a strategy during previous conflicts, such as the War of 1812 and World War I, the internment of Japanese Americans during World War II was the most notorious such incident in U.S. history.

See also: CIVIL RIGHTS MOVEMENT; CULTURAL GROUPS; ETHNICITY; HISTORICAL EVENTS; IMMIGRATION AND FOLKLORE; JAPANESE-AMERICAN FOLKLORE; PEARL HARBOR (REMEMBRANCE) DAY; PROTEST IN FOLKLORE; ROOSEVELT, FRANKLIN DELANO; WORLD WAR II.

For Further Reading:

Burton, Jeffery, Eleanor Roosevelt, and Irene J. Cohen. *Confinement and Ethnicity: An Overview of World War II Japanese American Relocation Sites.* Seattle: University of Washington Press, 2002.

Daniels, Roger. *Prisoners without Trial: Japanese Americans in World War II.* New York: Hill & Wang, 1993.

Fiset, Louis. *Imprisoned Apart: The World War II Correspondence of an Issei Couple.* Seattle: University of Washington Press, 1997.

Irons, Peter. *Justice at War: The Story of the Japanese Internment Cases.* New York: Oxford University Press, 1983.

McClain, Charles, ed. *The Mass Internment of Japanese Americans and the Quest for Legal Redress.* New York: Garland, 1994.

Okihiro, Gary. *Whispered Silences: Japanese Americans and World War II.* Seattle: University of Washington Press, 1996.

Taylor, Sandra. *Jewel of the Desert: Japanese American Internment at Topaz.* Berkeley: University of California Press, 1993.

Weglyn, Michi. *Years of Infamy: The Untold Story of America's Concentration Camps.* Seattle: University of Washington Press, 1996.

Jersey devil (legendary)   As an unexplained and potentially supernatural creature, the Jersey devil takes a place among the lore of such creatures as Bigfoot and the Loch Ness monster.

The folklore regarding the Jersey devil involves primarily orally transmitted tales. It is a folk legend of long standing, reputed to date back as far as the 18th century. Stories of the Jersey devil, while perhaps not as widely known as those of Sasquatch, have a similarly strong association with a geographic region. The Jersey devil has close ties to the Middle Atlantic states and, in particular, with the southern portion of New Jersey.

The creature is said to have emerged from mysterious circumstances. While accounts vary, the tale typically indicates that a woman named Jane Leeds, one so unconventional in her ways that some perceived her to be a witch, discovered to her distress that she was pregnant with her 13th child. Upon this discovery, she is reputed to have appealed to God to make this offspring not a human baby, but rather a "devil."

When the time arrived, the woman experienced a normal delivery. Shortly thereafter, however, the child underwent a fateful transformation, emerging as a frightening, massive, and violent beast. The creature then attacked the midwife and escaped the place of birth, only to wander the Pine Barrens terrifying all it encounters.

The appearance of the Jersey devil varies among storytellers but usually consists of a mythically hybrid form with such features as a hairy hide, wings, goat's limbs, and talon-sharp claws.

See also: BIGFOOT/SASQUATCH; CHANGE-LING; DEVIL, THE; FOLK HEROES/LEGENDARY FIGURES; MONSTERS; NORTHEASTERN REGIONAL FOLKLORE; REGION, FOLK; SUPERNATURAL.

For Further Reading:

Cohen, David. *Folklore and Folklife in New Jersey.* New Brunswick, N.J.: Rutgers University Press, 1983.
Girard, Geoffrey. *Tales of the Jersey Devil.* Moorestown, N.J.: Middle Atlantic Press, 2004.
McCloy, James. *Phantom of the Pines, More Tales of the Jersey Devil.* Moorestown, N.J.: Middle Atlantic Press, 1998.
McCloy, James, and Ray Miller, Jr. *The Jersey Devil.* Wallingford, Pa.: Middle Atlantic, 1976.
Martinelli, Patricia, and Charles Stansfield. *Haunted New Jersey: Ghosts and Strange Phenomena of the Garden State.* Mechanicsburg, Pa.: Stackpole Books, 2004.

Jewish-American folklore   Jewish-American folklore involves all those who identify themselves as Jewish, whether on the basis of faith, ethnicity, culture, or choice.

Jewish immigration to the United States, under way since the middle of the 17th century, peaked during the period 1880–1920. Jewish Americans settled throughout the country but concentrated initially in the northeastern states and major cities.

The central texts of Judaism are the laws as written, the Torah, and the orally transmitted laws of the Talmud. Within Jewish-American culture, there are several distinct subgroups, based largely on the ways members understand and practice their cultural identity. Hasidic and Orthodox Jews, for instance, adhere quite strictly to a set of practices and prohibitions based upon spiritual beliefs and historical memory. These expectations include maintaining a kosher home, a practice that involves specific foodways such as handling dairy and meat products separately. Reformed Jews also honor certain of these rules and ceremonies, but their forms of observance are not as stringent. Still other Jewish-identified people may not express this legacy through attendance at and participation in religious services and rituals. Nonetheless, they feel a close connection to a folk group that has survived historical adversities and religious persecution, most notably during the Holocaust.

Rituals and rites of passage among Jewish Americans help dramatize spiritual traditions and folk customs. Newborns, for instance, are welcomed with a ceremony such as the *bris* for males and the *simkhat bat* for females. Later, the bar mitzvah or bat mitzvah represents a coming of age for Jewish-American youth. The occasion of a bar mitzvah or bat mitzvah is a pivotal point in the individual's entry into adulthood within Judaism. These rites mark the point at which the youth becomes subject to the commandments of a faith, a heightened level of responsibility within religious life. The bar mitzvah, typically conducted when a boy is 13, is the tradition rite of passage for males. The preparations by the person initiated represent a signal of maturity and conviction. The presence of extended family and spiritual community conveys acceptance of the youth into religious adulthood. The service communicates the tradition by which Jewish heritage continues across generations. The bar mitzvah or/bat mitzvah is a traditional way of welcoming Jewish youth into the responsibilities of spiritual adulthood, while preserving the heritage of Judaism for future generations.

As with other folk groups, Jewish Americans have a distinctive set of practices surrounding holidays and observances. Examples include Passover, Rosh Hashonah, Yom Kippur, and

Hanukkah. Each of these points in the Jewish calendar represents a way of reinforcing and transmitting to a new generation a set of cultural beliefs, historical memories, and social values.

Passover is a seven-day seasonal festival within Judaism designed to celebrate freedom from bondage. This holiday occurs during the first month of the Jewish calendar, generally in March or April. On the first and seventh days of Passover, participants are to refrain from labor. The emphasis is on reaffirming family and communal identity through a series of symbolic meals, readings, and other rituals that help Jews fulfill the obligation to retell the story of exodus from Egypt. As with other Judaic calendar observances, Passover preserves and promotes historical memory and awareness as each generation learns about Jewish cultural identity.

Held in autumn each year, Rosh Hashonah represents a new year's observance within Judaism. The name of the observance means "head of the year." Rosh Hashonah is a communal rather than familial holiday, and so religious services and other shared public activities shape the observance. Readings from Scripture, group recitations, and other acts of devotion play a part in this occasion. The majority of the activity associated with Rosh Hashonah's confession and quest for forgiveness is conducted not in the household, but rather in the wider faith community. As a time of purification and repentance, Rosh Hashonah plays a central role in the spiritual lives of Jewish people.

Yom Kippur, a Day of Atonement within Judaism, occurs in autumn each year in accordance with the lunar calendar. As a spiritually based new year's observance, it is the single most solemn day of the religious year. Practices associated with Yom Kippur include fasting by all but the young and sick, abstinence from business or other work, and prayer in services available in temples and synagogues. Yom Kippur is the culmination of a 10-day period of penitence that commences with Rosh Hashonah. It establishes the value of beginning each year with contemplation and purification of the spirit.

Hanukkah is the name of an eight-day winter festival in Judaism, generally occurring during the month of December. Hanukkah remembers the shared past. In so doing, it honors practices and ideals of community among Jewish persons the world over. Customs surrounding this holiday are designed to promote awareness of the historical struggles of Jewish people, and in particular their efforts to keep intact their cultural and religious identity in the face of great challenges within and threats without.

Additional folk customs among Jewish Americans include those practices associated with weddings. The marriage ceremony usually takes place under a canopy (huppah), which symbolizes the welcoming place the couple's home is to be. At the end of the ceremony, it is also customary for the groom to step on a glass vessel, sometimes wrapped in cloth, until it breaks. This practice is symbolic, intended both to recall destruction of the Temple in Jerusalem and to promote the bride and groom's ability to weather difficulties together.

Furthermore, as often occurs when a collective's history involves so much hardship and oppression, Jewish-American folklore involves not only the legends and parables of sacred texts, but also an extensive connection to folk humor. These comedic traditions include a full spectrum of self-deprecating jokes. Such humor sometimes proves an effective antidote to ethnic jokes, such as anti-Semitic jokes, told at the expense of historically disenfranchised groups. In this way, humor shields a cultural group by deflecting hostility from others.

In addition to informal and local efforts to keep alive the folk traditions of Jewish Americans, there are sites established to forward that work on an institutional and national basis. Organizations dedicated to study and philanthropy related to Jewish-American culture include four New York–based groups: the American Jewish Committee, American Jewish Joint Distribution, Anti-Defamation League of B'nai B'rith, and American Section of the World Jewish Congress. Major collections of Jewish-American cultural material include Waltham, Massachusetts's, American Jewish Historical Society; Washington, D.C.'s U.S. Holocaust Memorial Museum; and New York's Jewish Museum.

Jewish-American folklore includes a wide array of forms, including folktales, proverbs, stories, holidays and observances, folk rituals, and foodways. In order to maintain cultural traditions, such as facility with Hebrew language, many families enroll their children in special instructional sessions where sons and daughters may learn the language and culture of their ancestors.

See also: BAR MITZVAH/BAT MITZVAH; COPLAND, AARON; CULTURAL GROUPS; ETHNICITY; HANUKKAH; IMMIGRATION AND FOLKLORE; PASSOVER; RELIGION, FOLK; ROSH HASHONAH; YOM KIPPUR.

For Further Reading:

Koppman, Steve, and Lion Koppman. *A Treasury of American Jewish Folklore*. Northvale, N.J.: Jason Aronson, Inc., 1996.

Mintz, Jerome R. *Legends of the Hasidim: An Introduction to Hasidic Culture and Oral Tradition in the New World*. Chicago: University of Chicago Press, 1968.

Rush, Barbara. *The Book of Jewish Women's Tales*. Northvale, N.J.: Jason Aronson, 1994.

Sherman, Josepha. *Jewish American Folklore*. Little Rock, Ark.: August House, 1992.

Shuldiner, David P. *Of Moses and Marx: Folk Ideology and the Folk History in the Jewish Labor Movement*. Westport, Conn.: Bergin & Garvey, 1999.

Slobin, Mark. *Tenement Songs: The Popular Music of the Jewish Immigrants*. Urbana: University of Illinois Press, 1982.

Sorin, Gerald. *Tradition Transformed: The Jewish Experience in America*. Baltimore: Johns Hopkins University Press, 1997.

Spalding, Henry D., ed. *Encyclopedia of Jewish Humor from Biblical Times to the Modern Age*. New York: Jonathan David, 1979.

Ungerleider-Mayerson, Joy. *Jewish Folk Art from Biblical Days to Modern Times*. New York: Summit Books, 1986.

Waskow, Arthur I. *Seasons of Our Joy: A Handbook of Jewish Festivals*. New York: Summit Books, 1986.

Joad, Tom (fictional)   Tom Joad is the fictional protagonist of John Steinbeck's classic novel of the Depression era. This saga recounts the experiences of a dust bowl family making the forced migration from Oklahoma to California, in search of work.

The Grapes of Wrath (1939), perhaps John Steinbeck's best-known literary work, follows the fate of Tom Joad, the story's protagonist. Having returned home from prison, Joad discovers that his family, as have many others, has lost its battle to continue farming land ravaged by dust storms and erosion. Displaced by the dust bowl and by the banks who repossess bankrupt family farms in Oklahoma and Arkansas, these "Okies," as they were known, load what possessions they can into vehicles and travel west in hopes of generating income. The tale of their struggles as itinerant laborers and downtrodden citizens captivates audiences with its poignancy.

In both Steinbeck's novel and the motion picture adaptation of the work for the screen, Tom Joad emerges as a character who, although born to misfortune, nonetheless transcends the petty and dehumanizing forces of poverty and social inequality. Tom Joad serves as the voice of an entire underclass, humbled but not cowed, by hard times and mistreatment.

In the film version of *The Grapes of Wrath*, Henry Fonda's Joad delivers a stirring speech about the cause of social justice. With his remarks, the character claims an immortality as he forms common cause with all have-nots and outcasts. It is the evocative power of this address that inspired songwriters from Woody Guthrie (who wrote and performed a song called "Tom Joad") and Bruce Springsteen (who released an album entitled *The Ghost of Tom Joad*) to pay tribute to this fictional character as a compelling folk hero and voice of the American people.

See also: DEPRESSION, THE GREAT; FOLK HEROES/LEGENDARY FIGURES; MIDWESTERN REGIONAL FOLKLORE; MUSIC, FOLK; PROTEST IN FOLKLORE; REGION, FOLK; ROOSEVELT, FRANKLIN DELANO; STEINBECK, JOHN; WESTERN REGIONAL FOLKLORE.

For Further Reading:

Elliott, Ramblin' Jack. *Hard Travelin': Songs by Woody Guthrie and Others.* Berkeley, Calif.: Fantasy, 1989.

Ford, John. *The Grapes of Wrath.* Fox Studios Classic Collection, 1940/2004.

Shindo, Charles L. *Dust Bowl Migrants in the American Imagination.* Lawrence: University Press of Kansas, 1997.

Steinbeck, John. *The Grapes of Wrath.* New York: Viking Press, 1939.

Johnson, James Weldon (1871–1938) As a writer, teacher, and civil rights advocate, James Weldon Johnson helped build a legacy for African-American writers concerned with preservation of folk narratives and traditions.

The child of two free black parents, James William Johnson was born in Jacksonville, Florida, on June 17, 1871. He changed his middle name to Weldon in 1913.

Johnson was accomplished at writing poetry, lyrics, essays, and fiction. Perhaps the book-length Johnson work most often read today is *Autobiography of an Ex-Colored Man* (1912). This text tells the fictional story of an African American who is so light-skinned that he can pass as a white person. The novel explores the protagonist's experiences across and between racial worlds. Johnson's other works include *Black Manhattan* (1930) and an autobiography, *Along This Way* (1933). In something of the manner that Paul Laurence Dunbar used, Johnson wrote dialect verse reminiscent of 19th-century folk speech. He aimed to portray a more accurate and dignified version of African-American speech than the era's minstrel shows ever provided.

For a 1900 commemoration of Abraham Lincoln's birthday, Johnson composed the verse for which he may be most widely known, "Lift Every Voice and Sing." Set to music, these lyrics first became an anthem for the National Association for the Advancement of Colored People (NAACP), and later an informal national anthem for African Americans more generally. The lyrics of this tune are uplifting and motivating to singers and listeners, as shown in the opening verse:

> Lift every voice and sing,
> Till earth and heaven ring,
> Ring with harmonies of liberty.
> Let our rejoicing rise
> High as the listening skies,
> Let it resound loud as the rolling sea.
> Sing a song full of the faith that the dark past has taught us,
> Sing a song full of the hope that the present has brought us.
> Facing the rising sun of our new day begun,
> Let us march on till victory is won.

In *God's Trombones: Seven Negro Sermons in Verse* (1927), a work with similar themes of racial uplift, Johnson seeks to capture the poetry of the pulpit, a spirited and musical form of expression that had not appeared on the page before this time. When Johnson died in 1938, a next generation of African-American writers stood poised to continue the literary work begun by Johnson and his contemporaries. Novelists from Richard Wright to Paule Marshall draw from the precedent of Johnson's fiction.

James Weldon Johnson devoted his writing to conveying to readers the creative richness of African-American folk culture.

See also: AFRICAN-AMERICAN FOLKLORE; CIVIL WAR; FOLKLORE IN AMERICAN LITERATURE; IBO LANDING; LINCOLN, ABRAHAM; MINSTRELSY; MUSIC, FOLK; RELIGION, FOLK; SLAVERY; SPEECH, FOLK.

For Further Reading:

Bone, Robert. *The Negro Novel in America.* New Haven, Conn.: Yale University Press, 1965.

Bronz, Stephen. *Roots of Negro Racial Consciousness, the 1920s: Three Harlem Renaissance Authors.* New York: Libra, 1964.

Egypt, Ophelia Settle. *James Weldon Johnson.* New York: Crowell, 1974.

Fleming, Robert. *James Weldon Johnson.* New York: Chelsea House, 1988.

———. *James Weldon Johnson and Arna Wendell Bontemps: A Reference Guide.* Boston: G. K. Hall, 1978.

Kostelanetz, Richard. *Politics in the African-American Novel: James Weldon Johnson, W. E. B. Du Bois, Richard Wright, and Ralph Ellison.* New York: Greenwood Press, 1991.

Levy, Eugene. *James Weldon Johnson: Black Leader, Black Voice.* Chicago: University of Chicago Press, 1973.

Tolbert-Rouchaleau, Jane. *James Weldon Johnson.* New York: Chelsea House, 1988.

Whalum, Wendell Phillips. "James Weldon Johnson's Theories and Performance Practices of Afro-American Folksongs," *Phylon* 32 (winter 1972): 383–395.

jokes   See HUMOR, FOLK.

Jones, John Luther (Casey) (1863–1900)

Born John Luther Jones in 1863, this folk hero took the name "Casey" Jones from the town in which he was raised, Cayce, Kentucky.

Jones had a fine reputation as a deft railroad engineer, celebrated in story and song. He worked the Cannonball Express, which ran between Chicago and New Orleans. One day in 1900, when that train crashed, Casey Jones died in service to the occupation at which he excelled. As the story has it, the man's body was found with one hand on the whistle and the other on the brake.

A 1909 popular song, entitled "Casey Jones (The Brave Engineer)," eulogized the railroad man who would in time become a well-known figure in occupational lore. As are most such heroes, Jones was not without detractors. For instance, in 1912, the labor movement songwriter Joe Hill penned and sang a parody of the 1909 homage to Jones. He called his version "Casey Jones the Union Scab," evidently to suggest that Jones was no friend to organized labor. In the lyrics of the Joe Hill tune, Casey Jones arrives in heaven only to take up as a scab during an angel strike, a decision that ultimately delivers him to hell.

For others, however, John Luther "Casey" Jones takes his place among many American folk figures, both historical and imagined, who prove memorable through their close association with their specific fields of endeavor, from John "Johnny Appleseed" Chapman to Paul Bunyan.

See also: BUNYAN, PAUL; CHAPMAN, JOHN (JOHNNY APPLESEED); FOLK HEROES/LEGENDARY FIGURES; HILL, JOE; HUMOR, FOLK; INDUSTRIALIZATION AND FOLKLORE; MUSIC, FOLK; OCCUPATIONAL FOLKLORE; PROTEST IN FOLKLORE; SOUTHERN REGIONAL FOLKLORE.

For Further Reading:

Cohen, N. *Long Steel Rail: The Railroad in American Folksong.* Urbana: University of Illinois Press, 1981.

Drummond, Allan. *Casey Jones.* New York: Frances Foster Books, 2001.

Farmer, Nancy. *Casey Jones' Fireman.* New York: Phyllis Fogelman, 1999.

Lee, Fred. *Casey Jones: Epic of the American Railroad.* Kingsport, Tenn.: Southern Publishers, 1939.

Jones, John Paul (1747–1792)

Honored for his role in the United States Navy, John Paul Jones became an icon in and beyond this branch of the nation's armed forces.

Jones was born as John Paul in Scotland on July 6, 1747. He assumed the surname of *Jones* later in life. As a boy, he became fascinated with ships, sailors, and the prospect of life on the sea. By age 13, Jones secured an apprenticeship as a seaman. At 17, he became active in the slave traffic but found the institution abhorrent and so switched to service on a cargo ship. Jones was only 21 when he was made a ship's captain for the first time.

John Paul became John Paul Jones when he moved to Virginia, seeking a refuge from murder charges stemming from his role in turning back a mutiny's leader. Once in the colonies, Jones took part in the American Revolution by joining the Continental Navy. His counsel became sought after, and Jones had dealings with figures such as Benjamin Franklin in this regard. Jones became an accomplished adviser on naval warfare. His most illustrious battle occurred on September 23, 1779. In a confrontation with two other vessels, Jones answered a call for him to surrender with a subsequently famous retort: "I have not yet begun to fight."

For his loyalty, bravery, and success in battle, John Paul Jones received many public recognitions, including a congressional expression of gratitude for the honor he gained for America's fleet. The celebrity Jones achieved extended beyond America, however, and lent an international cachet to the captain. His accomplishments were well known in such countries as England, France, Holland, and Russia.

Jones died July 18, 1792. His remains are located in a crypt at Annapolis Naval Academy, a tribute befitting his contributions to the navy.

See also: AMERICAN REVOLUTION; FOLK HEROES/LEGENDARY FIGURES; FRANKLIN, BENJAMIN; MARITIME FOLKLORE.

For Further Reading:

Bowsen-Hassell, E. Gorgon. *Sea Raiders of the American Revolution: The Continental Navy in European Waters.* Washington, D.C.: Naval Historical Center/Department of the Navy, 2003.

Ellsberg, Edward. *"I Have Just Begun to Fight!" The Story of John Paul Jones.* New York: Dodd, Mead, 1942.

Haugen, Brenda. *John Paul Jones: Father of the American Navy.* Minneapolis: Compass Print Books, 2005.

Morison, Samuel Eliot. *John Paul Jones: A Sailor's Biography.* Annapolis, Md.: Naval Institute Press, 1959.

Thomas, Evan. *John Paul Jones: Sailor, Hero, Father of the American Navy.* New York: Simon & Schuster, 2003.

Joseph, Chief (1840–1904) Chief Joseph distinguished himself as a Native American tribal leader and champion of harmony in relations between indigenous people and European Americans.

Born Hin-mah-too-yah-lat-kekt in Oregon's Wallowa Valley in 1840, Joseph became a well-known member of the Nez Percé. His name meant "thunder coming up over the land from the water," and true to the name he would become a powerful force. The name by which the man became widely known, Joseph, was derived from his father, who took the name *Joseph* when he converted to Christianity in 1838.

Both Joseph the Elder and Joseph the Younger had advocated peace with white populations. This outlook changed, however, when an 1860 gold rush caused the federal government to violate an 1855 treaty by seizing some 6 million acres of Nez Percé territory. This move had the effect of reducing the tribe's land by 90 percent. While they had cooperated with formation of a reservation, this dramatic tightening of its boundaries put an end to that support. As a consequence, Joseph the Elder rejected the treaty establishing the smaller version of a reservation and declined to relocate the group from their traditional hunting grounds.

As son succeeded father with Joseph the Elder's death in 1871, he became known as Joseph the Younger, or simply as Joseph. As his father had, Joseph resisted the federal government's attempts to commandeer land and constrict his tribe's available area. The tribe became engaged in the homeland wars, and their new chief helped lead Native American resistance. A long struggle ensued, during which the tribe held off a U.S. force nearly three times its own number, and the defiant tribe staged a long march—some 1,500 miles—toward Canada by way of Oregon, Idaho, Wyoming, and Montana. Finally, Joseph relented when he had reached a position less than 40 miles from the border. On October 5, 1877, he issued a formal surrender. His speech on this occasion proved memorable, most notably his declaration "I will fight no more forever."

After the surrender, Chief Joseph and his people were sent to a series of reservations, never to see their homeland again. Joseph remained outspoken about the historic injustice done to his tribe, pointing out the irony of an America that sought its own people's independence at the expense of another's. Although he even made his case to President Rutherford B. Hayes, Chief Joseph died while still confined on the Colville Reservation in Washington State in 1904. While he had been permitted to resume residence to the Pacific Northwest, Joseph was never allowed to revisit the ground that held the bones of his parents and other tribal ancestors.

Chief Joseph's protests against the U.S. government's mistreatment of Native Americans are still remembered by champions of human and civil rights.

See also: FOLK HEROES/LEGENDARY FIGURES; FRONTIER; GOLD RUSH, THE; NATIVE AMERICAN FOLKLORE; NORTHWESTERN REGIONAL FOLKLORE; REGION, FOLK.

For Further Reading:
Avery, Susan, and Linda Skinner. *Extraordinary American Indians*. Chicago: Children's Press, 1992.
Hines, Donald. *Tales of the Nez Percé*. Fairfield, Wash.: Ye Galleon Press, 1984.
King, David C. *First Facts about American Heroes*. Woodbridge, Conn.: Blackbirch Press, 1996.
Matson, Emerson, ed. *Legends of the Great Chiefs*. Nashville, Tenn.: T. Nelson, 1972.

Journal of American Folklore See AMERICAN FOLKLORE SOCIETY.

jumping the broom See WEDDING/MARRIAGE FOLKLORE.

jump rope rhymes Jump rope rhymes are the rhythmic lyrics sung while a jump rope game is in progress.

These familiar, and often fanciful or humorous tunes may be intoned by either the jumpers or turners; most typically, the jumper sings or leads the others if the rhyme is shared. Even in cases when rope turners sing along with the jumper, it is customary for the voices to sing a rhyme in unison in this context. The rhymes pattern movement and add enjoyment to the pastime, usually favored for play by girls.

The songs keep time, mark turns, and signal changes in the rate of a particular game. Such tempos are especially important in Double-Dutch, a pastime in which two jump ropes are turned in opposite directions simultaneously. Counts, riddles, and jokes may be incorporated within each tune. For the most part, their use is formulaic, and the chants are learned by rote and performed by memory. While it is true that some rhymes incorporate time-sensitive references to current events or popular culture, most change very little over the years.

Across regions, eras, and cultural groups, jump rope rhymes have been an enduring feature of American children's folklore.

See also: CHILDREN'S FOLKLORE; FOLKLORE IN EVERYDAY LIFE; GAMES/PASTIMES; RHYMES, FOLK; SPEECH, FOLK; TOYS, FOLK.

For Further Reading:
Abrahams, Roger D., ed. *Jump Rope Rhymes: A Dictionary*. Austin: University of Texas Press, 1969.
Beresin, Ann Richman. "Double Dutch and Double Cameras: Studying the Transmission of Culture in an Urban School Yard." In *Children's Folklore: A Source Book*, edited by Brian Sutton-Smith, 75–91. New York: Garland, 1995.

Cole, Joanna, ed. *Anna Banana: 101 Jump-Rope Rhymes.* New York: Morrow Junior Books, 1989.

Gaunt, Kyra D. "Dancin' in the Street to a Black Girl's Beat: Music, Gender, and the Ins and Outs of Double-Dutch." In *Generations of Youth: Youth Cultures and History in Twentieth-Century America,* edited by Joe Austin and Michael Nevin Willard, 272–292. New York: New York University Press, 1998.

Gaunt, Kyra D. "Translating Double-Dutch to Hip-Hop: The Musical Vernacular of Black Girls' Play." In *Language, Rhythm, and Sound: Black Popular Cultures into the Twenty-First Century,* edited by Joseph K. Adjaye and Adrianne R. Andrews, 146–163. Pittsburgh: University of Pittsburgh Press, 1997.

Goodwin, Marjorie Harness. "The Serious Side of Jump Rope: Conversational Practices and Social Organization in the Frame of Play," *Journal of American Folklore* 98, no. 389 (summer 1985): 315–330.

Juneteenth Juneteenth, also known as Jun-Jun Freedom Day, or National Freedom Day, is among the oldest African-American observances. This holiday is celebrated each year on June 19.

After the Civil War concluded and the Emancipation Proclamation was signed by President Abraham Lincoln, it took time for the "freedom message" to cross the country. The occasion of Juneteenth takes its name from a specific date in history—June 19, 1865, when news of the Emancipation Proclamation reached Galveston, Texas.

Although celebrations of this occasion occur primarily in Texas, the tradition is a means of marking with ritual the emergence of African Americans from a state of involuntary servitude. Other localities sometimes join in this, or related, acts of remembrance.

Customs for Juneteenth vary, but typical events include meals, picnics, parties, and public readings of key freedom documents, such as the Emancipation Proclamation. As does its companion holiday, Emancipation (Proclamation) Day, usually marked on January 1 each year, Juneteenth ensures that the indignities and injustices of American slavery are not forgotten. Juneteenth marks the historical moment that represented to slaves something analogous in a sense to what the Declaration of Independence meant to colonists. The meaningful difference, however is that although colonists experienced a lack of autonomy and representation, slaves endured torture and suffered a complete lack of liberty.

Each year, as celebrants remember the historical injustice of slavery, they also find in Juneteenth an opportunity for reflection, renewal, and rededication to the cause of human freedom.

See also: AFRICAN-AMERICAN FOLKLORE; CIVIL RIGHTS MOVEMENT; CIVIL WAR; EMANCIPATION DAY; HOLIDAYS/OBSERVANCES; LINCOLN, ABRAHAM; SLAVERY; SOUTHWESTERN REGIONAL FOLKLORE.

For Further Reading:

Abernathy, Francis Edward, ed. *Juneteenth Texas: Essays in African-American Folklore.* Denton: University of North Texas Press, 1996.

Anyike, James. *African American Holidays: A Historical Research and Reference Guide to Cultural Celebrations.* Chicago: Popular Truth, 1991.

Turner, Victor, ed. *Celebrations: Studies in Festivity and Ritual.* Washington, D.C.: Smithsonian Institution Press, 1952.

Wiggins, William. *O Freedom! Afro-American Emancipation Celebrations.* Knoxville: University of Tennessee Press, 1987.

K

Kansas folklore See CODY, WILLIAM F. (BUF-FALO BILL); DISNEY, WALTER ELIAS; EARHART, AMELIA MARY; FEBOLDSON, FEBOLD; FLOYD, CHARLES ARTHUR (PRETTY BOY); HICKOK, JAMES BUTLER (WILD BILL); LEWIS, MERI-WETHER, AND WILLIAM CLARK; MIDWESTERN REGIONAL FOLKLORE; ROBINSON, JACK ROOS-EVELT (JACKIE); SMITH, WINDWAGON.

Kentucky folklore See BOONE, DANIEL; CARSON, KIT; OZARKS FOLKLORE; SHAKER FOLKLORE; SOUTHERN REGIONAL FOLKLORE.

Key, Francis Scott See FLAG DAY; FLAG FOLKLORE; ROSS, BETSY.

Kidd, Captain William (1654–1701) Captain William Kidd was a Scottish sea captain whose maritime adventures yielded legends and ended in his death by hanging.

William Kidd was born in 1654. Not much is known concerning his early life, but tales of his exploits as an adult abound. Kidd lived in an era of privateering, an arrangement through which countries hired private vessels and their crews to attack enemy vessels. In this way, nations sought to protect assets and/or recover losses. Kidd was one of these seagoing mercenaries and spent his career accepting such employments.

His crews were not provided with a wage but instead received a cut of the ship's profits. Sailors sometimes referred to this practice of Kidd's privateering as "no prey, no pay," as it involved financial risks for crew members.

Although privateers were not pirates, their maritime adventures still evoked a certain cachet. Kidd's reputation was put to the test with a January 1698 attack on the *Quedah Merchant*, which yielded iron, opium, textiles, saltpeter, and sugar. The vessel's influential owner charged Kidd with piracy. As a result, Kidd fled, abandoned the *Quedah Merchant*, and ventured to New York City, where he enjoyed some potentially useful connections, to begin work on a pardon. In July 1699, Captain Kidd was detained in a Boston jail, then sent to England to stand trial. After a brisk two-day trial, Kidd was found guilty on charges of murder and piracy. For these crimes, he was hanged on May 23, 1701.

It has been rumored that prior to his capture, William Kidd may have stashed a gold-filled trunk somewhere in New York. Some accounts place the buried chest along the Connecticut River. Although the treasure has never been located, according to a legend, three people digging at 12 o'clock midnight with a full moon's light directly overhead can find it if they work in complete silence. It is reported that attempts of this kind have been made, but to no avail.

Whether a privateer or a pirate, Captain Kidd has entered American popular culture in numerous ways, including these legends of buried fortune, ship model kits manufactured to resemble his ship, swashbuckler films, and occasional comedies, such as *Abbott and Costello Meet Captain Kidd* (1952).

See also: FOLK HEROES/LEGENDARY FIGURES; MARITIME FOLKLORE; OCCUPATIONAL FOLKLORE.

For Further Reading:

Bonner, William Hallam. *Pirate Laureate: The Life and Legends of Captain Kidd*. New Brunswick, N.J.: Rutgers University Press, 1947.

Brooks, Graham, ed. *Trial of Captain Kidd*. New York: Gaunt, 1995.

Clifford, Barry, and Paul Perry. *Return to Treasure Island and the Search for Captain Kidd*. New York: William Morrow, 2003.

Reid, Van. *Cordelia Underwood, or, The Marvelous Beginnings of the Moosepath League*. New York: Viking, 1998.

Winston, Alexander Porter. *No Man Knows My Grave: Sir Henry Morgan, Captain William Kidd, Captain Woodes Rogers in the Great Age of Privateers and Pirates, 1665–1715*. Boston: Houghton Mifflin, 1969.

Zaks, Richard. *The Pirate Hunter: The True Story of Captain Kidd*. New York: Theia, 2002.

Kilroy (legendary)   Kilroy is a familiar graffiti icon for the U.S. military dating back to World War I.

The name *Kilroy* refers to a hand-drawn figure of a man peering over a wall. The drawing is of simple design. His face is visible only as a nose and pair of eyes behind the wall. Kilroy has dots for eyes, and his fingers extend over the flat surface of the wall before him. His appearance remains somewhat generic, rendering him a kind of everyman. This visual image, with or without the companion inscription, "Kilroy was here," completes the effect.

Kilroy has found his way everywhere members of the U.S. armed services travel, from Korea to Kuwait. His whimsical visage marks the presence of American soldiers. Kilroy lore calls for GIs to place drawings of the character in the most remote and unlikely locations, signifying the power and reach of the U.S. military. It is also customary for soldiers to claim that the marking was discovered rather than placed, making Kilroy always the first to arrive at a host of sites. He is rumored to adorn a range of places from the Statue of Liberty's torch to the surface of the Moon. According to some narratives, the Kilroy character was even called to the attention of Hitler when Nazi equipment was vandalized during World War II.

As early as the 1940s, people tried to track down the origin of this character and distinctive site-marking technique. There are several accounts of how this cartoon character originated. While the person behind Kilroy's signature doodle and slogan remains uncertain, the most likely claim belongs to James T. Kilroy, a U.S. ship inspector. As the story goes, his spot checks of riveting concluded with a distinctive marking inside the ship's hull, signaling a completed inspection. Subsequently other members of the military adopted the picture and message, using it to leave their own mark on behalf of the American armed forces.

This tradition is immediately recognizable to American GIs and civilians alike, and Kilroy's image still appears as a popular culture reference today. Indeed, versions of this item of graffiti have even made their way into cyberspace, as the following example shows:

```
        \V/
      -(@@)-
   --0O0—(_)—OO0--
```

See also: FOLK HEROES/LEGENDARY FIGURES; GRAFFITI; HISTORICAL EVENTS; LIBERTY, MISS; MARITIME FOLKLORE; WORLD WAR I; WORLD WAR II.

For Further Reading:

Beltrone, Art, and Lee Beltrone. *Vietnam Graffiti: Messages from a Forgotten Troopship*. Charlottesville, Va.: Howell Press, 2004.

Kilroy Was Here! The 1940s Revisited. Columbus: Ohio Historical Society, 2000.

Osgood, Charles. *Kilroy Was Here: The Best American Humor from World War II.* New York: Hyperion, 2001.

Panati, Charles. *Panati's Extraordinary Origins of Everyday Things.* New York: Perennial Library, 1989.

Kingston, Maxine Hong (1940–) As the nation's premier contemporary Chinese-American writer, Maxine Hong Kingston combines biography with history, autobiography with fiction, and myth with modern occurrences to produce fiction that is acclaimed by both critics and popular audiences.

Kingston was born October 27, 1940, in Stockton, California, to Chinese immigrant parents. Kingston attended University of California, Berkeley, an institution with which she was later associated as an author. Kingston was influenced by such American writers as Walt Whitman and William Carlos Williams. Her first book, *The Woman Warrior: Memoirs of a Girlhood among Ghosts* (1976), debuted to great and immediate acclaim. With this work, Kingston launched an illustrious literary career. Her other works include *Hawaii One Summer* (1978), *China Men* (1980), *Through the Black Curtain* (1987), *Tripmaster Monkey: His Fake Book* (1989), *To Be the Poet* (2002), and *The Fifth Book of Peace* (2003).

Kingston has become known for literary texts that explore issues of identity, heritage, and family for ethnic Americans. The author's works demonstrate a signature concern with cultural myths and oral traditions. She seems particularly fascinated with traditional storytelling, such as "talk stories." It is in this respect that Kingston's writing is indebted to both Chinese and Chinese-American folklore. Her name is particularly associated with intergenerational and multigenerational stories about the experiences and challenges of people of Chinese descent in America. In this regard, Kingston's writings often employ a nonlinear sense of time, creating a fictional world in which past, present, and future commingle. Kingston is also given to experiments with literary form that involve blending and justaposing distinct writing genres such as autobiography, history, and fiction. Finally, in addition to Kingston's imaginative synthesis of literary genres to create new hybrid forms, she often uses her writings to challenge attitudes concerning race, gender, and ethnicity.

Kingston's interests in social causes have caused her to turn toward writing and other forms of action that hold the power to influence the views of readers. As an activist and cultural critic, Kingston speaks out in interviews and, at times, her work, about the causes in which she is most involved, such as global feminism and pacifism.

Critics often draw comparisons between Maxine Hong Kingston and authors such as Paula Gunn Allen, Toni Morrison, Leslie Marmon Silko, and Amy Tan, all of whom share her interest in folk traditions.

See also: ALLEN, PAULA GUNN; CHINESE-AMERICAN FOLKLORE; CULTURAL GROUPS; ETHNICITY; FAMILY FOLKLORE; FOLKLORE IN AMERICAN LITERATURE; IMMIGRATION AND FOLKLORE; MORRISON, TONI; SILKO, LESLIE MARMON; WHITMAN, WALT.

For Further Reading:

Huntley, E. D. *Maxine Hong Kingston: A Critical Companion.* Westport, Conn.: Greenwood Press, 2001.

Kim, Elaine. *Asian American Literature: An Introduction to the Writings and Their Social Context.* Philadelphia: Temple University Press, 1982.

Kingston, Maxine Hong. "Personal Statement." (In *Approaches to Teaching Kingston's* The Woman Warrior, edited by Shirley Geok-lin Lim, 23–35. New York: Modern Language Association of America, 1991.

Simmons, Diane. *Maxine Hong Kingston.* New York: Twayne, 1999.

Skandera-Trombley, Laura, ed. *Critical Essays on Maxine Hong Kingston.* New York: G. K. Hall, 1998.

Wong, Sau-ling Cynthia. *Maxine Hong Kingston's* The Woman Warrior: *A Casebook.* New York: Oxford University Press, 1999.

kitsch   Kitsch is a category of cultural artifact that may be characterized as unsophisticated, but not necessarily without pretense.

The term usually refers to products of consumer culture in an industrial society. The appeal of such material is to the aesthetic of a population of consumers who wish to decorate their homes and other environments but do not necessarily have the same models of refinement that would impress the society's tastemakers.

Whereas high-end objects involve a labor-intensive presentation of uniquely wrought ornamentation, kitsch tends to look more like what it usually is—a mass-produced item that represents a knock-off derived from, but not fashioned in that same way as, the real thing. It reflects neither the best of regional or national culture, but rather a mélange of elements and styles that are crudely incorporated into an inferior object. It tends toward the commercial, the sentimental, and the obvious. No matter how ornate the piece may be, it lacks elegance. Examples of objects frequently invoked to portray kitsch as a genre are pictures of dogs playing poker and portraits of Elvis Presley painted on velvet.

If elite culture becomes labeled as "highbrow" and ordinary culture "lowbrow," then kitsch has an even lower station within this style hierarchy: "no brow." Its enduring aesthetic value, at least by traditional measures (such as elevation of the mind and ennobling of the outlook), is negligible; at best neutral in its effects, kitsch may even be deemed to have a negative influence. Such items do little to dignify folk culture.

Kitsch involves the guilty pleasures of objects that a design elite would deem common, coarse, or tacky.

See also: ART, FOLK; CULTURE, FOLK; FOLKLIFE; FOLKLORE IN EVERYDAY LIFE; MATERIAL CULTURE; VERNACULAR CULTURE.

For Further Reading:

Dorfles, Gillo, ed. *Kitsch: The World of Bad Taste.* New York: Universe Books, 1970.

Farkas, Eniko. "Authenticity and Kitsch: A Hungarian-American Revisits the Folk Art of Her Native Land." *New York Folklore Newsletter* 20, no. 2 (fall-winter 1999): 9, 12–13.

Gowans, Alan. "The Case for Kitsch: Popular/Commercial Arts as a Reservoir of Traditional Culture and Humane Values." In *Living in a Material World: Canadian and American Approaches to Material Culture*, edited by Gerald L. Pocius, 127–143. St. John's, Newfoundland, Can.: Institute of Social & Economic Research, Memorial University, 1991.

Kulka, Tomas. *Kitsch and Art.* University Park: Pennsylvania State University Press, 1996.

Ward, Peter. *Kitsch in Sync: A Consumer's Guide to Bad Taste.* London: Plexus, 1991.

Korean-American folklore   Korean-American folklore concerns the social life and customs among Korean immigrants to the United States and persons of Korean descent born in America.

Immigration to the United States from Korea was not common until the very end of the 19th century. At that point, most Korean immigrants were unmarried men or men who had traveled to the new land without their wives and families, seeking economic opportunities. The majority lived in Hawaii and California, where they worked on sugar plantations, practiced tenant farming, and worked in other agricultural settings. A few arrived in America in order to pursue higher education. During the early decades of the 20th century and, in particular, the 1920s, the United States placed a series of restrictions on immigration and naturalization. As a consequence, fewer Koreans were able to immigrate until the middle of the 20th century. The years following the Korean War changed that, as American soldiers arranged for their war brides and, in some cases, young children of such marriages to travel to the United States to join them.

Korean immigration to the United States was at it highest in the late 1980s.

Just as other immigrant groups formed ethnic enclaves in urban settings, Korean Americans sometimes found cultural continuity in areas such as Los Angeles's Koreatown. Many Korean Americans established themselves economically by starting small businesses. Especially in American cities such as Los Angeles and New York, they became proprietors of laundries, groceries, specialty shops, and restaurants featuring Korean cuisine. Events such as the race riots of 1992 in Los Angeles proved very damaging and discouraging to Korean-American entrepreneurs and small business owners who saw their businesses damaged and their merchandise looted.

Korean Americans have sought to strike a balance between preservation of folkways from their homeland and assimilation into the customs of the United States. Although crises such as the riots put the future of that balance in question, Korean-American folklore has proved a source of ethnic continuity and cultural survival during times of strife. With traditional practices ranging from shamanism and martial arts to ancestor worship, Korean Americans seek to triumph over such threats to security and prosperity.

See also: ATOMIC/NUCLEAR ERA FOLKLORE; CULTURAL GROUPS; ETHNICITY; IMMIGRATION AND FOLKLORE; INDUSTRIALIZATION AND FOLKLORE.

For Further Reading:

Barringer, Herbert. *Koreans in the United States: A Fact Book*. Honolulu: Center for Korean Studies/University of Hawaii, 1989.

Blair, Clay. *The Forgotten War: America in Korea, 1950–1953*. New York: Times Books, 1987.

Choy, Bong-Youn. *Koreans in America*. Chicago: Nelson-Hall, 1979.

Kim, Hyung-chan. *Korean American Pioneers*. Long Island City, N.Y.: Canaan Printing, 2002.

Kim, Ilpyong, ed. *Korean-Americans: Past, Present, and Future*. Elizabeth, N.J.: Hollym International, 2004.

Lee, Seong Hyong, and Tae-Hwan Kwak, eds. *The Koreans in North America: New Perspectives*. Seoul: Kyungnam University Press, 1988.

Patterson, Wayne, and Hyung-Chan. *The Koreans in America, 1882–1974: A Chronology and Fact Book*. Dobbs Ferry, N.Y.: Oceana Publications, 1974.

Takaki, Ronald. *From the Land of Morning Calm: The Koreans in America*. New York: Chelsea House, 1994.

Korean War See KOREAN-AMERICAN FOLKLORE.

Kwanzaa Kwanzaa is an annual winter celebration of African-American culture and heritage.

The holiday was conceived by Dr. Maulana Karenga during the 1950s in San Diego, California. The first observance of Kwanzaa was in 1966.

Karenga was a cultural nationalist, and consequently the focus within the holiday was on instilling in African Americans values for proper living, both individually and communally. The observance features seven symbols and seven principles invoked over the course of a weeklong celebration.

Similar to the menorah used in Hanukkah, a candle holder called a *kinara* is employed during Kwanzaa. This device holds seven candles. The center black candle is lit first, and the remaining green and red ones are illuminated in order from left to right, one candle each day. This lighting ritual is a shared activity intended to follow the family's evening meal. The candle-lighting custom represents the energy of the ancestors and the legacy of the past.

Other symbols of Kwanzaa include a straw mat (tradition), fruits and vegetables (collective labor), corn ears (children), a communal drinking cup (unity), and gifts (each marking commitments honored or goals achieved by participants).

The seven principles of Kwanzaa are the basis for the celebration: cultural unity, self-determination, collaboration, cooperative economics, resolve, creativity, and faith.

On the sixth evening, the Kwanzaa Feast of Karamu, an evening of food drink, and joyful time in company, is held. The seventh, final night of Kwanzaa finds the family sharing another meal, followed by a discussion of the seven principles and the exchange of gifts.

See also: AFRICAN-AMERICAN FOLKLORE; FAMILY FOLKLORE; HANUKKAH; HOLIDAYS/OBSERVANCES; RITUALS, FOLK.

For Further Reading:
Anyike, James C. *African American Holidays: A Historical Research and Reference Guide to Cultural Celebrations.* Chicago: Popular Truth, 1991.

Cohen, Hennig, and Tristram Potter Coffin, eds. *The Folklore of American Holidays.* Detroit: Gale, 1987.

Karenga, Maulana. *The African American Holiday of Kwanzaa: A Celebration of Family, Community, and Culture.* Los Angeles: University of Sankore Press, 1988.

McClester, Cedric. *Kwanzaa—Everything You Always Wanted to Know but Didn't Know Where to Ask.* New York: Gumbs & Thomas, 1990.

Myers, Robert. *Celebrations: The Complete Book of American Holidays.* Garden City, N.Y.: Doubleday, 1972.

Santino, Jack. *All around the Year: Holidays and Celebrations in American Life.* Urbana: University of Illinois Press, 1994.

Shannon-Thornberry, Milo. *The Alternative Celebrations Catalogue.* New York: Pilgrim Press, 1982.

L

Labor Day Celebrated on the first Monday of September each year since 1882, Labor Day honors the hard work performed by Americans all year long.

Labor Day had its beginnings in the height of the American labor movement and so was tied directly to the struggles of the industrial working class. Today, however, the holiday recognizes workers of every social station in America.

As were many U.S. national holidays, Labor Day was established through the devoted efforts of its champions. Organized labor supported the concept of acknowledging the contributions of workers to the American way of life; in particular, Peter J. McGuire and Matthew MacGuire, a labor leader and a machinist, saw to it that the Central Labor Union in New York City celebrated the first such occasion in 1882 with a parade, picnic, and other festivities. Two years later, the Knights of Labor called for Labor Day to gain the status of an annual observance. Individual states began to honor the day officially, starting with Oregon in 1887. Others followed, until all 50 states and the District of Columbia proclaimed Labor Day a legal holiday.

Early celebrations of Labor Day included speeches, processions, and other public festivities, some of which continue today. Religious services also marked the event in its original form, although that custom has waned somewhat over the years.

Today, Labor Day, as do other holidays tied to three-day weekends, carries an additional importance to Americans as a time when working parents may have more time with their children, students may embrace the final days of vacation before returning to school, and families have a day together on which to appreciate the close of the summer season and the approach of autumn. From its early associations with the causes of labor, such as the eight-hour day, to its modern-day role as a respite from work's demands, Labor Day is a holiday marked with picnics, clearance sales, and other simple pleasures of a working life in America.

See also: HOLIDAYS/OBSERVANCES; INDUSTRIALIZATION AND FOLKLORE; OCCUPATIONAL FOLKLORE; RELIGION, FOLK.

For Further Reading:

Aveni, Anthony F. *The Book of the Year: A Brief History of Our Seasonal Holidays.* New York: Oxford University Press, 2004.

Cohen, Hennig, and Tristram Potter Coffin, eds. *The Folklore of American Holidays.* Detroit: Gale, 1987.

Geoffrey, Scott. *Labor Day.* Minneapolis: Carolrhoda Books, 1982.

Mir Tamim, Ansary. *Labor Day.* Des Plaines, Ill.: Heinemann Library, 1999.

Myers, Robert. *Celebrations: The Complete Book of American Holidays.* Garden City, N.Y.: Doubleday, 1972.

Santino, Jack. *All around the Year: Holidays and Celebrations in American Life.* Urbana: University of Illinois Press, 1994.

Schuh, Mari C. *Labor Day.* Makato, Minn.: Pebble Books, 2003.

labor folklore   See OCCUPATIONAL FOLKLORE.

Latvian-American folklore   Latvians began to immigrate to the United States as early as the 17th century; several waves of immigration followed.

Latvia's difficult history and its struggle for self-determination have shaped Latvian-American folklore to a great degree. Folklorists who have examined Latvian-American folklore have paid special attention to *dainas*, a form of folk poetry that is often presented in the form of songs. These verses function in several ways for Latvian Americans: as an introduction to cultural heritage for youth, as guidance to adults, and entertainment to all. Taken together, these poems offer a portrait of Latvian cultural values such as serenity with nature. Frequent themes include relationships to others, to nature, and to one's country. In fact, *dainas* often portray the nation's worldview. For example, many assert cultural nationalism for Latvia.

Not surprisingly, one of the most important celebrations for Latvians, and for Latvian Americans who maintain dual citizenship, is Latvian Independence Day. This occasion is observed on November 18 each year. It remains a time to express support for autonomy and cultural preservation in Latvia.

Various organizations have been established to promote Latvian-American culture, including its folklore. Examples include the American Latvian Association, Republican National Federation, and American National Latvian League. Major collections of Latvian-American cultural information include Portland, Oregon

Association for the Advancement of Baltic Studies; Rockville, Maryland Latvian Museum; and Kalamazoo, Michigan Latvian Studies Center.

Along with Lithuania and Estonia, Latvia is a Baltic country. Its tales, ethnic theater, festivals, songs, and other folk traditions continue to inform the lives of Latvian Americans, both as individuals and as a collective.

See also: CULTURAL GROUPS; ETHNICITY; FOLKTALES; IMMIGRATION AND FOLKLORE; LITHUANIAN-AMERICAN FOLKLORE.

For Further Reading:

Bunkse, Edmunds V. "Latvian Folkloristics," *Journal of American Folklore* 92, no. 364 (spring 1979): 196–214.

Durham, Mae, Skaidrite Rubene-Koo, and Alan Dundes. *Tit for Tat and Other Latvian Folk Tales Retold.* New York: Harcourt, Brace & World, 1967.

Kārklis, Maruta, Līga Streips, and Laimonis Streips. *The Latvians in America, 1640–1973: A Chronology and Fact Book.* Dobbs Ferry, N.Y.: Oceana, 1974.

Kratins, Ojars. "An Unsung Hero: Krisjanis Barons and His Lifework in Latvian Folk Songs," *Western Folklore* 20 (1961): 239–255.

Neuland, Lena. *Motif-Index of Latvian Folktales and Legends.* Folklore Fellows' Communications 229. Helsinki: Suomalainen Tiedakatemia, 1981.

Straumanis, Alfreds. "Latvian American Theatre," *Ethnic Theatre in the United States,* edited by Maxine Schwartz Seller 277–318. Westport, Conn.: Greenwood Press, 1983.

Veidemanis, Juris. *Social Change: Major Value Systems of Latvians at Home, as Refugees, and as Immigrants.* Greeley: Museum of Anthropology/University of Northern Colorado, 1982.

Laveau, Marie   See VOODOO/HOODOO.

Lee, Robert E.   See DEATH.

legendary figures See FOLK HEROES/LEGEND-
ARY FIGURES.

legends, contemporary See URBAN LEGENDS.

legends, folk Folk legends are folktales in
which stories are woven into conversation in
such a way as to make them seem credible. They
usually deal with extraordinary events and phenomena (such as the supernatural), however, and
so warrant storytelling.

Legends are traditional stories, probably
derived from history. They are most often specific
to a locality, as was Washington Irving's literary
legend "The Legend of Sleepy Hollow." They
may include historical details, lending the ring of
truth to the tales. They are plot-driven stories,
which are delivered in a temporally sequential
manner. Legends rely upon a set of shared reference points between the legend's teller and
listeners. They must incorporate and affirm some
number of shared beliefs, experiences, or the like,
in order to be effective. Legends may be told as
either first-person or third-person accounts.

Contemporary legends, or urban legends
as they are better known, are among the most
studied forms of folk legend today. Urban legends are the contemporary stories traded in
conversation, often without any knowledge that
the stories have no basis in fact. The tales are
presented as true, and it is typical for the speaker
to take pains to establish that the story is true
rather than merely a rumor or a hoax. The teller
may in fact believe the story is true, because it
goes through so many retellings that few realize it is fiction. Although live oral transmission
is the most common route for dissemination
of urban legends, they may also travel via fax,
e-mail, or photocopy. Urban legends usually
have sensational content. They can be funny or
spooky; can point a moral or issue a warning.
The patterns across retelling for these contemporary legends are so pronounced that, apart
from sharing motifs, they can be described as
variations on a theme.

Whether contemporary or not, folk legends
represent an important form of American folklore, for students and scholars alike.

See also: FOLKTALES; IRVING, WASHINGTON;
SUPERNATURAL; URBAN LEGENDS.

For Further Reading:
Dégh, Linda, Henry Glassie, and Felix Oinas, eds.
Folklore Today: A Festschrift for Richard Dorson.
Bloomington: Indiana University Press, 1976.
Dorson, Richard. *American Folklore.* Chicago: Uni-
versity of Chicago Press, 1959.
———. *American Folklore and the Historian.* Chi-
cago: University of Chicago Press, 1971.
———. *America in Legend: Folklore from the Colo-
nial Period to the Present.* New York: Pantheon
Books, 1971.
Leeming, David, and Jake Page. *Myths, Legends,
and Folktales of America: An Anthology.* New
York: Oxford University Press, 1999.

legends, urban See URBAN LEGENDS.

Leprechauns See SAINT PATRICK'S DAY.

**Lewis, Meriwether, and William
Clark** (1774–1809, 1770–1838) The Corps
of Discovery expeditions of 1804–06, as conducted by its commanders, Meriwether Lewis
and William Clark, helped develop U.S. awareness of the the continent west of the Missouri
River.

In a document dated June 20, 1803, President Thomas Jefferson commissioned Lewis
Meriwether, then captain of the first regiment
of the U.S. Infantry, to lead an exploration of
the American West. The United States knew
relatively little about this region, and Jefferson
sought a remedy by authorizing a journey that
could accomplish several goals. First, the expedition would explore and document the territory, including its potential for settlement and
its natural resources. Second, the group would
create accurate maps of the region. Finally, and

most critical, Jefferson wished Lewis to identify a northwest passage, an efficient commercial water route between the Missouri River and the Pacific Ocean.

Meriwether Lewis secured the talents of William Clark, a lieutenant in the U.S. Army, as cocommander of the expedition. Clark had some crucial skills, among them experience as a riverman and a knowledge of both geography and cartography. Together, Meriwether Lewis and William Clark traveled some 3,700 miles during their quest to fulfill Jefferson's commission. Their journey lasted from 1804 through 1806.

Along the way, they encountered many groups of indigenous people. With rare exception, such as a clash with the Lakota, these contacts were hospitable ones. During their journey, Meriwether Lewis and William Clark presented the Indians they met with mementos of their meetings, such as flags, certificates, and Jefferson medals (also known as peace medals). They were greatly aided in their interactions with Native Americans by Sacajawea (c. 1786–1812?) a native woman who accompanied them on the trip as a guide and assistant.

Sacajawea was born the daughter of a Shoshone chief in approximately 1786. At the age of 10, she was kidnapped and made to marry a French-Canadian trapper named Toussaint Charbonneau. When Charbonneau became an interpreter for Meriwether Lewis and William Clark in 1804, Sacajawea was invited to travel with them. She was accompanied by her newborn son, Jean Baptiste Charbonneau. The explorers believed that Sacajawea's presence in their midst would signal their peaceful intentions to all they encountered. She also contributed numerous helpful skills. She spoke English, French, and a form of sign language. She taught her employers about plant lore and edible materials found along their way. She also helped them traverse the Continental Divide. During the journey, Sacajawea renewed her lost contact with her brother, Cameahwait, from whom Lewis sought to acquire horses for their travels.

Cameahwait had succeeded his father, who had died since Sacajawea's abduction, as Shoshone chief. Sacajawea and Charbonneau saw to it that Meriwether Lewis and William Clark reached their destination. Lewis and Clark caught sight of the water along the Washington coast on November 15, 1805. As the party traveled back east, Sacajawea and her husband split off from the expedition.

Meriwether Lewis and William Clark have long been celebrated for their travels and their contributions to knowledge. Together, they embody the spirit of pioneers, willing to take risks to advance the nation's growth and maturity. For that reason, Lewis and Clark are honored in various ways, including the National Park Service's designation of a National Historic Trail marking their passage to discoveries. This area includes portions of what are now the states of Iowa, Idaho, Illinois, Kansas, Missouri, Montana, Nebraska, North Dakota, Oregon, South Dakota, and Washington. In addition, in 2004, the bicentennial of their journey was celebrated with public events and educational programs.

See also: FOLK HEROES/LEGENDARY FIGURES; FRONTIER; HISTORIC PRESERVATION; NORTHWESTERN REGIONAL FOLKLORE; REGION, FOLK; SACAJAWEA; WESTERN REGIONAL FOLKLORE.

For Further Reading:

Ambrose, Stephen. *Undaunted Courage: Meriwether Lewis, Thomas Jefferson, and the Opening of the American West.* New York: Simon & Schuster, 1996.

Duncan, Dayton et al. *Lewis and Clark: An Illustrated History.* New York: Knopf, 1997.

Ronda, James, ed. *Voyages of Discovery: Essays on the Lewis and Clark Expedition.* Helena: Montana Historical Society Press, 1998.

Slaughter, Thomas. *Exploring Lewis and Clark: Reflections on Men and Wilderness.* New York: Knopf, 2003.

Snyder, Gerald. *In the Footsteps of Lewis and Clark.* Washington, D.C.: National Geographic Society, 1970.

Liberty, Miss (legendary) "Miss Liberty" is the name sometimes used to refer to the figural sculpture also known as the Statue of Liberty.

Along with Uncle Sam, Miss Liberty is the personification of the United States, and so her image is prevalent in American folk culture, from Independence Day trinkets to patriotic-themed quilts.

This monument and national icon has a rich history. The Statue of Liberty originated as a gift to the United States from France. It was offered as a symbol of friendship between the two nations, including in particular a kinship that dates back to the Revolutionary War. The statue was formally accepted as a gift by President Grover Cleveland, acting on behalf of the United States.

Frederic Auguste Bartholdi was the sculptor who developed the design for this enormous piece. The figure itself is just over 150 feet tall from head to foot, not including the platform on which it stands. As most Americans and countless people the world over know, the statue depicts a classically draped woman wearing a crown. In one hand, she grips a tablet, inscribed with the date July 4, 1776. In the other, she lifts above her head a lit torch. It is presumably for this reason that the sculpture bears the title *Liberty Enlightening the World*. In its immediate reference to 1776, the statue pays tribute to U.S. independence. The suggestion of this title for the piece, however, was that the American Revolution carried a message with worldwide implications for the cause of freedom.

The gift of the Statue of Liberty was intended to arrive in time for America's centennial celebration in 1876. Circumstances both in France and in the United States required a delay, however, and only a portion of the monument, the arm with its torch, appeared at the Centennial Exhibition. The full statue would not be open to visitors until its dedication on October 28, 1886. From the time it first welcomed the public up until the present, the statue has held many meanings for beholders.

Although the earliest documentation about the initial gift of the statue suggests that it was to represent international friendship, along with a commemoration of the Revolutionary War, alternative symbolisms have been posited for the monument. For example, the timing of the gift, during the years following America's Civil War, put many in mind of the issue of liberty granted to U.S. slaves by the Emancipation Proclamation. This impression of the statue is underscored by the broken shackles at the figure's feet. Rumors have also circulated, including some urban legends, that the model for the statue was a black woman and that the subtext of abolition was intended by the designers. Therefore, instead of conjuring images of the Revolutionary War, the statue reminds some viewers of the Civil War and the institution of slavery.

In the years since its dedication, the Statue of Liberty has also assumed an iconic importance for immigrants to the United States. This effect is due in part to the 1903 addition of an Emma Lazarus poem to the monument's base, opening with the familiar line of welcome to new arrivals, "Give me your tired, your poor." This inscription, along with the placement of the statue on Liberty Island, near Ellis Island, the historically an entry point for immigrants to the United States, led many to regard the statue's message of liberty as equally relevant to those who travel to America seeing refuge and freedom from persecution. Accordingly, the United Nations designated the Statue of Liberty as a World Heritage Site. The site of the Statue of Liberty is maintained as a landmark by the U.S. Department of the Interior's National Park Service. Included there is an attraction now known as the Ellis Island Immigration Museum.

Not only is there folklore concerning the statue itself, but the sculpture also appears in a great many examples of popular and folk expression. Replicas of Miss Liberty have been fashioned out of just about every possible construction materials grand or plain. She is also a motif or decorative image adorning many objects designed for other purposes, from quilts to sweaters.

Regardless of which form of freedom a viewer most associated with the Statue of Liberty, as a widely recognizable monument the world over, her image and nickname, Miss Liberty, have come to function as an emblem for the United States.

See also: CIVIL WAR; FOLK HEROES/LEGENDARY FIGURES; IMMIGRATION AND FOLKLORE; INDEPENDENCE DAY/FOURTH OF JULY; MUSEUMS, FOLK; REVOLUTIONARY WAR; SLAVERY; UNCLE SAM; URBAN LEGENDS.

For Further Reading:

Dillon, Wilson, and Neil Kotler, eds. *The Statue of Liberty Revisited.* Washington, D.C.: Smithsonian Institution Press, 1994.

Glassberg, David. *American Historical Pageantry: The Uses of Tradition in the Early Twentieth Century.* Chapel Hill: University of North Carolina Press, 1990.

———. Rethinking the Statue of Liberty: Old Meanings, New Contexts. Available online. URL: http://www.libertyellisplan.org/documents.asp. Accessed July 25, 2005.

Pauli, Herta, and E. B. Ashton. *I Lift My Lamp: The Way of Symbol.* New York: Appleton-Century-Crofts, 1948.

Yellin, Jean Fagin. "Caps and Chains: Hiram Powers' Statue of Liberty," *American Quarterly* 38 (winter 1986): 798–826.

Library of Congress   See AMERICAN FOLKLIFE CENTER; AMERICAN MEMORY PROJECT; ARCHIVE OF FOLK CULTURE.

Lincoln, Abraham (1809–1865)   As the president who saw the nation through a civil war, Abraham Lincoln is a figure surrounded by a good deal of mythology and lore.

In part, this lore developed because he embodies the ideologies of self-improvement and upward mobility. His rise from life in a log cabin to life in the White House proves a satisfying story to the American imagination. His success appears to affirm the idea that with effort and education, one can aspire to any goal or station in America.

As if this tale of the American dream and its fulfillment were not enough, the historical memory of Lincoln also attributes to the man other personal virtues, including honesty and humility. According to one piece of Lincoln lore, he once walked a great distance just to return a small overpayment on a minor transaction. Therefore, Lincoln seemed to combine ambition with honor.

Because Lincoln held the presidency at one of the country's times of greatest internal strife, the Civil War, he is also valorized for his part in keeping the union of states intact. In particular, Lincoln's 1893 signature of the Emancipation Proclamation earned him a place in history. To this day, Lincoln is associated with the reunification of North and South, as well as the abolition of slavery.

Further, the fact that Lincoln was the victim of an assassin's bullet made him an object of both mourning and myth. As Americans sought to sort out their feelings about the fallen president, they began to regard him as a martyr of sorts. His murder also inspired curiosity, and the public remains fascinated with the circumstances surrounding the assassination. No less than the poet Walt Whitman delivered Lincoln's eulogy, thereby contributing to Lincoln's mythic stature. Ford's Theater, where the shooting occurred, has become a national museum where visitors can learn more about Lincoln and his tragic death. Part of the lore surrounding Lincoln's death includes a legend that at midnight on April 27 each year, one can still see Lincoln's funeral train make its way to the burial site of Springfield, Illinois.

Americans have honored Lincoln with many public tributes. His countenance appears carved into the face of Mount Rushmore, alongside his fellow presidents Thomas Jefferson, George Washington, and Theodore Roosevelt. His image has adorned coins, currency, and stamps. Places where he lived or worked bear commemorative plaques and/or enjoy the status of historical sites. His name marks buildings and locations from Lincoln Center in New York City to Lincoln, Nebraska. Popular culture also bears Lincoln's mark, such as the composer Aaron Copland's "A Lincoln Portrait," and Walt Disney's exhibit, Great Moments with Mr. Lincoln, in which a robotic figure of Abraham Lincoln delivers an address combining excerpts from his writings and speeches.

The most famous tribute of all may be Washington, D.C.'s, Lincoln Memorial, which was completed on Memorial Day 1922. It consists of a classical marble building housing the Daniel Chester French sculpture of a seated Lincoln. This location has become associated with numerous key moments in the struggle for racial equality, including Marian Anderson's concert and Martin Luther King's "I have a dream" speech.

Lincoln's name has become synonymous with the causes of unity and equality, making him a larger than life figure from the American past.

See also: BROWN, JOHN; CIVIL WAR; CONSPIRACY FOLKLORE; EMANCIPATION (PROCLAMATION) DAY; FOLK HEROES/LEGENDARY FIGURES; GHOST STORIES; GREENFIELD VILLAGE, HENRY FORD MUSEUM AND; HISTORIC PRESERVATION; JUNETEENTH; MARTIN LUTHER KING DAY; MEMORIAL DAY; MUSEUMS, FOLK; NEW YEAR'S DAY/EVE; POLITICS AND FOLKLORE; PRESIDENTS' DAY; ROOSEVELT, THEODORE; SANDBURG, CARL; SLAVERY; THANKSGIVING; TRUTH, SOJOURNER; WASHINGTON, GEORGE; WHITMAN, WALT.

For Further Reading:

Bodnar, John. *Remaking America: Public Memory, Commemoration, and Patriotism in the Twentieth Century.* Princeton, N.J.: Princeton University Press, 1992.

Goodman, Ailene. *Abe Lincoln in Song and Story.* Washington, D.C.: Eliza Records, 1988.

Leeming, David, and Jake Page. *Myths, Legends, and Folktales of America: An Anthology.* New York: Oxford University Press, 1999.

Mieder, Wolfgang. *Proverbs Are the Best Policy: Folk Wisdom and Politics.* Logan: Utah State University Press, 2005.

Peterson, Merrill. *Lincoln in American Memory.* New York: Oxford University Press, 1994.

Sherwood, Robert. *The Lincoln of Carl Sandburg: His Monumental Work Has the Character of Folk Biography.* New York: New York Times, 1939.

Turner, Thomas Reed. *Beware the People Weeping: Public Opinion and the Assassination of Abraham Lincoln.* Baton Rouge: Louisiana State University Press, 1982.

Lincoln's birthday   See PRESIDENTS' DAY.

Lindbergh, Charles (1902–1974) Charles Lindbergh, pioneer of aviation, numbers among the most famous historical figures of American occupational folklore. Lindbergh was born in Detroit, Michigan, on February 4, 1902, the son of a congressman. He grew up fascinated with technology and air travel, in particular. These interests led him to become an airmail pilot. He would rise to fame, however, for his historic transatlantic flight from New York to Paris, a nonstop solo flight completed in 1927. For this achievement, Lindbergh was dubbed the "Lone Eagle." The Ryan aircraft monoplane Lindbergh used to make the journey, the *Spirit of St. Louis,* also became well known to the American public.

Lindbergh's flight was embraced as a national triumph, and it was celebrated in many ways. The crooner Rudy Vallee sang a song in the pilot's honor entitled "Lucky Lindy." In addition, a popular dance called the "Lindy hop" came into fashion. Lindbergh then served as an adviser while commercial flight was developing. He was also something of an environmentalist.

Lindbergh would reenter the public eye in 1932, when his two-year-old child disappeared from the family home. The kidnapping and murder was described in the press at the time as the crime of the century. It was in part as a consequence of this tragedy that kidnapping became designated as a federal crime in the United States.

When Lindbergh penned his autobiography, *The Spirit of St. Louis*, he received the Pulitzer Prize. Although his stance opposing U.S. entry into World War II was controversial, he went on to fly some 50 missions in support of the war effort. Lindbergh died in Hawaii on August 26, 1974.

Lindbergh's solo transatlantic flight ensured a place of distinction for him within the history of aviation, as well as within the American lore of technological progress.

See also: CONSPIRACY FOLKLORE, EARHART, AMELIA MARY; FLIGHT; FOLK HEROES/LEGENDARY FIGURES; OCCUPATIONAL FOLKLORE; WRIGHT BROTHERS

For Further Reading:

Berg, Scott. *Lindbergh*. New York: Putnam, 1998.

Burleigh, Robert, and Mike Wimmer. *Flight: The Journey of Charles Lindbergh*. New York: Philomel Books, 1991.

Davis, Kenneth Sydney. *The Hero: Charles A. Lindbergh and the American Dream*. New York: Doubleday, 1959.

King, David. *First Facts about American Heroes*. Woodbridge, Conn.: Blackbirth Press, 1996.

Lindbergh, Charles. *The Spirit of St. Louis*. New York: Scribner's, 1953.

Newton, James. *Uncommon Friends: Life with Thomas Edison, Henry Ford, Harvey Firestone, Alexis Carrel, and Charles Lindbergh*. San Diego: Harcourt Brace Jovanovich, 1987.

Pisano, Dominick. *Charles Lindbergh and the Spirit of St. Louis*. Washington, D.C.: Smithsonian/Abrams, 2002.

Ross, Walter. *The Last Hero: Charles A. Lindbergh*. New York: Harper & Row, 1976.

literature   See FOLKLORE IN AMERICAN LITERATURE.

Lithuanian-American folklore   Lithuanian-American folklore reflects the cultural heritage of immigrants to the United States from Lithuania, along with those born in American of Lithuanian ancestry.

Immigration to the United States from Lithuania has been occurring since the 17th century, most of it after 1860. Lithuanian Americans favored settlement in urban and undustrial centers of the Northeast and Midwest.

Lithuania-based traditions in folk expression take many forms, such as songs, legends, and tales. The process of cultural assimilation has made it necessary to take concerted measures, such as specialized instruction, to maintain Lithuanian language traditions in the United States. Otherwise, verbal lore will only be experienced in translation. Lithuanian-American cuisine features meat, potatoes, dark breads, and dairy products. One of the best-known Lithuanian-American artisans, Joseph Mender, drew pictures and fashioned decorated canes by carving tree branches. As is the case with other Baltic countries, such as Latvia and Estonia, Lithuanian-American folk traditions are closely tied to nationalism and the homeland's struggle for autonomy. Lithuanian Americans join their mother country in national celebrations such as Lithuanian Kingdom Day (September 8) and Lithuanian Independence Day (February 16).

Organizations dedicated to the preservation and study of Lithuanian-American culture include Chicago's Lithuanian American Council, Institute of Lithuanian Studies, along with New York's Lithuanian Alliance of America. Major collections of Lithuanian cultural material include Philadelphia, Pennsylvania Van Pelt Library; Putnam, Connecticut Lithuanian American Cultural Archives; and Chicago's Lithuanian American Culture Archives.

Folklore helps connect Lithuanian Americans to the people and culture of their homeland.

See also: ART, FOLK; CRAFTS, FOLK; CULTURAL GROUPS; ETHNICITY; FOLKLORISM; FOOD/FOODWAYS; HOLIDAYS/OBSERVANCES; IMMIGRATION AND FOLKLORE; LATVIAN-AMERICAN FOLKLORE; ORAL FOLKLORE.

For Further Reading:

Alilunas, Leo. *Lithuanians in the United States: Selected Studies.* San Francisco: R & E Research Associates, 1978.

Budreckis, Algirdas. *The Lithuanians in America, 1651–1975: A Chronology and Factbook.* Dobbs Ferry, N.Y.: Oceana, 1975.

Fainhauz, David. *Lithuanians in the U.S.A.: Aspects of Ethnic Identity.* Chicago: Lithuanian Library Press, 1991.

Gedmintas, Aleksandras. *An Interesting Bit of Identity: The Dynamics of Ethnic Identity in a Lithuanian-American Community.* New York: AMS Press, 1989.

Gieysator de Gorgey, Maria. *Art of Lithuanian Cooking.* New York: Hippocrene Books, 1998.

Gimbutas, Marija Alseikaite. *Ancient Symbolism in Lithuanian Folk Art.* Philadelphia: American Folklore Society, 1958.

Kantautas, Adam. *A Lithuanian Bibliography.* Edmonton, Canada: University of Alberta Press, 1975.

Kučas, Antanas. *Lithuanians in America.* San Francisco: R & E Research Associates, 1975.

Library of Congress, Archive of Folk Culture/American Folklife Center. Resettlement Administration Collection. Available online. URL: http://lcweb.loc.gov/spcoll/196.html. Accessed February 22, 2006.

Suziedelius, Simas, ed. *Encyclopedia Lithuanica.* 6 vols. Boston: Juozas Kapocius, 1970–78.

Little Canada See FRENCH-AMERICAN FOLKLORE.

Little Italy See CITY FOLKLORE; ETHNICITY.

"Little Mermaid, The" See "MERMAID, THE LITTLE."

Little Tokyo See CITY FOLKLORE; ETHNICITY.

living history museums Living history museums typically consist of areas of districts that combine historic buildings with restored or recreated cultural landscapes to offer to visitors the effect of walking into a historical setting.

Their goal is to produce the sensation of immersion in another era and its way of life, as though a time machine had transported one back through time to another place and another society.

While many museums have been influenced by the premises and techniques of living history, folklife museums and museums that make heavy use of living history programming are joined together through the Association for Living History, Farm and Agricultural Museums (ALHFAM). This organization was created to support such agencies in their efforts to bring history to life.

In other words, a living history museum's professionals are not content to collect, catalog, and display objects related to American folklore. Rather, they seek to provide visitors with insights into how that society might have felt to its members. Much of this effect relies upon compelling arrangements of physical space and accomplished interpreters, staff members who assume the roles of members of the historical society evoked by the museum. Such first-person informants spend their shifts conducting characteristic work and life activities, while interacting with tourists for both dramatic and educational purposes.

Exemplified by such sites as Colonial Williamsburg, Greenfield Village, Mystic Seaport, and Old Sturbridge Village, the living history museum is an important resource to those who wish to inquire into American folklore and folklife.

See also: ARCHITECTURE, FOLK; ART, FOLK; COLONIAL WILLIAMSBURG; FOLKLIFE; FOLKLIFE MOVEMENT; FOLKLORE IN EVERYDAY LIFE; GREENFIELD VILLAGE, HENRY FORD MUSEUM AND; HISTORIC PRESERVATION; MATERIAL CULTURE; MUSEUMS, FOLK; MYSTIC SEAPORT AND PRESERVATION SHIPYARD; NORTHEASTERN REGIONAL FOLKLORE; OCCUPATIONAL FOLKLORE; PUBLIC FOLKLORE; REGION, FOLK; STURBRIDGE VILLAGE, OLD.

For Further Reading:

Benson, Susan Porter, Steven Brier, and Roy Rosenzweig, eds. *Presenting the Past: Essays on History and the Public.* Philadelphia: Temple University Press, 1986.

Brochu, Lisa. *Personal Interpretation: Connecting Your Audience to Heritage Resources.* Fort Collins, Colo.: InterpPres, 2002.

Gardner, James B., and Peter S. LaPaglia, eds. *Public History: Essays from the Field.* Malabar, Fla.: Krieger, 1999.

Jameson, John H., Jr., ed. *The Reconstructed Past: Reconstructions in the Public Interpretation of Archaeology and History.* Walnut Creek, Calif.: Alta Mira, 2004.

Loewen, James. *Lies across America: What Our Historic Sites Get Wrong.* New York: New Press, 1999.

Roth, Stacy Flora. *Past into Present: Effective Techniques for First-Person Historical Interpretation.* Chapel Hill: University of North Carolina Press, 1998.

Llorona, La   See WEEPING WOMAN.

Locke, Alain Le Roy (1886–1954)   As a philosopher, writer, editor, critic, and educator, Alain Le Roy Locke opened new pathways for African Americans as he simultaneously celebrated their cultural traditions.

Locke was born September 13, 1886, in Philadelphia, Pennsylvania. He graduated from Harvard University in 1917. He became the first African American ever to receive the Rhodes Scholarship, with which he studied literature at Oxford University. Upon his return, Locke earned a Ph.D. in philosophy from Harvard University.

Locke became known for his concept of the "New Negro," a term for African Americans who embraced their racial and cultural identities and used that legacy to fuel their strivings for personal and collective advancement. In 1925, Locke edited, contributed to, and published a pivotal book, *The New Negro*, which collected writings by a variety of African-American authors of the day, such as James Mercer Langston Hughes, Countee Cullen, Jean Toomer, and Claude McKay. With this and other efforts, he became a proponent of a "talented tenth" theory, which relied upon the most gifted African Americans to lead the way to racial uplift and understanding. Locke did his part by becoming a professor of philosophy at Howard University in Washington, D.C., where he worked from 1918 until 1953. Locke died the following year in New York City, having reached countless students and readers with a message of hope and responsibility.

As a civil rights leader and tastemaker, Alain Locke made visible a host of African-American writers and artists, particularly those of the Harlem Renaissance. His influence can be felt in all the work that followed, especially the black arts movement of the latter 1960s.

See also: AFRICAN-AMERICAN FOLKLORE; FOLKLORE IN AMERICAN LITERATURE; HUGHES, JAMES MERCER LANGSTON; TOOMER, JEAN.

For Further Reading:

Favor, J. Martin. *Authentic Blackness: The Folk in the New Negro Renaissance.* Durham, N.C.: Duke University Press, 1999.

Harris, Leonard. *The Philosophy of Alain Locke: Harlem Renaissance and Beyond.* Philadelphia: Temple University Press, 1989.

Cain, Kofi, and Rudolph Alexander. *Alain Leroy Locke: Race, Culture, and the Education of African American Adults.* Amsterdam: Rudopi, 2003.

Linnemann, Russell, ed. *Alain Locke: Reflections on a Modern Renaissance Man.* Baton Rouge: Louisiana State University Press, 1982.

Locke, Alain. *The Cultural Temper of Alain Locke: A Selection of His Essays on Art and Culture*, edited by Jeffrey C. Stewart. New York: Garland, 1983.

Posnock, Ross. *Color and Culture: Black Writers and the Making of the Modern Intellectual.* Cambridge, Mass.: Harvard University Press, 1998.

logging   See BUNYAN, PAUL; CROCKETT, DAVY; OCCUPATIONAL FOLKLORE.

Longabaugh, Harry (Sundance Kid) (1867–1908) Along with his partner in crime, Butch Cassidy, the figure popular history tends to accord top billing, the Sundance Kid emerged as a legendary figure of the American West.

This notorious figure from American lore was born Harry Longabaugh. He was the second most famous member of Butch Cassidy's Wild Bunch, also known as the Hole-in-the-Wall Gang. Longabaugh is better remembered by his assumed persona (the Sundance Kid), coined in memory of an 1887–89 stint in the Sundance, Wyoming, jail on a charge of horse theft. The group also included Ben Kilpatrick (the Tall Texan), Will Carver, and Harvey Logan (Kid Curry). This band of criminals robbed trains, banks, and mines during the 1890s, hiding between jobs in remote areas in Wyoming and Utah. By the turn of the century the gang disbanded, but the two principal members, Cassidy and Sundance, continued their working partnership.

As the pursuit of Butch Cassidy and the Sundance Kid intensified, it is believed that they left the West for New York. They subsequently relocated to Argentina and Bolivia, where they engaged in cattle ranching and more robbery. Most accounts suggest that both were killed by police gunfire while in Bolivia, just after a payroll robbery in which they were believed implicated.

Historical memory is generous, perhaps overly so, to both Cassidy and Sundance. Folk histories tend to cast them as Robin Hood figures given to robbing the rich to benefit the poor. While such a notion is romantic, attributions of altruistic motives for their careers as criminals remain highly suspect. Similarly glossy tales surround other outlaws, such as Jesse James.

In addition to folktales and storybooks, the Sundance Kid was the subject of a popular 1969 Twentieth Century Fox film, *Butch Cassidy and the Sundance Kid*, in which Robert Redford portrayed him. Redford later established the Sundance Foundation, after the nickname of the character he portrayed in that film. The Sundance Foundation is best known for the Sundance Festival, an important venue for independent film. In the sense that Redford's foundation counters the commercialism of Hollywood film and promotes the efforts of unsung directors, the Sundance Kid does achieve something of a Robin Hood legacy.

As tricksters and adventurers, Butch Cassidy and the Sundance Kid stand as part of the history of the American West and its crime lore.

See also: FOLK HEROES/LEGENDARY FIGURES; JAMES, JESSE; OUTLAWS; PARKER, ROBERT LEROY (BUTCH CASSIDY); ROBIN HOOD; TRICKSTER.

For Further Reading:

Durer, Christopher S., ed. *American Renaissance and American West*. Laramie: University of Wyoming Press, 1982.

Painter, Larry. *In Search of Butch Cassidy*. Norman: University of Oklahoma Press, 1977.

Steckmesser, Kent. "Robin Hood and the American Outlaw," *Journal of American Folklore* 79, no. 312 (spring 1966): 348–355.

Steckmesser, Kent. *Western Outlaws: The "Good Badman" in Fact, Film, and Folklore*. Claremont, Calif.: Regina Books, 1983.

Longfellow, Henry Wadsworth (1807–1882) As one of the best-known poets of America's 19th century, Henry Wadsworth Longfellow had a deep appreciation for the nation's folkloric traditions.

Longfellow was born on February 27, 1807, in Portland. His choice of topics would include many subjects directly related to the colonial past of New England and maritime economy of Maine.

Longfellow graduated in 1825 from Maine's Bowdoin College, where he would later be employed as a professor. He was also a novelist, translator, and textbook writer of repute. It was for his literary works, however, that Longfellow is best remembered. In terms of themes, approach, and inspiration, American folklore greatly influenced Longfellow's body of work. It might be for this reason, an affinity for American lore, that he so admired the folk-styled stories and sketches of his fellow northeastern author Washington Irving.

As a writer, Longfellow, as had Irving, demonstrated an affinity for early American history and its tales. He put on the page a kind of poetry that approximated the form of the folk ballad and its sounded language rhythms.

Various selections by Longfellow commonly appear in anthologies of American literature, such as "The Wreck of the Hesperus" and "The Children's Hour." It is historical writing for which Longfellow is remembered. For instance, in an 1847 piece, *Evangeline: A Tale of Acadie*, Longfellow explored the plight of the Acadians, writing about the expulsion of these French Canadians from what is now Nova Scotia by the British. Many resettled in the coastal regions of the state of Louisiana, where they gave the United States a rich lore of Cajun culture. Other works, such as *The Song of Hiawatha* (1855) and *Courtship of Miles Standish* (1858), sought to capture the complexities of icons of American history.

While these and other verses from Longfellow were accomplished literary texts, it is another poem for which he is widely known, "Paul Revere's Ride," published in 1863 in *The Tales of a Wayside Inn*. This work is worded as the account of a storyteller addressing youth: "Listen, my children, and you shall hear / Of the midnight ride of Paul Revere." This particular poem has long been a favorite of schoolteachers, and so generations of children have been called upon to memorize and recite it as part of their studies.

Over time, Longfellow's work has helped acquaint readers with the narrative traditions of the United States. Even some of those not drawn to historical subjects find in literary treatments by Longfellow tales that engage and entertain. In that sense, his compositions have functioned as literary folklore. In his historical poems and works of fiction, Longfellow recorded a version of historical figures and events that has stood for, and sometimes even functions as, folk history.

Time has not been as generous to Longfellow as to other writers of his era, such as Walt Whitman. Longfellow's literary cachet has faded somewhat over the past 50 years, as critics have deemed his voice as sentimental and academics have regarded his verse as minor, especially when compared to that of the likes of Whitman. Nonetheless, there is no denying that Longfellow's popularity as a writer and influence as an interpreter of American lore and legend have made him a powerful force within the imaginations and reading lives of many.

See also: CAJUN FOLKLORE; FOLK HEROES/LEGENDARY FIGURES; FOLKLORE IN AMERICAN LITERATURE; HIAWATHA; IRVING, WASHINGTON; MARITIME FOLKLORE; NORTHEASTERN REGIONAL FOLKLORE; REGION, FOLK; REVERE'S RIDE, PAUL; REVOLUTIONARY WAR; WHITMAN, WALT.

For Further Reading:

Calhoun, Charles. *Longfellow: A Rediscovered Life*. Boston: Beacon Press, 2004.

Cameron, Kenneth Walter. *Longfellow's Reading in Libraries; The Charging Records of a Learned Poet Interpreted*. Hartford, Conn.: Transcendental Books, 1973.

Clarke, Helen Archibald. *Longfellow's Country*. New York: Baker and Taylor, 1909.

Ferguson, Robert. "Longfellow's Political Fears: Civic Authority and the Role of the Artist in *Hiawatha* and *Miles Standish*," *American Literature* 50 (March 1978): 187–215.

Gale, Robert. *A Henry Wadsworth Longfellow Companion*. Westport, Conn.: Greenwood Press, 2003.

Mathews, Joseph Chesley, ed. *Henry W. Longfellow Reconsidered: A Symposium*. Hartford, Conn.: Transcendental Books, 1970.

Moyne, Ernest. "Manabozho, Tarenyawagon, and Hiawatha," *Southern Folklore Quarterly* 29 (1965): 195–203.

Trachtenberg, Alan. *Shades of Hiawatha: Staging Indians, Making Americans, 1880–1930*. New York: Hill & Wang, 2004.

Wagenknecht, Edward. *Henry Wadsworth Longfellow: His Poetry and Prose*. New York: Ungar, 1986.

Louisiana folklore See CABLE, GEORGE WASHINGTON; FINK, MIKE; MARDI GRAS; SOUTH-ERN REGIONAL FOLKLORE.

Loup-Garou (legendary) The term *Loup-Garou* refers to the legendary figure of the werewolf.

Although many cultures have lore concerning wolves, Loup-Garou stories appear to be a specific form of supernatural tale introduced to the United States by French settlers and traders. They are a survival of French oral culture, transplanted to become part of folk culture in areas such as Vincennes, Indiana.

According to legend, the Loup-Garou is a human being who has been placed under a spell. The werewolf at the center of these tales is a human being who undergoes transformation into a wolf. Such creatures are purported to feed on human blood and flesh and so inspire fear in those who believe. Loup-Garou stories also occasionally feature people who become other animals, such as horses or cows, but wolves remain the most common metamorphosis.

The nature of the Loup-Garou, or bewitched figure, is to take a human shape during the day and change into animal form by night. Under cover of darkness, the Loup-Garou prowls the land until the spell is broken or concludes, generally after a specified length of time. In some stories that duration is 101 days. To break the spell, a human must recognize the person as a Loup-Garou and draw blood. Once this is done, both must not talk about the incident until the spell's original period has elapsed, or else the consequences for the bewitched individual will be even worse.

The image of the wolf is a staple of horror stories and even some fairy tales, such as "Little Red Riding Hood." The Loup-Garou stories take this dread one step further by suggesting that anyone might be turned into a wolf through enchantment.

See also: ANIMALS; CHANGELING; FOLK HEROES/LEGENDARY FIGURES; MONSTERS; "RED RIDING HOOD, LITTLE"; SUPERNATURAL; WEREWOLVES.

For Further Reading:
Casanova, Mary. *Curse of a Winter Moon.* New York: Hyperion, 2000.

Frost, Brian. *The Essential Guide to Werewolf Literature.* Madison: University of Wisconsin Press, 2003.

Fudge, Erica, ed. *Renaissance Beasts: Of Animals, Humans, and Other Wonderful Creatures.* Urbana: University of Illinois Press, 2004.

Gilmore, David. *Monsters: Evil Beings, Mythical Beasts, and All Manner of Imaginary Terrors.* Philadelphia: University of Pennsylvania Press, 2003.

Lover's Leap See COURTSHIP/DATING FOLKLORE.

luck/fortune In the United States, as in most nations, there is an extensive lore surrounding beliefs, objects, and practices related to concept of luck or fortune.

These folk notions usually consist of two aspects: those believed to yield good luck and those believed to result in bad luck.

Many holidays feature beliefs about luck. On Saint Patrick's Day, for instance, there is talk of the "luck of the Irish." At New Year's, there are various rituals believed to usher in good luck, prosperity, or health for the coming year. Birthdays are considered to be fortunate days, and accompanying celebrations involve rituals of luck, such as the birthday wish made silently before blowing out any candles on the birthday cake. Friday the thirteenth, on the other hand, regardless of the month in which it falls, is commonly regarded as an unlucky day. For that reason, the date is an object of considerable superstition.

There is also a traditional set of beliefs regarding prediction. For example, wedding lore continues to feature many long-standing practices believed to avert bad luck and summon good luck for the bride and groom. An example would be the prohibition on the groom's seeing the bride in her wedding dress prior to the ceremony. Similarly, there are folk beliefs surrounding pregnancy and childbirth. An example would be the placement of scissors under the woman's pillow to cut the pain of labor and delivery.

Furthermore, Americans have several beliefs about objects considered to confer luck, especially when carried on one's person. Examples include the rabbit's foot, four-leaf clover, and horseshoe.

The rabbit foot as a lucky object has its origins in African-American folklore, specifically the practices associated with hoodoo, or folk magic. A rabbit's foot is sometimes carried as a lucky charm, also known traditionally as a "hoodoo hand." The luckiest such object is the left hind foot of a rabbit killed in a graveyard during the correct phase of the Moon. Such amulets are also associated with conjuring traditions, in which a root or other charm is carried on the person. The rabbit's foot is believed not only to combat bad luck, but to produce good luck.

The four-leaf clover is another object considered to have lucky properties for the person who finds or carries it. The three-leaf clover is common; the four-leaf is a rare mutation valued for its novelty. According to folklore, each leaf has symbolism, and the fourth represents luck.

The idea of a horseshoe's being lucky dates back to a story about the archbishop of Canterbury. Also trained as a blacksmith, he secured a promise from the devil that he would never enter a structure where a horseshoe was displayed over the entrance. Since then, people have regarded the horseshoe as a lucky object.

As a form of everyday magic, folk beliefs about luck and fortune pervade American life.

See also: ALGER, HORATIO, JR.; BELIEFS, FOLK; BIRTHDAYS; BROWN, MARGARET TOBIN (UNSINKABLE MOLLY); CHILDBIRTH/PREGNANCY FOLKLORE; CHRISTMAS; CONJURE/CONJURING; EVIL EYE; FLOWERS; FOLKLORE IN EVERYDAY LIFE; FRIDAY THE THIRTEENTH; GOLD RUSH, THE; "GOLDEN GOOSE, THE"; HOBOES; MAGIC; NEW YEAR'S EVE/DAY; PREDICTION; SAINT PATRICK'S DAY; SUPERSTITION; TOOTH FAIRY; WEDDING/MARRIAGE FOLKLORE.

For Further Reading:

Ellis, Bill. *Lucifer Ascending: The Occult in Folklore and Popular Culture.* Lexington: University of Kentucky Press, 2004.

Gong, Rosemary. *Good Luck Life: The Essential Guide to Chinese American Celebrations and Culture.* New York: HarperResource, 2005.

Lears, T. J. Jackson. *Something for Nothing: Luck in America.* New York: Penguin Group, 2004.

Rescher, Nicholas. *Luck: The Brilliant Randomness of Everyday Life.* Pittsburgh: University of Pittsburgh Press, 2001.

lynching   See CLEMENS, SAMUEL LANGHORNE; LOCKE, ALAIN LE ROY.

M

Magarac, Joe (legendary) Joe Magarac was a legendary immigrant steel man from the region of Pittsburgh, Pennsylvania.

There is some debate over the question whether Magarac was an actual historical personage or an imagined hero, such as Paul Bunyan represents for lumberjacks or John Henry represents for railroad workers. This is some suspicion that the image of Magarac was created by the author Owen Francis. Nonetheless, the Magarac tales date back at least the 1930s in America, and he is a key figure in occupational folklore.

As are other such legendary characters, Magarac was remarkable for his superhuman performance. His capacity for work and his prowess as a steel laborer established him as an exemplar of the working man. He was reputed to be able to bend steel with his bare hands and work around the clock. He was also known as a changeling, able to transform his size and shape to suit the situation or task at hand. Many Magarac stories also laud his efforts to render aid to the citizens around him, suggesting his benevolent character.

Whether he is the product of history or not, whether folklore or fakelore, Magarac remains an emblem of the field of steelwork. He is usually featured within collections of America's tall tales.

See also: BUNYAN, PAUL; CHANGELINGS; FAKE-LORE; FEBOLDSON, FEBOLD; FOLK HEROES/LEG-ENDARY FIGURES; HENRY, JOHN; IMMIGRATION AND FOLKLORE, LEGENDS, FOLK; OCCUPATIONAL FOLKLORE.

For Further Reading:

Blair, Walter. *Tall Tale America: A Legendary History of Our Humorous Heroes.* New York: Coward-McCann, 1944.

Carver, George. "Legend in Steel," *Western Pennsylvania Historical Magazine* 27 (1944): 129–136.

Reutter, Clifford. "The Puzzle of a Pittsburgh Steeler: Joe Magarac's Ethnic Identity," *Western Pennsylvania Historical Magazine* 63 (1980): 31–36.

Richman, Hyman. "The Saga of Joe Magarac," *New York Folklore Quarterly* 9 (1953): 282–293.

Swetnam, George. *Devils, Ghosts, and Witches: Occult Folklore of the Upper Ohio Valley.* Greensburg, Pa.: McDonald/Sward, 1988.

magic Magic involves folk beliefs about ways to influence people, relationships, and events. Depending upon what definition is used, magic can include any action taken on the belief that it will help produce a desired outcome, despite the appearance that such a belief is irrational or unhelpful.

Generally speaking, magic represents human efforts to exert some measure of control over those natural forces that shape lives, such as weather, illness, misfortune, and death. Magic can include specific processes, such as spells, charms, and incantations. It can also be a more everyday occurrence, such as when wishing or willing something to happen despite all odds. A common example would be the custom of wedding guests' throwing rice at the newlywed couple to ensure their fertility.

Figures associated with magic are various; they include witches, wizards, voodoo priests and priestesses, sorcerers, conjurers, warlocks, shamans, healers, diviners, wisemen and wisewomen, and, of course, magicians. Although a great number of magical figures are female, there are also male figures traditionally regarded as possessing magical powers, from Merlin and Aladdin to the Pied Piper of Hamelin. Magical beings are linked to supernatural forces by their unusual abilities, such as their status as changelings.

Distinctions are sometimes made between white magic and black magic. While either force can have unfortunate effects, black magic often involves the attempt to cause intentional harm to the objects of one's practice. White magic includes most efforts to increase one's luck, so long as they are not at the expense of others. By contrast, malevolent magic may seek to manipulate the will of others, as would be the case in use of a voodoo doll, the placing of curses, the use of the evil eye, or the casting of evil spells. This form of magic was suspected in the 1692 witch trials held in Salem, Massachusetts. Today, magic persists in every form from the folk belief in horoscopes and astrology to the practice of modern white magic, such as Wicca.

Numerous American writers have incorporated magic in their writings, such as Frederick Douglass, Charles Waddell Chesnutt, and Toni Morrison. Whether fictional or nonfictional, magical characters and practices are a pervasive feature within American folklore.

See also: BELIEFS, FOLK; CHANGELINGS; CONJURE/CONJURING; DEVIL, THE; EVIL EYE; FOLKLORE IN EVERYDAY LIFE; HOUDINI, HARRY; "JACK AND THE BEANSTALK"; LUCK/FORTUNE; "PIED PIPER OF HAMELIN, THE"; PREDICTION; SUPERNATURAL; SUPERSTITION; WITCHCRAFT, SALEM; VOODOO/HOODOO.

For Further Reading:
Cantwell, Robert. "Conjuring Culture: Ideology and Magic in the Festival of American Folklife," *Journal of American Folklore* 104, no. 412 (spring 1991): 148–163.
Leone, Mark P., and Fry, Gladys-Marie. "Conjuring in the Big House Kitchen: An Interpretation of African American Belief Systems Based on the Uses of Archaeology and Folklore Sources," *Journal of American Folklore* 112, no. 445 (summer 1999): 372–403.
Mechling, Jay. "The Magic of the Boy Scout Campfire," *Journal of American Folklore* 93, no. 367 (winter 1980): 35–56.
Neubauer, Paul. "The Demon of Loss and Longing: The Function of the Ghost in Toni Morrison's *Beloved*." In *Demons: Mediators between This World and the Other: Essays on Demonic Beings from the Middle Ages to the Present*, edited by Ruth Petzoklt and Paul Neubauer, 165–174. New York: Peter Lang, 1998.
Roberts, Leonard W. "Magic Folktales in America." In *Our Living Traditions: An Introduction to American Folklore*, edited by Tristram Coffin, 142–153. New York: Basic Books, 1968.
Whitcomb, Bill. *The Magician's Companion: A Practical and Encyclopedia Guide to Magical and Religious Symbolism*. St. Paul, Minn.: Llwellyn, 1999.

Maine folklore   See LONGFELLOW, HENRY WADSWORTH; NORTHEASTERN REGIONAL FOLKLORE; PATRIOTS' DAY; SHAKER FOLKLORE; YANKEE DOODLE.

Mardi Gras   Mardi Gras is as much a series of events as it is a holiday in current American practice, conducted on the Tuesday before Ash Wednesday each year.

The holiday had its origins in a practice dating from the Middle Ages in which people confess their sins in anticipation of the religious season of Lent. Indeed, Mardi Gras's alternative name, "Shrove Tuesday," derives from the term for confession. Mardi Gras began, on some level, as a New Year's or seasonal festival, and in earlier days practices included burning an effigy of winter. By marking time's passage and welcoming the renewal of spring, Mardi Gras takes its place among a wide array of Carnival events.

In the United States, the definitive Mardi Gras celebration site is New Orleans, Louisiana, where the holiday's observance began in 1827 and continues to this day. In addition to providing residents of the region with an occasion to celebrate, each year's Mardi Gras observance in New Orleans attracts tourists from across the country and, indeed, around the world.

Since at least 1857, the streets of New Orleans have hosted a procession that proves both colorful and exciting. This parade is best known for its costume ritual, dancers, decorated floats, and tossing of tokens and trinkets (such as toy doubloons and strings of beads) to onlookers. Mardi Gras is associated in the public imagination with a suspension of usual standards of propriety and strictures of good taste. As with other costume rituals, it provides an opportunity to be playful and assume other identities for a time.

In this respect, Mardi Gras, as does Carnival elsewhere, represents a time of freedom, mischief, and fun. In something of the spirit of earlier observances of Mardi Gras, with their confessions and absolutions, today's participants in a more secular observance nonetheless exorcise their demons and find release through shared ritual.

See also: CAJUN FOLKLORE; FESTIVALS, FOLKLORE; HOLIDAYS/OBSERVANCES; PARADES; REGION, FOLK; SOUTHERN REGIONAL FOLKLORE.

For Further Reading:

Cohen, Hennig, and Tristram Potter Coffin, eds. *The Folklore of American Holidays.* Detroit: Gale, 1987.

Gaudet, Marcia G., and James C. McDonald, eds. *Mardi Gras, Gumbo, and Zydeco: Readings in Louisiana Culture.* Jackson: University Press of Mississippi, 2003.

Gulevich, Tanya. *Encyclopedia of Easter, Carnival, and Lent.* Detroit: Omnigraphics, 2002.

Kinser, Sam. *Carnival American Style: Mardi Gras at New Orleans and Mobile.* Chicago: University of Chicago Press, 1990.

Myers, Robert J. *Celebrations: The Complete Book of American Holidays.* Garden City, N.Y.: Doubleday, 1972.

Santino, Jack. *All around the Year: Holidays and Celebrations in American Life.* Urbana: University of Illinois Press, 1994.

maritime folklore Maritime lore is a long-standing tradition within American occupational folklore.

In many respects, American maritime folklore resembles such lore elsewhere. For example, there is the seafarer's ubiquitous reliance upon weather, hence weather lore. This set of beliefs includes ideas about portents and the predictive significance of the appearance of the sky, the Sun, the Moon, the water, or the waves. There are also the luck customs of christening a vessel before its maiden voyage and avoiding practices such as whistling while at sea.

Americans working the waterways also have some of their own legends, songs such as chanteys, hazing rituals, lingo, superstitions, stories, and disaster lore. America even has its mythic sea creatures, such as Lake Champlain's Chessie, a home-grown version of Scotland's Loch Ness monster.

After seagoing vessels no longer traveled under sail, the allure of maritime life subsided somewhat. Today's generation is most likely to encounter maritime folklore only in the context of living history museums or aboard docked ships that have become tourist sites. Among the nation's showcases for this purpose is the Mystic Seaport and Preservation Shipyard, located in Mystic, Connecticut.

Also the site of the Museum of America and the Sea, Mystic Seaport functions as a living history environment for the study of maritime lore. As do its living history counterparts, Colonial Willamsburg and Plimoth Plantation, Mystic Seaport attempts to provide visitors with a firsthand experience of another era in America's history. With a reconstruction of a 19th-century village, tourists and schoolchildren can enter the era of wooden shipbuilding. Assisting in this process are "role players," or staff members charged with first-person dramatization of life within the historic community.

With folklore-inspired works of American literature such as Herman Melville's *Moby-Dick* and Samuel Langhorne Clemens's *Huckleberry Finn* and legendary figures such as Mike Fink and Annie Christmas, water lore has remained an important aspect of American folktale traditions.

From traditions of music and the prediction of weather to the folk museums and folk heroes associated with the seas, America's maritime workers are considered to be part of a celebrated occupation with its own folklore, whether it be about Captain Kidd or Captain Ahab.

See also: BOLES, CHARLES E. (BLACK BART); KIDD, CAPTAIN WILLIAM; CHRISTMAS, ANNIE; CLEMENS, SAMUEL LANGHORNE; COOPER, JAMES FENIMORE; FINK, MIKE; LIVING HISTORY MUSEUMS; MELVILLE, HERMAN; MUSEUMS, FOLK; MYSTIC SEAPORT AND PRESERVATION SHIPYARD; NORTHEASTERN REGIONAL FOLKLORE; OCCUPATIONAL FOLKLORE; SMITH, WINDWAGON; STORMALONG, OLD.

For Further Reading:

Bartis, Peter. *Maritime Folklore Resources: A Directory and Index*. Washington, D.C.: American Folklife Center/Library of Congress, 1980.

Bassett, Fletcher. *Sea Phantoms; or, Legends and Superstitions of the Sea and of Sailors*. Chicago: Morrill Higgins and Co., 1892.

Beck, Horace. *Folklore and the Sea*. Middletown, Conn.: Wesleyan University Press, 1973.

Botkin, Benjamin, ed. *A Treasury of Mississippi River Folklore: Stories, Ballads, and Folkways of the Mid-American River Country*. New York: Crown, 1955.

Colcord, Joanna. *Sea Language Comes Ashore*. New York: Arno Press, 1977.

———. *Songs of American Sailormen*. New York: W. W. Norton, 1938.

Doerflinger, William Main. *Songs of the Sailor and Lumberman*. Glenwood, Ill.: Meyerbooks, 1990.

Hugill, Stan. *Shanties from the Seven Seas: Shipboard Work-Songs and Songs Used as Work-Songs from the Great Days of Sail*. New York: Dutton, 1984.

Jeans, Peter. *Seafaring Lore and Legend: A Miscellany of Maritime Myth, Superstition, Fable, and Fact*. Camden, N.J.: International Marine/McGraw-Hill, 2004.

Taylor, David. *Documenting Maritime Folklife: An Introductory Guide*. Washington, D.C.: Library of Congress, 1992.

marriage See WEDDING/MARRIAGE FOLKLORE.

Marshall, Paule See AFRICAN-AMERICAN FOLKLORE; HURSTON, ZORA NEALE; IBO LANDING; JOHNSON, JAMES WELDON; PROVERBS.

Martin Luther King Day Dedicated as a day of remembrance in honor of a distinguished leader in the Civil Rights movement, Martin Luther King Day is held annually on a selected Monday in January.

In the period following King's April 4, 1968, assassination in Memphis, Tennessee, many Americans wished to find a way to pay homage to the role he had played in the civil rights struggle and, more generally, as a proponent of nonviolent protest. For these noteworthy efforts, Dr. King received international acclaim with the 1964 Nobel Peace Prize. Efforts to create a King holiday began. In addition to renaming schools and streets in cities and towns throughout the nation, proponents of this annual observance sought to establish a national occasion for reflection.

During the immediate grief of King's loss, some Americans chose to mark King's birthday, while others felt the need to mark the date of his violent death. Over time, however, the birthday observances prevailed in most tributes. Initial observances of the King holiday were held on Martin Luther King's birthday, January 15. As a result of legislation that shifted numerous American holidays to Mondays in order to establish three-day weekends, the celebration of King's life and work is now observed nationally on a Monday during the month of January.

In keeping with the serious focus of the occasion, Martin Luther King Day typically includes memorials, speeches, plays, concerts, and other activities. As new generations join in the observance, the project increasingly involves educating youth about King's life and career. For this purpose, documentaries, spoken word recording, and other resources are featured within school- and community-based learning units. In recent years, a new custom has emerged, as those wishing to honor King's contributions to community elect to conduct volunteer work and service projects on or near this day.

Although establishment of the King holiday proved controversial and, to some extent, remains so for those who do not share the man's convictions, it is testament to King's importance to historical memory that he is the only African American so recognized nationally, and one of very few individuals honored by name within American holidays who have not held the office of the U.S. president. King's principled dissent, however, resonates with the nation's tradition and ideal of resisting tyranny and inequality.

See also: AFRICAN-AMERICAN FOLKLORE; CIVIL RIGHTS MOVEMENT; FESTIVALS, FOLKLORE; HOLIDAYS/OBSERVANCES; PARKS, ROSA; POLITICS AND FOLKLORE; PRISON FOLKLORE, PROTEST FOLKLORE.

For Further Reading:

Anyike, James. *African American Holidays: A Historical Research and Reference Guide to Cultural Celebrations.* Chicago: Popular Truth, 1991.

Cohen, Hennig, and Tristram Potter Coffin, eds. *The Folklore of American Holidays.* Detroit: Gale, 1987.

King, David C. *First Facts about American Heroes.* Woodbridge, Conn.: Blackbirch Press, 1996.

Myers, Robert. *Celebrations: The Complete Book of American Holidays.* Garden City, N.Y.: Doubleday, 1972.

Santino, Jack. *All around the Year: Holidays and Celebrations in American Life.* Urbana: University of Illinois Press, 1994.

Maryland folklore See APPALACHIAN FOLKLORE; DOUGLASS, FREDERICK; NORTHEASTERN REGIONAL FOLKLORE; TUBMAN, HARRIET.

Massachusetts folklore See ANTHONY, SUSAN BROWNELL; ATTUCKS, CRISPUS; BARTON, CLARA; BORDEN, LIZZIE; CHAPMAN, JOHN (JOHNNY APPLESEED); NORTHEASTERN REGIONAL FOLKLORE; PATRIOTS' DAY; REVERE'S RIDE, PAUL; REVOLUTIONARY WAR; STORMALONG, OLD; STURBRIDGE VILLAGE, OLD.

Massacre, Boston See ATTUCKS, CRISPUS.

material culture The term *material culture* refers to all human alterations to the natural environment.

The study of material culture, conducted by scholars including folklorists, seeks to know and understand a culture through its physical world. Consequently, such research involves everything from tools, furniture, and toys, to buildings, gardens, and household devices. Folklorists find in material culture a tangible record of the lives of ordinary Americans. By studying these traces and carefully interpreting their meanings, folklorists gain insights into the daily practices of the American past.

Therefore, while a specialist in material culture might pay attention to some of the same objects that might interest museum curators and private collectors, such a scholar would not be concerned with connoisseurship or provenance. Rather, material culture research looks for history in things, making their current market price or rarity irrelevant. Instead, material culture studies permit folklorists to see the daily texture of a way of life otherwise obscured by cultural distance, temporal remoteness, or both. For such researchers, a quilt represents more than a way to keep warm in winter. It is a medium of artistic expression for quilters. Quilting is a social act, involving communal processes such as quilting bees. The designs on quilts are not merely decorative. They are also culture bearers, encoding traditional motifs in design and values in family life. Since many quilts are linked to rites of passage, such as the birth of a baby or a marriage, quilts often convey attitudes about those experiences and relationships. Story quilts, often stitched with memorable bits of fabric or depicting key moments within a family's or culture's life, record and recount whole generational sagas.

Within the study of American material culture, then, artifacts are treated as cultural evidence rather than as art objects. A society's goods and products may be examined as clues to the nation's history as seen through its social life and customs. An expert on gravestones might determine when and why a trend toward winged death's heads or cherubs as decorative motifs in monument design subsides. A specialist in gender might explore how and when the marketing of action figures made it possible for more American boys to play with dolls, traditionally toys associated with girls. A student of the built environment might ask how it is that lawn ornaments became a popular form of domestic adornment. Someone interested in distinctive musical instruments might inquire into the history of the dulcimer. Whatever the category or vintage of object(s) examined, material culture invites scholars to take the props of everyday life seriously, finding in their construction, use, and display clues regarding what members of that cultural group considered necessary, true, and desirable.

As part of the movement toward an emphasis on folklife, material culture is a growing field within the study of folk culture.

See also: AGEE, JAMES; ARCHITECTURE, FOLK; ART, FOLK; ARTS AND CRAFTS MOVEMENT; CHILDBIRTH/PREGNANCY FOLKLORE; COLONIAL WILLIAMSBURG; CRAFTS, FOLK; FAMILY FOLKLORE; FAMILY PHOTOGRAPHY; FOLKLIFE; FOLKLIFE MOVEMENT; FOLKLORE IN EVERYDAY LIFE; HISTORIC PRESERVATION; HISTORY, FOLK; KITSCH; LIVING HISTORY MUSEUMS; MUSEUMS, FOLK; QUILT, AIDS; RITES OF PASSAGE; VERNACULAR CULTURE; WEDDING/MARRIAGE FOLKLORE.

For Further Reading:

Bronner, Simon. *American Material Culture and Folklife.* Logan: Utah State University Press, 1985.

Glassie, Henry. *Material Culture.* Bloomington: Indiana University Press, 1999.

Kingery, W. David., ed. *Learning from Things: Method and Theory of Material Culture Studies.* Washington, D.C.: Smithsonian, 1996.

Martin, Ann Smart, and J. Ritchie Garrison, eds. *American Material Culture: The Shape of the Field.* Knoxville: University of Tennessee Press, 1997.

Mayo, Edith. *American Material Culture: The Shape of Things around Us.* Bowling Green, Ohio: Bowling Green State University Popular Press, 1984.

Quimby, Ian. *Material Culture and the Study of American Life.* New York: W. W. Norton, 1978.

Schlereth, Thomas. *Material Culture: A Research Guide.* Lawrence: University Press of Kansas, 1985.

May Day This holiday, held on May 1 each year, dates from prehistoric rites of the new year's arrival, before the Roman calendar made January 1 the first day of the year.

While not a legal holiday, May Day is nonetheless observed through numerous folk customs. The iconic practice involves the maypole, a European tradition of a staff placed into the earth and used in the celebration. In traditional ceremonies, youth, especially girls, dance around the maypole, often while twining colored streamers or ribbons around it in the process. The tree from which the maypole is made is another symbol of the day, with its suggestions of fertility in keeping with the atmosphere for this spring festival.

Signaling as it does the arrival of spring's renewal, May Day inspires a variety of folk beliefs and practices. Over the years, this holiday has come to be known as a day of portents, particularly for females as they come of age. Any number of beliefs surround the day's power to reveal to such young women the identity of their future mate. Among children, May Day is celebrated with the fashioning of May baskets. Once filled with candy, flowers, and other treats, such baskets are left anonymously at the doors of friends and loved ones.

In addition to its long-standing link with spring rites, May Day has two other associations: It has ties to the labor movement in the United States, and in particular, the movement to establish an eight-hour workday. Since President Eisenhower's action in 1958, May 1 has also marked a national observance of Loyalty Day, an occasion to reaffirm allegiance to America.

See also: FESTIVALS, FOLKLORE; HOLIDAYS/OBSERVANCES; RITES OF PASSAGE; RITUALS, FOLK.

For Further Reading:

Aveni, Anthony F. *The Book of the Year: A Brief History of Our Seasonal Holidays.* New York: Oxford University Press, 2004.

Cohen, Hennig, and Tristram Potter Coffin, eds. *The Folklore of American Holidays.* Detroit: Gale, 1987.

Coker, Suzanne Weikert. "Go a-Maying," *Early American Life* 23, no. 3 (June 1992): 12–13.

Myers, Robert. *Celebrations: The Complete Book of American Holidays.* Garden City, N.Y.: Doubleday, 1972.

Santino, Jack. *All around the Year: Holidays and Celebrations in American Life.* Urbana: University of Illinois Press, 1994.

Zuckerman, Michael. "Pilgrims in the Wilderness: Community, Modernity, and the Maypole at Mercy Mount," *New England Quarterly* 50, no. 2 (June 1977): 255–277.

McCarty, William Henry (Billy the Kid, Kid, William H. Bonney) (c. 1859–1881)

As a mythic figure of the American past, Billy the Kid lives on in the nation's crime lore.

Romanticized by memory in the same way many notorious outlaws have been, Billy the Kid has been cast alternately as a historical villain and a folk hero. This mixed reception probably stems from the harsh circumstances of the man's beginnings. The individual known to history by his outlaw names (William H. Bonney, Billy the Kid, or simply Kid) was born William Henry McCarty circa 1859. While still an adolescent, Billy the Kid lost his mother. Because his father had died or disappeared years before, McCarty as an orphan lived in several foster homes. He emerged from these experiences and entered a criminal world that would make him famous, but for all the wrong reasons.

Although hardly fierce in his profile, indeed young and slight of build, Billy the Kid became a gunslinger of considerable reputation. According to lore, he killed 21 men in total, one for each of the years he lived. Stories cast him as a thrill killer, striking at random targets. Whether these tales are true or not, Billy the Kid never outlived his youthful appearance or moniker. If the circumstances of his birth were murky, those of his death proved all too clear. "Kid" was killed by Sheriff Pat Garrett in Fort Sumner, New Mexico, on July 14, 1881.

Since his demise, Billy the Kid has been the object of wide curiosity. At Fort Sumner's Billy the Kid Museum, for example, one can view vintage Americana and slip into the gift shop to purchase reproductions of the outlaw's wanted poster or postcards bearing photographs of his gravestone. Many ballads have been written about "Kid," including recent ones recorded by the popular artists Jon Bon Jovi ("Blaze of

Glory") and Billy Joel ("Ballad of Billy the Kid").
He was also the subject of a 1938 musical ballet
(*Billy the Kid*) by one of America's most distinguished composers, Aaron Copland, known for
incorporating folk motifs into his work.

Perhaps it is unsurprising that someone who
lived so boldly and died so young would capture
the popular imagination. In any case, "Billy the
Kid" takes his place in the pantheon of America's
fraternity of frontier outlaws.

See also: FOLK HEROES/LEGENDARY FIGURES;
FRONTIER; MUSIC, FOLK; MUSEUMS, FOLK; OUT-
LAWS; REGION, FOLK; SOUTHWESTERN REGIONAL
FOLKLORE.

For Further Reading:

Burns, Walter Noble. *The Saga of Billy the Kid*.
    Albuquerque: University of New Mexico Press,
    1999.
Nolan, Frederick. *The West of Billy the Kid*. Nor-
    man: University of Oklahoma Press, 1998.
Otero, Miguel Antonio, Jr. *The Real Billy the Kid*.
    Houston: Arte Público Press, 1998.
Siringo, Charles A. *History of "Billy the Kid."* Albu-
    querque: University of New Mexico Press,
    2000.
Tatum, Stephen. *Inventing Billy the Kid: Visions
    of the Outlaw in America, 1881–1981*. Tucson:
    University of Arizona Press, 1997.
Tuska, Jon. *Billy the Kid, His Life and Legend*. West-
    port, Conn.: Greenwood Press, 1994.

medical folklore   See MEDICINE, FOLK.

medicine, folk   Folk medicine involves all the
folk beliefs and practices relating to health, illness, injury, and healing. These systems of belief
vary widely across cultural and ethnic groups,
depending upon traditions of care specific to
those populations.

When a person has a minor or routine
health problem, the first approach may be to
turn to folk wisdom for results. Sayings these
as "Feed a cold; starve a fever" reflect these
practices. Although such advice might appear to

be merely common sense, the specific measures
taken—drinking fluids for a head cold, gargling
for a sore throat, and the like—have their origins
in folk wisdom.

Another common aspect of folk medicine are
home remedies, those informal treatments of specific health conditions used within households and
families. These cures and palliatives are typically
passed down from parent to child, and from one
generation to the next, through demonstration
rather than formal instruction. Tonics, medicinal teas, aloe vera gel, mustard plasters, or other
ingredients may be advised when a loved one
suffers symptoms of illness. When these home
treatments fail to resolve the problem, the affected
individual may look further for assistance.

Usually, this help is sought from a healer or
other practitioner, according to the individual's
cultural beliefs about wellness. For instance, a
root worker, herbalist, conjurer, shaman, medicine man or woman, or hoodoo priest or priestess may be consulted for this purpose. Such
figures are entrusted with examination, diagnosis, and treatment of ailments, although their
practices may or may not prove consistent with
modern medical science. Dancing, herbs, prayer,
massages, or other therapeutic techniques may
be employed as means to restore the individual's
health. Most alternative health care providers
who work outside the framework of Western
medicine may be regarded as practicing folk
medicine. If treatments of a folk healer do not
avail, then the services of a conventional medical
doctor may be engaged.

Folk illnesses are all those maladies whose
nature and origin are unaccounted for by Western medicine. While the patient's community
might have lore about the ailment, its source,
and the method for its resolution, the American
Medical Association would not recognize it as a
medical condition to be treated.

Folklorists take such an interest in the nuance
and persistence of folk medicine that the University of California at Los Angeles (UCLA) even
maintains a database in which healing methods
may be searched by ailment or ingredient.

See also: AGING AND FOLKLORE; BELIEFS, FOLK; BODYLORE; CHILDBIRTH/PREGNANCY FOLKLORE; CONJURE/CONJURING; DEATH; FAMILY FOLKLORE; FOLKLORE IN EVERYDAY LIFE; GARDENING; MAGIC; RELIGION, FOLK; VOODOO/HOODOO.

For Further Reading:

Baer, Hans. *Biomedicine and Alternate Healing Systems in America: Issues of Class, Race, Ethnicity, and Gender.* Madison: University of Wisconsin Press, 2001.

Bergner, P., and Hufford, D. *Folk Remedies: Healing Wisdom.* Lincolnwood, Ill.: Publications International, 1998.

Gaines, Atwood, ed. *Ethnopsychiatry: The Cultural Construction of Professional and Folk Psychiatries.* Albany, N.Y.: SUNY Press, 1992.

Hand, Wayland, ed. *American Folk Medicine: A Symposium.* Berkeley: University of California Press, 1976.

Hand, Wayland. *Magical Medicine: The Folkloric Component of Medicine in the Folk Belief, Custom, and Ritual of the Peoples of Europe and America.* Berkeley: University of California Press, 1980.

Helman, C. *Culture, Health and Illness.* Oxford: Butterworth-Heineman, 1990.

Huson, Paul. *Mastering Herbalism: A Practical Guide.* New York: Stein & Day, 1974.

Janos, Elizabeth. *Country Folk Medicine.* New York: Galahad Books, 1995.

Kinsley, D. *Health, Healing and Religion: A Cross-Cultural Perspective.* Englewood Cliffs, N.J.: Prentice-Hall, 1996.

O'Connor, Bonnie Blair. *Healing Traditions: Alternative Medicine and the Health Professions.* Philadelphia: University of Pennsylvania Press, 1995.

Rinzler, Carol Ann. *The Dictionary of Medical Folklore.* New York: Crowell, 1979.

Scarborough, John, ed. *Folklore and Folk Medicines.* Madison, Wis.: American Institute of the History of Pharmacy, 1987.

Steiner, Richard, ed. *Folk Medicine: The Art and the Science.* Washington, D.C.: American Chemical Society, 1986.

Weyler, Lena, ed. *Home Remedies: A Handbook of Herbal Cures for Common Ailments.* New York: Penguin Books, 1998.

Melville, Herman (1819–1891)

Probably best remembered for his epic novel *Moby-Dick, or The Whale* (1851), Herman Melville was a 19th-century American writer of literary work that both drew resource material from and at times itself emulated folklore.

Melville was born Herman Melvill on August 1, 1819, in New York City. Both of his grandfathers had achieved distinction in the events surrounding and during the American Revolution. Family finances made Melville's formal education somewhat patchy, but he was a voracious reader and learned a great deal on his own. He was greatly influenced by such writers as Washington Irving.

Melville ultimately completed a course in engineering and surveying but found jobs in other pursuits. Melville's employment history included time with the merchant service, the navy, and the whaling trade. These travels and seafaring experiences helped develop his interest in maritime lore. This concern would be manifested in several of Melville's literary works, such as *Moby-Dick*.

Considered by some to be the quintessential American novel, *Moby-Dick* tells the story of the heroic Captain Ahab in his quest to capture a great white whale. This tale of adventure was initially poorly received but has since found greater favor with audiences. He dedicated the epic to his good friend and colleague Nathaniel Hawthorne. Melville's works included a wide range of literature, from tales of the sea to psychologically rich short stories. His book-length published works include *Pierre; or, The Ambiguities* (1852), *The Confidence-Man: His Masquerade* (1857), *Battle-Pieces and Aspects of the War* (1866), and *Billy Budd, and Other Prose Pieces* (1924). Melville was also an accomplished writer of short stories. Perhaps the most famous of these are "Bartleby the Scrivener: A Story of Wall Street" (1853) and "Benito Cereno" (1855). Melville also wrote poetry, particularly during the latter years of his career; he is better known for his achievements in fiction.

Melville helped provide the iconic figures of the American literary imagination: the sea captain, the con man, and the embattled clerk or laborer. Melville died on September 28, 1891. As one of the writers most closely associated with the literary movement described as the American Renaissance, Herman Melville published works that provide insight into American culture and lore.

See also: CIVIL WAR; FOLKLORE IN AMERICAN LITERATURE; HAWTHORNE, NATHANIEL; IRVING, WASHINGTON; MARITIME FOLKLORE; OCCUPATIONAL FOLKLORE; REVOLUTIONARY WAR; YANKEE PEDDLER.

For Further Reading:

Dimock, Wai-chee. *Empire for Liberty: Melville and the Poetics of Individualism.* Princeton, N.J.: Princeton University Press, 1989.

Garner, Stanton. *The Civil War World of Herman Melville.* Lawrence: University Press of Kansas, 1993.

Hayes, Kevin J. *Melville's Folk Roots.* Kent, Ohio: Kent State University Press, 1999.

Higgins, Brian, and Hershel Parker, eds. *Herman Melville: The Contemporary Reviews.* New York: Cambridge University Press, 1995.

Robertson-Lorant, Laurie. *Melville, a Biography.* New York: Clarkson N. Potter, 1996.

Wenke, John. *Melville's Muse: Literary Creation and the Forms of Philosophical Fiction.* Kent, Ohio: Kent State University Press, 1995.

Memorial Day   As its name suggests, Memorial Day is a holiday of remembrance, particularly with respect to those who died in military service for their country.

This observance has been held since 1866, and while it was once fixed on May 30 each year, it has since changed to the last Monday in May.

Memorial Day had its origins in the era's deep grief over Civil War deaths. Henry C. Welles, a Waterloo, New York, pharmacist, made the suggestion that these graves be adorned annually with flower tributes. New York was the first to formalize the practice at the state level in 1873. Memorial Day has since been identified as a national day of remembrance for all men and women lost in service.

Customs associated with Memorial Day are accordingly patriotic ones. Parades, ceremonies, and reenactments at Civil War sites are usual. Each year, the U.S. president participates in a solemn recognition held at Arlington National Cemetery, a national burial site in Washington, D.C., dedicated to those who served the nation in the armed forces. At the local level, ceremonies honor the dead and flags or flowers decorate their resting places. Memorial Day is often linked in the popular mind with other patriotic celebrations, such as Veterans Day, Independence Day/Fourth of July, and Pearl Harbor (Remembrance) Day. On a less somber note, Memorial Day's placement within the calendar year also causes its association with the opening of the summer season, just as Labor Day is understood to mark the close of summer and, with it, children's commencement of a new school year.

See also: BURIAL CUSTOMS; CEMETERY FOLKLORE; CIVIL WAR; DEATH; FLOWERS; HOLIDAYS/ OBSERVANCES; INDEPENDENCE DAY/FOURTH OF JULY; LABOR DAY; PEARL HARBOR (REMEMBRANCE) DAY; VETERANS DAY.

For Further Reading:

Bodnar, John. *Remaking America: Public Memory, Commemoration, and Patriotism in the Twentieth Century.* Princeton, N.J.: Princeton University Press, 1992.

Cohen, Hennig, and Tristram Potter Coffin, eds. *The Folklore of American Holidays.* Detroit: Gale, 1987.

Myers, Robert. *Celebrations: The Complete Book of American Holidays.* Garden City, N.Y.: Doubleday, 1972.

Santino, Jack. *All around the Year: Holidays and Celebrations in American Life.* Urbana: University of
Illinois Press, 1994.

Shackle, Paul, ed. *Myth, Memory, and the Making of
the American Landscape.* Gainesville: University
Press of Florida, 2001.

memorial folklore See BURIAL CUSTOMS;
CEMETERY FOLKLORE; DEATH; MEMORIAL DAY.

mermaids Folk narratives have long portrayed mermaids as the embodiment of the
idea of temptation. Similarly to other mythical creatures such as the centaur, mermaids
represent a combination of life-forms. They
are part human and part aquatic creature, an
improbable mixture. For this reason, the mermaid cannot be fully at home on land or in the
water and seems doomed to be an outsider in
both worlds. As the name suggests, the mermaid is generally a female character. Mermen
do appear within folklore but are relatively
uncommon in American lore. They are also
said to be much less visually appealing than
mermaids.

Most folk narratives concerning mermaids
involve contact between a mermaid and her
human counterparts. Often, these are maritime
tales in which seafarers happen upon the creature in the course of their travels. The sight of
a mermaid is said to be striking, because of her
unusual, distinctive beauty and enchanting song.
Mermaids are reputed sirens, possessing such an
alluring call that they can lead otherwise resilient men astray.

It may be for this reason that a mermaid
sighting is frequently regarded as a portent of
imminent danger. The mermaid's influence is
not always unfortunate, however, and in some
cases she holds the power and disposition to
grant the sailor wishes. In fact, some folktales portray genuine and enduring connections
established between mermaids and humans. One
such example is the familiar Hans Christian
Andersen text "The Little Mermaid."

Anderson's narrative proceeds from the
premise that mermaids do not have immortal
souls. The mermaid in his tale, however, yearns
for a soul, and her conduct pivots around this
desire. Her dilemma occurs when she is forced
to choose between the human she loves and her
own ability to return to the sea.

As mythical beings, mermaids intrigue sailors
and other humans who encounter them. They
also capture the fancy of audience members,
who wish to learn more about these unusual
creatures.

See also: ANDERSEN, HANS CHRISTIAN; ANI-
MALS; CHANGELINGS; CHILDREN'S FOLKLORE;
FABLES; FAIRY TALES; MARITIME FOLKLORE; "MER-
MAID, THE LITTLE"; MONSTERS; MYTHS, FOLK;
OCCUPATIONAL FOLKLORE; SUPERNATURAL.

For Further Reading:

Bell, Elizabeth, Lynda Haas, and Laura Sells, eds.
*From Mouse to Mermaid: The Politics of Film,
Gender, and Culture.* Bloomington: Indiana
University Press, 1995.

Bettelheim, Bruno. *The Uses of Enchantment: The
Meaning and Importance of Fairy Tales.* New
York: Knopf, 1976.

Bredsdorff, Elias. *Hans Christian Andersen: An
Introduction to His Life and Works.* Copenhagen:
Hans Reitzels Forlag, 1987.

Wyman, Walker. *Mythical Creatures of the U.S.A.
and Canada.* River Falls: University of Wisconsin, River Falls Press, 1978.

"Mermaid, The Little" "The Little Mermaid" relates the poignant story of an impossible
romance between a creature of the sea and a
creature of the land.

In folklore, the mermaid has long embodied
the idea of temptation. Their hybrid form, part
fish and part human, fates them for crises of
identity and sorrows in relationships. Mermaids
are reputed sirens, possessing such an alluring
call that they can lead otherwise resilient men
astray. In Hans Christian Andersen's "The Little Mermaid," this power is put to the test.

The tale begins with a mermaid who, having discerned that only creatures with immortal souls are eligible to enter the afterlife, determines to achieve that end. Her initial plan involves becoming human and securing the affections of a prince, all with the thought that these measures would confer on her the divine blessing of a soul. Ultimately, this plan does not succeed.

The crestfallen mermaid then faces an intractable dilemma. Within the terms of this fictional world, her only means to return to her home in the sea calls for her to kill the prince. When her feelings for him prevent her from taking this action, the mermaid receives what she has desired all along, a soul that will ensure her immortality.

The message of sacrifice and loving others before oneself is fairly straightforward. If the plot seems familiar, it may be because Disney has produced two feature-length films adapted from this fairy tale: the animated *The Little Mermaid* (1989) and the live-action *Splash* (1984). Both recount versions of the classic fish-out-of-water story.

For centuries, audiences fond of unlikely romances have embraced retellings of this tale of a mermaid who starts out looking for a soul, and in the process finds her heart.

See also: Andersen, Hans Christian; children's folklore; "Emperor's New Clothes, The"; fables; fairy tales; mermaids; myths, folk; "Princess and the Pea, The"; "Ugly Duckling, The."

For Further Reading:

Ayres, Brenda, ed. *The Emperor's Old Groove: Decolonizing Disney's Magic Kingdom*. New York: Lang, 2003.

Bell, Elizabeth, Lynda Haas, and Laura Sells, eds. *From Mouse to Mermaid: The Politics of Film, Gender, and Culture*. Bloomington: Indiana University Press, 1995.

Sugarman, Sally. "Whose Woods Are These Anyhow? Children, Fairy Tales, and the Media." In *The Antic Art: Enhancing Children's Literary Experiences through Film and Video*, edited by Lucy Rollin, 141–151. Fort Atkinson, Wis.: Highsmith, 1993.

Wullschlager, Jackie. *Hans Christian Andersen: The Life of a Storyteller*. Chicago: University of Chicago Press, 2002.

Zipes, Jack. *Fairy Tales and the Art of Subversion: The Classical Genre for Children and the Process of Civilization*. New York: Wildman Press, 1983.

Mexican-American folklore See Chicano folklore.

Mexican War See Carson, Kit. (Christopher Houston Carson).

Michigan folklore See Greenfield Village and Henry Ford Museum; Lindbergh, Charles.

Midas, King (legendary) King Midas, a character in Greek and Roman mythology, has been an influence on figures appearing within American folklore.

Midas was king of Phyrgia during the eighth century. While there are several myths surrounding Midas, one resonates most with contemporary American narratives. Within this myth, it seems that Silenus, a teacher and father figure of sorts to Dionysus, has been drinking and becomes lost in his wanderings. When peasants find Silenus, they take him to King Midas. After spending some time to enjoy the man's stories, Midas returns Silenus to Dionysus. Out of gratitude for the mentor's safe return, Dionysus offers to grant Midas a wish. The king, greedy to a fault, decides that he would like to possess the ability to transform anything he touches into gold. Although Dionysus does not regard this as a wise use of the opportunity, after verifying that it is in fact still the king's wish, he makes it come true.

King Midas then discovers that his wish has been fulfilled, but with some surprising results. That is, he can turn objects to gold whenever he wishes, but he cannot do otherwise. When he tries to eat, he is thwarted as the food turns to gold. The same happens when he seeks to quench his thirst. Even the people he loves are susceptible to this transforming touch, and before realizing the consequences, Midas unthinkingly touches his daughter and turns her to gold.

Needless to say, Midas returns to Dionysus seeking a remedy. He is then permitted to wash away his golden touch in Pactolus River, a process that deposits gold throughout the riverbed and restores Midas to his original state.

This myth of the Midas touch is recalled in many subsequent narratives, including "Rumplestiltskin" and "The Golden Goose." In American culture, its echoes also can be heard in folk speech, such as the saying "Be careful what you wish for; you just might get it!"

The myth of King Midas and his golden touch warns against greed and thoughtlessness, and continues to provide an apt message as it appears in modified form in contemporary American folk speech and folk narratives, from sayings to tales of the gold rush.

See also: CHILDREN'S FOLKLORE; FABLES; FAIRY TALES; "GOLDEN GOOSE, THE"; GOLD RUSH, THE; MYTHS, FOLK; "RUMPLESTILTSKIN."

For Further Reading:

Banks, Lynne. *The Adventures of King Midas*. London: Bell and Hyman, 1958.

Craft, Charlotte. *King Midas and the Golden Touch*. New York: Morrow, 1999.

Green, Roger. *Old Greek Fairy Tales*. London: Bell and Hyman, 1958.

Midwestern regional folklore Sometimes referred to as America's heartland, the inland states of the Midwest represent an important folk region.

Since its inception, the study of American folklore has emphasized the concept of folk regions in the United States. Despite the claim that we now have an entirely global culture, local and regional variations continue to exist, and these are important objects of study for folklorists. In the United States, these regions are typically conceived of as clusters of nearby states with commonalities, such as populations, practices, or other attributes.

Although the American Midwest can be described and delimited in various ways, the Midwest as a folk region can generally be defined as including folklore of or relating to the states of Illinois, Indiana, Iowa, Kansas, Michigan, Minnesota, Missouri, Nebraska, Ohio, and Wisconsin.

As a region, the Midwest has its share of folk heroes and legendary figures. Examples include Paul Bunyan, Mike Fink, Johnny Appleseed, Hiawatha, and Wild Bill Hickok. In addition, numerous writers are associated with the Midwest, either personally or through the topics and settings of their work. These include Paul Laurence Dunbar, Carl Sandburg, Samuel Langhorne Clemens, and James Mercer Langston Hughes.

See also: BUNYAN, PAUL; CHAPMAN, JOHN (JOHNNY APPLESEED); CLEMENS, SAMUEL LANGHORNE; DUNBAR, PAUL LAURENCE; FINK, MIKE; HIAWATHA; HICKOK, JAMES BUTLER (WILD BILL); HUGHES, JAMES MERCER LANGSTON; SANDBURG, CARL.

For Further Reading:

Allen, Barbara, and Thomas J. Schlereth, eds. *Sense of Place: American Regional Cultures*. Lexington: University Press of Kentucky, 1990.

Dorson, Richard. *Bloodstoppers and Bearwalkers*. Cambridge, Mass.: Harvard University Press, 1952.

Dorson, Richard M., ed. *Buying the Wind: Regional Folklore in the United States*. Chicago: University of Chicago Press, 1964.

Koch, William. *Folklsong, Folklore, Folklife and Some History*. Manhattan: Kansas State University Press, 1985.

midwifery See CHILDBIRTH/PREGNANCY FOLKLORE; JERSEY DEVIL.

military folklore See CIVIL WAR; REVOLUTIONARY WAR; VIETNAM WAR; WORLD WAR I; WORLD WAR II.

Minnesota folklore See BABE THE BLUE OX; BUNYAN, PAUL; CLARK, ARIZONA DONNIE (MA BARKER); MIDWESTERN REGIONAL FOLKLORE.

minstrelsy Perhaps the most controversial form of folk drama or performance is minstrelsy, a genre that peaked in popularity in the United States during the period from 1850 to 1870.

In this genre of entertainment, companies of performers offered audiences caricatures of slavery. Often, these actors appeared wearing blackface, a technique in which performers' faces were covered with black greasepaint to achieve an exaggerated characterization of African Americans. Even black troupes engaged in minstrelsy often used blackface, a distinctive feature of the medium. Once on stage, minstrel shows featured jokes, dances, and songs. It is said that the popular slave dance called the cakewalk, itself a parody of elite Anglo-American culture, became known to white audiences as a direct result of minstrelsy.

For the most part, minstrel shows receded as a mass entertainment during the 20th century. While a few individual performers seeking to be comedic or provocative in recent times have attempted to reintroduce blackface on stage, such efforts have been largely unsuccessful because of changing social and political sensibilities.

With their caricatures of slavery and African-American life, minstrel shows emerged as a popular entertainment that would give audiences pleasure or offense, depending upon their perspectives on theater that took such a highly charged approach to a sensitive subject: race.

See also: AFRICAN-AMERICAN FOLKLORE; DRAMA, FOLK; FOLKLORE IN EVERYDAY LIFE; HUMOR, FOLK.

For Further Reading:

Cockrell, Dale. *Demons of Disorder: Early Blackface Minstrels and Their World.* New York: Cambridge University Press, 1997.

Lhamon, W. T., Jr. *Raising Cain: Blackface Performance from Jim Crow to Hip Hop.* Cambridge, Mass.: Harvard University Press, 1998.

Lott, Eric. *Love and Theft: Blackface Minstrelsy and the American Working Class.* New York: Oxford University Press, 1993.

Paskman, Dailey. *"Gentlemen, Be Seated!" A Parade of the American Minstrels.* New York: Crown, 1976.

Toll, Robert. *Blacking Up: The Minstrel Show in Nineteenth-Century America.* New York: Oxford University Press, 1974.

Mississippi folklore See FAULKNER, WILLIAM; FINK, MIKE.

Mississippi River See CHRISTMAS, ANNIE; CLEMENS, SAMUEL LANGHORNE; FINK, MIKE; MARITIME FOLKLORE.

Missouri folklore See BROWN, MARGARET TOBIN (UNSINKABLE MOLLY); CARSON, KIT (CHRISTOPHER HOUSTON CARSON); CLARK, ARIZONA DONNIE; (MA BARKER); CLEMENS, SAMUEL LANGHORNE; DISNEY, WALTER ELIAS; FLOYD, CHARLES ARTHUR (PRETTY BOY); HUGHES, JAMES MERCER LANGSTON; JAMES, JESSE; LEWIS, MERIWETHER, AND WILLIAM CLARK; MIDWESTERN REGIONAL FOLKLORE; OZARKS FOLKLORE; STARR, BELLE.

mistletoe See CHRISTMAS.

mojo See CONJURE/CONJURING.

Momaday, Navarre Scott (1934–) Navarre Scott Momaday is a contemporary writer of poetry, fiction, plays, stories, and essays inflected with Native American folklore.

Momaday was born in Lawton, Oklahoma, in 1934. He is of Kiowa, Cherokee, and Anglo descent. Momaday attended Augustus Military Academy and the University of New Mexico, and went on to earn a Ph.D. in literature from Stanford University in 1963. Early in his writing career, Momaday gained the public's attention when his novel *House Made of Dawn* received the Pulitzer Prize in fiction in 1969. Since then, he has been actively producing works of literature across genres, as well as serving on the faculties of such institutions as the University of California at Berkeley, Stanford University, and the University of Arizona at Tucson.

Momaday's volumes of poetry include *Angle of Geese, and Other Poems* (1974) *The Gourd Dancer* (1976), and *In the Presence of the Sun: Stories and Poems, 1961–1991* (1993). Momaday has written autobiographical works such as *The Journey of Tai-me* (1967), *The Way to Rainy Mountain* (1969), and *The Names: A Memoir* (1976). He has also published *House Made of Dawn* (1968), *Colorado: Summer, Fall, Winter, Spring* (1973), *The Colors of Night* (1976), *The Ancient* Child (1989), *In the Presence of the Sun: A Gathering of Shields* (1992), *Circle of Wonder: A Native American Christmas Story* (1993), *The Man Made of Words: Essays, Stories, Passages* (1997), and *In the Bear's House* (1999). His produced plays include *The Indolent Boys* (1994) and *Children of the Sun* (1997). In partnership with Richardson Morse, Momaday also prepared the script for a 1987 film adapation of his novel *House Made of Dawn*. As an academic, Momaday has also published literary criticism, including articles dealing with Native American literature such as "Navajo Place-Names" and "The Native Voice in American Literature." Some of the author's works also include his original artwork.

Throughout his work, Momaday inscribes Native American cultural legacies, including oral traditions, customs, chants, ceremonies, legends, and myths. For example, as the title of *The Journey of Tai-me* suggests, he is specifically concerned with practices surrounding the Sun dance and its use of the *tai-me*, a medicinal and ceremonial object. Other works, such as *House Made of Dawn*, span many generations and hundreds of years. Both thematically and topically, Momaday weaves such aspects of folklore into the fabric of his literary language. For instance, Momaday's short stories include references to the frontier legend of Billy the Kid. He not only references such traditions, but also extends them. In fact, during interviews, the author describes himself as engaged in myth making. In this respect, Momaday likens his overall project as a writer to the similarly ambitious work by William Faulkner to evoke the fullness and complexity of southern culture and folklore. For Momaday, cultural consciousness is a source of both self-understanding and agency, for both individuals and collectives.

Consequently, readers of Momaday's work encounter shamans, medicine women, shape shifters, and other characters of the magico-spiritual realm the author regards as central to his work with myth. As is the case with other contemporary Native American writers working today, such as Paula Gunn Allen and Leslie Marmon Silko, Navarre Scott Momaday recovers, preserves, and celebrates indigenous folklore traditions. He also acquaints a culturally diverse readership with the histories, myths, and worldviews of Native Americans.

See also: ALLEN, PAULA GUNN; FAULKNER, WILLIAM; FOLKLORE IN AMERICAN LITERATURE; McCARTY, WILLIAM HENRY; NATIVE AMERICAN FOLKLORE; SILKO, LESLIE MARMON; SOUTHWESTERN REGIONAL FOLKLORE.

For Further Reading:

Allen, Paula Gunn, ed. *Studies in American Indian Literature: Critical Essays and Course Designs.* New York: MLA, 1983.

Brumble, H. David III. *American Indian Autobiography.* Berkeley: University of California Press, 1988.

Roemer, Kenneth, ed. *Approaches to Teaching Momaday's "The Way to Rainy Mountain."* New York: MLA, 1988.

Scarberry-García, Susan. *Landmarks of Healing: A Study of "House Made of Dawn."* Albuquerque: University of New Mexico Press, 1990.

Schubnell, Matthias, ed. *Conversations with N. Scott Momaday.* Jackson: University of Mississippi Press, 1997.

Schubnell, Matthias. *N. Scott Momaday: The Cultural and Literary Background.* Norman: University of Oklahoma Press, 1985.

Swann, Brian, and Arnold Krupat, eds. *Recovering the Word: Essays on Native American Literature.* Berkeley: University of California Press, 1987.

Velie, Alan. *Four American Indian Literary Masters: N. Scott Momaday, James Welch, Leslie Marmon Silko, and Gerald Vizenor.* Norman: University of Oklahoma Press, 1982,

monsters   Folklore concerning unreal animals or beings, sometimes called monsters, is a popular field of inquiry.

As with other unexplained phenomena, such as crop circles or unidentified flying objects (UFOs), monsters both frighten and excite the popular imagination in America. Within the United States, any number of curious land or water creatures have been sighted and studied. Sea serpents comparable to Scotland's Loch Ness monster include Chesapeake Bay's Chessie and Lake Champlain's Champ or Champy. Examples of other strange creatures spotted in the nation are Dover, Massachusetts's; Dover Demon; Loveland, Ohio Loveland Lizard; and Point Pleasant, West Virginia Mothman. Among the most widely known mysterious beasts associated with regions in the United States are the Jersey devil, Bigfoot/Sasquatch, and Loup-Garou. In addition, Americans trade stories of monsters that are older than the nation itself, including narratives of witches, vampires, werewolves, and ghosts. All of these creatures are commonly associated with Halloween, as well. Americans also maintain and extend story traditions in terms of mythical creatures such as mermaids. Finally, there are monsters such as the "bogey" or "bogeyman," which are a perennial part of American children's folklore. It is said that these stories of an evil creature of indefinite appearance and active by night originated as a ploy by parents, who told their children to behave or the bogeyman would get them.

From cryptozoology, the study of hidden animals, to the spooky creatures perceived to be associated with the night, American narrative traditions feature many monsters.

See also: Bigfoot/Sasquatch; change-lings; children's folklore; devil, the; ghost stories; Halloween/All Hallow's Eve; haunted houses; Jersey devil; Loup-Garou; mermaids; vampires; werewolves;.

For Further Reading:

Blackman, W. Haden. *The Field Guide to North American Monsters: Everything You Need to Know about Encountering over 100 Terrifying Creatures in the Wild.* New York: Three Rivers Press, 1998.

Coleman, Loren. *The Field Guide to Bigfoot, Yeti, and Other Mystery Primates Worldwide.* New York: Avon, 1999.

———. *Mysterious America.* Boston: Paraview Press, 1983.

Eberhart, George M. *Monsters: A Guide to Information on Unaccounted for Creatures, Including Bigfoot, Many Water Monsters, and Other Irregular Animals.* New York: Garland, 1983.

Guiley, Rosemary Ellen. *Atlas of the Mysterious in North America.* New York: Facts On File, 1995.

Heuvelmans, Bernard. *On the Track of Unknown Animals.* Cambridge, Mass.: MIT Press, 1958.

Meurger, Michel, and Claude Gagnon. *Lake Monster Traditions: A Cross-Cultural Analysis.* London: Fortean Tomes, 1988.

Rose, Carol. *Giants, Monsters, and Dragons: An Encyclopedia of Folklore, Legend, and Myth.* Santa Barbara, Calif.: ABC-CLIO, 2000.

Schultz, Ted, ed. *The Fringes of Reason: A Field Guide to New Age Frontiers, Unusual Beliefs, and Eccentric Sciences.* New York: Harmony, 1989.

Sergent, Donnie, Jr., and Jeff Wamsley. *Mothman: The Facts behind the Legend.* Point Pleasant, W.Va.: Mothman Lives, 2002.

Montana folklore See Chinese-American folklore; ghost towns; Joseph, Chief; Lewis, Meriwether, and William Clark; Northwestern regional folklore.

Mormon folklore The Mormons are members of the faith community of the Church of Jesus Christ of Latter-Day Saints.

This religion began with a 19th-century New Yorker, Joseph Smith, Jr., whose revelations formed the basis for American Mormonism. His visions produced a key set of teachings among Mormons, now known as the *Doctrines and Covenants*. The sacred text used by believers in this evangelical faith is *The Book of Mormon*.

Many central narrative of the religion's origins feature the migrations westward during the 19th century, often referred to as the Mormon trek. As leader of the church, Smith directed his followers to travel west and seek converts for the faith. He wished to establish an exemplary community, a "New Zion." They spent some time in Ohio, Illinois, and Missouri, but Smith urged them to continue traveling west. For this reason, the Mormon church has a close assocation with the state of Utah and parts of Idaho, where most of the resulting settlements occurred. Mormonism is not an exclusively American phenomenon, however, and Mormon youth routinely go on missions internationally to share their faith in the service of others.

Non-Mormons often view Mormon practices as paradoxical. On one hand, Mormons are taught to conduct themselves according to scriptures, which include prohibitions of worldly influences such as use of tobacco, alcohol, caffeine, and other substances. They also believe that premarital sexual contact is a sin. On the other hand, Mormons are also known for such practices as plural marriage. In the popular imagination, this combination of restraint and excess seemed a contradiction. For many, the notion of polygamy was more than curious: It was a legal and moral offense. In fact, in 1844 Smith was murdered by a mob who broke into a jail where he was being held. Brigham Young, the man for whom today's Mormon-affiliated Brigham Young University is named, assumed leadership after Smith's death. During his term, the Mormons created their "New Zion" in Salt Lake City, Utah.

Customs such as a "Family Home Evening," a weekly family observance typically conducted on Monday evenings, promote families' spending time together for the purpose of spiritual instruction. Given the emphasis on family and shared worship, genealogy is a popular activity among members of the Church of Latter Day Saints. Many members have made detailed studies of their family history and family tree. This information assists in preserving the Mormon past and unifying the faith community. Even aspects of material culture, such as quilting, may take distinctive forms that strengthen family connections among the Mormons. Temple quilts, with designs that recall the site where a couple were married, are one such memento.

While folklore in use among Mormons may not be altogether different from that of other populations, its purpose is more explicitly to reinforce spiritual beliefs and bonds, for example, Mormon verbal lore features tales regarding the founder Joseph Smith, conversion narratives, Mormon trek survival stories, and anecdotes about triumph over religious intolerance. These narratives provide spiritual instruction as well as motivation. Folk stories and folktales are an important part of Mormon culture, especially in the context of spiritual instruction for children or converts. One set of stories concern a church elder named J. Golden Kimball. With his charmingly unsophisticated ways, Kimball functions as a kind of folk hero within this context.

Although the separateness of Mormon culture has sometimes resulted in stigma and religious persecution, Mormonism's steadfast devotion to the faith's teachings, as expressed through its folklore, has made it resilient to such external judgments.

See also: CULTURAL GROUPS; PARKER, ROBERT LEROY (BUTCH CASSIDY); REGION, FOLK; RELIGION, FOLK; WESTERN REGIONAL FOLKLORE.

For Further Reading:

Cheney, Thomas Edward, ed. *Mormon Songs from the Rocky Mountains: A Compilation of Mormon Folksong.* Austin: University of Texas Press, 1968.

Fife, Austin, and Alta Fife. *Saints of Sage and Saddle: Folklore among the Mormons.* Bloomington: Indiana University Press, 1956.

Graham, Joe Stanley. *The Dream Mine: A Study in Mormon Folklore.* New Haven, Conn.: Human Relations Area Files, 1977.

Griffith, James. *A Shared Space: Folklife in the Arizona-Sonora Borderlands.* Logan: Utah State University Press, 1995.

Lee, Hector. *The Three Nephites: Substance and Significance of Legend in Folklore.* Albuquerque: University of New Mexico Press, 1949.

Poulsen, Richard C. *The Pure Experiences of Order: Essays on the Symbolic in the Folk Material Culture of Western America.* Albuquerque: University of New Mexico Press, 1982.

A Selected List of References on Mormon Folklore and Folksong. Washington, D.C.: Archive of Folk Song, 1970.

Whittaker, David J. *Mormon Americana: A Guide to Sources and Collections in the United States.* Provo, Utah: Brigham Young University Studies, 1995.

Morrison, Toni

Morrison, Toni (1931–) Integral to the texture of Toni Morrison's prose is a set of cultural references to the African-American past and, in particular, folk culture.

As a novelist, essayist, critic, and educator, Toni Morrison positions herself as a scholar of American history and lore. Her works, such as *Tar Baby* (1981) and *Song of Solomon* (1977), make overt and key references to the folktales and beliefs of African Americans during the times in which these stories are set. In this way, Morrison both responds to and transmits elements of the folk tradition.

Perhaps the most complex of these efforts is Toni Morrison's Pulitzer Prize–winning 1987 novel *Beloved*. In this historical fiction, Morrison explores the portion of the African-American past related to American slavery. In writing *Beloved* Morrison conducted extensive research into the experiences of African Americans during this time. She looked not only at the indignities and suffering endured by slaves, but also at the responses slaves made to these offenses. She took particular note of acts of slave resistance.

The inspiration for her novel was a brief account of Margaret Garner, an escaped slave mother who was prepared to kill her children rather than let them be slaves again. In this act of defiance and spirit of fierce love, Morrison found the basis for the event at the center of her novel. During interviews, Morrison has suggested that as important as the work of historians of slavery might be, there are some elements of the human condition that only artists can capture. Her goal with *Beloved* was to bring this artistic and spiritual sensibility to bear on her subject matter.

Much has been made of the spiritual and supernatural elements of Morrison's work, and, indeed, she grew up in a family in which ghost stories and numerology played a role. She frequently employs supernatural images and violent death scenes to raise moral dilemmas and feelings of ambivalence. Allied to this feature of her work is the also often-discussed mythic and fabulistic content of Morrison's writing. At times, Morrison's work parodies the Western model of the fairy tale, replacing it with an alternative form. Readers of her work note the part myths, African tales, and even fables play. It is through such forms as African-American song and story that characters recover a cultural identity lost to them, and for which they grieve (consciously or unconsciously). In *Beloved*, it may be that the title character, as much as she may also function as a character in the story, on another level represents a personage—or identity—lost to the characters, and for which they grieve (consciously or unconsciously). She is a visual reminder of that for which characters yearn, and that which they feel they lack.

Within her own writings, Toni Morrison speaks in compelling ways as she constructs a rich narrative of the personal, spiritual, and social costs of American slavery. In doing so, she ennobles the cultural resources that sustained African Americans both during that time and since, from preaching to quilting. These folk traditions lend strength and continuity to African-American culture.

As an author, Toni Morrison incorporates aspects of folk culture within her accounts of the indomitable human spirit of the African-American people. For Morrison, these traditions are both the legacy of the past and the hope of the future.

See also: AFRICAN-AMERICAN FOLKLORE; FOLKLORE IN AMERICAN LITERATURE; GHOSTS; GHOST STORIES; HAUNTED HOUSES; PROTEST IN FOLKLORE; SLAVERY; SUPERNATURAL; TAR BABY.

For Further Reading:

Harris-Lopez, Trudier. *Fiction and Folklore: The Novels of Toni Morrison.* Knoxville: University of Tennessee Press, 1991.

Higgins, Therese. *Religiosity, Cosmology, and Folklore: The African Influence in the Novels of Toni Morrison.* New York: Routledge, 2001.

Middleton, David L., ed. *Toni Morrison's Fiction: Contemporary Criticism.* New York: Garland, 1997.

Mobley, Marilyn Sanders. *Folk Roots and Mythic Wings in Sarah Orne Jewett and Toni Morrison: The Cultural Function of Narrative.* Baton Rouge: Louisiana State University Press, 1991.

Weever, Jacqueline de. "Toni Morrison's Use of Fairy Tale, Folk Tale and Myth in *The Song of Solomon*," *Southern Folklore Quarterly* 44 (1980): 131–144.

Morton, J. Sterling   See ARBOR DAY.

Mose the Fireman (legendary)   As a tall tale figure comparable in some respects to

Pecos Bill, John Luther "Casey" Jones, and Old Stormalong, Mose the Fireman was a legendary firefighter associated with New York City.

It is believed that Mose the Fireman was modeled after a real person, Moses Humphrey, a newspaper printer and volunteer fireman. Mose traveled into lore as a colorful yet somewhat stereotypical figure. He was an Irish-American firefighter who kept a beer keg fastened to his belt.

Mose was as tall as the tales told about him, some eight feet or more in height. He performed superhuman feats in the conduct of his work as a fireman. These activities included lifting trolley cars full of passengers to save someone in the vehicle's path. He was known to swim area waters, such as the Hudson River, in just two or three strokes. In one of his most memorable adventures, Mose the Fireman is reputed to have extinguished a raging fire in the Bowery by tunneling to New Jersey and dousing the blaze with the Hudson River. As the stories go, the tunnels he dug are now passageways for the New York City subway system.

Mose reached his height of popularity during the first half of the 19th century and appeared as one of the heroic characters of storybooks and stage plays. These representations included Benjamin Baker's popular play *A Glance at New York*, a work that had been absent from the stage since the Civil War until revived on Broadway at the end of the 20th century. More recently, he was featured in a 1993 *American Heroes and Legends* book and videotape series for children, by Rabbit Ears Productions.

In something of the way Paul Bunyan was an icon of the lumbering trade and Mike Fink an icon of the seafaring life, Mose the Fireman became a figure in occupational lore, most notable for the fact that he is an example of the relatively rare use of urban figures in American tall tales and lore.

See also: BUNYAN, PAUL; CITY FOLKLORE; CIVIL WAR; FINK, MIKE; FOLK HEROES/LEGENDARY FIGURES; JONES, JOHN LUTHER; (CASEY); NORTHEASTERN REGIONAL FOLKLORE; OCCUPA-

TIONAL FOLKLORE; PECOS BILL; REGION, FOLK; STORMALONG, OLD.

For Further Reading:

Blair, Walter. *Tall Tale America: A Legendary History of Our Humorous Heroes.* New York: Coward-McCann, 1944.

Felton, Harold. *Big Mose, Hero Fireman.* Champaign, Ill.: Garrard, 1969.

Metaxas, Eric, and Everett Peck. *Mose the Fireman.* New York: Rabbit Ears Books, 1996.

"Mose the Fireman." In *American Heroes and Legends.* Told by Michael Keaton. New York: Rabbit Ears Productions, 1993.

Osborne, Mary Pope. *American Tall Tales.* New York: Knopf, 1991.

Mother Goose (legendary) Mother Goose, an icon of children's literature and storytelling, is most closely associated with the genre of nursery rhymes.

Depicted variously, Mother Goose typically appears in illustrations and on book covers as a goose with personifying details that establish her as a maternal figure, such as a bonnet, apron, and granny glasses. The overall visual effect is of a goose turned out as a nurse or nanny and carrying a distaff, an object that represents both femininity and weaving, as is consistent with the image of Mother Goose as a female spinner of yarns.

Over the years, scholars have made numerous efforts to identity the figure of Mother Goose with a specific historical personage. Several individuals with ties to storytelling and spinning have received consideration, from Queen Blanche to the queen of Sheba. It is more likely, however, that Mother Goose represents a conflation of the animal tale with the so-called old wives' tale, and so a goose becomes a matron and narrator.

In the United States, references to Mother Goose link her to nursery rhymes since at least the 18th century. Since then, there have been countless collections and recastings, both playful and parodic, of Mother Goose stories, from *The American Mother Goose* to *The Inner City Mother Goose.*

Mother Goose has to her credit many nursery rhymes and other writings for children, from "Hey Diddle Diddle" to "Humpty Dumpty."

See also: CHILDREN'S FOLKLORE; FABLES; FAIRY TALES; FAMILY FOLKLORE; FOLK HEROES/LEGENDARY FIGURES; MYTHS, FOLK; NURSERY RHYMES; RHYMES, FOLK.

For Further Reading:

Lewis, Philip. *Seeing through the Mother Goose Tales: Visual Turns in the Writings of Charles Perrault.* Palo Alto, Calif.: Stanford University Press, 1996.

Lobel, Arnold, ed. *The Random House Book of Mother Goose.* New York: Random House, 1986.

Merriam, Eve. *The Inner City Mother Goose.* New York: Simon & Schuster Books for Young Readers, 1996.

Opie, Iona, and Peter Opie, eds. *The Oxford Dictionary of Nursery Rhymes.* New York: Oxford University Press, 1997.

Wood, Ray. *The American Mother Goose.* New York: Frederick A. Stokes, 1940.

Mother's Day This annual holiday, held on the second Sunday in May, honors the virtues and contributions of the nation's mothers.

While it is not the first celebration of motherhood, Mother's Day has a distinctively American origin. At least two women are credited, separately, with originating the yearly observance.

The first of these, Julia Ward Howe, issued her own "Mother's Day Proclamation" in 1870. Howe, the poet who framed the lyrics to "The Battle Hymn of the Republic," had a history of activism in the antislavery and women's suffrage causes. Her proclamation of Mother's Day was a pacifist statement, issued in reaction to the Civil War and on behalf of mothers throughout the nation.

The second name associated with the emergence of Mother's Day is that of Anna Jarvis

(1864–1948), an individual who first conceived of the campaign as a way of carrying forward efforts by her mother, the Sunday school teacher Anna Reese Jarvis, to establish official recognition of America's mothers.

The first observance of Mother's Day, held on May 10, 1908, was therefore a tribute to her own mother, who had died three years earlier. The church service honored the character and accomplishments of Anna Reese Jarvis, and as a tribute to all mothers, those present received the fallen matriarch's favorite flower, the white carnation. As the holiday developed, while carnations remained the standard flower of the day, white flowers were used to honor deceased mothers and red carnations were presented to living ones.

After a sustained effort, complete with a letter-writing campaign and founding of a Mother's Day International Association in 1912, Anna Jarvis succeeded in establishing a national day of recognition for American motherhood. In 1914, President Wilson endorsed, and Secretary of State William Jennings Bryan proclaimed, a national observance of Mother's Day. By 1934, a U.S. stamp would commemorate the day's importance. Depicted on that stamp was a reproduction of a painting by James Abbott McNeill Whistler entitled *Arrangement in Grey and Black*. The work is more commonly known as "Whistler's Mother."

As the story has it, Jarvis would later take vigorous exception to the commercialization of Mother's Day. Her objections reached the level of legal action against profit-oriented celebrations, and Jarvis was even arrested at a convention where carnations were being sold in conjunction with Mother's Day. It is said that the woman behind Mother's Day became so outraged by the merchandising of the holiday that she would ultimately regret her involvement in its establishment. A day that had its beginnings in antiwar sentiment and reverence for maternity has since become associated in the national consciousness with sentimentality too often expressed through commerce.

Today, Mother's Day is the occasion for sons and daughters to remember their mother with visits, cards, flowers, meals, and gifts. It remains one of the highest-volume days for telephone communication, as well-wishers extend their compliments to mothers too far away to address in person.

See also: CIVIL WAR; FAMILY FOLKLORE; FATHER'S DAY; GRANDPARENTS DAY; HOLIDAYS/OBSERVANCES; PROTEST IN FOLKLORE.

For Further Reading:
Cohen, Hennig, and Tristram Potter Coffin, eds. *The Folklore of American Holidays.* Detroit: Gale, 1987.

Myers, Robert. *Celebrations: The Complete Book of American Holidays.* Garden City, N.Y.: Doubleday, 1972.

Santino, Jack. *All around the Year: Holidays and Celebrations in American Life.* Urbana: University of Illinois Press, 1994.

motif, folk Most stories, whether spoken or written, represent complex forms composed of many narrative elements. As familiar features recurring within traditional or tradition-influenced narratives, motifs represent details used within a story's composition or delivery. Motifs can be a wide array of images or references but typically involve recognizable forms associated with storytelling. For example, the motif of the ogre is well known to readers of fairy tales. The classification of the ogre can be further divided into subcategories such as witches, cannibals, and other malevolent creatures who commonly appear in stories.

Motifs can describe virtually any manner of detail marshaled by storytellers, whether from society or mythology. As figures within the language of storytelling, motifs pattern tales in such a way as to reward the attentive reader or listener who discerns the meaning behind such images or allusions. In this way, motifs become a shorthand that enables storytellers and their audiences to summon the repertoires of traditional narrative for each new occasion. For instance, motifs surrounding the topic of wisdom might involve not only the cautionary tale of the fool, but also warnings against deception, reminders of fate, and portents of fortune (whether good or ill).

Students of folklore can document the use and implication of motifs within folk narratives through use of a classificatory index, such as Stith's *Motif-Index of Folk-Literature*. With the help of such a resource, it becomes possible to catalogue tales by the motifs they employ. A sound knowledge of narrative motif helps folklorists see any given story within the wider context of a storyteller's time-honored vocabulary of references, images, and allusions.

See also: FABLES; FAIRY TALES; FOLKTALES; MYTHS, FOLK; TERMS.

For Further Reading:

Baughman, Ernest W. *Type and Motif-Index of the Folktales of England and North America.* Bloomington: Indiana University Press, 1966.

Bierhorst, John. "Hot Pepper Story: The Need for an Expanded Motif-Index," *Journal of American Folklore* 92, no. 366 (fall 1979): 482–483.

Limón, José. "Legendry, Metafolklore, and Performance: A Mexican-American Example," *Western Folklore* 42, no. 3 (July 1983): 191–208.

Stith, Thomson. *Motif-Index of Folk-Literature: A Classification of Narrative Elements in Folktales, Ballads, Myths, Fables, Mediaeval Romances, Exempla, Fabliaux, Jest-Books, and Local Legends.* Bloomington: Indiana University Press, 1993.

Mount Rushmore   See CRAZY HORSE; ROOSEVELT, THEODORE; WASHINGTON, GEORGE.

murals   See ART, FOLK; DEPRESSION, THE GREAT.

Museum of American Folk Art   See ART, FOLK.

museums, folk   Folk museums are generally considered those institutions that place their exhibition focus on local and/or regional culture.

In some countries, the term *folk museum* specifies an open-air museum, similar to what Americans call living history sites. The American appetite for such experiences probably has its origins in the turn-of-the-century popularity of folklore tableaux and, later, house and farm museums.

It is important to observe that while such locations create the illusion of time travel, they are simulations rather than full-scale survivals. These replicas of the American past tend to be selective and tend to focus on those aspects of the folk culture that are most affirmative to the sensibilities of the visitors. At their worst, folk museums nourish tourist misconceptions with composite pictures of past experience. At their best, they use sound research to reconstruct a particular place and time such that visitors can correct preconceptions and deepen their thinking about a specific cultural past.

Folk museums can be found throughout the nation, but especially in the Northeast. Examples in Massachusetts include Plimoth Plantation, where a 1627 Pilgrim village is recalled; Old Sturbridge Village, where the 1830s are revisited; and Salem, Massachusetts, where a 1630 village and fishing town is portrayed.

In the United States, folk museums typically strive to present their visitors with living history, a carefully arranged version of the past and its folk culture.

See also: AMERICAN FOLKLIFE CENTER; AMERICAN MEMORY PROJECT; ARCHITECTURE, FOLK; ARCHIVE OF FOLK CULTURE; ART, FOLK; ARTIFACTS, FOLK; ARTS AND CRAFTS MOVEMENT; BORDEN, LIZZIE; BROWN, MARGARET TOBIN (UNSINKABLE MOLLY); COLONIAL WILLIAMSBURG; EARP, WYATT BERRY STAMP; FESTIVALS, FOLKLORE; FOLKLIFE; FOLKLIFE MOVEMENT; FOLKLORE IN EVERYDAY LIFE; FOLKLORE STUDIES; GRAFFITI; GREENFIELD VILLAGE, HENRY FORD MUSEUM AND; GRIMM BROTHERS; HISTORIC

PRESERVATION; HISTORY, FOLK; INDUSTRIALIZA-
TION AND FOLKLORE; JAMES, JESSE; LIBERTY,
MISS; LINCOLN, ABRAHAM; LIVING HISTORY
MUSEUMS; MATERIAL CULTURE; McCARTY, WIL-
LIAM HENRY (BILLY THE KID); MYSTIC SEAPORT
AND PRESERVATION SHIPYARD; OCCUPATIONAL
FOLKLORE; REVERE'S RIDE, PAUL; "PRINCESS
AND THE PEA, THE"; PUBLIC FOLKLORE; SHEL-
LEY, KATE; SMITHSONIAN INSTITUTION; STUR-
BRIDGE VILLAGE, OLD; VERNACULAR CULTURE;
WITCHCRAFT, SALEM; WRIGHT BROTHERS.

For Further Reading:

Alanen, Arnold, and Robert Melnick, eds. *Preserv-
ing Cultural Landscapes in America*. Baltimore:
Johns Hopkins University Press, 2000.
Ames, Kenneth, Barbara Franco, and L. Thomas
Frye, eds. *Ideas and Images: Developing Interpre-
tive History Exhibits*. Nashville, Tenn.: American
Association for State and Local History, 1992.
Anderson, Jay. *Time Machines: The World of Living
History*. Nashville, Tenn.: American Associa-
tion for State and Local History, 1984.
Hall, Patricia, and Charles Seemann, eds. *Folklife
and Museums: Selected Readings*. Nashville,
Tenn.: American Association for State and
Local History, 1987.
Loomis, Ormond. *Sources on Folk Museums and Liv-
ing History Farms*. Folklore Forum Bibliograph-
ical and Special Series. Bloomington: Indiana
University Folklore Institute, 1977.

music, folk   Folk music is one of the best-
known manifestations of American folklore
today.

In its traditional sense, folk music is any
form of musical expression that is composed
and performed by ordinary people and transmitted orally to others. They in turn embellish,
perform, and transmit it once again through
song variations. Folk music is most commonly
vocal music with acoustic instrumentation. In
its oldest sense, folk music is performed live and
informally rather than by commercial means or
recording.

Such music is usually associated with preindustrial societies in which mass media and consumer culture have not overtaken regional and
local forms of musical expression. Traditional
folk music involves a participatory process that
unites the members of a community in shared
singing and/or instrumental performance. It has a
spontaneous rather than prepackaged property, as
it emerges from mutual need and contribution.

Folk music has many forms, including sea
chanties, spirituals, work songs, and ballads.
Such tunes are context-sensitive, emerging from
events, occupations, and emotions that the songs
express. Folk songs of this kind are generally
learned with the ear rather than with the eye, as
most are not written out as lyrics or in musical
notation. People learn by listening and singing
along with those who already knows the songs.
For this reason, most folksingers labored in
obscurity, and their most influential songs were
not seen in a proprietary manner since they
belonged to everyone.

The content of American folk music ranges
widely. Many of the best-loved folk tunes feature
folk heroes and legendary figures. Ballads about
Billy the Kid, Pretty Boy Floyd, John Luther
"Casey" Jones, and Joe Hill are examples. Other
folk songs are celebrations of aspects of the
nation's history, such as cowboy tunes of the
American frontier. Still others relate the experiences of American laborers. For instance, "I've
Been Working on the Railroad," "The Trail of
the Lonesome Pine," and "Clementine" all have
their origins in the toil of America's workers.

American folk music also has a long tradition
of protest. During the Great Depression, for
example, Woodrow "Woody" Guthrie wrote
and performed songs that reflected the hardships the era posed for the American people.
Guthrie is best known for such songs as "This
Land Is Your Land" and "This Train Is Bound
for Glory." As a composer/folksinger born in
Oklahoma, Guthrie was especially sensitive to
the plight of the "Okies." These farm families
were displaced by both poverty and the effects
of the dust bowl on the land. Many migrated

westward to California, where they worked as migrant farm workers. In dust bowl ballads about adversity, such as "Blowing down This Old Dusty Road," Guthrie protested the poor living and working conditions facing the laboring poor.

During the 20th century, American folk music developed a second definition, including a wider set of songs, performers, and performances. Any music bearing the influence of old-time and traditional music may, in this sense, be regarded as folk music. During the 1950s, for example, a major folk music revival was under way. Musicians such as Bob Dylan, along with activists/singers/songwriters such as Pete Seeger and Joan Baez, produced new music inspired by the work of more traditional folk musicians such as Woody Guthrie. This movement continued through the 1960s and 1970s, when folk music was a preferred genre for civil rights and antiwar songs, marches, and rallies.

Since that time, annual folk concerts such as the Festival of American Folklife and the Newport Folk Festival have become regular celebrations of folk musical traditions. American folk music remains a vibrant genre, from traditional tunes to folk-influenced forms such as folk rock, country, old-time music, contemporary folk, zydeco, bluegrass, and rockabilly.

See also: APPALACHIAN FOLKLORE; ARCHIVE OF FOLK CULTURE; BROWN, MARGARET TOBIN (UNSINKABLE MOLLY); BROWN, STERLING ALLEN; CAJUN FOLKLORE; CINCO DE MAYO; COWBOYS; FESTIVALS, FOLKLORE; FLOYD, CHARLES ARTHUR (PRETTY BOY); FOLKLIFE; FOLKLORE IN EVERYDAY LIFE; HILLBILLIES; HILL, JOE; HIPPIES; JOAD, TOM; JONES, JOHN LUTHER (CASEY); McCARTY, WILLIAM HENRY (BILLY THE KID); OAKLEY, PHOEBE ANNIE; OUTLAWS; PIED PIPER; POPLORE; PROTEST IN FOLKLORE; STARR, BELLE; TOOMER, JEAN; TURNER, NAT; UNDERGROUND RAILROAD.

For Further Reading:

Cantwell, Robert. *When We Were Good: The Folk Revival.* Cambridge, Mass.: Harvard University Press, 1996.

Denisoff, R. Serge. *Great Day Coming: Folk Music and the American Left.* Urbana: University of Illinois Press, 1971.

Lomax, Alan. *The Folk Songs of North America in the English Language.* Garden City, N.Y.: Doubleday, 1960.

Lomax, John, and Alan Lomax. *American Ballads and Folk Songs.* New York: Macmillan, 1934.

Lomax, John, and Alan Lomax. *Our Singing Country.* New York: Macmillan, 1941.

Lornell, Kip. *Introducing American Folk Music: Ethnic and Grassroots Traditions in the United States.* Boston: McGraw-Hill, 2002.

Netti, Bruno. *Folk Music in the United States.* Detroit: Wayne State University Press, 1976.

Rosenberg, Neil, ed. *Transforming Tradition: Folk Music Revivals Examined.* Urbana: University of Illinois Press, 1993.

Santelli, Robert, Holly George-Warren, and Jim Brown, eds. *American Roots Music.* New York: H. N. Abrams, 2001.

Sieling, Peter. *Folk Music.* Broomall, Pa.: Mason Crest, 2003.

Vassal, Jacques. *Electric Children: Roots and Branches of Modern Folkrock.* Translated by Paul Barnett. New York: Taplinger, 1976.

Yales, Janelle. *Woody Guthrie: American Balladeer.* Staten Island, N.Y.: Ward Hill Press, 1995.

Mystic Seaport and Preservation Shipyard Also the site of the Museum of America and the Sea, Mystic Seaport functions as a living history environment for the study of maritime lore.

This facility, located on the Mystic River in Connecticut and founded in 1929, covers some 17 acres. It houses a collection of some 500 historic seafaring vessels, including the *L. A. Dunton*, the *Joseph Conrad*, and the *Charles Morgan*, the last whaling ship afloat. In the Planetarium, visitors can learn about the role of stars and constellations in navigation. The on-site museum features artifacts such as scrimshaw and oral histories.

As do its living history counterparts, Colonial Willamsburg and Plimoth Plantation, Mystic

Seaport attempts to provide visitors with a firsthand experience of another era in America's history. With a reconstruction of a 19th-century village, Mystic Seaport enables tourists and schoolchildren to enter the era of wooden shipbuilding. Assisting in this process are "role players," or staff members charged with first-person dramatization of life within the historic community.

From folklore-inspired works of American literature such as Herman Melville's *Moby-Dick* and Samuel Langhorne Clemens's *Huckleberry Finn* to legendary figures such as Mike Fink and Annie Christmas, water lore has remained an important feature of American folktale traditions.

See also: ARCHITECTURE, FOLK; CHRISTMAS, ANNIE; CLEMENS, SAMUEL LANGHORNE; COLONIAL WILLIAMSBURG; FINK, MIKE; FOLKTALES; GREENFIELD VILLAGE, HENRY FORD MUSEUM AND; HISTORIC PRESERVATION; HISTORY, FOLK; LIVING HISTORY MUSEUMS; MARITIME FOLKLORE; MELVILLE, HERMAN; MUSEUMS, FOLK; OCCUPATIONAL FOLKLORE.

For Further Reading:

Beck, Horace. *Folklore and the Sea*. Middletown, Conn.: Wesleyan University Press, 1973.

Jeans, Peter. *Seafaring Lore and Legend: A Miscellany of Maritime Myth, Superstition, Fable, and Fact*. Camden, Me.: International Marine/Raggid Mountain Press, 2004.

Mallory, Philip. *Mystic Seaport and the Origins of Freedom*. New York: Newcomen Society in North America, 1954.

Taylor, David. *Documenting Maritime Folklife: An Introductory Guide*. Washington, D.C.: Library of Congress, 1992.

myths, folk   Folk myths are prose narratives that feature plots that address large and abstract issues.

There are many misconceptions about what folk myths are. Some believe myths are false ideas, though this is not the case. Others suppose myths represent attempts explain the unexplainable, and that also is not necessarily correct.

It might be more accurate to say that folk myths give people ways to contemplate the elusive. Many myths are stories of origins, retrospective tales about the way the world is (or how it came to be so).

As is the case with other folk narratives, myths are stories of events. Rather than focusing on people and animals, however, folk myths tend to feature gods and heroes as their principal characters. The stories typically deal in metaphor as a means to express ideas of cosmology.

In addition to functioning as stories in their own right, folk myths dealing with such figures as King Midas, Sisyphus, and Icarus also operate as a figurative language with which to speak to concepts that would otherwise remain ineffable.

See also: CHILDREN'S FOLKLORE; FABLES; FAIRY TALES; FOLKTALES; MIDAS, KING.

For Further Reading:

Campbell, Joseph. *Myths to Live By*. New York: Bantam, 1984.

Nodelman, Perry, ed. *Touchstones: Reflections on the Best in Children's Literature: Fairy Tales, Fables, Myths, Legends, and Poetry*. West Lafayette, Ind.: Children's Literature Association, 1987.

naming/names Names and naming are important within American culture, and the practices surrounding both are part of American folklore.

Place-names, for example, often reveal popular values, aesthetics, and ideals. When locations are named after well-known persons, either locally or generally, the gesture is usually construed as a tribute. For example, Washington, D.C., the District of Columbia, and Washington State both bear the name of the first president of the United States. City and town names can also reflect the esteem in which a public person is held, such as the naming of Columbus, Ohio, after Christopher Columbus or Lincoln, Nebraska, after Abraham Lincoln. In addition to formal names, many cities, states, or localities have informal monikers: Philadephia is known as the City of Brotherly Love, Seattle is the Emerald City, Connecticut is the Nutmeg State, Kennett Square, Pennsylvania, calls itself "the mushroom capital of the world," and so forth.

Personal names can also reflect cultural meanings and lore. For instance, when a newborn child receives a given name that is or echoes the name of a family member, especially one who is deceased, the practice is usually considered to be a way of honoring that ancestor. Even names not selected in this way usually carry historical associations or meanings that stem from the name's derivation. These connotations can include everything from biblical names to popular beliefs about the luck of a particular name.

Nicknames, or informal names given to friends or associates, are often chosen on the basis of their perceived aptness to describe the individual's attributes or characteristic behavior. Such names are most often used only among intimates who are familiar with the origin of a nickname or set of nicknames, as might be used within a sports team, fraternity, or other shared context of association. A few nicknames become more widely known, as with folk heroes and legendary figures. For example, few Americans today would recognize William Henry McCarty as the birth name of the notorious figure from American crime lore, Billy the Kid. In a few cases, a nickname effectively replaces the individual's name in public memory, as is the case with Pocahontas or John "Johnny Appleseed" Chapman.

Renamings can also be socially significant. Until the latter part of the 20th century, for example, it was customary for women to take the surname of the men they married. While this practice continues in some cases, it is no longer most common. These days, women may retain their surname, take the surname of their husband, or do neither. That is, some couples use both surnames, sometimes combined as hyphenates, upon marriage, while others choose a third surname to use as their new last name in marriage. Many people change their name for other reasons, such as adoption or divorce. Others seek to change their name, whether legally or informally, for different reasons. It is not uncommon, for instance, for writers to use a nom de plume, or pseudonym, under which they publish some or all of their works. This is the case for Samuel Langhorne Clemens, who typically published under the name Mark Twain, and Ann Sophia Stephens, who used the pen name Jonathan Slick. In still other cases, individuals modify the name they were given at birth. This is true of such people as Toni Cade Bambara, John Paul Jones, James Fenimore Cooper, and James Weldon Johnson. Others replace the name with which they were born, as when Isabella Baumfree shed her slave name and became Sojourner Truth.

The ability to give names is often regarded as powerful, even magical, in its implications. Traditional tales, such as "Rumpelstiltskin," dramatize the importance of names and the power conferred on a speaker when uttering another's name. It is considered an abuse of power and profound insult to call someone by another's name or the wrong name. Similarly, a person who insults another is said to have called that person "out of their name." This is likely because names are typically closely linked to identity, and so any manipulation or muddling of a name is seen as an act of disrespect.

Whether involving the proper or informal identifications of people or places, naming is a culturally laden process with many folkloristic nuances.

See also: FAMILY FOLKLORE; FOLKLORE IN EVERYDAY LIFE; SPEECH, FOLK.

For Further Reading:
Baker, Ronald L., ed. *The Study of Place Names.* Terre Haute: Indiana Council of Teachers of English/Hoosier Folklore Society, 1972.
Miller, Roscoe. *Amerigo and the Naming of America.* New York: Carlton Press, 1968.
Nicolaisen, W. F. H. "Names and Narratives," *Journal of American Folklore* 97, no. 385 (summer 1984): 259–272.
Nicolaisen, W. F. H. "Place-Name Legends: An Onamistic Mythology," *Folklore* 87 (1978): 146–159.
Thomas, Jeannie B., and Doug Enders. "Bluegrass and White Trash: A Case Study Concerning the Name 'Folklore' and Class Bias," *Journal of Folklore Research* 37, no. 1 (2000): 23–52.

narrative, folk   A folk narrative consists of any verbal text produced by and transmitted within a folk group.

Folk narratives may be oral or written. Examples of oral narratives include anecdotes, oral histories, interviews, conversations, stories, legends, jokes, and tales. Written folk narratives may include fables, fairy tales, myths, memoirs, and other works of literature. Whatever the form it takes, a folk narrative offers a great deal of information for the folklore scholar. It usually relates real or imagined events, implies a sequence or chronology, features one or more compelling characters, and tailors its presentation to the intended audience. From a folk narrative, a researcher may glean insights into cultural traditions, values, assumptions, and ideals.

Collectors of folk narratives may use them to inform studies of folk speech, folk humor, folktales, and a variety of other phenomena of interest to the folklorist. Folk orators, storytellers, and others skilled at narrative forms employ folk narratives for a range of purposes, including information transmission, education, socialization, moral instruction, and entertainment.

From interviews with former slaves to stories of legendary figures such as John Henry, American folklore is rich with narrative. If folklore is the spoken literature of a society, then the nation's folk narratives represent an important dimension of America's traditions of expression.

See also: FABLES; FAIRY TALES; FOLKLORE IN EVERYDAY LIFE; FOLKTALES; HUMOR, FOLK; MYTHS, FOLK; ORAL HISTORY; SPEECH, FOLK.

For Further Reading:

Bascom, William. "The Forms of Folklore: Prose Narratives," *Journal of American Folklore* 78, no. 307 (winter 1965): 3–20.

Bauman, Richard. *Verbal Art as Performance.* Prospect Heights, Ill.: Waveland Press, 1977.

Foley, John Miles. *The Theory of Oral Composition: History and Methodology.* Bloomington: Indiana University Press, 1988.

Stahl, Sandra Dolby. *Literary Folkloristics and the Personal Narrative.* Bloomington: Indiana University Press, 1989.

National Park Service See ELLIS ISLAND; LEWIS, MERIWETHER, AND WILLIAM CLARK; LIBERTY, MISS; TRANSCONTINENTAL RAILROAD; UNDERGROUND RAILROAD.

National Register of Historic Places See ARCHITECTURE, FOLK; HISTORIC PRESERVATION.

Native American folklore Native American folklore reflects the traditional customs and ways of American Indians and their descendants. It also describes the culture of Alaska natives, native Hawaiins, and Pacific Islanders.

For the most part, however, when folklorists refer to Native Americans, they mean American Indians. When the American Folklore Society was established in the late 19th century, part of its charter was to explore the folk traditions of Native America. Consequently, this population may be the best studied of all American folk groups. To be more precise, Native America represents many subgroups rather than a unified one. Each tribe has its own heritage and beliefs and must be studied accordingly.

Because of the embattled history of Native Americans, they have tended to shield their culture from the view of outsiders. That is, while tribes may display versions of their culture's rituals, dances, and crafts for the benefit of tourists, these exhibitions may serve to mask as much as to reveal the genuine beliefs and practices of indigenous peoples. The same is true for many of the craft objects marketed to visitors, including silver, turquoise, baskets, weaving, beading, and pottery. Since Native American folklore interweaves mythology and the sacred, it is no small matter to exhibit or sell it to outsiders. Ceremonies, weaving traditions, ritual objects, and the like, may be held as private and so kept secret from all but members of the community.

Storytelling traditions of Native Americans may nonetheless shed light on the population's worldview. Native American verbal lore is rich and varied. Creation/origin stories exist in most cultures, and some of the most closely studied creation stories are those of Native Americans. These accounts for the world's or human life's origin differ across tribes and regions. They may also detail the source of other natural phenomena such as the origin of fire, corn, or the thunderbird. Most embody fundamental beliefs that help form a folk group's worldview. Some even constitute central folk myths for a culture. For example, the figure of Grandmother Spider functions in a symbolic manner for Native Americans. Hopi tribes feature Grandmother Spider in stories in which she weaves the world out of her own web. Native American folk crafts also reflect this myth, such as the use of myth-driven designs for sandpainting rituals and textiles.

The figure of the trickster is a common one throughout American folklore, but is an especially frequently seen character in Native American tales. The trickster is an unlikely hero and appears even less likely to emerge as a victor, yet somehow prevails in a variety of situations portrayed within trickster tales. Tricksters are no strangers to comedy or mischief. They are known for pranks and other forms of misdirection. They often violate cultural taboos, sometimes muting such transgressions with clowning or other methods of ingratiating themselves to those who might otherwise exact punishment.

In addition to their use of whimsy and cunning, tricksters often possess unusual talents of intellect, wellness, foresight, or magic. The trickster typically triumphs through unexpected turns of events, whether by chance or design. On this basis, the trickster is related to other figures within folklore who rely upon subterfuge, such as outlaws, magicians, and changelings. Tricksters can defy, deflect, and defeat the host society's standards of common sense and right conduct. In so doing, they capture the interest of audiences satisfied by the inversions, power plays, and wit of such tales of contest.

Coyote, a figure who alternately assumes the shape of a man or wild canine, is an example of a trickster figure from Native American folklore. In much the manner that Raven is a trickster figure linked to Northwestern regional folklore, Coyote is connected to Southwestern regional folklore. As with other trickster figures, Coyote functions as a picaresque hero. He transgresses cultural expectations and societal rules, often with great effect. Tricksters are playful creatures, given to pranks and misdirection, and so their victories are often accomplished through deception and sly humor.

Although there are many variations, probably the most famous tale of Coyote involves the power of fire. Demonstrating the true spirit of a trickster, Coyote steals fire from the gods and gives it to humans. In this sense, Coyote exerts considerable power. He, as many tricksters do, operates as a creator figure rather than simply as a manipulator. Tricksters alter the human world with their feats of guile and strength. As an element of Native American folklore, Coyote continues to be featured within North American turnabout narratives.

Contemporary Native American writers often draw from folklore elements such as these for the cultural background and motifs of their work. Examples include Paula Gunn Allen, Louise Erdrich, Joy Harjo, Linda Hogan, Navarre Scott Momaday, and Leslie Marmon Silko.

Since 1968, when San Francisco State University began its program in Native American studies, similar programs have emerged at colleges and universities across the country. Through their efforts, such programs help scholars document, study, and teach about the history and culture of Native America, including its folklore.

See also: Allen, Paula Gunn; American Folklore Society; Bigfoot/Sasquatch; Cannary-Burke, Martha (Calamity Jane); conjure/conjuring; Coyote; Crazy Horse; cultural groups; Custer, George Armstrong; fables; folklore; Geronimo; gold rush, the; Hiawatha; Joseph, Chief; Lewis, Meriwether, and William Clark; Longfellow, Henry Wadsworth; Pocahontas; region, folk; Sacajawea; Seattle, Chief; Silko, Leslie Marmon; solstice; Southwestern regional folklore; trickster; worldview.

For Further Reading:

Bellfy, Phil. *Indians and Other Misnomers: A Cross-Referenced Dictionary of the People, Persons, and Places of Native North America*. Golden, Colo.: Fulcrum Press, 2001.

Bright, William. *A Coyote Reader*. Berkeley: University of California Press, 1993.

Cunningham, Keith. *American Indians: Folk Tales and Legends*. Ware, England: Wordsworth, 2001.

Dixon-Kennedy, Mike. *Native American Myth and Legend: An A–Z of People and Places*. London: Blandford, 1996.

Erodoes, Richard, and Alfonso Ortiz, eds. *American Indian Myths and Legends*. New York: Pantheon Books, 1984.

Furst, Peter T., and Leslie Furst. *North American Indian Art*. New York: Annellen, 1982.

Hazen-Hammond, Susan. *Spider Woman's Web: Traditional Native American Tales about Women*. New York: Berkeley, 1999.

Leeming, David A. *The Mythology of Native North America*. Norman: University of Oklahoma Press, 1998.

Taylor, Colin. *Native American Myths and Legends*. New York: Smithmark, 1994.

Williamson, Ray A., and Claire R. Farrer, eds. *Earth and Sky: Visions of the Cosmos in Native American Folklore*. Albuquerque: University of New Mexico Press, 1992.

Zitkala-Sa. *American Indian Stories, Legends, and Other Writings*. New York: Penguin Books, 2003.

nature   See ANIMALS; ARBOR DAY; EARTH DAY; FLOWERS; GARDENING; WEATHER FOLKLORE.

Nebraska folklore   See ARBOR DAY; FEBOLD-SON, FEBOLD; LEWIS, MERIWETHER, AND WILLIAM CLARK; LINCOLN, ABRAHAM; MIDWESTERN REGIONAL FOLKLORE; NAMING/NAMES.

needlework   See CRAFTS, FOLK.

Nevada folklore   See CARSON, KIT; GHOST TOWNS; GOLD RUSH, THE; WESTERN REGIONAL FOLKLORE.

New Deal   See DEPRESSION, THE GREAT; ROOSEVELT, FRANKLIN DELANO.

New Hampshire folklore   See ALLEN, ETHAN; NORTHEASTERN REGIONAL FOLKLORE; SHAKER FOLKLORE; YANKEE DOODLE.

New Jersey folklore   See COOPER, JAMES FENIMORE; EDISON, THOMAS ALVA; EINSTEIN, ALBERT; GREENFIELD VILLAGE, HENRY FORD MUSEUM AND; HISTORIC PRESERVATION; IMMIGRATION AND FOLKLORE; JERSEY DEVIL; MOSE THE FIREMAN; NORTHEASTERN REGIONAL FOLKLORE; WHITMAN, WALT.

New Mexico folklore   See ALLEN, PAULA GUNN; SILKO, LESLIE MARMON.

New Year's Eve/Day   In America, this holiday is celebrated at the close of one year and the opening of the next in accordance with the Roman calendar. New Year's Eve is a nighttime celebration taking place on December 31, and New Year's Day is observed all day on January 1 each year. The outgoing year finds its symbol in an aging, bearded figure bearing a staff ('Father Time"), while the incoming year is symbolized by a newborn ("Baby New Year").

People have been observing end-of-the-year rituals for centuries. Across time and cultures, New Year's celebrations perform ceremonial functions for societies, such as purification, remembrance of the dead, and banishing of evil spirits.

Early American customs associated with New Year's included home visits, open houses, and gift exchanges. Presidents from George Washington up until Franklin Delano Roosevelt held public receptions at the White House for the occasion. Lincoln's decision to sign the Emancipation Proclamation on January 1, 1863, precipitated a subsequent observance to be marked on the same day each year, especially by former slaves, as Emancipation (Proclamation) Day.

Food and entertainment continue to be a part of today's celebrations, but in the 21st century, participation is chiefly by invitation and so represents less of an obligation to complete social rounds within one's community. Today's New Year's Day customs include public events such as parades (most widely known among these may be Pasadena, California's Tournament of Roses Parade) and football bowl games (such as the annual Rose Bowl).

Today's celebrants in the United States concentrate their holiday energy on the night before January 1. They frequently mark the arrival of a new year at New Year's Eve parties and galas, toasting the transition, ringing bells, and exchanging kisses at the stroke of midnight. Typically, the song "Auld Lang Syne," whose words are a variation on a Robert Burns poem and whose theme of memory aligns with the event, is played at the moment the clock strikes 12:00. This moment of transition is often depicted visually with the figures of Father Time and Baby New Year, symbolizing the death of the old year and the birth of a new one.

While these customs are familiar, their origins may not be. Drinking at the arrival of a new year is a holdover of much older religious rites. The ringing of bells, or noise making of other sorts, recalls traditional practices for banishing evil spirits and keeping the devil at bay. Although practices such as the midnight kiss are newer, they seem to be in accord with the communal effort to summon good luck and make a sound start to the coming year.

Generally a way of marking the passage of time, as well as delineating a new beginning, the arrival of a new year offers cause not only for festivity, but also for reflection, fortune-telling, and goal setting. For that reason, other practices commonly associated with New Year's celebrations include making predictions and resolutions. Just as the calendar itself imposes order on human time, so does the impulse to forecast and direct human activity signal the desire to control or influence destiny. While this effort may involve wishful thinking, it also suggests a certain amount of superstition about the unknown. As Americans bid farewell to one year, they wish to usher in greater fortune with the next one.

See also: EMANCIPATION (PROCLAMATION) DAY; HOLIDAYS/OBSERVANCES; LUCK/FORTUNE; PARADES; PREDICTION; ROOSEVELT, FRANKLIN DELANO; SUPERSTITION; TOASTS/DRINKING; WASHINGTON, GEORGE.

For Further Reading:

Cohen, Hennig, and Tristram Potter Coffin, eds. *The Folklore of American Holidays*. Detroit: Gale, 1987.

Morgan, David, and Sally M. Promey, eds. *The Visual Culture of American Religions*. Berkeley: University of California Press, 2001.

Myers, Robert. *Celebrations: The Complete Book of American Holidays*. Garden City, N.Y.: Doubleday, 1972.

Santino, Jack. *All around the Year: Holidays and Celebrations in American Life*. Urbana: University of Illinois Press, 1994.

Sobchack, Vivian. "'Happy New Year and Auld Lang Syne': On Televisual Montage and His-

torical Consciousness." In *Reality Squared: Televisual Discourse on the Reel*, edited by James Friedman, 92–118. New Brunswick, N.J.: Rutgers University Press, 2002.

Walsh, Martin. "Shooting in the New Year: An Early American Instance," *New York Folklore* 12, nos. 3–4 (summer–fall 1986): 153–155.

Yoder, Don. *American Folklife*. Austin: University of Texas Press, 1976.

New York folklore   See ALGER, HORATIO, JR.; ANTHONY, SUSAN BROWNELL; COOPER, JAMES FENIMORE; IRVING, WASHINGTON; LABOR DAY; NORTHEASTERN REGIONAL FOLKLORE; PARADES; PATRIOT DAY; ROOSEVELT, FRANKLIN DELANO; ROOSEVELT, THEODORE; SAINT PATRICK'S DAY; SHAKER FOLKLORE; SPORTS FOLKLORE; STANTON, ELIZABETH CADY; SOJOURNER TRUTH; SUFFRAGE, WOMEN'S; THANKSGIVING; YANKEE DOODLE.

North Carolina folklore   See APPALACHIAN FOLKLORE; CHESNUTT, CHARLES WADDELL; FOLKLORE STUDIES; GOLD RUSH, THE; SOUTHERN REGIONAL FOLKLORE; WRIGHT BROTHERS.

North Dakota folklore   See LEWIS, MERIWETHER, AND WILLIAM CLARK; NORTHWESTERN REGIONAL FOLKLORE.

Northeastern regional folklore   As the area of the United States that includes most of the original colonies, the Northeast is an important folk region.

Since its inception, the study of American folklore has emphasized the concept of folk regions in the United States. Despite the claim that we now have an entirely global culture, local and regional variations continue to exist, and these are important objects of study for folklorists. In the United States, these regions are typically conceived of as clusters of nearby states with commonalities, such as populations, practices, or other attributes.

Although the American Northeast can be described and delimited in various ways, the Northeast as a folk region can generally be defined as including folklore of or relating to the states of Connecticut, Delaware, Maine, Maryland, Massachusetts, New Hampshire, New Jersey, New York, Pennsylvania, Rhode Island, and Vermont, along with the District of Columbia.

Authors connected to the Northeast, whether personally or in their subject matter, include James Fenimore Cooper, Washington Irving, Henry Wadsworth Longfellow, and Harriet Beecher Stowe. Numerous folk heroes and legendary figures have ties to America's Northeast. Examples would be Hiawatha, Paul Revere, Ethan Allen, Crispus Attucks, Yankee Doodle, the Yankee Peddler, Rip Van Winkle, and the Jersey devil.

See also: ALLEN, ETHAN; ATTUCKS, CRISPUS; COOPER, JAMES FENIMORE; HIAWATHA; IRVING, WASHINGTON; JERSEY DEVIL; LONGFELLOW, HENRY WADSWORTH; MARITIME FOLKLORE; REVERE'S RIDE, PAUL; REVOLUTIONARY WAR; STOWE, HARRIET BEECHER; VAN WINKLE, RIP; YANKEE DOODLE; YANKEE PEDDLER.

For Further Reading:

Allen, Barbara, and Thomas J. Schlereth, eds. *Sense of Place: American Regional Cultures.* Lexington: University Press of Kentucky, 1990.

Botkin, B. A., *Treasury of New England Folklore: Stories, Ballads, and Traditions of the Yankee Folk.* New York: Crown, 1965.

Browne, George. *Real Legends of New England.* Chicago: A. Whitman, 1930.

Dorson, Richard M. *America Begins.* New York: Arno Press, 1980.

Dorson, Richard M., ed. *Buying the Wind: Regional Folklore in the United States.* Chicago: University of Chicago Press, 1964.

Drake, Samuel. *A Book of New England Legends and Folk Lore, in Prose and Poetry.* Detroit: Singing Tree Press, 1901/1969.

Glassie, Henry. *Patterns in the Material Culture of the Eastern United States.* Philadelphia: University of Pennsylvania Press, 1969.

Hastings, Scott. *Miss Mary Mac All Dressed in Black: Tongue Twisters, Jump-Rope Rhymes, and Other Children's Lore from New England.* Little Rock, Ark.: August House, 1990.

Johnson, Clifton. *What They Say in New England: A Book of Signs, Sayings, and Superstitions.* Boston: Lee and Shepherd, 1896.

O'Neill, J. P. *The Great New England Sea Serpent.* Camden, Me.: Down East Books, 1999.

Ringel, Faye. *New England's Gothic Literature: History and Folklore of the Supernatural from the Seventeenth through the Twentieth Centuries.* Lewiston, N.Y.: E. Mellen Press, 1995.

Snow, Edward Rowe. *Fantastic Folklore and Fact: New England Tales of Land and Sea.* New York: Dodd, Mead, 1968.

Taft, Lewis. *A Profile of Old New England: Yankee Legends.* New York: Dodd, Mead, 1965.

Withers, Carl, ed. *What They Say in New England, and Other American Folklore.* New York: Columbia University Press, 1963.

North Star See DOUGLASS, FREDERICK; UNDERGROUND RAILROAD.

Northwestern regional folklore Sometimes described as the Pacific Northwest, the Northwest is an important folk region.

Since its inception, the study of American folklore has emphasized the concept of folk regions in the United States. Despite the claim that we now have an entirely global culture, local and regional variations continue to exist, and these are important objects of study for folklorists. In the United States, these regions are typically conceived of as clusters of nearby states with commonalities, such as populations, practices, or other attributes.

Although the American Northwest can be described and delimited in various ways, the Northwest as a folk region can generally be defined as including folklore of or relating to the states of Idaho, Montana, North Dakota, Oregon, South Dakota, and Washington.

Folk heroes and legendary figures associated with the Northwest include Coyote, Meriwether Lewis and William Clark, Sacajawea, Calamity Jane, and Bigfoot. The region is also part of the area involved in the gold rush.

See also: BIGFOOT/SASQUATCH; CANNARY-BURKE, MARTHA (CALAMITY JANE); COYOTE; GOLD RUSH, THE; LEWIS, MERIWETHER, AND WILLIAM CLARK; REGION, FOLK; SACAJAWEA.

For Further Reading:

Allen, Barbara, and Thomas J. Schlereth, eds. *Sense of Place: American Regional Cultures*. Lexington: University Press of Kentucky, 1990.

Bingham, Edwin, and Glen Love. *Northwest Perspectives: Essays on the Culture of the Pacific Northwest*. Eugene: University of Oregon Press, 1979.

Dorson, Richard M., ed. *Buying the Wind: Regional Folklore in the United States*. Chicago: University of Chicago Press, 1964.

Hilbert, Vi. *Haboo: Native American Stories from Puget Sound*. Seattle: University of Washington Press, 1985.

Judson, Katharine Berry. *Myths and Legends of the Pacific Northwest*. Chicago: Mcclurg, 1997.

Macdonald, Margaret Read. *Ghost Stories from the Pacific Northwest*. Little Rock, Ark.: August House, 1995.

Smelcer, John. *The Raven and the Totem: Traditional Alaska Native Myths and Tales*. Anchorage, Alaska: Salmon Run, 1992.

Thomas, Philip. *Songs of the Pacific Northwest*. Saanichton, Canada: Hancock House, 1979.

Norwegian-American folklore   Norwegian-American folklore belongs to immigrants to the United States from Norway, along with those born in America of Norwegian ancestry.

Immigration to the United States from this Nordic country began in the 17th century. Of all Scandinavian countries, Norway has had the highest rate of immigration to America. Place-names such as Norway, Michigan, and Norway, Iowa, signal areas with concentrations of Norwegian settlers. Accustomed to a rural culture, many of these newcomers remained in farming as a livelihood. They also continued to be a close-knit ethnic community.

Norwegian Americans are known for their verbal lore. Individuals with Norwegian heritage may also exchange jokes and folktales about such stereotypical characters as "Little Ole." Within these self-deprecating caricatures, Norwegian Americans appear guileless and even foolish. They also have a rich repertoire of proverbs for use in daily conversation, including such familiar sayings as "All that glitters is not gold."

Traditional Norwegian foodways are still practiced, particularly on holidays and special occasions. At Christmas, a preparation of dried cod fish, *lutefisk*, is a traditional dish and often served with thin pancakes. In addition to celebrating the usual American holidays, Norwegian Americans have strong traditions associated with functional folk crafts such as weaving and wood carving, as well as some decorative arts such as rose painting. Norwegian Americans observe Norwegian Independence Day, also known as Norwegian Constitution Day, each May 17. In areas with significant populations of Norwegian Americans, this annual celebration includes parades, music, and other forms of merriment. Annual festivals held in locations such as Decorah, Iowa, and Minot, North Dakota, celebrate and promote Norwegian-American folklore and folklife.

Organizations dedicated to the preservation and study of Norwegian-American culture include New York's American-Scandinavian Foundation and Northfield, Minnesota's, Norwegian-American Historical Association. Major collections of cultural material include Decorah, Iowa's Vesterheim Norwegian American Museum; Coon Valley, Wisconsin's Norskedalen Heritage and Nature Center; and Seattle, Washington's, Nordic Heritage Museum.

The folklore of Norwegian Americans helps promote unity within this folk group in the United States and continuity with the homeland.

See also: CULTURAL GROUPS; FINNISH-AMERICAN FOLKLORE; IMMIGRATION AND FOLKLORE; SWEDISH-AMERICAN FOLKLORE.

For Further Reading:

Anderson, Arlow W. *The Norwegian Americans.* Boston: Twayne, 1975.

Lovoll, Odd S., ed. *Nordics in America: The Future of Their Past.* Northfield, Minn.: Norwegian American Historical Association, 1993.

Lovoll, Odd. *The Promise Fulfilled: A Portrait of Norwegian Americans Today.* Minneapolis: University of Minnesota Press, 1998.

———. *The Promise of America: A History of the Norwegian American People.* Rev. ed. Minneapolis: University of Minnesota Press, 1999.

Nelson, Marion John, ed. *Material Culture and People's Art among the Norwegians in America.* Northfield, Minn.: Norwegian American Historical Association, 1994.

Nelson, Marion, ed. *The Norwegian Folk Art: The Migration of a Tradition.* New York: Abbeville Press, 1995.

Schultz, April. *Ethnicity on Parade: Inventing the Norwegian American through Celebration.* Amherst: University of Massachusetts Press, 1994.

nuclear folklore   See ATOMIC/NUCLEAR ERA FOLKLORE.

numbers   See LUCK/FORTUNE.

nursery rhymes   Nursery rhymes are familiar narratives specifically designed for the youngest audiences and intended to entertain with sound and story.

While most nursery rhymes did not originate in the United States, they are nonetheless standard aspects of an American child's narrative life. They are intended to be recited or read aloud. The characters and plots are fanciful, even nonsensical, and the rhymes make the tales more musical to the ear. Typical nursery rhymes are "Hickory Dickory Dock," "Mary Had a Little Lamb," "Little Miss Muffett," "Old King Cole," "Old Mother Hubbard," "Jack and Jill," and "The Old Woman Who Lived in a Shoe."

Mother Goose, a legendary figure and icon of children's literature, is most closely associated with the genre of nursery rhymes. Depicted variously, Mother Goose typically appears in illustrations and on book covers as a goose with personifying details that establish her as a maternal figure, such as a bonnet, apron, and granny glasses. The overall visual effect is of a goose turned out as a nurse or nanny and carrying a distaff, an object that represents both femininity and weaving, as is consistent with the image of Mother Goose as a female spinner of yarns. It is most likely that Mother Goose represents a conflation of the animal tale with the so-called old wives' tale, and so a goose becomes a matron and narrator.

In the United States, references to Mother Goose link her to nursery rhymes since at least the 18th century. Since then, there have been countless collections and recastings of Mother Goose stories. Nursery rhymes are constantly being updated in order to engage new audiences of youngsters in these folktales.

See also: CHILDREN'S FOLKLORE; FABLES; FAIRY TALES; FAMILY FOLKLORE; FOLKTALES; MOTHER GOOSE; MYTHS, FOLK.

For Further Reading:

Brunvand, Jan Harold, ed. *Readings in American Folklore.* New York: W. W. Norton, 1979.

Nodelman, Perry, ed. *Touchstones: Reflections in the Best in Children's Literature: Fairy Tales, Fables, Myths, Legends, and Poetry.* West Lafayette, Ind.: Children's Literature Association, 1987.

Opie, Iona, and Peter Opie, eds. *The Oxford Dictionary of Nursery Rhymes.* New York: Oxford University Press, 1951.

Reichertz, Ronald. "The Generative Power of Nursery Rhymes," *Children's Literature Folklore Quarterly* 19, no. 3 (fall 1994): 100–104.

Reid-Walsh, Jacqueline, and Ronald Reichertz. "Nursery Rhymes and Children's Songs," *Children's Literature Association Quarterly* 19, no. 3 (fall 1994): 99–117.

Wood, Ray. *The American Mother Goose.* New York: Frederick A. Stokes, 1940.

O

Oakley, Phoebe Annie (1860–1926)   Born in 1860 as Phoebe Annie Oakley Moses, this denizen of the American West is best remembered as Phoebe Annie Oakley.

Oakley prided herself on matching or besting her male counterparts in activities, such as shooting, long dominated by men. In those efforts, she often donned men's attire. It is not surprising, then, that Oakley became the subject of remark. She was both talented and unconventional, and people remembered her long after her death in 1926.

As the subject of folk stories and songs, Annie Oakley has a secure place within the lore of the Wild West. In this regard she joins the ranks of such frontier heroes as Kit Carson, William F. Cody (Buffalo Bill), and Wild Bill Hickok. Oakley even inspired a successful 1946 Irving Berlin musical, *Annie Get Your Gun*, which has been revived in many subsequent performances.

In sharp contrast to the iconic figure of the male gunslinger, women such as Annie Oakley and Calamity Jane demonstrated the contributions American women could make to frontier history and lore.

Phoebe Annie Oakley distinguished herself as a sharpshooter and a rodeo rider.

See also: CANNARY-BURKE, MARTHA (CALAMITY JANE); CARSON, KIT; CODY, WILLIAM F. (BUFFALO BILL); COWBOYS; FOLK HEROES/LEGENDARY FIGURES; FRONTIER; HICKOK, JAMES BUTLER (WILD BILL); PECOS BILL; REGION, FOLK; RODEO; WESTERN REGIONAL FOLKLORE.

For Further Reading:

Coffin, Tristan Potter. *The Female Hero in Folklore and Legend.* New York: Seaburg, 1975.

Glass, Andrew. *Bad Guys: True Stories of Legendary Gunslingers, Sidewinders, Fourflushers, Drygulchers, Bushwhackers, Freebooters, and Downright Bad Guys and Gals of the Wild West.* New York: Doubleday Book for Young Readers, 1998.

Havighurst, Walter. *Annie Oakley of the Wild West.* New York: Macmillan, 1954.

Kasper, Shirl. *Annie Oakley.* Norman: University of Oklahoma Press, 1992.

Riley, Glenda. *The Life and Legend of Annie Oakley.* Norman: University of Oklahoma Press, 1994.

occult   See GHOSTS; GHOST STORIES; SUPERNATURAL; WITCHCRAFT, SALEM.

occupational folklore   Occupational folklore includes all the narratives associated with the everyday working lives of Americans.

Workplace folklore is a universal phenomenon, perhaps because people spend so much of their time at work and rely upon it for the resources needed for family, household, leisure, and investment.

Practices associated with trades, professions, and other vocations are part of folklore, as are the jokes told among workers in each field.

Legendary figures, particularly those appearing as characters within tall tales, are among the best known figures of American occupational lore. Examples include John Chapman (Johnny Appleseed), Paul Bunyan, Annie Christmas, Mike Fink, John Henry, Joe Magarac, Mose the Fireman, Windwagon Smith, and Old Stormalong. Such characters usually portray exemplars in their fields of endeavor, if also somewhat fanciful ones. Narratives about them tend to deal in hyperbole to describe the legendary worker's acumen, not just to entertain the listener; but also to extoll the spirit and abilities of America's working people. The nation's cowboys, farmers, watermen, and lumberjacks, just to name a few, are mythic occupational figures of the American landscape.

Icons of hard work in America include Benjamin Franklin and the young protagonists featured in the stories and novels of Horatio Alger, Jr. In addition, many national heroes in the United States rose because of their prowess and/or pioneering roles within their work lives. Historical figures such as Orville Wright and Wilbur Wright, Charles Lindbergh, and Amelia Mary Earhart are examples of such names in the field of aviation. Railroad lore, to provide another example, includes such individuals as Casey Jones and Kate Shelley.

Key events within the pageant of American history have involved their own forms of occupational lore. For instance, the gold rush created a whole group of workers, such as prospecters, who had supported themselves through other means until that time. Another example of historical events that shaped occupational lore would be the building of the transcontinental railroad. This vast project of railway construction involved a workforce consisting of many immigrant laborers. Once again, a unique historical situation created a new population of workers.

Prominent figures, both living and literary, in the history of American protest are also a part of the nation's occupational lore. Examples include César Estrada Chavez, Susan Brownell Anthony, Joe Hill, and the protagonists of many works by John Steinbeck. Even American holidays, such as Labor Day and Administrative Professionals' Day/Secretaries' Day, are work-related observances.

Although the oldest elements of American occupational folklore primarily involve land-based and water-based forms of work, it is now at least as common for occupational lore to be tied to urban and industrial work. During the Great Depression, a good deal of federal collection of folklore took place, chiefly by the Works Progress Administration and the Federal Writers' Project. Within these efforts, particular emphasis was given to urban and industrial activities. Since then, *occupational folklore* is a term that has been used inclusively. During contemporary times, for example, new technologies associated with office work have produced some of the emerging forms of folklore, such as computer lore and Xerox/fax lore.

In fact, for many Americans, their only contact with agrarian and seafaring lore occurs at living history museums such as Colonial Williamsburg or other historical sites such as Mystic Seaport and Preservation Shipyard.

Although one of the slogans of the American labor movement was "Eight hours for sleep, eight hours for work, eight hours for what we will," it is still rare individuals in the United States who routinely can devote as many hours to "what they will" as they must devote to the paid work of employment or the unpaid work of a household. Therefore, occupational lore, whether pertaining to the practices, humor, stories, chants, chanteys, or work songs of American labor, accounts for the majority of the waking hours of the nation's workers.

See also: ADMINISTRATIVE PROFESSIONALS' DAY/WEEK; ALGER, HORATIO, JR.; ANTHONY, SUSAN BROWNELL; ARCHITECTURE, FOLK; AUCTIONS; BABE THE BLUE OX; BUNYAN, PAUL; CAMPUS FOLKLORE; CHAPMAN, JOHN (JOHNNY APPLESEED); CHAVEZ, CÉSAR ESTRADA; CHRISTMAS, ANNIE;

CITY FOLKLORE; COMPUTER FOLKLORE; COWBOYS; CRAFTS, FOLK; EARHART, AMELIA MARY; EARTH DAY; FEBOLDSON, FEBOLD; FINK, MIKE; FLIGHT; FOLKLORE IN EVERYDAY LIFE; FRANKLIN, BENJAMIN; GARDENING; GHOST TOWNS; GOLD RUSH, THE; HENRY, JOHN; HILL, JOE; IMMIGRATION AND FOLKLORE; INDUSTRIALIZATION AND FOLKLORE; JONES, JOHN LUTHER (CASEY); LABOR DAY; LINDBERGH, CHARLES; LIVING HISTORY MUSEUMS; MAGARAC, JOE; MARITIME FOLKLORE; MOSE THE FIREMAN; MUSEUMS, FOLK; MYSTIC SEAPORT AND PRESERVATION SHIPYARD; PROTEST IN FOLKLORE; SHELLEY, KATE; SMITH, WINDWAGON; STEINBECK, JOHN; STORMALONG, OLD; TELL, WILLIAM; TRANSCONTINENTAL RAILROAD; WASHINGTON, BOOKER TALIAFERRO; WEATHER FOLKLORE; WRIGHT BROTHERS; XEROX/FAX FOLKLORE.

For Further Reading:

Byington, Robert H., ed. *Working Americans: Contemporary Approaches to Occupational Folklife.* Los Angeles: California Folklore Society, 1978.

Coffin, Tristram Potter, and Hennig Cohen. *Folklore from the Working Folk of America.* Garden City, N.Y.: Doubleday, 1974.

Dewhurst, C. Kurt. "The Arts of Working: Manipulating the Urban Work Environment," *Western Folklore* 63 (1984): 192–211.

Green, Archie. *Calf's Head and Union Tale: Labor Yarns at Work and Play.* Urbana: University of Illinois Press, 1996.

Green, Archie. *Wobblies, Pile Butts, and Other Heroes: Laborlore Explorations.* Urbana: University of Illinois Press, 1993.

Oring, Elliott, ed. *Folk Groups and Folklore Genres: An Introduction.* Logan: Utah State University Press, 1986.

———, ed. *Folk Groups and Folklore Genres: A Reader.* Logan: Utah State University Press, 1989.

Reuss, Richard. *Songs of American Labor, Industrialization, and the Urban Work Experience: A Discography.* Ann Arbor: University of Michigan Press, 1983.

Schoemaker, George H., ed. *The Emergence of Folklore in Everyday Life: A Fieldguide and Sourcebook.* Bloomington, Ind.: Trickster Press, 1990.

Taylor, David. *Documenting Maritime Folklife: An Introductory Guide.* Washington, D.C.: Library of Congress, 1992.

ogres See ITALIAN-AMERICAN FOLKLORE; "JACK AND THE BEANSTALK"; MOTIF, FOLK; "RUMPELSTILTSKIN."

Ohio folklore See CHAPMAN, JOHN (JOHNNY APPLESEED); CUSTER, GEORGE ARMSTRONG; DUNBAR, PAUL LAURENCE; MIDWESTERN REGIONAL FOLKLORE; SHAKER FOLKLORE; SWEETEST DAY; WRIGHT BROTHERS.

Oklahoma folklore See DEPRESSION, THE GREAT; ELLISON, RALPH WALDO; FLOYD, CHARLES ARTHUR (PRETTY BOY); GERONIMO; JOAD, TOM; MOMADAY, NAVARRE SCOTT; SOUTHWESTERN REGIONAL FOLKLORE; STEINBECK, JOHN.

"Old Glory" See FLAG DAY; FLAG FOLKLORE; ROSS, BETSY.

Old Sturbridge Village See STURBRIDGE VILLAGE, OLD.

omens/portents See PREDICTION.

oral folklore Oral folklore includes all the categories of lore that involve speech.

Human voices bear the marks of folk group and region, from accents to dialects. As can cadences and rhythms, these speech differences can help the astute listener identify the geographical origin of a speaker.

Even ordinary conversation can prove a source of folk information. Examples include turn-taking behavior, expressions, and slang. Patterns of this kind can reveal the age, region, and class of participating speakers. The same is true for the preferred forms of gossip, rumors, insults, expletives, and boasts. Human speech is a rich source to mine for cultural information.

Spoken narratives, such as stories, jokes, toasts, anecdotes, and arguments, can also interest the folklorist of oral expression. Storytelling and other complex forms of utterance reveal the creativity, sociability, and oral traditions of the teller.

One of the ways folklorists collect and archive such information is through oral history, the method by which researchers record the speech of their informants so that it may be replayed and transcribed. As early as the Great Depression, fieldworkers of the Works Program Administration collected the spoken autobiographies of former slaves. Although there have been questions about how fully and frankly these narratives portray the experience of former slaves in the United States, they nonetheless represent one of the first federal efforts to document the experiences of ordinary Americans in their own sounded words.

Oral folklore studies, as distinct from artifactual or textual studies of folk tradition, attempt to hear the voices of the Americans they seek to document.

See also: DEPRESSION, THE GREAT; FIELD-WORK, FOLKLORE; FOLKLORE STUDIES; HISTORY, FOLK; ORAL HISTORY; SLAVERY; SPEECH, FOLK.

For Further Reading:

Greene, Ellin, and George Shannon. *Storytelling: A Selected Annotated Bibliography.* New York: Garland, 1986.

Jacobs, Claude. "Folk for Whom? Tourist Guidebooks, Local Color, and the Spiritual Churches of New Orleans," *Journal of American Folklore* 114, no. 453 (summer 2001): 309–330.

Kochman, Thomas, ed. *Rappin' and Stylin' Out: Communication in Urban Black America.* Urbana: University of Illinois Press, 1972.

Meade, Erica Helm. *Tell It by Heart: Women and the Healing Power of Story.* Chicago: Open Court, 1995.

Pellowski, Anne. *The World of Storytelling: A Practical Guide to the Origins, Development, and Applications of Storytelling.* New York: H. W. Wilson, 1990.

Tedlock, Dennis. *The Spoken Word and the Work of Interpretation.* Philadelphia: University of Pennsylvania Press, 1983.

Walls, Robert, and George Schoemaker, eds. *The Old Traditional Way of Life: Essays in Honor of Warren E. Roberts.* Bloomington, Ind.: Trickster Press/Indiana University Folklore Institute, 1989.

oral history   As one of the central fieldwork techniques available to the folklorist, oral history affords researchers a means to preserve and study the voices of the American people.

Oral history involves tape-recorded interviews that document the firsthand testimony of all the individuals who may serve as historical informants. Before oral history came into use as a field method, most first-person accounts of the American experience were those of the elite. Such evidence focused chiefly on those who were famous enough to be interviewed by journalists, studied in universities, and/or permitted to publish their autobiographies and memoirs.

With the advent of oral history, it became possible to widen the pool of potential witnesses to American history. Oral historians typically devote their energies to social history, or the documentation of daily experiences for ordinary citizens. Rather than concentrating on presidents and generals, then, oral historians find their subjects in the constituencies of such leaders.

Oral histories have contributed in important ways to the way the world perceives and understands the American past. Through oral history, the voices of former slaves, sharecroppers, mill workers, and homemakers help tell a fuller story of the nation's character and development. Oral history proceeds from an understanding that all people have a role to play in the unfolding of the past.

For folklorists, oral history confers dignity on the observations of craftspeople and practitioners, records oral traditions precisely as their tellers render them, and helps preserve the story of generations that attends the transmission of folk culture.

See also: FIELDWORK, FOLKLORE; FOLKLORE IN EVERYDAY LIFE; HISTORY, FOLK; ORAL FOLKLORE; RESEARCH, FOLKLIFE; TERMS.

For Further Reading:
Allen, Barbara, and William Lynwood Montell. *From Memory to History: Using Oral Sources in Local Historical Research*. Nashville, Tenn.: American Association for State and Local History, 1981.

Dunaway, David, and Willa Baum, eds. *Oral History: An Interdisciplinary Anthology*. Walnut Creek, Calif.: AltaMira Press, 1996.

Hoopes, James. *Oral History: An Introduction for Students*. Chapel Hill: University of North Carolina Press, 1979.

Ives, Edward D. *The Tape-Recorded Interview: A Manual for Field Workers in Folklore and Oral History*. Knoxville: University of Tennessee Press, 1995.

Ritchie, Donald. *Doing Oral History: A Practical Guide*. New York: Oxford University Press, 2003.

Oregon folklore See CHINESE-AMERICAN FOLKLORE; FESTIVALS, FOLK; FOLKLORE STUDIES; GOLD RUSH, THE; JAPANESE-AMERICAN INTERNMENT; JOSEPH, CHIEF; LABOR DAY; NORTHWESTERN REGIONAL FOLKLORE.

organizational folklore See OCCUPATIONAL FOLKLORE.

outlaws Within American folklore, one of the more curious figures is the heroic outlaw.

Perhaps because the nation's ideology is so steeped in defiance of authority, or perhaps because American audiences have always had an enthusiasm for sensational figures, the criminal represents a distinctive form of national hero. Although the public realizes that these individuals are engaged in unlawful and, often enough, violent activities, the outlaws somehow avoid functioning as villains in the minds of the public.

This effect may have something to do with the public's efforts to justify such figures' actions or, at least, to place those crimes in a wider context. Sometimes, criminals are glorified on the basis of the distastefulness of their victims. For example, thieves who steal from unsympathetic targets, such as banks and corporations, have often enjoyed comparisons to romantic figures such as Robin Hood. In a few cases, outlaws have in fact provided for the less fortunate with some of their ill-gotten resources. Other criminals prove so glamorous or their stories so captivating that the public overlooks the otherwise objectionable nature of their crimes. Still other criminals have been regarded as conscientious objectors, resisting unjust authority or misused power.

Americans have followed the exploits of famous "bad men" from Jesse James to John Dillinger and, in a few cases, women. In many instances, the outlaws at the center of this lore emerge as celebrities, regarded with affection despite—or perhaps because of—their notoriety. Otherwise, it would be difficult to explain the popularity of such tourist attractions as the Jesse James Bank Museum's robbery reenactments or such popular culture portrayals as Arthur Penn's 1967 feature-length film, *Bonnie and Clyde*.

Audiences not only seem curious about the sagas of America's outlaws, but also seem to take some measure of vicarious enjoyment from following their careers. Two major groups of outlaws deserve special notice in this regard. The first group, outlaws of the Wild West, includes individuals such as Jesse James, Butch Cassidy and the Sundance Kid, Wild Bill Hickok, and Billy the Kid. The second group features outlaws of the gangster era, such as Al Capone, Bonnie and Clyde, John Dillinger, and Pretty Boy Floyd. Indeed, many of the 20th century's gangsters idolized the 19th century's "bad men."

The outlaw, as does the figure of the trickster, entices the public imagination with the promise of adventure and the possibility of rapidly changing fortunes.

See also: ALLEN, ETHAN; CLARK, ARIZONA DONNIE (MA BARKER); BONNIE AND CLYDE; BRER RABBIT; CAPONE, ALPHONSE GABRIEL (AL); COMPUTER FOLKLORE; CONSPIRACY FOLKLORE; DILLINGER, JOHN; FLOYD, CHARLES ARTHUR (PRETTY BOY); FOLKLORE IN EVERYDAY LIFE; FRONTIER; HICKOK, JAMES BUTLER (WILD BILL); JAMES, JESSE; JOAD, TOM; LONGABAUGH, HARRY (SUNDANCE KID); McCARTY, WILLIAM HENRY (BILLY THE KID); MUSEUMS, FOLK; PARKER, ROBERT LEROY (BUTCH CASSIDY); REGION, FOLK; ROBIN HOOD; STAGOLEE; STARR, BELLE; TRICKSTER; WESTERN REGIONAL FOLKLORE.

For Further Reading:

Adams, Ramon. *Six-Guns and Saddle Leather: A Bibliography of Books and Pamphlets on Western Outlaws and Gunmen.* Norman: University of Oklahoma Press, 1969.

Erbsen, Wayne. *Outlaw Ballads, Legends, and Lore.* Asheville, N.C.: Native Ground Music, 1996.

Kooistra, Paul. *Criminals as Heroes: Structure, Power, and Identity.* Bowling Green, Ohio: Bowling Green State University Popular Press, 1989.

Roberts, John. *From Trickster to Badman: The Black Folk Hero in Slavery and Freedom.* Philadelphia: University of Pennsylvania Press, 1990.

Seal, Graham. *The Outlaw Legend: A Cultural Tradition in Britain, America, and Australia.* Melbourne, Australia: Cambridge University Press, 1996.

Ozarks folklore Although it is not a formally designated region, the area commonly known as the Ozarks has a close relationship to many genres of folklore.

The Ozarks represent an ill-defined region for most observers, with each describing its edges differently. By most accounts, however, the area includes portions of Arkansas, Missouri, Kansas, and Illinois. Some delineations of the Ozarks set its perimeter with the intersections among four rivers, the Missouri, Mississippi, Arkansas, and Neoshoa. Whatever the size or placement of the region, its people are well known for their folklore.

This area drew its population from several sources, including the wider phenomenon of westward expansion. Migrants from the states of Alabama, Kentucky, North Carolina, and Virginia were among the settlers. Other new residents were there taking advantage of land grants assured to them as descendants of soldiers of either the Revolutionary War or the War of 1812.

The people of the Ozarks enjoyed a primarily rural culture, in which lives and livelihoods remained close to the land. In many respects, the Ozarks region formed the precise conditions consistent with the classic definition of folklore, with its emphasis on agricultural, preindustrial populations in geographically remote or culturally isolated locations. Collectors have gathered Ozarks folk narratives since the latter part of the 19th century, and the region has achieved national visibility for its folklore in the years since the 1940s. This attention is due in large part to several amateur folklorists who devoted themselves to documenting Ozarks culture and lore.

Sometimes likened to the folklore of the Appalachian area, Ozarks folklore reflects a high degree of continuity in practice over time in a range of folk traditions, including ballads, narratives, songs, and crafts.

See also: APPALACHIAN FOLKLORE; BALLADS; CLARK, ARIZONA DONNIE (MA BARKER); CRAFTS, FOLK; CULTURAL GROUPS; FLOYD, CHARLES ARTHUR (PRETTY BOY); HILLBILLIES; MUSIC, FOLK; ORAL FOLKLORE; REGION, FOLK.

For Further Reading:

Blevins, Brooks. *Hill Folks: A History of Arkansas Ozarkers and Their Image.* Chapel Hill: University of North Carolina Press, 2002.

LaPin, Deirdre. *Hogs in the Bottom: Family Folklore in Arkansas.* Little Rock, Ark.: August House, 1982.

McNeil, W. K., and William Clements, eds. *An Arkansas Folklore Sourcebook.* Fayetteville: University of Arkansas Press, 1992.

McNeil, W. K., ed. *The Charm Is Broken: Readings in Arkansas and Missouri Folklore*. Little Rock, Ark.: August House, 1984.

McNeil, W. K. *Ozark Country*. Jackson: University Press of Mississippi, 1995.

Randolph, Vance. *The Devil's Pretty Daughter, and Other Ozark Folktales*. New York: Columbia University Press, 1955.

———. *Hot Springs and Hell: And Other Folk Jests and Anecdotes from the Ozarks*. Hatboro, Pa.: Folklore Associates, 1965.

———. *Ozark Superstition*. New York: Columbia University Press, 1947.

———. *The Ozarks: An American Survival of Primitive Society*. New York: Vanguard Press, 1931.

———. *Pissing in the Snow and Other Ozark Folktales*. Urbana: University of Illinois Press, 1976.

———. *We Always Lie to Strangers: Tall Tales from the Ozarks*. New York: Columbia University Press, 1951.

Tatham, Robert L. *Ozark Treasure Tales*. Raytown, Md.: R. L. Tatham, 1979.

P

parades As public displays and spectator events, parades are popular forms of entertainment in the United States and are often occasions with folk origins.

Most parades in America are celebratory; whether the tone be honorific or irreverent, parades amount to a kind of street theater for the benefit of an audience of ordinary people. In addition to providing entertainment, parades are spectacles that typically have narrative content. For example, when the soldiers returned from fighting World War II, there were hundreds of congratulatory parades in the United States. At such events, troops were honored as heroes and thanked for their sacrifices and courage. Accordingly, the parades had patriotic themes and messages relevant to the atmosphere of victory.

Some parades in the United States are devoted to celebrations of ethnicity and cultural heritage. Examples include the Irish focus of Saint Patrick's Day parades or the Italian focus of Columbus Day parades. Such events serve to reaffirm shared history and identity, honor cultural heroes, and reconnect members of ethnic groups.

Similarly, parades and marches often accompany protests calling for public recognition and acceptance. An example would be gay pride parades held throughout the nation, especially in larger cities. Such gatherings promote solidarity within a disenfranchised population and help publicize its desire for a more fully inclusive America.

Parades can also involve religious connections and occasions. For instance, while not overtly religious, the celebrations of Mardi Gras are timed to coincide with the last feast before Lent. Perhaps the most famous of Mardi Gras festivities are those of New Orleans, Louisiana. This event is a popular one with tourists as well as locals and represents a time of merriment and loosened restrictions on public behavior.

Holidays may also be observed with parades. On Independence Day/Fourth of July, for example, many communities gather for celebrations that begin with patriotic parades and culminate in evening displays of fireworks. At Halloween, it is common for costume parades to take place, especially those featuring children dressed up for trick-or-treating. Perhaps the best known of all holiday parades is the Macy's Thanksgiving Day Parade in New York City, a tradition that got its start in 1924. Timed to coincide with the height of the holiday shopping season and brimming with retail and corporate sponsors, it is also a good example of the way parades can also function as marketing vehicles. Televising of this and other parades widens the audience for such commercial appeals, as well as involving more Americans in the celebration.

From the Pasadena, California, Rose Parade at New Year's to the ticker-tape parades that greet celebrities visiting New York City, parades in America recall a whole range of folk traditions.

See also: COLUMBUS DAY; ETHNICITY; FESTIVALS, FOLKLORE; FOLKLORE IN EVERYDAY LIFE; HALLOWEEN/ALL HALLOWS' EVE; HOLIDAYS/OBSERVANCE; INDEPENDENCE DAY/FOURTH OF JULY; MARDI GRAS; NEW YEAR'S EVE/DAY; SAINT PATRICK'S DAY; THANKSGIVING; WORLD WAR II.

For Further Reading:

Davis, Susan. *Parades and Power: Street Theater in Nineteenth Century Philadelphia*. Philadelphia: Temple University Press, 1986.

Kugelmass, Jack. "Wishes Come True: Designing the Greenwich Village Halloween Parade." In *Of Corpse: Death and Humor in Folklore and Popular Culture*, edited by Peter Narváez, 171–196. Logan: Utah State University Press, 2003.

Macaloon, John, ed. *Rite, Drama, Festival, Spectacle: Rehearsals towards a Theory of Cultural Performance*. Philadelphia: Institute for the Study of Human Issues, 1984.

Manning, Frank, ed. *The Celebration of Society: Perspectives on Contemporary Cultural Performance*. Bowling Green, Ohio: Bowling Green State University Popular Press, 1983.

Ryan, Mary. "The American Parade: Representation of the Nineteenth Century Social Order." In *The New Cultural History*, edited by Lynn Hunt, 131–153. Berkeley: University of California Press, 1989.

Sussman, Mark. "Celebrating the New World Order: Festival and War in New York," *Drama Review* 39, no. 2 (summer 1995): 147.

Parker, Bonnie   See BONNIE AND CLYDE.

Parker, Robert Leroy (Butch Cassidy) (1866–1908)   Butch Cassidy is the archetypal outlaw of the American West.

This figure from American lore began life as Robert Leroy Parker in 1866. He was born in Beaver, Utah, as one of 13 children in a Mormon family. His exploits in the years to follow would take him far from his native Utah and his Mormon upbringing.

Parker assumed the alias Butch Cassidy as he began his career of crime. He borrowed the surname from a ranchhand who taught him how to shoot during his boyhood. Parker/Cassidy became the leader of the Wild Bunch, also known as the Hole-in-the-Wall Gang. The second most famous member of this group was Harry Longabaugh (the Sundance Kid), so named because of an 1887–89 stint in the Sundance, Wyoming, jail on a charge of horse theft. The group also included Ben Kilpatrick (the Tall Texan), Will Carver, and Harvey Logan (Kid Curry). This band of criminals robbed trains, banks, and mines during the 1890s, hiding between jobs in remote areas in Wyoming and Utah. By the turn of the century the gang disbanded, but the two principal members maintained their working partnership.

As the pursuit of Butch Cassidy and the Sundance Kid intensified, it is believed that they left the West for New York. They subsequently relocated to Argentina and Bolivia, where they engaged in cattle ranching and more robbery. Most accounts suggest that both were killed by police gunfire while in Bolivia, just after a payroll robbery in which they were believed implicated.

The lore surrounding Butch Cassidy includes rumors that he actually survived the shoot-out in Bolivia. There were numerous claimed sightings, and some believe he survived through the 1930s and lived under another assumed name in the United States. There are also stories worthy of pirate tales, claiming that a concealed treasure was left behind unclaimed.

Butch Cassidy was a figure of public interest and even sympathy, as is so often the case for American outlaws. Whether deservedly or not, Cassidy was identified as a Robin Hood figure, perceived as performing acts of benevolence toward ordinary people down on their luck. In one classic such tale, Cassidy intervenes on behalf of a widow about to be evicted by a heartless landlord. Similar tales exist surrounding other outlaws, such as Jesse James.

In addition to folktales and storybooks, he was the subject of a popular 1969 Twentieth Century Fox film, *Butch Cassidy and the Sundance Kid*, in which Paul Newman and Robert Redford played the leads. Newman, who portrayed Cassidy in the film, later named one of his charitable ventures after the bad man. At Newman's Hole in the Wall Gang Camp, children who have cancer and other diseases find sponsored recreation and respite from their cares. In an indirect sense, then, Cassidy did inspire some altruism of the kind attributed to Robin Hood.

As a trickster and adventurer, Butch Cassidy became part of American crime lore.

See also: FOLK HEROES/LEGENDARY FIGURES; JAMES, JESSE; LONGABAUGH, HARRY (SUNDANCE KID); OUTLAWS; REGION, FOLK; ROBIN HOOD; TRICKSTER; WESTERN REGIONAL FOLKLORE.

For Further Reading:

Betenson, Lula Parker, and Dora Flack. *Butch Cassidy, My Brother*. Provo, Utah: Brigham Young University Press, 1975.

Durer, Christopher S., ed. *American Renaissance and American West*. Laramie: University of Wyoming Press, 1982.

Painter, Larry. *In Search of Butch Cassidy*. Norman: University of Oklahoma Press, 1977.

Steckmesser, Kent. "Robin Hood and the American Outlaw: A Note on History and Folklore," *Journal of American Folklore* 79, no. 312 (spring 1966): 348–355.

———. *Western Outlaws: The "Good Badman" in Fact, Film, and Folklore*. Claremont, Calif.: Regina Books, 1983.

Parks, Rosa (1913–2005) Rosa Parks was one of the earliest and most prominent women within the United States Civil Rights movement. To many, she remains a hero for the wider cause of human rights.

The woman known to American history as Rosa Parks began her life on February 4, 1913, as Rose Louise McCauley. She was born in Tuskegee, Alabama, the daughter of a schoolteacher and a house builder. In 1932, she married Raymond Parks, a barber. Two years later, she received her high school diploma.

Parks had come of age during an era of legal segregation, and she was expected to comply with the unjust practices and policies that it entailed. In one such incident in 1943, Rosa Parks was ejected from a bus for refusing to board the coach from the rear entrance. She did not believe such rules were just and wished to demonstrate so through her refusal.

Later, on December 1, 1955, occurred the bus incident for which Parks is best known. While riding a bus in Montgomery, Alabama, Rosa Parks was arrested for declining to yield her seat to a white passenger just boarding the vehicle. Although at that time it was common practice on crowded buses for drivers to call on African-American passengers to rise and give their seats to any white passengers who were standing, Rosa Parks took a stand against this injustice.

While many accounts of Rosa Parks's actions on December 1, 1955, suggest that she remained seated on the bus chiefly because she was tired, such claims are unsupported by the historical evidence. Parks was a thoughtful opponent of segregation, and she had every intention of making a statement that day.

In response to both the arrest and the inequalities imposed by segregation, the African Americans in Montgomery organized a bus boycott that began on December 5 of that year. They would walk or share rides, but they would not use the buses. This action continued for 381 days. In 1956, the U.S. Supreme Court declared the practices of segregation on Montgomery buses to be unconstitutional. Although Rosa Parks had taken a chance that day in 1955 and had experienced death threats during the boycott, she drew attention to the problem of racial prejudice.

As did other organizers for civil rights, such as Martin Luther King, Jr., and Jo Ann Gibson

Robinson, Rosa Parks believed that direct action was required to effect social change. Parks was present at the 1963 Civil Rights March on Washington, D.C., at which King delivered his famous "I Have A Dream" speech, and she spent the subsequent years promoting unity and advocating for social justice. She was the cofounder of such organizations as the Rosa and Raymond Parks Institute for Self Development and Pathways to Freedom, both headquartered in Detroit, Michigan.

For her achievements, Rosa Park was recognized with many awards, such as the Spingarn Medal and the U.S. Medal of Honor. A bust of Parks stands in the Smithsonian Institution, and she has been the subject of many other honors, including musical concerts and recordings such as the 1995 "A Tribute to Mrs. Rosa Parks."

Rosa Parks occupies a place of honor among America's conscientious objectors, from Patrick Henry to Martin Luther King, Jr. Upon her death, Parks became the first woman ever to lie in state in the Capitol Rotunda.

See also: AFRICAN-AMERICAN FOLKLORE; CIVIL RIGHTS MOVEMENT; FOLK HEROES/LEGENDARY FIGURES; HENRY, PATRICK; MARTIN LUTHER KING DAY; PRISON FOLKLORE; PROTEST IN FOLKLORE.

For Further Reading:
Brinkley, Douglas. *Rosa Parks*. New York: Penguin, 2000.
Parks, Rosa. *Rosa Parks: My Story*. New York: Putnam, 1992.
Raines, Howell, ed. *My Soul Is Rested: Movement Days in the Deep South Remembered*. New York: G. P. Putnam's Sons, 1977.
Reed, Gregory J., ed. *Dear Mrs. Parks: A Dialogue with Today's Youth*. New York: Lee and Low Books, 1996.

Passover   Passover is a seven-day seasonal festival within Judaism designed to celebrate freedom from bondage.

This holiday occurs during the first month of the Jewish calendar, generally in March or April. On the first and seventh days of Passover, participants are to refrain from labor. The emphasis is on reaffirming family and communal identity through a series of symbolic meals, readings, and other rituals that help Jews fulfill the obligation to retell the story of the exodus from Egypt.

Food customs associated with Passover include abstinence from leavened bread, which is replaced by flat breads such as matzah. The Passover Seder, a dinner ceremony, represents an important part of the holiday's observance. It is a commemoration for adults and, for younger participants, a lesson. A set of symbolic foods are displayed or consumed at this meal, each helping to recall the story of the exodus. A roasted lamb shank recalls earlier observances in which lamb rituals were performed. Bitter herbs represent the experience of slavery and salt water the tears of slaves. Haroset, a dish combining nuts, apples, raisins, and cinnamon, symbolizes the mortar used to join bricks in Egypt. Roasted eggs and parsley suggest the arrival of spring and its renewal. By custom, a cup is placed at Seder for the prophet Elijah.

After the meal, participants recite blessings, share readings from psalms and legends, discuss the holiday's themes, sing, and conduct the "four questions" ritual, in which the youngest child present asks questions of an adult present, often the father, concerning the reasons for specific Passover customs.

As do other Judaic calendar observances, Passover preserves and promotes historical memory and awareness as each generation learns about Jewish cultural identity.

See also: FAMILY FOLKLORE; HOLIDAYS/ OBSERVANCES; JEWISH-AMERICAN FOLKLORE; RELIGION, FOLK.

For Further Reading:
Aveni, Anthony F. *The Book of the Year: A Brief History of Our Seasonal Holidays*. New York: Oxford University Press, 2004.
Fredman, Ruth Gruber. *The Passover Seder: Afikoman in Exile*. Philadelphia: University of Pennsylvania Press, 1981.

Gaster, Theodore H. *Festivals of the Jewish Year.* New York: William Sloane Associates, 1952.

———. *Passover: Its History and Traditions.* New York: Henry Schuman, 1949.

Greenspoon, Leonard J., and Ronald Simkins. *Spiritual Dimensions of Judaism.* Omaha, Nebr.: Creighton University Press, 2003.

Kaplan, Dana Evan. *The Cambridge Companion to American Judaism.* New York: Cambridge University Press, 2005.

Schauss, Hayyim. *The Jewish Festivals: History and Observance.* New York: Schocken Books, 1962.

Patrick's Day, Saint   See SAINT PATRICK'S DAY.

Patriot Day   Patriot Day is among the newest national observances in the United States, first signed into existence as Public Law No. 107–89 by President George W. Bush on December 18, 2001. This provision designates September 11 each year as Patriot Day and calls upon presidents to issue an annual proclamation of the occasion, (1) directing the people of the United States to observe a moment of silence in honor of the individuals who lost their lives in connection with attacks on September 11, 2001; (2) calling upon state and local governments to hold appropriate programs and conduct relevant activities; and (3) advising organizations and individuals to display the U.S. flag at half-staff on Patriot Day to honor those who died. It is, in other words, a government-sponsored observance.

Patriot Day, first observed on September 11, 2002, is wholly distinct from a similarly named regional observance, Patriots' Day, during which New Englanders recall Paul Revere's ride and the Revolutionary War's battle of Lexington and Concord.

An excerpt from the text of first presidential proclamation of Patriot Day serves to demonstrate the purpose of the newly designated commemoration:

On this first observance of Patriot Day, we remember and honor those who perished in the terrorist attacks of September 11, 2001. We will not forget the events of that terrible morning nor will we forget how Americans responded in New York City, at the Pentagon, and in the skies over Pennsylvania—with heroism and selflessness; with compassion and courage; and with prayer and hope. We will always remember our collective obligation to ensure that justice is done, that freedom prevails, and that the principles upon which our Nation was founded endure.

By using language and rhetoric similar to those applied to military days of remembrance, such as Memorial Day and Veterans Day, the proclamation appears to be an attempt to venerate the September 11 deaths, many of whom were civilians, in a similar fashion.

At present, popular references to this date still describe it as September 11 or 9/11, rather than calling it Patriot Day. It is not clear, then, whether the day's formal designation will change that, or whether folk practices will emerge in association with the day.

From the way yellow ribbons symbolized the homecoming welcome awaiting returned hostages and prisoners, to the artificial poppies used to raise funds to remember veterans, Americans have tended to favor symbols of national loss. On the other hand, over time, September 11 may be approached in the same way as Pearl Harbor (Remembrance) Day, chiefly at the sites of attack.

It does seem likely, though, given the scale of the tragedy and the strength of the public response to it, that some customs will take shape for the day's remembrance. It is possible that current individual acts of memory such as the wearing of flag label pins, along with collective responses such as construction of memorials at the World Trade Center and Pentagon Building, may provide some indication of the ways

Americans will in future choose to remember this day. It may be too soon, however, to assess the folklore associated with these tragic events.

See also: HOLIDAYS/OBSERVANCES; MEMO-RIAL DAY; NORTHEASTERN REGIONAL FOLK-LORE; PATRIOTS' DAY; REVERE'S RIDE, PAUL; PEARL HARBOR (REMEMBRANCE) DAY; REVOLU-TIONARY WAR; VETERANS DAY.

For Further Reading:

Calendar Updates Website. Patriot Day. Available online. URL: http://www.calendar-updates. com/Holidays/US/patriot.htm. Accessed February 22, 2006.

Colonial Flag Website. Public Law 107-89, Patriot Day. Available online. URL: http://www.colo-nialflag.com. Accessed February 22, 2006.

National Conference of State Legislatures. September 11 Commemorations. Available online. URL: http://www.ncsl.org/programs/ press/2001/freedom/911commemorations. htm. Accessed February 22, 2006.

Raising Our Kids Website. Patriot Day. Available online. URL: http://www.raisingourkids.com/ hol/pd6.shtml. Accessed February 22, 2006.

White House Press Release. Patriot Day Procla-mation. Available online. URL: http://www. whitehouse.gov/news/releases/2002/09/200209 04-10.html. Accessed February 22, 2006.

patriotic folklore   See INDEPENDENCE DAY/ FOURTH OF JULY; LIBERTY, MISS; ROSS, BETSY; UNCLE SAM.

Patriots' Day   Held on the third Monday in April since 1894, Patriots' Day commemorates the "shot heard round the world," which, on April 19, 1775, set in motion the Revolutionary War with the conflicts known as the battles of Lexington and Concord.

Because of its local origins, this observance remains centered in the state of Massachusetts. The holiday's establishment was championed by an organization known as the Sons of the American Revolution. It is a legal holiday in Massachusetts and Maine. The significance of the date is routinely marked with such events as parades and the running of the Boston Mara-thon. Reenactments of Paul Revere's ride, an event later immortalized in a poem of the same name by Henry Wadsworth Longfellow, have also coincided with Patriots' Day.

While the whole nation has cause to recall the key struggles that defined the Revolutionary War and occasioned the nation's independence, Patri-ots' Day is not observed as a national holiday as its counterparts such as Independence Day/Fourth of July are. Finally, Patriots' Day should not be confused with Patriot Day, a recent ceremonial renaming of September 11 as a day of remem-brance of the World Trade Center and Pentagon terrorist attacks of September 11, 2001. While the names of these observances are quite similar, Patriots' Day recalls a much earlier conflict.

See also: FLAG DAY; FOLKLORE IN AMERI-CAN LITERATURE; HOLIDAYS/OBSERVANCES; INDE-PENDENCE DAY/FOURTH OF JULY; LONGFELLOW, HENRY WADSWORTH; NORTHEASTERN FOLKLORE; PATRIOT DAY; REVERE'S RIDE, PAUL; REVOLU-TIONARY WAR.

For Further Reading:

Coffin, Tristram Potter. *Uncertain Glory: Folklore and the American Revolution.* Detroit: Folklore Associates, 1971.

Cummings, Thomas Harris. *Patriot's Day in Cam-bridge, Mass., April 19th, 1921: An Address on the First American Flag, Washington's Flag.* Cambridge, Mass.: Cambridge Tribune Press, 1921.

Santino, Jack. *All around the Year: Holidays and Cel-ebrations in American Life.* Urbana: University of Illinois Press, 1994.

Peaceable Kingdom   See ART, FOLK.

Pearl Harbor (Remembrance) Day   Pearl Harbor Remembrance Day is a tribute to those men and women of the armed services who died on December 7, 1941.

On this solemn occasion each year, Americans turn their thoughts to the unfortunate events of 1941, and the forces that threatened, and in some instances took, the lives of those serving in America's armed forces. in particular, the observance commemorates the contributions of those Americans who lost their lives during Japan's December 7, 1941, attack on the U.S. fleet at Pearl Harbor, Hawaii. A crew of more than 1,100 was killed when the *Arizona*, a U.S. battleship anchored in the harbor there, was destroyed by a bomb. At the site where the ship was once anchored, the nation erected a memorial. Here, visitors learn about the full set of events surrounding the attack, which resulted in the loss of more than 2,400 U.S. citizens in total.

Intended as a time to contemplate the contributions of those who died, Pearl Harbor Day calls for the U.S. flag to fly at half-staff, its position in mourning. Each year at this time, and especially on key anniversaries such as the 50th, Pearl Harbor Day is the occasion for reunions of other service members and survivors of those who perished. It is also a time for traditional acts of military memorial, such as the playing of "Taps," the song of farewell. Although Hawaii remains at the center of such observances, other localities honor the day in their own way. In San Francisco, for example, an aircraft beacon is illuminated on the summit of a mountain on the evening of December 7 each year.

Once described by President Franklin Delano Roosevelt as a day that will "live in infamy," December 7 weighs heavily on the national consciousness. In his 2002 proclamation of the day, President George W. Bush linked Pearl Harbor Day to the terrorist attacks of September 11, 2001. On both days thousands of U.S. citizens died, although the 2001 attack targeted mostly civilians. Pearl Harbor Day remains a time to salute the loyalty and reflect on the sacrifice of those killed in the 1941 attack. Although not a national observance on which schools and places of business close, Pearl Harbor Day nonetheless takes its place beside other such patriotic observances as Memorial Day and Veterans Day.

See also: DEATH; HOLIDAYS/OBSERVANCES; MEMORIAL DAY; PATRIOT DAY; ROOSEVELT, FRANKLIN DELANO; VETERANS DAY; WORLD WAR II.

For Further Reading:
Landy, Marcia. "America under Attack": Pearl Harbor, 9/11, and History in the Media. In *Film and Television after 9/11*, edited by Wheeler Winston Dixon, 49–100. Carbondale: Southern Illinois University Press, 2003.
Rosenberg, Emily S. *A Date Which Will Live: Pearl Harbor in American Memory*. Durham, N.C.: Duke University Press, 2003.

Pecos Bill (legendary) As an imagined rather than recalled figure from American history, Pecos Bill summons a mythic portrait of a cowboy from the era of westward expansion.

Many folklorists trace the beginnings of this figure to Edward O'Reilly in 1923. As were other figures in American legend, Bill was described as not entirely human. In his case, the reference to being half coyote is not just a characterization of his fierceness. It speaks of the portion of his childhood spent parentless on the untamed frontier of the American West.

According to the stories that survive, Pecos Bill was born in Texas in 1880 to a rather large family. When he, his parents, and his 13 siblings ventured west in a Conestoga wagon, Bill joined them in the cross-country journey. One day, however, the family's wagon struck a rock with such force that Bill fell out of the back of the wagon accidentally. Left behind mistakenly by a preoccupied clan of humans, Pecos Bill was left to the care of the creatures that surrounded him. He had always been one to befriend the animals of the world, and when he became separated from his human family, the coyotes raised Bill. Some say they still miss him. Bill came of age on the land, as wild a creature as the region ever knew.

As such a beginning might portend, Pecos Bill was a resilient individual. He not only survived the loss of his family, he thrived. He personified the cowboy of the American West. He is a favorite character of cowboy tales, and he is featured in many children's stories, tall tale anthologies, and the 1948 Disney feature *Melody Time.*

Many tales recount the ways in which Pecos Bill taught other cowboys how it was done. Stories depict him as performing amazing feats such as riding a cougar and using a snake for as a lasso. Bill is said to have "invented" the cattle drive, the signature activity of the now archetypal American figure of the cowboy. He is also reputed to have devised the six-shooter, the frontiersman's weapon of choice. Bill also fashioned a guitar, which he used to play tunes and sing by the campfire at night. As he reached adulthood, Bill fell in love with an outdoorsy woman named Slue-Foot Sue, and together they raised a family of cowboys and cowgirls. Accounts of his death and its cause, which vary widely include variations in which Pecos Bill falls prey to his own tendencies to be brash and a bit of a show-off.

Pecos Bill functions as an emblem of cowboy culture and its conquest of the American frontier.

See also: ANIMALS; COWBOYS; COYOTE; FAKE-LORE; FOLK HEROES/LEGENDARY FIGURES; FOLK-TALES; FRONTIER; REGION, FOLKS; SOUTHWEST-ERN REGIONAL FOLKLORE.

For Further Reading:

Boatright, Mody. *Tall Tales from Texas Cow Camps.* Dallas: Southern Methodist University Press, 1982.

Bowman, James Cloyd. *Pecos Bill, the Greatest Cowboy of All Time.* Chicago: A. Whitman, 1948.

Dary, David. *Cowboy Culture: A Saga of Five Centuries.* New York: Knopf, 1981.

Dobie, J. Frank, ed. *Texas and Southwestern Lore.* Austin: Texas Folklore Society, 1927.

Felton, Howard. *New Tall Tales of Pecos Bill.* New York: Prentice-Hall, 1958.

———. *Pecos Bill, Texas Cowpuncher.* New York: Random House, 1962.

Osborne, Mary Pope. *American Tall Tales.* New York: Knopf, 1991.

Pennsylvania Dutch/Pennsylvania German folklore The population sometimes known as the Pennsylvania Dutch are more accurately described as the Pennsylvania Germans.

The reference to them as Dutch is a misnomer, probably deriving from the German word for "German," *Deutsch.* Therefore, when people speak of Pennsylvania's "Dutch Country," they usually mean the state's residents of German ancestry. In particular, they often mean those subgroups of the Pennsylvania German whose folkways remain the most distinctive, such as the Amish and the Mennonites. These communities have held true to traditional ways and resisted the introduction of new technologies. With their horse and buggy transportation, the Amish represent otherwise lost or vanishing folkways.

The Pennsylvania Germans have been in North America since the 17th century. They have earned a wide reputation for signature folklore forms from folk art to folk architecture. Folk crafts associated with the Pennsylvania Germans include paper cutting, quilting, stenciling, manuscript illumination, and painting of furniture or other domestic objects. This folk group is responsible for several holiday customs observed by many Americans beyond their group, including the Easter Bunny, the adorned Christmas tree, and Groundhog Day. Perhaps the most famous of all Pennsylvania German traditions involve food customs and foodways. Popular dishes originating with the Pennsylvania Germans are pretzels, scrapple, sauerkraut, funnel cakes, and shoofly pie.

With the formation of recognition organizations such as the Pennsylvania German Society, founded in 1891, Americans paid tribute to the folk culture and traditions associated with this small but influential group. Pennsylvania German decorative motifs such as birds, flowers, hearts, and hex signs such as can be seen on traditional barns and farmhouses typify the look of Pennsylvania German handiwork.

See also: ARCHITECTURE, FOLK; CHRISTMAS; CULTURAL GROUPS; DUTCH-AMERICAN FOLKLORE; EASTER; EASTER BUNNY; FOOD/FOODWAYS; IMMIGRATION AND FOLKLORE; NORTHEASTERN REGIONAL FOLKLORE; REGION, FOLK; RELIGION, FOLK.

For Further Reading:

Beck, Ervin. *MennoFolk: Mennonite and Amish Folk Traditions.* Scottsdale, Pa.: Herald Press, 2004.

Brendle, Thomas Royce, and William S. Troxell. *Pennsylvania German Folk Tales, Legends, Once-upon-a-Time Stories, Maxims, and Sayings.* Norristown: Pennsylvania German Society, 1944.

Fogel, Edwin Miller. *Beliefs and Superstitions of the Pennsylvania Germans.* Philadelphia: American Germanica Press, 1915.

Hostetler, John A., ed. *Amish Roots: A Treasury of History, Wisdom, and Lore.* Baltimore: John Hopkins University Press, 1989.

Kirchner, Audrey. *In Days Gone By: Folklore and Traditions of the Pennsylvania Dutch.* Englewood, Colo.: Libraries Unlimited, 1996.

Korson, George, ed. *Pennsylvania Songs and Legends.* Philadelphia: University of Pennsylvania Press, 1949.

Kraybill, Donald B., and Carl F. Bowman. *On the Backroad to Heaven: Old Order Hutterites, Mennonites, Amish, and Brethren.* Baltimore: John Hopkins University Press, 2001.

Parsons, William T. *The Pennsylvania Dutch: A Persistent Minority.* Boston: Twanye, 1976.

Swank, Scott. *Arts of the Pennsylvania Germans.* New York: W. W. Norton, 1983.

Yoder, Don. *Discovering American Folklife: Studies in Ethnic, Religious, and Regional Culture.* Ann Arbor, Mich.: UMI Research Press, 1989.

Pennsylvania folklore See ART, FOLK; BOONE, DANIEL; CHAPMAN, JOHN (JOHNNY APPLESEED); CHRISTMAS; EASTER BUNNY; FOLKLORE STUDIES; FRANKLIN, BENJAMIN; GROUNDHOG DAY; MAGARAC, JOE; NAMING/NAMES; NORTHEASTERN REGIONAL FOLKLORE; PATRIOT DAY; PENNSYLVANIA DUTCH/PENNSYLVANIA GERMAN FOLKLORE; QUAKER FOLKLORE; ROSS, BETSY.

photography, folk Photography is an element of both material and popular culture. The commercialization and technological democratization of photography for nonelite consumption have made it a shared life experience and presence for many. If not from photography's arrival in 1839, certainly since the latter part of the 19th century with the introduction of the Kodak and the rise of amateur photography, photographs have chronicled the lives of common persons. As an artifact that occurs in a context, a literal and figurative frame, the photograph should be considered for both its surface qualities and the more subtle information it holds about the human condition.

By customarily treating photography as a flat art, photographic scholarship has often featured surface analysis, accomplished through scrutiny of the formal and compositional characteristics of the picture plane. While this is one appropriate level of appreciation and understanding of photos, to consider folk photography, it is equally necessary to come to terms with the methods for contextual study of photography.

Photographs may act as visual cues to the persons connected with those images: That is, they frequently encourage an intimate viewer to engage in a dialogue specifically corresponding to the imagery. Additionally, pictures may serve as a catalyst to viewer-listener sharing of a visual narrative, as is common in the ritual act of presenting the contents of a family album. Without such organization, with the passing years, family photographs risk becoming a pedestrian and meaning-devoid collection of depictions of persons and their circumstance, artifacts whose specific importance resides in their function within social and historical memory.

Because photography is a relatively new phenomenon, though, its human context remains in large part accessible. Often, the photographer or others linked directly to the photographic event are available to researchers. Interviews, oral histories, and other personal contact may then accompany visual scholarship. In this way, the student of photography can capture and preserve the interaction between persons and the material images.

While photography receives explanation and embellishment from verbal expression, it can also be seen as a language in itself. A photographic image has both a surface and a deep structure. The communication of a photographic message is coded and as such contains a subtle set of rules and methods for the transmission of information visually. People assign their own meanings to images, and yet, when viewed in large numbers, snapshots begin to resemble one another and fall into categories. Photographic images, in this regard, may become universalized in their outward patterns.

In this sense, the study of photographs concerns itself with the history of ordinary life. Once the hand camera freed photographers of some of the costly and cumbersome tripods and flash units once required, more travel and quicker exposures became possible. This revolution in technology had an impact on both the photographic subjects and the manner of their presentation. Pictures became affordable, and plentiful, and so less formal and posed. Scholars such as Marianne Hirsch and Jerald Maddox approach homemode photography as a folk medium, concerned more with document than technology or high art.

See also: ART, FOLK; FAMILY FOLKLORE; FOLKLIFE; FOLKLIFE MOVEMENT; FOLKLORE IN EVERYDAY LIFE; MATERIAL CULTURE; VERNACULAR CULTURE.

For Further Reading:

Coke, Van Deren, ed. *One Hundred Years of Photographic History*. Albuquerque: University of New Mexico Press, 1975.

Hirsch, Marianne, ed. *The Familial Gaze*. Hanover, N.H.: University Press of New England, 1999.

Hirsch, Marianne. *Family Frames: Photography, Narrative, and Postmemory*. Cambridge, Mass.: Harvard University Press, 1997.

Ohrn, Steven, and Michael Bell. *Saying Cheese: Studies in Folklore and Visual Communication*. Bloomington, Ind.: Folklore Forum Society, 1975.

"Pied Piper of Hamelin, The"

"The Pied Piper of Hamelin" is a medieval tale of a legendary figure capable of great influence on those around him, both for good and for ill.

A town plagued by rats wishes to be relieved of this blight. Responding to their predicament, a musician of unusual attire, the Pied Piper, uses his music to lure the rats to the river, where they then drown.

While the town's rat problem is resolved in this manner, another greater problem awaits. When payment for the piper's service is refused, he retaliates by using his skill as a piper to lead the town's children off just as he had the rats, on a journey from which they never return.

In this moralizing tale, the title character exacts a high price for an unpaid debt. The message is fairly plain: When accepting a completed service, it is imperative to compensate the provider of that service promptly and equitably. To refuse such payment is to risk reprisal, as the townspeople in this tale learn all too well.

Although it is not American in origin, the story of the Pied Piper is a staple of children's story culture in the United States. The figure of the piper symbolizes the power to charm, as well as the power to render consequences. The tale of the Pied Piper not only warns against being too ready a follower, but also about the dangers of failing to meet one's obligations to others. When people speak of the need to "pay the piper," they are recalling the lesson of this traditional tale.

The tale of the Pied Piper has been the subject of a poem by Robert Browning, as well as many retellings and satires.

See also: ANIMALS; CHILDREN'S FOLKLORE; FABLES; FAIRY TALES; FOLK HEROES/LEGENDARY FIGURES; MYTHS, FOLK.

For Further Reading:
Mieder, Wolfgang. "'To Pay the Piper' and the Legend of 'The Pied Piper of Hamelin,'" *Proverbium* 2 (1985): 263–270.

Seal, Graham. *Encyclopedia of Folk Heroes.* Santa Barbara, Calif.: ABC-CLIO, 2001.

Queenan, Bernard. "The Evolution of the Pied Piper," *Children's Literature* 7 (1978): 104–114.

piercing, body   See BODYLORE.

plant folklore   See CONJURE/CONJURING; FLOWERS; GARDENING; "JACK AND THE BEANSTALK."

Pledge of Allegiance   Most American children learn the Pledge of Allegiance by rote, accomplished through daily recitation in the classroom.

Few, however, know the story behind this ritual. Beyond knowing the words, though, and noticing its ubiquity in American culture, a folklorist might look at the source of the phenomenon.

Such an inquiry likely holds some surprises. For one thing, the pledge was first created by a socialist, Francis Bellamy. One early draft of the text ended with a reference not only to liberty and justice, but also to equality. That element was removed, however, presumably because the notion of equality was not universally held. Further, in its original form, the pledge made no reference to God or to religion. Therefore, while the Pledge of Allegiance is taken for granted as an affirmation, and it might be tempting to suppose has always existed and has not changed, its origin and evolution reveal some interesting shifts in public opinion.

Customs surrounding the Pledge of Allegiance are largely a product of the 19th century. By the 1890s, it became a daily practice for schoolchildren to recognize the flag each morning with the Pledge of Allegiance. Class members would stand, place their right hand over their heart, and recite in unison the pledge: "I pledge allegiance to the flag of the United States of America and to the Republic for which it stands, one Nation, indivisible, with liberty and justice for all."

The wording of this pledge has shifted several times over the years. For instance, it was not until the 1950s that the reference to deity was introduced; President Eisenhower's 1954 addition of the words *under God* between the words *Nation* and *indivisible*.

More recently, there have been legal challenges to the compulsory recitation of the pledge, particularly the pledge's mention of God. Invoking the principle of separation of church and state, plaintiffs haved sought to challenge the constitutionality of requiring people to participate in the pledge. They contend that, among other things, such a practice is tantamount to a public prayer. As yet, such challenges have not altered the pledge or its customs of recitation.

While reciting the Pledge of Allegiance might appear a straightforward act of loyalty to one's country, its related lore is largely unknown, and its recitation has been a matter of controversy.

See also: FLAG DAY; FOLKLORE IN EVERYDAY LIFE; RITUALS, FOLK; RELIGION, FOLK; ROSS, BETSY.

For Further Reading:
Baer, John. *The Pledge of Allegiance, a Centennial History, 1892–1992.* Annapolis, Md.: Free State Press, 1992.

Brandt, Nat. "To the Flag," *American Heritage* 22, no. 4 (June 1971): 72–75, 104.

Committee on the Judiciary. Subcommitttee on the Constitution, Civil Rights and Property Rights. *Beyond the Pledge of Allegiance.* Washington, D.C.: U.S. GPO, 2005.

Ellis, Richard. *To the Flag: The Unlikely History of the Pledge of Allegiance.* Lawrence: University Press of Kansas, 2005.

Pocahontas (c. 1595–1617) Pocahontas is a highly romanticized and somewhat mysterious figure from North America's 17th century.

Not many specific facts about her life are known. Most accounts must be based upon others' accounts, including the stories framed by Captain John Smith of Jamestown, Virginia.

Pocahontas was born the daughter of an Algonquin chief, Powhatan, in Virginia. *Pocahontas* was actually her nickname, suggesting that she was a spirited and playful girl. Her given name, however, was *Matoaka*. This Indian princess is reputed to have been a salutary influence in the relations between Anglo settlers and indigenous peoples throughout her life.

One such encounter was her first meeting with Smith. He had strayed from an expedition party and found himself among indigenous people. In what may or may not have amounted to a Native American ritual traditionally conducted with the arrival of strangers in their midst, the captain believed himself to be under attack. Whether interceding for his rescue or merely carrying out the custom of pretending to so do, Pocahontas stepped in and Smith was spared. This meeting was the first of many situations in which Pocahontas was perceived by Anglo settlers to be promoting peaceful understanding.

Pocahontas may or may not have had a first marriage to a fellow Indian, Kocoum. In any case, when Pocahontas was captured and held captive by the settlers, Kocoum failed to retrieve her, and thus, by tribal custom, dissolved any union. In 1614, Pocahontas converted to Christianity in order to marry John Rolfe. In 1615, they had a son, Thomas. The following year, Sir Thomas Dale included the Rolfe family in a party of Native Americans whom he transported to London, hoping for a favorable response from sponsors of the Virginia Company. Unfortunately, as Pocahontas reached the shore on the return voyage, she lost her battle with an illness that had afflicted her during the passage.

Hailed as an intermediary between two populations frequently in conflict, Pocahontas is the subject of many stories, legends, and popular images, including a historically fanciful 1995 Disney animated feature, *Pocahontas*.

See also: ALLEN, PAULA GUNN; FOLK HEROES/LEGENDARY FIGURES; NATIVE AMERICAN FOLKLORE.

For Further Reading:
Abrams, Ann Uhry. *The Pilgrims and Pocahontas: Rival Myths of American Origin.* Boulder, Colo.: Westview Press, 1999.

Mossiker, Frances. *Pocahontas: The Life and the Legend.* New York: Random House, 1976.

Rountree, Helen. *Pocahontas's People: The Powhatan Indians of Virginia: The Powhatan Indians of Virginia through Four Centuries.* Norman: University of Oklahoma Press, 1990.

Tilton, Robert. *Pocahontas: The Evolution of an American Narrative.* New York: Cambridge University Press, 1994.

poinsettia See CHRISTMAS.

Polish-American folklore Polish-American folklore pertains to immigrants to America from Poland, as well as those persons born in the United States of Polish heritage.

Immigration to the United States from Poland has been occurring since at least the 17th century. Most such immigrants arrived after 1830, as did many groups who relocated to America. Large populations of Polish immigrants took up residence in American cities such as Chicago, Detroit, and New York City.

Polish-American folklore takes many forms. Craft traditions cultivated in Poland, such as woodworking and glassmaking, entered America with Polish artisans. Folk beliefs among Polish Americans include concepts of good luck and concerns about malevolent forces such as the devil, witches, and the evil eye. Although it is not original to Poland, the polka is a folk dance commonly enjoyed at Polish-American festivities. Traditional foods include cabbage, sauerkraut, dark bread, dumplings, apple and potato pancakes, and sausage.

Polish Americans celebrate many of the same holidays other Americans do but sometimes incorporate Polish customs within their holiday practices. For example, just before the fasts of Lent begin, many Polish Americans enjoy filled doughnuts. This treat, while often purchased from bakeries now, once served the purpose of using up ingredients such as sugar that would not be used during the season of Lent. It is also customary to leave an empty chair at the holiday table for an unexpected visitor at Christmas and Easter.

Organizations dedicated to the preservation and study of Polish-American culture include Chicago's Polish National Alliance of the United States and Polish American Historical Association, Miami's American Institute of Polish Culture, and Washington, D.C.'s, American Council for Polish-Culture. Major collections of Polish-American cultural material include Chicago's Polish Museum of America, New York's Kosciuszko Foundation, and Miami's American Institute for Polish Culture.

By incorporating traditional elements of folklore in daily life, Polish Americans cultivate cultural awareness among the members of their communities, especially the young.

See also: CULTURAL GROUPS; DEVIL, THE; ETHNICITY; EVIL EYE; FOOD/FOODWAYS; HOLIDAYS/OBSERVANCES; IMMIGRATION AND FOLKLORE; SUPERSTITION.

For Further Reading:

Bukowszyk, John J. *And My Children Did Not Know Me: A History of the Polish Americans*. Bloomington: Indiana University Press, 1987.

Bukowczyk, John J., ed. *Polish Americans and Their History: Community, Culture, and Politics*. Pittsburgh: University of Pittsburgh Press, 1996.

Hodorowicz Knab, Sophie. *Polish Customs, Traditions, and Folklore*. New York: Hippocrene Books, 1996.

Lopata, Helena Znaniecka. *Polish Americans: Status Competition in an Ethnic Community*. 2d ed. New Brunswick, N.J.: Transactions, 1974.

Obidinski, Eugene, and Helen Stankiewicz Zand. *Polish Folkways in America*. Lanham, Md.: University Press of America, 1987.

Pula, James S. *Polish Americans: An Ethnic Community*. New York: Twayne, 1995.

Silverman, Deborah Anders. *Polish-American Folklore*. Urbana: University of Illinois Press, 2000.

politics and folklore In its participatory democracy, the United States has a long tradition of electoral politics and its associated lore.

America's political folklore has its origins in the American Revolution and the struggle for self-determination. Since then, Americans have taken great pride in the notion of a country promising the rights of "life, liberty, and the pursuit of happiness." Although African Americans and women would not win the vote for many years, such victories for civil rights have helped move the country closer to the national ideals of political equality.

Politics in a democracy involves a process in which all citizens participate in selecting leaders and, in so doing, shaping their own government. In fact, many of the nation's holidays and observances are in part celebrations of the democratic process. Examples include Independence Day/ Fourth of July, Election Day, and Inauguration Day. Even the political campaigns and political party conventions preceding elections have elements of patriotic pageantry. With their flags, buntings, imitation straw hats, placards, and campaign buttons, these events perform the symbolic work of linking candidates to positive national identity. Similarly, rallies and protests directed at campaigns and conventions dramatize the rights of assembly and free speech accorded to dissenters in America.

While the imagery of political engagement in a free society is strong, there is a simultaneous distrust of politicians as a group, whom ordinary Americans suspect of vanity, greed, and corruption by power.

In addition to electoral politics, there are a variety of other, more informal forms of political activity in which U.S. citizens may engage.

In some states, for instance, an initiative process permits citizens to use signed petitions to advance a matter of policy such as gas taxes or smoking prohibitions. Boycotts represent another way in which Americans make their displeasure known to manufacturers, distributors, and corporations. This form of political action is sometimes described as voting with one's pocketbook. When a proposed law or policy, domestic or foreign, excites controversy, it is also common for opponents to take to the streets to march in protest. In these and other contexts, folk music has often accompanied protests by unifying, informing, and voicing in public the sentiments of those who object to a measure, from reinstatement of the military draft to recall of an elected official.

Of course, not all Americans exercise their civic rights. Voting returns in national elections suggest that many citizens take their ballots and the powers that they confer for granted. Nonetheless, there remains a rhetoric of patriotism that extolls such political freedoms even when individuals decline to use them. In holidays and observances, material culture, and music, folklore has helped express the voice of the American people.

See also: CITIZENSHIP DAY; CIVIL RIGHTS MOVEMENT; COMPUTER FOLKLORE; ELECTION DAY; FOLKLORE IN EVERYDAY LIFE; INAUGURATION DAY; LINCOLN, ABRAHAM; MUSIC, FOLK; PLEDGE OF ALLEGIANCE; PROTEST IN FOLKLORE; ROOSEVELT, FRANKLIN DELANO; ROOSEVELT, THEODORE; WASHINGTON, GEORGE; WOMEN'S MOVEMENT; WOMEN'S SUFFRAGE.

For Further Reading:

Eliasoph, Nina. *Avoiding Politics: How Americans Produce Apathy in Everyday Life*. Cambridge: Cambridge University Press, 1998.

Kryzanek, Michael. *Angry, Bored, Confused: A Citizen Handbook of American Politics*. Boulder, Colo.: Westview Press, 1999.

Lawrence, John Shelton, and Robert Jewett. *The Myth of the American Superhero*. Grand Rapids, Mich.: W. B. Eerdmans, 2002.

Lieberman, Robbie. *"My Song Is My Weapon": People's Songs, American Communism, and the Politics of Culture, 1930–1950*. Urbana: University of Illinois Press, 1989.

Radner, Joan, and Susan Lanser. "The Feminist Voice: Strategies of Coding in Feminism and Literature," *Journal of American Folklore* 100, no. 398 (fall 1987): 412–425.

Reuss, Richard, and JoAnne Reuss. *American Folk Music and Left-Wing Music and Left-Wing Politics, 1927–1957*. Lanham, Md.: Scarecrow Press, 2000.

poltergeists   See GHOSTS.

poplore   The term *poplore* is a controversial one used to speak to the interstices of folk culture and popular culture in the United States.

The American studies scholar Gene Bluestein, who invokes the term in his 1994 book of the same name, advocates an approach to the study of United States culture that acknowledges and explores the intersections of folk and popular expression.

The controversy concerning poplore is, at its base, a debate about the definition of folklore itself. While the definitions of folklore in use by experts in the discipline vary widely, most have emphasized certain properties in common in establishing the central category of analysis.

Therefore, conventional folklore usually confines itself to traditional and often rural works/performances, items/events fashioned by the human hand or ordered by the human voice, and cultural expressions personally disseminated.

As opposed to marking a sharp and definitive boundary between folk and pop cultures, the study of poplore presumes the existence of important and interesting hybrids. Poplore scholars emphasize the sense in which folklore and popular culture are interdependent and, on some level, inseparable. In other words, poplore allows for the integration of commercial, mass-produced, and exactly repeatable cultural artifacts or expressions in tandem with conventional folk material.

There is little doubt that in today's information society, much of what Americans learn reaches them at least in part through electronic media rather than strictly through storytellers, direct observation, or apprencticeship to craftspeople. Still, much of what Americans encounter each day—even when mediated through consumer culture and the media of television, film, and the Internet—relates to folk traditions.

For example, very few Americans who are familiar with tales from American slavery, such as the Uncle Remus tales, have discovered them through oral culture. In fact, relatively few are even familiar firsthand with the transcriptions of such tales published by collectors such as Joel Chandler Harris. Many more have become acquainted with the Uncle Remus tales through popularized representations, such as Disney's feature-length film, *Song of the South* (1946), in which the Uncle Remus stories and characters were the focus. However, since that film has not been in distribution for many years, today's youth probably encounter the Uncle Remus tales indirectly, through storybook adaptations (which may themselves be influenced as much by the Disney version as by any earlier one) or by the Splash Mountain attraction at Disney theme parks in California, Florida, and Tokyo, where characters and scenes of *Song of the South* inspire the design. In the end, Walt Disney and Joel Chandler Harris may not function as folklorists, but their audiences nonetheless experience and understand folk content through their representations.

The challenge in embracing poplore, as in defining folklore, is related to one's expectations of authenticity and purity in cultural expression. In a postmodern world, a rigid model of what is genuine and worthy of study may ultimately exclude much lived-world experience. That is, while children may not consciously see the character of Roger Rabbit or Bugs Bunny as the logical successor of the character Brer Rabbit from the Uncle Remus tales, through these modern-day cartoons, they nonetheless understand a good deal about the meaning of the trickster figure in American culture.

A more expansive definition of lore may help keep traditional culture recognizable, if not intact, in a rapidly changing environment where conventional folk material must find its niche.

See also: BRER RABBIT; FAKELORE; FOLKLORE; FOLKLORE IN EVERYDAY LIFE; KITSCH; REMUS, UNCLE; TERMS; TRICKSTER.

For Further Reading:

Bluestein, Gene. *Poplore: Folk and Pop in American Culture.* Amherst: University of Massachusetts Press, 1994.

Cullen, Jim. *The Art of Democracy: A Concise History of Popular Culture in the United States.* New York: Monthly Review Press, 1996.

Dégh, Linda. *American Folkore and the Mass Media.* Bloomington: Indiana University Press. 1994.

Motz, Marilyn J., and Ray Broadus Browne, eds. *Eye on the Future: Popular Culture Scholarship into the Twenty-First Century.* Bowling Green, Ohio: Bowling Green State University Popular Press, 1994.

Narvaez, Peter, and Martin Laba, eds. *Media Sense: The Folklore-Popular Culture Continuum.* Bowling Green, Ohio: Bowling Green State University Popular Press, 1986.

Smith, Martin J., and Patrick J. Kiger. *Poplorica: A Popular History of the Fads, Mavericks, Inventions, and Lore That Shaped Modern America.* New York: Harper Resource, 2004.

portents   See PREDICTION.

Portuguese-American folklore   Portuguese-American folklore pertains to all immigrants to the United States from Portugal, along with American-born individuals of Portuguese heritage.

Although Portuguese explorers reached North America earlier, perhaps even before the arrival of Columbus, immigration from Portugal to the United States has been going on since the middle of the 19th century. This immigration reached its height in the first two decades of the 20th century. Literacy tests and immigrant quotas instituted during that era curtailed the process until 1965, when the annual quota system ended. Portuguese Americans tended to make their homes in port cities, such as those of New England. Especially large populations concentrated in particular cities such as New Bedford, Massachusetts. With the influence of the Homestead Act, some Portuguese Americans ventured west to new homes in states such as California. Once there, many entered agriculture. Civic clubs and fraternal organizations helped support the success and cultural identity of Portuguese Americans.

Folklore among Portuguese Americans spans many genres of personal and ethnic expression. Portuguese-American folk beliefs include fears of the devil, the evil eye, Fridays, and the number 13. Several proverbs in common use in America originate with Portuguese Americans, such as "Charity begins at home" and "Of evils, choose the least." Portuguese-American foodways feature shellfish, cod, and other seafood found in abundance in Portugal.

Portuguese Americans celebrate many of the usual holidays in America but often have their own distinctive practices. For example, at New Year's it is customary to pick and eat 12 grapes at the stroke of midnight to ensure joy in the coming year. Residents in Portuguese-American communities also celebrate feast days and festivals of their home country, including the Festival of the Blessed Sacrament, the Festival of the Holy Ghost, and the Senhor da Pedra Festival. Each event has religious origins but includes social and secular elements.

Well-known Portuguese Americans include John Philip Sousa, composer of patriotic soncs and marches such as "Stars and Stripes Forever." Portuguese Americans have historical heroes, as well. An example is Peter Francisco, a 16-year-old who enlisted and served in America's Revolutionary War.

Organizations dedicated to the preservation and study of Portuguese-American culture include New York's American Portuguese Society and Sacramento, California's, Portuguese Historical and Cultural Society. Major collections of Portuguese-American cultural material include the Oliveira Lima Library in Washington, D.C., and the Society for Spanish and Portuguese Historical Studies in Tucson, Arizona.

By maintaining the customs and traditions of their ancestors, Portuguese Americans honor both their ethnic heritage and their homeland.

See also: BELIEFS, FOLK; COLUMBUS, CHRISTOPHER; CULTURAL GROUPS; DEVIL, THE; EVIL EYE; FRIDAY THE THIRTEENTH; IMMIGRATION AND FOLKLORE; NORTHEASTERN REGIONAL FOLKLORE.

For Further Reading:
Cabral, Stephen L. *Tradition and Transformation: Portuguese Feasting in New Bedford.* New York: AMS Press, 1989.
Cardozo, Manoel da Silveira. *The Portuguese in America: 590 B.C.–1974: A Chronology and Fact Book.* Dobbs Ferry, N.Y.: Oceana, 1976.
Leder, Hans Howard. *Cultural Persistence in a Portuguese-American Community.* New York: Arno Press, 1980.
Mira, Manuel. *The Forgotten Portuguese.* Franklin, N.C.: Portuguese-American Historical Research Foundation, 1998.
Pap, Leo. *The Portuguese-Americans.* Boston: Twayne, 1981.
Pap, Leo. *The Portuguese in the United States: A Bibliography.* Staten Island, N.Y.: Center for Migration Studies, 1976.
Ribeiro, José Luís. *Portuguese Immigrants and Education.* Bristol, R.I.: Portuguese American Federation, 1982.
Wolforth, Sandra. *The Portuguese in America.* San Francisco: R & E Research Associates, 1978.

pottery   See CRAFTS, FOLK.

pranks/tricks   See HUMOR, FOLK.

prediction   In a wide range of folk beliefs and practices, Americans seek to forecast the future. In most cases, these efforts represent attempts to influence, foretell, or control forces that otherwise remain outside the exercise of human will.

Efforts at prediction, such as dowsing, divination, clairvoyance, palmistry, tea-leaf reading, and fortune-telling, all rely on folk beliefs for their potency. From strategies to locate water beneath the ground to attempts to determine a person's life expectancy, these prediction rituals aspire to advance knowledge of facts not in evidence, or to understand matters that cannot otherwise be researched or intuited. While throughout history such abilities have provoked suspicion and cast those regarded as psychic as witches or other dangerous beings, there continues to be a curiosity about the future and those who claim to be in closer contact with it.

In fact, many superstitions and notions of the supernatural include embedded concepts about the future. The most common of these items of folk wisdom include beliefs about ways to predict the happiness and productivity of an individual or couple's future, as is frequently desired at key moments in the life cycle, such as childbirth or marriage. Numerous aspects of wedding lore can be traced to long-standing beliefs about omens and portents. From interpreting the weather on the wedding day to preventing the groom from seeing the bride in her wedding dress, wedding folklore often represents the collective attempt to prevent misfortune and promote luck for the bride and groom. Similarly, at New Year's Eve/Day, many Americans try to behave in such a manner as to gain prosperity and good fortune during the coming year.

In addition, beliefs about magic, folk medicine, and folk religion can hinge on ideas of prediction. For instance, there are various folk beliefs about how to forecast whether an expected baby will be a boy or a girl. While such practices may rely upon informal theories about differences in how pregnant women carry a male or female fetus in utero, the sheer odds of a given case of such prediction would indicate at least a 50 percent

success rate, reinforcing the effectiveness of the ritual or other device used to arrive at a forecast.

Beyond the role prediction plays in daily life, there are several American holidays that involve some role for acts of prediction. The clearest such case involves animal rather than human powers of foreknowledge: Groundhog Day. Depending upon whether a groundhog sees his shadow on this occasion, the arrival of spring may be judged near or far. While many may regard such a prediction as unreliable, it continues to be recounted and reported as an annual ritual.

While there are many forces and variables at work in the ways the future takes shape, folk beliefs about prediction enable people to channel their energies into what they regard as the most fruitful approaches to its forecast.

See also: BELIEFS, FOLK; BODYLORE; CHILDBIRTH/PREGNANCY FOLKLORE; EVIL EYE; FOLKLORE IN EVERYDAY LIFE; GROUNDHOG DAY; LUCK/FORTUNE; MAGIC; MEDICINE, FOLK; RELIGION, FOLK; SAINT VALENTINE'S DAY; "SLEEPING BEAUTY"; SUPERNATURAL; SUPERSTITION; TOAST/DRINKING; VOODOO/HOODOO; WEATHER FOLKLORE; WEDDING/MARRIAGE FOLKLORE.

For Further Reading:
Gibson, Walter, and Litzka Gibson. *The Complete Illustrated Book of Divination and Prophecy.* New York: Doubleday, 1973.
Ikeya, Motoji. *Earthquakes and Animals: From Folk Legends to Science.* River Edge, N.J.: World Scientific, 2004.
Opie, Iona, and Moira Tatem, eds. *A Dictionary of Superstitions.* New York: Oxford University Press, 1989.
Pickover, Clifford. *Dreaming the Future: The Fantastic Story of Prediction.* Amherst, N.Y.: Prometheus Books, 2001.
Pollack, Rachel. *Practical Guide to Fortune Telling; Teach Yourself Fortune Telling: Palmistry, the Crystal Ball, Runes, Tea Leaves, the Tarot.* New York: H. Holt, 1986.
Winkleman, Michael, and Philip Peek, eds. *Divination and Healing: Potent Vision.* Tucson: University of Arizona Press, 2004.

pregnancy See CHILDBIRTH/PREGNANCY FOLK-LORE.

preservation, historic See HISTORIC PRESER-VATION.

Presidents' Day Presidents' Day is a fairly recent concept, and the proposed holiday's proponents aspire through this holiday to combine previously separate observances of the birthdays of Presidents Abraham Lincoln and George Washington. While at this point the holiday exists only as an informal designation, if formalized it would conjoin the solemn days of remembrance for two beloved U.S. presidents.

Lincoln's Birthday was first celebrated at the United States Capitol on February 12, 1866. The first state to observe the day as a holiday was Lincoln's home state of Illinois. Most states, with the exception of some from the Confederacy, followed suit with a day of remembrance of the Civil War era president. Customs for the day include placement of a mourning wreath at the Lincoln Memorial in Washington, D.C., and schoolchildren's participation in patriotic songs and pageants. Lincoln's birthday does not enjoy the status of a federal holiday in the United States but is celebrated annually nonetheless.

Washington's Birthday was observed for the first time, in accordance with a resolution of Congress, on February 22, 1800. Washington's Birthday has had the status of a federal holiday since 1885, when President Chester Arthur lent his signature to that designation. Washington's centenary in 1932 was an especially prominent act of memory and the occasion for many renamings of streets and localities in his honor.

As a result of the Mondays Holiday Act, passed by Congress in 1968, Washington's Birthday is now observed on the third Monday in February each year. The day is still marked by wreath laying at Washington's Mount Vernon gravesite. Plays, ceremonies, and reenactments of historic battles have also been scheduled as tributes to the nation's first commander in chief.

Presidents' Day is an unofficial holiday, regarded as a fusion of the observances of Washington's Birthday and Lincoln's Birthday, that occurs on the third Monday in February each year. Although many Americans now think of the third Monday in February as Presidents' Day, the formal designation of that day by law is as Washington's Birthday. This does not prevent states or businesses from terming the holiday Presidents' Day, and it is now commonplace for advertisements and commercials to feature both presidents when promoting sales set for the day each year.

See also: CIVIL WAR; HOLIDAYS/OBSERVANCES; LINCOLN, ABRAHAM; WASHINGTON, GEORGE.

For Further Reading:

Cohen, Hennig, and Tristram Potter Coffin, eds. *The Folklore of American Holidays.* Detroit: Gale, 1987.

Myers, Robert J. *Celebrations: The Complete Book of American Holidays.* Garden City, N.Y.: Doubleday, 1972.

Santino, Jack. *All around the Year: Holidays and Celebrations in American Life.* Urbana: University of Illinois Press, 1994.

"Princess and the Pea, The" (legendary)
"The Princess and the Pea" conveys the tale of a female traveler who, in seeking refuge from inclement weather, finds her future.

The tale begins, however, with the plight of a prince. Because of his desire to find love and marry, the prince travels throughout the world in search of a fitting spouse. While many women present themselves as princesses, he has reservations about each one he encountered. In time, he despairs of finding a mate and returns to the castle where his family resides. His homecoming is a melancholy one since he fears he will never find the princess he sought.

One stormy night, however, a woman stops at the castle, hoping to find shelter until the weather passes. The residents of the castle grant her request. Although her appearance upon arrival is far from regal, for she is rain soaked and travel worn, the stranger identifies herself as a princess. The queen doubts the veracity of this claim, however, and decides to administer a kind of test of her unexpected visitor. Unknown to the traveler, the queen has arranged the guest's bed in a way that she feels certain with reveal the true identity of the visitor. Beneath 20 mattresses and 20 featherbeds, the queen places a single pea.

When morning arrives, the guest wakes and indicates that she is bruised from some object in the bed that disturbed her slumber. Since this report satisfies the initially skeptical queen, the castle's occupants now accept the guest's claimed status as a princess.

With the impediment of such doubt removed, the visiting princess and the resident prince marry, and the single pea that confirmed her royal status is placed in a museum in the kingdom they now share.

The story underscores the central role social class plays within a hierarchical society and in particular as it pertains to marriage. The tale also portrays marriage as a bond to be approached only after careful reflection on the fitness of a match. Along the way, the prince's experience lends support to the supposition that love occurs best when it is not pursued as if a task to be accomplished by will alone.

This brief but memorable tale has been retold many times, perhaps most notably on the stage in the 1960 production *Once Upon a Mattress*. It also provides an analogy when people wish to suggest that someone has delicate sensibilities or overreacts, as the princess does to the pea.

Along with other tales rendered by Danish storyteller Hans Christian Andersen, such as "The Emperor's New Clothes," "Thumbelina," "The Ugly Duckling," and "The Little Mermaid," "The Princess and the Pea" figures among the most recognizable childhood tales derived from oral traditions of folk culture.

See also: ANDERSEN, HANS CHRISTIAN; CHILDREN'S FOLKLORE; FABLES; FAIRY TALES; MUSEUMS, FOLK; MYTHS, FOLK.

For Further Reading:

Bernheimer, Kate, ed. *Mirror, Mirror, on the Wall: Women Writers Explore Their Favorite Fairy Tales.* New York: Anchor, 1998.

Cashdan, Sheldon. *The Witch Must Die: The Hidden Meaning of Fairy Tales.* New York: Basic Books, 1999.

Esrock, Ellen J. "The Princess and the Pea: Touch and the Private/Public Domains of Women's Knowledge." In *Research in Science and Technology Studies: Gender and Work*, edited by Shirley Gorenstein, 17–29. Stamford, Conn.: JAI, 2000.

Levine, Gail Carson. *The Princess Test.* New York: HarperCollins, 1999.

Tatar, Maria, ed. *The Annotated Classic Fairy Tales.* New York: W. W. Norton, 2002.

prison folklore   Although it is an involuntary association, a prison population represents a distinctive folk community. Prison populations are communities by shared circumstance, and prison folklore involves both those traditions inmates introduce when they enter and those associated with prison life.

Such a folklore is rich, though often dark in its references and gallows humor. It has its own slang, ballads, work songs, stories, jokes, sayings, and informal rules of conduct. First-time inmates must acclimate to this environment by learning its lore. Prison folklore offers one of the most intact folk traditions, for while the nation romanticizes its outlaws, there has been little impulse to co-opt the culture of captivity. The fascination is with the fugitive, not the apprehended criminal. Consequently, the insular world of prison folklore has escaped some of the commercialization and falsification other folk traditions have undergone.

Prison life is framed by some common expectations among prisoners, including the notion of "honor among thieves." That is, an individual must demonstrate loyalty to peers and not inform on others. There are also fairly elaborate systems of power and status among inmates, including barter and protection practices. In addition, there is an extensive verbal culture, including boasts, warnings, insults, laments, toasts, terminology, and oral performance.

Prose narratives of prison life abound. These stories feature both everyday and exceptional episodes in captivity. There are, of course, stories of memorable figures, whether inmates, guards, or wardens. These characters dominate such tales. Some prison narratives recount incidents in which prisoners succeed at subterfuge or even escape. Such tales feature legendary figures including John Paul Scott, who was the first Alcatraz inmate to swim all the way to shore at Fort Point in 1962.

Prison culture is not devoid of folk crafts. Needless to say, however, the objects created must be confined to those materials readily available to prisoners. An example would be matchstick sculptures, some of which can still be seen on display. More elaborate cases would be musical instruments, such as makeshift banjos fashioned from tin cans, newspaper, and waistband elastic. A more prevalent and worrisome form of craft would be improvised objects such as tools and weapons. Hand-crafted hatchets, knives, and guns are among the items constructed behind bars. Also common are recipes for homemade "hooch," alcohol brewed by inmates. Most such methods involve alcohol made from fruit, such as Apple Jack or Pruno.

In a curious turn within tourism, several closed prisons and penitentiaries, as well as some still operating, have opened small museums featuring prison artifacts, including razor ribbon, shackles, and objects related to American crime lore, such as Clyde Barrow's semiautomatic. At one such facility in Texas, "Old Sparky," a decommissioned electric chair used in 361 executions during the 20th century, stands on exhibit. In an equally curious turn within consumerism, such locations may also boast gift shops where visitors can purchase everything from refrigerator magnets to mugshot cups bearing the likenesses of notorious inmates.

See also: DILLINGER, JOHN; FLOYD, CHARLES ARTHUR (PRETTY BOY); FOLKLORE IN EVERYDAY LIFE; GERONIMO; JOAD, TOM; MARTIN LUTHER KING DAY; MUSEUMS, FOLK; OUTLAWS; POLITICS AND FOLKLORE; PROTEST IN FOLKLORE; STAGOLEE

For Further Reading:

Burke, Carole. *Vision Narratives of Women in Prison.* Knoxville: University of Tennessee Press, 1992.

Jackson, Bruce. *In the Life: Versions of the Criminal Experience.* New York: Holt, Rinehart & Winston, 1972.

———. "Prison Folklore," *Journal of American Folklore* 78, no. 310 (fall 1965): 317–329.

———. *Wake Up Dead Man: Afro-American Worksongs from Texas Prisons.* Cambridge, Mass.: Harvard University Press, 1972.

———. "What Happened to Jody?" *Journal of American Folklore* 80, no. 318 (fall 1967): 387–396.

James, Joy, ed. *Imprisoned Intellectuals: America's Political Prisoners Write on Life, Liberation, and Rebellion.* New York: Rowman & Littlefield, 2003.

protest in folklore Insofar as it documents the culture of regular citizens, American folklore has long functioned as the voice of the nation's people. On many occasions, the power of this voice has been invoked for the purpose of protest, whether to challenge injustice or to promote social change.

Protest has been a part of American history since at least the Revolutionary War era, as the nation owes its origins to resistance against British rule without representation. For that reason, the national identity has been integrally connected to acts of individual and collective dissent. Since the American Revolution, virtually every social movement associated with protest has included a folklore component.

During the 19th century, for example, abolitionists opposed the institution of slavery in the United States. The Civil War was itself a protest, as the southern states seceded from the Union over the slavery question. Both sides of the conflict felt the need to defend their principles, and so the northern states and the southern states did battle over the kind of nation they wished to preserve. While the resolution of the Civil War ended legalized slavery, it would mark only the beginning of the Civil Rights movement, through which Americans would fight for the equality of status and rights accorded to people of color.

Similarly, the fight for women's suffrage was a protest against interpretations of the Constitution that excluded women from political participation and representation by denying them the vote. Activists struggled mightily until the Nineteenth Amendment extended the franchise to include women. Following on the heels of this victory, the women's movement of the mid- to late 20th century sought full legal equality for women in the United States.

Other protests, such as labor-based strikes, antiwar demonstrations, gay pride marches, and antinuclear rallies, are likewise a part of American culture and its lore. Folk heroes and legendary figures such as Martin Luther King, Jr.; César Estrada Chavez; and Rosa Parks are closely associated with the freedom to assemble and freedom of speech accorded by the U.S. Constitution. American folk music, with its celebration of such rights, has contributed greatly to many American protests. Examples include the use of slave songs and spirituals in the Civil Rights movement and the folk revival ballads employed in teach-ins during the Vietnam War.

From the sit-ins of the Civil Rights movement to the placards of contemporary pickets, folklore contributes to the folk traditions, methods, and symbolism of American protest movements.

See also: ANTHONY, SUSAN BROWNELL; BAMBARA, TONI CADE; BROWN, JOHN; CABLE, WASHINGTON GEORGE; CHESNUTT, CHARLES WODDEL; CHAVEZ, CÉSAR ESTRADA; CIVIL RIGHTS MOVEMENT; DEPRESSION, THE GREAT; DOUGLASS, FREDERICK; DUNBAR, PAUL LAURENCE; EARTH DAY; ELLISON, RALPH WALDO; EMANCIPATION (PROCLAMATION) DAY; FOLKLORE IN EVERYDAY LIFE; GAY/LESBIAN FOLKLORE; GERONIMO; HENRY, PATRICK; HILL, JOE; HIPPIES; HUGHES, JAMES MERCER LANGSTON; IBO LANDING; JOAD, TOM; JONES, JOHN LUTHER (CASEY); JUNETEENTH; LABOR DAY; MARTIN LUTHER KING DAY; MORRISON, TONI; MOTHER'S DAY; MUSIC, FOLK; OCCUPATIONAL FOLKLORE; PARKS, ROSA; POLITICS AND FOLKLORE; PRISON FOLKLORE; QUILT, AIDS; REMUS, UNCLE; REVOLUTIONARY WAR; SLAVERY; STANTON, ELIZABETH CADY; STEINBECK, JOHN; STOWE, HARRIET BEECHER; STYRON, WILLIAM; TELL, WILLIAM; TRUTH, SOJOURNER; TUBMAN, HARRIET; TURNER, NAT; UNCLE SAM; UNDERGROUND RAILROAD; VESEY, DENMARK; VIETNAM WAR; WOMEN'S MOVEMENT; WOMEN'S SUFFRAGE; YANKEE DOODLE.

For Further Reading:

Carawan. Guy. *Sing for Freedom: The Story of the Civil Rights Movement through Its Songs.* Bethlehem, Pa.: Sing Out Corporation, 1990.

Davis, Susan. *Parades and Power: Street Theaters in Nineteenth-Century Philadelphia.* Philadelphia: Temple University Press, 1985.

Ferraro, Pat, Elaine Hedges, and Julie Silber. *Hearts and Hands: The Influence of Women and Quilts on American Society.* San Francisco: Quilt Digest Press, 1987.

Fowke, Edith, and Joe Glazer. *Songs of Work and Protest.* New York: Dover, 1973.

Greenway, John. *American Folksongs of Protest.* New York: A. S. Barnes, 1960.

Pershing, Linda. *The Ribbon around the Pentagon.* Knoxville: University of Tennessee Press, 1996.

Rodnitzky, Jerome. *Minstrels of the Dawn: The Folk-Protest Singer as a Cultural Hero.* Chicago: Nelson-Hall, 1976.

Wiggins, William. *O Freedom: Afro-American Emancipation Celebrations.* Knoxville: University of Tennessee Press, 1987.

proverbs Proverbs represent an important part of oral culture and so deserve special note within the study of folk speech. As do other sayings, proverbs represent efforts at pithy statement and plainspoken insight. While it is difficult to establish a firm edge around this category of speech as a discrete genre, proverbs seek to convey communal knowledge among a group's members, particularly its young or uninitiated members.

Proverbs typically travel through sounded language transmission, although such lessons, and even their familiar wording, may also find reinforcement as messages recorded within written texts. The content of proverbs usually consists of traditional teachings, concisely phrased for the listener, for both immediate impact and retention through memory. Herein rests the paradox of the proverb, for while a speaker does not invent the saying, there is a personal art of integrating it within communication in such a way as to achieve the optimal effect. A conversationalist skilled in the use of proverbs, then, embodies this paradox, which may itself be expressed with a proverb: "The wit of one, the wisdom of many."

Indeed, proverbs are a common language phenomenon across cultures and frequently overlap cultures that might otherwise seem disparate. That is, while specific cultural beliefs vary widely, proverbs usually address themselves chiefly to aspects of the human condition that transcend national culture or historical reference. Familiar examples of proverbs conveying items of cross-culturally recognizable advice include "Forgive and forget" and "Forewarned, forearmed." Although it is true that some proverbs invoke notions that are culturally idiosyncratic or linguistically idiomatic, most can be understood across eras, communities, and tongues. In fact, some proverbs are appropriated from oral cultures or written sources and then incorporated into speech.

Although they generally have their origin in the spoken word, proverbs also appear in published literature. They seem especially common in the writings of historically disenfranchised populations, presumably because writers honor the vitality of oral culture. For example, in Zora Neale Hurston's novel *Their Eyes Were Watching God*, Janie confides in her friend, Pheoby, telling her of recent journeys, "It's uh known fact, Pheoby. You got tuh *go* there tuh *know* there" (Hurston, 285). Rather than the signature discovery of the individual speaker, a proverb is more like the voice a community uses to speak to its members. The subject *you*, as in Janie's statement, is simultaneously an implied *we*. This legacy of oral narrative offers a mobilizing force in the lives of both speakers and listeners. Proverbs inform the decisions of individuals in the present with the experiences of the collective past. Through this communication, the past helps shape, and sometimes safeguard, the future.

Recent African-American women's fiction also demonstrates countless ways in which mother wit, including such cultural survivals as proverbs, may contest an oppressive racial master narrative. How do the voices of ancestral spirits travel into such thoroughly contemporary writings? Consider the "men without skin" in Toni Morrison's *Beloved* or Paule Marshall's images of the Ibos' water walk in *Praisesong for the Widow*. Consider, too, the consciousness and copresence of the ancestor in Michelle Cliff's *No Telephone to Heaven*. Incorporation of proverbs, both in the context of character dialogue and the direct address to the reader, enables authors to invoke the shared wisdom that might otherwise be lost or overlooked.

Proverbs are more than a specialized interest for folklore scholars and a collection item for field researchers; they remain a staple of conversation and expression, helping new generations embrace the senses of cultural belonging and understanding only possible when one regards history as a story of generations rather than simply of individual episodes. For this reason, proverbs speak to widespread patterns of events, both deeds and outcomes, experienced over time.

See also: AFRICAN-AMERICAN FOLKLORE; FOLK-LORE IN AMERICAN LITERATURE; FOLKLORE IN EVERY-DAY LIFE; HURSTON, ZORA NEALE; IBO LANDING; MORRISON, TONI; SLAVERY; SPEECH, FOLK.

For Further Reading:

Atewa, E. Ojo, and Alan Dundes. "Proverbs and the Ethnography of Speaking Folklore," *American Anthropologist* 66 (1964): 70–85.

Collis, Harry. *101 American English Proverbs: Understanding Language and Culture through Commonly Used Sayings.* New York: McGraw-Hill, 1991.

DeCaro, Francis A., and W. K. NcNeil, eds. *American Proverb Literature: A Bibliography.* Bloomington, Ind.: Folklore Forum, 1970.

Kerschen, Lois. *American Proverbs about Women: A Reference Guide.* Westport, Conn.: Greenwood Press, 1998.

Norrick, Neal R. *How Proverbs Mean: Semantic Studies in English Proverbs.* New York: Mouton, 1985.

Prahlad, S. Anand. *African-American Proverbs in Context.* Jackson: University Press of Mississippi, 1996.

Trench, Richard Chenevix. *Proverbs and Their Lessons.* New York: E. P. Dutton, 1905.

public folklore Public folklore, also known as public sector folklore, reflects the efforts made outside the academy to promote, document, and display folklore.

While most folklorists are trained in colleges and universities, and many go on to work at such institutions as faculty and staff members, pubic folklorists conduct their work within the discipline of folklore at other sites. These locations include historical societies, humanities boards, art councils, community centers, cultural agencies, libraries, museums, and educational organizations such as primary and secondary schools. They may also apply their knowledge of folklore in other occupations, such as human resources management, environmental planning, and tourism.

Within these public contexts, the intent is not only to educate, but also to broaden both the participation in and the audiences for American folklore. Public folklorists involve the widest possible spectrum of collectors for folklore and viewers for the resulting exhibitions.

Some believe that public folklore in America dates back to the 1930s. At that time, in response to the national challenges posed by the Great Depression, President Franklin Delano Roosevelt created a host of federal agencies designed to hasten the nation's recovery from its financial setback. Several of these organizations concentrated on the arts and cultural expressions of the nation, including its legacies of folk tradition and customs. These efforts stimulated the interest in folklore and raised the visibility of the methods and purposes of folklore in America. Workers with the Farm Security Administration, Works Progress Administration, and Federal Writers' Project devoted their resources to revealing the variety and vitality of everyday America.

Since then, public folklorists have been conducting outreach, with the hope that the more Americans know about their heritage, the more they will benefit as a nation. Organizations such as the Smithsonian Institution's Office of Folklife Programs, the National Endowment for the Arts's Folk Arts Program, and the Library of Congress's Archive of Folk Culture have contributed to the growth of public folklore.

Public folklorists seek to raise the nation's consciousness of folklore and folklife and to promote a deeper appreciation of its importance to American culture.

See also: DEPRESSION, THE GREAT; FIELD-WORK, FOLKLORE; FOLKLORE STUDIES; LIVING HISTORY MUSEUMS; MUSEUMS, FOLK; TERMS.

For Further Reading:

Baron, Robert, and Nicholas Spitzer, eds. *Public Folklore.* Washington, D.C.: Smithsonian Institution Press, 1992.

Bronner, Simon. *Following Tradition: Folklore in the Discourse of American Culture.* Logan: Utah State University Press, 1998.

Dwyer-Shick, Susan. "The Development of Folklore and Folklife Research in the Federal Writers' Project, 1935–1943," *Keystone Folklore* 20, no. 4 (1975): 5–31.

Hufford, Mary, ed. *Conserving Culture: A New Discourse on Heritage.* Urbana: University of Illinois Press, 1994.

Loomis, Ormond. *Cultural Conservation: The Projection of Cultural Heritage in the United States.* Washington, D.C.: Library of Congress, 1983.

pumpkin See HALLOWEEN/ALL HALLOWS' EVE.

Quaker folklore   The Quakers, also known as the Religious Society of Friends, are a religious sect known for their distinctive way of life.

Quakerism in America dates back to the 17th century. The Quakers suffered from oppression in early America, and their members were subject to discrimination for their religious teachings and practices. They sought Inner Light, a sense of divinity they believed resided within all persons, through direct contact with God. They advocated equality and declined gestures of deference that were customary in New England at the time. As was the case with the Shakers, to whom they are sometimes compared, members of the Society of Friends became known as Quakers on the basis of the stirrings sometimes observed during their otherwise silent form of worship.

Since their worldview differed so greatly from that of the Puritans, the Friends were regarded with suspicion, judgment, and cruel treatment. Sometimes labeled witches, placed in jail, tortured, and deported, the Quakers were not accepted in 17th-century New England. Their belief that anyone might achieve salvation through right conduct and introspection was perceived as an affront to those who continued to belief in the existence of a religious elect. They also employed a consensus-based decision-making model that baffled those outside the tradition. The Quaker tenet of pacifism made

them even more suspect when the American Revolution took shape. Quaker persecution did not abate until the 18th century.

The 19th-century climate of social reform afforded the Quakers an opportunity for leadership and renewed influence. The Quaker values of equality made them advocates of women's rights and opponents of slavery. Quaker settlements throughout the country became preferred stops and destinations along the Underground Railroad. Quakers, from William Lloyd Garrison to Lucretia Mott, became active in the abolitionist and women's suffrage movements. The Civil War proved a test to Quaker beliefs, since they both favored emancipation of the slaves and opposed armed conflict. Many Quakers supported the Union effort, and some even fought in the war.

During the 20th century, the Quakers continued their efforts on behalf of social justice. They lent their support to the Civil Rights movement and the antiwar movement during the Vietnam conflict. Today, the Quakers have come to stand for strong convictions, expressed through such views as pacifism and social reform. Their traditions of plain attire, simple living, and personal restraint are portrayed in popular culture through such solemn icons as the Quaker Oats man.

Folklore for the Quakers is constrained by the customary prohibitions against painting, drama, and music. The aesthetic associated with

Quaker living, while visually appealing, is spare and austere. Nonetheless, figures such as the seamstress Betsy Ross and folk painter Edward Hicks have emerged as legendary figures in American folklore.

See also: ART, FOLK; CIVIL RIGHTS MOVEMENT; CIVIL WAR; CULTURAL GROUPS; PENNSYLVANIA DUTCH/PENNSYLVANIA GERMAN FOLKLORE; PROTEST IN FOLKLORE; RELIGION, FOLK; SHAKER FOLKLORE; SLAVERY; WOMEN'S MOVEMENT; WOMEN'S SUFFRAGE.

For Further Reading:

Bacon, Margaret Hope. *Mothers of Feminism: The Story of Quaker Women in America.* San Francisco: Harper & Row, 1986.

Barbour, Hugh, and J. William Frost. *The Quakers.* Philadelphia: Friends United Press, 1994.

Brinton, Howard. *Friends for 300 Years: The History and Beliefs of the Society of Friends Since George Fox Started the Quaker Movement.* New York: Harper, 1952.

Hamm, Thomas. *The Quakers in America.* New York: Columbia University Press, 2003.

Lapsansky, Emma Jones, and Anne Verplanck, eds. *Quaker Aesthetics: Reflections on a Quaker Ethic in American Design and Consumption.* Philadelphia: University of Pennsylvania Press, 2003.

Magida, Arthur, and Stuart Matlins, eds. *How to Be a Perfect Stranger: A Guide to Etiquette in Other People's Religious Ceremonies.* Woodstock, Vt.: SkyLight Paths, 1999.

Pushon, John. *Portrait in Grey: A Short History of the Quakers.* London: Quaker Home Service, 1984.

Soderlund, Jean. *Quakers and Slavery: A Divided Spirit.* Princeton, N.J.: Princeton University Press, 1985.

Quilt, AIDS By using a genre borrowed from folklore rather than figural sculpture, the AIDS Quilt represents a new form of memorial art.

In response to the widespread effects of the human immunodeficiency virus/acquired immunodeficiency syndrome (HIV/AIDS) crisis, the activist Cleve Jones and other individuals asso-ciated with an enterprise that would eventually become known as the NAMES Project wished to honor those lost to AIDS. With their work, the members of the NAMES Project sought a way to pay tribute to those who died, comfort those who survived, thank those who served as caregivers, educate those who might not yet have firsthand contact with the crisis, and remind those who participate in policymaking and decision making at the national level of the crisis.

In the communal tradition of the quilting bee, each square represents part of a collective product and statement. Squares within the quilt correspond to specified individuals felled by AIDS or AIDS-related complex (ARC). Each three-by-six-foot piece is individualized to reflect the person receiving tribute and recall that person's unique qualities and contributions. Whether fashioned by a single survivor or a group of loved ones, every square offers a tender document of the life lost.

As a metaphor, the quilt is an object of comfort and intimacy. The AIDS Quilt was designed to travel the country, literally taking the message home to Americans. It has been displayed in prominent public areas, such as on the Mall in Washington, D.C., where it first appeared in 1987. As the quilt has grown in size, it has become necessary in most cases to display the memorial in portions rather than in its entirety. The quilt is presented with an unfolding ceremony. When on view, the AIDS Quilt is arranged so that visitors can move through the piece and examine it in detail. It is customary for the exhibition to be accompanied by the reading aloud of the list of all names memorialized by the quilt.

Contemporary memorials, especially unconventional ones such as the Vietnam Wall and the AIDS Quilt, have proved controversial. This is probably the case because the stakes of historical memory and informed action are so high. Consequently, an act of memorial deemed objectionable can provoke protest.

Some of its critics regard the AIDS Quilt as an emblem of the "homosexual agenda" in American politics. Others of its detractors, by contrast, consider the AIDS Quilt insufficiently confrontational toward the institutions and systems of power that make it necessary.

While this memorial proves as controversial as it is captivating in its allusion to American folklore, the NAMES Project AIDS Memorial Quilt continues to inspire both reverence and thoughtful response among those who witness its force as a public statement of grief and outrage.

See also: CRAFTS, FOLK; DEATH; FOLKLORE IN EVERYDAY LIFE; FOLKLORISTICS; GAY/LESBIAN FOLKLORE; POLITICS AND FOLKLORE; PROTEST IN FOLKLORE; PUBLIC FOLKLORE; UNDERGROUND RAILROAD.

For Further Reading:
Bolcom, William, and William Parker. *The AIDS Quilt Songbook*. New York: Boosey & Hawkes, 1993.

Brown, Joe, ed. *A Promise to Remember: The NAMES Project Book of Letters*. New York: Avon Books, 1992.

Capozzola, Christopher. "A Very American Epidemic: Memory Politics and Identity Politics in the AIDS Memorial Quilt, 1985–1993," *Radical History Review* 82 (winter 2002): 91–109.

Jones, Cleve, and Jeff Dawson. *Stitching a Revolution: The Making of an Activist*. New York: HarperCollins, 2000.

Ruskin, Cindy. *The Quilt: Stories from the NAMES Project*. New York: Pocket Books, 1998.

Sturken, Marita. *Tangled Memories: The Vietnam War, the AIDS Epidemic, and the Politics of Remembering*. Berkeley: University of California Press, 1997.

quilting   See CRAFTS, FOLK.

rabbit's foot   See LUCK/FORTUNE.

railroad folklore   See HENRY, JOHN; JONES, JOHN LUTHER (CASEY); OCCUPATIONAL FOLKLORE; SHELLEY, KATE; TRANSCONTINENTAL RAILROAD.

Ramadan   Ramadan is a religious observance in Islam, held during the ninth month of the Islamic year. It commemorates the revelation of the Quran to the Prophet Muhammad.

During this month-long event, Muslims mark the occasion with several practices. Those who have reached puberty fast daily and refrain from designated activities, such as smoking, as an act of devotion. The fast is broken each night before evening prayer, preferably with dates and water. Ramadan is also the time for recitations and prayers related to the observance. Some spend the final 10 days of Ramadan in the mosque, conducting continuous contemplation. Ramadan concludes with a celebration.

See also: FAMILY FOLKLORE; FOOD/FOODWAYS; HOLIDAYS/OBSERVANCES; RELIGION, FOLK.

For Further Reading:

Armburst, Walter. "The Riddle of Ramadan: Media Consumer Culture, and the 'Christmasization' of a Muslim Holiday." In *Everyday Life in the Muslim Middle East*, edited by Donna Lee Bowen, 335–348. Bloomington: Indiana University Press, 2002.

Buitelaar, Marjo. *Fasting and Feasting in Morocco: Women's Participation in Ramadan*. Oxford: Oxford University Press, 1993.

Ghazi, Suhaib Hamid. *Ramadan*. New York: Holiday House, 1996.

Hoyt-Goldsmith, Diane. *Celebrating Ramadan*. New York: Holiday House, 2001.

"Rapunzel" (legendary)   As one of the fairy tales collected by the brothers Grimm, "Rapunzel" offers the story of an archetypal damsel in distress and maiden in the tower.

As the tale begins, a man and woman long to produce a child. The woman experiences a deep craving for the taste of a food (rampion, or rapunzel) found growing only in the garden of a dreaded enchantress. In some versions of the tale, this craving results from her pregnancy. She tells her husband that if she does not have it, she might die. Consequently, he surreptitiously enters the garden to fetch what his wife professes to require. He continues to do so without incident until he is caught stealing by the enchantress herself. Facing the witch's reprisals, the man tries to negotiate a solution. In return for the desired green from her garden, the enchantress seeks the promise of their firstborn child. The husband, fearful that his wife's very life might be at stake, assents to the demand.

When the child, a daughter, is born, her parents surrender her to the enchantress. The enchantress names the girl Rapunzel, after the green her mother so craved in anticipation of the birth. Once Rapunzel reaches the age of 12, the enchantress seals her in the topmost room of a tower that has neither stairs nor a door. The only access to Rapunzel's chamber, then, is by climbing the girl's long hair when it is extended from the open window. When the enchantress wishes to so do, she stands at the base of the tower and recites, "Rapunzel, Rapunzel, / Let down thy hair to me." The girl complies, holding her hair in such a way that the witch can scale it to the tower room.

Although the tower is somewhat remote, a king's son discovers Rapunzel through her beautiful singing. Lured to the tower again and again to listen to Rapunzel's song, he eventually witnesses the manner by which the enchantress gains access to Rapunzel. The witch visits by day, and the king's son calls in the evening and eventually asks Rapunzel for her hand in marriage.

When by chance the enchantress discovers this romance, however, she is horrified that the measures she has taken to isolate her young charge from the influences of the world have failed. She cuts Rapunzel's hair and casts her out of the tower. The witch then uses Rapunzel's hair to trick her suitor, confronting him with the news that his beloved is gone forever. The brokenhearted prince manages to escape.

Meanwhile, an equally heartsick Rapunzel finds herself in exile once again, this time alone in the desert. When the king's son learns of this fact, he searches for her and rescues her from a harsh fate.

Obviously enough, theft and deception are punished within this plot. Other lessons conveyed through this story share the theme of resisting temptation. Rapunzel's removal from her family represents one such caution, as her mother's appetites and her husband's indulgence of them led to the loss of the child they so longed to raise themselves. The romance plot between Rapunzel and the king's son suggests the dangers of satisfying other appetites prematurely. This message becomes even more emphatic in versions of the story that suggest that Rapunzel was pregnant by the king's son when she was cast out of the tower.

As do many fairy tales, the story of "Rapunzel" functions as an analogy. It is invoked in popular culture regularly when people wish to address parallel situations within the lived world. For instance, any deal exacting too great a price may be described as calling for the promise of one's "firstborn child." Similarly, romantic matches pursued despite the objections of the lovers' families are sometimes likened to the plight of Rapunzel and her suitor.

The tale of Rapunzel seems to resonate for children and adults alike as it elicits compassion for the young girl forced to live a life not of her own, or even her family's, choosing. In this regard, it echoes other tales in which innocent children's fates rest in the hands of violent and/or unscrupulous adults. Readers long to see Rapunzel flee the tower and the enchantress's captivity, while learning the importance of moderating one's desires.

See also: CHILDREN'S FOLKLORE; FABLES; FAIRY TALES; MYTHS, FOLK.

For Further Reading:

Bettelheim, Bruno. *The Uses of Enchantment: The Meaning and Importance of Fairy Tales.* New York: Knopf, 1976.

Radner, Joan Newlon, ed. *Feminist Messages: Coding in Women's Folk Culture.* Urbana: University of Illinois Press, 1993.

Tatar, Maria, ed. *The Annotated Classic Fairy Tales.* New York: W. W. Norton, 2002.

Tatar, Maria. *The Hard Facts of the Grimms' Fairy Tales.* Princeton, N.J.: Princeton University Press, 1987.

Ward, Donald. "The German Connection: The Brothers Grimm and the Study of 'Oral' Literature," *Western Folklore* 53, no. 1 (January 1994): 1–26.

"Red Riding Hood, Little" (legendary) "Little Red Riding Hood," the story of a girl's fateful visit to her grandmother's house in the forest, is another of the hundreds of fairy tales recorded by the Grimm brothers during the 19th century.

The first known written version of this story is from 1697, when Charles Perrault included it in one of his story collections as "The Little Red Hat." Perrault tended to recast traditional tales to make them more suitable to the sensibilities of his middle-class audience. Therefore, Perrault's rendition for the page is considerably more tame than the oral versions of "Little Red Riding Hood," which were more lurid in terms of violence and sexuality. For instance, the werewolf of earlier versions becomes the wolf common in today's tellings of the tale. The Grimm brothers represent another round in the story's evolution and they helped to produce the version of the fairy tale most Americans recognize today.

A girl known as Little Red Riding Hood because of her distinctive cloak was sent through the forest alone to pay a call on her ailing grandmother, who lived in a cottage there. At this point, some story versions have the girl wandering off the safety of the path into the unknown. In any case, a wolf takes note of Red Riding Hood, questions her, and unknown to the child, determines to make a victim of her.

First, he hurries ahead to the grandmother's house, where he murders the old woman. By the time Little Red Riding Hood reaches her destination, the wolf has donned the deceased woman's clothing and now poses as Red Riding Hood's grandmother. Initially, the girl seems to accept the wolf as her grandmother, and the visit commences.

In time, however, with a series of declarations Little Red Riding Hood begins to notice differences in her "grandmother's" appearance. Each time the girl makes such a remark, the disguised wolf is quick with an explanation intended to assuage the girl's fears. By the end of the questioning, however, when Little Red Riding Hood exclaims on her "grandmother's" big teeth, the answer comes back, "The better to eat you with!" The ruse is over, and Little Red Riding Hood must flee the wolf, who would make a meal of her.

While versions vary as to what happens next, in most accounts a passerby, a woodsman, rescues the girl from being devoured by the wolf. In some tellings, this Good Samaritan is also able to save the grandmother.

Whether or not the girl and grandmother survive the wolf's attacks, the tale of "Little Red Riding Hood" makes a stark lesson to its audience. There is no mistaking the dangers that may befall children who stray, talk to strangers, or mistrust their instincts when matters prove other than what they appear.

Most children in the United States are acquainted with the story of "Red Riding Hood," and find themselves urged by parents and teachers to exercise caution in their own lives, especially when alone and confronting the unknown. In today's popular imagination, when no one's personal safety is assured, Little Red Riding Hood is an emblem of imperiled innocence. By the same token, the image of the wolf stands in for a multitude of dangers modern children face within the lived world.

See also: CHILDREN'S FOLKLORE; FABLES; FAIRY TALES; GRIMM BROTHERS; MONSTERS; MYTHS, FOLK.

For Further Reading:

Bettelheim, Bruno. *The Uses of Enchantment: The Meaning and Importance of Fairy Tales*. New York: Knopf, 1976.

Bottigheimer, Ruth. *Grimms' Bad Girls and Bold Boys: The Moral and Social Visions of the Tales*. New Haven, Conn.: Yale University Press, 1987.

Douglas, Mary. "Red Riding Hood: An Interpretation from Anthropology," *Folklore* 106 (1995): 1–7.

Dundes, Alan, ed. *Little Red Riding Hood: A Casebook*. Madison: University of Wisconsin Press, 1989.

region, folk While it has become customary to speak of the world as a "global village," particularly given the unifying but also homogenizing effects of information technology and media, it is nonetheless true that the premise on which most folklore study is based is the belief in meaningful regional variations.

In fact, the foundational documents for such institutions of American folklore as the American Folklore Society and the *Journal of American Folklore*, make it clear that a good deal of the momentum for formalizing American folklore as a field arose from a fear that industrialization, urbanization, and other forces taking hold at the end of the 19th century threatened to erode or eradicate local differences and regional patterns within American folk culture. Therefore, while folklorists may specialize in particular forms (such as quilts) or populations (such as Amish culture), most also attend closely to both continuity and disjuncture within such bodies of folklore.

Within this encyclopedia, for example, as appropriate, entries are cross-referenced by the connections of that entry's framing concept, term, or form to one or more regions using a variant on the regional folklores described by Charles Haywood in his 1951 *Bibliography of North American Folklore and Folksong*: Midwest, Northeast, Northwest, Southern, Southwestern, and Western.

Within this scheme, Connecticut, Delaware, the District of Columbia, Maine, Maryland, Massachusetts, New Hampshire, New Jersey, New York, Pennsylvania, Rhode Island, and Vermont correspond to Northeastern regional folklore. Midwestern regional folklore includes the states of Illinois, Indiana, Iowa, Kansas, Michigan, Minnesota, Missouri, Nebraska, Ohio, and Wisconsin. Folklore for the Southern region features Alabama, Arkansas, Florida, Georgia, Kentucky, Louisiana, Mississippi, North Carolina, South Carolina, Tennessee, Virginia, and West Virginia. The states of California, Colorado, Hawaii, Nevada, Utah, and Wyoming coincide with Western regional folklore. Northwestern regional folklore refers to Alaska, Idaho, Montana, North Dakota, Oregon, South Dakota, and Washington. Finally, folklore associated with Arizona, New Mexico, Oklahoma, and Texas belongs to the Southwestern region of the United States.

One way that regional differences may become noticeable in oral expression is through such language markers as dialect, accent, sayings, slang, and idiosyncrasies of usage. A skilled sociolinguist can often place a speaker both geographically and culturally on a first meeting, using just observations of these signature features within an individual's speech. The same can be said about many other forms of folklore, including crafts, architecture, music, humor, and storytelling.

While regional identities do not account for all attributes in a folk object or performance, they remain meaningful categories of analysis within American folklore studies, even in a digital age.

Despite globalization of culture, there are still distinct folk regions in some regards. Local culture provides a sense of place. Mass culture poses a threat to the local but has not eclipsed area-specific folk cultures.

See also: BIGFOOT/SASQUATCH; CABLE, WASHINGTON GEORGE; CLEMENS, SAMUEL LANGHORNE; FOLKLORE IN EVERYDAY LIFE; JERSEY DEVIL; MIDWESTERN REGIONAL FOLKLORE; NORTHEASTERN REGIONAL FOLKLORE; SOUTHERN REGIONAL FOLKLORE; SOUTHWESTERN REGIONAL FOLKLORE; TERMS; WESTERN REGIONAL FOLKLORE.

For Further Reading:

Allen, Barbara, and Thomas J. Schlereth, eds. *Sense of Place: American Regional Cultures*. Lexington: University Press of Kentucky, 1990.

Cassidy, Frederic Gomes, and Joan Houston Hall. *Dictionary of American Regional English*. Cambridge, Mass.: Belknap Press, 1985.

Chamberlin, J. Edward. *If This Is Your Land, Where Are Your Stories? Reimaging Home and Sacred Space*. Cleveland, Ohio: Pilgrim Press, 2004.

Dorson, Richard M., ed. *Buying the Wind: Regional Folklore in the United States.* Chicago: University of Chicago Press, 1964.

Haywood, Charles. *A Bibliography of North American Folklore and Folksong.* New York: Greenberg, 1951.

Jones, Suzi. "Regionalization: A Rhetorical Strategy," *Journal of the Folklore Institute* 13 (1976): 105–120.

Whisnant, David. *All That Is Native and Fine: The Politics of Culture in an American Region.* Chapel Hill: University of North Carolina Press, 1983.

religion, folk Folk religion, sometimes also referred to as vernacular religion, involves the faith-based practices and beliefs of the members of an informal folk group.

Folk religion is not limited to, and sometimes not even linked to, formal religious doctrine or religious institutions. In this sense, it implies the layperson's worldview and worship rather than the clergy's, the real rather than the ideal. As such, folk religion pays closest attention to the daily presence of religion in people's lives instead of concentrating on sacred texts or dogma. The everyday awareness of distinctions between the sacred and the profane, good and evil, virtue and vice typically undergirds such a consciousness. Folk religion entails all the concepts, choices, and behavior that result from that awareness. By necessity, folklorists investigating folk religion often incorporate attention to folk beliefs and folk medicine as closely related phenomena.

Traditions of folk religion vary widely and often stand outside or cross standard denominational distinctions. For example, African Americans may carry forward traditions of the shouted sermon, or call and response, a model of worship remarkable for its interaction between the preacher and others worshiping during a religious service. These traditions may be seen and cherished as part of an embattled spiritual legacy, especially given prohibitions on literacy, assembly, and worship during American slavery. The folk sermon may also resonate in other forms of African-American oratory, such as when the verbal arts of the pulpit are translated to the podium in political addresses. Similarly, slave songs including spirituals have been revisited in political contexts, such as the Civil Rights movement. In this respect, protesters took strength and inspiration from the songs that helped slaves survive, and sometimes even escape, captivity.

Other aspects of folk religion may be manifested in the realm of material culture. In some ethnic cultures, for instance, home shrines and altars are common elements of domestic space. Using an assemblage of visual material and artifacts, individuals may construct designated areas for prayer and spiritual renewal within the home. Such spaces are foci of religious energy in the everyday life of families and folk groups, personalizing and supplementing other available places of worship.

Because religion represents such a focal point for folk beliefs, American folklorists have paid special attention to folk groups constituted around shared religious beliefs and practices. Several well-studied American populations have functioned in this way, including the Amish, the Shakers, and the Quakers. Inquiries into customs surrounding birth, marriage, healing, death, and the afterlife help illuminate the values connecting people observing a shared practice within folk religion.

By studying the rituals, rites of passage, scriptures, legends, jokes, stories, and folklife of practitioners of folk religion, folklorists strive to understand the principles behind a whole way of life that religions informs.

See also: AFRICAN-AMERICAN FOLKLORE; BAR MITZVAH/BAT MITZVAH; BELIEFS, FOLK; CHRISTMAS; DEVIL, THE; EASTER; EVIL EYE; FOLKLORE IN EVERYDAY LIFE; JEWISH-AMERICAN FOLKLORE; LUCK/FORTUNE; MAGIC; MEDICINE, FOLK; MONSTERS; MORMON FOLKLORE; PASSOVER; PENNSYLVANIA DUTCH/PENNSYLVANIA GERMAN FOLKLORE; PREDICTION; QUAKER FOLKLORE; RITES OF PASSAGE; RITUALS, FOLK; SAINT PATRICK'S DAY; SHAKER

FOLKLORE; SUPERNATURAL; SUPERSTITIONS; VOO-
DOO/HOODOO; WEDDING/MARRIAGE FOLKLORE;
WITCHCRAFT, SALEM; YOM KIPPUR.

For Further Reading:
Lippy, Charles H. *Being Religious, American Style: A
    History of Popular Religiosity in the United States.*
    Westport, Conn.: Pragaer, 1994.
Oring, Elliott, ed. *Folk Groups and Folklore Genres:
    An Introduction.* Logan: Utah State University
    Press, 1986.
Oring, Elliott, ed. *Folk Groups and Folklore Genres:
    A Reader.* Logan: Utah State University Press,
    1989.
Rosenberg, Bruce. *Can These Bones Live? The Art of
    the American Folk Preacher.* Urbana: University
    of Illinois Press, 1988.
Schoemaker, George H., ed. *The Emergence of Folk-
    lore in Everyday Life: A Fieldguide and Sourcebook.*
    Bloomington, Ind.: Trickster Press, 1990.
Yoder, Don. "Toward a Definition of Folk Reli-
    gion," *Western Folklore* 33 (1974): 2–15

Remus, Uncle (legendary) Uncle Remus
represents the legendary narrator of a series of
African-American stories from the Civil War
and Reconstruction South.

These animal tales and plantation stories
were based on oral narratives documented by
the journalist turned folklorist Joel Chandler
Harris. Harris, a member of the American Folklore Society, sought to record the dialect stories
told by slaves. He published his work with the
structure of a fictional storyteller, Uncle Remus.
In this sense, he was a popularizer of such tales,
especially for a white audience of readers.

Oral culture proves fundamental to folklore—whether as sermons, jokes, rumors and
gossip, stories, or speeches. Perhaps the best-
known American narrative genre is the tale.
Recent analysts of African-American folktales
have interpreted the form's functions variously.
Some see tales as vehicles for self-affirmation,
social protest, and psychological release. Others see folktales as reiterating, inculcating, and
complementing cultural values, although many
would warn against overly literal interpretation
of values as depicted in the stories, because of the
playful and frequently ironic tone of the stories.
For instance, many scholars believe that animal
tales, and the paradigms those tales provide, had
their origin in substitutions of animal names for
specific people's names. A literal approach, then,
could mask important subtextual meanings of
such texts.

For many readers today, it is unfortunately
still the case that all that is known of African-American storytelling traditions is filtered
through the work of people such as Joel Chandler Harris, whose book *Uncle Remus: His Songs
and Sayings* (1880) came to represent—or, one
might more accurately say, misrepresent—African-American storytelling traditions. It was
Harris's claim that in relating stories, he provided those stories in their original and unadul-
terated form. Harris's language proves revealing,
though, for when he refers to other people and
their cultures as "simple" or "picturesque," he
trivializes them. That is, he might not have
consciously set out to inscribe his own attitudes
about African Americans, but neither was he
self-conscious about the implications of a white
observer's serving up African-American culture
to a white audience, and all that that could mean.
Indicative of this lack of introspection is the
puzzlement Harris expressed about informant
reticence. In time, Harris adopted an approach
of telling a few stories to get a few others, but his
bafflement about the problem merely confirms
how little Harris understood the extent to which
the lore's shielding was, in part, testimony to its
enduring value.

Figures such as Joel Chandler Harris, with
his Uncle Remus stories, recorded African-
American tales but in the process embedded
their own stereotypical views of African-American narrative culture. The anthropologist Franz
Boas addresses this issue somewhat diplomatically, by suggesting that efforts such as those of
Harris fail to capture what he calls the intimate
setting of those tales.

See also: ANIMALS; BRER RABBIT; FIELDWORK, FOLKLORE; FOLK HEROES/LEGENDARY FIGURES; FOLKTALES; SOUTHERN REGIONAL FOLKLORE; TAR BABY; TRICKSTER.

For Further Reading:
Brasch, Walter M. *Brer Rabbit, Uncle Remus, and the "Cornfield Journalist": The Tale of Joel Chandler Harris.* Macon, Ga.: Mercer University Press, 2000.
Chang, Linda S. "Brer Rabbit's Angolan Cousin: Politics and the Adaptation of Folk Material," *Folklore Forum* 19, no. 1 (1986): 36–50.
Montenyohl, Eric L. "Joel Chandler Harris and American Folklore," *Atlanta Historical Journal* 30, nos. 3–4 (fall–winter 1986–1987): 79–88.
———. "The Origins of Uncle Remus," *Folklore Forum* 18, no. 2 (spring 1986): 136–167.
Walton, David. "Joel Chandler Harris as Folklorist: A Reassessment," *Keystone Folklore* 11 (1966): 21–26.

research, folklife   Folklife's story relies upon original inquiries conducted through research.

Typically, this work begins in the field rather than the library. Depending upon the questions a folklorist wishes to explore, a site or set of sites for research may be identified. Then, the folklorist develops a plan for how to proceed, usually consisting of a refined set of questions, a method for responding to those questions, and at least a tentative notion of what resources exist to support the researcher in answering those questions more fully.

Research involves careful investigation using evidence. Within folklife, that evidence usually consists of verbal lore, material lore, and/or customs. In some cases, collections of relevant evidence already exist within archives, historical societies, and museums. In other cases, the folklorist must collect such evidence at the outset of the research project. Either way, proper folklore involves both the material itself and documentation of its cultural and social context. That is, if the subject under study were quilting, it would be important to research not only the quilts as objects, but also the practices surrounding their construction and use, the customs of quilting bees, the history of quilting patterns and their symbolism, and so forth. In other words, if the goal is to understand the "folk" in folklore, it is not enough merely to gather the lore.

For this reason, folklife research often requires extensive research in order to lay the groundwork for its public products. In order to promote folklife and knowledge about it, such researchers may consult a wide spectrum of public presentations of folk culture, including craft demonstrations, battle and event reenactments, public lectures, books written for a lay audience, and collaborations with cultural informants conducted for the purpose of promoting and/or preserving folk practice.

Because the folklife movement is part of a larger trend toward public scholarship, there are many online resources available to support such work as it might be conducted by independent scholars, elementary and secondary school teachers, and interested others. These publications include guidelines for conducting interviews, collecting folklife, developing exhibitions, and undertaking related procedures that play a part in folklife research.

Through American folklife research, it is possible to learn a great deal not only about folk artifacts, but also about U.S. history, social life, and customs.

See also: ETHICS IN FOLKLORE; FIELDWORK, FOLKLIFE; FOLKLIFE; FOLKLIFE MOVEMENT; FOLKLORE STUDIES; FOLKLORISTICS; LIVING HISTORY MUSEUMS; MATERIAL CULTURE; MUSEUMS, FOLK; ORAL HISTORY; PUBLIC FOLKLORE; TERMS; VERNACULAR CULTURE.

For Further Reading:
Bartis, Peter, and Stephanie A. Hall, comps. Folklife Sourcebook: A Directory of Folklife Resources in the United States. Available online. URL: http://www.loc.gov/folklife/source/. Accessed on July 20, 2005.

Borden, Carla, ed. El Río: Do-Your-Own-Exhibition Kit. Available online. URL: http://www.folklife.si.edu/resources/pdf/elrioGUIDE_ALL.pdf. Accessed July 20, 2005.

Corsaro, Karen. *Folklore in Archives: A Guide to Describing Folklore and Folklife Materials.* Ithaca: New York Folklore Society, 1998.

Hunt, Marjorie. The Smithsonian Folklife and Oral History Interviewing Guide. Available online. URL: http://www.folklife.si.edu/explore/Resources/InterviewGuide/InterviewGuide_home.html. Accessed February 17, 2006.

Moran, Carol, and Catherine Hiebert Kerst. A Teacher's Guide to Folklife Resources. Available online. URL: http://www.loc.gov/folklife/teachers/index.html. Accessed February 17, 2006.

Smithsonian Institution. Artifacts and Analysis: A Teacher's Guide to Interpreting Objects and Writing History. Available online. URL: http://www.smithsonianeducation.org/idealabs/ap/index.htm. Accessed February 17, 2006.

Revere's ride, Paul

Revere's ride, Paul Although Paul Revere (1735–1818) made his living primarily as a skilled silversmith, it is the events of a single night—April 18, 1775—for which Revere will always be remembered.

This indelible image of Revere's midnight ride owes much to the work of the American author Henry Wadsworth Longfellow, who recounted the events of that night in a now-famous poem. As Longfellow's poem would have it, Revere single-handedly defended the national cause. Thanks to the poem, routinely heard and even memorized by school-age children, Revere's place in American folklore seems secure. It takes nothing from Revere's accomplishments to affirm, as historians have, that Revere had help in the form of fellow messengers.

In Revere's time, the colonists were deeply dissatisfied with their relationship to Britain and King George III. Often they found themselves taxed heavily, and the colonists considered this to be taxation without representation. They had no ready recourse if they wished to dissent. For that reason, the colonists took more drastic means to secure their rights as individuals and their autonomy as a society. This struggle culminated in the American Revolution.

Revere, as a champion of the colonists in their struggle for autonomy, bravely served as an express messenger for numerous key wartime communications among the patriots of Boston. His best-known message by far, however, was his warning to nearby towns of the approach of British combatants. The British general Thomas Gage meant to take Boston by surprise and seize the colonial arsenal, but word of their plan reached a few, including Revere.

He and two other riders set out not only to alert the Minutemen and other colonists of the danger, but also to advise them about the manner of approach. In case their efforts to convey the information on horseback were thwarted, Revere arranged for a signal to be placed in the steeple of an area church. One lantern would be set there if the British intended a land route, and two lanterns if they planned to approach by boat on the Charles River. Revere personally notified such prominent figures as John Hancock and Samuel Adams, both of whom were staying in a house in Lexington.

Revere had several close calls with the British that night. In one instance, he managed to outride the British soldiers pursuing him. In another case, Revere was questioned at gunpoint. When he revealed to the soldiers that no matter what they now did the word of their plan would travel widely, the soldiers left him behind, taking only his horse to limit his further activity that night. With the ensuing battles of Lexington and Concord, the American Revolution began in earnest.

Paul Revere's wooden house in Boston's North End is still intact. Operating as the Paul Revere House, it stands as one of the nation's oldest house museums. Visitors may conduct self-guided tours and, while on the property, examine examples of Paul Revere's skill as a silversmith.

See also: HISTORICAL EVENTS; LONGFEL-
LOW, HENRY WADSWORTH; NORTHEASTERN
REGIONAL FOLKLORE; PATRIOTS' DAY; PROTEST
IN FOLKLORE; REGION, FOLK; REVOLUTIONARY
WAR.

For Further Reading:

Fischer, David Hackett. *Paul Revere's Ride.* New
York: Oxford University Press, 1994.

Krensky, Stephen. *Paul Revere's Midnight Ride.*
New York: HarperCollins, 2002.

Longfellow, Henry Wadsworth. *Paul Revere's Ride.*
New York: HarperCollins, 2002.

Morgan, Edmund, ed. *Paul Revere's Three Accounts
of His Famous Ride.* Boston: Massachusetts Historical Society, 1968.

Revolutionary War From 1775 to 1783,
colonists fought a fierce war for American
independence from British rule. As part of the
nation's founding mythology, the Revolutionary
War is replete with symbolism and lore.

The war began as a struggle for control
over the colonies. British rule had alienated the
colonists by requiring compliance with laws and
taxes they had no opportunity to help shape.
The settlers had ventured to a new land for a
new start but found themselves subject to many
of the same structures they had tried to escape.
The British could not understand why the colonists resisted their mother country and its rule.

While some colonists remained loyalists, they
were overpowered by those who wished to rebel.
In defying British tyranny and seizing control of
the colonies, several participants assumed heroic
roles. Individuals such as Crispus Attucks, Paul
Revere, Nathan Hale, Ethan Allen, Betsy Ross,
and John Paul Jones became famous for their
part in the war.

New England was the setting for the earliest battles of the revolution. The Boston Massacre on March 5, 1770, was a memorable part
of the early phase of the conflict. On that day,
a clash between residents of the colonies and
British soldiers (or "redcoats," as they were

also called by colonists) escalated to a riot. By
the end of the skirmish, several were wounded
and five fatally so: Crispus Attucks, James
Caldwell, Patrick Carr, Samuel Gray, and
Samuel Maverick.

The remains of Crispus Attucks were interred
at the Old Granary Burial Ground on Boston's
Tremont Street and not far from where Attucks
was killed. He shares his resting place not only
with the others who died in the Boston Massacre, but with some of the best-known patriots
of his day, including Samuel Adams, John Hancock, and Paul Revere. As an African-American
patriot, Crispus Attucks represents more than
5,000 African-American soldiers who fought in
the battle for the nation's independence. Many
consider Attucks the first to die in the American
Revolution.

The Boston Tea Party of 1773 was another
key moment in the development of the war.
When a shipment of British tea arrived in Boston harbor, opponents of taxation without representation cast the tea into the water.

The indelible image of Paul Revere's midnight ride on April 18, 1775, owes much to the
efforts of the American author Henry Wadsworth Longfellow, who recounted the events
of that night in a now-famous poem. Revere, as
a champion of the colonists in their struggle for
autonomy, bravely served as an express messenger for numerous key wartime communications
among the patriots of Boston. His best-known
message by far, however, was his warning to
nearby towns of the approach of British combatants. The British general Thomas Gage had
meant to take Boston by surprise and seize the
colonial arsenal, but word of their plan reached
a few, including Revere.

He and two other riders set out not only to
alert the Minutemen and other colonists of the
danger, but also to advise them about the manner of approach. In case their efforts to convey
the information on horseback were thwarted,
Revere arranged for a signal to be placed in the
steeple of an area church. One lantern would be
set there if the British intended a land route, and

two lanterns if they planned to approach by boat on the Charles River. Revere personally notified such prominent figures as John Hancock and Samuel Adams, both of whom were staying in a house in Lexington.

Revere had several close calls with the British that night. In one instance, he managed to outride the British soldiers pursuing him. In another, Revere was questioned at gunpoint. When he revealed to the soldiers that no matter what they now did the word of their plan would travel widely, the soldiers left him behind, taking only his horse to limit his further activity that night. With the ensuing battles of Lexington and Concord, the American Revolution began in earnest.

As with most wars, in addition to legendary figures, the American Revolution gave rise to its share of tales, songs, ballads, and legends. Ethan Allen and his Green Mountain Boys inspired many songs and ballads, as did John Paul Jones. Even the song "Yankee Doodle" had its origins in the Revolutionary War. From "the shot heard round the world" to Ralph Waldo Emerson's tribute "Concord Hymn," the folklore of the American Revolution has become a crucial part of the nation's image of itself.

See also: ALLEN, ETHAN; ANGLO-AMERICAN FOLKLORE; ATTUCKS, CRISPUS; FRANKLIN, BENJAMIN; HISTORICAL EVENTS; IRVING, WASHINGTON; JONES, JOHN PAUL; LIBERTY, MISS; LONGFELLOW, HENRY WADSWORTH; HAWTHORNE, NATHANIEL; NORTHEASTERN REGIONAL FOLKLORE; PATRIOTS' DAY; REVERE'S RIDE, PAUL; ROSS, BETSY; WASHINGTON, GEORGE; YANKEE DOODLE; YANKEE PEDDLER.

For Further Reading:

Browne, Ray. "Superstitions Used as Propaganda in the American Revolution," *New York Folklore Quarterly* 17 (1961): 202–211.

Coffin, Tristram Potter. *Uncertain Glory: Folklore and the American Revolution.* Detroit: Folklore Associates, 1971.

Coleman, John. *Colonial Legends and Folklore.* New York: New York Society of the Order of the Founders and Patriots of America, 1910.

Dorson, Richard. *America in Legend: Folklore from the Colonial Period to the Present.* New York: Pantheon Books, 1973.

Hickerson, Joseph Charles. *A Brief List of References to Popular and Folk Music of the American Revolutionary War.* Washington, D.C.: Library of Congress/Archive of Folk Song, 1975.

Raphael, Ray. *Founding Myths: Stories That Hide Our Patriotic Past.* New York: New Press, 2004.

Rourke, Constance. *The Roots of American Culture and Other Essays.* New York: Harcourt, Brace, 1942.

Scheurer, Timothy. *Born in the U.S.A.: The Myth of America in Popular Music from Colonial Times to the Present.* Jackson: University Press of Mississippi, 1991.

Scott, John Anthony, and John Wardlaw Scott. *A Ballad of America: A History of the United States through Folk Song.* Holland, Mass.: Folksong in the Classroom, 2003.

Silverman, Kenneth. *A Cultural History of the American Revolution.* New York: T. Y. Crowell, 1976.

Rhode Island folklore   See NORTHEASTERN REGIONAL FOLKLORE.

rhymes, folk   As an element of children's folklore, folk rhymes play an important role in the narratives of music, game play, and other pastimes.

For the very young, nursery rhymes are a staple of folk culture. From the time they are cradled in a parent's arms to the time when they are able to say the rhymes along with adults, children use their imaginations to follow along, and they delight in the patterned sounds of nursery rhymes.

As children grow, rhymes take on additional significance within their lives. While nursery rhymes may still be fond memories, older boys and girls begin to recite or construct their own rhymes through play. As do riddles and tongue twisters, such rhymes provide entertainment and contribute to a range of childhood activities.

Perhaps the most elaborate rhymes accompany jump rope games, and jump rope rhymes can be set pieces or improvised songs to facilitate play. The songs keep time, mark turns, and signal changes in the rate of a particular game. Such tempos are especially important within Double-Dutch, a pastime in which two jump roles are turned in opposite directions simultaneously. Counts, riddles, and jokes may be incorporated within each tune.

Also widespread in American folk culture are counting-out rhymes, which children invoke for a variety of purposes. Counting-out rhymes such as the well-known "Eeny, Meeny, Miny, Mo" date back to the 18th century in America, and while many variations on the rhymes may emerge, their basic structures tend to persist. Counting-out rhymes such as "One potato, two potato" assist children in game selection, assignment of roles, player order, or determination of who will be "it" in a given game.

As the poetry of children's playgrounds, folk rhymes are a familiar and memorable aspect of folk culture for America's youth.

See also: BORDEN, LIZZIE; CHILDREN'S FOLK-LORE; FABLES; FAIRY TALES; FOLKLORE IN EVERY-DAY LIFE; GAMES AND PASTIMES; JUMP ROPE RHYMES; MYTHS, FOLK.

For Further Reading:

Abrahams, Roger, and Rankin, Lois. *Counting-Out Rhymes: A Dictionary*. Austin: University of Texas Press, 1980.

Arleo, Andy. "Counting Out and the Search for Universals," *Journal of American Folklore* 110, no. 438 (fall 1997): 391–407.

Butler, Francelia. *Skipping around the World: The Ritual Nature of Folk Rhymes*. Hamden, Conn.: Library Professional, 1986.

Delamar, Gloria. *Children's Counting-Out Rhymes, Fingerplays, Jump-Rope and Bounce-Ball Chants, and Other Rhythms: A Comprehensive Language Reference*. Jefferson, N.C.: McFarland, 1983.

Emrich, Duncan. *The Nonsense Book of Riddles, Rhymes, Tongue Twisters, Puzzles, and Jokes from American Folklore*. New York: Four Winds, 1970.

Knapp, Mary, and Herbert Knapp. *One Potato, Two Potato … : The Secret Education of American Children*. New York: W. W. Norton, 1976.

Withers, Carl. *A Rocket in My Pocket: The Rhymes and Chants of Young Americans*. New York: Holt, Rinehart & Winston, 1948.

riddles, folk   Riddles are a specific form of verbal play that involves the posing of fanciful or baffling questions. In this respect, riddles resemble jokes or puzzles. They proceed from a question and often culminate in tricky, humorous, or witty responses.

Joke-style riddles are a favorite among youth, who delight in their whimsy. For example, the query "Why was 6 afraid of 7?" can be met with the explanation, "Because 7 8 [ate] 9." As in this instance, riddles often rely upon wordplay or absurdity for their punchlines. Such riddles can also be grouped in a joke cycle, chain, or category. Among the most familiar themes involving riddles are joke cycles featuring elephants, bananas, and lightbulbs. Other, more controversial riddles fall into the sick joke category; these include ethnic jokes, disaster jokes, dead baby jokes, Helen Keller jokes, and the like. For instance, a well-known definition riddle poses the question "What do you call 500 lawyers at the bottom of the ocean?" and draws the reply "A good start."

Puzzle-style riddles are brain teasers, calling for the answer to a furnished question, rather than one that surfaces organically through conversation. Responding to such riddles involves the ability to think creatively about the solution to the riddle's question. For example, "Why is a fish like a piano?" might draw the reply "Because both have scales." This is an analogical riddle; other format, include descriptive and contrasting riddles. A typical contrast asks a questions like this one: "What is the difference between a dog and a flea?" To solve the puzzle, one must explain, "A dog may have fleas, but a flea cannot have a dog."

Riddles are a distinctive form of folk humor that, depending upon topic, involves old and young in the effort to summon the appropriate response to a playful interrogative. When approached by a folklorist, riddles hold the power to reframe or call attention to tacit understandings and beliefs within a population.

See also: FOLKLORE IN EVERYDAY LIFE; HUMOR, FOLK; SPEECH, FOLK.

For Further Reading:

Georges, Robert, and Alan Dundes. "Toward a Structural Definition of the Riddle," *Journal of American Folklore* 76, no. 300 (spring 1963): 111–118.

Hasan-Rokem, Galit, and David Shulman, eds. *Untying the Knot: On Riddles and Other Enigmatic Modes.* New York: Oxford University Press, 1996.

Köngäs-Maranda, Elli, ed. "Riddles and Riddling," *Journal of American Folklore* 89, no. 352 (spring 1976): 127–265.

McDowell, John Holmes. *Children's Riddling.* Bloomington: Indiana University Press, 1979.

Oring, Elliott, ed., *Folk Groups and Folklore Genres: An Introduction.* Logan: Utah State University Press, 1986.

———, ed. *Folk Groups and Folklore Genres: A Reader.* Logan: Utah State University Press, 1989.

Pepicello, W. J., and Thomas A. Green. *The Language of Riddles: New Perspectives.* Columbus: Ohio State University Press, 1984.

rites of passage   A rite of passage is an event that signals a life transition of consequence.

Rites of passage mark, often with ceremonies, movement between life stages. Such rites are generally experienced by individuals, whose landmark occasions are celebrated by and with intimate others. Parties, religious services, receptions, and presentation of gifts may accompany such events.

Many rites of passage involve the maturation steps of children. Because the very young learn, develop, and change rapidly, such transitions can be frequent. Examples include baptisms, birthdays, first haircuts, first day of school, pageants, and the like. Such events may involve gatherings and the taking of photographs to document the event.

As youth mature, rites of passage mark stages of movement toward adulthood. These rites can signal religious coming of age, as with first communion, confirmation, or bar mitzvah or bat mitzvah. Other rituals associated with this phase of life include menarche, prom, high school graduation, college commencement, and advanced study or professional certification. Rites can also function as adult initiations, such as those common in fraternities, military service, or other membership organizations.

Once individuals have reached adulthood, their rites of passage may include engagement, marriage, and childbirth. As they advance through life, landmark moments can involve birth of grandchildren, reunions, anniversaries, retirement, and death.

Throughout the life course, rites of passage represent the most memorable days and attainments. Folklorists are interested in the ways such transitions are customarily observed, as well as what the changes represent.

See also: AGING AND FOLKLORE; ANNIVERSARIES; BAR MITZVAH/BAT MITZVAH; BIRTHDAYS; DEATH; FOLKLORE IN EVERYDAY LIFE; GENDER AND FOLKLORE; RELIGION, FOLK; WEDDING/MARRIAGE FOLKLORE.

For Further Reading:

Davis-Floyd, Robbie. *Birth as an American Rite of Passage.* Berkeley: University of California Press, 1992.

Galambos, Nancy, and Jeffrey Jensen Arnett. *Exploring Cultural Conceptions of the Transition to Adulthood.* San Francisco: Jossey-Bass, 2003.

Gullo, Frank. *Wide Awake in America: The Emergence and Dissolution of American Ceremonial Rites of Passage.* Ottawa: National Library of Canada, 1997.

Huntington, Richard, and Peter Metcalf. *Celebrations of Death: The Anthropology of Mortuary*

Ritual. New York: Cambridge University Press, 1979.

Jenkins, Emyl. *The Book of American Traditions: Stories, Customs, and Rites of Passage to Celebrate Our Cultural Heritage.* New York: Crown, 1996.

Van Gennep, Arnold. *The Rites of Passage.* Chicago: University of Chicago Press, 1960.

rituals, folk   Rituals can be practices and events associated with special occasions in the lives of a community or its members.

Folk rituals include not only rites of passage, but also other events of consequence for both individuals and collectives. Religious landmarks account for many folk rituals, from christening to funeral services.

Not all folk rituals are solemn occasions, however, as anything from rodeos to Halloween trick-or-treating may function in this way. A folk ritual can involve any event in which a tradition is preserved through repetition, whether annually or on another basis.

Rituals associated with individuals can be baptisms, birthdays, and graduations. Rituals connected to group occasions include raising glasses for a midnight toast at New Year's, throwing rice at married couples as they exit the ceremony, and sitting down to a dinner feast with loved ones at Thanksgiving.

Whatever the occasion marked, folk rituals help connect the present to the past, new events and relationships to previous ones, and next prospects with time-honored traditions.

See also: FOLKLORE IN EVERYDAY LIFE; NEW YEAR'S EVE/DAY; RITES OF PASSAGE.

For Further Reading:

Browne, Ray Broadus. *Rituals and Ceremonies in Popular Culture.* Bowling Green, Ohio: Bowling Green State University Popular Press, 1980.

Frese, Pamela. *Celebrations of Identity: Multiple Voices in American Ritual Performance.* Westport, Conn.: Bergin & Garvey, 1993.

Gutiérrez, Ramón, and Genevieve Fabre. *Feasts and Celebrations in North American Ethnic Communi-*

ties. Albuquerque: University of New Mexico Press, 1995.

Jenkins, Emyl. *The Book of American Traditions: Stories, Customs, and Rites of Passage to Celebrate Our Cultural Heritage.* New York: Crown, 1996.

Smithsonian Institution, Office of Folklife Programs. *Celebration, A World of Art and Ritual.* Washington, D.C.: Smithsonian Institution Press, 1982.

Robin Hood (legendary)   Robin Hood, and his legend as an altruistic outlaw, enter American lore by way of British mythology.

While not original to American culture, Robin Hood is a fixture within the nation's lore. His image as a noble thief, loyal to his fellows and benevolent in his redistribution of his profits to those in need, has captured the fancy of a country priding itself on egalitarian ideals. The notion that Robin Hood "robbed from the rich to give to the poor" appealed to a nation suspicious of the wealthy as corrupt and undeserving.

Robin Hood tales are common in the United States. Just as numerous, and in some ways even more interesting, are the ways in which Americans have invoked Robin Hood as an icon or analogy for understanding homegrown criminals popular with the public. Such comparisons have been made in describing such renowned 20th-century "hoods" as John Dillinger and Pretty Boy Floyd. While there may not be much evidence that figures such as Floyd made magnanimous gestures with their criminal proceeds, their profoundly unpopular targets, such as banks, hardly evoked sympathy in the popular mind. In this way, criminals became recast as heroic or mythic, and their exploits were followed as if tales and the careers remembered as if myths.

While American representations of Robin Hood may have little in common with the British lore where he originated, this fact in no way undermines the power of his influence over an American folklore of the benevolent outlaw. He persists as a kind of trickster figure whose crimes are paradoxically regarded, at least in part, as the work of conscience.

See also: DILLINGER, JOHN; FLOYD, CHARLES ARTHUR (PRETTY BOY); FOLK HEROES/LEGENDARY FIGURES; JAMES, JESSE; LONGABAUGH, HARRY (SUNDANCE KID); OUTLAWS; PARKER, ROBERT LEROY (BUTCH CASSIDY); STARR, BELLE; TRICKSTER.

For Further Reading:

Harris, Percy Valentine. *The Truth about Robin Hood: A Refutation of the Mythologists' Theories, with New Evidence of the Hero's Actual Existence.* London: Linneys of Mansfield, 1955.

Knight, Stephen, ed. *Robin Hood: An Anthology of Scholarship and Criticism.* Rochester, N.Y.: D. S. Brewer, 1999.

Knight, Stephen. *Robin Hood: A Complete Study of the English Outlaw.* Cambridge, Mass.: Blackwell, 1994.

———. *Robin Hood: A Mythic Biography.* Ithaca, N.Y.: Cornell University Press, 2003.

Robinson, Jack Roosevelt (Jackie) (1919–1972)

As the first African-American player in the nation's major leagues of professional baseball, Jack Roosevelt "Jackie" Robinson became a cultural hero.

Robinson was born in Cairo, Georgia, on January 31, 1919. His grandfather had been a slave, and so even as a very young child, Jackie Robinson was well aware of the historical disenfranchisement of African Americans. He also saw firsthand the discrimination still experienced by people of color in the United States. While still a boy, Robinson discovered his talent for athletics. As a youth, he excelled at basketball, track, football, and baseball. He attended college for a time and was a successful member of the football team. In 1941, he went professional with the Honolulu Bears football team.

Shortly thereafter, Robinson was drafted into military service. While in the army, he collaborated with the boxer Joe Louis to contest unequal treatment of people of color in the service. When he emerged from the army,

Robinson joined the Negro League in baseball as a member of the Kansas City Monarchs. He became disenchanted with the sport's schedule and compensation. In 1945, however, he was signed to play on the Montreal Royals, a farm team for the Brooklyn Dodgers.

Although Jackie Robinson had found a place in baseball's major leagues in 1947 and became that season's Rookie of the Year, his troubles were far from over. As the first African-American player in the majors, Robinson encountered a great deal of resistance. In addition to suffering the indignity of racial segregation while traveling with his team, he was met with hostility in the sport. Players and fans alike opposed his entry into the majors, and many mistreated him out of prejudice.

Despite the abuse, Robinson distinguished himself as a baseball player and mentor to other players of color. In 1949, he was named Most Valuable Player (MVP). His sports career lasted until 1957, when the effects of diabetes forced Robinson into retirement. At this point, he became a successful businessman, vice president of a corporation, and force behind the Jackie Robinson Foundation, a charity to benefit America's youth. In 1962, Robinson was honored for his excellence in baseball by induction into the Hall of Fame. Robinson died in Connecticut on October 24, 1972.

Beyond his unusual skills as a fielder, hitter, and base stealer in baseball, Jack Roosevelt "Jackie" Robinson became a civil rights advocate and an emblem of racial desegregation in sport.

See also: AFRICAN-AMERICAN FOLKLORE; CIVIL RIGHTS MOVEMENT; FOLK HEROES/LEGENDARY FIGURES; PROTEST IN FOLKLORE; SPORTS FOLKLORE.

For Further Reading:

Allen, Maury. *Jackie Robinson: A Life Remembered.* New York: F. Watts, 1987.

Dorinson, Joseph, and Joram Warmund. *Jackie Robinson: Race, Sports, and the American Dream.* Armonk, N.Y.: M. E. Sharpe, 1998.

Rampersand, Arnold. *Jackie Robinson: A Biography.* New York: Knopf, 1997.

Robinson, Jackie, and Alfred Duckett. *I Never Had It Made*. New York: Putnam, 1972.

Robinson, Jackie, and Jules Tygiel. *The Jackie Robinson Reader: Perspectives on an American Hero*. New York: Dutton, 1997.

Tygiel, Jules. *Baseball's Great Experiment: Jackie Robinson and His Legacy*. New York: Oxford University Press, 1983.

Ward, Geoffrey, and Ken Burns. *Baseball: An Illustrated History*. New York: Knopf, 1994.

rodeo   As emblematic events to celebrate the figure and the life of the American cowboy, rodeos continue to attract attention to western folklore of the frontier.

The name *rodeo* derives from a Spanish word that refers to the cattle roundup. Today, a rodeo typically involves both demonstrations and contests of skills associated with cowboy culture, including riding, roping, and bronco busting. Such events had their origins in a festivity traditionally held on the Fourth of July, referred to as "Cowboy Christmas." These feats of bravado gave way to the spectator sport now known to the American public as rodeo. Rodeos are held throughout the West, including Wyoming and Texas. Perhaps the oldest continuous rodeo, established in 1888, occurs in Prescott, Arizona.

One of the great popularizers of cowboy culture and rodeo was William F. "Buffalo Bill" Cody. During the late 19th century, Cody's touring Wild West Show, featuring figures such as Phoebe Annie Oakley, whetted the nation's appetite for displays of cowboy skill and historical pageantry. In addition to showcasing tricks of the cowboy trade, Cody's shows featured fanciful reenactments of battles between cowboys and Indians. The rodeo helped cast the cowboy as a romantic figure within American lore, and no less a figure than President Theodore Roosevelt was an enthusiast for the "strenuous life." Since the days of Cody, other popular figures such as Gene Autry, Roy Rogers, and Hopalong Cassidy have kept the American interest in cowboy culture alive.

In recent times, rodeos have enjoyed a resurgence, as specialty shows, such as prison rodeos and gay rodeos, widen the circle of the first cattle round-ups associated with the form.

See also: ANIMALS; CHRISTMAS; CODY, WILLIAM F. (BUFFALO BILL); COWBOYS; FOLKLORE IN EVERYDAY LIFE; FRONTIER; INDEPENDENCE DAY/ FOURTH OF JULY; NATIVE AMERICAN FOLKLORE; WESTERN REGIONAL FOLKLORE.

For Further Reading:
Frederickson, Kristine. *American Rodeo: From Buffalo Bill to Big Business*. College Station: Texas A & M University Press, 1985.

Jordan, Bob. *Rodeo History and Legends*. Montrose, Colo.: Rodeo Stuff, 1994.

Woerner, Gail Hughbanks. *A Belly Full of Bedsprings: The History of Bronc Riding*. Austin, Tex.: Eakin Press, 1998.

Wooden, Wayne, and Gavin Ehringer. *Rodeo in America: Wranglers, Roughstock, and Paydirt*. Lawrence: University of Kansas Press, 1996.

Roosevelt,   Franklin   Delano (1882– 1945)   As America's 32nd president, Franklin Delano Roosevelt (FDR) had a remarkable influence on the ways the nation's people would understand the collective of which they were a part.

Roosevelt was born in 1882, a distant cousin of another president, Theodore Roosevelt. FDR came of age in affluence in Hyde Park, New York, but was raised to see himself as someone with a social responsibility. Roosevelt had the opportunity for a first-rate education, attending the Groton School, Harvard University, and Columbia Law School.

Roosevelt was positioning himself for a life in public office when, in 1921, he was stricken with poliomyelitis. While he survived polio, he emerged from the experience a paraplegic. Nevertheless, he continued with his plans for entering politics and was elected New York's governor in 1928. Not long after that, FDR ran a successful race for the U.S. presidency and served in that capacity from 1933 to 1945. These years proved some of the most trying in the nation's economic history.

FDR's years in office would be marked by memorable feats of rhetoric, and elements of Roosevelt's speeches became part of popular culture. With his references to a "New Deal" for the "Forgotten Man," and his radio talks presented as "fireside chats" to engage the citizenry, Roosevelt made a powerful appeal to the populace.

Therefore, although he inherited the problems resulting from the stock market crash and early phases of the national economic crisis later known as the Great Depression, Roosevelt projected images of hope and recovery. Toward this end, he enlarged the federal government's role in addressing the needs of Americans during this crucial time. His New Deal initiated many social and economic programs designed to improve the conditions in which the nation's people lived and worked. He set in place federal agencies for relief, employment, and national arts and heritage cultivation.

From the standpoint of folklorists, FDR made possible some of the documentation programs that would form both the basis and the inspiration for subsequent fieldwork. One such project was the photographic survey conducted by the Farm Security Administration (FSA), which yielded a vast archive of images chronicling the conditions of ordinary Americans in times of adversity. Another such project was the Works Progress Administration's (WPA's) Oral History Project, in which former slaves were interviewed about their experiences during and since slavery. Alongside the New Deal's arts projects that produced murals and other representations of American values and victories, the FSA and WPA documentation projects reflected the everyday obstacles people faced in their quest to achieve the American Dream as depicted in those murals and other public artworks.

From his programs to his epigrammatic phrases, such as "The only thing we have to fear is fear itself," Franklin Delano Roosevelt helped shape the way Americans thought about the nation's character and fortitude.

See also: AGEE, JAMES; ART, FOLK; DEPRESSION, THE GREAT; FOLK HEROES/LEGENDAY FIGURES; JAPANESE-AMERICAN INTERNMENT; JOAD, TOM; OCCUPATIONAL FOLKLORE; PUBLIC FOLKLORE; ROOSEVELT, THEODORE; SLAVERY; STEINBECK, JOHN.

For Further Reading:

Hamby, Alonzo. *For the Survival of Democracy: Franklin Roosevelt and the World Crisis of the 1930s.* New York: Free Press, 2004.

Kessler-Harris, Alice. *In Pursuit of Equity: Women, Men, and the Quest for Economic Citizenship in Twentieth Century America.* New York: Oxford University Press, 2001.

Robinson, Greg. *By Order of the President: FDR and the Internment of Japanese Americans.* Cambridge, Mass.: Harvard University Press, 2001.

Ward, Geoffrey. *A First-Class Temperament: The Emergence of Franklin Roosevelt.* New York: Harper & Row, 1969.

Roosevelt, Theodore (1858–1919) Theodore Roosevelt was born to privilege on October 27, 1858. He was educated at Harvard University and soon began a life in politics as a member of the New York State Assembly. He would go on to serve as assistant secretary of the navy under President McKinley.

Roosevelt, an avid hunter, outdoorsman, and advocate of the "strenuous life," participated in the Cuban War in 1898. His band of sportsmen and cowboys, the "Rough Riders," served admirably and contributed to Roosevelt's prominence. Soon thereafter, he was elected governor of New York, and later vice president of the United States. When McKinley was assassinated on September 14, 1901, Roosevelt assumed the presidency. He would remain in office through March 1909. Even after leaving office, he remained a patriot, and while his offer was refused, Roosevelt had volunteered to serve his country in World War I.

That is not to say that Roosevelt was a warmonger. He had long had a reputation as a reformer, and as president he continued that work. Roosevelt became an active proponent of the use of arbitration in international disputes. He became the first U.S. president to be honored with the Nobel Peace Prize, awarded in recognition of his role in the Russo-Japanese Treaty.

In addition to his career in politics, Roosevelt was a prolific author, publishing more than 26 books and a number of articles. His readers know him for the views espoused in his writing. He may be known by others, though, as the source of the term *teddy bear*. In 1903, he received as a present a stuffed toy in the shape of a bear, and as the story goes, stuffed bears ever since have been called teddy bears. He is also memorialized in Mount Rushmore. There, his visage is carved in the mountainside along with three other beloved American presidents: Thomas Jefferson, Abraham Lincoln, and George Washington.

Theodore Roosevelt, sometimes referred to simply as TR, is remembered as a rancher, hunter, statesman, and diplomat.

See also: FOLK HEROES/LEGENDARY FIGURES; GHOST STORIES; LINCOLN, ABRAHAM; TOYS, FOLK; WASHINGTON, GEORGE; WORLD WAR I.

For Further Reading:

Auchincloss, Louis. *Theodore Roosevelt*. New York: Times Books, 2001.

Brands, H. W. *T.R.: The Last Romantic*. New York: Basic Books, 1997.

Burns, James MacGregor, and Susan Dunn. *The Three Roosevelts: Patrician Leaders Who Transformed America*. New York: Atlantic Monthly Press, 2001.

Dalton, Kathleen. *Theodore Roosevelt: A Strenuous Life*. New York: Knopf, 2002.

Dolin, Eric Jay. *Smithsonian Book of National Wildlife Refuges*. Washington, D.C.: Smithsonian Institution Press, 2003.

Miroff, Bruce. *Icons of Democracy: American Leaders as Heroes, Aristocrats, Dissenters, and Democrats*. New York: Basic Books, 1993.

Morris, Edmund. *Theodore Rex*. New York: Random House, 2001.

Rauchway, Eric. *Murdering McKinley: The Making of Theodore Roosevelt's America*. New York: Hill & Wang, 2003.

roots   See CONJURE/CONJURING.

Rosh Hashonah   Held in autumn each year, Rosh Hashonah represents a new year's observance within Judaism. The name of the observance means "head of the year."

This occasion has been a part of the Jewish, or lunar, calendar for many centuries. Rosh Hashonah represents a time at which individuals are judged for their sins. The findings in this process become their destinies, and such are inscribed in the Book of Life. This new year's holiday, then, has major ethical and spiritual components for believers. Rosh Hashonah lasts one day for Reformed and Israeli Jews and spans two days among Orthodox and Conservative Jews.

The interval between Rosh Hashonah and Yom Kippur, a Jewish day of atonement, offers a time of additional reverence, during which prayer and reflection acknowledge one's shortcomings. Together, the two observances are linked to form a 10-day process of penitence described as the High Holy Days or Ten Days of Repentance.

Rosh Hashonah is a communal rather than familial holiday, and so religious services and other shared public activities shape the observance. Readings from Scripture, group recitations, and other acts of devotion play a part in this occasion. In addition, the blowing of the shofar (a ram's horn) symbolizes remembrance, honor to God, and the enduring practice of the horn's use each Rosh Hashonah. During a traditionally waterside ceremony of Tashlikh, worshipers say prayers, turn out their garment hems and pockets, and/or cast crumbs onto the water, in a manner symbolic of ridding themselves of sin.

In the home, those observing Rosh Hashonah have customs including dipping hallah bread into honey, symbolizing the hope for sweetness to follow in the new year. Many adult participants conduct morning fasts. The majority of the activity associated with Rosh Hashonah's confession and quest for forgiveness is conducted not in the household, but rather in the wider faith community.

As a time of purification and repentance, Rosh Hashonah plays a central role in the spiritual lives of Jewish people.

See also: HOLIDAYS/OBSERVANCES; JEWISH-AMERICAN FOLKLORE; NEW YEAR'S EVE/DAY; RELIGION, FOLK; YOM KIPPUR.

For Further Reading:

Cohen, Hennig, Tristram Potter Coffin, eds. *The Folklore of American Holidays.* Detroit: Gale, 1987.

Gaster, Theodor H. *Festivals of the Jewish Year.* New York: William Sloane Associates, 1952.

Greenspoon, Leonard J., and Ronald Simkins. *Spiritual Dimensions of Judaism.* Omaha, Nebr.: Creighton University Press, 2003.

Kaplan, Dana Evan. *The Cambridge Companion to American Judaism.* New York: Cambridge University Press, 2005.

Myers, Robert. *Celebrations: The Complete Book of American Holidays.* Garden City, N.Y.: Doubleday, 1972.

Schauss, Hayyim. *The Jewish Festivals: History and Observance.* New York: Schocken Books, 1962.

Ross, Betsy (1752–1836) Just as folklore may have overstated the role of Paul Revere in the American Revolution, so may it have exaggerated the part Betsy Ross played in creating the nation's first flag.

According to the popular myth, a Philadelphia seamstress named Betsy Ross, recently widowed, was commissioned by no less than Geroge Washington to create the first American flag. On this basis, Ross has taken on mythic importance in the history of this national icon. While it is true that Elizabeth Griscom Ross, granddaughter of a Quaker dissenter, sewed flags for the U.S. Navy, historians doubt that her fashioning of the first American flag, bearing a circle of 13 five-pointed stars on a blue field accompanied by red and white stripes, can be established through sufficient evidence.

Skeptics about the claim point out some of the reasons for holding the beloved myth suspect. These objections include the fact that the records of the Continental Congress, while detailing the colors and emblems to be used within the flag, make no mention of Ross as the banner's designer or even as its fabricator. Doubters also note that it was a descendent of Ross who made the first such claim.

Nonetheless, Betsy Ross is commonly held as a "founding mother" in the folklore of revolutionary America, and her memory is regarded accordingly. Her tiny residence in Philadelphia has been maintained, first as the "Betsy Ross House," then as the "Old Flag House," and most recently as the "American Flag House and Betsy Ross Memorial." Flag Day ceremonies are held on the premises, and actresses sometimes provide first-person dramatizations of Ross herself.

While it may not be possible to establish definitively the designer of the flag sometimes dubbed "Old Glory," Betsy Ross still captures the popular imagination as its mythic source.

See also: FLAG DAY; FOLK HEROES/LEGENDARY FIGURES; LEGENDS, FOLK; PLEDGE OF ALLEGIANCE; QUAKER FOLKLORE; REVOLUTIONARY WAR.

For Further Reading:

Kashatus, William. "Seamstress for a Revolution," *American History* 37, no. 3 (2002): 20–26.

Mastai, Boleslaw, and Marie-Louise D'Otrange Mastal. *The Stars and the Stripes: The American Flag as Art and as History: From the Birth of the Republic to the Present.* New York: Knopf, 1973.

McLean, Harvard. "Besty Ross Can Be Dangerous," *Social Studies* 70, no. 2 (1979): 71–75.

Stevens, William Oliver. *Famous Women of America*. New York: Dodd, Mead, 1950.

Varenne, Hervé, ed. *Symbolizing America*. Lincoln: University of Nebraska Press, 1986.

Rough Riders   See ROOSEVELT, THEODORE.

"Rumpelstiltskin"   "Rumpelstiltskin" is a Grimm brothers fairy tale whose title character is one of the magical yet dangerous little characters who inhabit the realm of folklore.

According to this tale, there was once a poor miller who had a beautiful daughter, who he claimed had the ability to spin gold from straw. The miller even boasts to the king of his daughter's rare talent. Learning of this unusual ability, the king summons her to his castle. He places the young lady in a room filled with straw, leaving her to fulfill her father's promise. He declares that she will either complete the task or die for failure to do so.

While she is kept in the room, a curious little man appears before the woman. He asks what she will give him if he transforms the straw into gold for her. She provides him with a necklace for this service. Satisfied with the offering, the little man sets to work. When he is done, the straw has vanished and in its place is only gold.

The king, suitably surprised with this result, furnishes a greater quantity of straw with the same demand as before. The young lady receives a second call from the little man. This time, he accepts a ring in exchange for complying with the king's request. Once again, he fulfills the king's desire.

Finding this to be the case, the king furnishes an even greater amount of straw to be rendered as gold. This time, the young lady has no more jewelry to give the little man, and in a moment of ultimate desperation, it is decided that she will give him her firstborn child in exchange for performing the task at hand. He completes the transformation a third time.

The king returns well pleased. The discovery of this woman's apparent gifts gives him another idea. Although the young woman is from a family of modest means, the king nonetheless concludes that a spouse with such lucrative abilities will prove priceless. On this premise, they marry.

Within a year, the queen bears the king a child. When the little man returns to claim the child as payment, the new mother refuses him. Always one to strike a bargain, the little man indicates that the queen has three days in which to guess his name. If successful, she may keep her baby and the little man will forgive the debt.

The frantic queen finds the naming task formidable, and she makes many unsuccessful attempts. Indeed, the little man is so certain that he will prevail that he cannot resist gloating, and as he shouts his own praises, a passing messenger overhears the little man calling out his own name.

This fateful message reaches the queen before the guessing period has concluded, and to the little man's shock and dismay, he must concede defeat when she finally identifies him correctly as Rumpelstiltskin. The little man becomes so enraged by this unexpected turn of events that he grabs hold of his own foot and tears himself asunder.

This fairy tale, as is typical of the narrative form, conveys moral messages to audiences. The story cautions against an array of vices, including boastfulness, pride, and greed. "Rumpelstiltskin," as "Rapunzel" does, centers on the ill-fated promise of a firstborn child to a stranger in return for a favor. In this sense, the tale also warns against expecting the impossible or promising the unthinkable.

Fairy tales are filled with characters—ogres, trolls, little people, and the like—who guard the way to treasures, strike devil's bargains, trick the innocent and the desperate, and manipulate their environment to their own advantage. In the end, Rumpelstiltskin joins the ranks of magical creatures who pose as helpers but actually constitute as great a threat as any villain encountered in fairy tales.

See also: CHILDREN'S FOLKLORE; FABLES; FAIRY TALES; MYTHS, FOLK; "RAPUNZEL."

For Further Reading:

Hallett, Martin, and Barbara Karasek. *Folk and Fairy Tales.* New York: Broadview Press, 2002.

Radner, Joan Newlon, ed. *Feminist Messages: Coding in Women's Folk Culture.* Urbana: University of Illinois Press, 1993.

Tatar, Maria, ed. *The Annotated Classic Fairy Tales.* New York: W. W. Norton, 2002.

Tatar, Maria. *The Hard Facts of the Grimms' Fairy Tales.* Princeton, N.J.: Princeton University Press, 1987.

Walker, Paul Robert. *Little Folk: Stories from Around the World.* San Diego: Harcourt Brace, 1997.

Ward, Donald. "The German Connection: The Brothers Grimm and the Study of 'Oral' Literature," *Western Folklore* 53, no. 1 (January 1994): 1–26.

Rushmore, Mount   See ROOSEVELT, THEODORE; WASHINGTON, GEORGE.

Sacajawea (Sacagewea) (c. 1786–1812?)
Sacajawea is best known as the Native American woman who aided the 19th-century explorers Meriwether Lewis and William Clark on their western expeditions.

Relatively little is known about her early life, including the exact date of her birth. Sacajawea was born the daughter of a Shoshone chief in approximately 1786. At the age of 10, she was kidnapped and made to marry a French-Canadian trapper named Toussaint Charbonneau. When Charbonneau became an interpreter for Meriwether Lewis and William Clark in 1804, Sacajawea was invited to travel with them. She was accompanied by her newborn son, Jean Baptiste Charbonneau. The explorers believed that Sacajawea's presence in their midst would signal their peaceful intentions to all they encountered. She also contributed numerous helpful skills. She spoke English, French, and a form of sign language. She taught her employers about plant lore and edible materials found along their way and helped them traverse the Continental Divide.

During the journey, Sacajawea again had contact with her brother, Cameahwait, from whom Lewis sought to acquire horses for their travels. Cameahwait had succeeded his father, who had died since Sacajawea's abduction, as Shoshone chief. Sacajawea and Charbonneau saw to it that Meriwether Lewis and William Clark reached their destination. As the party ventured back east, Sacajawea and her husband split off from Lewis and Clark. After this point, historians are less sure about the events of Sacajawea's life, and their biographies conflict. Some accounts describe her as returning to her husband's residence, where she perished in an 1812 epidemic. Others place her back with the Shoshone, living on a reservation until her death in 1884.

In terms of both her role in the successful expedition of Meriwether Lewis and William Clark and her somewhat mysterious life both before and after her dealings with them, Sacajawea has a legendary quality within American folklore.

See also: FOLK HEROES/LEGENDARY FIGURES; LEWIS, MERIWETHER, AND WILLIAM CLARK; NATIVE AMERICAN FOLKLORE; NORTHWESTERN REGIONAL FOLKLORE.

For Further Reading:
Ashby, Ruth, and Deborah Gore Ohrn. *Herstory: Women Who Changed the World.* New York: Viking Press, 1995.

Bruchac, Joseph. *Sacajawea: The Story of Bird Woman and the Lewis and Clark Expedition.* San Diego: Silver Whistle, 2000.

Howard, Harold. *Sacajawea.* Norman: University of Oklahoma Press, 1971.

Kessler, Donna. *The Making of Sacagawea, a Euro-American Legend.* Tuscaloosa: University of Alabama Press, 1996.

Milton, Joyce, and Shelley Hehenberger. *Sacajawea: Her True Story*. New York: Grosset & Dunlap, 2001.

Slaughter, Thomas. *Exploring Lewis and Clark: Reflections on Men and Wilderness*. New York: Knopf, 2003.

Thomasma, Kenneth, and Agnes Vincen Talbot. *The Truth about Sacajawea*. Jackson, Wyo.: Grandview, 1997.

Saint Nicholas   See SANTA CLAUS.

Saint Patrick's Day   This holiday on March 17 is named for Ireland's patron saint, Patrick. In addition to converting many to Christianity, Saint Patrick founded numerous churches and schools, making him a key religious figure in Ireland. Indeed, Saint Patrick's Day is a Catholic holy day there, marking his religious feast day and the anniversary of his death. In Ireland, Saint Patrick's Day began as a religious observance and a tribute to the miracles ascribed to him, such as driving the snakes from Ireland, but the holiday is now more often observed with secular festivities, such as gatherings in area pubs.

Saint Patrick's Day has been celebrated in America since 1737, when Boston became home to the holiday's new incarnation. In the United States, the observance of Saint Patrick's Day is as much secular as sacred, with revelry of several forms intended to honor the ethnic heritage of Irish Americans. The first Saint Patrick's Day parade took place in America in 1762; the first such event took place in New York City, where parades continue annually ever since. This parade route travels along Fifth Avenue and passes by New York's Saint Patrick's Cathedral. The New York parade remains the largest of those occurring in major cities across the nation. Additional holiday-themed events are associated with other cities, such as Chicago's tradition, begun in 1962, of temporarily tinting river water with green food coloring to celebrate the day.

Along with parades and public processions, parties, speeches, dinners, and dancing are typical practices conducted during American observances of Saint Patrick's Day. Only some of American traditions for this day derive from Irish culture. Others are U.S. inventions or appropriations of elements perceived to be Irish. The practice of wearing green attire is a part of the observance, and schoolchildren still pinch peers who fail to wear the color on March 17. Alcohol consumption is strongly associated with American traditions for the day, despite the belief that Saint Patrick himself abstained from drink. Many bars and pubs serve specialty beverages, such as green beer and Irish coffee, to accompany holiday festivities. Although bacon and cabbage might be more authentic Irish cuisine, corned beef and cabbage has become a customary American meal in celebration of Saint Patrick's Day.

Celtic symbols and images invoked in American celebrations of Saint Patrick's Day include the leprechaun (fairy) and the shamrock (used to represent and promote fertility in spring rites at this time in the calendar). The shamrock, or trefoil, has an additional connection to Saint Patrick through his use of the plant's three leaves to symbolize the Christian trinity and its stem to portray their unity in God.

Whereas in Ireland Saint Patrick's Day may provide a good way to promote tourism, in the United States, it functions as an opportunity for hedonism, especially in terms of reinforcing drinking culture.

See also: ETHNICITY; FOOD/FOODWAYS; HOLIDAYS/OBSERVANCES; IMMIGRATION AND FOLKLORE; PARADES.

For Further Reading:
Cohen, Hennig, and Tristram Potter Coffin, eds. *The Folklore of American Holidays*. Detroit: Gale, 1987.

Cronin, Mike, and Daryl Adair. *The Wearing of the Green: A History of St. Patrick's Day*. New York: Routledge, 2001.

Litwicki, Ellen. *America's Public Holidays, 1865–1920*. Washington, D.C.: Smithsonian Institution Press, 2000.

McCann, Jim, and Jeanne Benedict. *Celebrations: A Joyous Guide to the Holidays from Past to Present.* New York: HPBooks/Penguin, 2001.

Myers, Robert. *Celebrations: The Complete Book of American Holidays.* Garden City, N.Y.: Doubleday, 1972.

Santino, Jack. *All around the Year: Holidays and Celebrations in American Life.* Urbana: University of Illinois Press, 1994.

Saint Valentine's Day   On February 14 each year, Americans express affection for those they hold dear as part of the celebration of Saint Valentine's Day.

The origin of Saint Valentine's Day celebrations appears to date as far back as the Roman Lupercalia, a feast honoring Lupercus, a pastoral god. Within that celebration, women's names were placed into a box, from which men then drew names. After choosing lots in this manner, the male and female would be partnered for a year. In later observances, the procedure was Christianized such that one drew the name of a saint from the box and thereafter demonstrated the virtues associated with that figure. At some later point, the version of the pairing ritual was reinstated, and from this tradition arose the idea of Saint Valentine's Day as a day for romance.

The date of the celebration, February 14, has a context related to long-standing folk beliefs. Many people still uphold an old belief that this is the day on which birds identify their mates. The date is also supposed to be a rich one for prediction, especially where romance is concerned. For instance, some have contended that young women should marry the first eligible man they cast eyes on that day.

The exchange of paper greetings, now known as valentines, seems to derive from a variation of the drawn-lot ceremony in which mottoes were selected from a box. These mottoes appear to have given way to the verses we currently associate with the holiday. In the United States, valentine greeting cards were exchanged as early as the 17th century. It was not until the 18th century that homemade valentines became common, often aided by verse books that suggested language for both romantic overtures and replies. The advent of commercially produced valentine cards during the 19th century, along with the increased access to printing and postal service, helped establish more firmly the custom of sending valentine cards each year. Since its outset, the iconography of Saint Valentine's Day has remained fairly consistent over time and carries forward the theme of love, featuring hearts, lovers' knots, turtledoves, and images of Cupid with his arrow and bow.

Today, Saint Valentine's Day is observed chiefly as a secular occasion on which individuals honor their mates (or prospective ones), their friends, and their family members. The day is devoted to conveying the esteem in which such persons are held, and the tributes typically include cards, flowers, candy (often presented in heart-shaped boxes), gifts, and special activities conducted together, such as dining out. Schoolchildren join in Saint Valentine's Day fun through celebrations of friendship, typically marked by exchanging small greetings and gifts with their classmates.

As is true of Saint Patrick's Day, current Saint Valentine's Day practices seem largely remote from the lives of the church martyrs, but nonetheless continue to be holidays associated with these figures. In the case of Saint Valentine's Day, the general notion of a seasonal observance celebrating intimacy and anticipating the arrival of spring and with it, the renewal of life, seems to emphasize earthly love over its divine counterpart.

See also: CHILDREN'S FOLKLORE; COURTSHIP/DATING FOLKLORE; HOLIDAYS/OBSERVANCES; PREDICTION; SAINT PATRICK'S DAY; WEDDING/MARRIAGE FOLKLORE.

For Further Reading:

Aveni, Anthony F. *The Book of the Year: A Brief History of Our Seasonal Holidays.* New York: Oxford University Press, 2004.

Cohen, Hennig, and Tristram Potter Coffin, eds. *The Folklore of American Holidays.* Detroit: Gale, 1987.

Gair, Joseph, and Anne Marie Jauss. *Holidays around the World.* Boston: Little, Brown, 1953.

Genge, Ngaire. *Urban Legends: The As-Complete-as-One-Could-Be-Guide-to-Modern-Myths.* New York: Three Rivers Press, 2000.

McSpadden, J. Walker. *The Book of Holidays.* New York: Crowell, 1958.

Myers, Robert. *Celebrations: The Complete Book of American Holidays.* Garden City, N.Y.: Doubleday, 1972.

Santino, Jack. *All around the Year: Holidays and Celebrations in American Life.* Urbana: University of Illinois Press, 1994.

Staff, Frank. *The Valentine and Its Origins.* New York: Praeger, 1969.

Salem witchcraft   See WITCHCRAFT, SALEM.

Sandburg, Carl (1878–1967)   Carl Sandburg is among the most beloved of all American writers, in part because of his affection for incorporating the nation's lore within his works.

Sandburg was born in 1878 in Galesburg, Illinois, to parents who were immigrants from Sweden. The young Sandburg attended, but did not graduate from, Lombard College. He fought in the Spanish-American War and held various jobs, including spending time as a door-to-door salesman, before becoming well known as a writer emerging from America's Midwest.

Early on in his career, Sandburg became something of an independent scholar and folklorist in his own right. He would take various odd jobs and, while serving as a laborer, collect the folk songs and colorful tales of those he met. Toward this end, Sandburg followed the romance of the rails, traveling as a hobo might during the 1890s. His "songbag" books, published compilations of his findings accompanied with anecdotes about his experiences while gathering the tunes, proved popular. These vol-

umes included *American Songbag* (1927) and *New American Songbook* (1950).

In addition to collecting the traditional songs, he became a folk performer of some note, as well as studying various aspects of folk speech, such as sayings, proverbs, and slang. He went on to publish much of this material in a collection entitled *The People, Yes* (1936). Sandburg's interest in vernacular culture would continue throughout his life.

Sandburg's writing career was a long one and spanned numerous genres. For example, he worked in journalism, including a stint as a reporter for the *Chicago Daily News.* He edited collections of folklore. During the 1930s, he published a six-volume biography of President Abraham Lincoln, which was recognized with the Pulitzer Prize, one of two he would receive for his work. The other was awarded to his *Complete Poems* (1950), and it is as a poet that Sandburg is best remembered.

As a writer of verse, Sandburg was connected, at least in the minds of critics, to the Chicago Renaissance, a literary and artistic movement that followed the 1893 World's Fair held in Chicago. Such writers and artists celebrated Chicago as one of the nation's great cities and the Midwest as America's heartland. Indeed, the best known of Sandburg's poems may be his 1918 composition "Chicago." Other authors associated with the Chicago Renaissance include Theodore Dreiser and Edgar Lee Masters.

Sandburg's published poetry volumes include *Chicago Poems* (1914), *Cornhuskers* (1918), *Smoke and Steel* (1920), and *Slabs of the Sunburnt West* (1922). In these works, Sandburg expressed not only his enthusiasm for the American land, but his deep and abiding admiration for the nation's people. He placed his confidence in them to bring about needed social and political changes and it appears they reciprocated this high regard.

Sandburg was an immensely popular writer and remains a much-anthologized American poet. Sometimes compared to such poets as Robert Frost and Walt Whitman, Sandburg in his writings showed a parallel interest in Americana. Sandburg's name will be forever connected to the memory of the president about who he wrote so much and so well, Abraham Lincoln. His other interests as a writer and researcher are likely to remain in the background of the American public's mind when thinking of Sandburg's legacy.

See also: BROWN, STERLING ALLEN; FOLKLORE IN AMERICAN LITERATURE; LINCOLN, ABRAHAM; MIDWESTERN REGIONAL FOLKLORE; MUSIC, FOLK; PRESIDENTS' DAY; PROVERBS; SPEECH, FOLK; SWEDISH-AMERICAN FOLKLORE; WHITMAN, WALT.

For Further Reading:

Botkin, Benjamin, ed. *A Treasury of American Folklore: Stories, Ballads, and Traditions of the People.* New York: Bantam, 1981.

Callahan, North. *Carl Sandburg: Lincoln of Our Literature.* New York: New York University Press, 1970.

Mieder, Wolfgang. "Behold the Proverbs of a People: A Florilegium of Proverbs in Carl Sandburg's Poem 'Good Morning, America,'" *Southern Folklore Quarterly* 35 (1971): 160–168.

———. "Proverbs in Carl Sandburg's Poem 'The People, Yes,'" *Southern Folklore Quarterly* 37 (1973): 15–36.

Sandburg, Carl. *The American Songbag.* New York: Harcourt, Brace, and World, 1927.

Santa Claus (legendary) Santa Claus is the embodiment of the secular portion of America's celebration of Christmas.

Sources of the Santa figure as he is currently imagined are numerous and are drawn from the holiday lore of various countries. One such influence on the icon of Santa Claus is Saint Nicholas, a fourth-century bishop who was later identified as a patron saint of children, among others. His feast day traditionally falls on December 6. Kris Kringle, the German tradition in which the Christ child bears gifts each year by magically slipping through the keyhole of each home, also seems related. Father Christmas, a Reformation figure, also contributed in substantial ways to the development of Santa Claus. His Dutch name *Sinterklaas*, his red and white attire, and his annual visit on December 24 all seem to anticipate the arrival of Santa Claus on December 25.

The manner and appearance of Santa Claus as he is now known in the United States also owe much to two 19th-century men actively engaged in his portrayal on the page. Clement Moore's 1822 poem "A Visit from St. Nicholas" (also known by one of its phrases, "The Night before Christmas") became the basis for an extremely popular book that has helped shape reader visions of Santa as jolly. The other American who influenced perceptions of Santa in America was the political cartoonist Thomas Nast, whose drawings of Santa in *Harper's Weekly* from 1863 to 1886 established him as a plump individual.

Today, Santa Claus is understood as a mature and benevolent figure with an uncanny ability to determine the quality of children's conduct, and to direct the tokens of his annual visit accordingly. It is supposed that he maintains careful and comprehensive lists of conduct, and his all-seeing powers inform his selection of Christmas gifts. As the legend has it, children who have behaved well will be rewarded with gifts and toys to their liking, all reputed to be produced by an army of elves in a secret North Pole workshop. Children who have not met the conduct standard will either be left nothing or receive only a lump of coal, bespeaking the dark mark beside their name on Santa's list of good and bad children.

Although children could well be frightened by the prospect of such scrutiny and the resulting judgments, Santa is nonetheless regarded as a much-loved holiday icon. Each winter, many individuals assume the red and white attire of the beloved Santa so that they may greet boys and girls, inquire whether they have been good this year, and hear their holiday wishes. Since a great many of these individuals serve in the employ of retail establishments and/or shopping malls, such Santas are especially attuned to discerning children's hopes for specific store-bought, rather than North Pole–crafted, Christmas gifts.

See also: CHILDREN'S FOLKLORE; CHRISTMAS; FOLK HEROES/LEGENDARY FIGURES; HOLIDAYS/OBSERVANCES; TOYS, FOLK.

For Further Reading:

Coffin, Tristram Potter. *The Book of Christmas Folklore*. New York: Seabury Press, 1973.

Horsley, Richard, and James Tracy, eds. *Christmas Unwrapped: Consumerism, Christ, and Culture*. Harrisburg, Pa.: Trinity Press International, 2001.

Myers, Robert. *Celebrations: The Complete Book of American Holidays*. Garden City, N.Y.: Doubleday, 1972.

Restad, Penne. *Christmas in America: A History*. New York: Oxford University Press, 1995.

Santino, Jack. *All around the Year: Holidays and Celebrations in American Life*. Urbana: University of Illinois Press, 1994.

Sasquatch   See BIGFOOT/SASQUATCH.

Sawyer, Tom   See CLEMENS, SAMUEL LANGHORNE.

sayings, folk   See SPEECH, FOLK.

Scandinavian-American folklore   See DANISH-AMERICAN FOLKLORE; FINNISH-AMERICAN FOLKLORE; ICELANDIC-AMERICAN FOLKLORE; NORWEGIAN-AMERICAN FOLKLORE; SWEDISH-AMERICAN FOLKLORE.

Scottish-American folklore   Scottish-American folklore includes the folk heritage of immigrants to the United States from Scotland, along with persons born in America with Scottish ancestry.

Immigration to the United States from Scotland has occurred since the 18th century. Settlers felt especially drawn to the southern colonies, where many made their new homes.

Folklore forms most closely associated with Scottish Americans include ballads, folk dances, sporting events, and foodways. In fact, immigrant instrumentation of folk ballads such as "Barbara Allen" may have been a climate-setting influence for America's genre of country music. Fiddles and bagpipes are frequently featured instruments in Scottish folk music. The ritual dances of ancient Scottish history became the square dances of Scottish Americans. Traditional attire incorporates well known visual elements such as kilts, tartans, and tam-o'-shanters. These items of apparel, however, have more specific ties to Highland culture than to that of other regions within Scotland. Highland Games, still held today in New York and various other locations in the United States, showcase athletic competitions involving feats of skill and strength. Traditional Scottish foodways feature hearty foods such as potatoes, meat puddings, pastries, and shortbreads.

As is the case with many cultural groups, false perceptions and misconceptions of Scottish Americans abound. Outsiders may assume that Scottish people embody the characteristics associated with images in popular culture. For instance, they may mistake ethnic slurs for accurate characterizations, such as the accusation that Scottish people are excessively thrifty or "scotch." Such notions are merely stereotypes rather than accurate depictions of Scottish attributes.

Organizations dedicated to the preservation and study of culture include New York City's American Scottish Foundation; New Holland, Pennsylvania's Scotch-Irish Foundation; and Plymouth Meeting, Pennsylvania's Association of Scottish Games and Festivals. Major collections of cultural material include the Robert Louis Stevenson Collection at Yale University and the Robert Burns Collection at the University of South Carolina at Columbia.

From the folk hero Daniel Boone to the furniture craftsman Duncan Phyfe, Scottish Americans have contributed to a body of folklore that both recalls the past and revitalizes its traditions for new generations.

See also: APPALACHIAN FOLKLORE; BALLADS; BOONE, DANIEL; CULTURAL GROUPS; FESTIVALS, FOLKLORE; IMMIGRATION AND FOLKLORE; IRISH-AMERICAN FOLKLORE.

For Further Reading:

Dobson, David. *Scottish Emigration to Colonial America, 1607–1785*. Athens: University of Georgia Press, 1994.

Donaldson, Emily Ann. *The Scottish Highland Games in America*. Gretna, La.: Pelican, 1986.

Fischer, David Hackett. *Albion's Seed: Four British Folkways in America*. New York: 1989.

Jackson, Clayton. *A Social History of the Scotch-Irish*. Lanham, Md.: Madison Books, 1993.

Johnson, James E. *The Scots and Scotch-Irish in America*. Minneapolis: Lerner, 1991.

Lehmann, William C. *Scottish and Scotch-Irish Contributions to Early American Life and Culture*. Port Washington, N.Y.: Kennikat Press, 1978.

McWhiney, Grady. *Cracker Culture: Celtic Customs in the Old South*. Tuscaloosa: University of Alabama Press, 1988.

Newton, Michael Steven. *We're Indians Sure Enough: The Legacy of the Scottish Highlanders in the United States*. Chapel Hill, N.C.: Saorsa Media, 2001.

Thomson, James Casement. *Great Scots! The Scottish American Hall of Fame*. North Riverside: Illinois Saint Andrew Society, 1996.

seances See DEATH; SUPERNATURAL.

Seaport and Preservation Shipyard, Mystic See MYSTIC SEAPORT AND PRESERVATION SHIPYARD.

Seattle, Chief (c. 1790–1866) Seattle's birth date is uncertain but estimated at approximately 1790. This ambiguity may be due in part to the fact that he did not become a public figure until midlife. Seatttle developed into a formidable leader and warrior. He called the Pacific Northwest home, and one of the nation's most famous cities now bears his name.

During the 1840s, with the help of French missionaries, Seattle converted to Catholicism. It was at this point that he became an advocate of goodwill in relations with white Americans. Seattle earned a reputation as a gifted orator.

Some scholars question how accurate transcriptions of Seattle's famous addresses really are, at times suggesting that remarks made by others may have been attributed to Seattle as he emerged as a mythic figure. One of his most famous speeches took place in 1854, and its translation is freqeuently cited by the environmental movement. According to some research, this ecologically-minded version of the address actually originated with a 1971 documentary whose subjects included Chief Seattle.

Seattle's views, or at least those statements associated with his career as a speaker, came before the public in updated form in Disney's 1995 feature-length animated film *Pocahontas*.

Chief Seattle died June 6, 1866. His legacy lives on in Native American folklore and inspires environmental causes and occasions, such as Earth Day, when his speeches are frequently referenced.

See also: FOLK HEROES/LEGENDARY FIGURES; JOSEPH, CHIEF; NATIVE AMERICAN FOLKLORE; POCAHONTAS.

For Further Reading:

Bordewich, Fergus. *Killing the White Man's Indian: Reinventing of Native Americans at the End of the Twentieth Century*. New York: Doubleday, 1996.

Furtwangler, Albert. *Answering Chief Seattle*. Seattle: University of Washington Press, 1997.

Gifford, Eli. *How Can One Sell the Air? Chief Seattle's Vision*. Summertown, Tenn.: Book Publishing Company, 1992.

Joseph, James. *Remaking America: How the Benevolent Traditions of Many Cultures are Transforming Our National Life*. San Francisco: Jossey-Bass, 1995.

Kaiser, R. "Chief Seattle's Speech(es): American Origins and European Reception—Almost a Detective Story." In *Indians and Europe: An Interdisciplinary Collection of Essays*, edited by Christian F. Feest, 505–526. Lincoln: University of Nebraska Press, 1999.

Nerburn, Kent. *Wisdom of the Native Americans.* Novato, Calif.: New World Library, 1999.

Slemmons, Rod. *The Eyes of Chief Seattle.* Suquamish, Wash.: Suquamish Museum, 1985.

The Wisdom of the Great Chiefs: The Classic Speeches of Chief Red Jacket, Chief Joseph, and Chief Seattle. San Rafael, Calif.: New World Library, 1994.

Secretaries' Day   See ADMINISTRATIVE PROFESSIONALS' DAY/WEEK.

September 11   See PATRIOT DAY.

Shaker folklore   The Shakers practiced a folk religion with distinctive beliefs, practices, crafts, and way of life.

Formally known as the United Society of Believers in Christ's Second Appearing, this sect of millenarians called themselves Believers but became widely known as the Shakers because of observers' surprise at their movements during worship. The sect was founded in England during the 18th century. In an attempt to escape religious persecution, a small group of Shakers immigrated to New York, where they settled along the Hudson River Valley. Their elder leader, Mother Ann Lee, made prophecies and was regarded as a holy figure by the Believers. Shortly after arriving in America, though, the pacifism of this group made them suspect during the Revolutionary War, and their members were arrested, accused of witchcraft, and otherwise victimized.

The Shakers lived in religious communities with strict rules and a highly developed sense of order. They established settlements in Connecticut, New Hampshire, New York, Maine, and Massachusetts. The central community was located in New Lebanon, New York. Additional communities were formed in Kentucky, Indiana, and Ohio during the 19th century.

The Shaker communities were structured in such a way as to help ensure a simple and virtuous life. Individual members held no property, instead devoting their labors to the health and prosperity of the group. Gender equality was a central tenet within the group. Celibacy was practiced, and men and women resided separately. Objects of material culture, such as chairs and other furniture, embodied the principles of plain design the Shakers advocated. They also became known for their hymns and other music, religious dancing, foodways, medicinal herbs, and seed industry.

The Shaker movement reached the height of its popularity during the 1840s, when its members numbered approximately 6,000. With the rule of celibacy, the order relied upon a steady influx of new members. Membership declined during the 20th century, and fewer than 10 practicing Shakers remained at the opening of the 21st century.

Onlookers remain fascinated with the lives and folk practices of the Shakers. Some locations of communal villages now host visitors and provide gift shops, where cookbooks and crafts in the Shaker manner may be purchased. Shaker expression has inspired mainstream arts. An example would be the way the Shaker hymn "Simple Gifts" helped form the basis for Aaron Copland's 1944 ballet *Appalachian Spring.* Shaker design is still lauded for its spare and beautiful lines.

Often compared to the Quakers, the Amish, and the Pennsylvania Dutch, the Shakers were a small but influential force within American folk religion.

See also: CULTURAL GROUPS; PENNSYLVANIA DUTCH/PENNSYLVANIA GERMAN FOLKLORE; QUAKER FOLKLORE; RELIGION, FOLK.

For Further Reading:
Andrews, Edward. *The People Called Shakers: A Search for the Perfect Society.* New York: Dover, 1994.

Brewer, Priscilla. *Shaker Communities, Shaker Lives.* Hanover, N.H.: University Press of New England, 1986.

Heath, Alan. *Common Threads: Festivals of Folklore and Literature for Schools and Libraries.* Lanham, Md.: Scarecrow Press, 1996.

Sprigg, June. *By Shaker Hands.* New York: Knopf, 1975.

Stein, Stephen. *The Shaker Experience in America: A History of the United Society of Believers.* New Haven, Conn.: Yale University Press, 1992.

Whitson, Robley Edward. *The Shakers: Two Centuries of Spiritual Reflection.* New York: Paulist Press, 1983.

shamanism   See MAGIC.

shamrock   See SAINT PATRICK'S DAY.

shape shifters   See CHANGELINGS.

Shelley, Kate (1863–1912)   Kate Shelley's heroic story stands as an emblem of youthful altruism within both Iowa history and American lore.

On July 6, 1881, a storm overtook the Des Moines River valley. The creek near the Shelley home, where a railroad widow was raising Kate and four other children, began to flood. In the dark of the night, Kate Shelley heard an eerie crash as a steam train toppled and fell 184 feet as the Honey Creek Bridge collapsed. Realizing that a midnight express passenger train was due through that area shortly, Shelley recognized the danger posed to the crew and passengers of the next train if they attempted to traverse the same portion of track with its broken trestle.

Without concern for her personal safety, the teenager hastened to the nearest railroad station by crawling on her hands and knees across the 671-foot-long railroad bridge that spanned the Des Moines River. The crossing was slippery because of the storm and was made more perilous by the absence of planks. When Shelley reached the Moingona station, she was able to alert officials in time. She also insisted upon joining a rescue party sent to recover survivors of the earlier train wreck.

A grateful community rewarded Shelley with parades, medals, and gifts from the railroad company, including a half barrel of flour, a half load of coal, and a lifetime train pass.

After concluding her education, Shelley worked first as a teacher, and later as a depot agent at the station where she once issued her famous warning. When Shelley passed away, a special train bore her remains from her home to Boone, Iowa, her burial location. After her death on January 21, 1912, the Chicago and Northwestern Railway replaced the Des Moines River Bridge Shelley inched across that stormy night in 1881. They renamed the bridge after the young heroine who made the first bridge so memorable.

Shelley's railroad adventure is remembered with stories and poems. In Moingona, Iowa, the Kate Shelley Railroad Museum now stands at the previous site of the Moingona station.

See also: FOLK HEROES/LEGENDARY FIGURES; MIDWESTERN REGIONAL FOLKLORE; MUSEUMS, FOLK; OCCUPATIONAL FOLKLORE; REGION, FOLK.

For Further Reading:
Cooper-Mullin, Alison. *Once upon a Heroine.* New York: McGraw-Hill, 1998.

Porter, Wesley. *Kate Shelley and the Midnight Express.* New York: F. Watts, 1979.

San Souci, Robert. *Kate Shelley: Bound for Legend.* New York: Dial, 1995.

Wetterer, Margaret. *Kate Shelley and the Midnight Express.* New York: Carolrhoda Books, 1991.

Silko, Leslie Marmon (1948–)   Leslie Marmon Silko stands among the most celebrated Native American writers, and her work reflects a deep resonance with traditional culture and folk beliefs of indigenous peoples.

Silko was born Leslie Marmon on March 5, 1948, in Albuquerque, New Mexico, and grew up on New Mexico's Laguna Pueblo Reservation. She was a member of a storytelling family, and her father collected Laguna folk stories by recording them on tape. Silko's later work would reflect a respect for and understanding of the vitality of oral traditions. As some of her work reveals, the writer has a mixed-blood heritage, including Laguna Pueblo, Ango, and Cherokee ancestry. She attended the University of New Mexico, where she earned a B.A. in 1969. She then began law school but eventually shifted direction to pursue a life as a writer and educator. Toward that end, Silko has enjoyed affiliations with the University of New Mexico, Albuquerque, and the University of Arizona, Tucson. Today, she writes full time. The author became Leslie Marmon Silko with her 1971 marriage to a lawyer, John Silko.

Leslie Marmon Silko is associated with the 1970s Native American literary renaissance. Silko writes across genres, including poetry, fiction, and essays. She is best known, though, for her book-length fiction. Her published works include such fiction as *Ceremony* (1977), *Almanac of the Dead: A Novel* (1991), and *Gardens in the Dunes* (1999). She has also released short fiction and poetry, including *Storyteller* (1981), *Laguna Woman: Poems* (1974), *Sacred Water: Narratives and* Pictures (1993), and *Rain* (1996). Other titles she has issued include *After a Summer Rain in the Upper Sonoran* (1982) and *Yellow Woman and a Beauty of the Spirit: Essays on Native American Life Today* (1996). She has also published critical essays, helped write scripts, and made spoken word recordings. Most recently, she has published nonfiction, such as *Sacred Water* (1993). Her works are profoundly influenced by oral traditions among Native American people. They often have political overtones, especially in terms of racism in America. Silko's writing also demonstrates a keen attention to the social and cultural contexts her characters—and readers—occupy. Themes of fraught identiy, alienation, and estrangement thread through her work. Silko's works are often critical of the misdeeds perpetrated by European Americans on indigenous populations.

Although all of her works pay close attention to cultural considerations, *Ceremony* is among Silko's most mythic works and so is of special interest to the folklorist.

Critics have compared this Silko book to Navarrre Scott Momaday's *House Made of Dawn* (1968). In her writings, Silko incorporates traditional rituals, legends, myths, and tales. In these narratives, she believes, reside the power of a people's cultural and collective history. For instance, she retells Coyote stories, or trickster tales, in several of her texts. She also weaves myths, such as the story of "Yellow Woman" into her collaged volume, *Storyteller*. She also writes about historical personages such as Geronimo. *Ceremony* follows the life's journey of a half-blood Laguna protagonist who fights in World War II, only to reach the conviction that a Japanese soldier whose murder he witnesses is his uncle.

Often compared to her contemporaries among other Native American writers, such as Paula Gunn Allen and Navarre Scott Momaday, Leslie Marmon Silko depicts America's Southwest and the Laguna Pueblo people in a way that evinces a strong sense of the region and its landscapes as shapers of Native American experience.

See also: ALLEN, PAULA GUNN; ANIMALS; COYOTE; CREATION/ORIGIN STORIES; FOLKLORE IN AMERICAN LITERATURE; FOLKTALES; GERONIMO; LEGENDS, FOLK; MOMADAY, NAVARRE SCOTT; NATIVE AMERICAN FOLKLORE; SOUTHWESTERN REGIONAL FOLKLORE; TRICKSTER; WORLD WAR II.

For Further Reading:

Arnold, L., ed. *Conversations with Leslie Marmon Silko.* Jackson: University Press of Mississippi, 2000.

Beardslee, Karen. *Literary Legacies, Folklore Foundations: Selfhood and Cultural Tradition in Nineteenth and Twentieth-Century American Literature.* Knoxville: University of Tennessee Press, 2001.

Jaskowski, Helen. *Leslie Marmon Silko: A Study of the Short Fiction.* New York: Twayne, 1998.

Moore, David L., Louise K. Barnett, and James L. Thorson, eds. *Leslie Marmon Silko: A Collection of Critical Essays.* Albuquerque: University of New Mexico Press, 1999.

Preston, Cathy Lynn, ed. *Folklore, Literature, and Cultural Theory: Collected Essays.* New York: Garland, 1995.

Salyer, Gregory. *Leslie Marmon Silko.* New York: Twayne, 1997.

Seyersttad, Per. *Leslie Marmon Silko.* Boise, Idaho: Boise State University, 1980.

slavery   As one of the most tragic episodes in the nation's history, American slavery represented an ordeal for African Americans, and one that they sought to survive in part through the support of folk traditions.

Slaves lived under adverse circumstances that made it difficult, if not impossible, to pursue their folkways and customs. Crushing labor, inhumane hours, and deprivation made it hard for slaves even to endure their treatment. In addition, slave holders frequently prohibited teaching literacy, meeting for worship, and moving freely to visit family members at other plantations. These measures further threatened the educational, spiritual, and familial prospects for slaves.

Despite these challenges, some slaves managed to work around these restrictions. Some even managed to escape their plight. As the principal route by which American slaves sought to secure their freedom in the years leading up to the Civil War, the Underground Railroad is the network of connections, techniques, and locations that figure within this historical exodus. The Underground Railroad consisted of not one path but many, each leading from slave-holding states north to free states and/or to Canada. Slaves traveling the Underground Railroad relied upon specific cues placed on the ground. These signals could tip off a traveler whether or not there were safe

conditions in which to proceed. Such clues might take the form of a lantern or a hung quilt bearing the Jacob's Ladder design (later renamed the Underground Railroad design). The presence of such a sign could welcome fugitives, while its absence could alert them to danger or impediment.

A number of folk heroes emerged through the Underground Railroad, including Harriet Tubman, who helped lead many slaves to freedom in the North. Once they emerged from slavery, some former slaves also became orators and authors, taking their stories of emancipation to a national audience. Examples include Frederick Douglass and Sojourner Truth.

Meanwhile, some slaves led rebellions against the atrocities of American slavery. Indeed, the history of U.S. slavery suggests that there were many contemplated and attempted insurrections, and several of these were implemented. The 1831 rebellion in Southampton County, Virginia, led by Nat Turner was one such instance. Not all planned actions by slaves were so successful; some, such as the conspiracy led by Denmark Vesey in the Charleston, South Carolina, area some nine years before Turner's, were foiled before action could be taken. Tales of such rebellions, contemplated or realized, are a staple of African-American folk history, from music to oral culture.

Those who remained in slavery found ways to express both the folk traditions of their homelands and the customs their new situation inspired. For example, since slaves were often denied the right to marry, they devised a folk custom known as "jumping the broom" that recognized the unions slave masters forbade.

Folk and sacred music also provided a way for slaves to communicate with one another and, through song choice, sequencing, and tone, encode and transmit private information from slave to slave. For instance, lyrics could carry a double meaning. Therefore, whereas an outsider might hear merely a slave song, an insider might recognize a reminder about tools for celestial navigation.

Other practices, such as voodoo and conjuring, had their origins in West Indian and African folklore. These beliefs were adapted to the harsh environment created by American slavery. They helped to inspire, protect, and connect the lives of slaves whose circumstances might otherwise have isolated them even from one another.

Many of the customs and folkways of American slaves derived from their homelands throughout the African diaspora. Others of the traditions originated in the United States, with the slaves in captivity. Taken together, these elements of folklore form the cultural legacy of African Americans.

See also: AFRICAN-AMERICAN FOLKLORE; CIVIL WAR; DOUGLASS, FREDERICK; HARRIS, JOEL CHANDLER; LINCOLN, ABRAHAM; SOUTHERN REGIONAL FOLKLORE; TURNER, NAT; VESEY, DENMARK; WASHINGTON, BOOKER TALIAFERRO.

For Further Reading:

Botkin, B. A., and Jerrold Hirsch. *Lay My Burden Down: A Folk History of Slavery*. Athens: University of Georgia Press, 1945.

Burrison, John A., ed. *Storytellers: Folktales and Legends from the South*. Athens: University of Georgia Press, 1989.

Flusche, Michael. "Joel Chandler Harris and the Folklore of Slavery." *Journal of American Studies* 9 (1975): 347–363.

Govenar, Alan. *African American Frontiers: Slave Narratives and Oral Histories*. Santa Barbara, Calif.: ABC-CLIO, 2000.

Harris, James Henry. "Preaching Liberation: The Afro-American Sermon and the Quest for Social Change," *Journal of Religious Thought* 46, no. 2 (1989–90): 72–89.

Holloway, Joseph, ed. *Africanisms in American Culture*. Bloomington: Indiana University Press, 1990.

Siporin, Steve. *American Folk Masters*. New York: Harry N. Abrams, 1992.

Vlach, John Michael. *By the Work of Their Hands*. Ann Arbor, Mich.: UMI Press, 1991.

"Sleeping Beauty" "Sleeping Beauty" is a variation on an ancient folktale and cautionary story.

As the tale begins, a royal couple share a longing for a child. They love each other and eagerly envision parenthood. Then, one day, a frog appears, speaks to the queen, and tells her that her wish will be fulfilled within a year: The king and the queen will soon have a daughter.

With time, the frog's prediction is demonstrated to be true. The king and queen have a daughter so strikingly beautiful that the king plans a feast of celebration. To honor the birth of their first child, the mother and father host a party. They invite relatives, friends, and, because the king has only 12 gold plates with which to serve the kingdom's most venerable guests, 12 of the 13 wisewomen. The party is grand, and guests bestow many presents on the newly arrived princess. The wisewomen make such gifts as virtue, wealth, and beauty, ensuring that the child will have sound character and pleasing aspect.

The overlooked wisewoman, however, angered that she has not been included in the festivities, enters without invitation. She has arrived to exact revenge for this royal slight. The bitter wisewoman foretells that the child will die at age 15 of a spindle prick to her finger. With that said, she leaves. Another wisewoman modifies the spell, though she cannot lift it, to make the consequence of the finger prick a sleep of 100 years.

Needless to say, the king and the queen are deeply distressed by this turn of events. The party to celebrate their daughter's arrival in the world instead becomes a forecast of her departure from it. They resolve to do everything in their power to avert such a disaster.

In their attempt to protect their daughter, they issue a ban on spindles in the kingdom. All are to be destroyed by fire lest they harm the young princess.

The princess grows up with many blessings, including all the attributes bestowed upon her at the party that greeted her birth. She is beloved in the kingdom, and for good reason: She is kind, charming, and truthful. When her 15th birthday arrives, the princess is alone in the castle and cannot resist exploring its many chambers. In so doing, she comes upon an old woman spinning flax. The princess, who has never seen this technique before, draws near to inquire. In the process, she pricks her finger on the device and the evil spell is realized. Despite efforts made by the king and queen to prevent such a fate, the princess soon enters a deep sleep. When her parents return, they and everyone in the vicinity, including the animals, also fall asleep.

The castle falls still and silent. It becomes overgrown with briars, and around the kingdom word spreads of the lovely girl slumbering there. In such stories, the princess is referred to as Briar Rose. Several princes seek to enter the castle to gain access to her, but the briar hedge always stops them. They die gruesome deaths in the attempt.

Many years later, when nearly 100 years of court slumber had elapsed, a determined prince manages to gain entry to the castle.

The prince walks through the property, finding all asleep precisely where they must have been and doing what they must have been doing when the spell commenced. The prince finds Briar Rose in a tower, and she is so beautiful that he kneels to kiss her. When his lips touch the princess, she stirs and awakens. She and all the others are awakened. The prince and Briar Rose are then married, and they have a happy life together.

As do other traditional tales of sleepers, from "Rip Van Winkle" to "Snow White," "Sleeping Beauty" taps into related fears of sleep and death. Each tale plays out a scenario of what might happen if one were to fail to awaken, or to awaken only after such a duration as to be left in a world of strangers. In this sense, "Sleeping Beauty" is related to modern time travel narratives, from Edward Bellamy's *Looking Backward* to Woody Allen's *Sleeper*. The moral messages include the importance of extending uniform courtesy and the dangers of indulging curiosity.

"Sleeping Beauty" or "Briar Rose" is a tale frequently retold and recently challenged for its double conduct of standard. For example, the princess becomes inquisitive and is punished with 100 years of sleep. The prince explores in the same way and is immediately rewarded with a love match.

While in some sense the tale may not have aged perfectly, the story has lost none of its grip on youth culture. Most American children know the tale and have encountered some popularized version of it, such as Disneyland's signature theme park attraction Sleeping Beauty's Castle.

See also: CHILDREN'S FOLKLORE; FABLES; FAIRY TALES; MYTHS, FOLK; "SNOW WHITE"; VAN WINKLE, RIP.

For Further Reading:

Bernheimer, Kate, ed. *Mirror, Mirror, on the Wall: Women Writers Explore Their Favorite Fairy Tales.* New York: Anchor Books, 1998.

Cashdan, Sheldon. *The Witch Must Die: The Hidden Meaning of Fairy Tales.* New York: Basic Books, 1999.

Tatar, Maria, ed. *The Annotated Classic Fairy Tales.* New York: W. W. Norton, 2002.

Zipes, Jack. *The Brothers Grimm: From Enchanted Forests to the Modern World.* New York: Palgrave Macmillan, 2002.

Slick, Jonathan or Sam   See STEPHENS, ANN SOPHIA.

Smithsonian Institution   With its span of American arts, humanities, technology, and sciences, the Smithsonian Institution is a premier site for the study of the nation's culture.

This vast network of museums and research facilities, hubbed in the District of Columbia but supplemented with locations including New York City and Cambridge, Massachusetts, is considered one of the most prestigious cultural agencies in the country. In keeping with the organization's 1846 charter from the Congress, it is also an active collector, exhibitor, and publisher of materials related to American folklore.

The Smithsonian's cultural resources comprise quite a few facilities. These locations include the Anacostia Museum, the Arts and Industries Building, "The Castle" or Smithsonian Institution Building, the Center for African American History and Culture, the Cooper Hewitt National Design Museum, the Freer Gallery of Art, the Hirschorn Museum and Sculpture Garden, the National Air and Space Museum, the National Museum of African Art, the National Museum of American History, the National Museum of Natural History, the National Museum of the American Indian, the National Portrait Gallery, the National Postal Museum, the National Zoological Park, the Renwick Gallery, the Arthur M. Sacklet Gallery, and the Smithsonian American Art Museum. The Smithsonian also sponsors such ventures as the Center for Folklife and Cultural Heritage, of special interest to American folklorists.

Playfully referring to itself as the "nation's attic," in terms of the size and scope of its many and valuable collections, the Smithsonian is best known for its exhibitions, whether permanent, temporary, or traveling shows. Among its most beloved artifacts are some of the items associated with American icons. These holdings include the nation's first flag; Charles Lindburgh's plane, the *Spirit of St. Louis;* and Benjamin Franklin's printing press. While these objects may be centerpieces of the Smithsonian collections, there is much more to the place than these marquee items. In fact, although many objects are displayed, a considerable number of important pieces owned by the Smithsonian reside in its study collections or are retained in storage areas.

In addition to its holdings, the Smithsonian is active in educational events, cultural programs, and publication projects, intended to fulfill the larger purpose of the organization. These ventures include *Smithsonian* magazine, a popular title in circulation since 1970.

See also: ART, FOLK; FAMILY FOLKLORE; FESTIVALS, FOLKLORE; FLIGHT; FOLKLIFE; FOLKLIFE MOVEMENT; FRANKLIN, BENJAMIN; HISTORIC PRESERVATION; HISTORY, FOLK; LINDBERGH, CHARLES; LIVING HISTORY MUSEUMS; MATERIAL CULTURE; MUSEUMS, FOLK; PARKS, ROSA; POPLORE; PUBLIC FOLKLORE; ROSS, BETSY.

For Further Reading:

Bello, Mark. *The Smithsonian Institution, a World of Discovery: An Exploration of behind-the-Scenes Research in the Arts, Sciences, and Humanities.* Washington, D.C.: Smithsonian Institution Press, 1993.

Blatti, Jo, ed. *Past Meets Present: Essays about Historic Interpretation and Public Audiences.* Washington, D.C.: Smithsonian Institution Press, 1987.

Goode, G. Brown, ed., *The Smithsonian Institution, 1846–1896: The History of the First Half Century.* New York: Arno Press, 1980.

Henderson, Amy, and Adrienne Kaeppler, eds. *Exhibiting Dilemmas: Issues of Representation at the Smithsonian.* Washington, D.C.: Smithsonian Institution, 1997.

Lubar, Steven, and Kathleen Kendrick. *Legacies: Collecting America's History at the Smithsonian.* Washington, D.C.: Smithsonian Institution Press, 2001.

Oehser, Paul Henry. *The Smithsonian Institution.* Boulder, Colo.: Westview Press, 1963.

———. *Sons of Science: The Story of the Smithsonian Institution and Its Leaders.* New York: Schuman, 1949.

Smithsonian Institution. Center for Folklife and Cultural Heritage. Available online. URL: http://www.folklife.si.edu. Accessed March 10, 2006.

Smith, Windwagon (legendary) Windwagon Smith appears to be one of the unlikely characters contrived for use in America's tradition of tall tales.

Stories of Windwagon Smith appear in numerous collections of occupational lore and tall talls. The tale was featured in an animated short released by Disney in 1961 and entitled *The Saga of Windwagon Smith.* Smith was supposedly a 19th-century sea captain who found himself on the prairies of Kansas. While there, he constructed a covered wagon designed to operate on wind power. His Conestoga wagon was outfitted with a mast and sail, just as a seagoing vessel might be.

This improbable vehicle drew the attention of townspeople. Smith's innovation and economical design for transportation appealed to them, and the town's leaders decided to build a larger version of this windwagon for use to bear freight to Santa Fe, New Mexico. Unfortunately, while the hybrid vehicle combined elements associated with both land and water travel, it did not sufficiently reckon the wind's force across the prairie. In much the same way that *The Wizard of Oz*'s Dorothy, another Kansas-based protagonist, is carried away in a tornado, Smith's enhanced windwagon is destroyed by a twister.

Some accounts of the American gold rush allude to a historical figure known aqs "Wind-Wagon Thomas." With his aspiration to ferry prospectors in the 1849 California gold rush westward on a curious covered wagon powered by wind power, Thomas may have provided the basis for the figure now known as Windwagon Smith. On the other hand, Windwagon Smith, along with the better-known manufactured characters Febold Feboldson and Pecos Bill, may be a figure of American fakelore rather than folklore,

Whether historical, contrived, or some combination of the two, stories of Windwagon Smith's exploits nonetheless continue to entertain.

See also: FAKELORE; FEBOLDSON, FEBOLD; FOLK HEROES/LEGENDAY FIGURES; FOLKTALES; FRONTIER; GOLD RUSH, THE; MARITIME FOLKLORE; OCCUPATIONAL FOLKLORE; PECOS BILL; REGION, FOLK; SOUTHWESTERN REGIONAL FOLKLORE; WEATHER FOLKLORE; WESTERN REGIONAL FOLKLORE.

For Further Reading:
Calhoun, Mary. *High Wind for Kansas.* New York: Morow, 1965.

Maher, Ramona. *When Windwagon Smith Came to Westport.* New York: Coward, McCann, and Geoghegan, 1977.

Rees, Ennis. *Windwagon Smith.* New York: Prentice-Hall, 1966.

Schramm, Wilbur Lang. *Windwagon Smith and Other Yarns.* New York: Harcourt, Brace, 1947.

Shapiro, Edna. *Windwagon Smith.* Champaign, Ill.: Garrand, 1969.

sneezing   See SUPERSTITIONS.

snipe hunt   See HUMOR, FOLK.

"Snow White"   "Snow White" tells the tale of a young girl left to fend for herself in a harsh world of sordid human motives.

Across story variants, some plot elements remain fairly constant. A king's wife who is eager to have a child stands at a window, visualizing its preferred appearance. Looking out at the snow, she ventures several wishes in this regard, including her notion that a child as fair as the snow would be ideal.

When the child is born, she possesses all the attributes her mother envisioned. For obvious reasons, the woman names her newborn Snow White. Not long after childbirth, however, the mother dies.

In time, the king remarries and Snow White now has a stepmother. By the time Snow White reaches the age of seven, however, the new queen begins to envy Snow White's appearance and perceive the child as a beauty rival. So begins the familiar mirror ritual, in which the queen gazes into the looking glass and asks it who is "the fairest one of all?"

As tensions between the queen and Snow White escalate, the child is cast out of the household. Indeed, the queen orders a woodsman to do away with Snow White. When the hired man fails in that command, Snow White finds a home in a forest cottage occupied by seven dwarfs. In exchange for shelter, she takes care of them.

An angered queen, still resolute about removing her rival, assumes a disguise and tries to kill Snow White herself. After several attempts, a poisoned apple from the queen kills Snow White. The dwarfs, bereaved and unwilling to relinquish her, place Snow White in a crystal coffin where they may still cast fond eyes on her.

When a prince catches sight of Snow White, he kisses her lips, stirring the coffin in the process, and she awakens from what turns out to be a very deep sleep. They fall in love and marry.

For her evil deeds, the queen receives a deadly punishment. She is made to dance in extremely hot shoes until she perishes. While contemporary retellings of Snow White tend to stop at the happy ending for Snow White, omitting the details of the evil queen's demise, the morals of this tale remain. The story cautions readers against the dangers associated with envy, vanity, and violence against others.

See also: CHANGELINGS; CHILDREN'S FOLK-LORE; FABLES; FAIRY TALES; GRIMM BROTHERS; MYTHS, FOLK.

For Further Reading:

Bettelheim, Bruno. *The Uses of Enchantment: The Meaning and Importance of Fairy Tales.* New York: Vintage Books, 1989.

Cashdan, Sheldon. *The Witch Must Die: The Hidden Meaning of Fairy Tales.* New York: Basic Books, 1999.

Hallett, Martin, and Barbara Karasek. *Folk and Fairy Tales.* 3d ed. New York: Broadview Press, 2002.

Tatar, Maria, ed. *The Annotated Classic Fairy Tales.* New York: W. W. Norton, 2002.

solstice Both summer solstice and winter solstice are times of note, marking the times during the year at which the Sun is farthest north and south of the equator.

The summer solstice occurs on the first day of summer and provides the United States with the longest day of the year. As such, it is taken as a joyous time marking the season change and with it, June, the customary month for weddings.

This point of the year, falling as it does between planting and harvests, was thought to be the most opportune and fortunate time to marry.

The winter solstice provides the United States with the shortest day of the year. It falls in December, and festivities associated with this day often have the theme of rebirth, as celebrants anticipate the darkness of winter's giving way to the bright light of spring.

Many cultures mark summer solstice and winter solstice with rituals, celebrations, and ceremonies. Native Americans, for example, have traditionally constructed markers in the landscape where they could track the arrival of each solstice.

Although most residents of the United States do not approach solstice as a major holiday or observance, all are mindful of the change of seasons and all are affected to some degree by the cycle of the Sun's position relative to Earth.

See also: CHRISTMAS; GROUNDHOG DAY; HOL-IDAYS/OBSERVANCES; NATIVE AMERICAN FOLK-LORE; WEATHER FOLKLORE; WEDDING/MARRIAGE FOLKLORE.

For Further Reading:

Aveni, Anthony F. *The Book of the Year: A Brief History of Our Seasonal Holidays.* New York: Oxford University Press, 2004.

Clark, Toby. "Midwinter among the Penguins," *Talking Folklore* 10 (December 1990): 28–32.

Franco, L. N. "Newgrange and the Winter Solstice," *Parabola: Myth, Tradition, and the Search for Meaning* 21, no. 2 (summer 1996): 82–86.

Krupp, E. C. *Beyond the Blue Horizon: Myths and Legends of the Sun, Moon, Stars, and Planets.* New York: Oxford University Press, 1992.

Mayer, Bernadette. *Midwinter Day.* New York: New Directions, 1999.

Panati, Charles. *The Browser's Book of Beginnings: Origins of Everything under (and including) the Sun.* Boston: Houghton Mifflin, 1984.

"Winter Solstice and Christmas," *Seanchas* 2, no. 2 (1989–1990): 12–18.

South Carolina folklore See APPALACHIAN FOLKLORE; BABE THE BLUE OX; BUNYAN, PAUL;

IBO LANDING; SOUTHERN REGIONAL FOLKLORE; VESEY, DENMARK.

South Dakota folklore

See BABE THE BLUE OX; BUNYAN, PAUL; CRAZY HORSE; LEWIS, MERIWETHER, AND WILLIAM CLARK; NORTHWESTERN REGIONAL FOLKLORE; REGION, FOLK.

Southern regional folklore

The Southern states, known for distinctive speech patterns and other cultural practices, represent an important region for American folklore study.

Since its inception, the study of American folklore has emphasized the concept of folk regions in the United States. Despite the claim that we now have an entirely global culture, local and regional variations continue to exist, and these are important objects of study for folklorists. In the United States, these regions are typically conceived of as clusters of nearby states with commonalities, such as populations, practices, or other attributes.

Although the American South can be described and delimited in various ways, the South as a folk region can generally be defined as including folklore of or relating to the states of Alabama, Arkansas, Florida, Georgia, Kentucky, Louisiana, Mississippi, North Carolina, South Carolina, Tennessee, Virginia, and West Virginia.

See also: BOONE, DANIEL; BRER RABBIT; BROWN, JOHN; CABLE, GEORGE WASHINGTON; CHESNUTT, CHARLES WADDELL; CIVIL WAR; CLEMENS, SAMUEL LANGHORNE; CONJURE/CONJURING; CROCKETT, DAVY; FAULKNER, WILLIAM; HARRIS, JOEL CHANDLER; HENRY, JOHN; HURSTON, ZORA NEALE; IBO LANDING; JONES, JOHN LUTHER (CASEY); REMUS, UNCLE; SLAVERY; TRICKSTER; TURNER, NAT; VESEY, DENMARK; WASHINGTON, BOOKER TALIAFERRO.

For Further Reading:

Allen, Barbara, and Thomas J. Schlereth, eds. *Sense of Place: American Regional Cultures*. Lexington: University Press of Kentucky, 1990.

Botkin, B. A. *A Treasury of Southern Folklore: Stories, Ballads, Traditions, and Folkways of the People of the South*. New York: Crown, 1949.

Burrison, John, ed. *Storytellers: Folktales and Legends from the South*. Athens: University of Georgia Press, 1989.

Combs, Josiah Henry. *Folk-Songs of the Southern United States*. Austin: University of Texas Press, 1967.

Dorson, Richard M., ed. *Buying the Wind: Regional Folklore in the United States*. Chicago: University of Chicago Press, 1964.

Garrison, Webb. *Southern Tales: A Treasury of Stories from Virginia, North Carolina, South Carolina, Georgia, Florida, Alabama, Kentucky, Tennessee, and Mississippi*. New York: Galahad Books, 1997.

McNeil, W. K., ed. *Ghost Stories from the American South*. Little Rock, Ark.: August House, 1985.

Reed, John Shelton. *1001 Things Everyone Should Know about the South*. New York: Doubleday, 1996.

Southwestern regional folklore

As a distinctive landscape and culture, the American Southwest is an important region for folklore study.

Since its inception, the study of American folklore has emphasized the concept of folk regions in the United States. Despite the claim that we now have an entirely global culture, local and regional variations continue to exist, and these are important objects of study for folklorists. In the United States, these regions are typically conceived of as clusters of nearby states with commonalities, such as populations, practices, or other attributes.

Although the American Southwest can be described and delimited in various ways, the Southwest as a folk region can generally be defined as including folklore of or relating to the states of Arizona, New Mexico, Oklahoma, and Texas. Folk heroes and legendary figures associated with the Southwest include the Weeping Woman, Pecos Bill, Billy the Kid, Jesse James, and Belle Starr. Writers connected to the region include Navarre Scott Momaday, Paula Gunn Allen, and Leslie Marmon Silko.

See also: ALLEN, PAULA GUNN; JAMES, JESSE; JUNETEENTH; McCARTY, WILLIAM HENRY (BILLY THE KID); MOMADAY, NAVARRE SCOTT; OUTLAWS; PECOS BILL; SILKO, LESLIE MARMON; STARR, BELLE; WEEPING WOMAN.

For Further Reading:

Allen, Barbara and, Thomas J. Schlereth, eds. *Sense of Place: American Regional Cultures.* Lexington: University Press of Kentucky, 1990.

Boatright, Mody. *Folk Laughter on the American Frontier.* Gloucester, Mass.: Peter Smith, 1971.

Bordelon, Pamela, ed. *Go Gator and Muddy the Water: Writings by Zora Neale Hurston from the Federal Writers' Project.* New York: W. W. Norton, 1999.

Dorson, Richard M., ed. *Buying the Wind: Regional Folklore in the United States.* Chicago: University of Chicago Press, 1964.

Heisley, Michael. *An Annotated Bibliography of Chicano Folklore from the Southwestern United States.* Los Angeles: Regents of the University of California, 1977.

Lomax, John A., and Alan Lomax. *Cowboy Songs and Other Frontier Ballads.* New York: Macmillan, 1938.

Moore, Ethel, and Chauncey O. Moore. *Ballads and Folksongs of the Southwest.* Norman: University of Oklahoma Press, 1964.

space age folklore   See ATOMIC/NUCLEAR ERA FOLKLORE.

Spanish-American folklore   Spanish-American folklore pertains to immigrants to the United States from Spain, along with American-born persons of Spanish ancestry.

Immigration to the United States from Spain has occurred since colonial times, if not earlier. Early settlements were created in such locations as Florida, New Mexico, California, Arizona, and Texas. Later on, additional favorite destinations included New York City, the American West, and the industrial Midwest.

Although in the popular imagination Spanish-American customs are often conflated with regional folkways, such as the Andalusian practice of flamenco dancing, Spanish Americans do have a rich tradition of folk dance. In the American Southwest, for example, social and ceremonial dances of Spanish America can still be witnessed.

Several Spanish-American foodways are familiar to many Americans and are enjoyed across the nation. For example, gazpacho, a chilled vegetable soup, is a favorite among America's vegetarians. Paella, a stew made with rice, fish, and vegetables, is another popular meal at American restaurants.

In addition to celebrating many of the same holidays other Americans do, Spanish Americans have some holiday traditions of their own. For example, on January 6 each year, it is customary to exchange gifts in celebration of Dia de los Reyes Magos (the Day of the Three Wise Men), also known as Epiphany.

Organizations dedicated to the preservation and study of Spanish-American culture include New York's Hispanic Institute and Música Hispana. Major collections of Spanish-American cultural material include Los Angeles's Southwest Museum and New York's Hispanic Society of America.

The folk traditions of Spain, as transplanted and transformed in the United States, raise the cultural consciousness and cohesion of Spanish Americans as a group.

See also: CHICANO FOLKLORE; CULTURAL GROUPS; FOOD/FOODWAYS; HOLIDAYS/OBSERVANCES; IMMIGRATION AND FOLKLORE; MIDWESTERN REGIONAL FOLKLORE; SOUTHWESTERN REGIONAL FOLKLORE.

For Further Reading:

Espinosa, Aurelio Macedonio. *The Folklore of Spain in the American Southwest.* Norman: University of Oklahoma Press, 1985.

Fernández-Shaw, Carlos. *The Hispanic Presence in North America from 1492 to Today.* Translated by Alfonso Bertodano Stourton and others. New York: Facts On File, 1991.

Gómez, R. A. "Spanish Immigration to the United States," *The Americas* 19 (1962): 59–77.

McCall, Grant. *Basque Americans.* Saratoga, Calif.: R & R Research Associates, 1973.

Michener, James A. *Iberia: Spanish Travels and Reflections.* Greenwich, Conn.: Fawcett, 1968.

Pereda, Prudencio de. *Windmills in Brooklyn.* New York: Atheneum, 1960.

speech, folk   Folk speech involves patterns of speaking transmitted orally from one generation to the next.

Folk speech is typically fully integrated with other forms of social interaction. It is common, for example, to observe that Americans do not speak the same way they write. Few speakers use "the king's English" in the context of everyday conversation; in fact, few even employ the form of English a schoolteacher would endorse. That set of differences in spoken English versus written English represents folk speech.

Folk speech includes nearly any aspect of human speaking. All of the usual elements of conversation, including greetings, turn-taking behavior, and closing salutations, can reflect folk speech. In addition, folk speech can be present in such verbal practices as pronunciation, grammar, expressions, sayings, spoonerisms, malapropisms, figures of speaking, euphemisms, slang, word play, jokes, riddles, and limericks. The same is true for idiomatic vocabulary, usage, and terms. Even the language of conflict involves folk speech, such as insults, gossip, rumors, epithets, boasts, and cursing. It can even be an informality of speaking that involves knowingly incorrect conjugation, such as explaining that someone who gained access to a movie theater without purchasing a ticket "snuck in."

As with other aspects of folk culture, folk speech varies by region, and even by locality. It includes dialects and regional accents. An example would be the use of *y'all* to mean "all of you" among speakers native to the American South. It can also include variations in reference, such as calling a brown paper package for groceries a bag or a sack, or referring to a carbonated beverage as soda, pop, or soda pop. In fact, the astute listener or linguist can tell a great deal about people by hearing their nuances of spoken language, including area of origin and social class.

Of course, the more elaborate the form of spoken language, the more elements of folk speech it may entail. Storytelling, for instance, may employ anecdotes, poems, proverbs, parables, ballads, and even songs. Other examples of folk speech involve coded language (such as pig latin or other invented tongues), coded terms (as for confidential communication about contraband), graffiti, and folk say.

In a nation where speech is so widely influenced by the arrival of immigrants from a whole spectrum of other countries, American folk speech is in turn shaped by the patterns of speech associated with their homelands. For example, words and phrases from other languages may be featured in English, and there may be other ways in which hybridized language forms emerge as a consequence of either migration or immigration.

American folk speech combines personal expression with social process to produce communication of sufficient complexity to do much more than transmit information.

See also: CLEMENS, SAMUEL LANGHORNE; FOLKLORE IN AMERICAN LITERATURE; FOLKLORE IN EVERYDAY LIFE; GESTURES; GRAFFITI; HUMOR, FOLK; JUMP ROPE RHYMES; ORAL FOLKLORE; ORAL HISTORY; PROVERBS; RHYMES, FOLK; RIDDLES, FOLK; SPEECH, FOLK; TOASTS/DRINKING.

For Further Reading:
Abrahams, Roger. "A Rhetoric of Everyday Life: Traditional Conversation Genres," *Southern Folklore Quarterly* 32 (1968): 44–49.

Bauman, Richard. *Verbal Art as Performance.* Rowley, Mass.: Newbury House, 1977.

McDowell, John H. "The Poetic Rites of Conversation," *Journal of Folklore Research* 22, nos. 2–3 (May–December 1985): 113–132.

Nusbaum, Philip. "Storytelling and Conversation: Structural Relationships," *New York Folklore* 12, nos. 3–4 (summer–fall 1986): 69–86.

Rosnow, Ralph, and Gary Fine. *Rumor and Gossip: The Social Psychology of Hearsay.* New York: Elsevier, 1976.

Spitzer, Nicholas R. "Cultural Conversation: Metaphors and Methods in Public Folklore." In *Public Folklore*, edited by Nicholas R. Spitzer and Robert Baron, 77–103. Washington, D.C.: Smithsonian Institution Press, 1992.

Stahl, Sandra K. "Cursing and Its Euphemisms: Power, Irreverence and the Unpardonable Sin." *Midwestern Journal of Language and Folklore* 3 (1977): 54–68.

Wheeler, Will. "A Puzzling Conversation," *Folklore Forum* 17, no. 2 (fall 1984): 176–185.

spells See WITCHCRAFT, SALEM.

spiders See ANANSI.

spiritualism See SUPERNATURAL.

sports folklore As with most leisure activities popular in the United States, there is a fairly extensive folklore surrounding sports.

Whereas for professional players sports lore is a form of occupational folklore, for the rest of America sports are a recreation. Each sport has some of its own lore, but few if any rival the folklore of baseball, an American original. The sport was created in 1845 and since then has been considered America's national pastime. Complete with its own jokes, anecdotes, heroes, and turns of folk speech, baseball has also been a favorite subject among folklorists.

It was during the year of America's centennial celebrations, 1876, that baseball became a business as a professional sport. Since then, baseball games have figured among the most widely attended sporting events in the United States. Cities from Atlanta to Seattle have their own teams, and fans cheer for their favorites all season. In the World Series, the teams that have the best records for a given season face off in a best-of-seven playoff.

Over the years since baseball was devised as a sport, it has inspired not just spectators, but also writers and artists. Poems such as Ernest Lawrence Thayer's "Casey at the Bat," written in 1888, honor the sport and its heroes. Real-life players such as George Herman "Babe" Ruth, Jim Thorpe, and Jack Roosevelt "Jackie" Robinson have attained the status of cultural heroes for their prowess at the game. To honor the sport and its players' achievements, a Baseball Hall of Fame was erected in Cooperstown, New York. The best representatives of the sport's play may be inducted into a place of tribute in the Hall of Fame.

In the incident many regard as the darkest chapter in baseball's history, gangsters succeeded in persuading the Chicago White Sox to agree to throw the 1919 World Series. Because it besmirched the reputation of both the team and the sport, this event is sometimes referred to as the Black Sox scandal.

On balance, however, baseball has positive associations in America. Begun in an era of rapid urbanization and industrialization, baseball gave spectators the opportunity to go to the ball field or "park" to watch teams play a slow-paced, wholesome game. In this sense, the sport of baseball embodied pastoral ideals of wholesome outdoor family fun.

Of course, as with any competitive activity, baseball has its folk beliefs surrounding good and bad luck, its rituals such as the seventh-inning stretch, and its verbal lore. In fact, many phrases now common in American folk speech were coined in connection with baseball. When someone steps in when needed, that person is said to be "pinch hitting." When a person is inattentive or seems far away, he or she may be described as "out in left field." Many forms of slang associated with unsuccessful courtship also derive from baseball, including "struck out," "couldn't get to first base," and "out of my league." Folk sayings such as "Nice guys finish last" are linked to origins in baseball. In addition, some of the nation's best-known malapropisms are those of the baseball legend Lawrence Peter "Yogi" Berra. With remarks such as "You can observe a lot just by looking," Berra endeared himself not only to Yankee fans, but to a nation of listeners charmed by his way of expressing himself. In fact, the popular cartoon character Yogi Bear was inspired by Berra.

As an example of the richness of American sports folklore, baseball represents many of the values, aspirations, and folk traditions associated with the country where it got its start.

See also: FOLKLORE IN EVERYDAY LIFE; GAMES AND PASTIMES; ROBINSON, JACK ROOSEVELT (JACKIE).

For Further Reading:
Baldassaro, Lawrence, and Richard A. Johnson, eds. *The American Game: Baseball and Ethnicity.* Carbondale: Southern Illinois University Press, 2002.
Coffin, Tristram P. *The Illustrated Book of Baseball Folklore.* New York: Seabury, 1975.
———. *The Old Ball Game: Baseball in Folklore and Fiction.* New York: Herder & Herder, 1971.
Frank, Lawrence. *Playing Hardball: The Dynamics of Baseball Folk Speech.* New York: Peter Lang, 1984.
Rader, Benjamin. *Baseball: A History of America's Game.* Urbana: University of Illinois Press, 1992.
Rielly, Edward J., ed. *Baseball and American Culture: Across the Diamond.* New York: Haworth, 2003.
Simons, William, ed. *The Cooperstown Symposium on Baseball and American Culture, 2001.* Jefferson, N.C.: McFarland, 2002.
Umphlett, Wiley Lee. *American Sport Culture: The Humanistic Dimensions.* Lewisburg, Pa.: Bucknell University Press, 1985.

Stagolee (legendary) Known by several names, including "Stagalee" and "Stackerlee,"

Stagolee refers to a personage in African-American folk tradition.

This character appears in stories, songs, and toasts. According to the tales, as a youth Stagolee possessed supernatural talents. He sought to enhance these abilities and for that purpose sold his soul to the devil. In return, he received a magic hat that enabled him to shape shift.

There are many stories about Stagolee's adventures, but most portray his misuse of magical powers. For example, in some tales he uses these abilities to precipitate natural disasters. Toasts seem to focus instead on his sexual exploits. In the course of his exploits, Stagolee eventually shot a man, Billy Lyon. For that crime, he was tried and sentenced to hang. As the story goes, Stagolee went to hell, where he tried to take over the devil's realm.

Stagolee typifies the icon of the bad man and the trickster, as audiences enjoy the tall tales of his colorful life of crimes and misdeeds.

See also: AFRICAN-AMERICAN FOLKLORE; CHANGELING; DEVIL, THE; FOLK HEROES/LEGENDARY FIGURES; OUTLAWS.

For Further Reading:
Brown, Cecil. *Stagolee Shot Billy.* Cambridge, Mass.: Harvard University Press, 2003.
Bryant, Jerry H. *Born in a Mighty Bad Land: The Violent Man in African American Folklore and Fiction.* Bloomington: Indiana University Press, 2003.
Roberts, John W. *From Trickster to Badman: The Black Folk Hero in Slavery and Freedom.* Philadelphia: University of Pennsylvania Press, 1989.

Stanton, Elizabeth Cady (1815–1902) Elizabeth Cady Stanton is one of the most recognized figures in the launching of the women's movement in America.

Born to privilege in Johnstown, New York, in 1815, Stanton nonetheless concerned herself with inequality. Two areas of special concern for her in this regard were the plight of slaves and the status of women, irrespective of color. Stanton became a voice for change, both as an abolitionist and as an activist for women's rights.

In 1840, Elizabeth Cady Stanton married a fellow abolitionist and honeymooned at the World Anti-Slavery Convention held during that year. Her two causes were in conflict at this event, for while women were sent as delegates to the convention, by virtue of their sex, they were denied participation. Not without irony, women found themselves refused human rights even among those who prided themselves on progressive views on race. Experiences of this kind inspired many of those present, including Stanton, to respond to this predicament.

One such result was the Seneca Falls Convention of 1848, now famous for its pivotal role in the history of women's rights. From this meeting emerged a document, a "Declaration of Sentiments," which recalled the previous century's Declaration of Independence. This time, however, the language would pronounce all men and women created equal. The meeting's participants argued for better legal standing and social opportunity for women, from more equitable divorce laws to more ready access to the professions. A few years later, Stanton would meet someone who would become her lasting partner in this effort, Susan Brownell Anthony.

Stanton's greatest legacy may be her body of writing, which includes a history of women's suffrage, an autobiography, and the *Women's Bible*, modified to reflect a more dignified and inclusive depiction of women. For her accomplishments, Stanton is still honored. Some observe Elizabeth Cady Stanton Day each year on her birthday, November 19. Others visit the Seneca Falls, New York, site where she resided with her husband and children. This house, together with several other structures related to the 1848 meeting, has been designated as the Women's Rights National Historic Park.

As a lecturer, writer, and leader, Elizabeth Cady Stanton promoted the cause of women's equality that would secure the vote for women but not until some 18 years after Stanton's death in 1902.

See also: ANTHONY, SUSAN BROWNELL; CIVIL RIGHTS MOVEMENT; FOLK HEROES/LEGENDARY FIGURES; GENDER AND FOLKLORE; PROTEST IN FOLKLORE; SLAVERY; WOMEN'S SUFFRAGE.

For Further Reading:
Ashby, Ruth, and Deborah Gore Ohrn. *Herstory: Women Who Changed the World*. New York: Viking Press, 1995.

Banner, Lois. *Elizabeth Cady Stanton: A Radical for Women's Rights*. Boston: Little, Brown, 1980.

Miroff, Bruce. *Icons of Democracy: American Leaders as Heroes, Aristocrats, Dissenters, and Democrats*. New York: Basic Books, 1993.

Spruill, Marjorie Julian. *One Woman, One Vote: Rediscovering the Women's Suffrage Movement*. Troutdale, Ore.: New Sage Press, 1995.

Wellman, Judith. *The Road to Seneca Falls: Elizabeth Cady Stanton and the First Woman's Rights Convention*. Urbana: University of Illinois Press, 2004.

Starr, Belle (1848–1889)   Belle Starr was one of the legendary figures associated with the Wild West and was sometimes described as the female Robin Hood.

As did Calamity Jane and other larger-than-life women of the American frontier, Starr had a reputation for unconventional womanhood that was widely known. Nicknamed the "Bandit Queen" and the "Petticoat Terror of the Plains" for her misadventures, Belle Starr was notorious for her criminal exploits.

As the story goes, she was born in a log cabin in Missouri on February 5, 1848, and given the name Myra Belle Shirley. Some say that it was the loss of her brother in the Civil War that made Starr susceptible to a life of crime. Others say she herself was a Confederate spy near the close of the war. In any case, while still a young woman, Starr made the acquaintance of some legendary outlaws, including Jesse James and Thomas "Cole" Younger.

During her lifetime, Belle Starr took many lovers and had two children. The first, Rosie Lee (called "Pearl"), was fathered by Younger.

The second, a son named Edward, was fathered by Jim Reed. Both children spent time with relatives while Starr engaged in the activities for which she would ultimately become known: livestock theft and robbery. The name *Starr* appears to have resulted from her union with Sam Starr, a fellow criminal who died in an 1887 gunfight.

Belle Starr was an active outlaw for the rest of her adult life and had several turns before Judge Isaac C. Parker of Fort Smith, Arkansas (known as the "Hanging Judge"). While she eluded authorities for the most part, Starr completed at least one jail stint for her crimes. Starr's career as a livestock thief and robber concluded abruptly in 1889 when she was shot in the back during an ambush.

Starr has become the subject of many stories, both spoken and in print, and she was later memorialized by the folksinger Woodie Guthrie in a ballad that chronicled her biography as a female desperado.

See also: CANNARY-BURKE, MARTHA (CALAMITY JANE); CIVIL WAR; FRONTIER; JAMES, JESSE; McCARTY, WILLIAM HENRY (BILLY THE KID); MUSIC, FOLK; OUTLAWS; ROBIN HOOD; WESTERN REGIONAL FOLKLORE.

For Further Reading:

Block, Lawrence, ed. *Gangsters, Swindlers, Killers, and Thieves: The Lives and Crimes of Fifty American Villains.* New York: Oxford University Press, 2004.

Breihan, Carl, with Charles A. Rosamond. *The Bandit Belle.* Seattle: Hangman Press, 1970.

Etulain, Richard, and Glenda Riley. *With Badges and Bullets: Layman and Outlaws in the Old West.* Golden, Colo.: Fulcrum, 1999.

Shirley, Glenn. *Belle Starr and Her Times: The Literature, the Facts, and the Legends.* Norman: University of Oklahoma Press, 1982.

"Star-Spangled Banner"   See FLAG DAY.

Steinbeck, John (1902–1968) As one of America's most celebrated novelists, John Stein-beck also contributed to understandings of American folk culture.

Steinbeck was born in 1902, in the very Salinas, California, climate in which he would set some of his most important works of social fiction. Steinbeck would write about his native California in much the same way that the novelist William Faulkner would write about the American South and his fictional Yoknapatawpha County. In this agriculturally rich environment, Stein would find the setting for compelling stories of human striving such as *Of Mice and Men,* *In Dubious Battle,* and *The Grapes of Wrath.*

As a student writer, Steinbeck worked as a laborer in order to finance his coursework at Stanford University. In this process, he would gather labor experiences that would eventually figure in his proletarian novels. Although he did not complete his degree, Steinbeck worked as a freelance writer for a time. During this journalistic foray, Steinbeck learned more about the conditions faced by farmhands and migrant laborers. In fact, on at least one occasion, he is said to have refused payment from *Life* magazine for a piece prepared on this topic, unwilling to profit from accounts of their suffering. During the 1930s, Steinbeck went on to make a study of the situation. In this context, he conducted extended conversations with labor organizers, who helped him refine his understanding of the plight of agricultural workers.

The emergence of agribusiness in California had profoundly changed the nature of farming in the United States. Increasingly, farms were operating as factories and treating their workers about as well as did corporation of that era. At this point in American history, farm workers had few protections, and itinerant laborers enjoyed even fewer assurances of right treatment. When the dust bowl and Depression-era poverty cast out farm families from the Midwest, they, too, joined the forces of casual workers. They traveled the country, following the crops. In this way, they hoped to find work in the harvest season, picking each crop as it reached maturity. This army of unemployed and underemployed workers and their families would populate several of Steinbeck's most notable works of fiction, just as their predicament preoccupied his mind.

In Dubious Battle, based in part on Steinbeck's conversations with labor organizers of the era, told the story of a strike. The author claimed the novel offered a composite version, informed by several locations and the labor unrest associated with them. During the composition of *In Dubious Battle*, Steinbeck would do fieldwork to ensure that his dialogue effectively rendered worker speech mannerisms and accurately represented their habits in conversation. The book's stark images of life among the apple pickers suggested both the possibilities and the perils of collective action to effect social change.

Of Mice and Men went on to furnish a parable about the struggle for autonomy within the hearts of migrant workers, each struggling with both social conditions and his or her own human frailties. As two men attempt to form and maintain an enduring bond of friendship, they discover, with heartbreaking result, how relentless are the forces working against such loyalties.

With *The Grapes of Wrath*, Steinbeck produced his most epic version of the itinerant worker's story, here expressed as a generational saga. The Joads, who represent all the hardworking, hardscrabble families displaced by the dust bowl and by the banks who repossess bankrupt family farms in Oklahoma and Arkansas, venture west to find a new way of life. As emblems of the challenges faced by "Okies," the Joads give a human face to the hardships endured during the Great Depression.

John Steinbeck is remembered best for the political and social power of his literary works, as he, in much the manner as his colleague James Agee, painstakingly sought to document and convey the moving stories of regular Americans confronted by some of the harshest environmental and economic forces the nation's workers have ever faced.

See also: AGEE, JAMES; DEPRESSION, THE GREAT; FOLKLORE IN AMERICAN LITERATURE; JOAD, TOM; OCCUPATIONAL FOLKLORE; PROTEST IN FOLKLORE; ROOSEVELT, FRANKLIN DELANO; WESTERN REGIONAL FOLKLORE.

For Further Reading:

Daugherty, Tracy. *Five Shades of Shadow*. Lincoln: University of Nebraska Press, 2003.

DeMott, Robert, ed. *Working Days: The Journals of* The Grapes of Wrath, *1938–1941*. New York: Viking, 1989.

Fensch, Thomas, ed. *Conversations with John Steinbeck*. Jackson: University Press of Mississippi, 1988.

Hearle, Kevin, ed. *Beyond Boundaries: Rereading John Steinbeck*. Tuscaloosa: University of Alabama Press, 2002.

Johnson, Claudia Durst. *Understanding* The Grapes of Wrath: *A Student Casebook to Issues, Sources, and Historical Documents*. Westport, Conn.: Greenwood Press, 1999.

Owens, Louis. *John Steinbeck's Re-Vision of America*. Athens: University of Georgia Press, 1985.

Shillinglaw, Susan, and Jackson Benson, eds. *America and Americans, and Selected Nonfiction by John Steinbeck*. New York: Viking, 2002.

Stephens, Ann Sophia (1810–1886) Ann Sophia Stephens was a writer and editor by profession, often published under the pseudonym *Jonathan Slick*.

Stevens was born Ann Sophia Winterbotham in Connecticut. Her career as a writer began as a contributor to periodicals. She helped found *Portland Magazine* and edited *Portland Sketch Book*. She also wrote for such publications as *Ladies' Companion Magazine*, *Peterson's Magazine*, and *Graham's Magazine*. Later, in 1856, Stephens established a venue of her own: *Mrs. Stephens' Illustrated New Monthly*.

Stephens was a prolific writer of nonfiction, novels, short stories, and poetry. Her short stories, such as "The Patchwork Quilt" and "A Story of Western Life," reveal the author's enthusiasm for American folk culture. Her pen name was a fictitious identity, borrowed from Northeastern U.S. lore of the Yankee Peddler, also known as "Uncle Jonathan" and "Sam Slick." Stephens invoked this authorial identity chiefly when publishing humorous stories and works of serial fiction that would later be compiled and released as dime novels.

Her book-length works include *Maleska: The Indian Wife of the White Hunter* (1839), *Myra, the Child of Adoption* (1860), *Ahmo's Plot; or The Governor's Indian Child* (1863), *Pictorial History of the War for the Union* (1865), and several volumes about needlework.

See also: CIVIL WAR; FOLK HEROES/LEGENDARY FIGURES; NORTHEASTERN REGIONAL FOLKLORE; REGION, FOLK; WESTERN REGIONAL FOLKLORE; YANKEE PEDDLER.

For Further Reading:

Baym, Nina. "Ann Stephens, Mary Jane Holmes, and Marion Harland." In *Woman's Fiction: A Guide to Novels by and about Women in America, 1820–70,* edited by Nina Baym. 2d ed., 175–207. Urbana and Chicago: University of Illinois Press, 1993.

Gaul, Theresa Strough. "'Equal Communion': Racial Hierarchy and Gender Identity in Ann Stephens's *Malaeska*," *Prospects Annual* 27 (2002): 121–135.

Gemme, Paula. "Rewriting the Indian Tale: Science, Politics, and the Evolution of Ann S. Stephens's Indian Romances," *Prospects: An Annual of American Cultural Studies* 19 (1994): 375–387.

Papashvily, Helen Waite. *All the Happy Endings: A Study of the Domestic Novel in America.* New York: Harper, 1956.

Stern, Madeleine B. "The Author of the First Beadle Dime Novel: Ann S. Stephens, 1860." In *We the Women: Career Firsts of Nineteenth-Century America,* edited by Madeleine B. Stern, 29–54. New York: Schulte, 1962.

stork, the (legendary) The stork is the figure within folklore responsible for the arrival of babies.

A stork figures prominently within an alternative version of the origins of new life, one frequently told to small children deemed not yet ready for a scientific explanation of human reproduction. Within this tale, the stork delivers babies to the homes where they belong. The precious cargo they carry, often described as "bundles of joy," simply appear at a household when the time is right. Therefore, when children ask their parents where the new sibling came from, the adults reply that the stork brought him or her.

The image of the stork as a delivery agent for human infants has been a staple within American baby lore for quite a while. In keeping with this image, countless items designed for use in nurseries, from old-fashioned diaper pins to changing tables, have been decorated with pictures of storks. In addition, the stork sometimes appears at baby showers, parties at which a woman's pregnancy is celebrated by family and friends, especially female ones. Party ware and favors marketed for baby showers frequently incorporate the stork as a motif. Storks appear in the pastel colors favored for both showers and nurseries, particularly pink and blue, the colors associated with girls and boys, respectively.

The stork has come to symbolize a new arrival in the family.

See also: ANIMALS; CHILDBIRTH/PREGNANCY FOLKLORE; CHILDREN'S FOLKLORE; FAMILY FOLKLORE; FOLKLORE IN EVERYDAY LIFE; RITES OF PASSAGE.

For Further Reading:

Campbell, Marie. *Folks Do Get Born.* New York: Rinehart, 1946.

Davis-Floyd, Robbie E. *Birth as an American Rite of Passage.* Berkeley: University of California Press, 1992.

Franklin, Rosalind. *Baby Lore: Superstitions and Old Wives Tales from the World Over Related to Pregnancy, Birth, and Baby Care.* West Sussex, England: Diggory Press, 2005.

Roach, Joyce. "Baby Lore: The Why and Wherefore of It." In *2001: A Texas Folklore Odyssey,* edited by Francis Edward Abernathy and Shannon R. Thompson, 106–121. Denton: University of North Texas Press, 2001.

Stormalong, Old (legendary)

Stormalong, Old (legendary) Also known in folklore as Stormalong, Mister Stormalong, Stormy, or Old Stormy, Old Stormalong is an occupational hero of seafaring.

As is true for many figures featured within tall tales, the circumstances of Stormalong's life are not a matter of entirely clear consensus. Most accounts suggest that he was born in Massachusetts. In any case, the character came of age by the ocean. He was the son of another seafaring man. He was a larger-than-life figure whose size complicated his ambitions as a sailor. He was a hard-working ship hand, but one of uncommon appetite, and so a challenge to the cook. This was not the only challenge posed by Stormalong's dimensions. Although somehow he managed to serve on existing ships, he had to be careful not to capsize them with his body mass and his movements around the ship. Therefore, although he loved the sea, Old Stormalong yearned for a vessel with proportions suited to a sailor of his considerable size.

In time, he captained the *Courser*, a clipper ship made to accommodate his ample frame. Although the ship was initially used to move cargo, it eventually was transformed into a whaling ship. On this ship, Old Stormalong made many heroic journeys.

The character of Old Stormalong is closely associated with the traditions of wooden sailing vessels powered by wind. The advent of steamships seemed to threaten Old Stormalong's way of life. In a face-off that recalls John Henry's contest with new technology, Stormalong challenged a steam-powered ship to a race to see which craft would arrive at its destination, Boston, first. Although Stormalong's clipper ship prevailed, the legendary seaman died in victory.

Both songs and tall tales eulogize this mythical figure of the New England region, born Alfred Bulltop Stormalong. One such tale claims that Old Stormalong's ship went aground and, with its force alone, produced the Panama Canal. Another tale credits him with carving out the White Cliffs of Dover.

Even in the afterlife, Old Stormalong is said to be building ships in the sky, where he carries on his maritime career navigating the heavens rather than the oceans. For this reason, some tales explain that an eclipse is caused by the shadow cast by Old Stormalong's great ship, and shooting stars occur when they are struck by the movement of Stormalong's harpoon.

Old Stormalong stands as a mythic figure of America's Yankee culture and maritime lore.

See also: FOLK HEROES/LEGENDARY FIGURES; FOLKTALES; HENRY, JOHN; MARITIME FOLKLORE; NORTHEASTERN REGIONAL FOLKLORE; OCCUPATIONAL FOLKLORE; REGION, FOLK; YANKEE DOODLE.

For Further Reading:

Brown, Charles. *Old Stormalong Yarns: Small and Tall Tales of Alfred Bulltop Stormalong.* Madison, Wis.: C. E. Brown, 1933.

Carmer, Carl Lamson, and Elizabeth Hack Carmer. *The Hurricane's Children.* New York: McKay, 1937/1967.

Felton, Harold. *True Tall Tales of Stormalong: Sailor of the Seven Seas.* Englewood Cliffs, N.J.: Prentice-Hall, 1968.

Hugill, S. *Shanties from the Seven Seas.* London: Routledge and Kegan Paul, 1979.

Miller, Olive Beaupré. *Heroes, Outlaws and Funny Fellows of American Popular Tales.* New York: Doubleday/Doran, 1939.

Osborne, Mary Pope. *American Tall Tales.* New York: Knopf, 1991.

Walker, Paul Robert, and James Bernardin. *Big Men, Big Country: A Collection of American Tall Tales.* San Diego: Harcourt Brace Jovanovich, 1993.

storytelling See FOLKTALES; NARRATIVE, FOLK.

Stowe, Harriet Beecher

Stowe, Harriet Beecher (1811–1896) Stowe was born into an influential New England

family, the Beechers. Although she was a prolific author of essays, children's literature, and
sentimental fiction, Harriet Beecher Stowe is
probably most widely known for just one of her
novels, *Uncle Tom's Cabin; Or, Life among the
Lowly* (1852).

By her own accounts, Stowe's *Uncle Tom's
Cabin* was inspired by her opposition to the
Fugitive Slave Act of 1850. As the story has it,
Stowe maintained that God, rather than she,
had written *Uncle Tom's Cabin*. The work first
appeared in serial form in *The National Era*,
an abolitionist publication. Shortly thereafter,
it appeared in book form. Securing a book
publisher, however, was not simple; editors at
presses were reluctant to go to print with a novel
that addressed such controversial matters as
race, regional, and slavery.

Part polemic and part melodrama, *Uncle
Tom's Cabin* captivated readers in America and
the world over. Nonetheless, Stowe had detractors. It was largely for this reason that within
two years of the novel's appearance, Stowe went
on to publish *A Key to Uncle Tom's Cabin*, a volume intended to satisfy the need for evidence
of the conditions of slavery depicted in Stowe's
fiction.

The popularity of this antislavery novel with
its enthusiasts was deep and did not confine
itself to book purchases. Merchandise of various
sorts, such as card games, dolls, teaspoons, and
painted porcelain, was produced. Stowe received
no consideration for the adaptation of her work
for the stage, since the law in the United States
would not accord dramatic rights to authors of
fiction until 1856, but *Uncle Tom's Cabin* has
been staged countless times and ways since its
first publication as a novel.

Stowe had a complicated relationship to the
causes about which she cared, from women's
rights to abolition. While Stowe's abolitionist
writing exploded certain regional stereotypes
and complacencies in the American South, others persisted into and beyond the Reconstruction era, as evidenced by the works of such writers as Joel Chandler Harris and Thomas Dixon.

Some of Stowe's critics complained that she had
not done enough to challenge racial stereotypes
in *Uncle Tom's Cabin*.

Stowe died in 1896, but her work has gone
on to shape the feelings and perceptions of new
generations of American readers. By the middle
of the 20th century, Stowe became newly controversial when criticized by Civil Rights movement era figures such as James Baldwin. Her
work was found to contain too many images of
deferential and conciliatory slaves, most notably
the title character of the novel. Indeed, during
the 1960s, the term *Uncle Tom* emerged as an
epithet for any African American thought to
be pandering to white society and its attitudes
about other races.

Still, Harriet Beecher Stowe's works had an
amazing influence on readers and continue to
make a difference in their view of American folk
culture of the 19th century.

See also: Brer Rabbit; Civil Rights movement; Civil War; drama, folk; folklore in
American literature; Lincoln, Abraham;
minstrelsy; Northeastern regional folklore; politics and folklore; protest in
folklore; Remus, Uncle; slavery; Tar Baby;
Turner, Nat; Underground Railroad.

For Further Reading:

Gossett, Thomas. Uncle Tom's Cabin *and Ameri-
can Culture*. Dallas, Tex.: Southern Methodist
University Press, 1985.
Lowance, Mason, Ellen Westbrook, and R. C.
DeProspo, eds. *The Stowe Debate: Rhetorical
Strategies in* Uncle Tom's Cabin. Amherst:
University of Massachusetts Press, 1994.
Tompkins, Jane. *Sensational Designs: The Cultural
Work of American Fiction, 1790–1860*. New
York: Oxford University Press, 1985.
Wilson, Edmund. *Patriotic Gore: Studies in the Lit-
erature of the American Civil War*. New York:
Farrar, Straus & Giroux, 1962.

Sturbridge Village, Old   Sturbridge, Massachusetts, is home to Old Sturbridge Village, a

noteworthy example of America's living history museums.

The project began with a businessman, just as was the case with Henry Ford's Greenfield Village. In this case, it was A. B. Wells, founder of the American Optical Company, who initiated the activity that would eventually result in formation of Old Sturbridge Village. Wells was an American history enthusiast, and his growing collection of "primitives"—by which he meant simple objects from everyday life of the American past—needed a proper home. In 1935, Wells Historical Museum was developed to meet this purpose. Later, however, Wells became interested in displaying his folk artifacts in a different format, more similar to a living history museum than a traditional historical museum. The plan emerged to enlarge the attraction by arranging a suite of buildings around a common green, similar to the configuration and character of a preindustrial New England village.

During the 1830s, historical buildings were rescued by moving them to this location for restoration. Finally, on June 8, 1946, Old Sturbridge Village opened to visitors in the area. The structures include a parsonage, gristmill, store, cider mill, and tavern. In the environment Sturbridge Village recreates, visitors can begin to imagine what life might have been like in a New England country village. As is the case at other living history sites, such as Colonial Williamsburg and Mystic Seaport, staff members function as firsthand interpreters of ordinary life in such a place. Through training in the history and the region, such informants play the parts of community members and interact with visitors as a means to convey what it might mean to step back in time to the society as it then existed.

Old Sturbridge Village, while not a preservation of a single authentic historical village, nonetheless seeks to approximate the effect of one for the education of its visitors.

See also: ARCHITECTURE, FOLK; ART, FOLK; ARTIFACTS, FOLK; COLONIAL WILLIAMSBURG; GREENFIELD VILLAGE, HENRY FORD MUSEUM AND; HISTORIC PRESERVATION; HISTORY, FOLK; LIVING HISTORY MUSEUMS; MATERIAL CULTURE; MUSEUMS, FOLK; MYSTIC SEAPORT AND PRESERVATION SHIPYARD.

For Further Reading:

Fennelly, Catherine. *Life in an Old New England Country Village*. New York: T. Y. Crowell, 1969.

Lincoln, Crawford. *Preserving a Priceless Heritage of Old Sturbridge Village*. New York: Newcomen Society of the United States, 1984.

McCallum, Kent, and Thomas Neill, *Old Sturbridge Village*. New York: Harry N. Abrams, 1996.

Van Ravenswaay, Charles. *The Story of Old Sturbridge Village*. New York: Newcomen Society in North America, 1965.

Styron, William (1925–2006)   William Styron was the prizewinning author of essays, novels, and criticism on a range of subjects; of these topics Styron's depiction of the slave revolt leader Nat Turner has commanded most attention from folklorists.

In a much-debated novel, *The Confessions of Nat Turner* (1967), William Styron combined historical and fictional modes of storytelling to produce a book he described as a "meditation on history." Styron took as his subject for this volume the 1831 slave rebellion led by Nat Turner in Southampton County, Virginia.

Styron titled his work of fiction after the historic document of the same name written in 1931 by the attorney Thomas Gray, a text purportedly rendering the as-told-to memoir of the captured Turner. Gray's *Confessions*, though complicated by the circumstances and language in which they were rendered, were nowhere near as controversial as Styron's *Confessions*, with its psychological characterization of Nat Turner and its attribution of sexual motives to the slave leader, would later become. The debate became fierce: To whom does history—or its telling—belong?

By 1968, outcries against Styron's "meditation on history" were heard widely, and a volume of essays, *William Styron's* Nat Turner: *Ten Black Writers Respond*, appeared in response. According to Albert E. Stone, author of *The Return of Nat Turner: History, Literature, and Cultural Politics in Sixties America* (1992), Sherley Anne Williams was the first woman to engage this Nat Turner controversy in book-length print. In 1980, Williams published a text written during the early 1970s, calling it her own "Meditation on History." It would be in this short story about slavery that the 1986 novel, *Dessa Rose*, would have its beginnings. The short story corresponds in many respects to the portion of *Dessa Rose* entitled "The Darkey"; however, it is set in 1829, some 18 years earlier than the setting of Williams's novel.

In an important sense, Sherley Anne Williams's writing of *Dessa Rose* is her explicit and self-conscious response to the text by the white novelist Styron. In her "Author's Note" to *Dessa Rose*, Williams admits her outrage at Styron's presumptions in writing his novel about Turner. In fashioning her response to Styron, however, Williams did not write fiction directly addressing itself to the life and career of Nat Turner. Instead, Williams revisited slavery, this time viewing it through the perceptions of women—both African American and white. Williams devised a novel in which women's experiences of American slavery are visible, their voices in speaking to the issues of slavery are heard, and their deeds of survival are understood as heroic.

Williams also explains how her own research into African-American history, particularly through the writings of the scholars Herbert Aptheker and Angela Davis, inspired her to create an alternative historical-fictional narrative. She became interested in the historical figures of two women, both discussed by the historian Aptheker in *American Negro Slave Revolts* (1943). One was a female member of an 1829 slave coffle uprising in Kentucky. This pregnant slave was recaptured and sentenced to death by hanging but was kept alive until her baby was born. The other figure who caught Williams's atten-

tion was a white woman in 1830 North Carolina, a farmer who gave shelter and aid to runaway slaves. As Williams discovered these figures, she reflected on their lives, thinking it sad that these two women never met.

Her novel adapts these lives such that the two figures do participate in a symbolic meeting made possible only through the means of fiction. Remaining careful to prevent any misrepresentation of historical information, Williams calls her characters and their stories inventions, yet suggests that all are based on historical evidence concerning the daily lives of slaves. Therefore, although Williams only briefly alludes to Nat Turner's insurrection, through her blending of historical and literary narrative, *Dessa Rose* nonetheless signifies on the "factions" (works combining fact and fiction) of Thomas Gray and William Styron.

Williams's work stands as one of a number of African-American novels written since the publication of both the African-American writer Margaret Walker's novel of slavery, *Jubilee* (1966), and *Confessions of Nat Turner*, in which novelists invite readers to revisit the historical era of American slavery and to reclaim that history's telling on different terms than mainstream historical narratives have suggested. Other such revisionist texts include Octavia Butler's *Kindred* (1979), Barbara Chase-Riboud's *Sally Hemings* (1979), Ernest Gaines's *The Autobiography of Miss Jane Pittman* (1971), Charles Johnson's *The Oxherding Tale* (1982), Toni Morrison's *Beloved* (1987), and Ishmael Reed's *Flight to Canada* (1976).

After weathering the storm of debate that followed his fictional account of Nat Turner, including all the counterfiction written in its wake, William Styron would never underestimate the power of folk heroes to give meaning to people's lives and histories.

See also: CIVIL WAR; DOUGLASS, FREDERICK; FOLKLORE IN AMERICAN LITERATURE; FOLKLORISM; MORRISON, TONI; PROTEST IN FOLKLORE; SLAVERY; TUBMAN, HARRIET; TURNER, NAT; UNDERGROUND RAILROAD; VESEY, DENMARK.

For Further Reading:

Genovese, Eugene D. "William Styron's *The Confessions of Nat Turner:* A Meditation on Evil, Redemption, and History." In *Novel History: Historians and Novelists Confront America's Past (and Each Other)*, edited by Mark C. Carnes, 209–220. New York: Simon & Schuster, 2001.

Gross, Seymour L., and Bender, Eileen. "History, Politics and Literature: The Myth of Nat Turner," *American Quarterly* 23 (1971): 487–518.

Richardson, Thomas J. "Art and the Angry Times: Apocalypse and Redemption in William Styron's *The Confessions of Nat Turner*," *Mississippi Folklore Register* 19, no. 2 (fall 1985): 147–156.

Stone, Albert E. *The Return of Nat Turner: History, Literature, and Cultural Politics in Sixties America*. Athens: University of Georgia Press, 1992.

Williams, John A. "The Manipulation of History and of Fact: An Ex-Southerner's Apologist Tract for Slavery and the Life of Nat Turner; or William Styron's Faked Confessions." In *William Styron's Nat Turner: Ten Black Writers Respond*, edited by John Henrik Clarke, 45–49. Boston: Beacon, 1968.

suffrage, women's   The struggle to win the vote for women in the United States was also known as the battle for women's suffrage.

As recently as the 19th century, women had neither the right to vote nor the legal standing to hold property. In the 20th century, although a few states had extended the franchise to women, the majority of the nation's women were still being denied a vote. It was not until the Nineteenth Amendment to the U.S. Constitution passed in August 1920 that women were conferred voting rights on a federal level.

The movement for women's suffrage gained momentum during the 19th century. Although the Revolutionary War had freed the nation's men from taxation without representation, America's women did not benefit in the same way. By the middle of the 19th century, women

were speaking out about their plight. At the 1848 Seneca Falls Convention, held in Seneca Falls, New York, the suffrage advocate Elizabeth Cady Stanton presented a document entitled the "Declaration of Sentiments." With a title and message reminiscent of the Declaration of Independence, Stanton's text made the case for women's winning the vote.

Activist-minded women of the antebellum period promoted several causes, including temperance, abolition, and women's suffrage. During the Civil War, many such women found themselves torn between causes. Should most of their energies be devoted to supporting the Union forces, or should they concentrate on political and property rights for women? The moment found its crisis when the franchise was extended to African-American men, but still not to women of any race. Although many women activists had sought to end slavery and secure human rights for African Americans, it was difficult to be passed over once again for voting privileges.

In the years following the Civil War, Congress was asked annually to lend their support to the Susan B. Anthony Amendment, which would grant American women the vote. Organizations from the National Women's Party to the National American Woman's Suffrage Association pushed for endorsement of the amendment. The first two decades of the 20th century found women marching on Washington, D.C., and the White House in support of women's suffrage. In the process, their banners, sashes, songs, chants, and leadership all became part of the folklore of American protest. Women picketers were sometimes arrested on charges such as obstructing the sidewalk. Once in jail, some suffrage advocates began a hunger strike, only to be force fed as a result.

Despite efforts to dissuade the activists, women who were sometimes dubbed "suffragettes," their objective would soon be won. After considerable lobbying from suffrage proponents, President Woodrow Wilson, who personally hesitated to do so, nonetheless asked Congress to ratify the amendment.

This phase of American women's history, also known as the first wave of feminism, laid the groundwork for the women's movement of the 1960s and 1970s. The quest for women's suffrage also introduced to American folklore new heroes and images of political efficacy for the nation's women.

See also: ANTHONY, SUSAN BROWNELL; GENDER AND FOLKLORE; HISTORICAL EVENTS; POLITICS AND FOLKLORE; PROTEST IN FOLKLORE; STANTON, ELIZABETH CADY; TRUTH, SOJOURNER; WOMEN'S MOVEMENT.

For Further Reading:

Adams, Colleen. *Women's Suffrage: A Primary Source History of the Women's Rights Movement in America.* New York: Rosen Central Primary Source, 2003.

Baker, Jean H., ed. *Votes for Women: The Struggle for Suffrage Revisited.* New York: Oxford University Press, 2001.

Bausum, Ann. *With Courage and Cloth: Winning the Fight for a Women's Right to Vote.* Washington, D.C.: National Geographic, 2004.

DuBois, Ellen Carol. *Feminism and Suffrage: The Emergence of an Independent Women's Movement in America, 1848–1869.* Ithaca, N.Y.: Cornell University Press, 1978.

Frost-Knappman, Elizabeth, and Kathryn Cullen-DuPont. *Women's Suffrage in America.* New York: Facts On File, 2005.

Hannum, June. *International Encyclopedia of Women's Suffrage.* Santa Barbara, Calif.: ABC-CLIO, 2000.

Holton, Sandra Stanley. *Suffrage Days: Stories from the Women's Suffrage Movement.* New York: Routledge, 1996.

Keyssar, Alexander. *The Right to Vote: The Contested History of Democracy in the United States.* New York: Basic Books, 2000.

Purvis, June, and Sandra Stanley Holton. *Votes for Women.* New York: Routledge, 2000.

Sources for Songs of the Woman's Suffrage Movement with Library of Congress Call Numbers. Washington, D.C.: The Archive, 1969.

Stanton, Elizabeth Cady et al., eds. *History of Woman Suffrage.* 6 vols. Rochester, N.Y.: Source Book Press, 1881–1922.

Terborg-Penn, Rosalyn. *African-American Women in the Struggle for the Vote, 1850–1920.* Bloomington: Indiana University Press, 1998.

Sun   See SOLSTICE.

Sundance Kid   See LONGABAUGH, HARRY.

supernatural, the   As the name suggests, the supernatural involves all those phenomena that are not explained through natural causes or events.

Such phenomena are sometimes referred to as paranormal, because they fall so far beyond anything that could be accounted for under normal circumstances and forces. These otherworldly matters command the attention of folklorists concerned with folk beliefs and customs.

In early America, the supernatural was generally regarded as at least suspect and at most sinful. Since the natural was considered godly, the supernatural was perceived as the work of the devil. Within such a worldview, black magic and witchcraft represented threats to the spiritual order.

Perhaps one of the most notorious episodes in terms of the supernatural in American history would be the Salem witchcraft hysteria. Witch crazes and prosecutions have taken place for centuries and in many countries. The most concentrated activity of this kind, although not the only incidence in the United States, took place in Salem in the Massachusetts Bay Colony in the 17th century. During this era in colonial New England, many believed that witches could live within a society undetected. While doing so, witches could undermine the health of a community and its members. Believers considered witches to be shape shifters, transforming their appearance at will to harm or mislead others. Their chief activities were conducted under cover of night. Salem, Massachusetts's, witch trials of the 17th century demonstrated American folk beliefs about black magic and the supernatural.

American concern with the supernatural did not end with the witch trials in Salem. Especially during the decades following the Civil War, spiritualism emerged as a set of ideas embraced by quite a few Americans. Attempts to contact the deceased focused on spirit rappers, ghosts, séances, spirit paintings, and other practices. Perhaps because many soldiers had met untimely deaths during the war, an unprecedented number of Americans, particularly widowed women, sought to contact the dead. Belief in the supernatural helped such people to imagine that such possibilities as communication between the lived world and the spirit world might be pursued by those grieving.

During the 20th century, some Americans continued to be fascinated by the supernatural. Indeed, an entire genre of popular entertainments feature superstitions and other such phenomena. Horror tales, ghost stories, and movies about the supernatural all rely upon interest in the unearthly among audience members. Just as gothic themes had appealed in the 19th century, the 20th century yielded a new sensibility, sometimes called "goth," in which such dark forces resurfaced.

To a great extent, Americans' interests in the supernatural remain playful and/or seasonal. Each Halloween, for example, Americans attend costume parties and pageants dressed as ghosts, goblins, and witches. In addition, they tell ghost stories and spooky tales around bonfires and visit haunted houses and similar attractions.

Nonetheless, many Americans continue to believe in the dangers posed by supernatural forces, such as Friday the thirteenth and the evil eye.

See also: BELIEFS, FOLK; BIGFOOT/SASQUATCH; CAMP FOLKLORE; CHANGELINGS; CHESNUTT, CHARLES WADDELL; CONJURE/CONJURING; DEVIL, THE; EVIL EYE; FOLKLORE IN EVERYDAY LIFE; FRIDAY THE THIRTEENTH; GHOSTS; GHOST STORIES; GHOST TOWNS; HALLOWEEN/ALL HALLOWS' EVE; HAUNTED HOUSES; HOUDINI, HARRY; JERSEY DEVIL; LOUP-GAROU; LUCK/FORTUNE; MAGIC; MEDICINE, FOLK; MERMAIDS; MORRISON, TONI; PREDICTION; RELIGION, FOLK; STAGOLEE; SUPERSTITION; UFO FOLKLORE; URBAN LEGENDS; VAMPIRE; VOODOO/HOODOO; WEREWOLF; WITCHCRAFT, SALEM.

For Further Reading:

Abrahams, Roger D. et al., eds. *Fields of Folklore: Essays in Honor of Kenneth S. Goldstein.* Bloomington, Ind.: Trickster, 1995.

Edmundson, Mark. *Nightmare on Main Street: Angels, Sadomasochism, and the Culture of the Gothic.* Cambridge, Mass.: Harvard University Press, 1997.

Hufford, David. *The Terror That Comes in the Night: An Experience-Centered Study of Supernatural Assault Traditions.* Philadelphia: University of Pennsylvania Press, 1982.

Jordan, Rosan A. "Ethnic Identity and the Lore of the Supernatural," *Journal of American Folklore* 88, no. 350 (fall 1975): 370–382.

Kerr, Howard, and Charles Crow, eds. *The Occult in America: New Historical Perspectives.* Urbana: University of Illinois Press, 1983.

Walker, Barbara, ed. *Out of the Ordinary: Folklore and the Supernatural.* Logan: Utah State University Press, 1995.

superstitions The word *superstition* is a largely pejorative term to describe folk beliefs and attitudes, especially those related to do with portents, luck, magic, and the supernatural. It implies that superstitions are false beliefs or mistaken impressions. These beliefs need not be mistaken, however, and to judge them so is to dismiss the very folk culture one wishes to study. It may be fairer to say that ideas that are termed superstitions are those that involve matters about which there must remain some measure of doubt. They often result in behavior that is seemingly irrational. Beliefs labeled as superstitions include notions of what practices produce luck, whether good or bad. For example, conventional wisdom suggests that such acts as walking under ladders, breaking mirrors, or permitting a black cat to cross one's path are ways to generate bad luck. Tales, proverbs, and rituals (such as the need to toss a pinch of salt over one's shoulder after an accidental spill of salt) can all reveal folk beliefs about how to live well in the world.

Another category of beliefs frequently deemed superstitions involves the weather. Such notions typically involve ways of either predicting or interpreting meteorological phenomena. Weather lore employed by those in outdoor professions such as sailing and farming has many ways of forecasting based on the appearance of the natural environment or the conduct of creatures. Since weather can endanger the crops of farmers and the lives of mariners, knowing how to anticipate patterns and changes in the weather is important. Weather beliefs also extend to special occasions, such as weddings, and there are many ideas about what the weather on the day of a marriage ceremony portends.

Other so-called superstitions involve plant lore and folk medicine practices. From herbs and charms to incantations and hoodoo hands, flora are widely believed to possess magical properties. Still other superstitions have to do with calendar rituals, such as holidays and observances. At New Year's, for example, some Americans serve black-eyed peas to ensure a prosperous year ahead. Another date that is associated with superstitions is any Friday that falls on the 13th day of a month. Friday the thirteenth is often regarded as an unlucky day for all except those born on that day.

Some practices based on folk belief are more ambiguous, such as the notion of crossing fingers. Many Americans cross their fingers (or refer to doing so) in order to promote luck, avoid a jinx, or even signal a falsehood. Crossing fingers is a practice derived from the effort to "cross out" or neutralize evil or bad fortune. For tellers of white lies, crossed fingers are intended to fend off wickedness and spare the soul of the fibber.

Superstitions, as certain folk beliefs are characterized, represent a way to contend with those issues in life about which there can be no real certainty.

See also: BELIEFS, FOLK; CHESNUTT, CHARLES WADDELL; CHILDBIRTH/PREGNANCY FOLKLORE; CONJURE/CONJURING; DOUGLASS, FREDERICK; EVIL EYE; FOLKLORE; FOLKLORE IN EVERYDAY LIFE; FRIDAY THE THIRTEENTH; GHOSTS; GHOST STORIES; GROUNDHOG DAY; HALLOWEEN/ALL HALLOWS' EVE; HAUNTED HOUSES; LUCK/FORTUNE; MAGIC; MARITIME FOLKLORE; NEW YEAR'S EVE/DAY; PREDICTION; STORK, THE; SUPERNATURAL; UFO FOLKLORE; VAMPIRE; VOODOO/HOODOO; WEATHER FOLKLORE; WEDDING/MARRIAGE FOLKLORE; WEEPING WOMAN.

For Further Reading:
Clifton, Johnson. *What They Say in New England, and Other American Folklore.* New York: Columbia University Press, 1963.
Collis, Harry. *101 American Superstitions: Understanding Language and Culture through Superstitions.* New York: McGraw-Hill, 1998.
Dickson, Paul, and Joseph Goulden. *There Are Alligators in Our Sewers, and Other American Credos.* New York: Delacorte Press, 1983.
Ferm, Vergilius. *Lighting Never Strikes Twice (If You Own a Feather Bed): and 1904 Other American Superstitions from the Ordinary to the Eccentric.* New York: Gramercy, 1989.
Lorie, Peter. *Superstitions.* New York: Simon & Schuster, 1992.
Lys, Claudia de. *A Treasury of Superstitions.* New York: Philosophical Library, 1948.
Opie, Iona, and Moira Tatem, eds. *A Dictionary of Superstitions.* New York: Oxford University Press, 1989.
Rachleff, Owen S. *The Secrets of Superstitions: How They Help, How They Hurt.* Garden City, N.Y.: Doubleday, 1976.

Swedish-American folklore Swedish-American folklore involves immigrants to the

United States from Sweden, along with all those born in America of Swedish ancestry.

Immigration from Sweden to the United States has occurred since the 17th century. At that time, immigrants formed settlements in locations such as Delaware. Major immigration waves began during the latter half of the 19th century. Large populations of Swedish immigrants established residence in cities such as New York, Minneapolis, Chicago, and Seattle. Others entered the largely agricultural economy in the American Midwest.

Swedish Americans observe many of the holidays usual to the United States, often incorporating celebratory customs of their homeland. For example, at Christmas people of Swedish ancestry frequently serve a meal featuring *lutefisk*, baked cod. In addition to these American holidays, Swedish Americans conduct at least two additional celebrations of their own. In one of these celebrations, Midsummer's Day or Swedes' Day, members of this folk group observe the summer solstice on June 21 each year. Feasts, parades, picnics, and outdoor festivities are common on this occasion. Saint Lucia's Day or Luciafest, celebrated on December 13 each year, is another Swedish American holiday. On this day, Swedish Americans pay tribute to the saint credited with illuminating the world. At this time, it is typical for a female community member to honor Lucia by dressing in white garments, wearing a head wreath of candles, and leading people through town.

Organizations dedicated to the preservation and study of Swedish-American culture include the American Swedish Institute and the Swedish Council of America in Minneapolis, the Swedish-American Historical Society in Chicago, and the American Swedish Historical Foundation in Philadelphia. Major collections of Swedish-American cultural material include Chicago's Swedish American Museum Center, Philadelphia's American Swedish Historical Museum, and Minneapolis's American Swedish Institute Museum.

As one of the Nordic countries, Sweden and Swedish America have folk traditions that are closely related to Danish, Finnish, and Norwegian cultures. Swedish-American folklore represents a mixture of traditions from the old country and new customs established in the United States.

See also: CULTURAL GROUPS; DANISH-AMERICAN FOLKLORE; FEBOLDSON, FEBOLD; FINNISH-AMERICAN FOLKLORE; HILL, JOE; IMMIGRATION AND FOLKLORE; LINDBERGH, CHARLES; MIDWESTERN REGIONAL FOLKLORE; NORWEGIAN-AMERICAN FOLKLORE; SANDBURG, CARL; SOLSTICE.

For Further Reading:
Ander, O. Fritiof. *The Cultural Heritage of the Swedish Immigrant: Selected References.* New York: Arno Press, 1979.

Barton, H. Arnold. *The Search for Ancestors: A Swedish-American Family Saga.* Carbondale: Southern Illinois University Press, 1979.

Carlsson, Sten. *Swedes in North America 1638–1988: Technical, Cultural, and Political Achievements.* Stockholm: Streiffert, 1988.

Kastrup, Allan. *The Swedish Heritage in America.* St. Paul, Minn.: Swedish Council of America, 1975.

Klein, Barbro Sklute. *Legends and Folk Beliefs in a Swedish American Community.* New York: Arno Press, 1980.

Lovoll, Odd. *The Nordics in America: The Future of Their Past.* Northfield, Minn.: Norwegian American Historical Association, 1993.

Olsson, Christopher, and Ruth McLaughlin, eds. *American-Swedish Handbook.* Minneapolis: Swedish Council of America, 1992.

Winquist, Alan. *Swedish-American Landmarks: Where to Go and What to See.* Minneapolis: Swedish Council of America, 1995.

Sweetest Day This informal and secular holiday originated in the United States in 1922, when an employee of a Cleveland, Ohio, confectionary decided to set aside a day on which to recognize the companionship needs of those members of society who might otherwise be unnoticed. This individual, Herbert Birch Kingston, resolved to present tokens of care and appreciation to elders, invalids, orphans, and others, who might benefit from these special attentions. Early events included the screen star Theda Bara's presenting some 10,000 boxes of chocolates to patients in Cleveland hospitals. In time, the celebration became known, first regionally and later nationally, as Sweetest Day.

By custom, Sweetest Day falls on the third Saturday each October. It began as a day to perform good deeds and to raise the spirits of forgotten or underprivileged members of a community. Celebrations today still address these individuals, but also include general tributes to kindness, friendship, and love. Although it may be confused with Saint Valentine's Day for this reason, Sweetest Day is by no means reserved for romance. Rather, it is a time to honor family members, coworkers, friends, and acquaintances.

Today's participants in this annual event strive to acknowledge others with warm feeling and tokens of gratitude. Customary practices associated with the day include visits, cards, flowers, and other gifts. Given the name of the holiday and the profession of its inventor, the presentation of candy remains a favorite gesture for Sweetest Day celebrants. Observances of Sweetest Day are most prevalent in the Great Lakes area, where the holiday began, but national enthusiasm for the holiday may grow.

See also: FOOD/FOODWAYS; HOLIDAYS/OBSERVANCES; SAINT VALENTINE'S DAY.

For Further Reading:

Hallmark Press Room Sweetest Day Fact Sheet. Available online. URL: http://pressroom.hallmark.com/sweetest_day_fact_sheet.html. Accessed February 22, 2006.

Myers, Robert J. *Celebrations: The Complete Book of American Holidays*. Garden City, N.Y.: Doubleday, 1972.

Webb, Michael. Sweetest Day History and Facts. Available online. URL: http://www.theromantic.com/sweetestday.htm. Accessed February 22, 2006.

taboos   See FOLK BELIEFS.

Tar Baby (legendary)   Tar Baby is a figure who appears in traditional folktales, such as the Anansi and Uncle Remus stories.

In most cases, the Tar Baby is a simulated human figure, fashioned as a scarecrow and then coated with a sticky substance such as tar. Rather than fending off intruders in an area, such as a garden, the Tar Baby traps them. Would-be thieves and trespassers find themselves stuck to the tar figure and are found out by property owners.

In addition to appearing in traditional African-American folktales, the image of the Tar Baby reappears in contemporary African-American writing, such as the historically rich and culturally allusive fiction of the African-American authors Ralph Waldo Ellison and Toni Morrison. Morrison's 1981 novel *Tar Baby* references this figure from the African-American past.

See also: AFRICAN-AMERICAN FOLKLORE; ANANSI; ANIMALS; ELLISON, RALPH WALDO; FOLK HEROES/LEGENDARY FIGURES; MORRISON, TONI; REMUS, UNCLE; TRICKSTER.

For Further Reading:
Brasch, Walter. *Brer Rabbit, Uncle Remus, and the "Cornfield Journalist": The Tale of Joel Chandler Harris*. Macon, Ga.: Mercer University Press, 2000.

Brennan, Jonathan, ed. *When Brer Rabbit Meets Coyote: African-Native American Literature*. Urbana: University of Illinois Press, 2003.

Dussere, Erik. *Balancing the Books: Faulkner, Morrison, and the Economies of Slavery*. New York: Routledge, 2003.

Faulkner, William J. *The Days When the Animals Talked: Black American Folktales and How They Came to Be*. Trenton, N.J.: Africa World Press, 1993.

Reesman, Jeanne Campbell. *Trickster Lives: Culture and Myth in American Fiction*. Athens: University of Georgia Press, 2001.

tattooing   See BODYLORE.

teddy bear   See ROOSEVELT, THEODORE.

teeth   See TOOTH FAIRY.

Tell, William (legendary)   As a figure of 14th-century Swiss folklore, William Tell nonetheless reappears in American folklore, especially in legends and ballads.

The story begins with a tyrant who leads the Austrian occupation of Switzerland. He places his hat atop a pole in the town square, requiring residents to bow to it. When one townsman, William Tell, refuses to do so, the tyrant responds by making an alternative demand of him.

The despot directs William Tell, an archer, to use his skills with the bow to split an apple placed on Tell's son's head. When Tell succeeds at this challenge, the leader nonetheless calls for his arrest and imprisonment. En route to prison, William Tell eludes his captors, returns home, and kills the tyrant who sought to incarcerate him. An uprising ensues in which the occupiers are ousted and the Helvetian Confederation is established.

For many of the same reasons that William Tell stands as a national hero for Switzerland, his story figures among the most commonly retold to American children. Numerous animated cartoons, from *Mr. Peabody's Improbable History* to *Oswald the Lucky Rabbit*, have provided versions of the William Tell story. In still other children's fare, such as the familiar Looney Tunes cartoons, Gioacchino Rossini's musical composition the *William Tell* Overture is used to accompany various scenes of tension or suspense.

The story of William Tell is a straightforward one about an individual who stands up to an unreasonable leader. Those who show courage, as William Tell does in the story, will be rewarded. Those who abuse authority, as does the leader in this tale, will find due punishment.

See also: BALLADS, FOLK HEROES/LEGENDARY FIGURES; LEGEND, FOLK; OCCUPATIONAL FOLKLORE; PROTEST IN FOLKLORE.

For Further Reading:

Dundes, Alan. *From Game to War and Other Psychoanalytic Essays on Folklore.* Lexington: University Press of Kentucky, 1997.

Fiske, John. *Myths and Myth-Makers: Old Tales and Superstitions Interpreted by Comparative Mythology.* Boston: Houghton Mifflin, 1900.

Krall, Sarah. *100 Folk Heroes Who Shaped World History.* San Francisco: Bluewood Books, 1995.

Lee, Frank. *Folk Tales of All Nations.* New York: Tudor, 1930.

Nolan, Paul. *Folk Tale Plays Round the World: A Collection of Royalty-Free, One-Act Plays about Lands Far and Near.* Boston: Plays, Inc., 1982.

Small, Terry. *The Legend of William Tell.* New York: Bantam Books, 1991.

Untermeyer, Louis. *The World's Great Stories: Fifty-Five Legends That Live Forever.* Philadelphia: Lippincott, 1964.

Tennessee folklore See APPALACHIAN FOLKLORE; DEPRESSION, THE GREAT; MARTIN LUTHER KING DAY; SOUTHERN REGIONAL FOLKLORE.

terms Every discipline has some basic terminology that even novices find it helpful to understand.

At times, folklorists use some of the words, phrases, and categories of analysis employed in other social sciences. Such terms include *ethnicity* and *worldview*. In other instances, folklore scholars devise their own terms in order to articulate concepts more precisely or ideas specific to their work. These terms include *fakelore* and *poplore*.

Whatever the concept involved, terminology is intended to raise new and better questions about the nature of folklore study. What is the difference between folk culture and popular culture? How do scholars distinguish between folklore and folklife? How can fieldwork advance folklore scholarship? To what extent do internal and external perspectives on a folk society diverge? What does it mean to speak of folk traditions in an urbanized, industrialized, and digitized era? Where do new folk customs originate, and where could that be said to be happening now?

At their worst, such terms become jargon, limiting participation in disciplinary conversations. At their best, however, these terms help educate and involve more people in the field's study. Terms such as *folklife* and *urban legends* are among these.

See also: ART, FOLK; CULTURE, FOLK; DOCUMENTARY; ETHNICITY; FAKELORE; FIELDWORK;

FOLKLORE; FOLKLIFE; FOLKLIFE MOVEMENT; FOLKLORE; FOLKLORE STUDIES; FOLKLORISM; FOOD/FOODWAYS; HISTORY, FOLK; INSIDER/OUTSIDER; MATERIAL CULTURE; ORAL HISTORY; POPLORE; PUBLIC FOLKLORE; URBAN LEGENDS; VERNACULAR CULTURE; WORLDVIEW.

For Further Reading:

Bennett, Tony. *New Keywords: A Vocabulary of Culture and Society.* New York: Blackwell, 2005.

Feintuch, Burt. *Eight Words for the Study of Expressive Culture.* Urbana: University of Illinois Press, 2003.

Jobes, Gertrude. *Dictionary of Mythology, Folklore, and Symbols.* New York: Scarecrow Press, 1961–1962.

Williams, Raymond. *Keywords: A Vocabulary of Culture and Society.* New York: Oxford University Press, 1976.

Texas folklore   See BASS, SAM; BONNIE AND CLYDE; CAJUN FOLKLORE; JUNETEENTH; PECOS BILL; PRISON FOLKLORE; RODEO; SOUTHWESTERN REGIONAL FOLKLORE.

Thanksgiving   This distinctively American holiday, celebrating harvest and other blessings experienced by the Pilgrims, is celebrated nationally on the fourth Thursday of November each year.

As for other harvest festivals, Thanksgiving's timing is linked to the seasons, and in particular to the time when all crops have been harvested. The holiday punctuates the transition to winter by sending a reverent message of appreciation and rejoicing for plenty.

The first Thanksgiving in 1621 lasted three full days and featured games and skill displays, as well as feasting. Despite the later association of turkey with this holiday, the original observance called for venison, seafood, duck, and goose. It was only later that the turkey, the creature Benjamin Franklin believed would make a more suitable national symbol than the bald eagle, would become the standard entrée for the Thanksgiving feast. Thanksgiving did not immediately gain official status as a national holiday. In 1623, the Massachusetts governor Bradford proclaimed it a state observance. President George Washington declared a 1789 celebration, but given the religious overtones of Thanksgiving, the caution about separation of church and state impeded establishing a legal holiday for some years. It was not until a champion of the concept of a national holiday, Sarah Josepha Hale, devoted some 36 years to promoting the idea that President Lincoln proclaimed it so on October 3, 1863. Subsequent presidents declared the date each year until the 1940s, when Congress issued a joint resolution to fix the observance as annual.

Residual customs from earlier celebrations include activities related to the holiday feast, such as raffles for fowl and, latterly, turkey shoots. Other local celebrations of Thanksgiving include a reenactment of the first feast at its original site in Plymouth, Massachusetts. Sporting events of one sort or another have played a part in Thanksgiving celebrations from the beginning. Today's practice of scheduling football games on Thanksgiving, then, recalls the lawn sports engaged in at early celebrations of the day. A noteworthy modern addition to the observance is the holiday parade. The best known among these may be New York City's Macy's Thanksgiving Day Parade, in which marching bands, floats, giant balloon figures, celebrities, and troupes from Broadway shows entertain onlookers. As its sponsorship by a retailer suggests, the Macy's parade not only marks Thanksgiving, but signals the opening of the Christmas shopping season. Toward that end, the parade concludes each year with the arrival of Santa Claus.

Although as for many American holidays, the current practices of Thanksgiving are rather more secular than in the past, it remains a day on which families and friends gather to join in an ample meal and recognize all that for which they are grateful. A typical Thanksgiving combines such a feast with shared rest and recreation. At Thanksgiving, households and churches decorate with symbols of the holiday's origins, including images of turkeys, Pilgrims, Indians, and cornucopias.

See also: FOOD/FOODWAYS; FRANKLIN, BENJAMIN; HOLIDAYS/OBSERVANCES; LINCOLN, ABRAHAM; PARADES; WASHINGTON, GEORGE.

For Further Reading:

Aveni, Anthony F. *The Book of the Year: A Brief History of Our Seasonal Holidays.* New York: Oxford University Press, 2004.

Cohen, Hennig, and Tristram Potter Coffin, eds. *The Folklore of American Holidays.* Detroit: Gale, 1987.

Counihan, Carole M., ed. *Food in the USA: A Reader.* New York: Routledge, 2002.

Linton, Ralph, and Adele Linton. *We Gather Together: The Story of Thanksgiving.* New York: Henry Schuman, 1949.

Myers, Robert. *Celebrations: The Complete Book of American Holidays.* Garden City, N.Y.: Doubleday, 1972.

Santino, Jack. *All around the Year: Holidays and Celebrations in American Life.* Urbana: University of Illinois Press, 1994.

"Three Bears, Goldilocks and the" (legendary) American children are quick to recognize the characters and events depicted in the European fairy tale "Goldilocks and the Three Bears."

As happens so often in such tales, from "Hansel and Gretel" to "Little Red Riding Hood," a child ventures alone into the woods. While so engaged, she becomes curious about a house she passes during her travels. After determining that the house is unoccupied, Goldilocks enters.

The house belongs to three bears: a large bear, a medium-size bear, and a small bear. All three have stepped out of the house to give their breakfast porridge time to cool before they eat it.

Meanwhile, in the bears' absence, Goldilocks moves around the house sampling all it has to offer. First, she tastes the porridge the bears have prepared for breakfast. She finds the large bear's bowl too hot, the medium bear's too cold, but the little bear's just right. As a result, she finishes all the little bear's porridge.

Goldilocks then wishes to be seated. She finds the big bear's chair too hard and the medium bear's chair too soft, but the little bear's chair just right. When she sits down on it, however, the little bear's chair breaks.

Finally, Goldilocks goes to the bedroom for a rest. She tries the big bear's bed and finds its head too high. She tries the medium bear's bed and finds its foot too high. When she stretches out on the little bear's bed, though, she finds it just right. She settles in to sleep.

Sometime thereafter, the three bears return to the house to eat their breakfast. As they reach the table, the large and medium bears declared that someone has been eating their porridge. The little bear joins in, observing that someone has consumed his entire bowl of porridge.

Now aware of an intruder in the house, the bears notice other things out of place. They find evidence that someone has been sitting in their chairs, and that same someone has broken the little bear's chair.

When they continue their search, the bears find that their beddings are disturbed, and the little bear exclaims that a stranger is still sleeping in his bed.

Upon being so discovered, Goldilocks exits the house by a window, never to be heard from again.

This fairy tale carries a dual message to its audience. Those who are trusting enough to leave their homes unlocked may find that trust betrayed. In turn, those who exploit such a trust and invade the sanctity of another's home are likely to be found out. The harsher message of the two, however, is reserved for Goldilocks, as she trespasses, steals, and makes no amends for her misdeeds.

It is still true today that someone who acts finicky, spoiled, or greedy may draw comparisons to Goldilocks, who sees the world and its contents as available for her use, without consideration for others.

See also: ANIMALS; CHILDREN'S FOLKLORE; FABLES; FAIRY TALES; "HANSEL AND GRETEL"; MYTHS, FOLK; "RED RIDING HOOD, LITTLE."

For Further Reading:

Ashliman, D. L. *Folk and Fairy Tales: A Handbook.* Westport, Conn.: Greenwood Press, 2004.

Bacchilega, Cristina. *Postmodern Fairy Tales: Gender and Narrative Strategies.* Philadelphia: University of Pennsylvania Press, 1997.

Bernheimer, Kate, ed. *Mirror, Mirror, on the Wall: Women Writers Explore Their Favorite Fairy Tales.* New York: Anchor, 1998.

Ober, Warren, ed. *The Story of the Three Bears: The Evolution of an International Classic.* Delmar, N.Y.: Scholars' Facsimiles and Reprints, 1981.

Tatar, Maria, ed. *The Annotated Classic Fairy Tales.* New York: W. W. Norton, 2002.

Zipes, Jack. *Breaking the Magic Spell: Radical Theories of Folk and Fairy Tales.* Lexington: University Press of Kentucky, 2002.

Zipes, Jack, ed. *The Great Fairy Tale Tradition: From Straparola and Basile to the Brothers Grimm: Texts, Criticism.* New York: W. W. Norton, 2001.

"Three Billy Goats Gruff, The" (legendary)

"The Three Billy Goats Gruff" tells the familiar yarn of a contest of wits between animals and a potential predator.

The story, probably based on a Norwegian folktale, features three billy goats, all named Gruff. It is their goal to go up the hillside to feed. On the journey there, it is necessary to cross a bridge spanning a stream. Beneath the bridge is an ugly troll.

The first billy goat starts over the bridge. At this point, the troll demands to know his identity and business. This youngest of the three goats replies with a tiny voice, explaining that he is going up the hill to fill his belly. The troll then threatens to eat the goat, but the youngest goat persuades the troll to save his appetite for the next and larger goat.

The second billy goat approaches the bridge and is questioned in the same way by the bridge troll. The second goat convinces the troll to ignore his hunger and wait for the next and largest goat to come along.

The oldest billy goat arrives at the bridge, and the structure creaks beneath his girth. The troll questions this last of the three goats, and he answers in a large, hoarse voice. When the troll declares his intention to gobble up the goat, he responds fiercely and attacks the troll with great force.

The third billy goat then crosses the bridge and joins the others. There on the hillside, the billy goats gruff eat until they become so fat they can hardly move.

This fairy tale includes one of the stock figures of the genre, a troll who exacts a toll from all those who seek to pass. The story demonstrates the wile of the goats in deferring to their larger comrade, as well as the price of greed for the troll.

As in tales such as "Rumplestiltskin" or "The Golden Goose," this story presents a curious figure who must be appeased. In this respect, "The Three Billy Goats Gruff," one of the lesser known fairy tales today, resembles a trickster tale.

See also: ANIMALS; CHILDREN'S FOLKLORE; FABLES; FAIRY TALES; "GOLDEN GOOSE, THE"; MYTHS, FOLK; "RUMPLESTILTSKIN"; TRICKSTER.

For Further Reading:

Bettelheim, Bruno. *The Uses of Enchantment: The Meaning and Importance of Fairy Tales.* New York: Knopf, 1976.

Cashdan, Sheldon. *The Witch Must Die: The Hidden Meaning of Fairy Tales.* New York: Basic Books, 1999.

Tatar, Maria, ed. *The Annotated Classic Fairy Tales.* New York: W. W. Norton, 2002.

Velde, Vivian Vande. *Tales from the Brothers Grimm and the Sisters Weird.* San Diego: Harcourt Brace, 1995.

"Three Little Pigs, The" (legendary)

"The Three Little Pigs" is among the most readily

recognized tales for children in American culture.

The tale opens with a sow and her three little pigs, as suggested in the title. She cannot provide for all their needs, so she sends them out into the world to take care of themselves.

The first pig meets a man carrying a bundle of straw. The pig persuades the man to donate it to him for the purpose of building a shelter. The straw house is flimsy. When a wolf pays a call, although the pig tries to deny him entrance, the wolf blows the house down without much exertion and devours the pig.

The second pig meets a man with a bundle of sticks. This pig is likewise successful in finding a benefactor. Using the sticks given to him, the second pig constructs a house. Once again, a wolf arrives at the door. When the pig refuses to let him in, the wolf again manages to blow down the shelter and eat its occupant.

The third pig meets a man transporting a load of bricks. The pig talks the man into giving him the bricks. With them, he builds a sturdy house. When the wolf comes to call, he threatens the pig but is unable to topple the brick house.

Thwarted in this effort, the wolf engages in a series of ruses designed to draw the pig out of his home so the wolf might feed on him. Each time, the wolf promises to take the pig somewhere of mutual interest and benefit. Each time, the pig outsmarts the wolf by going on that trip alone and returning before the appointed time.

Finally, the wolf decides to try another approach by entering the house through the chimney. The pig discovers the plan, however, and devises a defense. He places a large pot of water into the lit fireplace. Just as the wolf makes his descent down the chimney, the pig lifts the cover and captures the wolf in the stew pot. There, the wolf is boiled, and, in a turnabout, the pig eats him for dinner.

This story is told for both amusement and educational purposes. It emphasizes the importance of good judgment, planning, and safety. It rewards the third pig for exercising skepticism about the wolf's offers of help, and it punishes the wolf for trickery and greed.

Retellings of "The Three Little Pigs" have tended to update the tale for modern audiences. During the Civil Rights movement and the era of the Black Panthers, for example, the author Toni Cade Bambara crafted a version she published as "The Three Little Panthers." More recently, John Scieskza released *The True Story of the Three Little Pigs*, a recasting of the tale, this time offered from the point of view of the wolf.

Through retellings the story of "The Three Little Pigs" seems to remain relevant to contemporary audiences, even in the face of social change. As other tales in which a wolf threatens, such as "Little Red Riding Hood," it bespeaks the importance of forethought and cautions against naïve ways of living in a dangerous world. In modern parlance, any threat to a household tends to be compared to "the wolf at the door."

See also: ANIMALS; BAMBARA, TONI CADE; CHILDREN'S FOLKLORE; CIVIL RIGHTS MOVEMENT; FABLES; FAIRY TALES; MYTHS, FOLK; "RED RIDING HOOD, LITTLE."

For Further Reading:
Bernheimer, Kate, ed. *Mirror, Mirror, on the Wall: Women Writers Explore Their Favorite Fairy Tales.* New York: Anchor, 1998.

Bettelheim, Bruno. *The Uses of Enchantment: The Meaning and Importance of Fairy Tales.* New York: Knopf, 1976.

Cashdan, Sheldon. *The Witch Must Die: The Hidden Meaning of Fairy Tales.* New York: Basic Books, 1999.

Tatar, Maria, ed. *The Annotated Classic Fairy Tales.* New York: W. W. Norton, 2002.

Titanic See BROWN, MARGARET TOBIN (UNSINKABLE MOLLY).

toasts/drinking There is an extensive body of lore surrounding beverages, from coffee to Chardonnay. These traditions and their meanings are largely contextual. The rituals help shape events, reinforce identity, and acknowledge major events in the life cycle of an individual, family, or other group.

Some such activities are chiefly social, such as the drinking games in use on college campuses. Other drinking customs involve attempts at divination, such as the reading of tea leaves at the bottom of a cup. Other drinking lore contributes to the festivity of formal occasions, such as weddings, anniversaries, and bar mitzvahs and bat mitzvahs. Probably the best-known element of drinking culture in this regard is the toast. Toasts are narrative acts associated with the consumption of alcoholic beverages at celebratory events. Toasts in America take two major forms.

In one form of toasting, the speaker leads fellow drinkers in a raised-glass ritual in which remarks suitable to the occasion, whether spontaneous or formulaic, precede the next sip of the beverage. Typically, the toast represents a tribute, which might be serious or humorous, to the host, the guest(s) of honor, or the occasion itself. For instance, the best man at a wedding usually makes a toast to the bride and groom during the reception. Such toasts, even when made in jest, are ways of wishing the person honored well. Wedding toasts do so most explicitly by expressings hopes that the couple will enjoy health, harmony, and the blessings of family life.

The other form of toasting in America often also accompanies drinking. In this context, particularly common among African Americans, the toast represents a verbal performance of a slightly different sort. Those toasting demonstrate in public ways their verbal style and prowess. Poems, recitations, and the like, are offered up, often in contest among participants. Such exchanges are friendly competitions, urged on by listeners for the enjoyment of all.

From the routines associated with brewing the perfect cup of coffee to the Champagne toast at New Year's, drinking lore helps plays a part in defining American social life.

See also: ANNIVERSARIES; BAR MITZVAH/BAT MITZVAH; CUSTOMS, FOLK; FOLKLORE IN EVERYDAY LIFE; FOOD/FOODWAYS; HOLIDAYS/OBSERVANCES; LUCK/FORTUNE; NEW YEAR'S EVE/DAY; PREDICTION; RITES OF PASSAGE; WEDDING/MARRIAGE FOLKORE.

For Further Reading:

Abrahams, Roger D. "The Toast: A Neglected Form of Folk Narrative." In *Folklore in Action: Essays for Discussion in Honor of MacEdward Leach*, edited by Horace D. Beck, 1–11. Philadelphia: American Folklore Society, 1962.

De Garine, Igor, and Valerie De Garine, eds. *Drinking: An Anthropological Approach*. New York: Berghahn Books, 2001.

Evans, David. "The Toast in Context," *Journal of American Folklore* 90, no. 356 (spring 1977): 129–148.

Jackson, Bruce. "Circus and Street: Psychological Aspects of the Black Toast," *Journal of American Folklore* 85, no. 336 (spring 1972): 123–139.

———. "The Titanic Toast." In *Veins of Humor*, edited by Harry Levine, 205–223. Cambridge, Mass.: Harvard University Press, 1972.

Marshall, Mac, ed. *Beliefs, Behaviors, and Alcoholic Beverages*. Ann Arbor: University of Michigan Press, 1979.

Smith, Andrew W. *Oxford Encyclopedia of Food and Drink in America*. New York: Oxford University Press, 2004.

Posey, Sandra. *Café Nation: Coffee Folklore, Magick, and Divination*. Santa Monica, Calif.: Santa Monica Press, 2000.

Walle, Alf H. "Two Possible Origins for the Term 'Toast,'" *Journal of American Folklore* 88, no. 308 (spring 1975): 418–419.

Toomer, Jean (1894–1967) As one of the authors associated with the Harlem Renaissance, an arts movement that spanned many media during the 1920s in America, Toomer earned a reputation as a writer with a keen awareness of folk culture and a distinctive ability to incorporate elements of its vitality within his work.

Probably the best known of his writings was *Cane*, which appeared in 1923. This book combined literary forms such as poetry and prose to create a hybrid form of novel. This text, with its strong associations to the American South and its distinctive culture, balances a respect for folk tradition with an energy for literary experimentation. Although he was a prolific writer, many consider *Cane* Toomer's greatest accomplishment.

Born Nathan Eugene Toomer in 1894, this author created works that captured nuances of turn-of-the-century race relations. As a light-skinned individual, Toomer claimed to have seen both sides of the color line.

Throughout his career, Toomer wove aspects of African-American folklore into his works. While he experimented with incorporating print forms of folklore such as legends, his characteristic choices as a literary artist emphasized acoustic influences of folk culture. He featured dialect that captured regional differences in voice. He also paid tribute to folk music, often writing pieces that recalled work songs and blues tunes.

Although the critically acclaimed *Cane* fell from notice for many years, its reissue in 1951 provided Toomer with a whole new audience. At this point, a next generation of authors sought to weave African-American folk culture into their writings. The Harlem Renaissance found its echo in the black aesthetic movement and the African-American women's renaissance.

In many respects, then, Toomer's folk-influenced literature established groundwork for later literary figures such as Ralph Waldo Ellison and Toni Morrison.

See also: AFRICAN-AMERICAN FOLKLORE; DuBois, W. E. B.; FOLKLORE IN AMERICAN LITERATURE; HUGHES, JAMES MERCER LANGSTON.

For Further Reading:

Cartwright, Keith. *Reading Africa into American Literature: Epics, Fables, and Gothic Tales*. Lexington: University Press of Kentucky, 2002.

Dixon, Melvin. *Ride Out the Wilderness: Geography and Identity in Afro-American Literature*. Urbana: University of Illinois Press, 1987.

Kramer, Victor, ed. *The Harlem Renaissance Re-Examined*. New York: AMS, 1987.

Scruggs, Charles, and Lee VanDemarr. *Jean Toomer and the Terrors of American History*. Philadelphia: University of Pennsylvania Press, 1998.

Tooth Fairy (legendary) The Tooth Fairy is a cherished figure in America's lore of childhood, marking with her visits the loss of each baby tooth as a child matures.

The Tooth Fairy may be described as a specialized sprite who possesses the power to discern when a boy or girl has lost a baby tooth. When a child loses a tooth, if he or she places it beneath the bed pillow (or, in some cases, a vessel specifically reserved for this occasion), the Tooth Fairy will visit while the child sleeps to reclaim the lost tooth. In exchange, the Tooth Fairy leaves behind a small payment for the tooth.

The Tooth Fairy's visit appears to compensate the youngster for maturation milestones, typically commencing at age five to seven, depending upon the individual child's developmental process. The Tooth Fairy also lends a bit of magic to the somewhat painful and distressing experience of having loose and absent teeth. The Tooth Fairy is not affiliated with any faith, nationality, or population. Her gifts vary in value depending upon the circumstances of each child. Since the Tooth Fairy does not need to reach every child in a single night as is the case with her holiday-specific counterparts Santa Claus and the Easter Bunny, she has the potential to visit every child on the special nights when restless sleepers wait for lost teeth to be transformed into legal tender.

Rather little is known regarding the specific origins of the legend of the Tooth Fairy as it is witnessed in American society, although it seems likely that the history of this figure originates in England or Ireland. Over the years, folk beliefs have held that children's milk teeth are a source of power or luck, and, in particular, that such an item in the hands of a witch could be dangerous.

For this reason, the disposition of baby teeth may have become a subject of special importance. Other than that, the Tooth Fairy remains a mystery, both in terms of where she originated and what she does with the teeth she collects.

Compared to other "wee folk" known in American lore, such as leprechauns, elves, and gnomes, the Tooth Fairy is more predictable and far less prone to mischief. Her visits are solely benevolent and seem to involve no special trick, beyond surrender of the tooth itself, to achieve a successful result.

See also: AGING AND FOLKLORE; BODYLORE; CHILDREN'S FOLKLORE; EASTER BUNNY; FOLK HEROES/LEGENDARY FIGURES; RITES OF PASSAGE; SANTA CLAUS.

For Further Reading:

Beeler, Selby B. *Throw Your Tooth on the Roof: Tooth Traditions from Around the World.* Boston: Houghton Mifflin, 1998.

Brill, Marlene Targ. *Tooth Tales from around the World.* Watertown, Mass.: Charlesbridge, 1998.

Carter, William et al. *Ethnodentistry and Dental Folklore.* Overland Park, Kans.: Dental Folklore Books of Kansas City, 1987.

Clark, Cindy Dell. *Flights of Fancy, Leaps of Faith: Children's Myths in Contemporary America.* Chicago: University of Chicago Press, 1995.

Opie, Iona, and Moira Tatum. *Dictionary of Superstitions.* New York: Oxford University Press, 1992.

Zipes, Jack. *The Oxford Companion to Fairy Tales.* New York: Oxford University Press, 2000.

"Tortoise and the Hare, The" (legendary) Few images of contest are more familiar to Americans than the scenes conjured by the Aesop fable "The Tortoise and the Hare."

The story begins with a boastful hare. He cannot refrain from extolling his own virtues. He is especially keen to brag about his speed when he wishes to taunt a tortoise for his slow pace.

The tortoise reminds the hare that anyone can be beaten in a contest and challenges the hare to a race. Once the race is under way, the hare takes pains to let the tortoise know that he will require little effort to outpace his sluggish opponent. Little effort is precisely what the hare invests, as he cannot resist capering along the race's course and teasing his rival. The hare dines, naps, and jokes throughout the race until he finally sees the tortoise nearing the finish line. The hare stirs from his languor but finds that he cannot overtake the tortoise in time. To the hare's amazement, he loses the contest.

This fable makes a simple point to its audience. No amount of physical strength or agility can offset a lack of discipline. Although the tortoise never accelerates, neither does he flag. The sustained effort of the tortoise proves more valuable in the end than the athleticism of the hare.

The moral of the tale, of course, has wider implications. In addition to cautioning against pride, sloth, and cruelty, the fable also reserves the spoils of victory for those who are capable of humility, steadfastness, and industry. The central characters are highly recognizable in contemporary U.S. culture and appear in storybooks, cartoons, comics, and other genres of popular expression.

"The Tortoise and the Hare" remains an emblem of the importance of a sound work ethic and the hazards of overconfidence in performance of one's tasks.

See also: ANIMALS; BRER RABBIT; CHILDREN'S FOLKLORE; FABLES; FAIRY TALES; MYTHS, FOLK.

For Further Reading:

Bader, Barbara. *Aesop and Company: With Scenes from His Legendary Life.* Boston: Houghton Mifflin, 1991.

Bennett, William J. *The Book of Virtues: A Treasury of Great Moral Stories.* New York: Simon & Schuster, 1993.

Lewis, Jayne Elizabeth. *The English Fable: Aesop and Literary Culture, 1651–1740.* New York: Cambridge University Press, 1996.

Rosenthal, Paul. *Yo, Aesop! Get a Load of These Fables.* New York: Simon & Schuster Books for Young Readers, 1997.

Temple, Olivia. *The Complete Fables of Aesop.* New York: Penguin Books, 1998.

toys, folk

Folk toys are handmade, traditional objects used as diversions, usually by youth.

Child-fashioned toys have been a perennial interest throughout American history. These toys are usually constructed with ordinary household items readily available to children. Examples include paper airplanes, fortune tellers, foosballs, cat's cradles, and slingshots. Other child-made amusements are seasonal in nature, such as snowmen and sandcastles.

Other folk toys are crafted by adults for children's enjoyment. These items include rag dolls, teddy bears, puzzles, tops, and skill games. While such toys are found in all regions of the United States, they are more common in rural and remote regions, such as Appalachia, where traditional craft traditions are more enduring and so folk toys are more plentiful.

In modern times, mass-produced and mass-marketed toys have nearly displaced folk toys in the lives of American children, except where accessibility and affordability of store-bought toys are limited. Nonetheless, folk toys are still being made and played with across the nation. In fact, today there is renewed interest in toys made in traditional ways using natural materials, such as wood. They are increasingly being marketed as classic, old-fashioned, and wholesome entertainments, even if the new folk toys are manufactured in factories.

See also: CHILDREN'S FOLKLORE; CRAFTS, FOLK; FOLKLORE IN EVERYDAY LIFE; GAMES AND PASTIMES; ROOSEVELT, THEODORE.

For Further Reading:

Ketchum, William C., Jr. *Toys and Games.* Washington, D.C.: Cooper-Hewitt Museum of the Smithsonian Instiution, 1981.

Knapp, Mary, and Herbert Knapp. *One Potato, Two Potato: The Secret Education of American Children.* New York: W. W. Norton, 1976.

McClary, Andrew. *Toys with Nine Lives: A Social History of American Toys.* North Haven, Conn.: Linnet Books, 1997.

O'Brien, Richard. *The Story of American Toys: From Puritans to the Present.* New York: Abbeville Press, 1990.

Page, Linda Garland, and Hilton Smith, eds. *The Foxfire Book of Toys and Games: Reminiscences and Instructions from Appalachia.* New York: E. P. Dutton, 1985.

Schmidt, Nancy J. et al. *African Children's Games for American Children.* Urbana: University of Illinois Press, 1975.

Sutton-Smith, Brian. "The Folk Games of the Children." In *Our Living Traditions: An Introduction to American Folklore,* edited by Tristram Potter Coffin, 179–191. New York: Basic Books, 1968.

Sutton-Smith, Brian. "Psychology of Childlore: The Triviality Barrier," *Western Folklore* 29 (1970): 1–8.

tradition, oral

Storytelling is an art form, and since most folk traditions involve oral transmission of narrative, storytellers are a major focus within the study of American folklore.

Oral tradition involves the narrative heritage of a folk group. Gifted speakers and performers command the attention of other community members. With their ability to summon the power of the word, storytellers and other verbal artists deliver tales, proverbs, tunes, sermons, lectures, parables, legends, myths, testimony, incantations, and other kinds of sounded texts.

All spoken or verbal art from poems to songs can be classified as oral tradition, but stories are the central form. Stories can inform, educate, inspire, and move their tellers' audiences of listeners. A traditional community's storyteller is the keeper of its memories and so plays an important role within the function of that group. In many societies, storytellers are revered as the source of wisdom, entertainment, and affirmation of collective identity.

See also: BELIEFS, FOLK; CUSTOMS, FOLK; FOLKTALES; LEGENDS, FOLK; MUSIC, FOLK; MYTHS, FOLK; ORAL FOLKLORE; TERMS.

For Further Reading:

Ben-Amos, Dan. "The Seven Strands of Tradition: Varieties in Its Meaning in American Folklore Studies," *Journal of Folklore Research* 21 (1984): 97–131.

Bronner, Simon. *Creativity and Tradition in Folklore: New Directions.* Logan: Utah State University Press, 1992.

———. *Folk Nation: Folklore in the Creation of American Tradition.* Wilmington, Del.: Scholarly Resources, 2002.

———. *Following Tradition: Folklore in the Discourse of American Culture.* Logan: Utah State University Press, 1998.

Feintuch, Burt, ed. *Eight Words for the Study of Expressive Culture.* Urbana: University of Illinois Press, 2003.

Glassie, Henry. "Tradition," *Journal of American Folklore* 108, no. 430 (autumn 1995): 395–412.

Hobsbawm, Eric, and Terence Ranger, eds. *The Invention of Tradition.* Cambridge: Cambridge University Press, 1992.

Kammen, Michael. *Mystic Chords of Memory: The Transformation of Tradition in American Culture.* New York: Knopf, 1991.

Williams, Raymond. *Keywords: A Vocabulary of Culture and Society.* New York: Oxford University Press, 1976.

transcontinental railroad As a landmark in American technological and transportation development, the transcontinental railroad, along with stories of its construction and completion, appears throughout folk histories.

The tracks laid to create this rail line were the first to span the area now known as the 48 contiguous states. As the route stretched across America, it symbolized not only the power of innovation, but also the concept of manifest destiny. The pathway was made possible by the Pacific Railroad Act of 1862. Because the project came to fruition in the year of America's centennial, not long after the end of the Civil War, the transcontinental railroad also represented national unity and connection.

What is most remarked in folklore related to the transcontinental railroad is the rather unusual process of its construction. Because the task of building across the nation was so vast, the labor needed for the construction project was considerable. Former soldiers and officers from the Civil War played a part, as did many immigrants from China and Ireland. The plan involved two railroad companies' working simultaneously and on opposite ends of the anticipated line. The Union Pacific Railroad worked the eastern section of the new line, while the Central Pacific assumed responsibility for the western end. They would compete to win land and cash sums provided as incentives for each mile-long portion of the track completed. Through such an arrangement, Congress challenged the two railroad concerns to finish the track by July 1, 1876. If the builders did not meet this deadline, they would lose all interests, monetary or otherwise, in the transcontinental railroad. The drama of this competition lent additional interest to the venture.

As it turned out, feverish work by both railroads led to the line's completion on May 10, 1869. In a ceremony to mark the meeting point of the two railroad segments, held in Promontory Point, Utah, a gold spike was used to join the two portions of the line. The event is commemorated by the Golden Spike National Historic Site, a facility now maintained by the National Park Service at the location of the golden spike.

The tale of the transcontinental railroad joins other grand stories of the rails, such as those of John Henry and John Luther "Casey" Jones, in American occupational folklore.

See also: CHINESE-AMERICAN FOLKLORE; CIVIL WAR; CODY, WILLIAM F. (BUFFALO BILL); FRONTIER; GHOST TOWNS; GOLD RUSH,

THE; HENRY, JOHN; HISTORICAL EVENTS; IMMI-GRATION AND FOLKLORE; INDUSTRIALIZATION AND FOLKLORE; IRISH-AMERICAN FOLKLORE; OCCUPATIONAL FOLKLORE; WESTERN REGIONAL FOLKLORE.

For Further Reading:

Ambrose, Stephen. *Nothing Like It in the World: The Men Who Built the Transcontinental Railroad.* New York: Simon & Schuster, 2000.

Billington, Ray Allen, and Martin Ridge. *Westward Expansion: A History of the American Frontier.* Albuquerque: University of New Mexico Press, 2001.

Botkin, B. A. *A Treasury of Railroad Folklore: The Stories, Tall Tales, Traditions, Ballads, and Songs of the American Railroad Man.* New York: Crown, 1953.

Cadbury, Deborah. *Dreams of Iron and Steel: Seven Wonders of the Nineteenth Century.* New York: Fourth Estate, 2004.

Chang, Iris. *The Chinese in America: A Narrative History.* New York: Penguin, 2004.

trees See ARBOR DAY; CHAPMAN, JOHN (JOHNNY APPLESEED); CHRISTMAS.

trickster The figure of the trickster is a common one throughout American folklore, especially in Native American and African-American tales.

The trickster is an unlikely hero and appears even less likely to emerge as a victor, yet somehow prevails in a variety of situations portrayed within trickster tales.

Tricksters are no strangers to comedy or mischief. They are known for pranks and other forms of misdirection. They often violate cultural taboos, sometimes muting such transgressions with clowning or other methods of ingratiating themselves with those who might otherwise exact punishment.

In addition to their use of whimsy and cunning, tricksters often possess unusual talents of intellect, willness, foresight, or magic. The trickster typically triumphs through unexpected turns of events, whether by chance or design. On this basis, the trickster is related to other figures in folklore who rely upon subterfuge, such as outlaws, magicians, and changelings.

Folk figures from Anansi to Brer Rabbit to Coyote dramatize the agency of the trickster. In contemporary American culture, Bugs Bunny is likely the most recognizable trickster character, always eluding the hunter or rival.

Tricksters can defy, deflect, defeat the host society's standards of common sense and right conduct. In so doing, they capture the interest of audiences satisfied by the inversions, power plays, and wit of such tales of contest.

See also: AFRICAN-AMERICAN FOLKLORE; ANANSI; ANIMALS; BRER RABBIT; PARKER, ROBERT LEROY (BUTCH CASSIDY); CHANGELING; CHESNUTT, CHARLES WADDELL; COMPUTER FOLKLORE; COYOTE; FABLES; FAIRY TALES; FOLK HEROES/LEGENDARY FIGURES; FOLKTALES; HARRIS, JOEL CHANDLER; LONGABAUGH, HARRY (SUNDANCE KID); MYTHS, FOLK; NATIVE AMERICAN FOLKLORE; OUTLAWS; POPLORE; REMUS, UNCLE; ROBIN HOOD; SOUTHERN REGIONAL FOLKLORE; STAGOLEE; TAR BABY; "THREE BILLY GOATS GRUFF, THE"; YANKEE PEDDLER.

For Further Reading:

Davidson, Hilda. *The Hero in Tradition and Folklore.* London: Folklore Society, 1984.

Doucet, Sharon Arms. *Lapin Plays Possum: Trickster Tales from the Louisiana Bayou.* New York: Farrar, Straus & Giroux, 2002.

Jurich, Marilyn. *Scheherazade's Sisters: Trickster Heroines and Their Stories in World Literature.* Westport, Conn.: Greenwood Press, 1998.

Radin, Paul. *The Trickster: A Study in American Indian Mythology.* New York: Philosophical Library, 1956.

Reesman, Jeanne Campbell. *Trickster Lives: Culture and Myth in American Fiction.* Athens: University of Georgia Press, 2001.

Roberts, John. *From Trickster to Badman: The Black Folk Hero in Slavery and Freedom.* Philadelphia: University of Pennsylvania Press, 1990.

Smith, Jeanne Rositer. *Writing Tricksters: Mythic Gambols in American Ethnic Literature.* Berkeley: University of California Press, 1997.

Wilson, William. "Trickster Tales and the Location of Cultural Boundaries: A Mormon Example," *Journal of Folklore Research* 20 (1983): 55–66.

Truman, Harry   See CITIZENSHIP DAY.

Truth, Sojourner (1797–1883)   Sojourner Truth is the name adopted in 1843 by a well-known antislavery activist and public speaker.

In 1797, she was born into slavery as Isabella Baumfree in Hurley, New York. She had 12 brothers and sisters. As a young slave, she was sold numerous times. She experienced hardship and cruelty from several masters but relied on her religious faith to sustain her. In 1814, at the age of 17, she married another slave, named Thomas, with whom she would have five children. By 1828, Isabella Baumfree was granted her freedom, permitting her to devote more of her time and energy to the abolitionist cause. In 1850, she published a memoir, *The Narrative of Sojourner Truth: A Northern Slave*, detailing her experiences as an American-born slave.

As her career fighting slavery continued, Sojourner Truth rose to prominence within the antislavery movement. In 1864, she met President Abraham Lincoln and during that same year joined the National Freedmen's Relief Association. Truth knew that emancipation did not remedy all the living conditions for former slaves, and so she worked diligently to render aid to freed men and women. She also became an orator of note on a variety of subjects, including women's suffrage. It was in this context that she became known for the question she posted on behalf of African-American females: "Ain't I a woman?"

Although Truth died in 1883, her legacy as a strong African-American woman lives on in stories, poems, and the deeds of all those who find courage in the memory of her heroism.

See also: AFRICAN-AMERICAN FOLKLORE; CIVIL WAR; FOLK HEROES/LEGENDARY FIGURES; GENDER AND FOLKLORE; LINCOLN, ABRAHAM; PROTEST IN FOLKLORE; SLAVERY; WOMEN'S SUFFRAGE.

For Further Reading:

Bernard, Jacqueline. *Journey toward Freedom: The Story of Sojourner Truth.* New York: Feminist Press at CUNY, 1990.

Fitch, Suzanne Pullon, and Roseann M. Mandziuk. *Sojourner Truth as Orator: Wit, Story, and Song.* Westport, Conn.: Greenwood Press, 1997.

Narrative of Sojourner Truth: A Northern Slave. Chapel Hill, N.C.: Academic Affairs Library, 2000.

Newhouse, Susan Mabee. *Sojourner Truth: Slave, Prophet, Legend.* New York: New York University Press, 1993.

Painter, Nell Irvin. *Sojourner Truth: A Life, a Symbol.* New York: W. W. Norton, 1996.

Tubman, Harriet (1820–1913)   Harriet Tubman was an antislavery activist and lifelong proponent of human rights.

Tubman was born a slave in 1820 in Maryland. She escaped slavery in 1849, although doing so required that she leave others behind. In order to win her freedom, Tubman was separated from her family, including her husband, John.

Once she fled slavery, Harriet Tubman led more than 300 slaves to freedom in northern states or Canada. Tubman made some 19 trips back into the slave South to accomplish this work. In this way, she functioned as a "conductor" on the Underground Railroad, an informal network of individuals who dedicated themselves to assisting fugitive slaves to find their way to freedom. On this basis, Tubman was dubbed the "Moses of her people," as she faithfully led them out of captivity.

Tubman went on to become a prominent champion for the abolitionist cause. For example, she met with the antislavery activist John

Brown and is reputed to have helped him plan his famous raid on the Harpers Ferry arsenal. During the Civil War, Tubman also supported the Union army as a nurse, scout, and spy.

After the war's conclusion, Tubman proved an indefatigable advocate for the success of former slaves. She established institutions for that specific purpose, including a school for freed slaves and a home for the elderly.

For these heroic deeds and sacrifices, Tubman found a place within the annals of history and lore. She is the subject of many biographies, films, and books for children.

See also: AFRICAN-AMERICAN FOLKLORE; FOLK HEROES/LEGENDARY FIGURES; PROTEST IN FOLKLORE; SLAVERY; UNDERGROUND RAILROAD.

For Further Reading:

Bradford, Sarah. *Harriet, the Moses of Her People.* Chapel Hill: University of North Carolina at Chapel Hill, 1995.

Clinton, Catherine. *Harriet Tubman: The Road to Freedom.* New York: Little, Brown, 2004.

Humez, Jean. *Harriet Tubman: The Life and the Life Stories.* Madison: University of Wisconsin Press, 2003.

Larson, Kate Clifford. *Bound for the Promised Land: Harriet Tubman, Portrait of an American Hero.* New York: Ballantine, 2004.

Turner, Nat (c. 1800–1831)   Although life as a 19th-century slave in Southampton County, Virginia, might have rendered Nat Turner anonymous to history, his decision to mobilize a group of slaves in resisting involuntary servitude earned Turner a place among legendary figures of the African-American past.

Turner was born in 1800, and as a child, he dazzled those around him with his intelligence and gifts of prophecy. He felt destined for something greater than the life of a slave, and so he devoted himself to his studies and his spiritual development in the hope of realizing that promise. Whatever his talents, Turner

still found himself subject to circumstances he, and other slaves, could not control. At age 12, Turner faced the reality of all slave children, as he began a life of unremunerated toil. Work was hard and treatment harsh, but that was only the beginning. Owners traded their human chattel at will, separating family members and often severing such ties forever through distance, death, and adversity. Turner saw his mother, and later his wife, sold and sent away.

While Nat Turner's personal restraint and religious outlook gave him the reputation of a trustworthy slave, he privately resented the constraints placed upon his liberty. As his father had before him, Turner became a fugitive slave at one point. Unlike his father, though, Nat Turner voluntarily returned 30 days later on the basis of what he considered divine guidance, urging him to help others escape captivity. Eventually, after the death of his owner, Turner found himself the property of a minor child of a slave master. Surely this could not be an easy thing for a thoughtful and freedom-loving adult to bear. With time and additional phenomena Turner identified as messages from God, he turned his energies toward organizing a rebellion.

His 1831 insurrection not only disproved the notion of slavery as a benevolent institution; it also sparked fears of further unrest and violence throughout the slave-holding South. In the wake of the trial and execution of participants in the uprising, slave legislation produced even more restrictions on any behavior whites considered a threat to the order, such as movement, assembly, and even literacy, since it helped slaves communicate freely among themselves.

With his reported final words "I am ready," uttered just prior to his public hanging, Turner ended his life as he had lived it: brave and resolute. In the American tradition of the patriot Patrick Henry, who vowed liberty or death in fighting to gain liberty, Turner gave his life in his effort to expose the hypocrisy of slave trade within a democracy. In part because of his profile as a conscientious objector to slavery and its curtailment of human rights, Turner has been the subject of countless stories, poems, plays, songs, and images. By interpreting and supplementing the historical record, artistic representations of the Southampton insurrection keep Nat Turner's historical memory vibrant. Fictional treatments of Turner's life include such works as Harriet Beecher Stowe's *Dred: A Story of the Great Dismal Swamp* (1856), Daniel Panger's *Ol' Prophet Nat* (1967), and William Styron's *The Confessions of Nat Turner* (1967). Poetry inspired by the incidents in Southampton abounds, particularly among African-American poets. Examples include Sterling Allen Brown's "Remembering Nat Turner," Robert Hayden's "The Ballad of Nat Turner," Alvin Aubert's "Nat Turner in the Clearing," and Ophelia Robinson's extended verse "Nat Turner." The same historical subject informs numerous plays written for the stage, from Randolph Edmond's *Nat Turner* to Robert O'Hara's *Insurrection: Holding History*. The story of Nat Turner also captures the imagination of musicians, as in the case with Corey Coke's spoken word performance on "mastablasta," a cut on his 1999 compact disc *Coreyography*.

These portraits of Nat Turner and the raid that made him famous have often inspired controversy, as writers, dramatists, artists, and composers approach the topic in their own ways and take liberties with the subject. A great deal is at stake, however, when a cultural icon is depicted, as people may regard him differently depending upon their perspectives. Nat Turner has been called a prophet, a fanatic, a criminal, an avenger, a leader, a visionary, a dissenter, and a rebel. However he may be viewed, he is not likely to be forgotten. Nat Turner continues to exert an influence on memories of the American past and its lore.

See also: AFRICAN-AMERICAN FOLKLORE; BROWN, STERLING ALLEN; FOLK HEROES/LEGENDARY FIGURES; HENRY, PATRICK; SLAVERY; SOUTHERN REGIONAL FOLKLORE; STOWE, HARRIET BEECHER; STYRON, WILLIAM; VESEY, DENMARK.

For Further Reading:

Davis, Mary Kemp. *Nat Turner before the Bar of Judgment: Fictional Treatments of the Southampton Slave Insurrection.* Baton Rouge: Louisiana State University Press, 1999.

Foner, Eric, ed. *Nat Turner.* Englewood Cliffs, N.J.: Prentice-Hall, 1971.

French, Scot. *Remembering Nat Turner: The Rebellious Slave in American Thought, 1831 to the Present.* Boston: Houghton Miffllin, 2003.

Greenberg, Kenneth S., ed. *Nat Turner: A Slave Rebellion in History and Memory.* Oxford: Oxford University Press, 2003.

Oates, Stephen B. *The Fires of Jubilee: Nat Turner's Fierce Rebellion.* New York: HarperPerennial, 1975.

Stone, Albert E. *The Return of Nat Turner: History, Literature, and Cultural Politics in Sixties America.* Athens: University of Georgia Press, 1992.

Twain, Mark   See CLEMENS, SAMUEL LANGHORNE.

Tylor, E. B.   See FOLK CULTURE.

UFO folklore   As most unexplained phenomena do, unidentified flying objects (or UFOs) are the subject of considerable American folklore.

From stories and urban legends to popular films and fiction, UFO lore helps people make sense of experiences for which science offers no definitive answers. The first stories on this topic in the United States tended to feature alien spacecraft that had the appearance of flying saucers. These stories of extraterrestrials became common during the mid-20th century in America. In an era during which Americans had to contend with dangers posed by human-made threats, such as atomic and nuclear bombs, these tales of disklike vessels visiting the Earth from faraway space now seem almost quaint by comparison. Nonetheless, there may be a subconscious connection between the images of spacecraft filled with creatures from Mars and the prospect of air raids and bombings.

For decades now, one of the clusters of UFO stories has focused on the so-called Area 51. This six- by 10-mile region of a military base located in Nevada, also known as Groom Lake, was the setting for whole sets of such tales. According to the lore, Area 51 held important discoveries and secrets about UFOs, but this information was being withheld from the citizenry by the military. As do other conspiracy theories and urban legends, this tale enjoys remarkable persistence in American culture. Narratives treating this and other UFO sitings continue to command the public's attention and pique its curiosity.

Stories, rumors, and beliefs about alien abductions and visits to Earth from other worlds still circulate today.

See also: ATOMIC/NUCLEAR ERA FOLKLORE; CONSPIRACY FOLKLORE; FOLKLORE IN EVERYDAY LIFE; SUPERNATURAL; SUPERSTITION; URBAN LEGENDS.

For Further Reading:

Bullard, Thomas E. "UFO Abduction Reports: The Supernatural Kidnap Narrative Returns in Technological Guise," *Journal of American Folklore* 102, no. 404 (spring 1989): 147–170.

Curran, Douglas. *In Advance of the Landing: Folk Concepts of Outer Space.* New York: Abbeville Press, 2001.

Peebles, Curtis. *Watch the Skies: A Chronicle of the Flying Saucer Myth.* Washington, D.C.: Smithsonian Institution Press, 1994.

Rojcewicz, Peter M. "The 'Men in Black' Experience and Tradition: Analogues with the Traditional Devil Hypothesis," *Journal of American Folklore* 100, no. 396 (spring 1987): 148–160.

Vallee, Jacques. *Passport to Magonia: On UFOs, Folklore, and Parallel Worlds.* Chicago: H. Regnery, 1969.

"Ugly Duckling, The" (legendary) "The Ugly Duckling," a tale popularized by the storyteller Hans Christian Andersen, recounts the experiences of a misfit.

In a glorious countryside, a mother duck sits on her nest, atop her eggs. She grows impatient waiting for them to hatch, because she misses the company and freedom of movement she knows that other ducks enjoy.

The mother duck persists, though, and in time she notices the ducklings breaking out of their shells. All but one egg, the largest of the brood, opens to reveal a beautiful little duckling.

Soon, an old duck stops by the nest to pay the mother duck a visit. When the visitor learns of her predicament, she advises the mother that the remaining egg is a turkey's egg rather than a duck's egg. The elder duck advises her not to bother with it.

The mother decides to permit the large egg a bit more time to hatch. When it does, she confronts a curious sight. The last hatchling is odd in appearance and in no way resembles the others.

When the mother takes her young for their first swim, their uniform success in that lesson reassures her that her youngest is not a turkey. Still, the last-born duckling is roundly ridiculed by others, even its siblings, for its unusual appearance.

The ugly duckling feels misunderstood and cannot fathom why it is so difficult to find his rightful place in the world. He remains quite lost until catching a glimpse of a group of elegant birds that seem strangely familiar, even kindred, to him. After those birds continue on their way, the ugly duckling endures a long, harsh winter before seeing their like again.

As spring arrives, the ugly duckling vows to find more of the elegant birds he observed before, whatever the consequences. Accustomed as he is to taunting, the ugly duckling fully expects the pretty swans to reject him, but he determines that even this fate is preferable to his current circumstances. To his surprise and delight, however, the swans welcome him as one of their own. They not only accept him as he is, they regard him as the most beautiful of all. In this way, the once ugly duckling begins a joyous new life among the swans.

As other entertaining tales presented by Hans Christian Andersen do, "The Ugly Duckling" conveys valuable advice. The story warns against judging others, especially on the basis of appearance. It decries mistreatment, particularly when the basis for that conduct is physical attractiveness. The tale also holds out the promise of redemption for everyone who feels out of place, misperceived, or spurned.

References today to this story tend to invoke its title character as an icon of someone who has been unfairly appraised.

See also: ANDERSEN, HANS CHRISTIAN; ANIMALS; CHILDREN'S FOLKLORE; FABLES; FAIRY TALES; MYTHS, FOLK.

For Further Reading:

Bernheimer, Kate, ed. *Mirror, Mirror, on the Wall: Women Writers Explore Their Favorite Fairy Tales.* New York: Anchor, 1998.

Bredsdorff, Elias. *Hans Christian Andersen: An Introduction to His Life and Works.* Copenhagen: Hans Reitzels Forlag, 1987.

Cashdan, Sheldon. *The Witch Must Die: The Hidden Meaning of Fairy Tales.* New York: Basic Books, 1999.

Rossel, Sven Hakon, ed. *Hans Christian Andersen: Danish Writer and Citizen of the World.* Amsterdam: Rodopi, 1996.

Tatar, Maria, ed. *The Annotated Classic Fairy Tales.* New York: W. W. Norton, 2002.

Uncle Remus   See REMUS, UNCLE.

Uncle Sam (legendary) As an emblem of the folklore of national identity, Uncle Sam represents the United States and, in particular, the country's branches of the selective service.

Although there are slight differences in his representations, Uncle Sam is typically depicted as a tall, slender male with white hair and whiskers. The look of his costume takes its inspiration from the U.S. flag, adding to the patriotic effect. He wears red and white striped slacks, a blue jacket, and a top hat, often adorned with a band of stars. The visage and distinctive attire of Uncle Sam help make him a widely recognizable national symbol for Americans.

Despite some uncertainty concerning the precise origins of this beloved figure, most accounts of Uncle Sam's history date to the early 19th century. A beef supplier to the United States Army during the War of 1812 was known as Samuel "Uncle Sam" Wilson (1766–1854). According to folklore, the marking on packages for meat shipments to the military included the abbreviation *U.S.* When queried about the label, the distributor's reply indicated that the letters stood for *Uncle Sam* (rather than *United States*), hence the conflation of an individual and the country he supplied with rations.

The notion of Uncle Sam as a personification of the nation took hold readily with the American public. During the 20th century, for example, recruitment posters for the world wars featured him prominently. These posters were of simple design. A large picture of Uncle Sam, posed with index finger extended in the direction of the viewer, appeared beside the caption "I WANT YOU." In smaller print, the sentence reads, "for the U.S. Army/Enlist Now." The poster achieved iconic status and has since become synonymous with a wide range of messages involving analogous directives. Some are related to the theme of recruitment as applied to other ventures ("I Want You to Help Congress Find Waste, Fraud, and Abuse," and "I Want You for Sigma Alpha Epsilon"), while others aspire to comedy ("I Want You in Prison" and "I Want You to Bend Over as I Proceed with This Digital Examination"). A few variants even seem to play on Uncle Sam's recognition value for purposes of inversion, such as when an antiwar group designed a ban-

ner to read, "Uncle Sam Wants You to Stop the Warmongers."

Apart from his original link to the service, the character of Uncle Sam refers more generally to the United States, as do other icons from the American flag to the Statue of Liberty. Uncle Sam now appears in a multitude of contexts, and he is even impersonated by costumed figures in parades and at events related to patriotic occasions, such as Independence Day.

See also: FOLK HEROES/LEGENDARY FIGURES; HUMOR, FOLK; INDEPENDENCE DAY/FOURTH OF JULY; LIBERTY, MISS; PARADES; PROTEST IN FOLKLORE; WORLD WAR I; WORLD WAR II.

For Further Reading:

Browne, Ray Broadus. *Frontiers of American Culture*. West Lafayette, Ind.: Purdue University Studies, 1968.

Horwitz, Elinor. *The Bird, the Banner, and Uncle Sam: Images of America in the Folk and Popular Art*. Philadelphia: Lippincott, 1976.

Johnson, Linda Carlson. *Our National Symbols*. Brookfield, Conn.: Millbrook Press, 1992.

Ketchum, Alton. *Uncle Sam: The Man and the Legend*. New York: Hill & Wang, 1959.

Varenne, Hervé, ed. *Symbolizing America*. Lincoln: University of Nebraska Press, 1986.

West, Delno. *Uncle Sam and Old Glory: Symbols of America*. New York: Atheneum Books for Young Readers, 2000.

Underground Railroad As the principal route by which American slaves sought to secure their freedom in the years leading up to the Civil War, the Underground Railroad is the network of connections, techniques, and locations that figure within this historical exodus.

The Underground Railroad consisted of not one path but many, each leading away from slave-holding states to free states in the North and Canada. The network was sustained by a coalition of people who opposed slavery and the Fugitive Slave Act. These participants included free blacks, former slaves, white abolitionists, and even entire spiritual communities, such as the Quakers, who were like-minded on this issue. A number of folk heroes emerged through the Underground Railroad, including Frederick Douglass, Sojourner Truth, and Harriet Tubman.

Of interest to the folklorist is the figurative turn of language used to characterize this system of support for fugitive slaves in the United States. Although the quest for freedom among slaves often inspired references to flight, the Underground Railroad was spoken of in terms of a whole set of metaphors related to rail travel. Slaves on the run were called cargo or, occasionally, passengers. The safe hourses or other hiding places slaves used during their journeys were labeled stations. Those who provided direct aid to fugitives and, in particular, those who led them to freedom, were described as conductors. Others who lent aid were termed agents. This set of analogies helped participants visualize the process by which they would make a stealthy escape to northern states or to Canada. This language was also a code used to protect communications about the movement of fugitives, accomplished by shielding the true content with encoded messages. The masking of such signals was highly effective, and even today there are people who have taken the reference to an Underground Railroad so literally that they hope to spots remnants of its tracks and rails. Others expect to find tunnels or buried passageways. Travel of this kind, however, was typically completed over land on foot or by wagon.

In addition to the railroad metaphor, those involved with the Underground Railroad relied upon folk music as a resource. Just as folk and sacred music had provided a way for slaves to communicate with one another and, through song choice, sequencing, and tone, encode and transmit private information from slave to slave, spirituals contributed to the success of the Underground Railroad. For instance, lyrics that directed listeners to "follow the drinking gourd" could carry a double meaning; in this case, the subtext would be to look for the Big Dipper and Little Dipper, constellations that helped fugitives traveling under cover of night find the direction of true north. Therefore, whereas an outsider might hear merely a slave song, an insider might recognize a tool for celestial navigation.

Furthermore, slaves traveling the Underground Railroad relied upon specific cues placed on the ground. These signals could tip off a traveler whether or not it was safe to proceed. Such clues might take the form of a lantern or a hung quilt bearing the Jacob's Ladder design (later renamed the Underground Railroad design). The presence of such a sign could welcome fugitives, while its absence could alert them to danger or impediment.

In recognition of this portion of America's historical legacy, in 1998, Public Law 105–203, the National Underground Railroad Network to Freedom Act, established a division within the National Park Service to commemorate the Underground Railroad and educate Americans about its contributions to the nation's development.

See also: AFRICAN-AMERICAN FOLKLORE; BROWN, JOHN; CIVIL WAR; CRAFTS, FOLK; DOUGLASS, FREDERICK; FOLKLORISTICS; HISTORICAL EVENTS; LIVING HISTORY MUSEUMS; MUSEUMS, FOLK; MUSIC, FOLK; POLITICS AND FOLKLORE; PROTEST IN FOLKLORE; QUAKER FOLKLORE; SLAVERY; TRUTH, SOJOURNER; TUBMAN, HARRIET.

For Further Reading:

Blight, David, ed. *Passage to Freedom: The Underground Railroad in History and Memory.* Washington, D.C.: Smithsonian Books, 2004.

Bordewich, Fergus. *Bound for Canaan: The Underground Railroad and the War for the Soul of America.* New York: Amistad, 2005.

Gara, Larry. "The Underground Railroad: Legend or Reality?" *Proceedings of the American Philosophical Society* 105, no. 3 (1961): 334–339.

Potter, James E. "Fact and Folklore in the Story of 'John Brown's Cave' and the Underground Railroad in Nebraska," *Nebraska History* 82, no. 2 (2002): 73–88.

Savage, Beth, ed. *African American Historic Places.* New York: Wiley, 1996.

Still, William. *The Underground Rail Road.* Medford, N. J.: Plexus, 2005.

urban folklore   See CITY FOLKLORE.

urban legends   Urban legends are the contemporary stories traded in conversation, often without any knowledge that they have no basis in fact.

The tales are presented as true, and it is typical for the speaker to take pains to establish that they are true rather than merely a rumor or a hoax. The teller may in fact believe the story is true, because it goes through so many retellings that few realize it is fiction. In fact, urban legends usually forward a truth claim by including a believable premise. In addition, the stories often indicate that the experience must be real because it happened to a friend or, more commonly, a "friend of a friend." As a result, the listener tends to believe the story being shared.

Although live oral transmission is the most common route for dissemination of urban legends, they may also travel via fax, e-mail, or photocopy. Urban legends usually have sensational content. They can be funny or spooky, can point a moral or issue a warning. The patterns across retelling for these contemporary legends are so pronounced that, apart from sharing motifs, they can be described as variations on a theme.

An example of such a theme would be the disgruntled customer or employee who seeks revenge against a company or retail concern by distributing a trade secret. In one version of this core idea a customer comes into possession of a proprietary piece of information, such as a prized corporate recipe. Variations on this tale involve the Waldorf-Astoria's recipe for red velvet cake, Neiman-Marcus cookies, and Mrs. Fields' cookies. Within each of these tales, someone who claims to be a mistreated customer tries to exact retribution by revealing important information.

Whether relating the tale of the fate that befalls a hitchhiker or the prophecy of a pending disaster, urban legends command the listener's attention.

See also: CAMP FOLKLORE; COMPUTER FOLKLORE; FABLES; FAIRY TALES; FOLKLORE IN EVERYDAY LIFE; FOLKTALES; FOOD/FOODWAYS; INDUSTRIALIZATION AND FOLKLORE; LEGENDS, FOLK; MYTHS, FOLK; OCCUPATIONAL FOLKLORE; SPEECH, FOLK; URBAN FOLKLORE; XEROX/FAX FOLKLORE.

For Further Reading:

Cunningham, Keith. "Reflections and Regurgitations upon the Well-Known Urban-Belief Tale: The Red Velvet Cake," *Folklore Forum* 5 (1972): 147–148.

Donovan, Pamela. *No Way of Knowing: Crime, Urban Legends, and the Internet.* New York: Routledge, 2004.

Dorson, Richard M. "Is There Folk in the City?" In *The Urban Experience and Folk Tradition*, edited by Americo Parades and Ellen J. Stekert. 22–64. Austin: University of Texas Press, 1971.

Genge, N. E. *Urban Legends: The As Complete as One Could Be Guide to Modern Myths.* New York: Three Rivers Press, 2000.

Roeper, Richard. *Urban Legends: The Truth behind All Those Deliciously Entertaining Myths That Are Absolutely, Positively, 100 Percent Not True.* Franklin Lakes, N.J.: Career Press, 1999.

Turner, Patricia. *I Heard It through the Grapevine: Rumor in African-American Culture.* Berkeley: University of California Press, 1993.

Utah folklore   See FOLKLORE STUDIES; GHOST TOWNS; GOLD RUSH, THE; JAPANESE-AMERICAN INTERNMENT; LONGABAUGH, HARRY (SUNDANCE KID); MORMON FOLKLORE; PARKER, ROBERT LEROY (BUTCH CASSIDY); TRANSCONTINENTAL RAILROAD; WESTERN REGIONAL FOLKLORE.

V

Valentine's Day, Saint See SAINT VALENTINE'S DAY.

vampire While hardly original to the United States, the dark figure of the vampire is nonetheless prominent among the monsters populating American folk narratives.

Typically, depictions of the vampire reference a reanimated corpse that surfaces at night to feed on human blood. Vampires belong to a wider category of figures associated with the folklore of human blood, including Bloody Mary. Such tales typically associate fear with the sight and/or loss of human blood.

While most readers might associate the vampire with Bram Stoker's 1897 novel, *Dracula*, folk beliefs and legends of the vampire precede this work considerably. Along with scary stories of the vampire's activities is a rich lore of protection from the vampire's threats. These beliefs include both temporary measures, such as warding-off techniques, and more permanent solutions, such as strategies for killing the undead figure. Perhaps the most familiar act of prevention is the wearing of garlic, somehow supposed to shield the wearer from a vampire's approach. Ending the power of the vampire usually calls for more extreme action, such as driving a stake through its heart, presumably while the vampire is at rest and between feedings.

The vampire began as an image of horror within folktales but later permeated popular culture to such an extent that depictions of vampires are commonplace in America, especially surrounding the celebration of Halloween/All Hallows' Eve and other costume rituals.

See also: BELIEFS, FOLK; BLOODY MARY; CHANGELINGS; FOLKLORE IN EVERYDAY LIFE; HALLOWEEN/ALL HALLOWS' EVE; LEGENDS, FOLK; MONSTERS; SUPERNATURAL; SUPERSTITION; URBAN LEGENDS; WEREWOLF.

For Further Reading:

Bell, Michael. *Food for the Dead: On the Trail of New England's Vampires.* New York: Carroll & Graff, 2001.

Dundes, Alan. *Bloody Mary in the Mirror: Essays in Psychoanalytic Folkloristics.* Jackson: University Press of Mississippi, 2002.

Houppert, Karen. *The Curse: Confronting the Last Unmentionable Taboo: Menstruation.* New York: Farrar, Straus & Giroux, 1999.

Knapp, Mary, and Herbert Knapp. *One Potato, Two Potato … : The Secret Education of American Children.* New York: W. W. Norton, 1976.

Schoemaker, George H., ed. *The Emergence of Folklore in Everyday Life: A Fieldguide and Sourcebook.* Bloomington, Ind.: Trickster Press, 1990.

Sutton-Smith, Brian, and Jay Mechling, eds. *Children's Folklore: A Sourcebook.* Logan: Utah State University Press, 1999.

vanishing hitchhiker See BLOODY MARY; LEGENDS, URBAN.

Van Winkle, Rip (legendary) The title character of Washington Irving's classic and fablelike yarn "Rip Van Winkle" awakens from a nap only to realize that fully 20 years have passed during the time of his rest.

Rip Van Winkle is a family man well regarded in his Catskills community. He helps neighbors and entertains area children with his stories. Although his relationship with his wife is somewhat contentious, Rip finds respite in trips to the Village Inn, where he joins in story sessions with other similarly disposed men. His other retreat is to take his gun and his dog and go hunting in the countryside.

On one such occasion, Rip makes the acquaintance of a stranger who addresses him by name. After helping the stranger transport a keg of liquor, Rip observes a game of ninepin played by a group of men who, as the first stranger does, wear antiquated Dutch attire. They pass some time partaking of the spirits, until Rip withdraws from the group to nap beneath a tree back where he first happened upon the burdened stranger. When Rip wakes, he gradually realizes from his own appearance and that of his environment that his nap was of inordinately long duration. He emerges from sleep to find his friends gone and his wife deceased. Rip goes to live with one of his daughters, now an adult. He subsequently resumes his regular place at the Village Inn, now with an even more remarkable story to offer his listeners.

In addition to functioning as the protagonist of a beloved story, the character of Rip Van Winkle has come to symbolize someone who resists change and clings to the past. His curious fate serves as a light-handed but cautionary tale of what awaits someone who avoids conflict and retreats from change. The story of Rip Van Winkle has been retold and recast countless times to dramatize this point in a manner that meets the needs of each era.

See also: AGING AND FOLKLORE; DUTCH-AMERICAN FOLKLORE; FABLES; FOLK HEROES/LEGENDARY FIGURES; FOLKLORE IN AMERICAN LITERATURE; FOLKTALES; GAMES AND PASTIMES; GENDER AND FOLKLORE; HORSEMAN, HEADLESS; HUMOR, FOLK; IRVING, WASHINGTON; NORTHEASTERN REGIONAL FOLKLORE; REGION, FOLK.

For Further Reading:

Blakemore, Steven. "Family Resemblances: The Texts and Contexts of 'Rip Van Winkle,'" *Early American Literature* 35, no. 2 (2000): 187–212.

Haberly, David T. "Form and Function in the New World Legend." In *Do the Americas Have a Common Literature?* edited by Gustavo Pérez Firmat, 42–61. Durham, N.C.: Duke University Press, 1990.

Seelye, John. "Root and Branch: Washington Irving and American Humor," *Nineteenth-Century Fiction* 38, no. 4 (March 1984): 415–425.

Wells, Robert V. "While Rip Napped: Social Change in Late Eighteenth-Century New York," *New York History* 70, no. 1 (January 1990): 5–23.

Vermont folklore See ALLEN, ETHAN; NORTHEASTERN REGIONAL FOLKLORE; REVOLUTIONARY WAR; YANKEE DOODLE.

vernacular culture Vernacular culture bridges the distance between traditional folklore and pop culture.

That is, when American folklore study began, the emphasis was almost entirely on rural and preindustrial customs and patterns of social life. Since that time, many folklorists have revised their working definitions of folklore such that urban, industrial, and even, in some cases, mass cultural examples may be included. In something of the way that the folklife movement stretched scholars' thinking about the legitimate objects of study within American folklore, vernacular culture challenges them to rethink assumptions about American folklore as chiefly agrarian in character, remote in time, and entirely hand-wrought in fabrication or use.

Such matters prove controversial, as some folklorists prefer to keep folklore study more tightly focused than others. Among those who are currently most enthusiastic about the concept of vernacular culture are researchers in American folk architecture. In particular, members of the Vernacular Architecture Forum (VAF) embrace the notion of the vernacular as a field of multidisciplinary explorations conducted by folklorists and interested others. While much of their work addresses the traditional purview of the folklorist, the organization's configuration permits inquiry into more modern topics in the field, such as the cultural significance of garden-planting patterns, the history of linoleum flooring, and the preservation of ethnic neighborhoods, such as Chinatowns.

As is the case with American folklore, vernacular culture has its roots firmly in local values and customs, but in choosing objects of study, vernacular culture scholars do not restrict themselves to remote, rural, and preindustrial folk practices.

See also: ARCHITECTURE, FOLK; ART, FOLK; CHINESE-AMERICAN FOLKLORE; CITY FOLKLORE; CULTURE, FOLK; ETHNICITY; FLOWERS; FOLKLIFE; GARDENING; HISTORIC PRESERVATION; INDUSTRIALIZATION AND FOLKLORE; KITSCH; LIVING HISTORY MUSEUMS; MATERIAL CULTURE; MUSEUMS, FOLK; PHOTOGRAPHY, FOLK; TERMS.

For Further Reading:

Alanen, Arnold R., and Robert Z. Melnick, eds. *Preserving Cultural Landscapes in America*. Baltimore: John Hopkins University Press, 2000.

Brown, Fahamisha P. *Performing the Word: African American Poetry as Vernacular Culture*. New Brunswick, N.J.: Rutgers University Press, 1999.

Green, Archie. *Torching the Fink Books and Other Essays on Vernacular Culture*. Chapel Hill: University of North Carolina Press, 2001.

Upton, Dell, and John Michael Vlach. *Common Places: Readings in American Vernacular Architecture*. Athens: University of Georgia Press, 1986.

Vesey, Denmark (c. 1767–1822) Denmark Vesey is one of numerous U.S. slaves who participated in plans to rebel against, not merely seek escape from, their involuntary servitude.

Although it is impossible to know the inner lives led by members of America's slave population, it is difficult to imagine that any slave endured a lifetime of captivity and violent mistreatment without entertaining thoughts of escape or retaliation. Indeed, the history of U.S. slavery suggests that there were many contemplated and attempted insurrections, and several of these were implemented. The 1831 rebellion in Southampton County, Virginia, led by Nat Turner was one such instance. Not all planned actions by slaves progressed that far; some, such as the conspiracy led by Denmark Vesey in the Charleston, South Carolina, area some nine years before Turner's, were foiled before action could be taken.

As was Turner, Vesey was a slave who, despite the adverse conditions of slavery, managed to learn to read and write. Everything he read, from the Declaration of Independence to the Bible, strengthened his opposition to slavery and his arguments for its abolition. He attempted to sharpen a resolve among the slaves of Charleston, both urban and rural, that they would no longer endure such treatment. The insurrection he helped design was intended as a culmination of this resistance and was to involve hundreds of African Americans from the region. Objectives for the action involved seizure of the Charleston arsenal.

As was the case with quite a few such efforts, the Vesey plans were betrayed by fearful coconspirators. Nonetheless, word of the intended action spread quickly, through slave and slave-holder populations alike. Among whites, it inspired tighter restrictions on slaves and increased vigilante-style enforcement. Among African Americans, it appears to have inspired thoughts of possibilities that, while not realized in 1822 Charleston, would nonetheless find their moment in the fullness of time. Tales of such rebellions, contemplated or realized, are a staple of African-American folk history, from music to oral culture.

Therefore, while some slaves confined their hopes to sheer survival or plans of escape, such as through the Underground Railroad, others turned their energies toward plots of resistance, made more bold by the efforts of figures such as Gabriel Prosser, Nat Turner, and Denmark Vesey.

See also: CIVIL WAR; CONSPIRACY FOLKLORE; FOLK HEROES/LEGENDARY FIGURES; MUSIC, FOLK; ORAL FOLKLORE; PROTEST IN FOLKLORE; SLAVERY; SOUTHERN REGIONAL FOLKLORE; TURNER, NAT; UNDERGROUND RAILROAD.

For Further Reading:

Aptheker, Herbert. *American Negro Slave Revolts.* New York: Columbia University Press, 1943.

Egerton, Douglas. *He Shall Go out Free.* Madison, Wis.: Madison House Press, 1999.

Robertson, David. *Denmark Vesey.* New York: Knopf, 1999.

———. *Denmark Vesey: The Buried Story of America's Largest Slave Rebellion and the Man Who Led It.* New York: Vintage, 2000.

Veterans Day Veterans Day was first dedicated as a recognition of those who contributed national service through the armed forces during World War I.

This holiday was established by President Woodrow Wilson on November 11, 1919. While Veterans Day was originally observed on November 11 each year, its present observance occurs on the fourth Monday in October. The timing of the original day was initially intended to mark the anniversary of the armistice of World War I. Indeed, Veterans Day was once known as Armistice Day.

Early practices associated with the occasion include observing two minutes of shared silence at 11:00 A.M., recalling the ceasefire for World War I. In a related action, Arlington National Cemetery established the tomb of America's Unknown Soldier in 1921. This burial site entombed an unidentified serviceman from the conflicts associated with World War I. This memorial symbolized the many who perished and could never be identified or returned to their families. Establishment of the Tomb of the Unknown Soldier dramatized the sense in which the nation became the family to any member of the American service meeting this fate. In 1927, the custom of flag display on Armistice Day was formalized. It became a legal holiday in the nation's capital on May 15, 1938.

On June 1, 1954, President Dwight Eisenhower renamed the observance Veterans Day to make it more inclusive of those men and women who had served at any time in the nation's life. On such national days of remembrance as Memorial Day and Veterans Day, ceremonies such as wreath placement are conducted at the Tomb of the Unknown.

Today, Veterans Day typically involves parades, ceremonies, placement of small flags or other tributes on the graves of veterans, and other acts of respect for those who have served the United States.

See also: BURIAL CUSTOMS; CEMETERY FOLKLORE; CIVIL WAR; FLAG DAY; HOLIDAYS/OBSERVANCES; MEMORIAL DAY; PARADES; REVOLUTIONARY WAR; VIETNAM WAR; WORLD WAR I; WORLD WAR II.

For Further Reading:

Cohen, Hennig, and Tristram Potter Coffin, eds. *The Folklore of American Holidays.* Detroit: Gale, 1987.

Festivals and Holidays. New York: Macmillan Library Reference USA, 1999.

Moehn, Heather. *World Holidays: A Watts Guide for Children.* New York: F. Watts, 2000.

Myers, Robert. *Celebrations: The Complete Book of American Holidays.* Garden City, N.Y.: Doubleday, 1972.

Santino, Jack. *All around the Year: Holidays and Celebrations in American Life*. Urbana: University of Illinois Press, 1994.

Sechrist, Elizabeth Hough. *Red Letter Days: A Book of Holiday Customs*. Philadelphia: Macrae Smith, 1965.

Sorensen, Lynda. *Veterans Day*. Vero Beach, Fla.: Rourke Press, 1994.

Spies, Karen Bornemann. *Our National Holidays*. Brookfield, Conn.: Millbrook Press, 1992.

Vietnam War   Although the war was never officially declared, America's involvement in the Vietnam conflict, especially during the years from 1961 to 1975, is routinely described today as the Vietnam War.

As with other armed conflicts in which the United States has been involved, the Vietnam War had comparable military folklore, complete with cadence chants, decorated helmets, and jokes told at the expense of the government's red tape or the commanding officers' failings. Unlike other wars, however, that in Vietnam was the subject of unprecedented levels of ambivalence for Americans at home. Rather than receiving complete home front support for the war effort, Vietnam War soldiers and veterans knew that many of their fellow citizens questioned the rightness of the war or America's involvement in it. In fact, some of the soldiers and veterans themselves shared these misgivings and objections, expressed through such organizations as Vietnam Veterans against the War.

Before soldiers even entered the war zone, they underwent a process of induction and training that was itself the subject of lore. Since many soldiers entered combat through the military draft, there was also a population of draft-age individuals who sought to elude military service. Sometimes called draft dodgers, these potential soldiers failed to report for duty, often because they had fled the country for destinations such as Canada. Other reluctant draftees traded tips about how to fail the physical examination required for induction in the military, whether on physiological or psychological grounds.

Those who went to fight in Vietnam were confronted with a harsh set of combat realities, whose results were often expressed as a "kill ratio." Oral histories conducted with Vietnam War soldiers reveal the uncertainties of such an existence. This tension resulted in a tendency to demonize the enemy, whom soldiers commonly referred to as the "VC" (for Viet Cong) or "Charlie." These antagonisms were also evident in the treatment of the bodies of fallen opponents, which were sometimes mutilated and severed body parts such as ears taken and worn as trophies of kills.

Under these circumstances, soldiers were more than usually eager to conclude their tours of duty. There were numerous terms to describe this situation, including keeping track of "DEROS": *date of estimated return from overseas.* Those who were nearing the end of their terms were described as "short." Such slang served as a shorthand among those in combat and formed the basis of other verbal lore, such as graffiti, jokes, and sayings. In addition, participants in the conflict frequently kept countdown calendars that recorded the number of days of service remaining for an individual.

Complicating the reentry period for veterans was the fact that the country was not accustomed to emerging from war without clear victory. The opposition to the war at home made it even more difficult for soldiers returning home. Whereas people returning from earlier wars received a hero's welcome and ticker tape parades, veterans of the Vietnam War were greeted unceremoniously. In some cases, they were even taunted by those stateside who had opposed the war and America's involvement in it. This hostility was the source of the folk figure of the "spitting hippie." According to stories, soldiers stepped off the plane in America only to be spit upon by antiwar youth.

The brutality of combat and the length of time soldiers spent overseas also left many soldiers with profound posttraumatic stress.

Perceptions of these aftereffects resulted in the image of the volatile Vietnam War veteran. This image was responsible for even more difficulties for veterans returning home from the war, as they were regarded with suspicion and fear.

See also: HIPPIES; HISTORICAL EVENTS; HUMOR, FOLK; PARADES; PROTEST IN FOLKLORE; SPEECH, FOLK; VETERANS DAY.

For Further Reading:

Burke, Carol. *Camp All-American, Hanoi Jane, and the High-and-Tight: Gender, Folklore, and Changing Military Culture.* Boston: Beacon Press, 2004.

Dewhurst, C. Kurt. "Pleiku Jackets, Tour Jackets, and Working Jackets: The Letter Sweaters of War," *Journal of American Folklore* 101, no. 399 (winter 1988): 48–52.

Fish, Lydia. "General Edward G. Lansckle and the Folksongs of Americans in the Vietnam War," *Journal of American Folklore* 102, no. 406 (fall 1989): 390–411.

Heineman, Kenneth J. *Campus Wars: The Peace Movement at American State Universities in the Vietnam Era.* New York: New York University Press, 1993.

Lembcke, Jerry. *The Spitting Image: Myth, Memory, and the Legacy of Vietnam.* New York: New York University Press, 1998.

O'Brien, Tim. *If I Die in a Combat Zone: Box Me Up and Ship Me Home.* New York: Delacorte Press, 1992.

Schechter, Harold, and Jonna G. Semeiks. "Leatherstocking in 'Nam: Rambo, Platoon, and the American Frontier Myth," *Journal of Popular Culture* 24, no. 4 (1991): 17–25.

Stevens, Michael E. *Voices from Vietnam.* Madison: State Historical Society of Wisconsin, 1996.

Village, Greenfield   See GREENFIELD VILLAGE HENRY FORD MUSEUM, AND.

Village, Old Sturbridge   See STURBRIDGE VILLAGE, OLD.

Virginia folklore   See APPALACHIAN FOLKLORE; BOONE, DANIEL; BROWN, JOHN; BROWN, STERLING ALLEN; CIVIL WAR; COLONIAL WILLIAMSBURG; EMANCIPATION (PROCLAMATION) DAY; HENRY, PATRICK; JONES, JOHN PAUL; POCAHONTAS; SOUTHERN REGIONAL FOLKLORE; STYRON, WILLIAM; TURNER, NAT; WASHINGTON, BOOKER TALIAFERRO.

voodoo/hoodoo   Most commonly associated with the city of New Orleans, American voodoo traditions have intrigued folklorists since the days of Zora Neale Hurston.

Although many may think of it as witchcraft, voodoo is actually a folk religion. It has its origins in African and Haitian belief systems. Enslaved Africans performed rituals that honored both nature and the spirits of the dead. When slaves were transported to the United States, they carried their spiritual traditions along with them. In places such as New Orleans, voodoo practitioners had to contend with slave holders who felt threatened by their religious beliefs. Some slaves were forbidden their forms of worship, while others were made to convert to other faiths such as Catholicism.

Among the best-known voodoo figures in New Orleans was Marie Laveau, a free black born in 1794 in Santo Domingo. Considered by many to be the queen of voodoo, Laveau was responsible for blending African traditions with Catholic ones. Although she was a hairdresser and later a bar owner by trade, Laveau became known for her powers and the ceremonies she conducted as a voodoo priestess until her death in approximately 1881. People from all walks of life called upon her for help in achieving their goals and fulfilling their desires. Even today, many visit her gravesite in Saint Louis Cemetery, leaving offerings and seeking blessings from Laveau. She is rumored to haunt a variety of locations around New Orleans, including her residences in life. Some believe her ghost rises each year to lead the Saint John's Eve ceremony, which coincides with the summer solstice.

Folklorists have long been interested in uncovering voodoo beliefs and practices. During her activities in folklore studies, the writer Zora Neale Hurston studied it long enough to complete the process of becoming a voodoo priestess. Hurston recorded her experiences in this regard in publications such as *Mules and Men* and *Tell My Horse*. Many other scholars have researched the topic since.

With their graveyard rituals and nighttime ceremonies, voodoo practitioners have figured among the most sensational figures in American folk religion.

See also: CABLE, WASHINGTON GEORGE; CAJUN FOLKLORE; CEMETERY FOLKLORE; CHESNUTT, CHARLES WADDELL; CONJURE/CONJURING; DEATH; FOLKLORE IN EVERYDAY LIFE; GHOSTS; GHOST STORIES; HURSTON, ZORA NEALE; IBO LANDING; MAGIC; MEDICINE, FOLK; PREDICTION; RELIGION, FOLK; SLAVERY; SUPERSTITION; WITCHCRAFT, SALEM.

For Further Reading:

Cosentino, Donald. "Who Is That Fellow in the Many-Colored Cap? Transformations of Eshu in Old and New World Mythologies," *Journal of American Folklore* 100, no. 397 (summer 1987): 261–275.

Hyatt, Harry Middleton. *Hoodoo-Conjuration-Witchcraft-Rootwork.* Hannibal, Mo.: Western, 1974.

Jacobs, Claude F. "Folk for Whom? Tourist Guidebooks, Local Color, and the Spiritual Churches of New Orleans," *Journal of American Folklore* 114, no. 453 (summer 2001): 309–330.

Mitchell, Faith. *Hoodoo Medicine: Gullah Herbal Remedies.* Columbia, S.C.: Summerhouse Press, 1999.

Pelton, Robert W. *The Complete Book of Voodoo.* New York: G. P. Putnam's Sons, 1972.

Snow, Loudell F. "Con Men and Conjure Men: A Ghetto Image," *Literature and Medicine* 2 (1983): 45–78.

Snow, Loudell F. "'I Was Born Just Exactly with the Gift': An Interview with a Voodoo Practitioner," *Journal of American Folklore* 86, no. 341 (summer 1973): 272–281.

Speisman, Barbara. "Voodoo as Symbol in Jonah's Gourd Vine," In *Zora in Florida*, edited by Steve Glassman and Kathryn Lee Seidel, 86–93. Orlando: University of Central Florida, Press, 1991.

Walker, Alice See BAMBARA, TONI CADE; HURSTON, ZORA NEALE.

war and folklore See CIVIL WAR; REVOLUTIONARY WAR; VIETNAM WAR; WORLD WAR I; WORLD WAR II.

War of 1812 See ANGLO-AMERICAN FOLKLORE; CROCKETT, DAVY; GHOST STORIES; IRVING, WASHINGTON; OZARKS FOLKLORE; UNCLE SAM.

Washington, Booker Taliaferro (1856–1915) Booker Taliaferro Washington was a late 19th- and early 20th-century leader in the African-American struggle for civil rights.

Remembered today as Booker T. Washington, he was born into slavery on a Virginia tobacco farm on April 5, 1856. He was the child of a union between a slave mother and a white father who never claimed his son. Washington came of age in the era of America's Civil War and its aftermath. While slavery was no longer legal in the United States, the conditions for African Americans remained arduous during Reconstruction as newly freed former slaves battled to achieve economic security and political autonomy.

Washington's contributions to this endeavor involved espousing a philosophy of self-help through education and professional development. Washington acted on that philosophy, attending Hampton Institute from 1872 to 1875. This experience positioned him for various careers in which he participated over his lifetime, including teaching and public speaking.

Washington advocated practical education for African Americans so that they might find more and better employment and the opportunities it would create. Toward that end, Washington established a school designed to promote such learning. On July 4, 1881, a date that recalls the nation's independence, he founded what was then called the Tuskegee Normal and Industrial Institute in Alabama. This institution is now known as Tuskegee University.

At the center point of the campus stands a monument to Washington, entitled *Lifting the Veil*. This figural sculpture shows a man raising a cloth from over the eyes of a crouching man. This statue symbolizes the view of education as itself a form and vehicle of emancipation. Inscribed on this monument are the following words of tribute: "He lifted the veil of ignorance from his people and pointed the way to progress through education and industry."

Washington's legacy is also noted in an array of folk and popular forms. In 1940, for example, Washington became the first African American to appear on a United States postage stamp. Not all such allusions are entirely celebratory because some have found Washington's stance too accommodationist, because they favor protest and confrontation of racial inequality. One such perspective appears in African-American literature. Ralph Waldo Ellison's novel *Invisible Man* features a campus similar to Tuskegee, a statue like *Lifting the Veil*, and a character called "The Founder" who closely resembles Washington. The presence of the literary portrait is significant, even if its message is not entirely flattering.

While his views on race and class proved distinct from those of other leaders, such as W. E. B. DuBois, Booker Taliaferro Washington emphasized the sense in which education is one possession that cannot be stripped away by oppression.

See also: AFRICAN-AMERICAN FOLKLORE; CIVIL RIGHTS MOVEMENT; CIVIL WAR; DUBOIS, W. E. B.; ELLISON, RALPH WALDO; FOLK HEROES/ LEGENDARY FIGURES; OCCUPATIONAL FOLKLORE; PROTEST IN FOLKLORE; SLAVERY; SOUTHERN REGIONAL FOLKLORE; TRICKSTER.

For Further Reading:

Denton, Virginia Lantz. *Booker T. Washington and the Adult Education Movement.* Gainesville: University Press of Florida, 1993.

McElroy, Frederick. "Booker T. Washington as Literary Trickster," *Southern Folklore* 49, no. 2 (1992): 89–107.

Washington, George (1732–1799) As the first president of the United States and the purported "Father of Our Country," George Washington is a figure surrounded by considerable American folklore.

Indeed, Washington has assumed a nearly mythic status among America's presidents, due largely to the honorific accounts of a host of historians and biographers. Chief among these champions was Mason Locke "Parson" Weems, a former minister and book salesman whose 1800 biography originated some of the central tales surrounding Washington's character.

These include the by-now ubiquitous story about Washington's cutting down the cherry tree, his tossing of a silver dollar across the Potomac River, and his assertion "I cannot tell a lie." With the efforts of writers such as Weems, Washington assumed a place of lasting honor in American history and lore.

Although his career was more controversial than his current state of national veneration might suggest, tributes to him are legion. In a manner almost royal, Washington's birthday was celebrated even during his lifetime. February 22, 1800, just a few months after his death, was proclaimed a national day of mourning. In 1832, the centenary of Washington's birth was the subject of an extended celebration, spanning February 22 until Thanksgiving. The centennial also resulted in the renaming of many streets and squares in Washington's honor. After construction delays due to the Civil War and the like, the Washington Monument, a 555 1/2-foot tall Egyptian obelisk designed by the architect Robert Mills, was dedicated on February 21, 1885. Construction had begun in 1848 but did not conclude until 37 years later.

In addition to national observances of George Washington's Birthday, various other customs recognize the first president's memory. Each Christmas, for example, there is a pageant to dramatize Washington's historic crossing of the Delaware River. On Washington's Birthday, it is usual for the U.S. Senate to read Washington's Farewell Address. Also on this day, the Massachusetts governor has been known to participate in a five-hour-long handshaking ritual, with the greetings extended in Washington's honor.

While the accuracy of these representations of Washington may not be consistent, the respect for the man and his career seems as solid as Washington's countenance carved into the face of Mount Rushmore, alongside those of Abraham Lincoln, Thomas Jefferson, and Theodore Roosevelt.

See also: CHRISTMAS; DEATH; FOLK HEROES/LEGENDARY FIGURES; LINCOLN, ABRAHAM; PRESIDENTS'

Day; Revolutionary War; Roosevelt, Franklin Delano; Roosevelt, Theodore.

For Further Reading:

Kahler, Gerard Edward. "Washington in Glory, America in Tears: The Nation Mourns the Death of George Washington, 1799–1800," *Dissertation Abstracts International, Section A: The Humanities and Social Sciences* 64, no. 5 (November 2003): 1722. [DA3091430, College of William and Mary, 2003].

Meyers, Jeffrey. *America's Famous and Historic Trees: From George Washington's Tulip Poplar to Elvis Presley's Pin Oak.* Boston: Houghton Mifflin, 2001.

Myers, Robert J. *Celebrations: The Complete Book of American Holidays.* Garden City, N.Y.: Doubleday, 1972.

Washington's Birthday   See Presidents' Day.

Washington folklore   See Bigfoot/Sasquatch; Chinese-American folklore; Father's Day; Japanese-American internment; Joseph, Chief; Lewis, Meriwether, and William Clark; Northwest regional folklore; Washington, George.

weather folklore   Although it is not the product of human effort or expression, weather forms the focus of a rich array of American folklore.

Most of these bits of lore consist of individual and collective efforts to forecast, interpret, and in some cases influence local climate.

Some professions and trades have an exceptionally close relationship to weather and weather changes, and so members of these groups have a disproportionate interest in the topic. Farming, seafaring, and similarly weather-influenced occupations each have some lore of this kind. For example, within maritime folklore, there are numerous proverbs and sayings about what certain weather signs indicate. One such instance is the familiar rhyming proverb "Red sky at night, sailors' delight. / Red sky at morning, sailors take warning." Those whose livelihoods, and sometimes lives, depend upon an awareness of the environment and weather pass on their insights and beliefs to others with folk speech of this sort.

For farmers, weather is an integral part of the planting, growth, and harvesting schedules. Sharp variations in light, wind, or moisture conditions can compromise the crops and with them, the farmer's income and community's food supply. As a consequence, farmers have many beliefs about how subtle cues in the natural world serve as portents of weather conditions or changes. The appearance of the sky, the behavior of animals, and even the postures of plants are believed to foretell weather conditions of importance to the land's cultivators. Because of the importance of rain to agriculture, lore surrounding the portents of rain (such as a ringed Moon) prove especially important, and there are even some rituals used to summon needed rain. In addition, it is customary for farmers to produce or use almanacs, published annually, suggesting how long and harsh the coming winter may be, and how dry or small the year's yield may be.

American holidays and observances reflect this preoccupation with the land, including Groundhog Day, an annual occasion for predicting the time of winter's end and spring's arrival. Similarly, customs and beliefs associated with other holidays and ceremonies involve notions of luck and fortune based upon weather events. Examples include the beliefs surrounding the implications of fair or foul weather on one's wedding day.

In addition, some folk beliefs specify that bodily symptoms can effectively forecast weather. For example, those who have achy joints (a condition sometimes described as rheumatism) sometimes sense changes in the coming weather because of shifts in their pain levels.

While weather lore is hardly unique to America, the nation does have its share of both transplanted and homegrown ideas about how the weather affects people's lives and predicts their prospects. From proverbs to rituals, American folklore regarding weather is a rich narrative tradition. Indeed, in a saying often attributed to Samuel Langhorne Clemens, the speaker remarks, "Everybody talks about the weather, but nobody does anything about it."

See also: APRIL FOOL'S DAY; BELIEFS, FOLK; EASTER; FOLKLORE IN EVERYDAY LIFE; FRANKLIN, BENJAMIN; GROUNDHOG DAY; LUCK/FORTUNE; MARITIME FOLKLORE; PREDICTION; PROVERBS; SUPERSTITION; WEDDING/MARRIAGE FOLKLORE.

For Further Reading:

Basgöz, Ilhan. "Frogs, Toads, and Rain Rituals." In *Folklore on Two Continents: Essays in Honor of Linda Dégh*, edited by Nikolai Burlakoff et al., 104–111. Bloomington, Ind.: Trickster Press, 1980.

Davis, Hubert, ed. *A January Fog Will Freeze a Hog, and Other Weather Folklore.* New York: Crown, 1977.

Inwards, Richard. *Weather Lore: The Unique Bedside Book.* New York: Rider, 1950.

Long, Eleanor R. "How the Dog Got Its Days: A Skeptical Inquiry into Traditional Star and Weather Lore," *Western Folklore* 43, no. 4 (October 1984): 256–264.

Resnick, Abraham. *Due to the Weather: Ways the Elements Affect Our Lives.* Westport, Conn.: Greenwood, 2000.

Sloane, Eric. *Folklore of American Weather.* New York: Duell, Sloan & Pearce, 1963.

Strauss, Sarah, and Ben Orlove. *Weather, Climate, Culture.* New York: Berg, 2003.

Watson, Benjamin A. *Acts of God: The Old Farmer's Almanac Guide to Weather and Natural Disasters.* New York: Random House, 1993.

Widdowson, John D. A. "Form and Function in Traditional Explanations of Weather Phenomena." In *Folklore Studies in Honour of Herbert Halpert: A Festschrift*, edited by Kenneth S. Goldstein et al., 353–376. St. John's: Memorial University of Newfoundland, 1980.

Wolff, Barbara. *Evening Gray, Morning Red: A Ready-to-Read Handbook of American Weather Wisdom.* New York: Macmillan, 1976.

Wurtele, M. G. "Some Thoughts on Weather Lore," *Folklore* 82 (1971): 292–303.

weather vanes   See ART, FOLK.

weaving   See FOLK CRAFTS.

wedding/marriage folklore   Few moments in the life cycle carry the symbolic weight of ritual and custom in America of the occasion of marriage. From the engagement phase, to the prenuptial activities, to the ceremony itself, wedding lore is a rich cultural tradition in the United States.

The process begins with a couple's agreement to wed, at which point they are engaged to be married. It is customary for the groom-to-be to present the bride-to-be with an engagement ring as a gift in contemplation of marriage. Diamond rings are the most common form. Later, when the betrothed pair marries, each wears a wedding band on the third finger of the left hand, where the engagement ring is also worn. These rings symbolize a noble and everlasting bond.

Between the engagement and the sealing of marriage vows, several other events may help recognize the importance of the occasion, such as a bridal shower or a bachelor's party. With such celebrations, the bride's and groom's friends and relatives mark the transition into married life.

Many superstitions or taboos surround the wedding day. Most of these folk beliefs concern notions of what will produce luck, prosperity, harmony, or fertility for the bride and groom. The groom should not see the bride in her wedding dress or see her at all prior to the ceremony on their wedding day. The bride should not make her own wedding cake, sew her own gown, assume her married name before the wedding, or model her gown prior to the service.

Additional folk beliefs are used to interpret the portents of the wedding couple, whether good or bad. For example, thunder during the wedding ceremony is said to mean that the couple will produce no children. Rain on the wedding day, however, is believed to be lucky for the bride and groom's future.

Other customs include wedding attire. Traditional brides were white gowns and veils over their faces. The color of the dress symbolizes the bride's purity, and the veil is believed to be a means of protection against the evil eye. It is considered good luck for the bride to include in her outfit "something old, something new, something borrowed, and something blue." In some cases, the bride places a coin inside one of her shoes to ensure the couple's wealth and/or sugar in one of her gloves to promote a sweet relationship.

Location and timing of ceremony are important, and weddings are usually conducted within faith communities. During the ceremony, bride and groom exchange vows and then rings, symbolizing endless union. Depending upon the couple's cultural beliefs, they may engage in other rituals. African Americans may engage in such traditions as "jumping the broom," a practice dating back to slavery days when formal weddings were not permitted among slaves. Similarly, Jewish American grooms may break a glass at the service's end to symbolize luck and longevity for the marriage. As the couple leaves the wedding site, it is customary for guests to throw uncooked rice at them to usher in a fertile and prosperous marriage. In modern weddings, the traditional rice is sometimes replaced with bird seed or soap bubbles.

After the ceremony, the wedding party and their guests typically gather for a reception, at which all celebrate the joyful occasion. Food, drink, toasts, and dances add to the festivities, with the first dance reserved for the wedding couple. Other rituals associated with the wedding reception include the bride's tossing her bouquet over her shoulder to an assembled group of unmarried women in attendance, with the suggestion that the one who catches the bridal bouquet will be the next woman to marry. In another traditional practice, the couple join to

cut the first slice of the wedding cake and then take turns feeding it to each other. This shared act represents the spirit of collaboration between bride and groom.

After marriage, the occasion of a couple's wedding is recalled annually with wedding anniversaries, observances that echo the deeply held folk beliefs about fidelity, family, and love that characterize wedding/marriage folklore.

See also: ANNIVERSARIES; BELIEFS, FOLK; CHILDBIRTH/PREGNANCY FOLKLORE; COURTSHIP/DATING FOLKLORE; EVIL EYE; FAMILY FOLKLORE; FLOWERS; FOLKLORE IN EVERYDAY LIFE; FOOD/FOODWAYS; LUCK/FORTUNE; MATERIAL CULTURE; PREDICTION; RELIGION, FOLK; RITES OF PASSAGE; SAINT VALENTINE'S DAY; SOLSTICE; SUPERSTITION; TOASTS/DRINKING; WEATHER FOLKLORE.

For Further Reading:
Baker, Margaret. *Wedding Customs and Folklore.* Vancouver, Canada: David and Charles, 1977.
Dundes, Alan. "'Jumping the Broom': On the Origin and Meaning of an African American Wedding Custom," *Journal of American Folklore* 109, no. 433 (summer 1996): 324–329.
Franklin, Rosalind. *The Superstitions Bride: A Book of Wedding Lore.* West Sussex, England: Diggory Press, 2005.
Jones, Leslie. *Happy Is the Bride the Sun Shines on: Wedding Beliefs, Customs, and Traditions.* Chicago: Contemporary Books, 1995.
Pershing, Linda. "'His Wife Seized His Prize and Cut It to Size': Folk and Popular Commentary on Lorena Bobbitt," *NWSA Journal* 8, no. 3 (fall 1996): 1–36.
Post, Elizabeth L. *Emily Post's Complete Book of Wedding Etiquette.* New York: HarperCollins, 1991.
Reuning, Sarah. "Seven Brides for a Single Gown: Communicating through Clothing," *North Carolina Folklore Journal* 47, no. 2 (2000): 135–151.
Vickers, Carol. "Something Old, Something New: Folklore in Matrimony," *Mississippi Folklore Register* 19 (1985): 61–65.

Zeitlin, Steven J. "The Wedding Dance." In *A Celebration of American Family Folklore: Tales and Traditions from the Smithsonian Collection*, edited by Steven J. Zeitlin, Amy J. Kotkin, and Holly Cutting Baker, 213–221. New York: Pantheon, 1982.

Weems, Mason Locke "Parson" See WASHINGTON, GEORGE.

Weeping Woman (legendary) The figure of the Weeping Woman, also known as "La Llorona," is a well-known character within Chicano folklore.

As this legend of the American Southwest would have it, the character at the center of this story was a widow who, in her eagerness to remarry, went to the river and drowned her children from her first marriage. Now a ghost herself, the Weeping Woman is said to be a restless spirit one can still encounter at the side of a river. It is said that in her everlasting regret and grief, she goes looking for her lost children.

In folklore, the figure of the Weeping Woman is both a morality tale for women and a cautionary tale for children. According to the lore, mothers warn their sons and daughters not to linger by the river after dusk, for it is at night that the Weeping Woman searches by the river for her own children, and there is no telling what she might do if she found children who were not her own.

Generally speaking, a sighting of the Weeping Woman by adults is regarded as a portent of sorrow, misfortune, or even death. She is an emblem of evil, and so a glimpse of her can cause harm to the viewer. Spoken rituals are sometime used to fend off ill effects of the Weeping Woman.

In the same way that receiving the evil eye can prove risky, just an inadvertent glimpse of the Weeping Woman can be perilous for the beholder.

See also: CHICANO FOLKLORE; EVIL EYE; FAMILY FOLKLORE; FOLK HEROES/LEGENDARY FIGURES; GENDER AND FOLKLORE; GHOSTS; GHOST STORIES; LEGENDS, FOLK; LUCK/FORTUNE; OUTLAWS; PREDICTION; REGION, FOLK; SOUTHWESTERN REGIONAL FOLKLORE; SUPERSTITION.

For Further Reading:
Abernethy, Francis Edward, ed. *Legendary Ladies of Texas*. Dallas: E-Heart, 1981.

Arora, Shirley L. "La Llorona: The Naturalization of a Legend," *Southwest Folklore* 5, no. 1 (winter 1981): 23–40.

Barakat, Robert A. "Aztec Motifs in 'La Llorona,'" *Southern Folklore Quarterly* 29 (1965): 288–296.

Bennett, Gillian, and Paul Smith, eds. *Contemporary Legend: A Reader*. New York: Garland, 1996.

George, Philip B. "The Ghost of Cline Avenue: 'La Llorona' in the Calumet Region," *Indiana Folklore* 5 (1972): 56–91.

Jones, Pamela. "'There Was a Woman': La Llorona in Oregon," *Western Folklore* 47, no. 3 (July 1988): 195–211.

Villarino, Jose, and Arturo Ramírez, eds. *Chicano Border: Culture and Folklore*. San Diego: Marin, 1992.

Walraven, Ed. "Evidence for a Developing Variant of 'La Llorona,'" *Western Folklore* 50, no. 2 (April 1991): 208–217.

werewolf The image of the werewolf is a familiar one within horror narratives in the United States.

A werewolf is a human being who falls victim to a condition in which she or he undergoes involuntary transformations. In this metamorphosis, the individual takes on attributes of a wolf or wolflike creature. Entering this state releases "the beast within," for both animal urges and suppressed human desires surface as the individual changes. In this context, tales of werewolves roughly parallel folk stories concerning wolves, such as "Little Red Riding Hood," in which the wolf exhibits predatory behavior.

Werewolves are not original to, or specific to, American folklore. Changelings of this sort appear in spoken and written narratives across cultures, countries, and eras. Within these accounts, there are considerable variations in detail. Nonetheless, some patterns emerge. The transformed individual displays an altered appearance, as well as unusual behavior, including aggressive conduct associated with wolves as they exist in nature. Werewolves typically emerge after nightfall, and especially when the moon is full.

The onset of such a condition can be explained through several means, including a bite from a wolf, a curse from a shaman or sorcerer, demonic possession, and consumption of the meat of a rabid wolf. In some cases, the situation, according to the narrative, is the result of a person's being conceived during a full moon.

In a similar but unrelated condition, lycanthropism, an individual becomes convinced that he or she is in fact a wolf. This perception is the product of a psychological disorder, however, and does not coincide with any physical changes in the affected individual. A werewolf, however, is a fabulous creature, rather than the manifestation of a mental illness.

Folklore concerning werewolves features numerous descriptions of potential cures for the problem. One such approach is to address the werewolf by his or her human name, thus restoring the original state. Another remedy involves collecting drops of the werewolf's blood. Some also believe that if the werewolf can abstain from attacking others for a prolonged period, sometimes indicated as nine years, it will no longer be subject to the transformations. Finally, there are some tales that posit that a werewolf can be killed with a silver bullet.

There are similarities between lore related to werewolves and that dealing with vampires. For instance, it is said that once a werewolf tastes human blood, the individual's soul is lost irretrievably. Both werewolves and vampires represent fears of dangerous impulses and loss of restraint. As with the figure of the vampire, werewolves surface in popular culture references to such monsters as the wolfman or manwolf,

including the 1941 Universal Pictures film *The Wolf Man*.

The werewolf remains a mysterious shape shifter and a staple of the horror and suspense genres of American folklore.

See also: ANIMALS; CHANGELINGS; FOLKLORE IN EVERYDAY LIFE; HALLOWEEN/ALL HALLOWS' EVE; LOUP-GAROU; MONSTERS; "RED RIDING HOOD, LITTLE"; SUPERNATURAL; WITCHCRAFT, SALEM.

For Further Reading:

Gardiner, Muriel, ed. *The Wolf-Man and Sigmund Freud.* London: Hogarth Press, 1972.

Hall, Jamie. *Half Human, Half Animal: Tales of Werewolves and Related Creatures.* Bloomington, Ind.: First Books, 2003.

Summers, Montague. *The Werewolf in Lore and Legend.* New York: Dover, 2003.

Zenko, Darren. *Werewolves and Shapeshifters.* Edmonton, Canada: Ghost House Books, 2004.

Western regional folklore   The American West, with its lore of the frontier, outlaws, and rodeo, represents an important region for folklore study.

Since its inception, the study of American folklore has emphasized the concept of folk regions in the United States. Despite the claim that we now have an entirely global culture, local and regional variations continue to exist, and these are important objects of study for folklorists. In the United States, these regions are typically conceived of as clusters of nearby states with commonalities, such as populations, practices, or other attributes.

Although the American West can be described and delimited in various ways, as a folk region it can generally be defined as including folklore of or relating to the states of California, Colorado, Nevada, Utah, and Wyoming.

Historical personages associated with the West include Ma Barker, Billy the Kid, Bonnie and Clyde, Daniel Boone, Kit Carson, Robert Leroy Parker (Butch Cassidy), William

F. Cody (Buffalo Bill), Martha Cannary-Burke
(Calamity Jane) , Crazy Horse, Charles Arthur
(Pretty Boy) Floyd, Geronimo, James Butler
(Wild Bill) Hickok, Jesse James, Meriwether
Lewis and William Clark, Harry Longabaugh
(Sundance Kid), Sacajawea, Wyatt Berry Stamp
Earp, Chief Joseph, and Phoebe Annie Oakley.
The West's many legendary figures include
John (Johnny Appleseed) Chapman, Bigfoot,
Paul Bunyan, Febold Feboldson, Pecos Bill,
Belle Starr, and Sally Ann Thunder Ann Whirl-
wind. Writers who described the region in
literature included John Steinbeck and Zane
Grey.

See also: Bigfoot; Bonnie and Clyde;
Boone, Daniel; Bunyan, Paul; Cannary-
Burke, Martha (Calamity Jane); Carson,
Kit; Chapman, John (Johnny Appleseed);
Clark, Arizona Donnie (Ma Barker); Cody,
William F. (Buffalo Bill); cowboys; Crazy
Horse; Earp, Wyatt Berry Stamp; Febold-
son, Febold; Floyd, Charles Arthur (Pretty
Boy); folktales; frontier; Geronimo; ghost
towns; gold rush, the; Hickok, James
Butler (Wild Bill); James, Jesse; Joseph,
Chief; Lewis, Meriwether, and William
Clark; Longabaugh, Harry (Billy the Kid);
McCarty, William Henry (Sundance Kid);
Mormon folklore; Oakley, Phoebe Annie;
outlaws; Parker, Robert Leroy (Butch Cas-
sidy); Pecos Bill; region, folk; rodeo; Sacaja-
wea; Starr, Belle; Steinbeck, John; trans-
continental railroad; Whirlwind, Sally
Ann Thunder Ann.

For Further Reading:

Alexander, Kent. *Legends of the Old West: Trailblaz-
errs, Desperadoes, Wranglers, and Yarn-Spinners.*
New York: Friedman/Fairfax, 1994.
Botkin, Benjamin, ed. *A Treasury of Western Folk-
lore.* New York: Crown, 1951.
Cunningham, Keith, ed. *The Oral Tradition of the
American West: Adventure, Courtship, Family,
and Place in Traditional Recitation.* Little Rock,
Ark.: August House, 1990.
Erdoes, Richard, ed. *Legends and Tales of the Ameri-
can West: Tales from the American Frontier.* New
York: Pantheon, 1998.
Etulain, Richard. *Myths and the American West.*
Manhattan, Kans.: Sunflower University Press,
1998.
Greenway, John. *Folklore of the Great West.* Palo
Alto, Calif.: American West, 1970.
Rosenberg, Bruce. *The Codes of the West.* Bloom-
ington: Indiana University Press, 1982.
Walker, Dale. *Legends and Lies: Great Mysteries of
the American West.* New York: Forge, 1997.

West Virginia folklore See Appalachian
folklore; Father's Day; Grandparents
Day; Henry, John; monsters; Southern
regional folklore.

Whirlwind, Sally Ann Thunder Ann
(legendary) As one of relatively few female
figures of America's tall tales tradition, Sally
Ann Thunder Ann Whirlwind is a memorable
character of the nation's lore.

Whirlwind was, as the surname implies,
a forceful individual described in stories as
strong, loud, savvy, and fearless. She also had
a distinctive look, even among the eccentric
tastes known among America's legends. She is
said to have worn a beehive hat and bearskin
dress and picked her teeth with a bowie knife.
Despite her bravery, Whirlwind was known for
a measure of restraint. She neither bragged nor
picked fights, although she could certainly hold
her own if she needed to do so. According to the
stories, Whirlwind married another legend of
the American frontier, Davy Crockett. In fact,
numerous stories feature both Whirlwind and
Crockett, a well-matched pair in terms of their
pluck and love for adventure.

While she is most likely a fanciful construct
and figure of storytelling imagination, like Old
Stormalong and Paul Bunyan, Sally Ann Thunder Ann Whirlwind stands out as a frontiers-
woman in a western folklore more typically
dominated by male characters.

See also: Bunyan, Paul; Crockett, Davy; folk heroes/legendary figures; folktales; frontier; gender and folklore; region, folk; Stormalong, Old; Western regional folklore.

For Further Reading:

Cohen, Caron Lee, and Ariane Dewey. *Sally Ann Thunder Ann Whirlwind Crockett.* New York: Greenwillow Books, 1985.

Kellogg, Steven. *Sally Ann Thunder Ann Whirlwind Crockett: A Tall Tale.* New York: HarperTrophy, 1999.

Osborne, Mary Pope. *American Tall Tales.* New York: Knopf, 1991.

San Souci, Robert D. *Cut from the Same Cloth: American Women of Myth, Legend, and the Tall Tale.* New York: Philomel Books, 1993.

Sattler, Anne, Edwin Vandermeulen, and Bruce Miles. *I Ride Panthers for Fun.* Scottsdale, Ariz.: Remedia, 2003.

Shore, Amy, and Wendy Chang. *Tall Tales.* Huntington Beach, Calif.: Teacher Created Materials, 1997.

White House   See Arbor Day; Christmas; Easter; ghost stories; Inauguration Day; Lincoln, Abraham; Patriot Day; suffrage, women's.

Whitman, Walt (1819–1892)   As one of the 19th century's most renowned writers, Walt Whitman both celebrated and collected American folk narratives.

Whitman was born in West Hills, Long Island, on May 31, 1819. He was a member of a Quaker family with nine children and was largely self-educated. Whitman had six years of education in Brooklyn's public schools and learned a great deal by reading voraciously as a youth, including such authors as James Fenimore Cooper and Henry Wadsworth Longfellow. He began working at the age of 11 as a printer's devil and became a journeyman printer at 16. Whitman went on to teach school for a time, although writing would become his calling.

Whitman wrote fiction and began publishing his stories during the 1840s. He also became active in journalism, an experience that would shape his subsequent literary efforts. Whitman found his way into an illustrious career as a poet. His first works were quite conventional, but by the height of his career, Whitman had emerged as a highly experimental writer of verse.

Whitman was one of several prestigious writers associated with the American Renaissance in literature, including Ralph Waldo Emerson, Henry David Thoreau, Nathaniel Hawthorne, and Herman Melville.

Hailed as the poet of democracy in America, Whitman is best known for such works as *Leaves of Grass* (1856). *Leaves of Grass* went through numerous editions, the first of which was published at Whtiman's own expense. When it was ready, he sent a copy to Emerson. *Leaves of Grass* was reissued nine times, each in a different form. In a sense, the text's many iterations chart the development of Whitman's vision. *Leaves of Grass* proved a controversial work with the public, especially in terms of its frank treatment of sexuality, and at one point was banned in Boston. Sections such as "From Pent-up Aching Rivers," "A Woman Waits for Me," and "To a Common Prostitute" were deemed obscene.

As an abolitionist and promoter of the Free Soil Party, Whitman took an interest in the events of the Civil War. His interest became even more personal when his brother was wounded at Fredericksburg in 1862. Whitman initially traveled to tend to his brother and then started to care for other injured soldiers. Whitman recorded his observations of the conflict and retold the stories of its soldiers in *Specimen Days* (1882–83) and *Hospital Sketches* (1883). Whitman's other Civil War writings include *Drum Taps* (1865), *Sequel to Drum Taps* (1965), and his elegy to Abraham Lincoln, "When Lilacs Last in the Dooryard Bloom'd." In his work, Whitman struggled to show audiences the realities of war.

During the 1870s, Whitman traveled and delivered lectures on subjects such as Abraham Lincoln. He also gave readings of his poetry. Whitman suffered a stroke in 1873, after which he went to live with a brother in Camden, New Jersey. He died of tuberculosis and other complications on March 26, 1892, and was buried in Camden's Harleigh Cemetery. The final version of *Leaves of Grass* appeared that same year.

Walt Whitman rejoiced in America's folk traditions at the same time that he challenged social mores. In his writings, Whitman echoed Emerson's notion of America as itself a great poem. Whitman's body of work eventually cast him as the people's poet. During his penultimate year, Whitman wrote a piece entitled "Have We an American Literature?" In that essay, he responded in the negative. In works such as *Democratic Vistas* (1870), however, Whitman helped build a national literature worthy of the name, and a fitting tribute to the American people. He has been celebrated countless times in literary and popular culture, such as the 1989 feature film *Dead Poets' Society*.

See also: CIVIL WAR; COOPER, JAMES FENIMORE; FOLKLORE IN AMERICAN LITERATURE; FOLKTALES; HAWTHORNE, NATHANIEL; LINCOLN, ABRAHAM; LONGFELLOW, HENRY WADSWORTH; MELVILLE, HERMAN; QUAKER FOLKLORE.

For Further Reading:

Greenspan, Ezra, ed. *The Cambridge Companion to Walt Whitman*. Cambridge: Cambridge University Press, 1995.

Grossman, Jay, and Betsy Erkkila, eds. *Breaking Bounds: Whitman and American Cultural Studies*. New York: Oxford University Press, 1996.

Kummings, Donald D., and J. R. LeMaster, eds. *Walt Whitman: An Encyclopedia*. New York: Garland, 1998.

Morris, Roy, Jr. *The Better Angel: Walt Whitman in the Civil War*. New York: Oxford University Press, 2000.

Myerson, Joel, ed. *Walt Whitman: A Documentary Volume*. Detroit: Gale Group, 2000.

Reynolds, David, ed. *A Historical Guide to Walt Whitman*. New York: Oxford University Press, 2000.

Reynolds, David. *Walt Whitman's America: A Cultural Biography*. New York: Knopf, 1995.

Wilderness Road   See BOONE, DANIEL.

Williamsburg, Colonial   See COLONIAL WILLIAMSBURG.

Windwagon Smith   See SMITH, WINDWAGON.

Wisconsin folklore   See BABE THE BLUE OX; BUNYAN, PAUL; MIDWEST REGIONAL FOLKLORE.

wishbone   See LUCK/FORTUNE; PREDICTION.

witchcraft   See BELIEFS, FOLK; CHRISTMAS; DEVIL, THE; EVIL EYE; FROG PRINCE/FROG KING, THE; GRIMM BROTHERS; HALLOWEEN/ALL HALLOWS' EVE; "HANSEL AND GRETEL"; HAWTHORNE, NATHANIEL; HISTORICAL EVENTS; IRVING, WASHINGTON; ITALIAN-AMERICAN FOLKLORE; JERSEY DEVIL; LOUP-GAROU; MAGIC; MOTIFS, FOLK; MUSEUMS, FOLK; POLISH-AMERICAN FOLKLORE; PREDICTION; QUAKER FOLKLORE; "RAPUNZEL"; SHAKER FOLKLORE; SUPERNATURAL; VOODOO/HOODOO.

witchcraft, Salem   Salem's witch trials of 1692 demonstrated American folk beliefs about black magic and folk ideas about the supernatural.

Witch crazes and prosecutions have taken place for centuries and in many countries. The most concentrated activity of this kind, although not the only incidence in the United States, took place in Salem, Massachusetts Bay Colony, in the 17th century. During this era in colonial New England, many believed that witches could live within a society undetected. While doing so, they could undermine the health of a community and its members. Believers considered witches to be shape shifters, transforming their appearance at will to harm or mislead others. Their chief activities were conducted under cover of night. It was believed that a witch could ride people as they slept, hence the term *nightmare* for fitful or disturbed sleep. They also were supposed to engage the help of familiars, small animals possessed by demonic spirits that furthered the work of witches. Witches were believed to consort with evil spirits, including the devil. Some considered witches to be possessed by the devil.

Americans fearful of witches and the dangers they posed had numerous ideas about how best to prevent harm or remedy it if it occurred. Examples of such measures included carrying amulets or horseshoes. They also experimented with techniques to subdue witches. For instance, some believed that a straight pin placed on the seat of a chair would hold a witch in place.

Residents of Salem Village had many hardships, so much so that they began to attribute their adversities to malevolent practices of magic or witchcraft. Accusations continued into the 18th century on a sporadic basis, but when historians refer to Salem witchcraft, the reference is usually to events that took place during the latter half of the 17th century. As community members charged one another with misdeeds, the situation escalated into a form of hysteria. Neighbors were accused of killing livestock or making creatures sick, infertile, or unproductive. They were held responsible for poor crop yields or ill health in the community. Citizens of Salem contended that such misfortunes could be traced to practitioners of witchcraft.

As the craze continued, many were suspected of being witches. While most of those tried were women, men were also tried, including a minister. The drama of the witch trials unfolded in a series of accusations and counteraccusations that culminated in the convictions and deaths of 19 individuals. Perhaps the best known of the suspects was Tituba, a West Indian slave who was accused not only of practicing witchcraft, but also of teaching this craft to several girls in Salem. It is possible that Tituba was simply engaging in folk practices, such as voodoo, that were unknown to the people of Massachusetts Bay Colony. All but one of the death sentences occurred by hanging. When an 80-year-old farmer by the name of Giles Corey refused to enter a plea, he was pressed to death for his defiance. As the story goes, Corey's final words were "More weight."

In fact, there are many theories about what caused the Salem witch craze, particularly concerning reasons behind accusations made of specific individuals. One of the most interesting of these perspectives involves a notion that at least the first people targeted were those deemed unconventional and those living on the outskirts of Salem, and so outlandish in both senses of the word. They were elderly, impoverished, of foreign birth, given to curious behavior such as muttering, or otherwise out of the ordinary. In any case, once the hysteria subsided, those being held on suspicion of witchcraft were released and cleared of all charges.

Whatever the nature and origin of this episode in New England history, its unfolding demonstrates telling aspects of American folklore, including concerning religion and the supernatural. Literary retellings of this event from folk history have also appeared in the works of such American authors as Arthur Miller and Nathaniel Hawthorne.

See also: CHANGELINGS; CONJURE/CONJURING; DEVIL, THE; FOLKLORE IN AMERICAN LITERATURE; FOLKLORE IN EVERYDAY LIFE; GENDER AND FOLKLORE; HAWTHORNE, NATHANIEL; HISTORICAL EVENTS; HISTORY, FOLK; LUCK/FORTUNE; MAGIC; MEDICINE, FOLK; NORTHEASTERN REGIONAL FOLKLORE; SLAVERY; SUPERNATURAL; SUPERSTITION; VOODOO/HOODOO.

For Further Reading:

Boyer, Paul, and Stephen Nissenbaum. *Salem Possessed: The Social Origins of Witchcraft.* Cambridge, Mass.: Harvard University Press, 1974.

Demos, John. *Entertaining Satan: Witchcraft and the Culture of Early New England.* Oxford: Oxford University Press, 1982.

Elliott, Emory. *The Cambridge Introduction to Early American Literature.* New York: Cambridge University Press, 2002.

Godbeer, Richard. *Escaping Salem: The Other Witch Hunt of 1692.* New York: Oxford University Press, 2005.

Hill, Francis. *The Salem Witch Trials Reader.* Cambridge, Massachusetts: Da Capo Press, 2000.

Norton, Mary Beth. *In the Devil's Share: The Salem Witchcraft Crisis of 1692.* New York: Knopf, 2002.

Oldridge, Darren, ed. *The Witchcraft Reader.* New York: Routledge, 2002.

Reis, Elizabeth. *Spellbound: Women and Witchcraft in America.* Wilmington, Del.: Scholarly Resources, 1998.

women's movement The campaign for women's rights and gender equality has been a long-standing one, with its own history and lore.

The first major push of the women's movement occurred during the 19th century, at which time a cadre of women activists led the fight for women's suffrage. Figures such as Susan Brownell Anthony, Lucretia Mott, and Elizabeth Cady Stanton emerged as leaders of the struggle and became early feminist icons. This era in the women's movement not only sought to extend the franchise to include America's women, but also advocated such rights as increased access to work in the professions, comparable pay for employment, and the extension of property rights to married women. In generating public support for change, women pointed out the irony of a nation forged in a rhetoric of freedom of equality, yet denying privileges and protections to its female population.

Many of the same Americans who advocated women's rights were also active in the movement to end slavery in the United States. For this reason, when the Civil War began, a good deal of energy went into supporting the war efforts and tending to the immediate needs of Union troops. After the war ended, the Fourteenth and Fifteenth Amendments widened voting rights but did nothing to make women voters. While most women's rights movements supported those measures, they were disappointed to find that the amendments, as the Constitution itself, made no provisions for improving the standing of women of any race in America.

Efforts for women's suffrage intensified during the postbellum period, and by August 1920, the Nineteenth Amendment passed, granting American women the vote. While women still sought equality on other fronts, they could finally participate in selecting the people who formed the laws to which they would be subject.

During the latter part of the 20th century, American women continued the fight for equality. One manifestation of this campaign was the effort to pass an Equal Rights Amendment (ERA). Although the attempt was not successful, its participants drew attention to the status of women in the United States. By the 1960s and 1970s, the women's movement was perceived to be reaching its peak, in terms of levels of visibility and participation. Movement culture in general, from the Civil Rights movement to the gay rights movement, was arguably at its most vital at this time in America.

At the opening of the 21st century, American women still fight gender bias, discrimination, and inequality. While more women hold elected office and positions of power within the professions, the fight for such rights as comparable compensation persists.

See also: ANTHONY, SUSAN BROWNELL; CIVIL WAR; GENDER AND FOLKLORE; HISTORICAL EVENTS; POLITICS AND FOLKLORE; PROTEST IN FOLKLORE; STANTON, ELIZABETH CADY; TRUTH, SOJOURNER; WOMEN'S SUFFRAGE.

For Further Reading:
Baxandall, Rosalyn F., and Linda Gordon, eds. *Dear Sisters: Dispatches from the Women's Liberation Movement.* New York: Basic Books, 2000.

Berkeley, Kathleen C. *The Women's Liberation Movement in America*. Westport, Conn.: Greenwood Press, 1999.

Flexner, Eleanor. *Century of Struggle: The Woman's Rights Movement in the United States*. New York: Atheneum, 1972.

Freedman, Estelle. *No Turning Back: The History of Feminism and the Future of Women*. New York: Ballantine, 2002.

Gluck, Sherna Berger, and Daphne Patai, eds. *Women's Words: The Feminist Practice in Oral History*. New York: Routledge: 1991.

Hawthorne, Susan, and Renate Klein, eds. *Cyberfeminism: Connectivity, Critique, and Creativity*. North Melbourne, Australia: Spinifex Press, 1999.

Prahlad, Ahnand. "'You Took the Words Right out of My Mouth': Proverbial Expressions, Feminist Perspectives, and the Fetish in the Work of Janet Davidson-Hues," *Journal of American Folklore* 117, no. 463 (winter 2004): 22–54.

Radner, Joan Newlon, ed. *Feminist Messages: Coding in Women's Folk Culture*. Urbana: University of Illinois Press, 1993.

Rosen, Ruth. *The World Split Open: How the Modern Women's Movement Changed America*. New York: Viking, 2000.

Tanner, Leslie B., ed. *Voices from Women's Liberation*. New York: Signet, 1970.

women's suffrage   See SUFFRAGE, WOMEN'S.

woodworking   See CRAFTS, FOLK.

worldview   The term *worldview* refers to a person's or, more commonly, a population's full set of beliefs about how to live in the world.

Sometimes described as a group's philosophy, the term more rightly describes the overarching premises on which people within a particular group ground their existence. A worldview typically encompasses a whole set of understandings and assumptions members of a group hold to be true; it includes their outlook, beliefs, expectations, and values. For this reason, a worldview is sometimes characterized as a form of collective consciousness.

In many cases, when a folklorist alludes to a worldview, the emphasis within that reference is on items of faith within a cultural or subcultural group. For example, a religious faith that organizes believers around strong central principles, tenets, and practices may have a formative effect on the worldview of its followers. Studies of Native American folklore, for example, often remark the alignment of cultural beliefs with everyday practices. They also tend to note the integration of spirituality in all aspects of life, including one's relationship to the Earth and its creatures.

More generally, though, a worldview is synonymous with a set of common answers to questions of consequence. Such questions involve the origins of human life, the meaning of existence, the source of such values as virtue, and the prevailing beliefs about mortality.

Within their worldview, the members of a group understand the world and express their proper place and right conduct within it.

See also: ALLEN, PAULA GUNN; BELIEFS, FOLK; CREATION/ORIGIN STORIES; NATIVE AMERICAN FOLKLORE; TERMS.

For Further Reading:

Naugle, David. *Worldview: The History of a Concept*. Grand Rapids, Mich.: William B. Eerdmans, 2002.

Sire, James. *Naming the Elephant: Worldview as a Concept*. Downers Grove, Ill.: InterVarsity Press, 2004.

Stewart, Polly, ed. *Worldviews and the American West*. Logan: Utah State University Press, 2000.

Woodhouse, Mark. *Paradigm Wars: Worldviews for a New Age*. Berkeley, Calif.: Frog Ltd., 1996.

World War I   Every war contributes its share of folklore, and that is certainly true for World War I.

Numerous terms entered popular speech as a direct consequence of the war. These words and phrases emerged from the experiences of members of the armed forces. In an adaptation of the earlier term *Yankee*, used to refer to Americans in general, members of the American troops in World War I became known as Yanks. Enlisted men became known as doughboys, so named for the biscuit flour in use to feed the soldiers. Other terms, such as *meat wagon* for ambulance, while not household words, became widely understood references to the war.

Folk speech was not the only aspect of World War I folklore. Music also played a part in expressive culture among American soldiers of this era. In addition to listening to and singing popular war-themed songs issued stateside, soldiers invented alternative lyrics, often playfully or satirically, such that "Over There" became the comical "Underwear." There were also ritual objects used by soldiers who believed they were lucky items that would help protect them. One example included items such as Bibles tucked or pinned over the portion of a uniform covering the soldier's heart. Another example involved images of black cats sewn onto the uniform to attract good luck, contrary to the usual superstitions about black cats' causing misfortune.

In addition, World War I involved many of the expressive forms usually present in the folklore of war. There were jokes about the lives of enlisted people and jokes at the expense of commanding officers. There were tales about boot camp as indoctrination, cadence calls and chants for marching soldiers while drilling, stories about the home front, legends of combat, and tales of survival.

Military folklore unites whole groups of people who assemble for a term of service, ones who might otherwise have little in common. The folklore of World War I continued to bind together veterans long after the conflict itself ended.

See also: FOLKTALES; HISTORICAL EVENTS; HUMOR, FOLK; KILROY; LEGENDS, FOLK; LUCK/ FORTUNE; MEMORIAL DAY; MUSIC, FOLK; SPEECH, FOLK; VETERANS DAY; YANKEE DOODLE.

For Further Reading:

Ben-Ami, Issacher. "Miraculous Legends of Wartime." In *Folklore Studies in the Twentieth Century*, edited by Venetia J. Newell, 123–127. Totowa, N.J.: Rowman & Littlefield, 1978–80.

Cleveland, Les. "Soldiers' Songs: The Folklore of the Powerless," *New York Folklore* 11 (1985): 79–97.

Corbin, David A. "Folklore as Wartime Propaganda," *New York Folklore* 2, nos. 3–4 (1976): 225–228.

Fiedler, Leslie A. "Mythicizing the Unspeakable," *Journal of American Folklore* 103, no. 410 (fall 1990): 390–399.

Jackson, Bruce. "The Perfect Informant," *Journal of American Folklore* 103, no. 410 (fall 1990): 400–416.

Kenagy, S. G. "Sexual Symbolism in the Language of the Air Force Pilot: A Psychoanalytic Approach to Folk Speech," *Western Folklore* 37 (1978): 89–101.

Sandels, Robert. "The Doughboy: The Formation of a Military Folk," *American Studies* 24 (1983): 69–88.

Wallrich, William. *Air Force Airs: Songs and Ballads of the United States Air Force, World War One through Korea.* New York: Duell, 1957.

World War II   As with any military event of consequence in the nation's history, World War II had its share of folklore.

Some of its practices, customs, and traditions were survivals of previous conflicts, such as World War I. Other elements were the product of the distinctive circumstances of this particular war.

American military lore is rich with items of folk speech, slang, and lay terminology. World War II was no exception, adding such abbreviations as *SOP* (standard operating procedure) and *GI* (government issue) to the lexicon. The parachute jumper's by-now familiar cry of

"Geronimo" also dates from this period. Other terms and practices, such as care packages and rationing, were the result of wartime scarcity of goods and materials.

Graffiti were another element of World War II folklore, and perhaps the best-known item of graffiti from this era was the phrase "Kilroy was here," accompanied by a sketch of the popular character. The name *Kilroy* refers to a hand-drawn figure of a man peering over a wall. The drawing is of simple design. His face is visible only as a a nose and pair of eyes behind the wall. Kilroy has dots for eyes, and his fingers extend over the flat surface of the wall before him. His appearance remains somewhat generic, rendering him a kind of everyman. This visual image, with or without the companion inscription, "Kilroy was here," completes the effect. His whimsical visage marks the presence of American soldiers. Kilroy lore calls for GIs to place drawings of the character in the most remote and unlikely locations, signifying the power and reach of the U.S. military. It is also customary for soldiers to claim that the marking was discovered rather than placed.

The Second World War also produced a number of popular songs, enjoyed by soldiers and their families alike, such as "Don't Sit under the Apple Tree" and "Gee, Mom I Wanna Go Home." The latter tune persisted long after the war, becoming a perennial at camps, where modified lyrics still suit the sentiments of today's homesick campers or those willing to feign dissatisfaction for entertainment purposes.

No war is fought without superstitions, especially beliefs and practices surrounding lucky and lucky behavior. Those fighting in the war had superstitions about acts they supposed would keep them safe, alive, or out of the service altogether.

Since the dawn of military aviation, war folklore has featured unexplained phenomena such as ghost planes, along with the more traditional ghost ships. These phantom vehicles are featured in war stories of encounters that cannot be accounted for any other way. Such ghostly

vehicles, as well as some ghostly figures, seem to appear at times of crisis to proffer mysterious help or deepen dangers in the war efforts.

Along with stories of benevolent forces during wartime, there were rumors of their malevolent counterparts: spies, traitors, and saboteurs. These individuals gave a face to the enemy and even warned soldiers against the enemy who poses as an ally. World War II also gave rise to another curious set of accounts. Allied bomber pilots reported seeing flying saucers or orbs of light as they flew missions in Japan and Germany. These unidentified flying objects were dubbed *foo fighters* after a line from the popular comic strip of the time *Smokey Stover*. At the time, these sights were presumed to be secret weapons deployed by enemy forces but were later written off as the product of combat stress.

Gestures were another popular aspect of World War II folklore, from variations on the traditional military salute to the "V for victory" gesture, in which extended fingers form the letter *V*.

Meanwhile, on the home front, Americans "kept the home fires burning" by conserving scarce materials and purchasing war bonds. Women filled in for their male counterparts in the factories, hoping to lend support to the war effort. The fictional character "Rosie the Riveter" was emblazoned on prowar posters, urging women to do their part by maintaining production while American men were away at battle. Gold stars signified families that had lost a family member to battle.

Several American holidays/observances refer to World War II, most notably Pearl Harbor (Remembrance) Day, which commemorates the December 7, 1971, Japanese attack on the anchored battleship U.S.S. *Arizona*. Although this is the central observance specific to the experience of World War II, the event is also recalled in ceremonies and observances associated with Memorial Day (which originally paid tribute to Civil War dead) and Veterans Day (which was set in place to honor those who fought in World War I). In addition, at

Arlington National Cemetery in Washington, D.C., there stands the Tomb of the Unknown Soldier, which symbolizes all those who were lost or rendered unidentifiable by the brutalities of war. At this site, one burial from each of several wars, including World War II, represents all those from the conflict whose bodies were never recovered or whose remains could not be returned to next of kin.

From slang to visual culture, World War II inspired Americans to develop new or modify old customs related to war.

See also: BURIAL CUSTOMS; CAMP FOLKLORE; CEMETERY FOLKLORE; CIVIL WAR; GENDER AND FOLKLORE; GERONIMO; GESTURES; GRAFFITI; HISTORICAL EVENTS; HOLIDAYS/OBSERVANCES; JAPANESE-AMERICAN INTERNMENT; KILROY; MEMORIAL DAY; MUSIC, FOLK; PEARL HARBOR (REMEMBRANCE) DAY; SPEECH, FOLK; UFO FOLKLORE; VETERANS DAY; WORLD WAR I.

For Further Reading:

Ben-Ami, Isaacher. "Miraculous Legends of Wartime." In *Folklore Studies in the Twentieth Century*, edited by Venetia J. Newall, 123–127. Totowa, N.J.: Rowman and Littlefield.

Blum, John Morton. *V Was for Victory: Politics and American Culture during World War II*. New York: Harcourt Brace Jovanovich, 1976.

Cleveland, Les. "Military Folklore and the Underwood Collection," *New York Folklore* 13, nos. 3–4 (1987): 87–103.

Holsinger, Paul, and Mary Anne Schofield, eds. *Visions of War: World War II in Popular Literature and Culture*. Bowling Green, Ohio: Bowling Green State University Popular Press, 1992.

Miller, William Marion. "Two Stories from World War II," *Journal of American Folklore* 59, no. 231 (spring 1946): 198.

Yates, Norris. "Some 'Whoppers' from the Armed Forces," *Journal of American Folklore* 62, no. 244 (spring 1949): 173–180.

Worth, Mary   See BLOODY MARY.

Wounded Knee   See CRAZY HORSE.

Wright brothers (Orville, 1871–1948; Wilbur, 1867–1912)   The Wright brothers enjoy the distinction of being the first Americans to achieve air flight.

Avid inventors and aviators, Orville and Wilbur Wright secured their place in the histories of technology and transportation when they successfully manned a controlled flight on a powered glider called the *Flyer*. This historic event in aviation took place at Kitty Hawk, North Carolina, on December 17, 1903.

The story of the Wright brothers began, however, with their births in Dayton, Ohio. They became part of a progressive family that lent active support to causes from women's rights to abolition. They also encouraged the life of the mind, and while the Wright brothers would not become scholars they would develop great ideas. Because of their prominent role as inventors, Dayton is considered by many to be the birthplace of flight. Wright Field, a site where subsequent test flights have taken place, stands as a tribute to their ingenuity.

Orville and Wilbur Wright worked together in several other endeavors before venturing into aviation. In 1890, they launched a printing business. Three years later, they added a bicycle business that would lend technological inspiration to their later experiments in flight. Fascinated as both men were by vehicles, and enticed by the prospect of human flight, they fashioned a wind tunnel and began to research the idea. By 1900, their flight experiments began in earnest. They devised several versions of their aircraft before arriving at the one that made that memorable 1903 journey. Although that first flight lasted only 12 seconds and spanned only 120 feet, its implications extended far beyond the time or distance traveled.

Because the Wright brothers triumphed in this effort without benefit of high school diplomas, training in engineering, or subsidies of any kind, their story has taken on symbolic importance within American folklore. They are hailed as heroes reminiscent of the protagonists in Horatio Alger stories, by prevailing chiefly through persistence and conviction. Their aircraft now hangs on display in the Smithsonian Institution. In addition, at the Wright Brothers National Monument, a 60-foot granite pylon unveiled in 1932 pays homage to their accomplishments. In 2003, the centennial of their Kitty Hawk success was celebrated.

Observances of Wright Brothers Day on December 17 each year serve as reminders of the role the Wrights played in American technology and popular imagination.

See also: ALGER, HORATIO, JR., EARHART, AMELIA MARY; FLIGHT; FOLK HEROES/LEGENDARY FIGURES; GREENFIELD VILLAGE, HENRY FORD MUSEUM AND; INDUSTRIALIZATION AND FOLKLORE; LINDBERGH, CHARLES; MUSEUMS, FOLK; OCCUPATIONAL FOLKLORE; SMITHSONIAN INSTITUTION.

For Further Reading:

Crouch, Tom. *First Flight: The Wright Brothers and the Invention of the Airplane*. Washington, D.C.: Harpers Ferry Center National Park Service, 2002.

Great People of the Twentieth Century. New York: Time Books, 1996.

Hellman, Hal. *Great Feuds in Technology: Ten of the Liveliest Disputes Ever*. Chichester, England: John Wiley & Sons, 2004.

Howard, Fred. *Wilbur and Orville: A Biography of the Wright Brothers*. New York: Knopf, 1987.

Walsh, John Evangelist. *One Day at Kitty Hawk: The Untold Story of the Wright Brothers and the Airplane*. New York: Crowell, 1975.

Wyoming folklore See JAPANESE-AMERICAN INTERNMENT; JOSEPH, CHIEF; LONGABAUGH, HARRY (SUNDANCE KID); RODEO; WESTERN REGIONAL FOLKLORE.

X

Xerox/fax folklore Whether as prank or hoax, the story of each falsehood spread through means of the now-common devices of the digital age—the photocopy and fax machines—adds to contemporary lore.

Xerox and fax folklore are closely related to computer folklore in the sense that many rumors and jokes are recirculated on the Internet or via e-mail. These copycat, clone, and parody messages keep the stories alive and distribute them more widely than might otherwise be possible.

Because the equipment involved in these folk practices is still more common to workplaces than to households, Xerox and fax lore tend to be associated with the workplace. Such technology makes it possible to disseminate information more rapidly, widely, and—where it is desired—anonymously than in the post. Consequently, it makes a nearly perfect medium for spoofs, jokes, and urban legends.

One example of such lore is the message of caution, which purports to alert the recipient of a dangerous situation. Typical indications that the message involves an urban legend are communications that proclaim "this is not a joke" and attest to the veracity of the content by offering testimony that a "friend" or a "friend of a friend" had an experience demonstrating the warning to be necessary. Such elements, along with noticeable errors of spelling and usage, are tells that the message is a contemporary legend rather than a spontaneous and genuine word to the wise.

In one such incident, the "Lights Out" rumor of 1993, faxes alerted recipients to a danger for motorists. The message claimed that would-be gang members were involved in an initiation ritual that involved their driving around after dark with their car lights off. According to the warning, these potential gang members could earn standing with their peers by killing the first driver to flash headlights at them, signaling that their car lights were off. People who peel such cautionary communications off the fax or machine or see them photocopied and posted on the bulletin board or lounge are left to determine what to make of these messages that arrive not over the transom, but over the network or modem.

Whether it involves items of advice, attempts at humor, or stories of another sort, Xerox/fax folklore is a pervasive aspect of office culture and urban folklore.

See also: COMPUTER FOLKLORE; FOLKLORE IN EVERYDAY LIFE; HUMOR, FOLK; INDUSTRIAL FOLKLORE; LEGENDS, FOLK; OCCUPATIONAL FOLKLORE; SPEECH, FOLK; URBAN LEGENDS.

For Further Reading:
Currie, Leslie. "Open University Photocopy Lore," *Talking Folklore* 4, no. 9 (August 1990): 50–51.

Dundes, Alan. *Never Try to Teach a Pig to Sing: Still More Urban Folklore from the Paperwork Empire.* Detroit: Wayne State University Press, 1991.

———. *When You're Up to Your Ass in Alligators: More Urban Folklore from the Paperwork Empire.* Detroit: Wayne State University Press, 1987.

Dundes, Alan, and Carl R. Pagter, eds. *Work Hard and You Shall Be Rewarded: Urban Folklore from the Paperwork Empire.* Bloomington: Indiana University Press, 1978.

Preston, Michael J. "Xerox-Lore," *Keystone Folklore* 19 (1974), pp. 11–26.

Roemer, Danielle M. "Photocopy Lore and the Naturalization of the Corporate Body," *Journal of American Folklore* 107, no. 423 (winter 1994): 121–138.

Smith, Paul. "An Interim Bibliography of Studies and Collections of Photocopy-Lore," *Talking Folklore* 1, no. 2 (winter 1986–1987): 15–17.

———. "Models from the Past: Proto-Photocopy-Lore." In *The Other Print Tradition: Essays on Chapbooks, Broadsides, and Relaxed Ephemera,* edited by Cathy Lynn Preston and Michael J. Preston, 183–222. New York: Garland, 1995.

Y

Yankee, Connecticut The figure of the Connecticut Yankee is a character from the folk-influenced stories of Samuel Langhorne Clemens, who published under the pen name Mark Twain.

Stories of King Arthur and the Round Table have fascinated audiences for many years. The original legend is rich with heroism, magic, and romance. It is no wonder, then, that American storytellers have attempted to capture some of the magic of those tales of Avalon in updated narratives prepared for American listeners and readers.

Adaptations of Arthurian tales include T. H. White's *The Sword in the Stone* (1938) and Marion Zimmer Bradley's *The Mists of Avalon* (1982). Among the most effective retellings of the legend is Samuel Langhorne Clemens's *A Connecticut Yankee in King Arthur's Court* (1889). Based on the Arthurian legend, Clemens's story of the Connecticut Yankee is a retelling of a much older tale. In this newer work, a protagonist named Hank Morgan experiences time travel. Clemens's version of Arthurian legend has in turn been adapted into mass media entertainments such as a Bugs Bunny cartoon entitled *A Connecticut Rabbit in King Arthur's Court* (1978) and the Disney full-length feature *A Kid in King Arthur's Court* (1995).

Narratives of noble quests, such as the search for the Holy Grail, recur throughout American folklore. Although initially readers did not warm to Clemens's Connecticut Yankee, the story of *A Connecticut Yankee in King Arthur's Court* has since been embraced as a modern classic.

See also: CLEMENS, SAMUEL LANGHORNE; FOLK HEROES/LEGENDARY FIGURES; FOLKLORE IN AMERICAN LITERATURE; FOLKTALES; LEGENDS, FOLK; NORTHEASTERN REGIONAL FOLKLORE.

For Further Reading:
Lupack, Alan, and Barbara Tepa Lupack. *King Arthur in America.* Cambridge, England: D. S. Brewer, 1999.
Mancoff, Debra, ed. *King Arthur's Modern Return.* New York: Garland, 1998.
Thompson, Raymond. *The Return from Avalon: A Study of the Arthurian Legend in Modern Fiction.* Westport, Conn.: Greenwood, 1985.

Yankee Doodle (legendary) The familiar patriotic figure of Yankee Doodle is most closely associated with a traditional song of the same name dating from the 1750s.

It is said that this character was originally framed in song by Dr. Richard Shuckburgh, a British army physician, as a mockery of the unpolished appearance of New England armed forces confronting the British army. Indeed, it appears to have been employed for this purpose since the era of the French and Indian Wars.

British troops joined in its singing during the course of battle and through its taunts asserted a superior attitude over their colonial counterparts.

Although the derivation of the term *doodle* is unknown, *Yankee* is a term of long standing in American history. *Yankee* was a name used first to describe New Englanders in general. During the Civil War era, the name was used to characterize Northerners. Typically, this term refers to New Hampshire, New York, Vermont, and the southern portion of Maine. In the 20th century, British onlookers used the term *Yanks* to refer to all Americans.

Despite the fact that the lyrics of "Yankee Doodle" were intended to insult colonial forces, in a strange turnaround or act of resistance, the song was subsequently embraced by the New England army and became something of a colonial and revolution anthem. It is said that at the close of the 1775 battle of Lexington and Concord, American soldiers played "Yankee Doodle" on fife and drum in triumph and defiance.

Although counts differ, there appear to be close to 200 verses to the tune, along with countless parodies, featuring military figures from George Washington on. During the 19th century, children sang a well-known English nursery rhyme ("Lucy Locket") to the tune of "Yankee Doodle." In 1942, a film about the life of the patriotic composer George M. Cohan bore the related title, *Yankee Doodle Dandy*.

As they learn of the nation's past, schoolchildren still learn to recite the whimsical lyrics of "Yankee Doodle" and, in so doing, come into contact with the enduring power of American patriotic lore.

See also: CIVIL WAR; FOLK HEROES/LEGENDARY FIGURES; MUSIC, FOLK; NORTHEASTERN REGIONAL FOLKLORE; PATRIOTS' DAY; REGION, FOLK; REVOLUTIONARY WAR; WASHINGTON, GEORGE.

For Further Reading:

Agay, Denes. *Best Loved Songs of the American People*. Garden City, N.Y.: Doubleday, 1975.

Chalk, Gary. *Yankee Doodle*. New York: DK, 1993.

Ditsky, John. "The Yankee Insolence of Ethan Allen," *Canadian Review of American Studies* 1 (1970): 32–38.

Hoyt, Edwin P. *The Damndest Yankees*. Brattleboro, Vt.: Stephen Green Press, 1976.

Kellogg, Steven. *Yankee Doodle*. New York: Aladdin, 1996.

McNeil, Keith, and Rusty McNeil. *Colonial and Revolution Songbook*. Riverside, Calif.: WEM Records, 1996.

Scott, John Anthony. *The Ballad of America*. New York: Grosset & Dunlap, 1967.

Yankee Peddler (legendary) The Yankee Peddler is a recurring image within American folktales. As part of a larger myth of the New England region, the Yankee, this figure exemplifies stereotypes of Northeastern character and culture.

While today the image of a "Yank" may be used to characterize any American, a Yankee more typically hails from the northern states. Such a reference was both commonly and pejoratively applied during the Civil War. During this era of sectional crisis, Confederates vowed to emerge triumphant over the North. Even today, Southerners may playfully refer to those residing north of the Mason-Dixon line as Yankees. The term *Yankee*, however, dates back as far as the Revolutionary War. During this historical period, the term was an epithet British troops applied to New England's colonists. In this sense, the usage relates closely to the now-familiar patriotic ditty "Yankee Doodle."

Within American folklore, the figure of a Yankee Peddler (often one bearing the name Jonathan Slick or Sam Slick) plays a prominent part in many cautionary and humorous tales. The Yankee Peddler is a genial, even charming, individual. Often an impressive talker, singer, and storyteller, this stock character is notable chiefly for his waggish sense of humor. In plying his trade, the peddler is given to pranks and practical jokes that manipulate people and circumstances to his own advantage. In this regard, he is a trickster. Given to disguises and subterfuge, the Yankee Peddler swindles or tricks customers and then is on his way, sometimes before his victims figure out they have been had. He anticipated the character of the confidence man, or con-man, who would later appear in the writings of such authors as Herman Melville and Samuel Langhorne Clemens. Even today, stories and jokes concerning traveling salesmen abound.

Therefore, while effective as a salesman, the folk figure of the Yankee Peddler is better remembered for his guile and wit, particularly by those who fall prey to his trickery.

See also: ANGLO-AMERICAN FOLKLORE; CIVIL WAR; CLEMENS, SAMUEL LANGHORNE; FOLK HEROES/LEGENDARY FIGURES; FOLKTALES; MELVILLE, HERMAN; NORTHEASTERN REGIONAL FOLKLORE; OCCUPATIONAL FOLKLORE; REGION, FOLK; REVOLUTIONARY WAR; TRICKSTER; YANKEE, CONNECTICUT; YANKEE DOODLE.

For Further Reading:
Hoyt, Edwin P. *The Damndest Yankees.* Brattleboro, Vt.: Stephen Green Press, 1976.

Jaffee, David. "Peddlers of Progress and the Transformation of the Rural North, 1760–1860," *Journal of American History* 78, no. 2 (September 1991): 511–535.

Jones, LuAnn. "Gender, Race, and Itinerant Commerce in the Rural New South," *Journal of Southern History* 66, no. 2 (May 2000): 297–320.

Peck, Catherine. *A Treasury of North American Folktales.* New York: W. W. Norton, 1999.

Rourke, Constance. *American Humor: A Study of the National Character.* Tallahassee: University Presses of Florida, 1986.

Yeti See BIGFOOT/SASQUATCH.

Yom Kippur Yom Kippur, a Day of Atonement within Judaism, occurs in autumn each year in accordance with the lunar calendar.

As a spiritually based new year's observance, it is the single most solemn day of the religious year. Practices associated with Yom Kippur include fasting by all but the young and sick, abstinence from business or other work, and continued prayer through services available in temples and synagogues. Yom Kippur is the culmination of a 10-day period of penitence that commences with Rosh Hashonah. It establishes the value of beginning each year with contemplation and purification of the spirit.

During this observance, believers join in an earnest process of introspection and a concerted appeal to God's forgiveness.

See also: FAMILY FOLKLORE; HOLIDAYS/OBSERVANCES; JEWISH-AMERICAN FOLKLORE; NEW YEAR'S EVE/DAY; RELIGION, FOLK; ROSH HASHONAH.

For Further Reading:
Caroza, Arlene Rossen. *Jewish Family Celebrations: The Sabbath, Festivals and Ceremonies.* New York: St. Martin's Press, 1982.

Gaster, Theodor H. *Festivals of the Jewish Year.* New York: William Sloane Associates, 1952.

Greenspoon, Leonard J., and Ronald Simkins. *Spiritual Dimensions of Judaism.* Omaha, Nebr.: Creighton University Press, 2003.

Kaplan, Dana Evan. *The Cambridge Companion to American Judaism.* New York: Cambridge University Press, 2005.

Schauss, Hayyim. *The Jewish Festivals: History and Observance.* New York: Schocken Books, 1962.

Trepp, Leo. *The Complete Book of Jewish Observance.* New York: Summit Books, 1980.

Yule/Yuletide See CHRISTMAS.

STARTING POINTS
FOR RESEARCHING
AMERICAN FOLKLORE

In preparing this book, I have had the enviable services of a library system that one of its reference specialists aptly described as "muscular"—in terms of both the depth and range of its holdings, and the access through electronic, consortia, and interlibrary resources; however, most folklore enthusiasts must rely chiefly if not exclusively on the collections and services available to them locally. I urge you to be resourceful, then, in optimizing your opportunities. What follow are some tips for those embarking on American folklore research.

- **Get to know your librarians.** They are devoted researchers and powerful allies.
- **Test the limits of your wider library system.** If you work with a branch library, find out what the county, city, or regional system affords you.
- **Be persistent.** If you have difficulty finding a particular piece of scholarship, see what else that author has published that is available to you. For example, most book-length studies and monographs begin as articles or dissertations. When one is out of print or out of reach, see whether you can turn up the other.
- **Do not be afraid of database searching.** If you have access to the Internet through a library or school interface, you probably also have the ability to conduct targeted searches within reference, index, and subject bibliography resources. While this approach may take a bit more patience than the standard search engine provided with your Web browser, it will yield results of a higher quality and degree of relevance. Conducting searches through

a database also increases the likelihood that you can locate a full-text version of a source electronically when it does not appear in hard copy at your home library. For folklore study, the *MLA Bibliography*, *America: History and Life*, and *Expanded Academic Index* are among the most helpful.

- **Remember that published scholars share your interests in the subject matter.** When you have a need or a question that cannot be addressed through library or archival research, you might weigh the option of contacting the author(s) who are most knowledgeable about the topic. While you do not wish to impose on a scholar's time or exploit the person's expertise, you can certainly address yourself to a scholar or fellow folklore enthusiast. So long as your requests are reasonable, specific, and respectfully framed, there is a good chance that a folklorist will respond to the occasional e-mail or letter. Many authors enjoy hearing from their readers, so there is little harm in thanking them for their work and/or asking for a clarification or tip for your own work.
- **Consider contributing sources as well as using existing ones.** Many folklorists collect as well as analyze material, so why not you? With some preparation (courses, training, reading, and the like) you might preserve evidence or collect information available to you. This can begin with an interview, photographic documentation, or other technique. After all, where would the study of American folklore be if no one felt qualified to enrich the archive of folk material?

- **Ask chewy questions.** Having worked as a teacher for many years, I can say that a compelling guide question often accounts for the difference between mediocre research and groundbreaking research. This approach requires you to be somewhat bold, attempting something at which you may not, at least at the outset, be certain you can prove successful. Be daring anyway. While it is true that you should not overreach, in this context, it is better to attempt something difficult or subtle and fall slightly short of the goal than to attempt something easy and obvious and succeed utterly. Those who take on the most challenging questions will achieve the greatest outcomes.

So, what is a chewy question and how does one go about arriving at one? Here are some thoughts I would offer as starting points.

A chewy question:

is specific—

It lends itself to targeted research that both restricts your assignment to a manageable scale and plays to the strength of available evidence, particularly the two featured sources.

(Watch out for a question so broad that it could be answered with generalities, surmises reached without evidence, or application of common sense alone.)

is open-ended—

It benefits from a discovery-based approach, justifies discussion, and requires argumentation.

(Avoid one that can be answered fully with a short answer, and by all means eschew one that might be resolved with a "yes," "no," or even the safe-but-dreary-dull standby, a "yes and no" answer.)

ultimately demands that you take a stand—

It will soon enough become necessary for you to form your own response and communicate your conclusions about its importance. In other words, it would never be enough for a researcher to report what others—including the so-called experts—have found, said, or concluded regarding your question or one similar to it.

(Beware of a question that invites mere summary or review of existing scholarship.)

requires you to arrive at an insight—

It calls upon you to address a gap or deficiency in the existing scholarship. While your insight need not be elaborate or grand, it should nonetheless contribute something new to our understanding of the topic.

(Stay away from a question that, while it may be one you feel confident you can resolve, will yield an answer that surprises no one, including you.)

incurs some degree of intellectual risk taking—

It should be possible for reasonable and informed people to disagree with your response to the question—typically on the basis of the way you have interpreted evidence.

(Steer clear of any question that addresses a matter of unambiguous record and utter consensus across sources/perspectives/populations/media.)

asks about the implications of history—

It stimulates analysis of historical phenomena rather than straightforward reconstruction of them—usually by posing questions about "how," "why" and "with what result."

(Move beyond a question that aims no higher than to determine "what," "who," or "when.")

approaches evidence in an investigative way—

It demonstrates your prowess as historian-detective, all the while governing that energy with a keen sense of the need to substantiate all claims.

(Be provocative in the question you pursue, but be equally scrupulous in marshalling support for your findings.)

tackles an issue of real consequence—

It sets in motion an inquiry that matters both to you and to your audience.

(Guard against a question that, while meticulously researched and impeccably answered, could be legitimately greeted by the reader with a frank retort of "So what?")

proves undeniably relevant to a human(e) purpose—

It serves the common good as well as gratifies the author's own need to know. It is attentive to the benefits such inquiry can afford an actual audience of readers. Before you consider a project finished, ask yourself the two chewiest questions of all about the implications of your findings: "So what?" and "Now what?")

(Guard against a product that ignores or fails to address the needs, interests, and pleasures of your immediate audience.)

- **Keep asking chewy questions.** Why stop at one? Every folklorist's career began with a really intriguing question. (Ask one and you can see for yourself.) Good questions lead to better, more meaningful ones. In an important sense, this is how research proceeds—through the refinement of an issue of investigation, expressed as an urgent but as yet unanswered question.
- **Involve others in your discoveries.** Help other people benefit from your research, but—as important—stimulate them to find their own chewy questions. In this way, you give back to folklore studies and help the process deepen and continue.

SELECTED BIBLIOGRAPHY OF AMERICAN FOLKLORE

While some specifically relevant resources appear in the "For Further Reading" portion of every individual entry in this encyclopedia, there are many other works—both scholarly and popular—that influenced this book's writing. They may also prove helpful to your explorations of American folklore. Items in this bibliography are arranged by format category: Bibliographies, Dictionaries, Encyclopedias, Guides, Treasuries, Monographs, Articles, and so forth. See which of these materials are available through your own library, and see where the research leads you.

BIBLIOGRAPHIES

Carnes, Pack. *Fable Scholarship*. New York: Garland, 1985.

Coughlan, Margaret. *Folklore from Africa to the United States: An Annotated Bibliography*. Detroit: Omnigraphics, 1999.

De Caro, Frank. *Women and Folklore: A Bibliographic Survey*. Westport, Conn.: Greenwood Press, 1983.

Flanagan, Cathleen, and John T. Flanagan. *American Folklore: A Bibliography, 1950–1974*. Metuchen, N.J.: Scarecrow Press, 1977.

Gillian, Bennett, and Paul Smith. *Contemporary Legend: A Folklore Bibliography*. New York: Garland, 1993.

Haywood, Charles. *A Bibliography of North American Folklore and Folksong*. New York: Greenberg, 1951.

Hickerson, Joseph. *American Folklore: A Bibliography of Major Works*. Washington, D.C.: Library of Congress/Archive of Folk Song, 1975.

Hickerson, Joseph. *A Tentative Beginning toward a Bibliography on the History of American Folkloristics and the American Folklore Society*. Washington, D.C.: Library of Congress/Archive of Folk Song, 1973.

Jones, Steven Swann. *Folklore and Literature in the United States: An Annotated Bibliography of Studies of Folklore in American Literature*. New York: Garland, 1984.

Ramsey, Eloise, and Dorothy Mills Howard. *Folklore for Children and Young People: A Critical and Descriptive Bibliography for Use in the Elementary and Intermediate School*. New York: Kraus Reprint, 1970.

DICTIONARIES

Axelrod, Alan, and Harry Oster, with Walton Rowls. *The Penguin Dictionary of American Folklore*. New York: Penguin Reference, 2000.

Cassidy, Frederic, and Joan Hall. *Dictionary of American Regional English*. Cambridge, Mass.: Belknap Press, 1985.

Fergusson, Rosalind, comp. *The Facts On File Dictionary of Proverbs*. New York: Facts On File, 1983.

James, Edward T. *Notable American Women, 1607–1950, a Biographical Dictionary*. Cambridge, Mass.: Belknap Press, 1971.

Jobes, Gertrude. *Dictionary of Mythology, Folklore, and Symbols*. 2 vols. New York: Scarecrow Press, 1962.

Jones, Alison. *Larousse Dictionary of World Folklore*. New York: Larousse, 1995.

Kutler, Stanley, ed. *Dictionary of American History*. New York: Scribner's Sons, 2003.

Leach, Maria. *Funk and Wagnalls Standard Dictionary of Folklore, Mythology and Legend*. New York: Funk and Wagnalls, 1949.

Leeming, David A., and Margaret Leeming. *A Dictionary of Creation Myths*. New York: Oxford University Press, 1995.

Mieder, Wolfgang, ed. *A Dictionary of American Proverbs*. New York: Oxford University Press, 1992.

Opie, Iona, and Moira Tatem, eds. *A Dictionary of Superstitions*. New York: Oxford University Press, 1989.

Pickering, David. *A Dictionary of Folklore*. New York: Facts On File, 1999.

Pyatt, Sherman, and Alan Johns. *A Dictionary and Catalog of African American Folklife of the South*. Westport, Conn.: Greenwood Press, 1999.

Sicherman, Barbara et al. eds. *Notable American Women: The Modern Period, a Biographical Dictionary*. Cambridge, Mass.: Belknap Press, 1980.

Tallman, Marjorie. *Dictionary of American Folklore*. New York: Philosophical Library, 1960.

Taylor, Archer, and Bartlett Jere Whiting. *A Dictionary of American Proverbs and Proverbial Phrases, 1820–1880*. Cambridge, Mass.: Belknap Press, 1967.

Ware, Susan. *Notable American Women: A Biographical Dictionary Completing the Twentieth Century*. Cambridge, Mass.: Belknap Press, 2004.

ENCYCLOPEDIA

Americans at War: Society, Culture, and the Homefront. Detroit: Macmillan Reference USA, 2005.

Asante, Molefi, and Ama Mazama, eds. *Encyclopedia of Black Studies*. Thousand Oaks, Calif.: Sage, 2005.

Bortman, Marci et al., eds. *Environmental Encyclopedia*. Detroit: Gale, 2003.

Breslow, Lester, ed. *Encyclopedia of Public Health*. New York: Macmillan, 2002.

Briggs, Kathrine. *An Encyclopedia of Fairies*. New York: Pantheon Books, 1976.

Brunvand, Jan Harold. *American Folklore: An Encyclopedia*. New York: Garland, 1998.

———. *Encyclopedia of Urban Legends*. Santa Barbara, Calif.: ABC-CLIO, 2001.

Carson, Thomas, and Mary Bonk, eds. *Encyclopedia of U.S. Economic History*. Detroit: Gale, 1999.

Cooper, J. C. *Symbolic and Mythological Animals*. London: HarperCollins, 1992.

Cullen-DuPont, Kathryn. *The Encyclopedia of Women's History in America*. New York: Facts On File, 1996.

Dynes, Wayne, ed. *Encyclopedia of Homosexuality*. New York: Garland, 1990.

Flynn, Roger, ed. *Computer Sciences*. New York: Macmillan, 2002.

Green, Thomas, ed. *Folklore: An Encyclopedia of Beliefs, Customs, Tales, Music, and Art*. Santa Barbara, Calif.: ABC-CLIO, 1997.

Guiley, Rosemary. *The Encyclopedia of Ghosts and Spirits*. New York: Facts On File, 1992.

Guthrie, James, ed. *Encyclopedia of Education*. New York: Macmillan, 2002.

Hirschfelder, Arlene, and Paulette Molin. *Encyclopedia of Native American Religions*. New York: Facts On File, 2000.

Kastenbaum, Robert. *Macmillan Encyclopedia of Death and Dying*. New York: Macmillan, 2003.

Lauer, Josh, and Neil Schlager, eds. *Science and Its Times: Understanding the Social Significance of Scientific Discovery*. Detroit: Gale, 2000.

Lehman, Jeffrey, ed. *Encyclopedia of Multicultural America*. Detroit: Gale, 2000.

MacDonald, Margaret Read. *The Folklore of World Holidays*. Detroit: Gale, 1992.

Nilsen, Alleen Pace, and Don Nilsen. *Encyclopedia of 20th-Century American Humor*. Phoenix: Oryx, 2000.

Pendergast, Sara, and Tom Pendergast, eds. *St. James Encyclopedia of Popular Culture*. Detroit: St. James Press, 2000.

Ponzetti, James J., Jr., ed. *International Encyclopedia of Marriage and Family*. New York: Macmillan, 2003.

Radford E., and M. A. Radford. *Encyclopaedia of Superstitions*. Westport, Conn.: Greenwood Press, 1969.

Resch, John, ed. *Americans at War*. Detroit: Macmillan, 2005.

Roof, Wade Clark. *Contemporary American Religion*. New York: Macmillan, 1999.

Rose, Carol. *Spirits, Fairies, Gnomes, and Goblins*. Santa Barbara, Calif.: ABC-CLIO, 1996.

Rosenberg, Bruce, and Mary Ellen Brown. *Encyclopedia of Folklore and Literature*. Santa Barbara, Calif.: ABC-CLIO, 1998.

Sader, Marion, ed. *Storytelling Encyclopedia: Historical, Cultural, and Multiethnic Approaches to Oral Traditions Around the World*, Phoenix, Ariz.: Oryx Press, 1997.

Sax, Boria. *The Mythical Zoo: An Encyclopedia of Animals in World Myth, Legend, and Literature*, Santa Barbara, Calif.: ABC-CLIO, 2001.

Scribners Reference Shelf. *Encyclopedia of American Cultural History*. New York: Scribners, 1999.

Seal, Graham. *Encyclopedia of Folk Heroes*. Santa Barbara, Calif.: ABC-CLIO, 2001.

Setnam, George. *Devils, Ghosts, and Witches: Occult Folklore of the Upper Ohio Valley*. Greensburg, Pa.: McDonald/Sward, 1988.

Sifakis, Carl. *The Encyclopedia of American Crime*. New York: Smithmark, 1992.

Smelser, Neil, and Paul Baltes. *International Encyclopedia of the Social and Behavioral Sciences*. New York: Elsevier, 2001.

Snodgrass, Mary Ellen. *Encyclopedia of Fable*. Santa Barbara, Calif.: ABC-CLIO, 1998.

Snodgrass, Mary Ellen. *Encyclopedia of Frontier Literature*. Santa Barbara, Calif.: ABC-CLIO, 1997.

———. *Encyclopedia of Southern Literature*. Santa Barbara, Calif.: ABC-CLIO, 1997.

Solomon, H. Katz, ed. *Encyclopedia of Food and Culture*. New York: Scribner's Sons, 2003.

Spalding, Henry. *Encyclopedia of Black Folklore and Humor*. New York: Jonathan David, 1978.

Stein, Marc, ed. *Encyclopedia of Lesbian, Gay, Bisexual and Transgendered History in America*. Detroit: Gale, 2004.

GUIDES/DIRECTORIES

Anyike, James. *African American Holidays: A Historical Research and Resource Guide to Cultural Celebrations*. Chicago: Popular Truth, 1991.

Ashliman, D. L. *A Guide to Folktales in the English Language*. New York: Greenwood Press, 1987.

Baker, Holly Cutting, Amy Kotkin, and Margaret Yocom. *Family Folklore: Interviewing Guide and Questionnaire*. Washington, D.C.: Smithsonian Institution/Folklife Program, 1978.

Bartis, Peter. *Folklife and Fieldwork: A Layman's Introduction to Field Techniques*. Washington, D.C.: Library of Congress/American Folklife Center, 1980.

Bartis, Peter, and Hillary Glatt. *Folklife Sourcebook: A Directory of Folklife Resources in the United States*. Washington, D.C.: U.S. Government Printing Office, 1994.

Bartis, Peter, and Mary Hufford. *Maritime Folklife Resources: A Directory and Index*. Washington, D.C.: American Folklife Center/Library of Congress, 1980.

Bartis, Peter, and Paddy Bowman. *A Teacher's Guide to Folklife Resources for K–12 Classrooms*. Washington, D.C.: American Folklife Center/Library of Congress, 1994.

Coe, Linda C. *Folklife and the Federal Government: A Guide to Activities, Resources, Funds, and Services*. Washington, D.C.: U.S. Government Printing Office, 1977.

Corsaro, James, and Karen Taussig-Lux. *Folklore in Archives: A Guide to Describing Folklore and Folklife Materials*. New York: New York Folklore Society, 1998.

Davidson, Levette. *A Guide to American Folklore*. Denver: Sage Books, 1951.

Dorson, Richard M., ed. *Handbook of American Folklore*. Bloomington: Indiana University Press, 1986.

Guiley, Rosemary Ellen. *Atlas of the Mysterious in North America*. New York: Facts On File, 1995.

Hickerson, Joseph Charles. *Folklore and Folk Music Archives and Related Collections in the United States and Canada*. Washington, D.C.: Library of Congress/Archive of Folk Song, 1978.

Kerschen, Lois. *American Proverbs about Women: A Reference Guide*. Westport, Conn.: Greenwood Press, 1998.

Lloyd, Timothy, and Hillary Glatt. *Folklife Resources in the Library of Congress*. Washington, D.C.: American Folklife Center, Library of Congress, 1994.

Mood, Terry Ann. *American Regional Folklore: A Sourcebook and Research Guide*. Santa Barbara, Calif.: ABC-CLIO, 2004.

Schoemaker, George H., ed. *The Emergence of Folklore in Everyday Life: A Fieldguide and Sourcebook*. Bloomington, Ind.: Trickster Press, 1990.

South, Malcolm, ed. *Mythical and Fabulous Creatures: A Source Book and Research Guide*. New York: Greenwood Press, 1987.

Spratford, Becky Siegel, and Tammy Hennigh Clausen. *The Horror Readers' Advisory: The Librarian's Guide to Vampires, Killer Tomatoes, and Haunted Houses*. Chicago: American Library Association, 2004.

Steinfirst, Susan. *Folklore and Folklife: A Guide to English-Language Reference Sources*. New York: Garland, 1992.

Taylor, David Alan. *Documenting Maritime Folklife: An Introductory Guide*. Washington, D.C.: Library of Congress, 1992.

Thomas, Inge. *Handbook of American Popular Culture*. New York: Greenwood Press, 1989.

White, John. *Catalog of Folklore, Folklife, and Folk Songs*. Boston: G. K. Hall, 1964.

ARCHIVES

Corsaro, James, and Karen Taussig-Lux. *Folklore in Archives: A Guide to Describing Folklore and Folklife Materials*. Schenectady: New York Folklore Society, 1998.

Davidson, Levette. *A Guide to American Folklore*. Denver: Sage Books, 1951.

Folk Heritage Collections in Crisis. Washington, D.C.: Council on Library and Information Resources, 2001.

Folklife Sourcebook: A Directory of Folklife Resources in the United States. Library of Congress. Available online. http://lcweb.loc.gov/folklife/source/. Accessed March 2, 2006.

Hall, Stephanie. *Ethnographic Collections in the Archive of Folk Culture.* Washington, D.C.: American Folklife Center, 1995.

Lloyd, Timothy. *The Archive of Folk Culture: The National Collection of American and World Folklife.* Washington, D.C.: American Folklife Center/ Library of Congress, 1992.

Steinfirst, Susan. *Folklore and Folklife: A Guide to English-Language Reference Sources.* New York: Garland, 1992.

TREASURIES

Battle, Kemp P. *Great American Folklore: Legends, Tales, Ballads and Superstitions from All across America.* New York: Doubleday, 1986.

Botkin, B. A., ed. *The American People in Their Stories, Legends, Tall Tales, Traditions, Ballads and Songs.* London: Pilot Press, 1946.

Botkin, Benjamin, ed. *A Civil War Treasury of Tales, Legends, and Folklore.* New York: Random House, 1960.

———. *Lay My Burden Down: A Folk History of Slavery.* Athens: University of Georgia Press, 1989.

Botkin, Benjamin. *Sidewalks of America: Folklore, Legends, Sagas, Traditions, Customs, Songs, Stories, and Sayings of City Folk.* Indianapolis: Bobbs-Merrill, 1954.

———. *A Treasury of American Anecdotes: Sly, Salty, Shaggy Stories of Heroes and Hellions, Beguilers and Buffoons, Spellbinders and Scapegoats, Gagsters and Gossips, from the Grassroots and Sidewalks of America.* New York: Bonanza Books, 1957.

Botkin, B. A., ed. *A Treasury of American Folklore: Stories, Ballads, and Traditions of the People.* New York: Crown, 1944.

Botkin, Benjamin. *A Treasury of Mississippi River Folklore: Stories, Ballads, and Folkways of the Mid-American River Country.* New York: Crown, 1955.

———. *A Treasury of New England Folklore: Stories, Ballads, and Traditions of the Yankee People.* New York: Crown, 1947.

Botkin, Benjamin, ed. *A Treasury of Railroad Folklore: The Stories, Tall Tales, Traditions, Ballads, and Songs of the American Railroad Man.* New York: Crown, 1953.

———. *A Treasury of Southern Folklore: Stories, Ballads, Traditions, and Folkways of the People of the South.* New York: Crown, 1949.

———. *A Treasury of Western Folklore.* New York: Crown, 1951.

Clarkson, Atelia, and Gilbert Cross. *World Folktales.* New York: Charles Scribner Sons, 1980.

Cohn, Amy L., ed. *From Sea to Shining Sea: A Treasury of American Folklore and Folk Songs.* New York: Scholastic, 1993.

Courlander, Harold. *A Treasury of Afro-American Folklore: The Oral Literature, Traditions, Recollections, Legends, Tales, Songs, Religious Beliefs, Customs, Sayings, and Humor of Peoples of African Descent in the Americas.* New York: Crown, 1976.

Davis, Hubert, ed. *A January Fog Will Freeze a Hog, and Other Weather Folklore.* New York: Crown, 1977.

De Lys, Claudia. *A Treasury of American Superstitions.* New York: Philosophical Library, 1948.

Emrich, Duncan. *The Hodgepodge Book: An Almanac of American Folklore: Containing All Manner of Curious, Interesting, and Out-of-the-Way Information Drawn from American Folklore, and Not to Be Found Anywhere Else in the World; As Well as Jokes, Conundrums, Riddles, Puzzles, and Other Matter Designed to Amuse and Entertain—All of It Most Instructive and Delightful.* New York: Four Winds, 1972.

Fleming, Robert Loren, and Robert F. Boyd, Jr. *The Big Book of Urban Legends: Adapted from the Works of Jan Jarold Brunvand.* New York: Paradox Press, 1994.

Lys, Claudia de. *A Treasury of American Superstitions.* New York: Philosophical Library, 1948.

Ruggoff, Milton Allan. *A Harvest of World Folk Tales.* New York: Viking Press, 1949.

Wood, Ray. *The American Mother Goose.* New York: Frederick A. Stokes, 1940.

Yolden, Jane. *Favorite Folktales from around the World.* New York: Pantheon Books, 1986.

OTHER BOOKS

Abernethy, Francis Edward, ed. *Juneteenth Texas: Essays in African American Folklore.* Denton: University of North Texas Press, 1996.

Abrahams, Roger D., ed. *African American Folktales: Stories from Black Traditions in the New World*. New York: Pantheon Books, 1985.

Abrams, Ann Uhry. *The Pilgrims and Pocohontas: Rival Myths of American Origin*. Boulder, Colo.: Westview Press, 1999.

Ambrose, Stephen E., and Douglas Brinkley. *Witness to America: An Illustrated Documentary History of the United States from the Revolution to Today*. New York: HarperCollins, 1999.

Bartis, Peter. *Folklife and Fieldwork: A Layman's Introduction to Field Techniques*. Washington, D.C.: Library of Congress, 2002.

Bascom, William. *African Folktales in the New World*. Bloomington: Indiana University Press, 1992.

Bascom, William, ed. *Frontiers of Folklore*. Boulder, Colo.: Westview Press, 1977.

Battle, Kemp. *Hearts of Fire: Great Women of American Lore and Legend*. New York: Harmony Books, 1997.

Bauman, Richard. *Story, Performance, and Event: Conceptual Studies of Oral Narrative*. New York: Cambridge University Press, 1986.

Bauman, Richard, and Américo Paredes, eds. *Toward New Perspectives in Folklore*. Austin: University of Texas Press, 1972.

Becker, Jane, and Barbara Franco, eds. *Folk Roots, New Roots: Folklore in American Life*. Lexington, Mass.: Museum of Our National Heritage, 1988.

Beckwith, Martha Warren. *Folklore in America: Its Scope and Method*. Poughkeepsie, N.Y.: Vassar College/Folklore Foundation, 1931.

Bell, Bernard. *The Contemporary African American Novel: Its Folk Roots and Modern Literary Branches*. Amherst: University of Massachusetts Press, 2004.

Ben-Amos, Dan, ed. *Folklore Genres*. Austin: University of Texas Press, 1976.

Ben-Amos, Dan, and Kenneth S. Goldstein, eds. *Folklore: Performance and Communication*. The Hague: Mouton, 1975.

Bendix, Regina. *In Search of Authenticity: The Formation of Folklore Studies*. Madison: University of Wisconsin Press, 1997.

Bennett, Gillian. *Tradition of Belief: Women, Folklore, and the Supernatural*. New York: Penguin Books, 1987.

Berger, Harris, and Giovanna Del Negro, eds. *Identity and Everyday Life: Essays in the Study of Folklore, Music and Popular Culture*. Middletown, Conn.: Wesleyan University Press, 2004.

Bettelheim, Bruno. *The Uses of Enchantment: The Meaning and Importance of Fairy Tales*. New York: Knopf, 1976.

Bierhorst, John. *The Mythology of North America*. New York: William Morrow, 1985.

Billingslea-Brown, Alma. *Crossing Borders through Folklore: African American Women's Fiction and Art*. Columbia: University of Missouri Press, 1999.

Blair, Walter. *Tall Tale America: A Legendary History of Our Humorous Heroes*. New York: Coward-McCann, 1944.

Blau, Judith. *The Shape of Culture: A Study of Contemporary Cultural Patterns in the United States*. New York: Cambridge University Press, 1989.

Bluestein, Gene. *Poplore: Folk and Pop in American Culture*. Amherst: University of Massachusetts Press, 1994.

———. *The Voice of the Folk: Folklore and American Literary Theory*. Amherst: University of Massachusetts Press, 1972.

Bogart, Barbara Allen. *Sense of Place: American Regional Cultures*. Lexington: University Press of Kentucky, 1990.

Boller, Paul F., Jr., *Not So! Popular Myths about America from Columbus to Clinton*. New York: Oxford University Press, 1995.

Bredsdorff, Elias. *Hans Christian Andersen: An Introduction to His Life and Works*. Copenhagen: Hans Reitzels Forlag, 1987.

Bronner, Simon. *American Folklore Studies: An Intellectual History*. Lawrence: University Press of Kansas, 1986.

Bronner, Simon, ed. *Folklife Studies from the Gilded Age: Object, Rite, and Custom in Victorian America*. Ann Arbor, Mich.: UMI Research Press, 1987.

Bronner, Simon, *Folk Nation: Folklore in the Creation of American Tradition*. Wilmington, Del.: Scholarly Resources, 2002.

———. *Following Tradition: Folklore in the Discourse of American Culture*. Logan: Utah State University Press, 1998.

———. *Grasping Things: Folk Material Culture and Mass Society in America*. Lexington: University Press of Kentucky, 1986.

Brown, Bill, ed. *Things*. Chicago: University of Chicago Press, 2004.

Brown, Carolyn. *The Tall Tale in American Folklore and Literature.* Knoxville: University of Tennessee Press, 1987.

Brunvand, Jan Harold. *The Choking Doberman.* New York: W. W. Norton, 1984.

———. *Folklore: A Study and Research Guide.* New York: St. Martin's Press, 1976.

———. *On the Teaching of American Folklore.* New York: W. W. Norton, 1970.

Brunvand, Jan Harold, ed. *Readings in American Folklore.* New York: W. W. Norton, 1979.

Brunvand, Jan Harold. *The Study of American Folklore: An Introduction.* New York: Penguin Reference, 2000.

———. *The Vanishing Hitchhiker: American Urban Legends and Their Meanings.* New York: W. W. Norton, 1981.

Bryant, Jerry. *Born in a Mighty Bad Land: The Violent Man in African American Folklore and Fiction.* Bloomington: Indiana University Press, 2003.

Burrison, John. *Storytellers: Folktales and Legends from the South.* Athens: University of Georgia Press, 1989.

Butler-Evans, Elliott. *Race, Gender, and Desire: Narrative Strategies in the Fiction of Toni Cade Bambara, Toni Morrison, and Alice Walker.* Philadelphia: Temple University Press, 1989.

Camp, Charles, ed. *Time and Temperature: A Centennial Publication of the American Folklore Society.* Washington, D.C.: American Folklore Society, 1989.

Cantwell, Robert. *Ethnomimesis: Folklife and the Representation of Culture.* Chapel Hill: University of North Carolina Press, 1993.

Carter, George E., and James R. Parker. *Afro-American Folklore: A Unique American Experience.* La Crosse: Institute for Minority Studies, University of Wisconsin-La Crosse, 1977.

Carvalho-Meto, Paulo de. *The Concept of Folklore.* Coral Gables, Fla.: University of Miami Press, 1971.

Cashdan, Sheldon. *The Witch Must Die: The Hidden Meaning of Fairy Tales.* New York: Basic Books, 1999.

Cashion, Gerald, ed. *Conceptual Problems in Contemporary Folklore Study.* Bloomington, Ind.: Folklore Forum Society, 1974.

Chambers, Wiche, and Spring Asher. *The Celebration Book of Great American Traditions.* New York: Harper & Row, 1983.

Chase, Richard. *The Jack Tales.* Boston: Houghton Mifflin, 1943.

Clements, William, ed. *One Hundred Years of American Folklore Studies: A Conceptual History.* Washington, D.C.: American Folklore Society, 1988.

Clough, Ben C., ed. *The American Imagination at Work: Tall Tales and Folk Tales.* New York: Knopf, 1947.

Coffin, Tristram Potter. *The Female Hero in Folklore and Legend.* New York: Seabury Press, 1975.

Coffin, Tristram Potter, ed. *Our Living Traditions: An Introduction to American Folklore.* New York: Basic Books, 1968.

Coffin, Tristram Potter, and Hennig Cohen, eds. *Folklore in America.* Garden City, N.Y.: Doubleday, 1966.

———. *The Parade of Heroes: Legendary Figures in American Lore.* Garden City, N.Y.: Anchor Press/ Doubleday, 1978.

Coleman, Loren, *Mysterious America.* New York: Paraview Press, 1983.

Counihan, Carole M., ed. *Food in the USA: A Reader.* New York: Routledge, 2002.

Cullen, Jim. *The Art of Democracy: A Concise History of Popular Culture in the United States.* New York: Monthly Review Press, 1996.

Cussler, Margaret, and Mary L. de Give. *'Twixt the Cup and the Lip: Psychological and Socio-Cultural Factors Affecting Food Habits.* New York: Twayne, 1952.

Daily, Don. *The Classic Treasury of Aesop's Fables.* Philadelphia: Courage Books, 1999.

Dance, Daryl Cumber, ed. *From My People: 400 Years of African American Folklore.* New York: W. W. Norton, 2002.

Dance, Daryl Cumber. *Shuckin' and Jivin': Folklore from Contemporary Black Americans.* Bloomington: Indiana University Press, 1978.

Danet, Brenda. *Cyberplay: Communicating Online.* Oxford: Berg, 2001.

De Caro, Frank, and Rosan Augusta Jordan. *Re-Situating Folklore: Folk Contexts and Twentieth-Century Literature and Art.* Knoxville: University of Tennessee Press, 2004.

Dégh, Linda. *American Folklore and the Mass Media.* Bloomington: Indiana University Press, 1994.

Dégh, Linda, Henry Glassie, and Felix Oinas, eds. *Folklore Today: A Festschrift for Richard M. Dorson.* Bloomington: Indiana University, Research Center for Language and Semiotic Studies, 1976.

De Onis, Harriet. *The Golden Land: An Anthology of Latin American Folklore in Literature*. New York: Knopf, 1948.

Dilworth, Leah. *Acts of Possession: Collecting in America*. New Brunswick, N.J.: Rutgers University Press, 2003.

Donald, David Berbert. *Lincoln Reconsidered: Essays on the Civil War Era*. New York: Knopf, 1956.

Dorson, Richard M. *America Begins*. New York: Arno Press, 1950.

———. *America in Legend: Folklore from the Colonial Period to the Present*. New York: Pantheon Books, 1973.

———. *American Folklore*. Chicago: University of Chicago Press, 1959.

Dorson, Richard M. *American Folklore and the Historian*. Chicago: University of Chicago Press, 1971.

———. *America Rebels: Narratives of the Patriots*. New York: Pantheon, 1953.

———. *Bloodstoppers and Bearwalkers: Folk Traditions of the Upper Peninsula*. Cambridge, Mass.: Harvard University Press, 1952.

Dorson, Richard M., ed. *Buying the Wind: Regional Folklore in the United States*. Chicago: University of Chicago Press, 1964.

Dorson, Richard M. *Folklore and Fakelore: Essays toward a Discipline of Folk Studies*. Cambridge, Mass.: Harvard University Press, 1981.

Dorson, Richard M., ed. *Folklore and Folklife: An Introduction*. Chicago: University of Chicago Press, 1972.

Dorson, Richard M. *Folklore and Traditional History*. The Hague: Mouton, 1973.

———. *Folklore in the Modern World*. The Hague: Mouton, 1978.

———. *Folklore Research around the World: A North American Point of View*. Bloomington: Indiana University Press, 1961.

———. *Folklore: Selected Essays*. Bloomington: Indiana University Press, 1972.

Dorson, Richard M., ed. *Folktales Told around the World*. Chicago: University of Chicago Press, 1975.

Dorson, Richard M., ed. *Handbook of American Folklore*. Bloomington: Indiana University Press, 1983.

Dorson, Richard M. *Jonathan Draws the Long Bow*. Cambridge, Mass.: Harvard University Press, 1946.

———. *Land of the Millrats*. Cambridge, Mass.: Harvard University Press, 1981.

———. *Man and Beast in American Comic Legend*. Bloomington: Indiana University Press, 1982.

———. *Negro Folktales in Michigan*. Cambridge, Mass.: Harvard University Press, 1956.

———. *Negro Tales from Pine Bluff, Arkansas, and Calvin, Michigan*. Millwood, N.Y.: Kraus Reprint, 1975.

Douglass, Mary. *Natural Symbols: Explorations in Cosmology*. New York: Pantheon, 1982.

Dundes, Alan. *Analytic Essays in Folklore*. The Hague: Mouton, 1975.

———. *From Game to War and Other Psychoanalytic Essays on Folklore*. Lexington: University Press of Kentucky, 1997.

Dundes, Alan, ed. *International Folkloristics: Classic Contributions by the Founders of Folklore*. Lanham, Md.: Rowman & Littlefield, 1989.

Dundes, Alan. *Interpreting Folklore*. Bloomington: Indiana University Press, 1980.

Dundes, Alan, ed. *Mother Wit from the Laughing Barrel: Readings in the Interpretation of Afro-American Folklore*. Jackson: University Press of Mississippi, 1990.

Dundes, Alan. *The Study of Folklore*. Englewood Cliffs, N.J.: Prentice-Hall, 1965.

Edmonds, Margot. *Voices of the Wind: Native American Legends*. New York: Facts On File, 1989.

Edmonson, Munro. *Lore: An Introduction to the Science of Folklore and Literature*. New York: Holt, Rinehart & Winston, 1971.

Elsner, John, and Roger Cardinal. *The Cultures of Collecting*. Cambridge, Mass.: Harvard University Press, 1994.

Emrich, Duncan. *Folklore in the American Land*. Boston: Little, Brown, 1972.

Farrer, Claire R., ed. *Women and Folklore*. Austin: University of Texas Press, 1975.

Feintuch, Burt, ed. *The Conservation of Culture: Folklorists and the Public Sector*. Lexington: University Press of Kentucky, 1988.

Ferris, William. *Afro-American Folk Arts and Crafts*. Jackson: University of Mississippi Press, 1983.

Fife, Austin, Alta Fife, and Henry H. Glassie, eds. *Forms upon the Frontier: Folklife and the Folklife and Folk Arts in the United States*. Logan: Utah State University Press, 1969.

Fishwick, Marshall. *Probing Popular Culture: On and Off the Internet*. New York: Haworth, 2004.

Foley, John Miles, ed. *Teaching Oral Traditions*. New York: Modern Language Association, 1998.

Frank, Diana, and Jeffrey Frank, eds. *The Stories of Hans Christian Andersen*. Boston: Houghton Mifflin, 2003.

Freccero, Carla. *Popular Culture: An Introduction*. New York: New York University Press. 1999.

Gardner, Ralph D. *Horatio Alger, or, The American Hero Era*. Mendota, Ill.: Wayside Press, 1964.

Geist, Valerius. *Buffalo Nation: History and Legend of the North American Bison*. Stillwater, Minn.: Voyageur Press, 1996.

Glazer, Mark, ed. *Flour from Another Sack and Other Proverbs, Folk Beliefs, Tales, Riddles, and Recipes*. Edinburg, Tex.: Pan American University, 1982.

Goss, Linda, and Marian E. Barnes. *Talk That Talk: An Anthology of African-American Storytelling*. New York: Simon & Schuster, 1989.

Green, Archie. *Wobblies, Pile Butts, and Other Heroes: Laborlore Explorations*. Urbana: University of Illinois Press, 1993.

Hallett, Martin, and Barbara Karasek. *Folk and Fairy Tales*. 3d ed. New York: Broadview Press, 2002.

Hamilton, Virginia. *The People Could Fly: American Black Folktales*. New York: Knopf, 1985.

Harris, Joel Chandler. *Told by Uncle Remus: New Stories of the Old Plantation*. New York: Grosset & Dunlap, 1903.

Hatch, Jane M., ed. *The American Book of Days*. 3d ed. New York: H. W. Wilson, 1978.

Hausman, Gerald. *Turtle Island Alphabet: A Lexicon of Native American Symbols and Culture*. New York: St. Martin's Press, 1992.

Hollis, Susan Tower, Linda Pershing, and M. Jane Young, eds. *Feminist Theory and the Study of Folklore*. Urbana: University of of Illinois Press, 1993.

Hufford, Mary, ed. *Conserving Culture: A New Discourse on Heritage*. Urbana: University of Illinois Press, 1994.

Hughes, Langston, and Arna Bontemps, eds. *The Book of Negro Folklore*. New York: Dodd, Mead, 1958.

Humphrey, Theodore C., and Lin T. Humphrey, eds. *"We Gather Together": Food and Festival in American Life*. Ann Arbor, Mich.: UMI Research Press, 1988.

Jackson, Bruce. *Folklore and Society: Essays in Honor of Benjamin A. Botkin*. Hatboro, Pa.: Folklore Associates, 1966.

Jackson, Bruce, Judith McCulloh, and Marta Weigle, eds. *Folklore and Folklife*. Washington, D.C.: American Folklore Society, 1984.

Jacobs, Melville. *The Anthropologist Looks at Myth*. Austin: University of Texas Press, 1966.

Jacoby, Mario, Verena Kast, and Ingrid Riedel. *Witches, Ogres, and the Devil's Daughter: Encounters with Evil in Fairy Tales*. Boston: Shambhala, 1992.

Jarmon, Laura. *Wishbone: Reference and Interpretation in Black Folk Narrative*. Knoxville: University of Tennessee Press, 2003.

Jones, Michael Owen, ed. *Putting Folklore to Use*. Lexington: University Press of Kentucky, 1994.

Jordan, Rosan A., and Susan J. Kalcik, eds. *Women's Folklore, Women's Culture*. Philadelphia: University of Pennsylvania Press, 1985.

Joyner, Charles. *Shared Traditions: Southern History and Folk Culture*. Urbana: University of Illinois Press, 1999.

Kimmel, Eric, and Mordicaai Gerstein. *The Jar of Fools: Eight Hanukkah Stories from Chelm*. New York: Holiday House, 2000.

King, David. *First Facts about American Heroes*. Woodbridge, Conn.: Blackbirch Press, 1996.

Kyvig, David E., and Myron A. Marty. *Nearby History: Exploring the Past around You*. Nashville, Tenn.: American Association for State and Local History, 1982.

Lake-Thom, Bobby. *Spirits of the Earth: A Guide to Native American Nature Symbols, Stories, and Ceremonies*. New York: Plume, 1997.

Langellier, Kristin M., and Eric E. Peterson. *Storytelling in Daily Life: Performing Narrative*. Philadelphia: Temple University Press, 2004.

Leeming, David, and Jake Page, *Myths, Legends, and Folktales of America: An Anthology*. New York: Oxford University Press, 1999.

Leonard, William. *Masquerade in Black*. Metuchen, N.J.: Scarecrow, 1986.

Lhamon, W. T., Jr., ed. *Jump Jim Crow: Lost Plays, Lyrics, and Street Prose of the First Atlantic Popular Culture*. Cambridge, Mass: Harvard University Press, 2003.

Life, editors of. *The Life Treasury of American Folklore*. New York: Time, 1961.

Lightning inside You: And Other Native American Riddles. New York: Morrow, 1992.

Lind, Michael. *Vietnam, the Necessary War: A Reinterpretation of America's Most Disastrous Military Conflict.* New York: Free Press, 1999.

Lomax, John, and Alan Lomax. *American Ballads and Folk Songs.* New York: Macmillan, 1934.

Lyons, Mary. *Raw Head, Bloody Bones: African-American Tales of the Supernatural.* New York: Scribner's, 1991.

Lyons, Mary E. *Sorrow's Kitchen: The Life and Folklore of Zora Neale Hurston.* New York: Scribner's, 1990.

Macdonald, Margaret Read. *The Storyteller's Sourcebook: A Subject, Title, and Motif Index to Folklore Collections for Children.* Detroit: Gale, 2001.

Major, Clarence. *Juba to Jive: A Dictionary of African American Slang.* New York: Penguin Books, 1994.

Marcatante, John, and Robert R. Pottter. *American Folklore and Legends.* New York: Globe Book, 1975.

Marling, Karal Ann. *The Colossus of Roads: Myth and Symbol along the American Highway.* Minneapolis: University of Minnesota Press, 1984.

Martin, Patricia Preciado. *Songs My Mother Sang to Me: An Oral History of Mexican American Women.* Tucson: University of Arizona Press, 1992.

Mead, Margaret, and Martha Wolfenstein, eds. *Childhood in Contemporary Culture.* Chicago: University of Chicago Press, 1955.

Meese, Elizabeth A. "The Languages of Oral Testimony and Women's Literature." In *Women's Personal Narratives: Essays in Criticism and Pedagogy,* edited by Leonore Hoffman and Margo Culley, 18–26. New York: Modern Language Association of America, 1985.

Morton, Patricia. *Discovering the Woman in Slavery: Emancipating Perspectives on the American Past.* Athens: University of Georgia Press, 1996.

Muthukumaraswamy, M. D. *Voicing Folklore: Careers, Concerns, and Issues: A Collection of Interviews.* Chennai, India: National Folklore Support Centre, 2002.

Myers, Robert. *Celebrations: The Complete Book of American Holidays.* Garden City, N.Y.: Doubleday, 1972.

Mylius, Johan de, Aage Jorgensen, and Viggo Hjornager Pedersen, eds. *Hans Christian Andersen: A Poet in Time.* Odense: Odense University Press, 1999.

Narvaez, Peter, and Martin Laba, eds. *Media Sense: The Folklore–Popular Culture Continuum.* Bowling Green, Ohio: Bowling Green State University Popular Press, 1986.

Oring, Elliott, ed. *Folk Groups and Folklore Genres: An Introduction.* Logan: Utah State University Press, 1986.

Oring, Elliott, ed. *Folk Groups and Folklore Genres: A Reader.* Logan: Utah State University Press, 1989.

Oring, Elliott, and James Durham, eds. *Perspectives on Folklore and Education.* Bloomington: Indiana University Press, 1969.

Piacentino, Edward J., ed. *The Humor of the Old South.* Lexington: University Press of Kentucky, 2001.

Places of Folklore and Legend. Pleasantville, N.Y.: Reader's Digest, 1997.

Plant, Deborah. *Ebery Tub Must Sit on Its Own Bottom: The Philosophy and Politics of Zora Neale Hurston.* Urbana: University of Illinois Press, 1995.

Pozzetta, George E., ed. *Folklore, Culture and the Immigrant Mind.* New York: Garland, 1991.

Price, Charles Edwin. *A Student Guide to Collecting Folklore.* Johnson City, Tenn.: Overmountain Press, 1996.

Radner, Joan Newlon, ed. *Feminist Messages: Coding in Women's Folk Culture.* Urbana: University of Illinois Press, 1993.

Ramsey, Eloise, and Dorothy Mills Howard. *Folklore for Children and Young People: A Critical and Descriptive Bibliography for Use in the Elementary and Intermediate School.* New York: Kraus Reprint, 1970.

Redfield, Robert. *The Little Community and Peasant Society and Culture.* Chicago: University of Chicago Press, 1967.

Roberts, Warren Everett. *Viewpoints on Folklife: Looking at the Overlooked.* Ann Arbor, Mich.: UMI Research Press, 1988.

Ronda, James. *Finding the West: Explorations with Lewis and Clark.* Albuquerque: University of New Mexico Press, 2001.

Rossel, Sven Hakon, ed. *Hans Christian Andersen: Danish Writer and Citizen of the World.* Amsterdam: Rodopi, 1996.

Ryden, Kent. *Mapping the Invisible Landscape: Folklore, Writing, and the Sense of Place.* Iowa City: University of Iowa Press, 1993.

Santino, Jack. *All around the Year: Holidays and Celebrations in American Life.* Urbana: University of Illinois Press, 1994.

Scharnschula, Eleonore. *A Pioneer of American Folkore: Karl Knortz and His Collections.* Moscow: University of Idaho Press, 1996.

Schoemaker, George H., ed. *The Emergence of Folklore in Everyday Life: A Fieldguide and Sourcebook.* Bloomington, Ind.: Trickster Press, 1990.

Schwartz, Alvin. *Witcracks: Jokes and Jests from American Folklore.* Philadelphia: Lippincott, 1973.

Schwartz, Alvin, and Sue Truesdell. *Unriddling: All Sorts of Riddles to Puzzle Your Guessery.* New York: J. B. Lippincott, 1983.

Seal, Graham. *The Outlaw Legend: A Cultural Tradition in Britain, America and Australia.* New York: Cambridge University Press, 1996.

Smith, Jeanne. *Writing Tricksters: Mystic Gambols in American Ethnic Literature.* Berkeley: University of California Press, 1997.

Smith, Martin J., and Patrick J. Kiger. *Poplorica: A Popular History of the Fads, Mavericks, Inventions, and Lore That Shaped Modern America.* New York: Harper Resource, 2004.

Smithsonian Institution Office of Folklife Programs. *Celebration: A World of Art and Ritual.* Washington, D.C.: Smithsonian Institution Press, 1982.

Sumner, William Graham. *Folkways: A Study of the Sociological Importance of Usages, Manners, Customs, Mores and Morals.* Boston: Ginn, 1906.

Tatar, Maria, ed. *The Annotated Classic Fairy Tales.* New York: W. W. Norton, 2002.

Toelken, Barre. *The Dynamics of Folklore.* Boston: Houghton Mifflin, 1979.

Tulea, Tad. *Curious Customs: The Stories behind 296 Popular American Rituals.* New York: Harmony Books, 1987.

Turner, Patricia. *I Heard It through the Grapevine: Rumor in African American Culture.* Berkeley: University of California Press, 1993.

Turner, Victor. *Celebration: Studies in Festivity and Ritual.* Washington, D.C.: Smithsonian Institution Press, 1982.

Tylor, Edward. *Primitive Culture: Researches into the Development of Mythology, Philosophy, Religion, Language, Art, and Custom.* 7th ed. New York: Brentano's, 1924.

Vlach, John Michael. *By the Work of Their Hands: Studies in Afro-American Folklife.* Ann Arbor, Mich.: UMI Research Press, 1991.

Walls, Robert E., and Geroge H. Schoemaker with Jennifer Livesay. *The Old Traditional Way of Life: Essays in Honor of Warren E. Roberts.* Bloomington: Trickster Press, Indiana University Folklore Institute, 1989

Warner, Marina. *From the Beast to the Blonde: On Fairy Tales and Their Tellers.* New York: Farrar, Straus & Giroux, 1994.

West, John. *Mexican-American Folklore.* Little Rock, Ark.: August House, 1988.

Wiggins, William H., Jr. *O Freedom: Afro-American Emancipation Celebrations.* Knoxville: University of Tennessee Press, 1987.

Williams, Raymond. *Keywords: A Vocabulary of Culture and Society.* New York: Oxford University Press, 1976.

Wittke, Carl. *Tambo and Bones: A History of the American Minstrel Stage.* Durham, N.C.: Duke University Press, 1930.

Wolf, Joan. *The Beanstalk and Beyond: Developing Critical Thinking through Fairy Tales.* Englewood, Colo.: Teacher Ideas Press, 1997.

Yoder, Don, ed. *American Folklife.* Austin: University of Texas Press, 1976.

Zipes, Jack. *Breaking the Magic Spell: Radical Theories of Folk and Fairy Tales.* Lexington: University Press of Kentucky, 2002.

———. *The Complete Fairy Tales of the Brothers Grimm.* New York: Bantam Books, 1992.

Zipes, Jack, ed. *The Great Fairy Tale Tradition: From Straparola and Basile to the Brothers Grimm: Texts, Criticism.* New York: W. W. Norton, 2001.

Zumwalt, Rosemary. *American Folklore Scholarship: A Dialogue of Dissent.* Bloomington: Indiana University Press, 1988.

ARTICLES

Abrahams, Roger. "Playing the Dozens," *Journal of American Folklore* 75, no. 297 (summer 1962): 297.

Aman, Reinhold. "Challenger Shuttle Jokes," *Maledicta: The International Journal of Verbal Aggression* 10 (1988–1989): 167–181.

Bascom, William. "Four Functions of Folklore," *Journal of American Folklore* 67, no. 266 (fall 1954): 333–349.

de Caro, Francis A., and Elliott Oring. "JFK Is Alive: A Modern Legend," *Folklore Forum* 2 (1969): 54–55.

Dundes, Alan. "Texture, Text, and Context," *Southern Folklore Quarterly* 28 (1964): 251–265.

Friedman, Albert. "Grounding a Superstition: Lactation as Contraceptive," *Journal of American Folklore* 95, no. 376 (spring 1982): 200–208.

Handler, Richard, and Jocelyn Linnekin. "Tradition, Genuine or Spurious." *Journal of American Folklore* 97, no. 385 (summer 1984): 273–290.

Morrow, Patrick. "Those Sick *Challenger* Jokes," *Journal of Popular Culture* 20 (1987): 175–184.

Redfield, Robert. "The Folk Society," *American Journal of Sociology* 52 (1947): 293–308.

Sheldon, Glenn. "Crimes and Punishments: Class and Connotations of Kitschy American Food and Drink," *Studies in Popular Culture* 27, no. 1 (October 2004): 61–72.

Simons, Elizabeth Radin. "The NASA Joke Cycle: The Astronauts and the Teacher," *Western Folklore* 45 (1986): 261–277.

Smyth, Willie. "*Challenger* Jokes and the Humor of Disaster," *Western Folklore* 45 (1986): 243–260.

ENTRIES BY CATEGORY

Entries within this volume are arranged alphabetically rather than thematically, but the work takes its shape from the following categories of folklore inquiry:

FOLK HEROES/LEGENDARY FIGURES

American folklore contributes a host of memorable characters, both real and imagined. From Paul Bunyan to Yankee Doodle, these personages surface in stories, songs, and other lore. Their persistence suggests that each is a resonant figure for the people of the United States.

FABLES/FAIRY TALES/ FOLK MYTHS

While not all of these narratives originate in the United States, each is a staple of the country's folklore. Particularly in the lives of children, these texts, from "Little Red Riding Hood" to "The Princess and the Pea," appear prominently. Later in life, one sees these familiar tales reworked countless times in ways specific to narrative occasions.

FOLKLORE IN AMERICAN LITERATURE

American literature has always been attentive to folklore's narratives, and today's readers may first encounter elements of American folklore through the retellings such stories receive in the pages of American literature. Other authors do more than record folktales; they also modify, add to, and generate them. For example, Washington Irving's legend of Rip Van Winkle is widely read, retold, and incorporated in other cultural practices or stories.

FOLKLORE RELATED TO HISTORICAL EVENTS

While folklore implies an ongoing set of processes, some specific events, such as the Civil War and the gold rush, stimulate an unusual volume of folk stories, many of which recur in later narratives.

TERMS

Folklore, as does every academic discipline, employs some basic terminology that even novices find it helpful to understand. Terms such as *folklife* and *urban legends* are examples and can accompany readers in their exploration of folklore as a field of investigation.

HOLIDAYS/OBSERVANCES

While we may not think of the calendar as a culture bearer, all of the customs associated with holidays and observances represent a familiar form of folklore in practice. Information about new and old occasions (from colonial times to the present, from Patriot's Day, which commemorates the Revolutionary War's "shot heard round the world," to Patriot Day, which recalls the attacks of September 11, 2001) can be found here.

FOLKLORE IN EVERYDAY LIFE

Just as holidays reveal cultural beliefs and values, so do our everyday activities and common understandings. From foodways to jokes, folklore permeates our daily lives, including our customs (Why do we bless someone who sneezes, but not someone who coughs or chokes?), attempts to forecast events and their consequences (Why is it that Friday the thirteenth is perceived as an unlucky day, but on March 17 we all enjoy "the luck of the Irish"?), premises that help us interpret our experiences, both as individuals and as a collective (Why do we celebrate the offspring on a birthday, rather than the person who gave birth?).

CULTURAL GROUPS

Since there is not one single and uniform American culture, it becomes necessary to consider how members of various cultural groups (by region, religion, race, or ethnicity) relate to folklore. Whether studying one's own cultural heritage or someone else's, knowledge of patterns within folk practice and narrative proves important. Through entries concentrating on particular cultural and subcultural groups, it becomes possible to examine more specific and distinctive, rather than general and pervasive, folklore practices and responses.

FOLK REGIONS

While it has become customary to speak of the world as a "global village," particularly given the unifying but also homogenizing effects of information technology and media, it is nonetheless true that the premise on which most folklore study is based is the belief in meaningful regional variations. Within this encyclopedia, as appropriate, entries are cross-referenced by the connections of that entry's framing concept, term, or form to one or more regions by using a variant on the regional folklores described by Charles Haywood in his 1951 *Bibliography of North American Folklore and Folksong:* Midwestern, Northeastern, Northwestern, Southern, Southwestern, and Western.

OTHER ENTRIES

Readers will find it helpful to have a few entries about major organizations/agencies involved in

both preserving and advancing American folklore traditions. Entries on cultural sites such as Colonial Williamsburg, organizations such as the Smithsonian Institution, and relevant items of legislation, such as the American Folklife Preservation Act, can assist in this regard.

FOLK HEROES/LEGENDARY FIGURES

Alger, Horatio, Jr.
Allen, Ethan
Anansi
Anthony, Susan Brownell
Appleseed, Johnny (See Chapman, John)
Attucks, Crispus
Babe, the Blue Ox
Barker, Ma (See Clark, Arizona Donnie)
Barton, Clara
Bass, Sam
Bigfoot /Sasquatch
Billy the Kid (See McCarty, William Henry)
Bloody Mary
Boles, Charles E. (Black Bart)
Bonnie and Clyde
Boone, Daniel
Borden, Lizzie
Brer Rabbit
Brown, John
Brown, Margaret Tobin (Unsinkable Molly Brown)
Bunyan, Paul
Calamity Jane (See Cannary-Burke, Martha)
Cannary-Burke, Martha (Calamity Jane)
Capone, Alphonse Gabriel (Al)
Carson, Kit
Cassidy, Butch (See Parker, Robert Leroy)
Chapman, John (Johnny Appleseed)
Chavez, César Estrada
Christmas, Annie
Clark, Arizona Donnie (Ma Barker)
Cody, William F. (Buffalo Bill)
Columbus, Christopher
Copland, Aaron
cowboys
Coyote
Crazy Horse
Crockett, Davy

FABLES/FAIRY TALES/MYTHS

supernatural
superstition
tattooing (See bodylore)
toasts/drinking
toys, folk
UFO folklore
vampire
voodoo/hoodoo
war and folklore (See Civil War, etc.)
weather folklore
weaving (See crafts, folk)
wedding/marriage folklore
werewolf
wishbone (See luck/fortune; prediction)
witchcraft (See witchcraft, Salem)
woodworking (See crafts, folk)
Xerox/fax folklore

CULTURAL GROUPS

Acadian and Creole folklore (See Cajun folklore)
African-American folklore
Amish folklore (See Pennsylvania Dutch/ Pennsylvania German folklore)
Anglo-American folklore
Appalachian folklore
Cajun folklore
Chicano-American folklore
Chinese-American folklore
Danish-American folklore
Dutch-American folklore
Filipino-American folklore
Finnish-American folklore
French-American folklore
German-American folklore
Greek-American folklore
Hungarian-American folklore
Icelandic-American folklore
Irish-American folklore
Italian-American folklore
Jamaican-American folklore
Japanese-American folklore

Jewish-American folklore
Korean-American folklore
Latvian-American folklore
Lithuanian-American folklore
Mexican-American folklore (See Chicano-American folklore)
Mormon folklore
Native American folklore
Norwegian-American folklore
Ozarks folklore
Pennsylvania Dutch/Pennsylvania German folklore
Polish-American folklore
Portuguese-American folklore
Quaker folklore
Scottish-American folklore
Shaker folklore
Spanish-American folklore
Swedish-American folklore
Folk Regions
Midwestern regional folklore
Northeastern regional folklore
Northwestern regional folklore
Southern regional folklore
Southwestern regional folklore
Western regional folklore

OTHER ENTRIES

American Folklife Center
American Folklife Preservation Act
American Folklore Society
American Memory Project (Historical Collections for the National Digital Library, Library of Congress)
Archive of Folk Culture
arts and crafts movement
Colonial Williamsburg
Greenfield Village, Henry Ford Museum and Mystic Seaport and Preservation Shipyard
Sturbridge Village, Old
Smithsonian Institution

INDEX